Nineteenth-Century Printing Practices & the Iron Handpress

Plate 20. Printing office with a handpress in an acorn frame, ca. 1836. The printer on the far right is waiting for the roller boy to ink the form. (Source: Edward Hazen, *Hazen's The Panorama of Professions and Trades*, 1836, p. [180].)

NINETEENTH-CENTURY PRINTING PRACTICES AND THE IRON HANDPRESS

with Selected Readings

Richard-Gabriel Rummonds
Foreword by Stephen O. Saxe

VOLUME TWO

OAK KNOLL PRESS & THE BRITISH LIBRARY | 2004
IN ASSOCIATION WITH FIVE ROSES PRESS

First Edition published 2004 by Oak Knoll Press & The British Library

Oak Knoll Press, 310 Delaware Street, New Castle, DE , 19720 USA
The British Library, 96 Euston Road, St. Pancras, London, NW1 2DB, UK

Library of Congress Cataloging-in-Publication Data

Rummonds, Richard-Gabriel, 1931 –
    Nineteenth-century printing practices and the iron handpress / Richard-Gabriel Rummonds. — 1st ed.
        p.   cm.
    Includes bibliographical references and index.
    ISBN 1-58456-088-6 (hbk.) — ISBN 1-58456-100-9 (pbk.)
    1. Printing, Practical — Great Britain—19th century. 2. Printing, Practical —United States—19th century.
3. Printing — History — 19th century. 4. Printing equipment and supplies — History — 19th century.
5. Handpresses — History — 19th century. 6. Printing — History — Sources — Bibliography I. Title.
Z124.R86 2004
686.2´09´034— dc21   2003045960

British Library Cataloging-in-Publication Data available from The British Library

ISBN: 1- 58456-088-6 (Oak Knoll hard cover)
ISBN: 1- 58456-100-9 (Oak Knoll soft cover)
ISBN: 0-7123-4867-0 (The British Library hard cover)

Publishing Director: J. Lewis von Hoelle
Technical Editor: Stephen O. Saxe
Copyeditor: Donna Giordano
Typography: Bradley Hutchinson
Endpapers (hard cover): John DePol

All inquiries should be addressed to:
Oak Knoll Press, 310 Delaware St., New Castle, DE 19720
Web: http://oakknoll.com

Author's e-mail address: rummonds@letterspace.com

This work was printed in the United States of America on 60# archival acid-free paper
meeting the requirements of the American Standard for Permanence
of Paper for Printed Library Materials.

Contents

Appendices

Bibliographies

Indexes

List of Plates

Nineteenth-Century Printing Practices & the Iron Handpress

VOLUME TWO

Plate 21. Collingridge's Printing Works with Columbian and Albion presses, 1865. One of the pressmen has a roller boy helping him. Note that on the left-hand side of the partition a warehouseman is pressing sheets on a rolling press. (Source: *Collingridge's Guide to Printing and Publishing*, [1865], recto of the 24th leaf following p. 36.)

CHAPTER SEVENTEEN

Black Ink

The basic ingredients for making printing ink are few, although certain additives can alter the ink's composition, often rendering the recipe more complex. Prior to the twentieth century, most inks were nothing more than a combination of varnish (the vehicle or binding agent) and pigment (the coloring matter). To these, small quantities of mineral or vegetable substances were often added in order to modify its color or consistency.

Moxon mentions inkmakers in his manual (1683, pp. 7, 75–77, 361), which indicates that inkmaking was already well-established as a separate trade in his day. About sixty years later, Ephraim Chambers, in his *Cyclopædia: or, An Universal Dictionary of Arts and Sciences* (1741–1743, s.v. *Printing*), noted that the art of making ink was "now rekonded no part of the printers['] business, but usually furnished them by other hands . . ." Some printers continued to doctor commercial inks to improve their appearance and workability.

The first book written exclusively about ink and its manufacture was *On the Preparation of Printing Inks* (1832) by William Savage. Readings 17.5, 17.6, and 18.1 on pp. 494, 501, and 512, respectively, are taken from this book. It was not until the twentieth century that another book on ink, *A History of Printing Ink, Balls and Rollers, 1440–1850,* (1967) by Colin H. Bloy, would challenge Savage's authority. Bloy's book – which many printers consider the definitive work on handpress inks – contains sixty-nine recipes for pre-twentieth-century printing inks. All of Bloy's citations below are taken from this work. Both Savage's and Bloy's texts contain a few minor errors, which I have noted as they occur in these readings.

Making ink was hard, tedious, and sometimes dangerous, work. All pigments were ground with a hand muller similar to the one shown in **Fig. 17.1** on p. 487, although power-grinding machines were already in use as early as the mid-1820s. In the days when printers still made their own varnish, they preferred to do it out-of-doors – usually outside the city walls – since the boiling oil, which also had to be ignited during the process, could be a fire hazard (see the second footnote on p. 491, in Reading 17.3).

Around 1754, William Blackwell founded the oldest European ink manufactory to survive into the twentieth century. Blackwell was asked to supply the ink that was used to print the first issue of the *Daily Universal Register* in 1785. This newspaper later changed its name to *The Times* in 1788. It was first printed on an array of wooden presses, which were replaced at the turn of the century by cast-iron Stanhope presses. These iron presses were also supplanted in 1814 when the publisher changed over to steam-driven cylinder printing machines. Savage, on p. 504 in Reading 17.6, describes doctoring Blackwell's ink in order to create what he considered to be a superior printing ink. Bloy (p. 84) says that by 1850 "the printer who made his own inks became a rarity."

The raw materials used in inkmaking remained fairly constant until the second half of the twentieth century when rubber-base inks began to replace oil-base inks for certain types of work. Most of these rubber-base inks were created specifically for offset and high-speed printing. In the *Proceedings of the Fine Printing Conference at Columbia University, Held May 19–22,*

1982 (1983, p. 52), Jack Power of the Van Son Holland Ink Company said, "In the case of rubber-base ink, the varnish is made from a resin that is actually like cyclosized rubber – it's a plastic-like resin."

Savage describes in detail the raw materials for making ink in Reading 17.5 on p. 494.

Reading 17.1
Printing Ink
from *The Printer's Grammar* by Caleb Stower (1808, pp. 512–513).

Stower assumes from the outset that the printer is not going to make his own ink, but purchase it from a commercial inkmaker. Therefore, he does not give any recipes for making it. Instead he appends at the back of his manual "A List of the Articles Used in the Printing Business, and Their Present Prices." Under "printing inks, one pound," on p. 517, he records six grades of ink, ranging in price from 10s 6d to 1s 4d. This ink was sold in cans or metal drums that held from half a pound upwards. In addition, on p. 518, he singles out seven London inkmakers, one of whom is Blackwell. It is unlikely that the lists of inkmakers published in printers' manuals in the first quarter of the nineteenth century reflected the total number of those actually plying their trade in the city at the time.

Of the twelve inkmakers on Mason's list (1823, p. 33), only one – Blackwell, which had by that time been taken over by Colvil, whom Bloy (pp. 68, 74–75) refers to as *Colvin* – is repeated from Stower's list of 1808. A year later, Johnson (1824, vol. II, p. 652) identifies seven inkmakers, or their agents, in London. Comparing Johnson's list with Mason's, we see that four were dropped in one year, an indication that this particular trade was in a state of flux.

Printing ink of every sort should be of a smooth and mellow quality, such as will work clear, free from picks, distribute well on the balls, and soon dry; the beauty and strength of the colour varying of course according to the price. It should be so manufactured as perfectly to unite the oil and colouring matter, otherwise it soon turns of a yellow-brown dingy hue, which has been too generally found to be the case with the common ink of most of the manufacturers. The finer sorts should be of a more solid consistence, but perfectly free from a pitchy quality.

Very considerable improvements have been made in the superior sorts of printing ink by several of our most eminent master printers; but the common ink with which three-fourths of the works published in this country [England] are printed, has remained for a long period at nearly the same standard. Mr. [Beale] Blackwell [d.1790] has, unquestionably, for many years produced better fine as well as common ink than any of his competitors; but an improvement is still wanting, as to colour, in the common ink. We understand however from several respectable printers, that a Mr. [P.] Anstie has lately made an ink of this desirable quality which is likely to be much used by the trade. Mr. Blackwell from his long and extensive practice in this art, must, we think, be pretty well acquainted with the necessary qualities of every description of printing ink, and the best mode of manufacturing it; but as there are many competitors in this as well as in every other art, he will do well to endeavour to preserve that celebrity he has so long and justly obtained.

Reading 17.2
Black Ink
from *Practical Hints on Decorative Printing* by William Savage (1822, p. 100).

Savage was the first printer to aggressively investigate the properties of ink. He was also the most vocal of any pre-twentieth-century manual writer in promoting a non-oil-base varnish for printing inks. Capivi – the vehicle in the recipe below – was also known as *copaiba balsam*. It is defined on p. 499. This ink was used to print both the letterpress and the plates in the above-mentioned work. It is curious to note that as late as 1822, Savage opted for composition balls – which he notes were made by Benjamin Foster – to ink his forms.

Savage eventually had to give up this project, turning it over to John Johnson, the printer and manual writer, who finished it. It is easy to see why the backers and subscribers of this project would become frustrated. Savage began printing the book in 1818, and even though 1822 is given on the title page as the date of publication, the work was not issued until 1823. The plates were all printed from wood engravings and were editioned separately and tipped in. One of these, "Ode to Mercy," required twenty-nine blocks and thirty colors to achieve the final color print. In an edition of 227 copies, this translates into 6,810 impressions just for this one plate! Altogether there were twenty-six plates printed in color, seven in black, two type specimens, two decorative headpieces each appearing three times and also printed in color, six tables of color specimens, and nine defaced impressions. Savage's was the first printers' manual to display specimens of colored inks.

[Savage's recipe for a black ink without an oil-base varnish:]

Balsam Capivi	8 oz	Indian Red	¾
Best Lamp Black	3	Turpentine Soap Dried	3
Prussian Blue	1½		

Ground on a Marble or Stone Slab with a Muller [**Fig. 17.1**], to an impalpable fineness. These ingredients will make rather more than 1 lb. in weight, and form the same Ink that the first part of this work is printed with; it has received the unequivocal approbation of the Pressmen who have used it, as working perfectly free and clean, and washing easily off the types; as much or more so, than any strong Inks they had ever used, and they had been accustomed to Fine Works.

Fig. 17.1. *Ink stone with muller and palette knife* – from MacKellar (1878, p. 285)

Reading 17.3

On Printing Ink

from *Typographia* by Thomas Curson Hansard (1825, pp. 715–718, 721–733).

Hansard, like most early-nineteenth-century manual writers, lamented the disreputable state into which English commercial inkmaking had fallen by the end of the eighteenth century. Since the materials used in making ink were very expensive, inkmakers, as well as printers, would often use inferior materials or doctor their inks in order to make them go further. Ink, like paper, was usually purchased for the job in hand. Weak ink was used for ephemeral works, such as circulars; good ink, for general printing and regular book work; and fine ink, for the best quality work, which included wood engravings.

Eventually, Hansard found the firm of Thomas Martin & Co. of Birmingham whose inks satisfied most of his requirements, so much so that he used their inks when printing his manual. In a section at the back of his book, Hansard included four ink specimens from Martin– a first for a printers' manual.

By the 1820s, commercial inkmakers had reached such a level of proficiency and dependability that printers no longer needed to make their own inks. And if they did, they could rarely match the superior quality of the manufactured product. This change was brought about by two things: (1) a better way to accumulate lampblack and (2) improvements in grinding the pigments.

All fine printers in the nineteenth century praised John Baskerville's ink. Hansard, however, was the first to publish Baskerville's recipe, which will be found below on p. 491. Hansard also noted that Baskerville set his ink aside for several months in order to let it mature. As all modern handpress printers know, the finer the pigments and the stiffer the ink, the more effort the pressman must take to make it print well.

Even though Stower, on p. 486 in Reading 17.1, has already mentioned the firm of Blackwell, Hansard adds some new information about the company when it was under the direction of Beale Blackwell, who died in 1790. Bloy (p. 68) says that Beale was "probably William's son."

In speaking of this preparation, so essential, as regards its quality, to good printing, it is my intention to go somewhat more into detail than any of those who have hitherto written on the subject of printing. Notwithstanding all the efforts which have been made in this country [England], there is still a wide field open for further improvement in this article, and though many makers have from time to time started into notice, none of them have been hitherto fortunate enough to attain perfection.

Mr. Beale Blackwell was the first maker of ink of any note in this country; he established considerable works for the supply of the trade, and for a long time kept all competitors at a distance . . . [At] length Messrs. Martin and Co. erected their works at Birmingham, and it is but justice to those gentlemen to say, they have been the means of making greater improvements in the manufacture than any who preceded them. The writer of this has tried most of the inks which have been recommended to the trade, from a desire of encouraging competition and finding a better article, but has constantly found those trials only confirmatory of his opinion in favour of that supplied by the firm just mentioned, and is perfectly willing to let his credit, in his profession, rest upon the use of their ink, in competition with any ink, or improved ink, made in this kingdom. . . .

Few printers, of any eminence, in this country attempt to be entire makers of their own ink,* the improvement of the manufacturer's ink being the most that has been attempted by any printer of much practice, with the exception of Mr. [William] Bulmer, and this has been effected by re-grinding, or mixing, the article with such additions as they thought might give a better colour, or a tint more congenial with their taste. I do not pretend to be possessed of their secrets – I never could perceive any such difference in that quality of their work as to induce me to bestow a single hour in trying experiments to find them out: nor, if I knew them, would I practice them. I believe, some few years ago, the article manufactured for sale was at so low an ebb as to make it desirable to try any means of improvement: the matter is now reversed, and if I wanted ink to have the purpleish blush which has by some been fancied as adding beauty to printing, I could have it immediately made to my mind. But that is not my idea of fine print-ing: black, as perfect as blackness can be, is, in my judgment, the true criterion of good ink. The lamp-black of commerce is too coarse and impure to effect this, as the manufacture has, for a long time, been confined to individuals who have had more profitable speculations in view, and who only made the article to get rid of the refuse substances lying about their works, with-out any attention to quality or cleanness, quantity being the principal object of those who are thus engaged.

Black, in this impure state, for a long time satisfied the makers of printing ink, which, dur-ing a period of nearly 200 years, received little or no further improvement, and it was not until the days of the celebrated Baskerville . . . that any attention was turned to this most essential article. His scrutinising eye was always on the search after improvement, and his mind, quick as his vision, ready to mature the first idea. It was reserved for him to discover, after such a lapse of time, a superior kind of black for the purpose required, and to this success may be attributed, in a great measure, the superiority of his printing, which is still justly admired, even in the present further improved state of the art. His success gave a stimulus of rivalry to others in the trade, and a few, out of many, attempts, were in course of time partially successful. . . . Some added indigo or prussian blue to the common ink of the makers, and thus considerably improved their colour; but the difficulty of working inks containing these pigments, and the impossibility of bringing off clear impressions from wood cuts or small type, without very considerable labour and great loss of time, were such drawbacks on the improvement as to render it almost useless. Other printers procured samples of black from the continent, and, in some few instances, suc-ceeded in finding a better colour; but the imperfect knowledge possessed by the printer of the entire art was always a stumbling block in these experiments too difficult to be entirely over-come, and though he might succeed in one point, a fresh obstacle generally arose to thwart him in another. . . .

Of the fine black manufactured by [Messrs. Thomas Martin & Co.] I have now some before me, and have no hesitation in pronouncing it the finest smoke-black made in this country. I understand it is produced from coal gas, burnt in a peculiar way, and the smoke collected in a similar manner as for the spirit-black described in their patent [British Patent No. 4601, 1821]. The complex nature of this apparatus, and the great extent of building requisite to carry on the same, render it impossible to give, by verbal description alone, any clear idea of this manufac-ture, nor indeed would it be right to lay open to the world an invention which has cost so much expense, time, and labour to perfect.

From these persevering exertions in the pursuit of this art, I am induced to hope the profes-sion will be supplied with superior inks, calculated for the various purposes of the press,

---

* Even those who make their own ink are glad to obtain the black of the manufacturer now spoken of.

combining beauty and richness of colour with clearness of impression, and freedom of working with quickness of drying, in quality so much improved, and at prices so much reduced, as totally to obviate the necessity of master-printers employing a portion of their valuable time, and risking the safety of their property, in the pursuit of an art that but few can attain, and if attained, where they have so much to risk and so little to gain.

In throwing out these observations to the trade, which I have been induced to do from motives of general utility, I would not be understood as wishing to damp the ardour of the speculative mind, or crush the spirit of inquiry in the pursuit of perfection; but I would suggest the advantages which might be obtained, if the printer and ink-maker would go hand in hand in their research after improvement, instead of endeavouring to render every part of their respective knowledge mysterious and undefined. There is likewise a second and more powerful motive for this union, as it would tend to do away that system of bribery and corrupt influence carried on between the ink-maker and the journeymen, and now become so prevalent in most printing-offices as to amount to an actual demand of a five, and frequently of a seven and a half, per cent on the consumption. This growing evil requires the immediate attention of the trade, as all must be aware no manufacturer can sacrifice so large a portion of his fair profits, and, consequently, that he must materially reduce the quality of the article manufactured, to meet this imposition. . . .

Good ink requires the possession of a variety of qualities, some of which seem to be at variance with each others. By the fineness of the black, the softness of the varnish, and the power of the mill in triturating [pulverizing] and mixing the ingredients, it should be made perfectly impalpable. To the eye it should appear of a clear black tint; not glaring or glossy, nor yet so mellow as to want an agreeable tone and strength of colour. The finer sorts should be made of that degree of stiffness, that the same inequalities of surface, even to fine pointed hillocks, and twisted forms, will be found to have retained their shapes, if the can had not been opened for twelve months after any part was taken away by the ink-slice [**Fig. 17.2**]; neither must it form any film or skin, or suffer any decomposition of its parts. Yet it must not have any tendency to dry while kept in the can or cask, or be too cohesive for distributing with tolerable ease on the balls or rollers. It must have such an affinity to the paper, as to adhere firmly to the surface from the moment it receives the impression; but it must not possess such tenacity as to remain upon the face of the type, and tear off the fibre of the paper, which would then be gathered upon the balls or rollers, and again conveyed to the type, filling up the face, and casting little blots, technically called picks, upon the subsequently printed sheets; but much of this must depend upon the texture of the paper.*

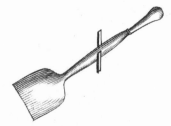

Fig. 17.2. *Ink slice* – from Moxon (1683, plate 7 facing p. 56), courtesy of Rochester Institute of Technology

---

* I would here wish the printer to notice particularly this point, as inks are too frequently complained of as being foul and gritty, and the ink-maker condemned, when it is wholly caused by the tenderness of bleached and cotton paper, and the earthy particles used in its manufacture.

Various receipts have at different times been published on this subject, but none that I have hitherto seen seem calculated to produce the effect; it would be therefore a folly to insert them here: the one I shall introduce, which has never before been published, has been given me as the mode practiced by Mr. Baskerville, which a careful examination of his printing will fully prove to have stood the test of time.

He took of the finest and oldest linseed oil* three gallons, this was put into a vessel capable of holding four times the quantity, and boiled with a long-continued fire till it acquired a certain thickness or tenacity, according to the quality of the work it was intended to print, and which was judged of by putting small quantities upon a stone to cool, and then taking it up between the finger and thumb; on opening which, if it drew into a thread an inch long or more, it was considered sufficiently boiled. This mode of boiling can only be acquired by long practice, and requires particular skill and care in the person who superintends the operation, as, for want of this, the most serious consequences may occur, and have very frequently occurred.† The oil thus prepared was suffered to cool, and had then a small quantity of black or amber rosin dissolved in it, after which it was allowed some months to subside; it was then mixed with the fine black, before named [smoke-black], to a proper thickness, and ground for use. [Editor's note: Savage (1832, p. 79) says that "This black was collected from glass-pinchers' and solderers' lamps."]

This method, with very little modification, I have every reason to suppose, was pursued by Mr. Bulmer in the making of his ink for the [Boydell] Shakespeare [1792–1802] and some other fine works printed in the early part of his practice: and I have it from the best authority, that when the boiling of the oil is properly managed and the black well mixed and ground, no finer or better working ink can be made....

Mr. Savage, in his work on Decorative Printing, recently published [1822], would seem to contradict this theory, as he insinuates that no ink can be depended upon where oil forms the base of the varnish; he has, in consequence, pointed out a new mode of making ink, entirely divested of oil [for Savage's formula, see p. 487 in Reading 17.2]....

These ingredients, when ground, seem to have formed an ink of good colour, as exhibited in the body of his work; but on a careful examination of its general appearance throughout the whole, it carries evident marks of not distributing well, or spreading freely on the types, and being equal to the quality of the paper. This I have no doubt will be found the case by any person who chooses to try the working of it, as I am fully convinced that all inks containing so large

---

* The linseed oil generally in the market, is totally unfit for the purpose of ink-making, being too frequently mixed with seeds of an inferior, drying, quality, or expressed from those which are damaged or unripe, and very often overheated in the steam-kettles in order to force out an additional quantity of oil; this excess of heat invariably causes a large portion of the mucilage to combine with the oil, and till that has subsided it is unfit for use. This mucilaginous combination is, in fact, more or less in all seed oils, which renders it necessary they should stand a very considerable time to subside, before being converted into varnish, which can only be regulated according to the quality of the oil, but in no case should it be used before twelve months old, and if kept longer will be considerably improved: good oil may, in some measure, be known by its appearance, the best being of a pale straw colour. This varnish, after being brought to its proper consistence, requires to stand for at least two months, that the decomposed mucilage and other matter may subside to the bottom, it will then be fit for use. Some makers add to their varnishes boiled turpentine; others rosin, and, not unfrequently, soap; these are useful in some instances, particularly in rendering the type easier to be cleaned, as, without something of this kind, the ink will be difficult to wash off, but only in this particular can they be of service.

† If flame once communicates to the oil in this state, nothing can extinguish it but instantly closing the pot or vessel, so that no air can draw in to feed the flame. One of the most tremendous fires that happened in this metropolis a few years since [ca. 1820] was thus occasioned; no making of varnish should ever be attempted within the walls of a printing-office.

a portion of prussian blue, however fine it may be ground, will invariably work foul; nor do I think the capivi balsam a good varnish for lamp-black, as the least exposure to the air on the ink-block would cause it to become thicker and more glutinous, and, in a few hours, destroy altogether the freeness of working....

Every workman ought to be aware that the thin weak ink, at eighteen-pence per pound, is only intended to produce a very pale black, for quick working and setting; the two-shilling a shade deeper; three-shilling, if good, is well calculated for the general purposes of book-printing, when there are no fine cuts introduced, and, with care, will even answer for those purposes: the six-shilling is suitable for all the uses of fine printing, and will produce, in its present improved state, as much effect as can be produced from the finer inks recently sold at nine and twelve shillings per pound. The colour of the work can be increased only by the quality of the ink; the better the quality of the ink the more time it will take the pressman to work it, and the better may be the paper; it is impossible to work fine ink upon bad paper, and no employer can expect his work to look a fine and rich colour, if either the printer or stationer be straightened in the price of their respective commodities.

The requisites of being very stiff without strong adhesion; of keeping always soft and mellow, but drying quickly and without loss of colour as soon as it is on the paper; of adhering strongly to the paper, but not to the type; are qualities much to be desired, but difficult to be attained, even by those who have been long practised in the art of ink-making; nor indeed, do I know of any maker who has wholly succeeded in obtaining them. That of drying quickly without being made too glutinous for working freely, would, indeed, appear to be an advantage utterly unattainable, as what induces the drying quality has hitherto been found to prevent, in equal ratio, the freedom of working, and tending, also, to deteriorate the colour. I have not hitherto found any means of approaching this object, but by keeping strong inks in tin cans, in a warm room for a considerable time, twelve months at least, which I then find become much mellowed, and to work soft and well.

Many efforts have been made to conquer these difficulties; many printers have thought themselves possessed of this *aurum potabile* [literally, drinkable gold; metaphorically, a highly desirable object]: many have been the trials made by printers of newly-set-up ink-makers, with a view, from their pretensions, of obtaining this object alone; but I have found that instead of general improvement, if this object was in any degree attained, the other qualities seemed to retrograde in proportion. I have, however, some hopes that it is, at last, in a great measure effected; some experiments made by [Messrs. Thomas Martin & Co.], seem to have brought the article nearest the desired degree of perfection; and, if experience should prove this to be the case, there is not, in my opinion, any thing further to be wished for in the art of ink-making.

Reading 17.4
For Black Ink
from "Printing Ink" in *The Cyclopædia* by Abraham Rees (1819, vol. 28) as reprinted in *Typographia* by Thomas Curson Hansard (1825, pp. 724–725).

Hansard had an encyclopedic interest in the history and practice of printing. He was always eager to present and discuss innovations relating to the printing trade in his manual. Therefore, he did not hesitate to include lengthy articles from works by other authors, of which the following reading is an excellent example. Abraham Rees's *Cyclopædia* (1819) contains many articles on printing and its allied arts, as well as information and diagrams about the latest inventions in those fields. As is the case here, Rees himself relied heavily on previously published works. He liberally quotes and paraphrases two articles on ink taken from eighteenth-century sources, without the benefit of quotation marks.

The first of these was written by André-François Le Breton, who was printer to the king of France, Louis XV (1715–1774) . Le Breton conceived, together with three associates, the idea of a French encyclopedia along the lines of Chambers's well-known English *Cyclopædia* (1741–1743). Their collective efforts resulted in the *Encyclopédie, ou dictionnaire raisonné des sciences, des arts et des métiers* (1751–1780), which was edited by Denis Diderot (1713–1784) and Jean le Rond d'Alembert (1717–1783). Le Breton's article appears in vol. 5, s.v. *Encre Noire*, which was published in 1755.

The second article was written by William Lewis whose comments on ink are taken from his *Commercium philosophico-technicum; or, The Philosophical Commerce of Arts* (1763, pp. 371–374). Rees refers to it as *Lewis's Commerce of Arts*.

In the recipe below, coarse bread and onions are added to the boiling oil, a practice first encountered in Moxon (1683, p. 80).

A hundred pounds of nut or linseed oil, being reduced, by boiling, to the consistence of a syrup, are cleansed and purified by throwing into them two pounds of coarse bread, and about a dozen onions. Nut oil is supposed to be the best, and is accordingly preferred for the black ink, though the darker colour which it acquires from the fire makes it less fit for the red. This oil is boiled in an iron pot, capable of holding at least half as much more, because it swells very much; when it boils it is kept stirring with an iron ladle; and if it does not itself take flame, it is kindled with a piece of lighted paper, or burning wood, in order to increase its consistence and tenacity, and to diminish its greasiness. The oil is suffered to burn for half an hour or more; and the flame being then extinguished by covering the vessel close, the boiling is afterwards continued, with a gentle heat, till the oil appears of a proper consistence; in which state it is called varnish; of which there should be two kinds, one more and another less boiled; or a thicker and thinner, to be used for different purposes, and in different weathers. The oil is said to lose in being boiled into thick varnish from a tenth to an eighth part of its weight; but different oils, and perhaps the same oil in different states, differ in this respect. The design of adding the bread and onions is more effectually to destroy the greasiness; but Dr. Lewis doubts, whether additions of this kind are of much use. They then boil thirty or thirty-five pounds of turpentine apart, till such time as they find, upon its cooling on paper, that it breaks clean, like glass, without pulverizing; for if it pulverize easily, it is a sign it is burnt. The oil and turpentine being thus prepared, the first is gently poured, half cold, into the latter; and the two stirred together with a stick till they be well mixed: after which the boiling is repeated and the composition is set by, to be used occasionally. The turpentine is used in order to give a greater body to the varnish, and to increase its drying quality; and with some artists, litharge [an oxide of lead] has in this intention been a secret. M. [Le] Breton, in the Encyclopédie, observes, that when very old oil is used, neither turpentine nor litharge are needful; but that when the oil is new, some turpentine ought to be employed, because, without it, the smearing of the paper, by the spreading or coming off of the ink, cannot be avoided; and he adds, that it is much more eligible to use old oil than to have recourse to this correction of the new: both turpentine and litharge, particularly the last, making the mixture adhere so firmly to the types, that it is scarcely to be got entirely off by the ley, whence the eye of the letter is soon clogged up.

Now to proceed to make ink, they take a quantity of this mixture, and add to it a certain quantity of lamp-black, working it up with a kind of wooden mallet, or brayer, till the whole be incorporated, and reduced into a kind of pulp; which is the ink for use.

Where, note, that its thickness or strength is always to be proportioned to that of the paper, and the warmth of the weather; strong paper and hot weather, requiring strong ink: and that the strength or weakness of the ink depends on the greater or the less degree of coction of the varnish. According to M. [Le] Breton, two ounces and a half of the lamp-black are sufficient for sixteen ounces of the varnish. – *Lewis's Commerce of Arts*, p. 371.

Reading 17.5
On the Materials and Implements for Making Printing Ink
from *On the Preparation of Printing Inks* by William Savage (1832, pp. 105–123).

Savage's work synthesizes all the knowledge regarding the craft of making ink that he acquired firsthand or that he could glean from English and French printers' manuals and encyclopedias. Lynch (1859, pp. 175–187) reprinted both the reading below and Reading 17.6 on p. 501 in his manual, adding his own comments to Savage's. In these readings, Lynch's observations have been inserted between brackets at the points where they appear in his text.

Both Savage (1832, p. 50) and Bloy (1967, pp. 106, 138) have stated that Le Breton's recipe for ink was taken from the *Encyclopédie méthodique*, giving 1751 as its date of publication; however, neither the source nor the date are correct since this particular encyclopedia was not published until 1783–1784. As I mentioned in my introductory note to Reading 17.4 on p. 493, Le Breton's article on ink appeared in the *Encyclopédie, ou dictionnaire raisonné des sciences, des arts et des métiers* (1751–1780). The article on ink in the *Encyclopédie méthodique: Commerce* (1783, vol. 1, p. 69) is only seven lines long and does not include any recipes for making ink.

Savage mentions the addition of soap in some of his ink recipes. Soap appears to have been regarded as a "secret" ingredient in some English printers' inks, although fatty soaps had been used earlier in the century for making lithographic inks. Savage also decries the horrid practice of putting water over the ink in the cans to prevent the ink from skinning.

Curiously, Savage only describes in detail two black pigments: lampblack and ivory black. The former was made from both mineral and vegetable materials; the latter, obtained from burning pieces of ivory, which is, of course, no longer available. Several other organic blacks, which would have been known to Savage but not mentioned by him, are still being manufactured today, such as bone black, vine black, and Frankfurt black.

It could safely be said that Savage was an ink fanatic and a compulsive perfectionist, but in my mind, his inks and his printing would amply justify his single-mindedness. He maintained throughout his career that the hallmark of a superior ink is its ability to retain the most density from the thinnest film of ink with the least amount of pressure as it is transferred from the type to the paper.

Printing Ink is a composition, formed of two articles; namely, Varnish and Colouring Matter.

The varnish may be either in its natural state, as the vegetable balsams; or a compound, as generally used, formed of oil, rosin, and soap.

The colouring matter varies in black Ink, according to the quality of the Ink; and in coloured Inks, according to the tinct [archaic term for *color*] required.

In the following pages I shall enumerate the ingredients, with observations on their properties; the method of preparing the varnish; the preparation of black Ink of different qualities, and a variety of coloured Inks; with an enumeration and description of the necessary implements.

Linseed Oil

Linseed oil is so generally used as the basis of the varnish, and answers so well for general purposes, when properly prepared, that it does not appear necessary to speculate on the properties of other oils for this purpose. It is generally allowed that the older it is the better, for making varnish.

It will be observed, that in the receipts for making Printing Ink which have been published, and which I have given in [ibid., pp. 23–104], the French prefer nut oil to linseed oil, but they do not specify in what particulars its superiority consists; and as nut oil is not in this country an article of commerce in a large way, it might not always be procurable with facility. They also mention rape oil, hemp oil, and other vegetable oils as worthless for making varnish for Printing Ink.

[Joseph] Moxon [1683], in the Dutch method of making Printing Ink, mentions linseed oil only, which he says should be old, the older the better; [Martin-Dominique] Fertel says [in *La science pratique de l'imprimerie*, 1723, p. 283] "there are but two sorts of oil which are proper for making varnish; namely, linseed oil and nut oil," and he does not express any opinion of a preference to either; [Le] Breton, in speaking of the qualities of nut oil and linseed oil, is not consistent – in one place [*Encyclopédie* (1755, vol. 5, fol. 633r)] he says, "Linseed and nut oils are the only proper ones for making good varnish for printing; that of nuts merits the preference in every respect." In another place [on the same folio] "The weak varnish can be made at the same fire as the strong, but in a separate vessel: we can thus employ, and it is my advice, for this varnish linseed oil; because that in preparing *it keeps a clearer colour, and clogs less than nut oil*." Subsequent writers have not noticed this discrepancy, but have continually given the preference to nut oil, on his authority in his first assertion, without further examination. In my opinion his second passage is decisively in favour of linseed oil – for that varnish must be the best, ceteris paribus [other things being equal], that is of the clearest colour and clogs the letter the least in working, two qualities essential to good Printing Ink.

Rosin

The rosin that is used in making varnish for Printing Ink is either black rosin or amber rosin, but amber rosin is the most generally employed, as being more common in the market than the other.

It is an important article in the composition of good Ink, as by melting it in the oil, when that ingredient is sufficiently boiled and burnt, the two articles combine and form a compound approximating to a natural balsam, which, perhaps, is the best varnish for Printing Ink that can be used. It prevents the oil separating from the colouring matter and staining the paper, and gives a binding quality to the Ink which prevents its smearing; and this tenacious quality may be qualified to any degree, as will be observed under the next article.

I noticed in my Observations on Fertel's method of preparing Printing Ink, where he says the turpentine after it is done is full of little grains of sand, which never mix with the varnish, but rest at the bottom of the pot, and fill up the letters of the form, that I thought they were deceived by appearances, and that the oil did not boil, otherwise it would have been completely melted by the heat of the oil; I am confirmed in this opinion by the following passage: – "Resin fuses at 276° Fahrenheit; is completely liquid at 306°, and at about 316° bubbles of gaseous matter escape, giving rise to the appearance of ebullition [boiling]. By distillation it yields empyreumatic oils [i.e., oils obtained by the decomposition of organic substances at high temperatures.]: in the first part of the process a limpid oil passes over, which rises in vapour at 300° F., and boils at 360°; but subsequently the product becomes less and less limpid, till towards the close it is very thick. This matter becomes limpid when heat is employed, and boils at about 500°F." – [Edward] *Turner's Elements* of *Chemistry, p. 723. 3d edit.* 1831.

Linseed oil requires a heat of 600° F. to raise it to the boiling point, so that it appears evident that rosin, which becomes completely liquid at 306° must entirely dissolve in boiling linseed oil, – and turpentine prepared in the manner described becomes rosin, – and that when these grains are in the varnish the oil could not have been so hot as even 306° when the rosin was mixed with it. My reason for dwelling on this point is to observe, that the varnish should not be kept on the fire at this great heat longer than is necessary to unite the rosin with the oil perfectly, otherwise it will become too strong, owing to the evaporation which would take place from the rosin.

Soap

This is a most important article in the preparation of Printing Ink, and what is surprising, it is not noticed in any of the old receipts that have been published; the Encyclopædia Britannica [1797, 3rd. ed.] is the only work I have seen that mentions it; and the use of it in England is kept a profound secret.

It may be fairly presumed, that neither Moxon, when he published the detailed account of the Dutch method of making Printing Ink, nor any of the French writers, knew the use and value of this material; and this presumption explains why the old printers were obliged to knock up their balls so often; why they were obliged to wash their forms so frequently and with hot lie; and why they directed water to be put over their Ink, to prevent it skimming over: – for the want of soap in the preparation would cause all these imperfections – without it the Ink would accumulate on the face of the types, so as to completely clog it up after a comparatively few impressions were printed; it would dry so hard on the types as to require to be frequently washed with *hot* lie to clean it, which would be attended with great trouble and delay; and would cause the Ink to skin over, which would occasion waste, and also cause picks in the form in working, that would spoil the appearance of the work and give great trouble to the workmen; and would also harden the balls in such a manner, as to make it necessary to take the pelts off and steep them every dinner time and every night when the pressmen gave over work, which was the custom when Ink was prepared without it. In fact, without soap Printing Ink at the present day could not be used. I have only reasoned on printing by means of presses; with machines, which require a weaker Ink than presses, it would be totally impossible to use it.

Its properties are – to cause the Ink to adhere uniformly to the face of the type, and to give it a complete coating with the smallest quantity; to cause the Ink to leave the face of the type clean, and attach itself to the damp paper by the action of pressure, and during the process of printing to continue to do this through innumerable impressions; also to cause the Ink to wash easily off the type; and to prevent the Ink skinning over, however long it may be kept.

For black and dark coloured Inks the best yellow or turpentine soap may be used; but it should be well dried. For light and delicate coloured Inks curd soap is preferable, which is white, and does not affect their tincts.

If too great a proportion be used, it has a tendency to render the colour unequal where a large surface is printed; to spread over the edges of the types, so as to give them a rough appearance; and to prevent the Ink drying quickly, and to set off when pressed. The proper proportion is when the Ink will work clean, without any accumulation or clogging on the surface of the types or engraving, and then the impression will be clear; if the proportion be greater, the effect just described will be produced. It thus corrects, to any extent required, the binding quality of the rosin in the varnish.

[Lynch's observations: Although soap has the qualities above stated, it can not be used, with advantage, when printing most light colors, on account of the alkali, which is one of its components, having a tendency to alter their shades.]

It appears to me that the use of this article in the preparation of Printing Ink, which is now indispensable, is a modern addition, and a great improvement; for I am persuaded both Moxon and [Jean-Michel] Papillon [in *Traité historique et pratique de la gravure en bois* (1766)] would not have omitted to mention it if they had been acquainted with its valuable properties, from the frankness and openness with which they both communicated their information, the one, in all that was connected with printing in his day; and the other, in what related to engraving on wood, and the process of printing the subjects when engraved.

Lamp Black

This article varies very much in quality, and equally so in the proportion that is required for a given quantity of Ink; so that any directions must be fallacious which do not specify the kind of lamp black to be used.

There are two kinds; *Mineral Lamp Black,* and *Vegetable Lamp Black.*

Mineral lamp black is much the heaviest, and it requires a much larger proportion of it, by weight, to make an Ink of the same consistency than it does of vegetable lamp black, and is not suitable for Ink of a fine quality; but I have found in practice that it answers very well in certain proportions for inferior Ink.

It looks blacker in the powder than the vegetable black, but is not so when mixed with the varnish. It is in general foul, having extraneous matters in it, owing, I suppose to the material from which it is made, and to the process, and also to the lowness of the price not allowing the manufacturer to be at the trouble of cleaning it.

Vegetable lamp black is much lighter than the mineral, and that which is the lightest is estimated as the best. This article varies much in the proportions that are requisite to make Ink of the same strength; I have found that that which is sold in firkins [i.e., a quarter of a barrel] takes by far the most varnish, and it is said to be the best that is made as an article of commerce. The price of this sort will allow it to be used only for fine Ink. There are still higher priced lamp blacks, which of course would be restricted to very select Inks.

If more [than] a just proportion of lamp black be used it will cause the Ink to smear, however long it may have been printed, and also set off under the bookbinder's hammer; and this effect must of consequence take place if the quantity be more than the varnish can bind: this fact shows that the thickest Inks are not always the best.

The process of making lamp black may be seen in Fertel's receipt [1723, pp. 287–289], in that translated from the Encyclopédie, and also in that from the Printer's Manual [i.e., *Manuel de l'imprimerie* (1817, pp. 19–21) ascribed to Joseph-Gaspard Gillé], a French publication. In England they line the chamber in which it is made with coarse green baize or flannel, instead of sheep's skins with the wool on, as is recommended by the French writers.

Ivory Black

Ivory Black is too heavy to be used alone as the colouring matter for black Printing Ink, but it may be used with great advantage, in a certain proportion, which may be ascertained by adding it after the Ink is made, and grinding it on the stone, taking care not to use too much at the first, for select purposes; for instance, if an engraving on wood is required to be printed in a very superior manner with black Ink, so as to produce the best effect that is possible, then ivory black, with the other ingredients necessary for the composition of fine Ink, will be found valuable. A difficulty, however, arises, of how it is to be procured, for the ivory black of commerce is not of sufficient blackness to produce this effect; and the printer will not be able to purchase an article that will answer the purpose.

The process by which this article, of the most intense blackness, may be prepared, and I have made it from this receipt, when it was as superior to the very best that could be bought as that very best was to the common ivory black of commerce, I shall now describe.

Provide a crucible, of a size proportioned to the quantity of black that may be required, and fill it with small pieces of ivory, which may be procured at table-knife cutlers, and are sold by the pound; the finest grained ivory I have observed makes the best black; close the top of the crucible with a cover that fits close, and that will bear a strong heat, or, in lieu of such a cover, close it with well-tempered clay; then place it in the middle of a hot fire, where every part of the crucible may be exposed to as equal a heat as possible, and let it remain till it is burnt to a charcoal to the centre; it should then be taken out of the fire and suffered to cool gradually. When the ivory is taken out of the crucible, it will be found that the outside of those pieces next to the sides will be burnt too much, and will be white, but the inside of them and that in the middle of the crucible will be of the most intense blackness. As the different pieces may vary in the intensity of the blackness, the most perfect should be picked out, any whiteness or discoloration on the outside be scraped off, and that selected reduced to a powder, when an article the most perfectly black that perhaps it is possible to make will be produced.

If it should happen to be wanted in a situation where a crucible could not conveniently be procured, enveloping the pieces of ivory with clay, and burning it as above described, will produce the same effect.

Prussian Blue

This article used sparingly greatly improves Printing Ink, by giving it a greater depth of colour; but if the due proportion be exceeded it gives the Ink a coldish appearance. The best will be found to be the cheapest, as it goes further and produces a better tone than the common. It does not affect the working of black Ink, either in the smoothness or clearness of the impression, but it requires a great deal of grinding to make it fine.

Indigo

This article produces the same effect as prussian blue, and may be substituted for it; or equal quantities of both may be used, which mixture, I think, produces a blacker Ink than when used separately. I am aware of the evils arising occasionally from the mixing of colours, but I have not perceived any bad effects from these two colours being used together in Printing Ink. I have not observed that indigo any more than prussian blue affects the Ink in its quality of working well.

Indian Red

To give a rich tone to black Printing Ink, and to take away the cold appearance of the black when prussian blue and indigo are used, some additional colouring matter is necessary; and I have found that Indian red has answered the purpose remarkably well: it possesses a depth of colour of a purplish reddish-brown, which with prussian blue or indigo adds considerably to the intensity and richness of appearance of the Ink. It works free and clean, and the price of it is moderate.

Carmine or lake might perhaps produce a superior effect, but their high price precludes their use; and besides the lake of commerce does not possess sufficient depth of colour to give a richness of appearance to an intensely black Ink. This I shall notice when I come to treat of coloured Printing Inks [see pp. 514–515 in Reading 18.1], and give a receipt for making a lake of greater intensity of colour.

Balsam of Capivi

This is a most valuable article, without any preparation, as a varnish for Printing Ink; but then it must be old, and pure. With this balsam, a due proportion of soap and colouring matter, and a stone and muller, any printer may at the moment make Ink of the most superior quality without any risk, and with very little trouble; the knowledge of which he may find of great service when he has any thing to print in a peculiarly neat manner.

It may not be improper to mention, to avoid disappointment, that I never purchased any balsam of capivi at an apothecary's shop that I could use as a varnish for Printing Ink: it was always thin and weak, and would not work clean; and the same complaint has been made to me by others who have used it on my recommendation. That which I purchased at Mr. Allen's, Plough Court, Lombard Street, London, never failed me; it was always of the same consistence, uniformly appearing to be the genuine balsam improved by age.

In the second volume of [Arthur] Aikin's Chemistry [i.e., *A Dictionary of Chemistry and Mineralogy*, 1807, p. 274], Article RESIN, is the following account of it.

> Balsam of Capivi or Copaiba is a clear yellowish resinous juice, about the consistence of thin treacle [British term for molasses], which flows in considerable quantity from incisions made in the bark of a large tree of South America, the *Copaifera Officinalis*.
>
> This balsam has a very agreeable smell and a pungent bitterish taste. It grows stiffer by long keeping, but never concretes into a solid. It dissolves totally in alcohol. When distilled with water it yields nearly half its weight of essential oil, and a brittle inodorous resin is left. It appears therefore to be a natural combination, simply of resin and essential oil.

This natural balsam possessing such valuable properties as a varnish in the preparation of Printing Ink, appears to point out to us that the next best composition for a varnish for this purpose, is that which approaches the nearest to it in quality; and our present varnish, when properly prepared, seems to approximate sufficiently near to answer every necessary purpose.

[Lynch's observations: It will often avoid disappointment if the printer will remember that the article sold by the druggists as balsam of copaiva is generally so much adulterated that it is of no value as a varnish for making printing-ink – being thin and weak, when it should be strong and viscid. – Editor's note: Copaiva is another spelling of *copaiba*.]

Canada Balsam

This is also a natural balsam, and may be useful to a certain extent in the preparation of Printing Ink, but not so generally as balsam of capivi, as its properties are a little varied. It is much thicker, and dries sooner, than that balsam, which properties would prevent its being adopted alone as a varnish; but for a strong Ink, a small proportion may, perhaps, be mixed with balsam of capivi to advantage, and also with the regular varnish.

These natural balsams have so little colour that they do not affect the Inks whose tincts are light and delicate, and they also dry slowly, on which account there is no danger of the Ink made with them, skimming over. This property, whatever opinions may be held to the contrary, is an advantage; for smearing is not attributable to this cause, but to too great a quantity of Ink being used, and that Ink containing too great a proportion of colouring matter, and also not being impressed on the paper with a sufficient power to fix it firmly on the surface, and this deficiency of power obliging the workmen to use a greater quantity to produce the desired colour: but, when the materials are duly proportioned, it requires only a very small portion of Ink to coat the surface of the type, and when that Ink is firmly impressed on the paper by means of sufficient power exerted by the press or machine, the impression will not smear when it is just printed, in the usual way of handling it. Master printers are anxious at the present day to procure an Ink that will dry immediately, but if this property were given to it, they would be again disappointed, for the Ink would work foul, and the workmen would neither be able to produce good work, nor to proceed with despatch, as the form would require to be washed frequently, as was the case before soap was used – in short, I hold that it is impossible to produce an Ink that will dry very quickly and also work clean to enable the pressman to proceed with his usual quickness.

I use the word machine, as implying cylindrical printing, with steam as the moving power generally, in contradistinction to press, which is worked by manual labour.

Implements

It is necessary to have an iron boiler, of a capacity to contain at least double the quantity of oil that is meant to be boiled; as I would never venture to make varnish with the boiler more than half full of oil, on account of the risk incurred of its rising and boiling over the top; in fact, one third full would be safer, and cause the oil to be more manageable in case of an accident.

The iron boiler must have three feet, and may be set on three bricks, to raise the bottom from the ground, so as to enable the fire to burn, and surrounded by a circle of bricks, to keep the fuel from spreading about, and to confine the fire under the boiler; it should also have two lugs, either to suspend it over the fire by means of a bow, or to lift it off the fire by means of iron hooks when set on bricks, when it is necessary. It may be suspended over the fire by the bow with a hook at the end of a chain affixed to a triangle.

The boiler should have a cover made to fit close but not tight, so that it may be put on and taken off with facility. It should have a handle at the top, by which it may be taken off with a stick; for after remaining on the boiler some time, for the purpose of extinguishing the flame, it will be found too hot for the hand. This cover may be made either of ironplate or tinplate.

An iron spatula should be provided, to stir up the oil during the process, as well as to take out a few drops, from time to time, when it is necessary to try its consistence, and to stir it up when the rosin and soap are added; as also to mix the colouring matter with the varnish.

It will also be necessary to have an iron ladle, large in proportion to the quantity of oil boiled at one time, with a long handle, to take out a portion if the oil should rise and be in danger of running over, from having too brisk a fire, as I shall describe in treating of boiling the oil [see Reading 17.6 below]; and it will also be requisite to lade the varnish out of the boiler, when it is completed.

A stick, about a yard long, with a cleft in one end will be found useful, when the oil is in a state to burn; as by putting a piece of paper in the cleft the oil may be set fire to without any risk of burning the hands or face.

Neither should a piece of slate, a plate, a tile, or a few oyster shells be forgotten, to put a few drops of the oil on occasionally, in order to ascertain when the oil is sufficiently boiled and burnt.

Reading 17.6
On the Preparation of Black Printing Ink of Different Qualities
from *On the Preparation of Printing Ink* by William Savage (1832, pp. 124–139).

> Savage, in another part of the above-mentioned work (pp. 23–104), includes nine recipes for making black ink that he has taken from English and French printers' manuals and encyclopedias. He also comments extensively on them, evaluating their properties, as well as their density of color. In the end, he dismisses all of them, claiming – and truthfully so – that he is the "first person who has treated this subject in a practical way." He alone seems to have understood the vigorous requirements necessary to make a superior black ink.
>
> Savage reiterates the claim that it is the ink that makes the printer, and as an example immodestly describes one of his own projects, *The British Gallery of Engravings* (1807) by Edward Forster (1769–1828) for which he printed the first two-thirds of the letterpress. He is not noted, however, as the printer on the title page; this honor going to James Moyes who completed the work after Savage was forced to withdraw from the project. For the text, Savage doctored a commercial black ink made by Blackwell (see p. 504 below).
>
> For me, one of the most fascinating and impressive qualities about Savage as a person was his willingness to share normally coveted information with other printers. His generosity should have had more of an influence on nineteenth-century printing, although, I seriously doubt that he changed many minds. The narrow-mindedness he encountered in the printing community of his day existed well into the twentieth century, even among a number of eminent handpress printers.

After having thus gone through the preliminary matter which appeared to me necessary to clear the way to the subject of making Printing Ink, including the directions of those who had previously written on the subject, which the reader will perceive are of no value, but which will enable him to give them a trial if he thinks proper, I shall now proceed to give the results of my own experiments; and I feel justified in saying that I am the first person who has treated this subject in a practical way, and laid before the Public the qualities of the different articles, and the process by which Printing Inks may be prepared – from that which is proper for book work generally, to that of the finest quality – without disguise or reserve. . . .

Printing Ink for General Purposes, Superior to That Usually Sold at Two Shillings and Sixpence a Pound
Having previously described the materials, and the apparatus necessary for boiling the oil, I shall now proceed to the process of making the varnish, and afterward to preparing the Ink; taking the proportions for a small quantity that would be easily managed, and would be convenient to printers in general.

A boiler being placed upon three brickbats, and surrounded by a circle of bricks, to confine the fire, placed a little apart from each other, to admit a current of air to the fuel, put into it six quarts of linseed oil, then light a coal fire, using plenty of wood in order to make it burn briskly, and keeping it up lively and steady, but not very violent. After the oil has been some time on the fire, it begins to simmer, and small bubbles arise; it soon after has the appearance of boiling, and the bubbles increase in number; but as the oil gets hotter this appearance ceases; the bubbles disappear, and the surface becomes smooth and unruffled: after this it begins to emit smoke; it begins to boil, and it smells very strong; and if the boiling be prolonged a scum arises: it should now be carefully attended to, and frequently tried with a piece of lighted paper, to see if it will take fire, which it will not do in this state, unless the flame of the paper be carried down to the surface of the oil.

It is a considerable time before it will take fire, but after the smoke begins to arise it should be tried frequently, as it is more manageable when taken as soon as it will burn. When the vapour begins to be inflammable, it takes fire with a few flashes, which may be distinctly heard, although not seen, and these flashes immediately clear away the smoke. In a little time these flashes become stronger, may be seen, and continue flashing a short time: I would now advise that it should be taken off the fire and placed on the ground, set on fire and kept stirring with an iron spatula, which exposes fresh surfaces to the atmosphere, and keeps the flame in. This burning increases the heat of the oil, and also increases the flame, so that it will be necessary to cover it occasionally, for the purpose of extinguishing the flame, and trying its consistence. This may be done by dipping the spatula into the oil, and dropping a little on an earthen plate, &c. which will soon cool. If it do not draw out into strings, on touching it with the finger, set fire to it again, and keep repeatedly trying it, and continually stirring it up with the spatula; when it will draw into strings about half an inch long, on touching it with a finger and withdrawing it from the plate, it is burnt enough for an ink sufficiently good for book work generally; the cover should then be placed on the boiler, and the flame extinguished.

If the oil be pushed to a violent boiling heat in the first instance, without trying if it will take fire, the probability is that it will froth so much and rise up in the pot, as to take fire spontaneously by contact with the atmosphere, and become unmanageable, and baffle all attempts to extinguish it, endangering the safety of the building, if within one, and the adjacent ones, and the wasting of the oil. Under these circumstances, when they occur, a large sized ladle will be found peculiarly serviceable, as a large portion of the oil may be taken out of the pot into the cool ladle, and by taking some out and pouring it into the pot again repeatedly it will rapidly cool, and the oil may thus be saved; and if a few small pieces of soap can safely be introduced without making the oil run over the top of the boiler, it will cause the rising to subside, and thus prevent loss and danger.

I have used a wooden cover to a boiler, made to fit very close, which answered the purpose very well two or three times; but at one time, boiling the oil with a strong fire, it suddenly burst into a violent flame, which set all my endeavours to extinguish it at defiance; for it burnt so furiously, that it boiled over, set the wooden cover on fire, and the ground was covered all round the boiler, with a liquid fire, spreading in all directions in a most alarming manner. I had, as soon as the cover was put on, got it off the fire, by putting a long piece of wood through the bow, and two people lifting it on the ground; throwing water on the burning oil caused it to burn more violently, so I poured water on the ground plentifully, and surrounded the oil with it, so as to prevent the fire spreading, and it thus burnt itself out, without doing any other harm than wasting the oil. The residuum, when cold, had the appearance of Indian rubber, was very sticky and elastic, very tough, and was very difficult to cut with a knife.

I mention this circumstance more particularly, to show how necessary it is to be cautious in boiling oil; how difficult it is to extinguish it when it is burning violently; and the necessity of great care and attention in this part of the process; and that the cover should be made to fit accurately, and be always at hand; for if such an accident were to take place within a building, it must inevitably be destroyed.

When the cover is taken off again there is a great quantity of smoke, that has a powerfully disagreeable smell, and a deal of froth: when this froth has subsided by stirring it well together, six pounds weight of amber rosin, or black rosin, should be gradually put into the oil, and stirred up: if it were put in at once the effervescence would be so great, that the oil would run over the top of the boiler.

When this is done, and the rosin dissolved, which the heat of the oil will do, there should be added one pound and three quarters of dry brown or turpentine soap of the best quality, cut into slices: this also should be put in gradually and with caution, for it causes a violent ebullition, and as the soap dissolves it is thrown up to the top, and forms a kind of froth to a great extent. When all the soap is put in, and the ebullition has ceased, it may be replaced over the fire till it boil, which it will soon do, and the varnish will be completed.

While the rosin is being put in, it is advisable to keep stirring the oil with the spatula; the same when the soap is put in, and also when over the fire for the last time, that the whole may be intimately and uniformly incorporated.

Then take five ounces of the best prussian blue or indigo, or equal weights of each to the same amount, reduced to a powder, and put into an earthen pot or a tub, large enough to contain the whole quantity of Ink when all the ingredients are mixed together.

Into this vessel also put four pounds of the best mineral lamp black and three pounds and a half of good vegetable lamp black, then add the varnish, little by little, while warm, and keep stirring it well together, till the whole of the varnish is put in; the stirring of the ingredients together should be continued till they are well mixed and no lumps remain: it should then be submitted to the levigating mill or to the stone and muller, and ground to an impalpable fineness, and the Printing Ink will be fit for use.

It will be found that if the varnish be cold, when the lamp black is added, a great deal of trouble and loss of time will be occasioned by the difficulty of mixing them; but if the varnish be warm or tolerably hot they may be mixed much more readily and with comparatively little trouble.

This Ink has been compared with the Ink of commerce of a celebrated manufacturer at Five Shillings a pound, both as to working and colour, and was pronounced to be fully equal to it in both particulars.

A Fine Printing Ink Prepared from the Best Ink of Commerce

Among other fine and splendid works entrusted to me to print, was "The British Gallery of Engravings, by the Rev. Edward Forster," and I was required to execute this work at least equal, but if possible superior, to any work that had been produced in England. This was in 1807. I then found it necessary, in order to satisfy this requisition, to turn my attention seriously to the improvement of Printing Ink; for no fine Ink was to be purchased from the manufacturers, their best being comparatively of an inferior colour, and of a weak consistence. The finest printers in England had obtained their celebrity solely, in my opinion, by the superior quality of their Ink, – for there were others who possessed as good practical knowledge in the art; – and these fine printers, as they were termed, for they were few in number who had obtained this distinguished appellation, were in the habit of improving the Ink of commerce, which improvement they kept a profound secret. In this state was the art of printing when I commenced my researches, and instituted a series of experiments for the improvement of this article, the results of which are detailed in these pages.

As the basis to work upon, I took Blackwell's best Ink, for which I paid five shillings a pound; and, after repeated experiments, I made the following mixture, which I shall copy from my original Memorandum, made at the time; viz. on the 12th of July 1808....

> 1 lb. of Blackwell's Ink, at 5s. a pound.
> 1¼ oz. of the best prussian blue.
> ¼ oz. of mastich varnish.
> ½ oz. of balsam of capivi.

These ingredients were ground on a marble with a muller, till they were intimately blended and made as fine as possible; and I have never seen any Ink superior to it; in my opinion, either for colour, for producing a fine clear impression, or for working clean, for fine work.

This observation, it will be recollected, was made in 1808.

The execution of this [i.e., Forster's] and other splendid works raised the productions of my press to at least a level with the best contemporary printers; and I have had the gratification of witnessing my employers comparing my printing with that of those who had acquired the highest name, and awarding to me the superiority.[*] I thus, by perseverance, completely succeeded both as to Ink and workmanship; the latter of which was executed at a wooden press of the common construction, the platen being enlarged, so as to make it a one-pull press.

I am perfectly aware that what may be styled egotism pervades this book; but when I consider that I am laying before the public the results of my own practice and experience; that I am criticising the receipts of others; and that I am the first who has treated at any length on this subject, I feel that I could only write in the first person; for, as I am neither theorizing nor availing myself of the knowledge of others, I wish to impress upon the minds of my readers that the subject on which I am treating is one to which I have devoted a great deal of application.

Printing Ink of a Very Superior Quality, without Oil or Rosin in its Composition

After persevering in making experiments for a series of years, I at last accomplished, the object which I long had in view, of making Printing Ink of the most superior character without any oil in its composition; thus getting clear of the imperfections of inferior or adulterated oil; of over boiling or under boiling; of inaccurate proportions of rosin; and of the trouble and danger of boiling the oil.

The Ink which the following receipt is for producing, is a fine and intense black, and works as freely and clean, looking at it as a strong ink, as can well be wished for; and washes easily off the types. It received the free admiration of Messrs. Bensley and Son, who had a supply of it for their very finest work. [Editor's note: In 1817, Bensley used this ink when he printed the "first book ever printed by machinery," that is, John Elliotson's translation of Johann Friedrich Blumenbach's *The Institutions of Physiology*.] This Ink surpasses by far any that I have ever seen manufactured for sale, lying smooth on the surface of the paper – not sinking through the paper, nor tinging it in any way, – not spreading at the edges – and retaining its intense black-

---

[*] It may not be irrelevant to give the following extract from the Monthly Magazine, for 1807 [i.e., 1808], vol. 24, p. 585 [i.e., 586], which formed part of the review of the British Gallery of Engravings: – "The Letter-press of this work is in the most superb style, and rivals the celebrated Horace by [Pierre] Didot [1730–1853]. It is from the press of Mr. W. Savage of Bedfordbury, and does him the highest honour."

ness; for I have some before me that has been printed fifteen years which is unchanged, and has precisely the same appearance as when it first issued from the press.

Proportions for One Pound of Superfine Printing Ink, without Oil or Rosin

Balsam of capivi	9	oz.
Lamp black	3	oz.
Indigo or prussian blue, or, equal		
quantities of both	1¼	oz.
Indian red	¾	oz.
Turpentine soap, dry	3	oz.
	17	oz.

To be ground upon a stone with a muller to an impalpable fineness, when it will be fit for use.

The lamp black to be of the best quality; I used that which is sold in firkins. . . .

This receipt for making a Printing Ink of a very superior quality, without either oil or rosin in its composition, will I believe be found of importance to every master printer who executes fine work, or highly-finished engravings on wood, as he may prepare it himself without the least risk, and with no more trouble than would be equal to grinding a little oil paint, and thus keep a small quantity in a tin can ready for use at any time; or in case of emergency it can be prepared in half an hour.

[Lynch's observations: The objectionable smell which balsam of copaiva has may be entirely removed by putting three or four drops of kreosote in the above quantity of ink. – Editor's note: Kreosote is an alternate spelling of *creosote*, a distillation of wood-tar oil.]

[Lynch continues: The writer of this work has been informed by a person who did most of the press-work on Savage's "Decorative Printing," that the black ink used in printing the part before page 53 was made according to the above recipe; and, upon examination, he finds that the outlines of the types are more definite and the surface blacker, in that portion, than in the remainder of the volume.]

Printing Ink of a Superior Quality, the Varnish Made with Oil

Balsam of capivi having a peculiar smell, which the Ink made with it will retain for years, and becoming more powerful when held near the fire, some persons may prefer a fine strong Ink without any peculiar scent; in which case it will be necessary to boil and fire the oil to a higher degree than I have described for an Ink intended for general book work, so as to make a stronger varnish to prevent any fear whatever of the oil separating from the colouring matter and staining the paper. This varnish will of course require a small proportion more of soap to make it work well and clean. Substituting this varnish for the balsam of capivi, the receipt will stand with regard to the articles and their quantities precisely the same as the last.

There are various reasons why strong varnish is used in fine Ink for superior work: – the oil being well boiled and fired, acquires a tenacity that, when combined, with rosin, prevents its spreading and staining the paper; the form requires to be well beat with it, that the face of the type or engraving may be completely coated, which it will thus be with the least possible quantity of Ink; the surface only is thus coated, and no superfluous quantity is present to squeeze or run over the edges and disfigure the work, and an impression is obtained of the surface only of a full rich colour, which should always be the object in fine work. It acts also as a preservative to the colour of the Ink, and thus continuing unimpaired the beauty of the workmanship. . . .

[Editor's note: At this point, Savage describes his observations after having examined several examples of early incunabula, noting the freshness and brilliance of their black and red inks.]

It appears to me that the cause of this preservation of colour arose from those early printers using a stronger varnish than we do in Ink for general use; and I draw this conclusion from the appearance of the works themselves, which tends to corroborate the opinion I have just expressed in the reasons for using strong varnish for fine Ink.

Reading 17.7
Good Ink
from *The Printers' Practical Every-Day-Book* by Thomas Shaw Houghton (1841, pp. 134–135).

Without a doubt, superiority of ink has always been regarded as a distinctive and recognizable feature in the work of all the great printers from Johannes Gutenberg to William Morris (1834–1896). Houghton, like Savage, believed that ink was the defining quality in fine presswork. In this reading, Houghton holds up several pre-nineteenth-century printers as examples of excellence, lamenting the fact that the production of many printers working in the first quarter of the nineteenth century was inferior, and that the printers themselves exhibited little effort or interest in emulating their illustrious predecessors. Because of the large number of persons mentioned by Houghton below, I have not added their first names or dates; however, this information will be found in the Name Index.

[Good ink,] of all materials used in printing, is, perhaps, the most important. It must be of excellent colour. Formerly, this was deemed to consist in an exceeding dark hue, not exactly black, but black enriched with a hue of the darkest blue or purple. This gave indescribable effect to the works for which it was used, a richness, a gorgeousness, which it is impossible to describe; but the works of Baskerville and Bulmer, especially the Milton of the latter, afford the best specimens. Now, we hold perfection to consist in the intensest black, and all the resources of chemistry and the arts have been sought to attain this end. It must stand for ever; but here we have miserably failed. Compare the productions of the old printers with those of twenty years back. What a difference! The works of the Aldi [i.e., Aldus Manutius and his grandson Aldus Manutius II – Houghton uses the Latin plural of *Aldus*] and Elizevirs, of Plantinus [Plantin], Caxton, Pynson, and Grafton, preserve their colour as intense as the day they were printed; there is no yellowness or brownness, no foxiness, whilst the books of those of 1810–1820 are wretchedly discoloured. Where fine printing has been required and paid for, the modern ink is no whit inferior to the ancient. Witness the . . . works of Bulmer, Macklin, Ritchie, Bowyer, Baskerville, and others; but certain it is that the ink in general use twenty years ago was of very inferior quality. It must be perfectly mixed, and ground until it is absolutely impalpable, otherwise it will speedily clog the type and inking apparatus; it must adhere to the paper and not to the type, or it will tear off the face of the former, and clog up the latter; it must be sufficiently thick; it must keep perfectly undried when in large masses, and dry very quickly when it is distributed in thin surface. Such constitutes good ink.

Reading 17.8
Printing Inks
from *Harpel's Typograph* by Oscar Henry Harpel (1870, pp. 45–46, 233).

Toward the end of the nineteenth century, commercial inkmaking had become very sophisticated. It relied more and more on scientific and chemical analysis to make better and more specialized inks. Early in the century, the first real challenge for inkmakers was to produce inks specifically for the new printing machines. Because of their speed, they required a thinner ink, yet one that would cover well and dry fast. In addition, there were many new types of paper, such as wood-pulp newsprint and clay-impregnated art papers, for which new inks had to be formulated that would print well on these new surfaces.

Harpel was one of the first manual writers to mention aniline coloring matter, which became available as a pigment for printing inks around 1860. Definitions for the chemicals and other ingredients in this reading will be found in the Glossary/Index.

Black and [colored] inks, as well as the varnishes, and other preparations used for tempering, reducing, drying, and brightening them as needed, should be matters of grave consideration. Formerly it was considered a part of the knowledge of a complete pressman to understand how to mix the inks he used. But the manufacture of printing inks, etc., has now become a distinct branch of business, employing great chemical and other scientific intelligences. Without entering into all the minutiæ of ink making, we will give a brief list of some of the most important agents employed in doing so.

The ingredients of ordinary good printing inks, – except some of those containing [aniline] coloring matter, in which are employed shellac, alcohol, turpentine, kreosote, glycerine, and other [fugitive] agents, – are principally burnt linseed oil (called varnish), resinous matter, small quantities of soap, gum arabic, Venice turpentine, balsams fir and copaiba, and pure coloring matter. For blacks the universal pigment is lampblack, obtained from a variety of sources and in many degrees of fineness. Carbonized ivory, or bone-black, when sufficiently pure and fine, also answer well. The brown tinge that is found in lampblacks is neutralized by the use of Prussian-blue, indigo, etc. . . .

In the choice of printing inks due regard should be paid not only to their depth of color and working qualities, but to their adaptability to the various kinds of paper, etc. to be printed with them. The grades of black inks now offered to printers by manufacturers are so numerous, and vary so much in quality and price, that it will require not only an experienced judgment in their selection as to quality, but some knowledge of their proper consistency and other necessary properties, according to price.

As a general rule, we have found that those inks which possess a bright, jet-black, satin-like lustre; that are soft and buttery to the touch, and deposite [archaic spelling of *deposit*] themselves upon the finger when they are touched softly and evenly, drawing from the main body only a short silky thread; that dry moderately fast; that distribute themselves smoothly and freely; that, when laid upon the type, print the edges and hair-lines sharply and cleanly, yet yield an abundance of rich, glossy color; and, finally, that may be washed off from the rollers or form without hard rubbing; are always good and reliable, according to their grades, in every sort of weather.

Inks that possess dirty or gritty sediment; that are oily and offensive in odor; that are stringy or gummy; that print dirtily and cling tenaciously to everything they touch, yet dry very slowly; are to be guarded against and prevented from ever entering a press room if possible.

Inks that clog up type, and distribute badly over the rollers when the latter are in good order, and do not wash off readily from the forms by means of good potash ley, should always and at once be discarded.

In the more costly grades of black inks one would suppose that few or none of the defects noticeable in the common qualities should be found. But price does not always secure the best qualities in an ink, although the best ingredients and most careful labor may have been used to make an article that cannot be afforded for less money than is asked for it. Nevertheless, for the want of proper proportions, or the addition or absence of something, the ink may not print well. It is harsh and raw, or dreggy [with sediment], or does not dry for a long time, and in all probability "sets off," which is the worst fault in the eyes of a painstaking and capable pressman.

A well-made ink will offset but little in ordinary cases. Very glossy, hard-surfaced papers or card-boards are liable to soil easily with most inks, unless preventatives are used . . . [Editor's note: Harpel (ibid., p. 234) says that these papers and boards "should be laid out thinly upon a drying rack," or that "slip-sheets of thin, cheap paper" should be placed "between the printed sheets."] But really fine printing qualities cannot exist in any ink that smears and offsets on surfaces not highly polished.

A good way to ascertain the relative fineness and difference of color in black inks of various grades, when more extended experiments are not convenient, is to spread them quite thinly with a small palette-knife [**Fig. 17.1** on p. 487] on the surface of a clean ink-stone, one against another, and then press a sheet of calendered paper upon them with the hand. Hang this up over night where the air can act upon the adhering inks, and the following morning will show very obviously their difference. These hints apply as well to colored inks.

[Aniline] colors, which fade easily, should not be employed except on the most ephemeral work. They are very showy, but ought not to be used on important work intended for preservation. . . .

When colored inks are dull, tough, dry, or work badly, they may be softened, improved, and brightened by using different articles. Here are recipes for making some of the best:

A Liquid for Brightening Common Qualities of Black or Colored Inks
[Damar] Varnish 1 ounce; Balsam Fir ½ ounce; Oil Bergamot 25 drops; Balsam Capaiba 35 drops; Kreosote 10 drops; Copal Varnish 50 drops. Use in small quantities.

This has been sold for some time under a variety of names, such as "Indispensable," "Pre-requisite," etc.

The whites of fresh eggs are also brighteners of colored inks; but they must be applied a little at a time, as they dry very hard, and are apt to take away the suction of rollers if used for any extended period.

A Good Reducing Dryer
Brown's (genuine) Japan. Use in small quantities.

Hardening Gloss for Inks
Gum Arabic dissolved in Alcohol or a weak dilution of Oxalic Acid. Use in small quantities, and mix with the ink as the latter is consumed[.]

Reading 17.9
The Care of Inks
from *The Practical Printer* by Henry Gold Bishop (1889, p. 118).

> Since inks were expensive, it is not surprising to find that some manual writers found space to include instructions for the care of inks. Bishop warns against the wasteful practice of opening a fresh can of ink when there is still some ink left in a previously opened can. In order to keep the ink from drying up, he suggests pasting a strip of paper around the lid edge to keep the can air-tight. Today, various types of adhesive tapes are used to seal the cans; and some printing inks, like rubber-base ones, are also available in tubes with plungers.

Inks should also have much more care bestowed upon them than they usually get, and should be kept in cupboards where dust cannot reach them. Lids ought always to be kept on the cans that are not in constant use and a strip of paper should be pasted around the part where they open, just as it is when first received from the ink manufacture. It is impossible to estimate the immense amount of loss occasioned by leaving ink cans and barrels lying about the pressroom with no covering over them – allowing dust and other matters to fall into them *ad libitum* [freely]. Not only is the ink affected thereby, but the particles of dust are carried onto the face of the form, and the type or cuts are injured thereby. Many a valuable cut has become covered with "pin-hole" spots from this cause, and many a font of delicate-faced type has been destroyed in the same way.

Where ink has been standing unused for a length of time, it is a good plan, before using, to turn it all out onto a slab and well mix with an ink-knife.

Pressmen should always make sure that a former can of ink has really been all used up before opening a fresh one, as the neglect of this precaution results in having several cans of the same ink in use at the same time. A good plan is to see that the empty can is thrown away or otherwise disposed of before opening a new one.

Plate 22. Horse-drawn wagon with a handpress in an acorn frame, 1876. The *St. Paul Dispatch* set up this printing press on a wagon to print facsimiles of the Declaration of Independence during a Fourth of July parade. (Courtesy of Minnesota Historical Society.)

CHAPTER EIGHTEEN
Colored Ink

The first book to be printed with colored inks was a Latin Psalter issued by Johann Fust (ca. 1400–1466) and Peter Schöffer (ca. 1425–ca. 1502) at Mainz in 1457. The text was printed in black and red, and the 292 two-color initials along with their arabesque backgrounds were printed in red and blue or red and gray. Adding color to the printed page was just another conscious effort on the part of early printers to imitate the manuscript codex, including its use of rubricated and illuminated embellishments.

This chapter addresses the materials and implements for making colored inks. Chapter 22 discusses the various methods for printing texts in multiple colors. Information regarding printing illustrations in color will be found in Chapter 24. Colored inks were frequently used in job printing; therefore, it was imperative that these printers – as well as any others who specialized in color work – be knowledgeable about the pigments and the procedures for making them. Colored inks were also much more difficult to make than black, which was made from fine smoke soot or pulverized charcoal. The pigments for colored inks were hard and coarse and often difficult to grind.

Prior to Savage's *Practical Hints on Decorative Printing* (1822), very few printers had been able to successfully produce color prints using multiple blocks. Ten years later, he published *On the Preparation of Printing Ink* (1832), which was the first printers' manual devoted entirely to making inks. Another early reference work on color theory, *The Principles of Harmony and Contrast of Colours* (1854) – an English translation by Charles Martel of *De la loi du contraste simultané des couleurs* (1839) by Michel Eugène Chevreul – is mentioned by both Harpel (1870, p. 235) and Southward (1900, vol. II, pp. 13, 14, 172). Later in the century, three other manuals played an important role in helping printers select and use colored inks in decorative or ornamental printing. They are Frederick Noble's *The Principles and Practice of Colour Printing Stated and Explained* (1881) and John Franklin Earhart's *The Color Printer* (1892) and his *The Harmonizer* (1897).

Unfortunately, throughout the nineteenth century, the meanings of certain terms related to colored inks varied from writer to writer and from country to country. Four such terms – *tones, tints, hues,* and *shades* – will be found in the following readings. In most cases, their significance will be clear within the context of the writer's discussion. Southward (1900, vol. II, pp. 6–7) defines them thus:

> *Tones*, degrees of density, such as light and dark green;
> *Tints*, admixtures with white;
> *Hues*, admixtures with other colors, such as red-violet;
> *Shades*, admixtures with black.

He says, "It is common enough to speak of hues and shades and of tones and tints as almost synonymous and interchangeable; yet their respective meanings are distinct, and a confusion in the signification attached to them leads sometimes to very inconvenient mistakes." To add to the confusion, in Moxon's time, *tinct*, the archaic spelling of *tint*, was also the generic term for *color*.

Definitions for the chemicals and other inkmaking ingredients in the following readings will be found in the Glossary/Index.

Reading 18.1

On Coloured Printing Inks

.from *On the Preparation of Printing Ink* by William Savage (1832, pp. 140–158).

Savage describes the various pigments that were available for making colored printing inks in his day. Aniline dyes, which were frequently used in ink making later in the century, were not introduced until the 1860s. Lynch (1859, pp. 187–197) reprinted this reading in his manual, adding his own comments to Savage's text. Lynch's observations have been inserted between brackets at the points where they appear in his text.

Colored inks had a short shelf life. Savage, like most manual writers, recommended mixing up small amounts of colored inks as needed. Lynch (1859, p. 175) also notes that it is uneconomical to procure "cans of different colors, when an ounce of each is not required."

Curiously, Savage includes only one recipe for colored inks – a red lake – in this section of his book; it is given below on pp. 514–515. He was the first to mention reducing colors in pure varnish to make transparent tints. The use of transparent tints meant that one color could overlap another to produce a third color. Prior to Savage's transparent varnish tints, tints were obtained by adding lead white to the base color, which had certain undesirable consequences since it was not permanent and with time had a tendency to darken if exposed to air. Lynch, on p. 519 below, suggests using oxide of zinc, also known as *zinc white* instead of lead white. Tints made with zinc and lead whites are opaque.

With the increased fashion for multicolor printing in the nineteenth century, especially for such items as posting bills, circulars, and other ephemeral pieces, the printer had to give some serious thought to the problem of fleeting or fugitive colors when selecting his inks. In addition, some colored inks would seep through the paper and stain its backside. This may not have been a detriment when printing individual color prints that were usually seen only from the front, but it became worrisome when prints were bound into books since the stain could also migrate to the adjacent pages of text and spoil them as well.

Savage was a fervent advocate of adding soap to ink, claiming that it made the inks work free and clean. He lamented the secrecy that surrounded the use of soap in ink manufacture. Even though soap appears in many recipes for both black and colored inks, and was added to stiff inks to make them more pliable, little was written about it as an ingredient in ink prior to Savage's experiments with it.

In one of printing history's little oddities, Lynch recommends on p. 517 below, steeping Prussian blue pigment in urine to facilitate grinding it. Urine was also used to soften the pelt of balls; see p. 534 in Reading 19.2.

I come now to a portion of my subject that invariably baffled all Printing Ink makers and printers who attempted any letterpress in colours, where the workmanship was required to be of good quality, until my work on "Decorative Printing" was published, which caused a great revolution in this department of the art.

I know of two instances which occurred before that period, where two printers in London, eminent for their skill and abilities, were completely baffled, and could not print some subjects in a brown Ink, to meet the authors wishes, to their great disappointment, and the printers mortification; the difficulty has been removed by the appearance of that work; but as the number printed was small, and the work expensive, it is not generally in the hands of printers.

It will be found that different colours will require different proportions of soap ground up with them, to cause them to work free and clean; and the utility and absolute necessity of this article in Printing Ink having been kept a profound secret by the few persons who manufactured the article for sale, and were interested in keeping the secret, prevented any great competition; and also prevented many ingenious printers from ornamenting their productions with colours, as the varnish which is sold was found not to be sufficient of itself to make even vermilion, the colour most commonly used, to work clean, and beyond this there was no resource; for self interest locked up closely the only known remedy.

[Lynch's observations: Although Mr. Savage recommends the use of soap in the preparation of printing-inks, still it must be evident to any person who gives the subject a moment's consideration, that its application to this purpose will have a bad effect, on account of the non-drying oil which it always contains, it being absurd to burn the oil to get rid of its greasy principle, and afterward to add the same thing in a far worse form. The way to obviate this is simple: to add the alkali, in its pure state, to the varnish, using bicarbonate of ammonia for the light and bicarbonate of soda for the deeper colors. The quantity of either article used, should be about one-tenth of the amount of soap recommended for a given amount of ink.]

[Lynch continues: During the manufacture and printing of light-colored inks, care should be taken that no metal, which is easily oxidized, such as iron or copper, comes in contact with them, because it will deaden the appearance of the color. For this reason a metal spatula should not be used while the ink is on the stone; neither should type-metal nor copper be employed to make an impression from. As an illustration of this, let the pressman take an electrotype-plate and pull an impression of it with the finest red ink he can make or procure, and he will find that the color will be nearer to a brown than to a red. The best thing to do in such a case is, to use a wooden block on which the design has been engraved. Type-metal may be used for the ordinary kinds of work, as it is less liable than copper to affect the color; but, if it should be necessary, at any time, to use the latter metal, a thin coating of silver should be deposited on it by the galvanic process, as the red or any other light color is less affected by this than by the inferior metals.]

Another reason for this deficiency of decorating the productions of the printing press by its own powers; appears to me to proceed from the general want of knowledge among printers and Printing Ink makers of colours and their application to imitating works of art by means of the press; and this formed an additional shackle which required to be broken.

I have seen coloured Inks offered for sale with high-sounding pretensions, which betrayed a complete ignorance of the subject on the part of the preparer: for instance the blue was made from prussian blue; and all the lighter shades were produced by the addition of white lead, in smaller or larger proportions according to the shade required: now I have found in practice that mixing white with any colour to produce a lighter tinct [archaic spelling of *tint*] invariably deadens the colour and destroys its liveliness and brilliancy, when it comes under the pressure of the platen; and it is a notorious fact that white lead is not a permanent white, but on the contrary, for the metal revives by exposure, and changes to a black hue; and I have some proofs by me of engravings on wood that were touched by the artist with white lead, as directions to the engraver, that have the appearance of being daubed with palish writing ink, owing to the revivification of the metal.

These Inks also skinned over after standing a few days, similar to oil paint, owing to a want of soap in their composition; the preparer of them being evidently ignorant of the necessity of its presence to cause the Inks to work clean. The result was that the Inks dried up and could not be used.

This is one among others that I have witnessed of the complete failures that have taken place in consequence of following the directions given by [André-François Le] Breton, [Jean-Michel] Papillon, and those who have ignorantly republished their receipts for making Printing Ink with undeserved commendation, without having taken the trouble of ascertaining their merits or demerits.

I would advise printers to have in readiness a small marble slab and a small muller, with some good Printing Ink varnish; they may thus immediately prepare a coloured Printing Ink when wanted with little trouble or inconvenience, and of any colour or tinct that is required, by reference to the following list; and if they find any Ink accumulate on the face of the type so as to clog it up and prevent it working clean, a little soap rubbed into the Ink with the muller will immediately remedy the defect. I would recommend curd soap for this purpose, for being white it will not affect the colour where a delicate tinct is required.

When a light washy tinct is required, I would strongly impress on the printer not to reduce the colour by the admixture of any white with it, which will take away all its liveliness, and produce dullness; but to thin it with varnish to the point required; to beat the subject with very little Ink; and to apply a very strong pressure, by which means any tinct may be produced that the colour is capable of, still retaining all its spirit: –

I have found in practice, that, whatever varnish may be used, some colours sink through the paper and stain the back of it more than others; this is owing to the solubility of the colouring matter in the varnish, which thus penetrates through the paper. It is therefore advisable in imitating drawings to avoid such colours as much as possible, and where it is not possible, to print on India paper, and mount them; for where it happens it disfigures them greatly, whether they are bound in a book or preserved in a portfolio. It is a curious fact that this action does not take place in thin white India paper, the back remaining unaffected.

After having premised thus much, I shall now proceed to enumerate the different colours that may be used for Printing Ink, describe their properties and the manner of preparing them, and add some observations that may be useful to those who have work to execute in colours.

Red

The best contrast with Red is Green.

Carmine. – This is a more brilliant colour than lake, and possesses more depth; it is readily ground into a fine Ink. I should strongly recommend balsam of capivi [also known as *copaiba*] to be used as a varnish when carmine is employed as a Printing Ink, on account of its paleness, as I should be afraid of the deeper shade of printing ink varnish deteriorating its brightness. Carmine is too expensive to be used as a Printing Ink except for very particular purposes. I have been accustomed to pay for the best two guineas an ounce.

Lake. – There are two sorts of lake in commerce – crimson lake and purple lake; the crimson lake is the richest colour, and is to be preferred, for a purplish tinge may easily be given to it when required, but the crimson tone could not be given to the purple lake. It is easily reduced to a fine Ink with the muller; it works clean, and does not require more soap than varnish contains. It is a colour that does not possess much depth.

As it may be necessary sometimes to use this colour of a deeper tone than that which the lake of commerce possesses, I think I shall be doing a service by giving a receipt, which has not, to my knowledge been published before, for making a very superior lake, of a much more powerful colour than can be purchased.

Take one ounce of the best cochineal, powder it, and boil it in one quart of water, till the colouring matter is extracted; then let the cochineal subside, and pour the liquid into another vessel; when cold, pour into this decoction gradually some muriat of tin, and keep stirring it; the muriat of tin immediately changes the decoction into a most beautiful colour; be cautious in the first instance of not putting in too much of the muriat of tin: let it subside, and if the supernatant liquor be nearly colourless, there is a sufficient quantity of the muriat of tin. If it still retains any considerable portion of colouring matter, a small quantity more must be added, but I would not advise so much as to precipitate every portion of the colour in the supernatant liquor; when this is done, add a little powdered alum, and assist its dissolution by occasionally stirring. Let it subside, then pour off the greatest part of the liquor, and wash the colour well in three or four waters; this is done by adding a considerable portion of the purest water you can obtain, stirring it up well each time, and when the colour has subsided pouring as much water off as you can without disturbing the colour; as the colour subsides, keep pouring off the water; by this process the colour is divested of the acid in the muriat of tin; then dry the precipitate gradually with as little heat and dust as possible, and a lake will be produced far deeper in colour and superior to any that can be purchased in the market – in fact it may be termed a fine carmine.

During the process of making it the addition of salt of tartar will give it a purple tinge.

Vermilion. – This colour is generally employed as the colouring matter for red Ink that is used for jobs of a neater appearance than common, and for title lines in books. Its properties and appearance vary much in different specimens. Chinese vermilion is estimated to be the best, and it is the brightest. It requires a large proportion of soap ground up with it to make it work clean, and Chinese vermilion more than the vermilion of commerce; but the exact proportion can only be ascertained at the press side when using it, as different specimens require different proportions: if it does not leave the type clean after a few impressions, but begins to accumulate and clog the face, a little more soap should be rubbed in; if the surface of the type be left clean, but the Ink spreads over the edges, there is too much soap in it, and a little more colour and varnish should be added; by attending to these suggestions, red Ink formed with vermilion may be made to work as clean and well as black Ink, as I have repeatedly experienced in my own practice.

Preceding writers on this subject have recommended the addition of lake to vermilion, for the purpose of producing a brighter colour than vermilion alone would produce; but I have invariably found that instead of brightening it injured both the colours, and produced a brick-dust dull effect. A much brighter red will be produced by taking Chinese vermilion and adding a small portion of chromate of lead. But the greatest improver of a colour is a good contrast. This colour is apt to turn black by exposure to the atmosphere.

Red Lead. – This article is inferior to vermilion, but is much used in posting bills, where cheapness is required; it may also be found useful where a variety is wanted of a paler colour. It requires a greater proportion of soap than is in the varnish, to cause it to work clean. It soon changes colour, and turns black.

Indian Red. – This colour is of a deep reddish brown with a purplish cast; it is tedious to grind it smooth, being hard and refractory under the muller, but when ground to the proper fineness it makes a good Ink of a rich tone, and works well. It is valuable in its combinations with other colours, both in mixture and contrast, as well as in its unadulterated state. It is capable of much intensity, and would, in my opinion, be superior in many instances to vermilion for effect, and would prove a good variety for jobs, titles, head lines, &c. The colour is permanent.

Venetian Red. – This colour is easily ground into a smooth Ink, and does not require much more soap than varnish generally contains. It makes a red Ink not of much intensity, but not without its value, as affording a variety of colour at but little expense.

Rose Pink. – This is a very cheap colour, and its cheapness may induce some printers to try it where economy is requisite; but except they succeed better than ever I was able to do, they will lose the colour, the varnish, and their time; for I have tried it in every way that I could think of, and I could never make it work clean, nor even make decent work with it. The result is, that I pronounce it to be a worthless colour for Printing Ink. It is also a very fleeting colour. I only mention it as a caution to prevent disappointment.

Orange

The best contrast with Orange is Blue.

Orange Chromate of Lead. – This variety makes decidedly the best orange coloured Ink. It is ground smooth with very little trouble, and forms a good working Ink of a brilliant hue, and capable of producing a most showy effect when happily contrasted with other colours.

Orange Lead. – This is a paler but warmer colour than red lead, and may be useful as a variety in large bills where economy in the price of the Ink is necessary. It requires an additional quantity of soap to what is contained in the varnish. It is by no means a permanent colour. None of the preparations of lead are to be depended on, as they all change colour.

Burnt Terra di Sienna. – This is a useful article where a warm yellow tint is required, or to shade yellows with. It works clear and clean, but requires an additional portion of soap. It is a permanent colour, and makes a smooth Ink; but it must be remembered that as this is a transparent colour rather than a body colour, its use is more appropriate in imitations of drawings or ornamental productions than with types.

Yellow

The best contrast with Yellow is Purple.

Chromate of Lead. – This is the brightest yellow as a body colour that is yet known. It is easily ground into a fine Printing Ink, and it works freely and well, and requires little or no addition of soap beyond what is contained in the varnish. There are different shades of this article, from a pale yellow to an orange colour. This colour united with indigo makes a powerful green; with prussian blue a brighter, but less intense; with Antwerp blue a brilliant green; all of them working well. It must always be kept in memory that the purest yellow, that is, that yellow which has least of the orange tinge, will produce by far the brightest green.

Indian Yellow. – It is a transparent colour; and will be useful in glazing, and where a rich mellow tone is required in imitating a coloured drawing of a landscape.

Gall Stone. – It is a transparent yellow of a peculiar warm tinct, and will be found useful in glazing rich mellow tones in landscapes. It is a concretion taken from the gall-bladder of cattle that are slaughtered; and the great supply is obtained from the government yards. It is apt to fly [fade].

Gamboge. – Although a bright yellow as a water colour, yet gamboge used as a Printing Ink possesses no merit, except in imitating drawings, when it may be used as a light washy tint where much effect is not wanted; but for a full yellow it will not answer. The colour stands well.

King's Yellow. –This is by no means a bright colour, and it has besides a disagreeable smell; yet it was the only article used where yellow Printing Ink was required till I introduced chromate of lead as the colouring matter, which is so much superior that king's yellow is entirely superseded. Does not stand.

Patent Yellow. – This is a colour that will not be of much use as a Printing Ink, possessing little body and that of a dull hue. Where bright tints are required it is worthless.

Roman Ochre. – It possesses a deeper tone than yellow ochre, with which it may be used as a shade in representing stone buildings, and in foregrounds of landscapes. It is dearer than yellow ochre, but the latter article may be easily brought to the same shade by burning.

Yellow Ochre. – In the representation of stone buildings, yellow ochre will be found a useful colour. It is easily ground into a fine Ink. It is dull, but stands well.

Green
The best contrast with Green is Red.

Verdigrise. – This article makes an Ink of a bright green colour with a very slight bluish tinge, which may be useful in large bills, where variety, show, and effect are required for temporary purposes; but care should be taken that the verdigrise be of a good quality. It does not form a good working Ink; in fact it would be almost impossible to produce an even surface, though when seen at a distance it produces a dashing effect. It is a very fleeting colour, and on these accounts unfit for general purposes.

Green. – Green Ink may be made with an admixture of blue and yellow, and the choice of the materials must depend on the shade and tinct of green that is wanted. Prussian blue and chromate of lead make a good rich green; indigo and the same yellow a deeper duller colour; Antwerp blue with it forms a brilliant and rich green; and thus greens of every hue may be formed with different blues and different yellows. It is necessary to observe that the purest yellow chromate of lead must be selected if a bright green be required; for that which is of an orange or reddish tint will invariably produce a dull green colour. The colour of any green Ink may be deadened by the addition of a little lake.

Blue
The best contrast with Blue is Orange.

Indigo. – This substance is a deep blue, but does not possess much brightness; it is a powerful colour, and may be used as a shade to prussian blue, for when it is printed upon that colour it appears like a deep blue black. It requires a great deal of grinding to make a smooth Ink. It is a cold but permanent colour.

Prussian Blue. – This is a deep bright colour, and makes a good Ink for large bills where variety is wanted for the sake of effect, and also to form deep greens. It requires a great deal of grinding to make a fine Ink, and an addition of soap to the varnish to make it work well and clean. This blue is far superior to either indigo or Antwerp blue, – being free from their greenish tinct, – in the composition of the various shades of peach, violet, and plum colours, and purple.

[Lynch's observations: Prussian-blue being of a hard gritty character, is not easily dissolved by the varnish; but, if it be steeped in urine, until it ceases to be acted upon, which will happen in between three and five minutes' time, it can be ground into a printing-ink as easily as chrome-yellow or any other color of that kind.]

Light Prussian Blue. – When this article is procured of a good quality, it forms an Ink of a bright blue, and of a lighter tint than prussian blue, as its name implies. It makes a good Ink as a variety in large bills; and for other purposes where the colour is suitable. It may be distinguished from Antwerp blue by not having the green tinge which always identifies that colour.

Antwerp Blue. – This is a bright light blue colour with a slight tinge of green; it forms a good Ink, works clean and well, and is easily ground to a proper degree of fineness; and makes a good contrast where a lively appearance is required: I have already said that it produces when mixed with chrome yellow a green of great brilliancy.

Cobalt Blue. – In the powder this is a most beautiful and rich blue, but when made into an Ink it loses all its brilliancy under the platen and produces a dull colour that is of little worth.

[Lynch's observations: Ultramarine. – Since Mr. Savage's work was published, the above-named color has been manufactured by chemical means (Editor's note: Lynch is referring here to aniline dyes), and the price has become nominal to what it was formerly; consequently it is now much used as the coloring-matter when a fine light blue ink is wanted. It is one of the hardest colors known, under the muller; and, for this reason, no pains should be spared in grinding it to an impalpable fineness. It is a permanent color.]

Purple

The best contrast with Purple is Yellow.

Purple Inks of different shades and tincts may be made by grinding together carmine, or lake, (purple lake for this purpose is the best,) with prussian blue. Indigo or Antwerp blue produce a far inferior colour. . . .

Brown

Bistre. – Bistre forms a useful brown, in the ground, in trunks of trees, and in shades. It is an obstinate colour under the muller, and requires a great deal of grinding to make a smooth Ink. [John Baptist] Jackson [1701–1780] used it extensively in his large Scripture prints which he copied from the pictures of the old masters in the churches in Italy, and engraved on wood, on blocks *en suite*. It is prepared from the soot of chimneys in which wood has been burnt, and well washed. It stands well.

Raw Umber. – This is not so warm a brown as burnt umber, but is more of an earthy colour; and is useful in foregrounds of pictures and as a shade, and in many other cases. It stands well.

Burnt Umber. – This is browner than either bistre or raw umber, and is useful by itself as well as to mix with other colours where a lively tone is not required. It works well, has more intensity than bistre, and is permanent.

Sepia. – This is a colour that is much used in water colour drawings in preference to Indian ink; possessing more richness and depth than that article. This brown has a tinct peculiarly its own, which cannot be successfully imitated by a compound colour. It makes a good working Ink, and may be used with advantage and effect both in the imitation of drawings, and as a variety where black is not required.

Brown. – In addition to bistre, raw umber, burnt umber, and Venetian red, deep and rich browns may be compounded of other colours far superior to any of these: – vermilion and black Printing Ink make a very good brown, which can be varied to any tinct that may be wanted; lake and burnt umber make a peculiarly rich brown; but the richest that I have ever seen in a Printing Ink, and I am not aware that any person but myself has formed it, may be made of lake prepared according to the receipt given in this chapter under the article *Lake*, Indian red, a small proportion of indigo, it being a powerful colour, and a little chromate of lead. For finely executed engravings on wood I think this brown Ink, when the different articles are well proportioned, produces a superior effect to the best black Ink, for richness and delicacy.

Prussiate of Copper. – This is a rich brown in oil painting, but the pressure of the platen destroys all its richness; and as a Printing Ink it becomes an inferior dull brown.

I am convinced by the result of innumerable experiments made during my long practice in this department of the art of printing, that every colour that is applicable to oil painting may be used as a Printing Ink; but it will be found that the great pressure applied in the process has the effect of making the colour duller than it would be in painting, either in oil colours or water colours.

[Lynch's observations: It will be seen, by an examination of the paragraphs quoted from Mr. Savage, in this chapter, that he is not in favor of using white to lighten the color, when it is necessary to print a tint-block or any work of that kind. The reason he assigns is, that white-lead, the article used generally, would become darkened by exposure to the air, and spoil the color of the tint. But, if the coloring-matter be mixed with varnish until the required shade is attained, there is a likelihood of the varnish spreading, if it should be thin, or remaining on the surface of the paper without drying, and being liable to become smutted by handling, if too thick. When it is required to make an ink of this kind, it would be better, instead of thinning the color with varnish, as he recommends, to use oxide of zinc, which, when pure, is as permanent as any color used in making printing-inks. This article, like the other colors, is often adulterated, which can be easily ascertained if any work in which it has been used be exposed a few minutes to a stream of sulphuretted-hydrogen, when, should the color not be pure, it will become dull and darkened.]

Reading 18.2
Mixing and Grinding Colors with Vanish
from *Typographia* by Thomas F. Adams (1837, p. 308–309).

Adams appropriated Stower's (1808, pp. 369–370) text, adding to it only a brief mention of rollers. The application and care of colored inks had their own requisites. Printing with them demanded much more attention than was needed for printing with black ink alone. Colored inks dried faster on the type and rollers, as well as on the ink slab and in the can. This meant that both the type and rollers had to be washed or cleaned frequently. The best colored inks were made from pigments that were ground perfectly smooth into a fine powder.

In the last line of this reading, Adams reminds his readers of the old adage from Moxon (1683, p. 331) that "The fittest Colours therefore for Printing, are such as are of the lightest Body and the Brightest Colour."

Varnish is the common menstruum [vehicle] adopted for all colors in printing. Red is the color generally used with black. Vermillion, with a small portion of lake, produces a beautiful red, which should be well ground with a muller on a marble slab, till it be perfectly smooth. If it be in the smallest degree gritty, it clogs the form, and consequently produces a thick and imperfect impression; no pains should therefore be spared to render it perfectly smooth; it may then be made to work as clear and free from picks as black. A cheaper red, but not so brilliant, may be prepared with orange mineral, rose pink, and red lead. The Prussian blue makes also an excellent color, and will require a good deal of time and labor to make it perfectly smooth. It is also ground with the best varnish, but made considerably thicker by allowing a greater portion of color with the same quantity of varnish, than the red; it will then work clear and free from picks. As this color dries rather rapidly, the rollers or balls will require to be frequently washed.

Other colors may be made, viz. lake and indian red, which produce a deep red; verditure and indigo, for blues; orpiment, pink, yellow ochre, for yellows; verdigris and green verditure, for green, &c. All these colors should be ground with soft varnish, being in themselves dryers, or they will so choke up the form, as to require it to be frequently washed, as well as dry and harden the rollers, and so render them useless.

In working the above colors there will be a great deal of difficulty unless they are ground perfectly smooth; too much care and labor cannot therefore be bestowed upon them.

The best colors for printing, are those of the lightest body and brightest color.

Reading 18.3

Coloured Inks

from *Practical Printing* by John Southward (1882, pp. 513–522).

By the 1880s, as Southward points out, there was an abundance of commercially made colored inks available to the printer; however, every printer needed to know how to make his own, especially if a specific color was needed on short notice, since most printing offices did not keep large quantities of any color other than red on hand. Southward makes a distinction between *dry colors* and *dusting colors*. The former are used as pigments for making colored inks; the latter are powders that are dusted over a varnished or inked impression similar to the bronzing process described in Reading 23.6 on p. 643. He also emphasizes the importance of matching the consistency of the ink to the type of work to be printed.

In modern color theory, *shades* are colors to which black has been added and *tints* are those to which white has been added. Most nineteenth-century manual writers used both terms interchangeably. However, Southward gives very specific instructions below for making shades and tints. For shades, the black ink is always added, a little at a time, to the colored ink; for tints, the colored ink is gradually added, in small quantities, to the white or tint base. When making hues, that is, mixing two colored inks together, the smaller quantity of color should be added to the larger quantity regardless of the color's intensity. It is important to remember that not all pigments weigh the same, which means that the percentage of varnish will vary with each pigment.

Southward includes a few helpful hints for printers. Among them, he suggests adding fresh egg whites to brighten colors. Unlike Lynch, on p. 517 in Reading 18.1, Southward recommends grinding very hard pigments in turpentine instead of urine. If cheap ink is too weak, it can be stiffened by adding some of a better quality to it; and if the printed impression is too light, it can be touched up by dusting it with dry color. He also mentions using benzine to remove stubborn colored inks from type.

The amount of color work produced in a large printing office can be imagined from the following remark that Southward makes at the end of this reading, "One person grinding can supply a hand-press in full work."

167. Although nearly every kind of coloured ink is now manufactured on a large scale by those who devote their entire attention and a special plant to the matter, and the printer may obtain from such firms nearly all the ink be requires, at a lower price, and perhaps of a better quality, than if he made it for himself, we yet think it desirable to give our readers some practical instructions on the processes of coloured ink making – partly in order that, on an emergency, they may be independent of external aid, and partly because those who know how a thing is made generally have a more intelligent idea how it ought to be used.

Materials Required. – The printer provides himself with the following – a marble slab . . . a muller, of marble or stone; and a palette knife. The materials required for making the inks are – (1) the varnish; (2) the colours, or "dry colours," as they are called. They must not be confused with "dusting" colours, however.

Dry Colours are those intended to be mixed with varnish, and the ink thus prepared is used like ordinary black ink.

Dusting Colours are in powder. The forme is printed in an invisible or "white" varnish, and these colours are dusted over it with a broad hair-brush, a clean hare's foot, or a little wool. The colours adhere to the paper only where it is coated with varnish, and when the latter is well dried the superfluous powder is brushed off.

We will [now] describe the use of dry colours … The raw colours may be purchased from the drysalters [dealers in chemical products] or oilmen. Several of the printing material dealers, however, supply colours specially prepared for printers' use. They ought to be of the best quality. The "printers' varnish"* may be had from the ink-makers.

Coloured inks should always be mixed on a slate or marble slab, with a stone or glass muller, and never upon an iron or other metallic table. This slab must, before beginning to mix, be thoroughly clean, and perfectly free from the slightest soil or trace of other inks.

No more ink should be mixed at a time than is required for the job in hand.

The colours are generally in various-sized lumps, which must be well ground on the slab by the use of the muller. Even the powder received from the oilman must be carefully ground in this way. Everything depends upon the grinding. If the smallest lumps are left, they will spoil the ink, clog the type, change the colour, and destroy the appearance of the job.

Small colour-grinding mills are now manufactured at a low cost, which will be found very useful and economical by the printer who has frequently to make up coloured ink, but the muller and slab will be quite sufficient for all practical purposes if patience is used, and cleanliness observed, and the grinding done thoroughly.

Next, mix up the colour with the varnish, by using the palette-knife. The requisite consistency is attained by gradually adding more powder. The same rules that apply to black ink are applicable to coloured ink in this respect. A large, heavy job, such as a placard, will require thin ink, while a card or a wood engraving will require a thick ink. The quantity of varnish used, of course, determines the consistency of the ink.

Some of the tints which are exceedingly light require an admixture of some white powder to make the ink thick enough for printing the required job. Whiting is suitable for thin colours, and dry flake white for the heavier ones. Either must be added in the process of mixing.

If two colours are to be mixed together, the darker tint should be first mixed with the varnish, and the lighter one added, in small quantities, gradually. Thus, if the colour be a dark green, the blue should be mixed up first, and the yellow added; but if it be a very light green, then the yellow should be first applied, and the blue added afterwards.

The best method of mixing cannot be very clearly described in words, but will soon be found out after a little practice. The material should be scraped into a corner of the slab, and a very small portion of it spread with the palette-knife, and well ground with the muller, until no specks or lumps appear. This portion should then be scraped up and placed in another corner. White lead especially requires this treatment, as it will be found that every little lump when crushed will produce a white streak upon the slab.

Lumps of any kind, in any sort of ink, not only clog the type, but alter the tint; hence, they must be very carefully avoided. The aim of the grinder should be to get a quite impalpable powder.

When the mixture is complete, it ought to be brayed out with the muller, and not with the ordinary brayer,† as any remains of black ink that might be upon it would spoil the ink colour.

---

* Common painters' varnish is unsuitable for printing, but it may be used on an emergency if a quarter of a pound of soft soap be added to every pound of colour.

† We may here remark that for working coloured inks the roller should not be too hard, and should possess a good "lug." When a roller is required to be used for another colour, it must be carefully cleaned with turpentine, and a moist sponge afterwards passed over its face to remove the turpentine. It must be kept until it is thoroughly dry before being used. The ink must be well distributed, and the forme rolled with extra care.

168. We will now enumerate the different colours, and the inks which may be made from them, pointing out the special recommendations or defects of the several substances: –

For *Red.* – Orange lead, vermilion, burnt sienna, Venetian red, Indian red, lake vermilion, orange mineral, rose pink, and red lead.

Yellow. – Yellow ochre, gamboge, and chromate of lead.

Blue. – Cobalt, Prussian blue, indigo, Antwerp blue, Chinese blue, French ultramarine, and German ultramarine.

Green. – Verdigris, green verditer, and mixtures of blue and yellow.

Purple. – A mixture of those used for red and blue.

Deep Brown. – Burnt umber, with a little scarlet lake.

Pale Brown. – Burnt sienna; a rich shade is obtained by using a little scarlet lake.

Lilac. – Cobalt blue, with a little carmine added.

Pale Lilac. – Carmine, with a little cobalt blue.

Amber. – Pale chrome, with a little carmine.

Pink. – Carmine or crimson lake.

169. *Shades and Tints.* – A bright red is best got from pale vermilion, with a little carmine added; dark vermilion, when mixed with the varnish, produces a dull colour. Orange lead and vermilion ground together also produce a very bright tint, and one that is more permanent than an entire vermilion colour. The pigments are dear; when a cheap job is in hand, orange mineral, rose pink, and red lead may be used.

Yellow. – Of the materials named, the chromate of lead makes the brightest colour. If a dull yellow be wanted, yellow ochre may be used; it grinds easily, and is very cheap.

Blue. – Indigo is excessively dark, and requires a good deal of trouble to lighten it. It makes a fine showy colour where brightness is not required. Prussian blue is useful, but it must be thoroughly ground. It dries very quickly, hence the roller must be frequently cleaned. Antwerp blue is very light, and easily worked. Chinese blue is also available. As already said, the shade may be varied with flake white. There is this objection to Prussian, Antwerp, and Chinese blues, that they are hard to grind, and likely to turn greenish with the varnish when used thin. A bright blue is also to be got from cobalt, or French or German ultramarine. This is cheap, easily ground, and works freely. Lime blue may also be used.

Green. – Any of the yellows and blues may be mixed. Gamboge, a transparent colour, is very useful in mixture with Prussian blue; or chromate of lead and Prussian blue may be used. The varnish, having a yellow tinge, has an effect upon the mixture, and should be taken into account. With a slight quantity of Antwerp blue, varnish in itself will produce a decidedly greenish tint. Verdigris and green verditer also give greens. If Chinese blue be added to pale chrome, it gives a good green, and any shade can be obtained by increasing or diminishing either colour. *Emerald* green is got by mixing pale chrome with a little Chinese blue, and then adding the emerald until the tint is satisfactory.

Brown. – Sepia gives a nice tint, and burnt umber a very hot tint. Raw umber gives a brighter brown, bistre a brighter still.

Neutral tints are obtained by mixing Prussian blue, lake, and gamboge.

In using painters' colours, it is advisable to avoid as much as possible the heavy ones.

Several of the painters' technical handbooks would be found very useful to the printer in mixing up his colours. . . .

Pink. – Carmine or crimson lake gives a good, bright pink.

Scarlet. – Carmine with a little deep vermilion gives a very deep colour.

Black Ink. – The following is a recipe for a black ink to be used with various coloured inks; but ink of a quality better than the printer can make can, as a rule, be had from the manufacturers: Burn ordinary lamp-black in an old frying-pan. Ivory black, with a little indigo or Prussian blue, and Indian red, is well adapted for woodcuts. When the latter are printed with it on a toned ground, it gives the appearance of an Indian ink drawing or an etching. Vegetable and drop black are easy to work, and require no preparation, hence are useful when the ink is wanted in a hurry.

170. *General Hints on Making Coloured Inks.* – The following is a recipe for making varnish: Four ounces of boiled linseed oil, and six ounces of yellow resin; or four ounces of neat's foot oil, and six ounces of yellow resin. Mix in a small earthenware pipkin [cooking pot] over a slow fire. The varnish is ready for use when cold. Care mast be taken that it does not boil over. The materials must be of the best quality, otherwise the varnish will be a failure. Clear resin is, perhaps, preferable. Let the oil stand until all the floating particles of fat have settled at the bottom and top of it. A small quantity of litharge expedites this process.

The printer must constantly bear in mind that some colours require less oil in the varnish than others, or he may make ink that will be practically useless.

Light-weighing colours, such as Chinese, Prussian, and Antwerp blues, chromes, patent yellow, rose pink, emerald green, and Brunswick green, suit such jobs as broadsides best when there is little of the resin in them.

Red, for most purposes, is certainly best bought from the ink-makers; but for the finer kinds, especially tints required to show up other tints, it is best when made up by the printer, as wanted.

For fine work, a little Canada balsam of the consistency of honey makes a good varnish, of great purity. The coarser but similar Venice turpentine may also be used with effect when time is precious and purity of tint not indispensable. A little soft soap may be added to the Venice turpentine.

If the work be coarse, and varnish not at hand, a little oak varnish and soft soap form a good substitute.

Savage gives as ingredients for varnish balsam of copaiba and Castile soap. It is an excellent mixture, and works clear, if well ground, but is most objectionable on account of its smell.

"Fine printers' varnish" is nearly the same as the burnt linseed oil used by ink manufacturers; hence, the latter may be used instead of varnish. The oil may be burnt and boiled in the open air, and the addition of a little resin is no detriment.

Prussian and Chinese blue, which are only variations of the same material, form excellent tints to work in contrast with or on vermilion, where it looks black. Covers of magazines are sometimes done in this way with only two colours, yet a variety of tints are obtained.

Vermilion, being a very dear colour, is often adulterated, and there are numerous substances passed off for it.

Red lead is a heavy colour, of a light orange tint, and is very difficult to work, even on the commonest paper.

Venetian and Indian reds are really reddish brown on paper.

Good rose pink is a cheap substitute for the crimson and scarlet lakes, which, however, should be used for good work. It may be lightened with any good light red, which will give it body.

Patent yellow is the cheapest material for yellow ink. Its tint may be heightened by a little orange chrome or a little vermilion. It forms a good foundation for green ink when mixed with Prussian or Chinese blue.

The Brunswick greens, of three shades, are very useful for making green ink, and comparatively cheap.

Brown ink is really red and black. Burnt umber, Spanish brown, and vandyke brown are useful, but the last is hard to grind.

Purple and mauve inks are better bought.

Where colour is very hard to grind with varnish on a muller and slab, it may be first ground with turpentine and then mixed with the varnish. The turpentine quickly evaporates, and leaves the colour thoroughly mixed and ready to work.

Common qualities of coloured inks may be brightened by using the whites of fresh eggs, but they must be applied a little at a time, as they dry very hard, and are apt to take away the suction of rollers if used for any lengthened period.

171. A hardening gloss for inks may be made by dissolving gum arabic in alcohol or a weak solution of oxalic acid. This mixture should be used in small quantities, and mixed with the ink while it is being consumed.

A bronze or changeable hue may be given to inks with the following mixture: Gum shellac, 1½ lb., dissolved in one gallon of 95 per cent. alcohol or Cologne spirits for 24 hours. Then add 14 ounces aniline red. Let it stand for a few hours longer, when it will be ready for use. When added to a good blue, black, or other dark inks, it gives them a rich hue. The quantity used must be very carefully apportioned.

In mixing the materials, add the dark colour sparingly at first, for it is easier to add more, if necessary, than to take away, as in making a dark colour lighter you increase its bulk considerably.

If a colour when worked does not look as full as you could wish, dust it over while wet with its own dry colour, which will wonderfully intensify it, using cotton wool or a camel's hair brush for the purpose, just as you would in bronzing.

If it is necessary to keep coloured inks, the best way of preserving them, so that they shall be workable after standing some time, is to pour a little colza oil on the top and securely close the vessel containing them. This oil will not generally rob the ink of any of its colour, and even if it is not all poured off afterwards, its presence can do no great harm. Some colours will not keep at all, and others deposit at the bottom of the can almost all their solid ingredients. It is not easy to alter this, but colza oil will at least prevent the surface skinning over.

Red and some other coloured inks are often found to become so hard in a few weeks after the can has been opened that the knife can scarcely be got into them, and they cannot be got to work at all. Oil, varnish, and turpentine are of no use in such a case; the remedy is paraffin oil mixed well up with the old ink. Indeed, many prefer paraffin oil rather than boiled oil or turps [short for *turpentine*] for thinning down both black and coloured inks.

Benzine is a powerful chemical preparation, which may be used to remove coloured inks when lye and turpentine fail[.] It should, however, not be used after dark, as it is very inflammable, and it should be kept out of doors if possible.

When ink is put out for a job, the pressman must consider not only whether it is the right shade, but whether it is too stiff or heavy, or too thin, and liable to spread on the impression. Every office should be provided with at least two kinds of varnish, as well as boiled oil, thick and thin. If the ink, from the effects of cold or any other cause, is too heavy to distribute freely, add the varnish or oil – the varnish for fine, the oil, for ordinary work – in small quantities, and mix well until the ink is reduced to a proper consistency for distribution, without making it so thin as to deaden the colour or cause it to spread.

If a thin, cheap ink is being used, and it is found to be too thin for the work in hand, a small quantity of a better quality of ink should be mixed with it, to give the necessary body to produce a clean impression.

Besides the two questions named above, the pressman must also consider whether his ink will dry fast enough, or will dry too fast. Every printer should have a good drying preparation. In using it, the pressman must exercise his judgment in regard to the extent to which the ink should be mixed with it, as no rule can be given to suit all contingencies which may arise where such dryers are necessary. The following are recipes for dryers: –

No. 1. – *For Fine Job Work:* Damar varnish, 6 ounces; bergamot, 2 drachms [archaic spelling of *drams*]; balsam copaiba, 2 drachms; balsam of fir, 3 ounces; creosote, 1 drachm; copal varnish, 1 drachm. Where an extra quick dryer is desired, add a few drops of dissolved gum arabic to the ink after it has been mixed with the dryer. In all cases mix well with the ink before applying to the rollers.

No. 2. – *For News and Poster Ink:* Spirits of turpentine, 1 quart; balsam copaiba, 6 ounces. Add a sufficient quantity to the ink to thin it to a proper consistency for working. This compound is one of the best that can be used as a dryer, and to brighten coloured inks and make them work free.

No. 3. – *A Quick Dryer:* Japanese gold size, 2 parts; copal varnish, 1 part; elber powder (radix carlinæ, carline thistle), 2 parts. Incorporate well together with a small spatula, and use in quantities to suit the consistency of the ink employed and the rapidity with which it is desired to dry. The usual proportion is a small teaspoonful of the dryer to about an ounce of average good ink.

The following is translated from [Henri] Fournier's new work on printing [*Traité de la typographie* (1870)], and is written by the late M. [Henri Rodolphe Gustave] Silbermann, of Strasburg, the most eminent typographic colour printer on the Continent: –

The principal labour in printing in colours is the preparation of the coloured inks, for those made beforehand are frequently defective, some drying too soon, and becoming pasty.

The choice of colours is of the greatest importance, as upon it depends success. It is necessary to select those of the first quality, and avoid those of a heavy specific gravity, as they are too easily precipitated, and do not combine completely with the varnish.

The varnish is also an essential matter. It must be pure, limpid, and of a strength proportionate to the work contemplated and the colour employed. Frequently strong varnishes must be avoided, as they render the ink too thick, and should be used only as mordants. For ordinary work very weak varnishes are suitable, and for more delicate impressions the varnish should be increased in strength. That made of linseed seems to be the most useful.

The inks are made by successively amalgamating the colours with the varnish, by grinding with a stone upon marble. The quality of the ink depends much upon this labour, which should be a work of patience, so as to combine the colours and varnish into a consistence equal to that of the fine black inks; for it is with other colours as with black – the better and more thoroughly the colour is mixed with the varnish, the better the ink.

When a large number of impressions are to be produced the colours should be prepared in proportion to the requirements, for some condense so rapidly that they soon become unserviceable, especially when the varnish is strong. One person grinding can supply a hand-press in full work.

Reading 18. 4
White Ink
from *The Principles and Practices of Colour Printing Stated and Explained* by Frederick Noble (1881) as edited and reprinted in *Practical Printing* by John Southward (1900, vol. II, pp. 21–23).

White ink was generally used only for making tints of darker colors. It was rarely used as a printing ink by itself. The color white was usually expressed, as it is today, by the absence of ink – in other words, by the color of the paper. Printing text in white, also referred to as *drop out* or *reverse printing*, was achieved by engraving the text on a block whose surface would later be printed as a solid area.

Noble discusses the pros and cons of lead (flake) and zinc whites. He also warns the printer that inks mixed with white will turn to powder and rub off when printed on some enamel papers.

The text below was revised by Noble in 1893–1894. Southward included it in his manual, noting that it is "now slightly edited."

A good white ink is difficult, if not impossible, to obtain, and yet it is constantly required by colour printers. The substance almost universally used for this purpose is an oxidised carbonate of lead, and is known to the trade as "flake white." It may be bought of any colour merchant at about 6d. per lb. Flake white has one radical defect – it oxidises on exposure to the air; therefore coloured inks made of it and exposed are liable to lose their brilliancy and purity. This is, no doubt, a serious defect, but, taking things as they are, this pigment is on the whole the best and almost the only one available for the printer. Other pigments have been tried, but they have all, for one reason or another, resulted in failure. Amongst the most successful, however, is zinc white, which possesses the inestimable advantage of being absolutely permanent in character, and in this respect is superior to flake white; but it is inferior to the latter in body, and when made into printing ink it does not cover well, which is an insuperable objection to its use.

In preparing a white ink for printing everything depends upon the most thorough cleanliness. If it be intended to make it in large quantities for use at machine, the flake white should be thoroughly pulverised in a large stone mortar, mixed stiff in the middle or thin varnish, and passed two or three times through a colour-grinding mill. It does not require much grinding, as it is an extremely soft pigment. It is not recommended to make a larger quantity of this ink than will be required for speedy use, as it rapidly skins and spoils. This ink may be reduced for the purposes of machine printing with thin varnish. No driers need be used with it.

It not unfrequently happens that the white ink forms the largest proportion of many pale coloured inks, and being from its nature very heavy, it separates from the varnish and does not clear the forme. When this occurs at press the printer may generally correct it by always grinding in strong varnish, which holds the colour together and causes it to adhere to the paper. At machine, however, it is, as a rule, not possible to use strong varnish. We must therefore meet the difficulty in another way. A little white curd soap, perfectly dry, should be scraped in very fine shreds and thoroughly ground up with the colour. We are now speaking of inks which have white for their basis. It is necessary to caution the reader that it is not safe to use soap with all coloured inks, for the alkali it contains changes the character of some colours and militates against the drying of all. In colours which are compounded of flake white it may he used in small quantity with safety; it is not recommended as a constant ingredient of this ink, but as an expedient for removing a difficulty which frequently occurs with it. In using flake white ink at press the most satisfactory way of dealing with it for fine work is to grind it stiff in strong varnish and use it in that condition; but as this makes an ink which gives the pressman very hard work to distribute, especially if he is dealing with a large solid block, it may be desirable in this and similar cases to thin the ink, and if the colour does not clear the forme, a small quantity of soap – a piece the size of a Spanish nut to half a pound of ink – may be added.

This white ink is also the basis of all the body tints used in printing. Tints made with white are opaque colours, but this opacity depends upon the amount of white (or body) the tinted ink contains. If, for example, we wished to make a pale blue opaque tint – the blue inclining more to green than to purple – the white should be mixed very stiff and Chinese blue added; if we wished to preserve the same tone but required a semi-opaque effect, some varnish would be added to the first colour; if the same tone were required, but it was necessary that the tint should be a transparent one, the white would he omitted altogether and the colouring matter only mixed with the varnish.

The considerations which govern the question when we are to use white and when varnish for our tints must be determined by the character and incidence of the particular work to be dealt with. In certain circumstances white is indubitably beneficial; for instance, suppose we are dealing with a set of blocks which shall represent a design with a black background and a gold outline as a last working. We will assume, for the sake of argument, that the intermediate colours of the ornaments consist of two pale tints, a pale blue and a bright pink, and one positive colour, carmine. The tints in this case should be made with white. In the first place, there is no objection to an opaque colour, while it is an all-important consideration that the inks of which the tints are made should dry hard and dry quickly: this attribute white possesses – we are, therefore, right to use it.

When white is used as a body tint on some sorts of enamel [paper] it frequently exhibits the vices peculiar to lead driers – it powders, and the colour may be wiped off in a dust. The only way to deal with this is to use the strongest litho varnish, or, if it be admissible, change the body colour for a transparent one.

Plate 23. Printing office with three Columbian presses, ca. 1850. The roller boy is charging the roller on an inking appliance. Note that the paper bank is placed at an angle to the pressman who is pulling the bar. (Source: Wood & Sharwoods leaflet, n.d., courtesy St. Bride Printing Library.)

CHAPTER NINETEEN

Balls, Rollers, and Inking Apparatus

Prior to the nineteenth century, all forms were inked with balls, also known as *pelt balls* (see Reading 19.2 on p. 533) or *skin balls* (see Reading 19.3 on p. 535), depending on the material that was used to cover them. About 1809, Benjamin Foster introduced his composition-covered canvas balls to British printers. This new material, generally known as *composition*, or *compo* for short, was basically a mixture of little more than glue and molasses. Compo balls are discussed in Readings 19.4 and 19.5 on p. 536. Mason (1823, facing the title page) has a tipped-in, claret-colored advertising leaf for Foster's composition balls and rollers.

The transition from balls to composition rollers – which were originally called *cylinders* – took place over a number of decades beginning in the 1820s. Even after composition rollers had become readily accessible, they were not immediately or universally accepted by all pressmen, many of whom actively resisted the change.

Johnson (1824, vol. II, p. 532) was the first manual writer to describe composition rollers, although from his brief comments on p. 540 in Reading 19.8, it is doubtful that he ever used them. Up to 1835, every apprentice and journeyman in England still had to learn how to ink with balls; on the other hand, in America, rollers – from their first appearance in the mid-1820s – quickly established themselves as the inking implement of choice; balls were seldom used after 1850. Therefore, it is not surprising to find that balls were still being recommended as late as the 1840s for fine work, such as woodcuts and wood engravings, and the practice of inking with them for certain types of jobs continued well into the 1880s.

The basic tools needed for inking a form were few: the brayer, shown in **Fig. 19.4**, LEFT, on p. 532, the slice, shown in **Fig. 19.4**, RIGHT, on p. 532, and a pair of balls like the one shown in **Fig. 19.1**. The ink brayer – which should not be confused with the roller brayer in **Fig. 19.2**, RIGHT – was a round wooden muller with a flat bottom. It was used to bray or rub out ink, working it up until it was pliable enough for the balls to pick it up off the ink block, which was a three-sided shelf with a usable surface of about 9 x 13 inches. It was attached to the rear post and rail of the wooden press. Illustrations of them will be found in **Figs. 3.4** and **3.5** on pp. 105 and 106, respectively. The ink slice – which should not be confused with the galley slice illustrated in **Fig. 7.55** on p. 267 – was a metal ink knife with a small projection on each side of the handle to keep the flat edge of the knife out of the ink.

Ink balls were pelt- or skin-covered cushions resembling dabbers. They were always used in pairs. Moxon (1683, pp. 306–312) has a detailed description of their construction and how *to knock them up*, the printers' term for assembling them. Moxon's instructions were frequently repeated in the nineteenth century even though, by that time, pelts had ceased to be a viable covering material.

When the German printing press manufacturers Friedrich Gottlob Koenig and Andreas Friedrich Bauer brought the first steam-powered cylinder printing machine to England in 1812, a new system for inking the form had to be devised since balls were deemed impractical due to the configuration and potential high speed of these machines. The first rollers were leather-covered wooden cylinders. There had been earlier attempts to cover wooden cylinders with leather and skins, but all of these efforts had failed. Their biggest drawback was the seam that ran along the length of the roller at the point where the two ends of the leather were joined. Since the technology for composition balls already existed, it was only logical that the same technology could also be applied to making rollers.

Because the iron handpress did not have a built-in ink block like the wooden press did, a small table, topped with a marble slab measuring about 14 x 20 inches, was set up on the left-hand, near side of the press. This table evolved into the brayer inking table shown in **Fig. 19.17** on p. 569. Pressmen referred to both of these implements as *inking* or *ink tables*. Hansard Jr. (1851, p. 104) notes, "On the left front [i.e., near side] of the press stands the inking table. This is a table of mahogany (which is best) or iron, about four feet high and three feet four inches wide; at the back is a slightly elevated stage [ledge] with a recess at each end, in one of which is the ink, in the other stands the brayer or muller, by which the ink is spread out in a thin layer upon the front of the stage." Inking tables are illustrated in **Plates 6** and **25** on pp. 100 and 592, respectively.

Rollers were either hand-held, such as the one shown in **Fig. 19.2**, LEFT, or attached to an *inking apparatus*, the generic term for a variety of inking devices designed to be used in tandem with the iron handpress. Hand-held rollers distributed the ink over the surface of an inking table, such as the one shown in **Fig. 19.19** on pp. 571. In the 1820s, a distributing cylinder, such as the one shown in **Fig. 19.20** on p. 571, was added to the inking table in order to charge the roller manually. A small roller – called a *brayer* like the one in **Fig. 19.2**, RIGHT – replaced the wooden brayer for spreading ink out on the table or slab. Since rollers came in different lengths, an adjustable iron frame with two handles, called a *roller-handle bridge* and illustrated in **Fig. 19.3**, was used to accommodate rollers of various sizes.

Fig. 19.1. *Ink ball* – from Jacobi (1890, p. 159)

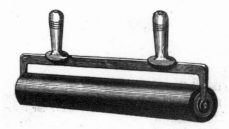

Fig. 19.2. LEFT, *Composition roller with two handles;* RIGHT, *Brayer* (composition roller with one handle) – from Jacobi (1890, pp. 158 and 159, respectively)

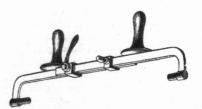

Fig. 19.3. *Adjustable roller-handle bridge* – from Jacobi (1890, p. 159)

Hansard Jr. (ibid., p. 114) notes that the traditional double-handle rollers were nicknamed "rolling-pins." This is curious because unlike lithographic rollers, letterpress rollers were not in the shape of a rolling pin.

Even though rollers were available for sale or rent from commercial firms, manual writers continued well into the twentieth century to give instructions for making them on the premises. Needless to say, the pressmen could not make them as perfect as those made in factories where the ingredients in the mixture were carefully selected and measured and the molds were precision turned. In addition, commercial rollers were better made since the liquid composition was forced up into the molds from the bottom, thus eliminating any bubbles that might occur when the composition was poured.

Because of atmospheric conditions, variant recipes were offered for casting rollers for summer, winter, and fall/spring use. As the manufacture of composition became more scientific, the ingredients also varied; for example, glycerine was added after 1854, and whiting and tar were dropped. Handpress rollers required less glue and more molasses than printing machine rollers.

Today, handpress printers seldom use composition rollers, although they are still available commercially from Tarheel Rollers in Clemmons, NC 27012. In the early 1970s I took a composition roller with me to Italy; but before I had a chance to use it, the composition, which was made of glue and molasses, mildewed, melted, and was eventually devoured by mice. Materials such as rubber and polyurethane have long since superseded composition.

There were several types of manual and automatic inking apparatus available to printers throughout the nineteenth century. Their widespread use would imply that they were employed to increase production and to reduce labor costs by eliminating the roller boy. Along with several manual writers, I have my doubts that these devices ever lived up fully to the claims made by their manufacturers, since the pressman's rhythm was seriously impaired and slowed by their complexity. For a more detailed account of them, see my introductory note to Reading 19.23 on p. 566. Inking apparatus are illustrated in **Plates 23** and **27** on pp. 528 and 632, respectively.

Colin H. Bloy has a short, but informative, chapter on ink balls, and rollers, as well as manual and automatic inking apparatus in his *A History of Printing Ink, Balls, and Rollers: 1440–1850* (1967, pp. 53–65).

Reading 19.1
Inking Accessories
from *The Printer's Grammar* by Caleb Stower (1808, pp. 336–337).

Stower describes and gives the dimensions of the ink brayer, the ink slice, the ball stocks – the foundation upon which the balls were formed – and the ball racks that held the balls when they were not in use. The ball rack was fastened to the near cheek of the wooden press. His instructions for knocking up the balls will be found in Reading 19.2 below.

Later in the same century, Ringwalt (1871, p. 220) illustrated another ink slice, or knife, shown in **Fig. 19.5**, that was used primarily for "taking ink out of kegs, casks, or tubs, and putting it on blocks, stones, or in fountains, etc." Because of its width, it probably was not used to mix inks. The modern, flexible ink knife most likely did not appear until the twentieth century; or at least, if it were known before then, it was not illustrated in any of the pre-twentieth-century printers' manuals.

The long, round-tipped printers' palette knife, shown in **Fig. 17.1** on p. 487, was used for mixing colors in the nineteenth century, and possibly even earlier. MacKellar (1878, p. 292) was the first to illustrate a printers' palette knife, although he does not mention it in his text.

The Brayer and Slice

The brayer [**Fig. 19.4**, LEFT] is . . . made of beech, and turned round on its sides, and flat on the bottom; its length, including the handle, is about seven inches long, and the bottom part about two inches and a half in diameter.

The slice [**Fig. 19.4**, RIGHT] is a small iron shovel, the broadest part about four inches, and about the eighth of an inch thick. Its length, including the handle, is about eight inches long.

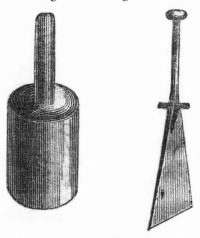

Fig. 19.4. LEFT, *Brayer* (muller); RIGHT, *Slice* (ink knife)

Fig. 19.5. *Slice* (ink knife) – from Ringwalt (1871, p. 220)

The Ball Stocks and Ball Racks

The ball stocks [**Fig. 19.6**, LEFT] are made of dry, well-seasoned elm, and turned hollow, of a conical form; their greatest diameter five inches and a quarter, and their length four inches. The handle of the stock is made of beech, four inches and a half long, and an inch in diameter.

The racks [**Fig. 19.6**, RIGHT] are also made of elm and beech, the sockets of which are elm, and the pins beech. The sockets of the first rack . . . two feet nine inches and a half from the bottom, is nine inches wide, and four and a half long; that end of it which receives the pins is one inch and a half thick, the opposite end only half an inch thick. The pins are nine inches long, and distant from each other three inches.

Fig. 19.6. LEFT, *Ball rack;* RIGHT, *Ball stock*

Reading 19.2
Knocking Up Balls
from *The Printer's Grammar* by Caleb Stower (1808, pp. 366–367).

Prior to the introduction of materials such as dressed sheepskins and composition, ink balls were covered with pelts. Pelts required a considerable amount of preparation before they could be attached to the ball stocks and a great deal more care once they were assembled since they frequently had to be cleaned or scraped during the day to keep them in optimum working order.

First, the pelts had to be degreased, and then they were softened by soaking them in urine. This was an unpleasant and nauseous task which pressmen were required to perform since each was responsible for knocking up his own balls. At night or when not otherwise in use, the balls were *capped*, which means that they were wrapped up in urine-soaked blankets and left in a sink until needed again.

Savage (1841, p. 94) mentions the rather perverse practice of "Capping a Man" which involved wrapping "one of the blankets with which the pelt balls are capped about a man's head, and tying it around his neck. This most filthy and disgusting punishment is very rarely inflicted in a press room."

Stower gives a detailed description for preparing the pelts and assembling the balls. After the pelts had been saturated in urine and rinsed in clean water, he suggests treading on them in order to extract any remaining water. The balls had to be perfectly dry or the ink would not adhere to them or transfer to the type. He explains, step-by-step, how to nail the leather pelts to the wooden ball stocks and the correct way to overlap the cardings of wool when stuffing them. The amount of wool was critical since too little would eventually cause the pelt to wrinkle, and too much would make the ball too hard. The care with which the pressman knocked up his balls had a direct effect on his performance as a beater. The only illustration in a printers' manual showing a pressman knocking up an ink ball comes from Moxon (1683); it is shown below in **Fig. 19.7.**

Fig. 19.7. *Pressman knocking up an ink ball* – from Moxon (1683, plate 30, in the section of plates following p. 394), courtesy of Rochester Institute of Technology

Johnson was the first manual writer to include an illustration of an ink ball. Hansard (1825, p. 414) describes the shape of pelt balls as having "the shape and appearance of a large round-headed mallet, such as is used by stone-masons, except that their surface is much broader and rounder." Even though Johnson's ball appears to have a flatter surface, it is very similar to Jacobi's, which is shown in **Fig. 19.1** on p. 530. The finished ball measured about seven inches in diameter. Larger balls were needed for newspaper work.

Pelts are used for this purpose, and such are chosen as have a strong grain, and the grease well worked out of them. They are purchased either wet or dry; if dry, they are put to soak in chamber-lie [urine]. One skin generally makes two proper sized balls. When the skin has soaked sufficiently, which will require about fourteen or fifteen hours, it is taken out of the lie, and *curried;* that is, by putting the skin around the currying iron, or any upright post, and taking hold of each end of it, and drawing it with as much force as possible, backwards and forwards, against the post, which discharges a good deal of the water and lime, and renders it more pliable; he then cuts the skin exactly in two, and puts them under his feet, and continues to tread them till he is unable to discover the smallest particle of water, or till it sticks to the foot in treading. The skin is then laid on a wetting board, or a vacant press stone, and stretched, by rubbing the ball stock on it, as much as possible. He then places a lining, (which is a worn-out skin, and which has been previously soaked, but not trodden), on the skin, and nails them with one nail to the ball stock; he then proceeds to lay the different cardings of the wool one upon the other, crossways, till he has sufficient for the ball; he then takes it up by the bottom corners, and grasps it into a circular form, with which he fills the ball stock, then brings the skin opposite the part already nailed, and makes that also fast with another nail. He then puts two nails immediately opposite each other between the fastenings already made, and proceeds to put the skin in plaits [folds and tucks], about an inch wide; through each plait a nail is driven; the superfluous skin should then be cut off, within half an inch of the nails. Balls are well knocked up when the wool is so placed, as to form a full even face, that every part of the skin may bear upon the letter; not rising in hillocks, or falling into dales; not having too much wool in them, for that will render them soon hard and uneasy for the pressman to work with; or too little, for that will make the skin, as the wool settles with working, soon flap, and wrap over into wrinkles, so that he cannot so well distribute the ink on his balls.

Having knocked up the balls, he dips them into the chamber-lie, and immediately scrapes them with the ball knife [usually an old table knife], in order to make them perfectly clean; he then procures a clean sheet of stout paper, and puts it on the ball, and continues rubbing and patting it till the ball is perfectly dry, which is considered in that state when it will readily take the ink on every part of it. Having thus dried the balls, he proceeds to take ink; but if he finds that scarcely any of the skin is black, they are not sufficiently dry; he then returns again to drying it with paper, or burns a piece of waste paper, and waves his ball to and fro over the flame of it [Editor's note: This procedure is called *flaring the balls*.], but so quick and cautiously that he neither scorches the leather nor dries it too much; in winter time, when a fire is at hand, he dries it gently by the fire.

If the balls are greasy, they should be frequently rubbed up with the pelt blankets, and well scraped; and dried, as before, with paper.

Reading 19.3
Knocking Up Skin Balls
from *The Printers' Guide* by Cornelius S. Van Winkle (1818, pp. 180–181).

> The use of oil-dressed sheepskins as an alternate covering material for balls was an inter-mediate step between pelt balls and composition balls. Even though Moxon (1683, p. 306) mentions sheepskin balls, it was not until the beginning of the nineteenth century that they replaced pelt balls in America. Just a few years later, skin balls would succumb to composi-tion balls (see Reading 19.4 below).
>
> Skin balls required half the labor of pelt balls and lasted longer. The skin covering was applied to the ball stock in the same manner that pelts were. Van Winkle also suggests rub-bing a little ink on the back of the skin to make it adhere better to the lining. But more importantly, skin balls eliminated many of the ills associated with pelt balls, such as the nauseous stench of urine that was used for cleaning and preserving the pelts.

Pelts were formerly used for balls, but have, within these few years, been entirely laid aside. The oil-dressed [sheep] skin has been substituted, and found to answer a much better purpose. They are got ready to knock up with less than half the labour, and last longer in working. They are not subject to putrefaction in hot weather, nor to being destroyed by maggots; consequently, printing offices are free from that nauseous stench to which they were formerly subject from the use of pelts.

The skin must be washed in clean water, and wrung dry; then stretched on a board, and a lit-tle ink rubbed on it to make the lining adhere to it; some rub oil on it, but this, by finding its way through the pores of the skin, which in this state are very open, may mix with, and injure the ink; the lining (which is generally a skin that has been wore out) is then laid smooth on the skin, and both nailed, with one nail, to the ball stock . . . [Editor's note: From here on, the procedures were the same for both pelt and skin balls (Reading 19.2 above).]

Reading 19.4
Composition Balls
from *Typographia* by John Johnson (1824, vol. II, pp. 531–532).

Johnson mentions that several printers in the early 1820s were still using pelt balls, although composition balls were more practical. When composition balls were first introduced around 1815, they were rejected by some master printers as well as many pressmen; however, by 1824, the year that Johnson's manual was published, they were in general use.

Composition balls were nothing more than a piece of canvas covered with a thin coating of composition that was then nailed to the ball stocks in the same manner as pelts. Johnson is the first manual writer to mention the ingredients used in making the composition: molasses, glue, and tar, although he does not give any proportions. Throughout the nineteenth century, the ingredients and their proportions varied slightly.

One great advantage of composition balls was their low maintenance. They could be washed with a solution of weak lye and then rinsed in clear water. Their only liability was a susceptibility to atmospheric changes, which necessitated altering the recipe seasonally.

About the year 1815, composition balls were introduced at Weybridge, by Mr. B. Foster, a compositor: upon their introduction into London they were opposed by some masters and also by many pressmen, but they gradually came into pretty general use; there are yet a few who still adhere to the old mode. These balls are made of molasses, glue, and a portion of tar, which are boiled together to a proper consistency, it is then poured upon a piece of [canvas] cloth, and when sufficiently cold is knocked up according to the rules [in Readings 19.2 on p. 533]; by this means the nuisance of the pelt pot and its attendant filth is dispensed with. Should these balls be hard, when dirty, they may be washed with a little weak lye, and rinsed with water; if soft, a little ink might be put on them, and then scraped: but the pressman must use his own judgment in this respect, because composition will vary so much from the boiling, and likewise the weather, that no decisive rule can be laid down.

Reading 19.5
Compo-Balls
from *Typographia* by Thomas Curson Hansard (1825, pp. 623–626, 628–629).

Hansard was the first manual writer to provide recipes with exact proportions for the composition, adjusting them for seasonal changes. He was also the first to mention adding Paris-white or whiting to the composition, and gives explicit instructions for making the composition, as well as detailed descriptions of the necessary tools and materials. He notes that the composition should be about a quarter of an inch thick at the center on the face of the ball.

A wide variety of glues were used; however, Hansard says that the best glue was made from parchment or vellum cuttings, which were soaked and then cooked in a double boiler. He suggests giving the inside of the canvas a coat of paint to prevent the composition from coming into contact with the wool stuffing. As an alternative, he recommends, using a separate lining similar to those used when knocking up pelt balls.

An early variation on the list of ingredients is mentioned by Timperley (1838, p. 109) who says that some "persons only use the simple glue and treacle, while others use a small quantity of isinglass [fish gelatin], or a few drops of sweet oil."

Hansard recommends using a shallow copper bowl as a mold. A quarter of a century later, his son Thomas Curson Hansard Jr. (1851, p. 121) notes "When the proper apparatus [i.e., metal mold] is wanting, small balls for wood-cuts or single pages may be made upon an earthen palette, or even upon a smooth dinner-plate."

The changes in paper technology mentioned in Chapter 16 presented serious problems for the beater since the new papers generated a considerable amount of flying lint or fuzz, also known as *flue*. This would clog the counters of the type and settle on the surface of the balls and inking table, requiring the balls to be scraped as many as four times a day.

Washing balls with turpentine would harden them; washing them with water would soften them. Turpentine mixed with water or pearl-ash lye was also used to remove ink from the balls. Composition balls – and later composition rollers – could be recycled, although frequent remeltings would impoverish the composition.

The composition (but which for shortness shall be called in future compo) consists principally of glue and molasses, or treacle. I have seen various receipts of ingredients and proportions, some possessing the recommendations which distinguish the recipes of ancient physicians; namely, a vast variety of articles with counteracting properties. But the simple prescription which my experience has proved best, is, to provide *glue* of the finest quality, made from the cuttings of parchment or vellum; fine green [sorghum] *molasses*, pure as from the sugar refiner, at least not adulterated for the bakers' or grocers' shops; and a small quantity of the substance called Paris-white [chalk],* and you will have every ingredient requisite for the compo. The proportions have been so variously stated, and so different from what I have found to be eligible, that I am wholly at a loss to account for such differences.

	Pounds of		
	Glue.	Molasses.	
One receipt which now lies before me *in print,* says	2	1	
Another, MS	2	3	
I find a mixture of	2	6	or 2 [to] 7

and about half a pound of the Paris-white, will make the compo of a superior quality to any other proportions, and will be sufficient for two demy rollers. The great disparity which appears in these receipts may perhaps be attributed to a difference in the quality of the materials, and to the mode of management....

[Compo is made in a] *melting kettle* [**Fig. 19.8**]. This must be a double vessel like a glue-kettle, so that the compo in the interior may be melted by the heat of the boiling water in the exterior. For this purpose a strong boiler may be the best or readiest thing found, into which let a tin vessel be fitted, with a flanch [archaic form of *flange*] to rest on the rim, so as to leave one or two inches clear under it. This vessel may be six or eight inches above the top of the boiler, so that the lid of the one may fit the other; and it must have a large lip for pouring out the compo.

---

* This is the carbonate of barytes, *terra ponderosa*, or ponderous earth; the most active of alkaline earths; and acts upon the animal economy as a violent poison. It is found in combination either with the sulphuric acid, forming the native sulphate of barytes, or heavy-spar[.] It is supplied from Yorkshire. It is chiefly used in adulteration of paint, giving a body almost equal to white lead. It is very difficult to be obtained pure, being often substituted with Spanish-white of the oil shops, which is nothing more than a finer kind of whitening.

Fig. 19.8. *Melting kettle*

Being thus prepared, put the glue into a little water for a few hours to soak. Pour off all the liquid, and put the glue into the inner vessel, the boiler having in it as much water as it will contain when the inner vessel is in its place. Put it on the fire and boil the water as quick as you please, the heat of which will soon cause the glue to dissolve, and evaporate part of the water. When the glue is all melted (supposing 4 lb.), add 14 lb. of the molasses, and let them be well incorporated together for at least an hour, receiving heat from the boiling water, which is a uniform degree that cannot exceed 212°. Then with a very fine sieve, mix the white powder, frequently stirring the compo. In another hour, or less, it will be fit to pour off; and when it is, take the inner vessel out of the boiler, and pour the mixture gently into the mould ...

In order to make the *compo-balls*, a mould will be required. This I have had made from a circular plate of copper nicely planished [polished], and beaten concave so as to sink in the centre about half an inch; which is turned over a wire at the circumference, and supported to a level by three little feet. Then, as the compo is not required to be more than a quarter of an inch thick in the centre of the face of the ball, I have a board made the same diameter as the mould, and convex to a quarter of an inch, in order to give the compo a shape approaching to the convexity of the ball without too much stretching its component parts. Upon this convex board I strain a square piece of coarse canvas by turning over its corners, and fastening them with a small tack or cords. Then, the compo being made hot, and the copper mould being made warm also, I pour about half-a-pound from the kettle, taking care that none of the condensed steam drops on the mould, and pressing the canvas with a half-hundred weight, let the whole cool gradually, and it will possess a face as smooth as the planished copper, the compo growing thinner and thinner from the centre towards the circumference, which contrivance renders it more convenient for plaiting when knocking up into balls. It may be adviseable to give the inside of the canvas a coat of paint, in order to prevent the compo from pressing quite through and adhering to the wool, or hair, or lining, if any should be used; or using an inner lining of finer canvas or linen.

This compo, if it possesses every desirable quality for the purpose here described, will yet be found to draw the dirt or flue from off the face of the type, and to retain it, in spite of the *distributing* on the table, with far more tenacity than inferior stuff. It will therefore be necessary to clean and scrape the ... ball, two, three, or four times a day, according to the foulness of the paper. This is best done by keeping some refuse ink on a spare table; and, covering the ... ball with a thick coat, scrape the whole off with a knife.

To wash the ... balls made with this compo, nothing more is requisite than the application of water, in cold frosty weather a little warmed, but cold as possible in warm weather, which needs only be used with the hand. Before they are worked again after washing, an hour's drying will be necessary. Sometimes, if from the effect of bad ink they show an appearance of grease, and make friars (white spots, or white-friars), a mixture of spirits of turpentine and water will be necessary; or a little pearl-ash lie. If becoming soft by a sudden change in the atmosphere, a washing in spirits of turpentine will harden them. If by a cold or dry night they are found too hard at first getting to work in the morning, a few turns at a moderate distance from the fire, or over the flame of a burning sheet of paper will be the remedy. Sometimes they will get into such a state as to require the flame of a candle to be passed over the whole face, which must be done with the greatest care and patience....

If you have old compo remaining, and find it necessary to renew either balls or rollers, a small portion of the fresh material must be incorporated with it; but, as the rules already given can alone determine the proportions requisite to make the compo harder or softer, it will not be possible to lay down the precise quantities of the respective ingredients that may in such cases be proper. The molasses, or vegetable substance, will certainly evaporate and become impoverished by frequent meltings: the glue, or animal substance, will grow harder: the earthy substance will retain its quality: but a little addition of new spar [gypsum or chalk] will be necessary to clear and bind the whole together.

Reading 19.6
Composition Balls
from *Typographia* by Thomas F. Adams (1844, p. 258).

> Adams repeated the following paragraph in each edition of his manual between 1844 and 1864. His approach to making composition balls varies from all other descriptions. First, he knocks up the ball, using the raw canvas covering, and then repeatedly dips the ball into the melted composition until a sufficient thickness of it has accumulated on the surface of the canvas. I personally find this method quite ingenious and wonder why it was not mentioned by any other writer.

Composition Balls are made [in the same manner as pelt balls], substituting instead of the skin, a cotton cloth; the ball being properly knocked up, must then be dipped into the melted composition, and held in the hand till it forms a smooth surface on the face, and is perfectly cool, after which we repeat the dipping until a sufficient thickness of composition is obtained, when it will require the same treatment laid down for rollers. [See Reading 19.9 on p. 541.]

Reading 19.7
Advantages of Composition Rollers
from *An Abridgment of Johnson's Typographia* by John Johnson, edited and with a new appendix by Thomas F. Adams (1828, pp. 310–311).

> Adams, who is clearly a proponent of composition rollers and wants to dispel certain prejudices against them, suggests that Johnson (1824, p. 684) – whose negative remarks about rollers Adams quotes below – was speaking from a lack of any practical experience with them. On the other hand, Adams does not acknowledge Johnson's praise of rollers elsewhere in his manual (see p. 540 in Reading 19.8).
>
> Adams lists three advantages that rollers have over balls: (1) they work cleaner than balls, which means that the pressman does not have to interrupt his work as often to clean the rollers and the form – in fact, they can often be worked all day without having to be washed;

(2) they require very little maintenance; and (3) they are cheaper since they waste less ink. The softness and delicacy of composition rollers also made them ideal for inking the fine hair strokes of type that were often worn down when beaten with balls.

Rollers, like most other improvements, have met with considerable opposition; yet their superiority must certainly be acknowledged by all who have become perfectly acquainted with them: but prejudice, in favour of Balls, has [deterred] many from giving the Rollers a fair trial – what we mean by a fair trial, is to study the nature of the composition, and pay particular attention to the manner of working them.

Notwithstanding the hand rollers in London turn off very handsome work, and are generally adopted, yet Mr. [John] Johnson seems to be prejudiced against them; we say *prejudiced*, and shall only quote his own words to prove it: he says . . . "with respect to the Rollers, our ideas still remain the same, having pronounced (long before we had seen them in action) that they would not execute the work equal to the Balls." From this it appears evident that Mr. Johnson did not possess a practical knowledge of the rollers; but he certainly must have been gifted with great foresight and penetration to discover the inability of a mechanical operation, *long before he had seen it in action*.

We shall now endeavor to point out a few of the advantages to which composition rollers are justly entitled: the first, and most important, is that of doing clean work; in this respect they are decidedly better than balls, as it is seldom necessary to take out picks, or clean the head lines; and a roller is frequently worked all day without the necessity of cleaning it. The next consideration is in point of cheapness, when compared with balls. The pressman will also find that they require but little attention when he has become perfectly acquainted with them. The softness and delicacy of the composition render it less liable, than balls, to injure the fine hair strokes of the letter – this consideration alone, is sufficient to warrant an experiment. The great saving of ink is also an object, worthy of attention; as it cannot penetrate the surface of the composition, there can be but very little wasted.

Reading 19.8
Rollers
from *Typographia* by John Johnson (1824, vol. II, p. 532).

> In this reading, Johnson appears to be in favor of using rollers, especially for heavy work, and notes that rollers for handpresses were first introduced to the printing trade in 1819. He says that they rapidly came into general use soon afterwards. Adams, above in Reading 19.7, implies that Johnson disapproved of rollers.

In 1814, the Times newspaper was first printed by a Steam Engine, consequently, from its being a cylindrical power, rollers were indispensably necessary; these were made of a composition of molasses, glue, and tar . . . [In] the following year the composition balls were brought into use; and in 1819, hand rollers were introduced to the notice of the profession, which very rapidly came into general use, and are likely to continue: they are manufactured of composition similar to the above, and are made in the form . . . shewn [in **Fig. 19.2**, LEFT, on p. 530]: they are excellently adapted for heavy forms, but not so much for light ones: they are likewise subject to the changes of the weather as well as the balls, and should be treated in a similar manner; but as they vary so much in the nature of the composition, we recommend the pressmen to study the best mode of treating them, as no general rule can here be laid down.

Reading 19.9
Composition Rollers
from *Typographia* by Thomas F. Adams (1837, p. 314–315).

Adams's recipe – the first to specify the amount of tar to be used in the composition – is for a roller twenty-seven inches long with a diameter of three and a half inches; its composition covering is half an inch thick. Throughout the nineteenth century, the diameters of both the roller and the core, as well as the thickness of the covering, varied slightly.

The composition is made of the following ingredients, viz. For a Medium roller,

> Three lbs. of best Glue.
> Three pints of sugar-house Molasses.
> One table-spoonful of Tar.

This is calculated for approaching cold weather, but it is necessary to reduce the quantity of molasses to one quart for summer heat; and in proportion for any intermediate temperature. The mould best calculated to receive the composition, should be made of brass, copper or iron, with the interior well polished. The above quantity of composition is intended for a roller of twenty-seven inches in length, and four inches diameter, with a wooden cylinder of three inches diameter, which will give half an inch thickness of composition. The thickness of the composition may be varied according to the size of the wooden cylinder [core].

Reading 19.10
Making Rollers
from *Typographia* by Thomas Curson Hansard (1825, pp. 622–627, 629–631).

Hansard describes the unsuccessful attempts of Charles, third Earl Stanhope, at the beginning of the nineteenth century to make *revolving cylinders* – an early term for rollers – for the iron handpress. However, by the late teens, composition rollers were quite common, due to the ease with which they could be cast in metal molds of various lengths and diameters. Hansard emphasizes the saving in money and labor that resulted from the adoption of rollers in the pressroom. He advocates their use for every type of work: for all sizes of type, for light and heavy forms, and for strong or weak ink.

Hansard illustrates a two-piece mold along with all its parts, which are shown in **Fig. 19.9**. Jacobi (1890) illustrated another mold, which is illustrated in **Fig. 19.10**; its construction varies slightly in the open and closed depictions of it. He also recommends a vertical, one-piece mold, shown in **Fig. 19.11**, for small rollers.

The late earl Stanhope, when he invented the Printing-Press which will bear his name to posterity, coupled with his object an idea of inking the forme on the press by means of a revolving cylinder; and in pursuit of this plan, spared no expense in endeavouring to find a substance with which to cover his rollers. He had the skins of every animal which he thought likely to answer the purpose, dressed by every possible process; and tried many other substances, as cloth, silk, &c. without success. The necessary seam down the whole length of the roller was the first impediment; and next the impossibility of keeping any skin or substance then known, always so soft and pliable as to receive the ink with an even coat, and communicate the same to the forme with the regularity required. All the presses of his early construction had, at each end of the table, a raised flanch, type high, for the purpose of applying his rollers; but the obstacles interposed by nature herself totally baffled and defeated his lordship's plans in this respect....

. . . The inventors of printing *machinery* soon caught the idea, and by running the composition as a coat upon wooden cylinders, produced the apparatus so long and unsuccessfully sought by lord Stanhope, and without which, no machine-printing would ever have succeeded....

As this composition has now become one of the most essential requisites of a printing-office, and as many printers may be desirous of making their own balls and *rollers* (which plain name seems to have been generally adopted for the revolving cylinder), I shall take some pains to describe such proportions of the ingredients [see Reading 19.5 on p. 536] as I have found to answer best in my work, as also the apparatus required both for balls, hand-rollers, and machinery, and the process by which the whole is manufactured....

. . . I shall state, minutely, my apparatus and process.

First, it is necessary to procure a mould very accurately made, and well finished. Mine [shown in **Fig. 19.9**] is made of brass, in two parts, adjusted to each other with rebates [rabbets], the inside being finely turned and polished, and having flanches [*a*] projecting by which the parts are screwed together by the screw and lock-burr [*b*]. To each end is also fitted a collar, *c*; and a circular plate of iron, *d* . . . is accommodated with great precision to the bore of the mould, having a projection in its centre to enter a cylinder of wood about which the compo is to attach itself, and to hold it exactly in the centre of the mould, and the other end of which is kept in a corresponding position by means of a brass piece [identified as the *brass keeper* below], *e*, to allow of the compo passing down between the interior surface of the mould and the wooden cylinder. The little projections on the sides of the mould, *f*, serve as feet to support each half in a steady position while lying upon a table or elsewhere . . . Previous to joining, the parts of the mould must be nicely cleaned and oiled; and the greatest care taken that no particle of compo, grit, or dirt, remain in the rebate. The parts being carefully placed on each other, and the wooden cylinder fixed inside, the screws must be put into their respective places in the flanches as marked, and when all is properly made tight the mould is to be set upright for receiving the stuff.

. . . A, represents the mould placed ready for receiving the compo from the kettle; B, shows the same in section; [C,] shows one-half, with the mode of fixing the core, or wood cylinder; [D,] the corresponding half; [E,] sections: the reference letters applying to each figure....

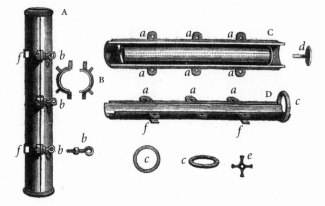

Fig. 19.9. *Roller mould.* KEY: A, mould in place to receive the compo; B, cross-section of the mould; C, one-half of the mould; D, the corresponding half; *a*, flanches; *b*, screw and lock-burr; *c*, collar; *d*, circular rim plate; *e*, brass keeper; *f*, feet. NOTE: The key letters have been reset.

Fig. 19.10. LEFT, *Two-piece mold, open;* RIGHT, *Two-piece mold, closed* – from Jacobi (1890, p. 162)

Fig. 19.11. *One-piece mold* – from Jacobi (1890, p. 161)

[When the compo is ready,] take the inner vessel out of the boiler, and pour the mixture gently into the mould through the opened brass keeper [*e*]. In about an hour, if the weather be dry and favorable, you may take the roller out of the mould; hang it in a cool, dry situation, or lay it horizontally in a rack made for the purpose, and the next day it will be sufficiently hardened for use. As there will be rather more of the compo at each end of the cylinder than would work clear of the frame in which it is to revolve, cut off from each extremity about half an inch, by encircling it with a piece of fine twine.

To keep the rollers thus made in good condition for working, a place should be chosen where the air has free circulation, without being subject to the extreme heat of the sun in Summer, or the freezing damp air in Winter: in short, in as even a temperature as possible. It will be necessary to keep a stock of more rollers than are at work; as it is frequently found, when a roller is *sick*, or greasy, or soft, or you do not know what is its ailment, that washing it clean and hanging it to rest for a time, restores it to as good a state as ever....

The cylinder upon which the compo is cast is made of alderwood, turned to a diameter of two inches; so that the coat of compo which it receives is half-an-inch. The cylinder is perforated through its centre, having a brass bush, or collar, driven into each end, through which is passed an iron rod, as an axis, with an enlarged head at one end, and tapped with a screw at the other. This axis is received in corresponding holes at the angle-turned ends of the frame, and is there secured by a nut fitted to its screw-end. To the upper bar of the frame are fixed two handles of turned wood, having considerable circular projections for keeping the handles from coming in contact with the ink upon the table [see **Fig. 19.2** LEFT on p. 530]....

[The invention of compo balls and rollers] was at once the means of getting rid of the nauseous, filthy process in the pelt-house, and rendering a press-room as free from offensive effluvia as any other part of the office. A great annual expense was also saved in skins and wool; and a vast deal of the precious time of the men. Upon the introduction of the balls I calculated that the saving to each man was half a day in a week; and I conceive that still more is saved by the rollers. But what is above every other consideration, the quality of the work is materially improved; and the labour is reduced to comparative ease by rolling over a forme instead of beating it.

It is curious to contemplate the various changes which have taken place in a press-room, as far as regards manual labour, within a very few years. Previous to the introduction of lord Stanhope's press, the *beating* was the lighter labour, and *pulling* the heavier; to the latter of which an apprentice was seldom put, except for very light-work, for the first twelve months. Then pulling became the lighter – the stronger beat, and the weaker pulled. But when the rollers were introduced, the stronger again took the bar, and the weaker rolled: and a well-grown lad was capable of taking both parts in the first month of his service. The pulling is now the only hard labour; the rolling requiring only a due degree of adroitness and attention to colour.

The rollers are found to answer for every description of work – for the largest or smallest type – the lightest or heaviest forme – all solid type, or all rule work – for the strongest or weakest ink – for black, or red, or any colour; and indeed, upon the whole, the introduction of the invention constitutes a new era in the art of printing.

Reading 19.11
Making Composition Rollers
from *The Practical Printers' Assistant* by Theodore Gazlay (1836, pp. 109, 113–120).

Just as early handpress printers had to knock up their own ink balls, it would appear from nineteenth-century printers' manuals that pressmen, who did not procure composition rollers from a commercial vendor, were also responsible for casting their own rollers. Gazlay notes that the rollers should be as long as the platen and were often referred to by the name of the format of the press, for example, folio, foolscap, super royal, imperial, etc. The thickness of Gazlay's composition covering is three-quarters of an inch. He gives a recipe for a pair of rollers twenty-nine inches long; and another, for a pair of rollers thirty-six inches long. A roller the length of the latter would have been used for posters and newspapers. It would also have been quite heavy. The composition alone for a 36-inch winter roller would have weighed around twelve pounds. That does not, of course, include the handles and frame or the wooden core and metal axle. Present-day handpress printers often place two sets of roller bearers in large forms, which allows them to ink each side of the form separately with a shorter roller.

For seasonal rollers, Gazlay gives the following proportions of molasses to be added to each pound of glue: summer, one pint; spring and fall, one and a half pints; and winter, one quart. He was the first to mention adding glycerine to the glue and molasses mixture in order to prevent the moisture in the glue from evaporating.

Gazlay also discusses how to keep rollers in good working order, the treatment of new rollers, and the maintenance of seasoned ones. There have always been makeshift remedies in printing houses; among them is one for mending rollers by melting the composition with a heated iron poker. Rollers were usually recast when they no longer functioned properly; however, it was not recommended to recast them more than twice.

He discusses washing rollers in lye with a sponge and then rinsing them in clean water. He warns about using too much water since the rollers will dissolve if they get too wet. For immediate use, he suggests applying oil by hand. Even though other manual writers also mentioned it, this practice is hard to imagine, since the pressman's hands would, as a result, be covered with ink and need to be cleaned. Fortunately, the inker did not handle the paper, which was done by the puller. Gazlay, like many of his predecessors, mentions using paper to wipe the roller clean after it has been washed with oil. I find this practice rather strange since paper could roughen up the delicate surface of the composition.

British and American printers preferred to store their rollers horizontally in cabinets in which air could circulate freely. Gazlay describes two arrangements for storing rollers in an enclosed box or closet. In the first, the rollers are stored horizontally in tiers of two or three deep; in the second, they are stored one deep. In both, he places lead-lined boxes or trays filled with water in order to keep the rollers moist. Rollers should also be stored so that they do not touch or they will stick together. Pasko (1894, p. 491) illustrates a German contrivance for storing rollers vertically (see **Fig. 19.12**). It has a metal cover that slides down over the rollers.

Composition rollers are cast in moulds from three and a fourth to three and a half inches in diameter, on wooden cylinders from one and a half to two inches in diameter, with iron journals, leaving the composition about three-fourths of an inch thick on the cylinders. The rollers should be as long as the platen of the press for which they are intended.

Moulds are made of copper, or cast-iron, type-metal, tin, and wood. Copper moulds cast whole are preferred, and are in general use. For a small roller a large sheet of tin, bent exactly circular, may answer a temporary purpose. The mould should have an iron or wooden *bottom-piece* made to fit precisely, to prevent the composition from escaping, with a hole in the centre to receive the journal of the cylinder; and a *centre-piece* to hold the journal at the top, which must slip easily into the mould; it must be scolloped to allow the composition to pass freely down into the mould. . . .

Glue

Rollers are made either of *Russian* or *American glue*, and *sugar-house*, or *thick West India molasses*.

Rollers made of Russian glue, are stronger than those made of the common American glue, and if used properly will last longer; they are best for fine book work. But, taking into consideration the numerous accidents to which rollers are liable, such as being torn, the face worn by hard washing, the surface hardened by exposure, &c., those made of American glue will, under ordinary circumstances last as long as those made of Russian, and being much cheaper, are generally used. Russian glue, however, makes the best rollers in very warm weather, or for fine work when strong ink is used.

Proportions

Different qualities of glue require more or less molasses than the ordinary proportions, which difference can only be ascertained by experiment: glue that soaks very easily, and is soft when soaked, will require less molasses than glue that soaks hard, and is firm when soaked.

The following proportions will generally be found to make rollers of the proper consistency: –

For Summer use, to each pound of glue,	1	pint of molasses.
Spring and fall use,	1½	[pints of molasses.]
Winter use,	1	quart of molasses.

Sugar-house molasses [i.e., the dregs from the sugar-refining molds], when convenient, is best.

In extreme warm weather, some glue will not require more than three-fourths of a pint to a pound, and sometimes not more than half a pint to a pound. And in very cold weather some qualities of glue will bear three pints of molasses to a pound, or even more.

Quantity of Composition

For a pair of super royal or imperial rollers, 29 inches long, 3½ inch mould, composition on cylinders ¾ inch thick,

Winter strength,	5 lbs. glue,	5 qts. mol.
Same rollers, summer strength,	7	3
spring and fall use,	6	4

For a pair of double medium or mammoth rollers, three feet in length, same size,

Winter use,	6 lbs. glue,	6 qts. mol.
Spring and fall use,	7	5
Summer use,	8	4

Soaking Glue

Place the glue in a bucket, and cover it completely with clean water.

Thick glue, the pieces of which average about *one-fifth* of an inch thick, should stand covered in water from three to five hours;[*] the water should be drained off, and the glue covered, and suffered to remain from six to twelve hours, and it will be in order for melting. Some qualities of very thick, hard glue, will require six hours soaking, or more; and some will require less than three.

Thin glue, the pieces of which are but little thicker than pasteboard, generally requires soaking in water only from twenty to thirty minutes; the water may be drained off, and it should remain covered three or four hours, and it will be in order for melting; it would be better, however, to let it remain all night covered, particularly in cold weather. Different qualities of glue of this thickness will require more or less soaking.

To ascertain if glue is sufficiently soaked, take a piece out of the water, and break it; if the water shall have penetrated one-fourth of the thickness of the glue each way, leaving one-half soaked, and one-half in the centre dry, the water should be poured off, and the glue suffered to stand the prescribed time, and it will be in good order.

The less water there is in the glue, the better, provided it will melt freely. The object of letting the glue stand after the water is drained off, is to allow the water time to penetrate to the centre of the glue, and to cause the superabundant water to evaporate from the surface. If the glue should stand in water until it was completely soaked through, there would be more water in it than is required to melt it, and the outside of the glue would be rotten, and the roller dead and *spongy*. Glue, when in order for melting, is as pliable as a piece of buckskin or soaked sole-leather, and can be doubled without cracking or coming in pieces, yet tough and dry, not sticking to the fingers when handled. If glue will not bear soaking without becoming soapy, or melting, it will not make a good roller.

Boiling Composition

A kettle large enough to hold a pair of mammoth rollers, should be about *fourteen inches deep,* and eight inches diameter at top and bottom, and may be made of copper or tin. Another kettle of cop-

---

[*] In very warm weather glue will soak much quicker than in cold weather, and allowance for this difference must be made.

per or tin may be constructed, about twelve inches in diameter, to receive the inner kettle, with a mouth fitting close to the inner kettle, which has a shoulder to prevent its sinking quite to the bottom of the large kettle. The composition is placed in the small kettle, which should be put in the large one. There should be water enough in the large kettle to completely surround the small one. After these directions have been attended to, the kettles may be placed over the fire.

Sometimes a common dinner kettle partly filled with water is placed in an arch, or hung over the fire, and an ordinary tin bucket containing the composition is placed in it. The bucket should be kept from standing on the bottom of the kettle, or the composition will burn. The water may be kept boiling.

The glue should be boiled till completely melted, which will require an hour or an hour and a half, and more if the water in the large kettle be not kept continually boiling. The molasses may then be added, and well mixed with the glue, by frequent stirring, and the composition boiled an hour or an hour and a half longer, and it may be poured into the moulds.

If, by accident, too much water should be in the glue, it may be boiled two or three hours before the molasses is added.

The composition should be poured slowly to allow the air to escape.

Preparation of the Moulds, &c.

Great care should be taken to have the moulds clean, and perfectly free from any particles of composition that may have remained from previous castings. If this be not observed, wherever a piece of old composition remains, the roller will invariably adhere.

The mould should be well oiled with a swab, smaller than the mould; if it fit tightly, it will not allow sufficient oil to adhere to the surface of the mould. The oil should cover the surface of the mould, as thick as it is possible to make it, without causing it to run. A roller cast in a mould oiled sufficiently, will come out by starting [loosening] it, and holding up the end of the mould.

In cold weather the mould should be warmed immediately before oiling by holding a piece of burning paper underneath it, and allowing the flame to draw through the mould: this should be done immediately before casting, after the composition is ready to pour. When the mould is cold it stiffens the composition before the face of the roller is formed, and makes the roller rough, if it does not prevent the mould from filling.

After the mould is warmed and oiled, the cylinder should be put in it, and firmly fastened down, by placing a stick on the centre-piece, and tying it down with twine, or it will rise in the mould. Care should be taken that the composition is cleaned from the centre-piece, or it will scrape the oil from the mould as it goes up.

The ends of the cylinders may be dipped in the melted glue before the molasses is put in: the clear glue being harder than composition will prevent the water from penetrating between the composition and the wood, which frequently causes the ends of the roller to start from the cylinder. Sometimes, particularly in warm weather, the composition will leave the cylinder in many places, so as to spoil the roller. This may be prevented by boiling the cylinder in water, till clean, (if it be an old one,) and covering it all over with melted glue. The glue, of course, must be suffered to become hard before the cylinder is put in the mould.

After the roller has been taken out of the mould, the oil may be wiped off with paper, and the roller suffered to remain in the air, (if in the summer, in as cool a place as possible) for one or two days, to allow the composition to acquire sufficient firmness. If the weather be very warm, or the roller quite soft, it may require longer exposure to the air, before it will be sufficiently strong to bear the operation of distributing.

Using New Rollers

When new rollers are to be used, the remaining oil and dust should be wiped off with paper, if in summer, and the roller be soft; if in winter, they may be washed in *lie* as usual, sometime before using. They should when quite new, be used as long as possible without washing, or until they become so dirty as to require it: washing a new roller before the composition acquires strength, unless done very carefully, injures the face. After they have been used several times they may be washed every night or oftener, if they become dirty, or loose their adhesion.

Washing Rollers

Rollers should be washed in *lie*, with a soft sponge, and rinsed perfectly clean with water and wiped dry with another sponge, or the same one, cleaned and squeezed dry. If the roller be new, it should be washed quickly, and with as little rubbing as possible, to take off the ink, or the composition will dissolve. A new roller, if the weather be warm, should not be used until sometime after washing.

A roller may be cleaned for immediate use with oil, if it is too soft to bear washing. Take a small quantity of oil in the hand, and rub it over the roller till the ink becomes loosened; wipe it off clean with paper. If it should not come clean at the first attempt, perform the same operation again. New rollers, in summer, if too soft to bear lie and water, may be cleaned in this manner till they acquire sufficient firmness.

Keeping Rollers

If the room be dry, rollers should be suspended in a tight box, containing water. A box of the length of the rollers and wide enough to hold as many rollers as necessary, two or three tiers deep, and lined in the bottom with sheet lead, and covered tightly, is as cheap and convenient as any. If a great number of rollers are in use, a closet may be constructed, as wide as the longest roller is long, about eight inches deep, and high enough to contain as many rollers as wished. If it should be six or eight feet high, it will require two or three doors, moving perpendicularly on hinges, to get at the rollers conveniently. And two or three leaden boxes may be placed at intervals, to contain water to keep the air moist. A box constructed in this manner, is more convenient than the other, and takes up much less room.

Fig. 19.12. *German contrivance for storing rollers –* from Pasko (1894, p. 491)

Keeping Rollers in Working Order

Rollers, to do good work, should be as adhesive as possible, without causing them to tear, or rendering it impossible for the boy to distribute them conveniently. This quality is essential to good rollers, as without it they will not perform the required operation. Good rollers, when new, have enough of the adhesive quality; but as they grow older, they gradually lose it, till they no longer cling to the form, and are therefore unfit for use. To keep rollers in order, it should be remembered, that *water or moist air always softens the roller,* or renders it adhesive; and that *air invariably hardens it*. The irregularities in the temperature of the weather, and the natural imperfections of the composition, may by strict attention to this rule, be in a measure, counteracted. *Therefore,* if rollers be too soft, they may be cleaned with oil, or left exposed to the air till they acquire the desired quality of adhesiveness. If too hard, they may be softened by frequent washing and close confinement in a moist box.

When rollers have become so old as to have lost much of their adhesive quality, they may be dampened with a *moist* sponge immediately before using. They may be soaked in water for several minutes, if extremely hard, till they acquire adhesion. But when rollers require this, they are of little use and must be re-cast.

Re-casting Rollers

When it is wished to re-cast a roller, soak it in water an hour or less, and scrape off the outside skin with a knife; cut it in small pieces, and put it in a kettle, as was directed for new composition. Add enough molasses to give it the proper consistence, which must be determined by the quality of the old composition. A roller made in winter, to be re-cast in summer, will require little or no molasses. A roller made in summer to be re-cast for fall or winter use, will require from one to two quarts of molasses, according as it was before melting, more or less hard.

Rollers are stronger after re-casting than before, but generally not as smooth; as the composition will not melt so thin as at first, the air bubbles cannot escape. If well used, rollers may be *re-cast twice;* after that there is no certainty of their melting: Some glue will not re-cast but once. Rollers have been made by soaking old composition in water in the same manner as new glue, and casting it. There is no certainty in it, and the success will not, [on] an average[,] warrant the trouble.

A roller may, if thought proper, be faced by cutting off the surface a quarter of an inch deep, evenly all around, and putting it in the mould, and filling it with new composition. The composition must be cut off smoothly, or the roller will be harder in some places than others. This method of recasting requires, of course, much less composition than a new roller.

Mending Rollers

If a roller should be torn by taking it out of the mould, or in any other way, it may be mended by applying a smooth iron poker, sufficiently warm to melt the composition, but not hot enough to burn it. The iron must be cleaned and re-heated several times if much mending is required. The ends of rollers are frequently soldered when new, to prevent their starting from the cylinder. If they have started, they may be soldered, in this way, till they are again fast. Rollers that come out of the mould quite rough, may, if care be taken, rendered smooth; and rollers that have lost their face, by using when new, or when the weather is very warm, may again be faced by a judicious application of a warm poker, or smooth iron rod.

Reading 19.12
Rollers
from *The Pressmen's Guide* by Richard Cummins (1873, pp. 17–19)

Cummins gives instructions for making rollers, and provides a source where pressmen can buy prepared composition. Even though he is describing rollers for cylinder presses, I have included this reading because it points out how durable composition rollers were despite their reputation for being temperamental. He mentions that he had a pair of rollers running at a speed of 1500 impressions an hour for a week in the summer.

Surprisingly, he did not wash his rollers at the end of the day but stored them in a cool place overnight. When he did wash them, he used benzine or turpentine. By the 1860s, benzine was widely used as a replacement for turpentine to clean rollers. It had first been extracted from coal tar in 1848 by Charles Bickford Mansfield (1819–1855). The earliest reference to benzine in a printers' manual was made by Harpel (1870, p. 42), who mentioned using benzine and a sponge to clean rollers, then wiping them well with another sponge containing a little water.

A new roller, coming from the mould, should be wiped clean of the loose oil, and hung up in a dry place to season, say about a week, then use, after making sure to raise it enough to allow it to touch the form. Do not set it up too tight against the distributor, as it often cracks it on the ends in Winter, and in Summer is sure to melt it.

I have used a pair of composition rollers on a newspaper press, running 1500 an hour a week in Summer, taking them out, and hanging them in a cool, dry place every night, not washing them. When I did wash them, it was with benzine or turpentine.

If they have not enough suction, why sponge them very lightly, and let them remain awhile near the air. When they get very dry, or old, wash them in lye, and quickly with a soft sponge and water wash off the lye, and do not use them for at least one hour after leaving them exposed to the air.

Great care should be taken not to allow any water to remain on the rollers, as it causes blistering.

For those who wish to make their own rollers, a prepared composition can be obtained at the American Printer's Warehouse, who will send complete directions for using the same.

Directions for Casting Rollers

To cast a roller, say for a temperature of about 70 degrees, use Cooper's No. 1 glue, and the purest extra syrup you can get. Let the proportion be one pound of glue to one quart of syrup. Steep the glue over night, and when it is soft enough it will bend without cracking. Drain the water off and let it stand awhile. . . .

The water should be kept at a boiling point, until the glue is melted, which generally takes about an hour. Then put in the syrup, and keep stirring till the composition is cooked, the water all the while keep steadily boiling. This generally occupies about an hour and a half. If the original softening of the glue was accomplished in 25 minutes, then the cooking may be done in 90 minutes, but if it took 10 minutes to soften the glue, then it will take only an hour to cook it.

To aid in the calculation of quantities for one or more rollers, the following table will be found very beneficial [for hand presses] . . .

Medium Roller,	Nine Pounds.
Super-Royal,	Ten Pounds.

Reading 19.13
Roller Moulds
from *Practical Printing* by John Southward (1882, p. 387)

> Southward describes two types of molds for casting rollers: the split mold, shown in **Fig. 19.10** on p. 543, and the tubular mold, shown in **Fig. 19.11** on p. 543. The latter was used primarily for casting small rollers and brayers. Southward notes that the split mold had to be perfectly machined in order to avoid any leaks where the two sections of the mold were joined; otherwise, unwanted raised lines would be cast on the surface of the rollers. This is never a problem with present-day rollers when they are made of rubber or polyurethane, since they are ground and polished after casting.

53. Roller moulds are of two kinds, open or *split* roller moulds and *tubular* ones.

54. *Split Roller Moulds* are made in two parts, which fit closely together, and are kept in contact by strong iron clamps, or (as they are called) dogs, secured with screws.

     The advantage of this kind of mould consists in the readiness with which the roller can be withdrawn after it is cast[.] There is a counterbalancing disadvantage, however, in the fact that rollers cast in such moulds invariably have a seam projecting from their surface, corresponding to the part where the two sections of the mould come together. This seam becomes, as the tube is used, continually more prominent, and materially interferes with the quality of the roller.

55. *Tubular moulds* consist simply of tubes, perfectly true and polished on the inside. They should be proportioned to the size of the roller to be cast. A mould, for instance, 18 inches long, should be about ⅝ of an inch thick and, 1½ inch diameter. Moulds of this kind are supplied with several printing machines. They are made of cast iron, and are very smooth.

     Roller moulds are sometimes made of brass, instead of iron, but their prime cheapness is their only recommendation. The printer will lose in the end by purchasing them, except for very small rollers. Zinc tubes should on no account be used.

Reading 19.14
Composition Rollers
from *The American Printer* by Thomas MacKellar (1866, p. 224).

> It is interesting to note that MacKellar included below, almost verbatim, these instructions on how to cast rollers for the handpress in every edition of his manual, the last of which was published in 1893. The notable exception is his substitution of the word *benzine* for *camphene* in the last paragraph in all editions from 1878 on. He mentions that handpress rollers are less susceptible to hard use and wear-and-tear than cylinder-press rollers since the former never had to be subjected to the high speeds of printing machines.

For *hand-press rollers* more molasses should be used, as they are not subject to so much hard usage as *cylinder-press rollers*, and do not require to be as strong; for the more molasses that can be used the better will be the roller. Before pouring a roller, the mould should be perfectly clean, and well oiled with a swab, but not to excess, as too much oil makes the face of the roller seamy and ragged. The end pieces should then be oiled, and, together with the cylinder, placed in the mould, the upper-end piece being very open, to allow the composition to pass down between the interior of the mould and the cylinder. The cylinder must be well secured from rising, before the composition is poured in, by placing a stick upon the end of it, sufficiently long to reach above the end of the mould, and be tied down with twine. The composition should be poured very slowly, and in such a manner as to cause it only to run down *one side* of the cylinder, allowing the air to escape freely up the other.

If the mould is filled at night, the roller may be drawn the next morning; but it should not be used for at least twenty-four hours after, except in very cold weather.

To determine when a roller is in order for working, press the hand gently to it: if the fingers can be drawn lightly and smoothly over its surface, it may be said to be in order; but should it be so adhesive that the fingers will not glide smoothly over its surface, it is not sufficiently dry, and should be exposed to the air.

Rollers should not be washed immediately after use, but should be put away with the ink on them, as it protects the surface from the action of the air. When washed and exposed to the atmosphere for any length of time, they become dry and skinny. They should be washed about half an hour before using them. In cleaning a *new* roller, a little oil rubbed over it will loosen the ink: and it should be scraped clean with the back of a case-knife [sheath knife]. It should be cleaned in this way for about one week, when *ley* may be used. New rollers are often spoiled by washing them too soon with ley. Camphene may be substituted for oil; but, owing to its combustible nature, it is objectionable, as accidents may arise from its use.

Reading 19.15
Excellent Recipes for Making Rollers
from *Harpel's Typograph* by Oscar Henry Harpel (1870, pp. 43–44)

Harpel gives four recipes for composition, three of which call for glycerine. The first is for summer rollers, with an adjustment for winter rollers; the second, for "middle weather" when the temperature was between 60 and 70 degrees. The third recipe is of special interest since it contains a small amount of rubber shavings.

Three later attempts at covering rollers with a rubber material were described by Southward (1882, pp. 405–406); "A few years ago Messrs. Forster & Taylor patented a new kind of roller composed of india-rubber sponge. It was claimed that they had a permanent elasticity, just enough to give them that soft, yielding surface so necessary for perfect work; and further that they were not affected by heat, cold, or damp, and hence were equally useful in all weathers and in every climate. These sponge rollers were intended to be covered with a thin coat of a gelatinous compound made by the patentees, or with the ordinary composition, which was said to give them a perfectly smooth surface, and one which readily took the ink. They were tested by Messrs. Clay, Son, & Taylor, and, testified to work with satisfaction. The sponge base was said to be an important saving, being very durable, and requiring only one-fourth part of the composition to form the surface. We have seen a circular which was well printed with one of these sponge rollers that had been in use for three years. The only treatment necessary was to wash them at the close of the day's work, and on commencing work on the following morning to pass over them a damp sponge. They were not to be scraped. . . .

"Of all substitutes for the ordinary composition roller, the most successful is the invention of Mr. R. Lanham. By specially treating vulcanised india rubber he has produced a roller equally adapted to lithographic and letter-press work. These 'Lanham rollers,' as they are named, are especially useful in hot machine rooms or on very fast machines, as they are not affected by temperature and are almost indestructible. They are cleaned with turpentine, after which they are washed over with water and rubbed dry with a clean cloth. This is all the treatment they require. Should the face by any chance lose its 'tack' it may be restored, we are assured, by boiling the roller, an operation which is said to have no ill effect upon the roller itself.

"Notice may also be made of the 'Moss Rubber' roller brought out by Messrs. Moulton & Co., of Bradford, Wilts, some years ago, and which, though we know it to have worked well, was not much adopted, probably on account of the remoteness of the manufactory."

Pasko (1898, p. 571) also mentioned an alternative to composition called Vallee's Elastic Roller Gum. He says that it "had such tenacity it was impossible to tear it." This may have been an early version of a rubber covered roller.

No. 1. – *For Summer.* – 2 lbs. Cooper's No. 1 Glue; 2 lbs. Baeder's Glue; 1 gallon best Sugar House Molasses; ½ pint Glycerine. *For Winter*, reduce each glue ¼ to ¾ of a lb.

DIRECTIONS: – First soak the glues, wrapped up separately in woolen cloths, until the pieces bend easily without snapping, which will generally take from two and a half to three hours. Boil the molasses for forty-five or fifty minutes, and skim it thoroughly. Then put in the glues, drained of superfluous water. Boil the whole for fifteen or twenty minutes. At last put in the glycerine; and after three to five minutes boiling and stirring, pour off.

The above composition may be cut into small pieces from time to time, as rollers require renewal, and be remelted several times, adding a little good-bodied molasses each time.

No. 2. – *Strong Middle Weather Rollers.* – 8½ lbs. Cooper's best Glue; 2 gallons best Extra Syrup; 1 pint Glycerine; 2 ounces Venice Turpentine.

DIRECTIONS: – Steep the glue in rain water until pliant, and drain it well. Then melt it over a moderate fire, but do not "cook" it. This will take from fifteen to twenty-five minutes. Next put in the syrup, and boil for about three-fourths of an hour, stirring it occasionally, and removing any impurities that arise upon the top of the composition. Add the other ingredients, a few minutes before removing the boiler from the fire, and pour slowly.

N.B. – If the glycerine and turpentine are to be omitted, reduce the quantity of syrup one pint.

The above makes excellent strong rollers for fast printing when the thermometer ranges from 60° to 70°. Slightly reduce or increase the glue as the weather becomes colder or warmer.

No. 3. – 10½ lbs. genuine Irish or Buffalo Glue; 2½ gallons Black Sugar House or best Maple Molasses; 1 lb. India-rubber Gum Shavings; 2 ounces Carolina Tar; 12 ounces Glycerine; 4 ounces strong Vinegar.

DIRECTIONS: – Soak glue over night, and drain in the morning by means of a *covered* [colander.] Boil molasses, and skim for twenty minutes. Add India-rubber chips, and stir until it combines with the molasses. Add glue, and boil for forty minutes, occasionally stirring the mass. Put in tar and glycerine, boil six or seven minutes, and pour.

This is the recipe for making the mysterious "Black Composition" so durable and elastic, and known to but very few persons until recently. If properly handled, it cannot be excelled, and contains every element required in a roller. Caution must be taken that only purified rubber gum is used. When this cannot be procured, add a pound and a half more glue, and four ounces more glycerine.

No. 4. – 4½ lbs. White Shell or Bonnet Glue; ¾ gallon Strained Wild Honey; 1 quart Sugar House Molasses; 2 ounces Burgundy Pitch.

    Directions: – Soak glue twenty minutes, or until pliant, and drain, but keep from air. Boil honey and molasses three-quarters of an hour. Add glue and pitch, boiling half an hour longer. Stir the mass, and skim well during process.

    A small quantity of this composition dropped on a board or iron plate will indicate when it is properly cooked. A shorter or longer time than is given above for boiling, as may be found sufficient or necessary, will sometimes happen. This makes a clear and durable roller.

Reading 19.16
General Directions for Working Rollers
from *Typographia* by Thomas F. Adams (1837, pp. 319–320).

    Adams discusses the use and care of rollers below. He warns about exposing rollers to the sun since they will melt when overheated and wrinkle if washed before they have had a chance to cool down. Since rollers reacted adversely to atmospheric conditions, it was necessary to test them before using them. Adams describes these tests and how to resolve any problems arising from them. Keeping the rollers in good working order was one of the pressman's main concerns.

    He also mentions how to store rollers. He suggests keeping them horizontal in a large, upright, air-tight box or closet – contrary to other writers who recommended putting holes in the box so the air could circulate freely.

    As noted in many nineteenth-century printers' manuals, both the puller and the beater – the latter eventually being replaced by the roller boy – were expected to check over the printed sheets for defects and consistency of color. This would probably account for why they continued to work on the same side of the press throughout the handpress period, although it has also been suggested that it was done to save floor space in the pressroom. However, once inking apparatus were introduced, the form was inked from the off side of the press.

    Rollers were not for every sort of work. Adams says that balls were still used for cards, single cuts, and light forms.

To determine when a roller is in order for working, we press the hand gently to it, to discover whether it is adhesive or not, if so, and the fingers can be drawn lightly and smoothly over its surface, it may then be said to be in order, but, should it be adhesive, and the fingers will not glide smoothly over its surface, it is then not sufficiently dry, and should be exposed to the air until it possesses the above qualities: a roller well washed at night, and put into an air tight box till morning, will generally be found in good order for working. For that purpose every pressroom should be furnished with a large upright box or closet of sufficient size to contain all the rollers in an horizontal position, resting on their axle on supporters at the end of the box.

    To wash the rollers nothing more is requisite than the application of water, after rolling them in the dust, in cold frosty weather a little warmed, but cold as possible in warm weather, which needs only be used with the hand or a sponge; some pressmen, however, prefer washing them with lie, after which they should be well rinsed with clean water.

    In very warm weather the rollers should be occasionally changed, to prevent them from getting too soft, or from melting; it is frequently found when a roller is *sick*, or soft, or you do not know what is its ailment, that washing it clean, and hanging it to rest for a time, restores it to as good a state as ever, but it should not be washed till after it has cooled a little, as the cold water has a tendency to wrinkle it very much when over-heated. Great care should also be taken to keep them from the effects of the sun, as they are so easily melted, and in warm weather they should be kept in as cool a place as possible during the night. Should any accident happen to the roller, to injure its surface, it may be melted again and re-moulded as before.

Notwithstanding the general use of these rollers, balls will be found sometimes necessary to vary the mode of work. Cards, single cuts, light forms, &c. may require the experience at least, of a change.

Reading 19.17
Preparing Rollers
from *The Printers' Practical Every-Day-Book* by Thomas Shaw Houghton (1841, pp. 87–89).

> Houghton also describes the care of rollers, emphasizing that they should be checked for flaws before the form is ready for press. With slightly different proportions, his recipe for the composition is very similar to Hansard's. Houghton offers various solutions to the problems that may arise from faulty rollers. He also recommends cleaning rollers by rolling them in floor dust – also noted by Adams in Reading 19.16 above. Houghton was the first to mention scrubbing rollers down with a piece of woolen cloth saturated with clean water. He maintains that this is a better method than washing rollers with lye.

For working a forme well, much depends on the state of the roller. It should be perfectly dry, and yet have sufficient suction to take a necessary quantity of ink without smearing the outer edges of the type, which always looks bad. In short, a roller that will not retain ink, when in contact with the forme, is unfit for use, and should be either replaced with another, or the work be delayed till it is washed and in order. That such delay may be avoided, however, it is necessary that the state of the rollers should be examined and prepared before a forme is ready for press.

Rollers may be unfit for working from several causes, for some of which it is difficult to account. If, however, they be kept in a dry situation, out of the sun, where the air freely circulates, an unknown cause of a roller not working will not frequently occur. Amongst the principal causes for bad rollers are, first, being too hard, which may arise from having too much glue in the composition, being too old, or being too cold; second, being washed and kept out of use too long, which produces a kind of skin over the face; third, being used too soon after being washed; fourth, being dirty and too long in use without cleaning, &c.

The first cause will require the roller to be recast, and the ingredients, of which it is made, brought as near as possible to the [following] proportions [of "two pounds and a half of the finest glue to six pounds of the best molasses, to which is added a half or three quarters of a pound of Paris-white, and a penny-worth of neatsfoot oil."– Houghton (ibid., p. 90)] . . . If, however, it be too cold from the effects of the preceding night, a few turns before the fire will obviate it. Passing the roller quickly through the flame of a candle, or the flame of a sheet of paper, is an excellent mode of putting on a new face.

The second cause will be obviated by rubbing the roller with a damp sponge, five or six minutes before it is wanted.

The third cause will require the roller to be hung up again, or, as before noticed, turned at a moderate distance from the fire, until it is properly dry.

The fourth cause must be obviated by the roller being cleaned, which may be done two ways, namely, by washing or scraping. It must depend upon circumstances which should be preferred. If the roller be getting hard, it is the best to wash it, in the following manner: – first let it be well rolled in dust, (if there can be as much scraped up in all the office to do it,) and then washed off with a piece of woollen cloth and clean water. This method is much better than using lye, and preserves rollers from cracks much longer. But if the roller be nearly new, or wanted for use immediately, the best way to clean it will be to scrape it. This may be done either with fresh lard or with common ink, by taking a quantity on the roller and scraping it clean off. After this, it should be rolled on a dry sheet of waste paper, till its ends are perfectly clean. This done, it is then ready for use.

If the roller be only wanted for a rough job, such as posters, &c., of course, it will not require that care and attention which it does for the finer description of work.

Reading 19.18
Skin Rollers
from *An Abridgment of Johnson's Typographia* by John Johnson, edited and with a new appendix by Thomas F. Adams (1828, pp. 309–310).

Even though skin rollers predate composition rollers – Lord Stanhope had experimented with them at the beginning of the nineteenth century – they seem to have been widely used in America. In the appendix to the above work, Adams describes how skin rollers were made. From his description, they would appear to have been quite heavy and clumsy. Because of their weight, they were generally charged on a cylinder inking table like the one in **Fig. 19.13**. The surface would not have been particularly smooth since the skin was stitched at the point where it overlapped, creating a seam along the length of the roller. They were never considered as good as balls.

It appears that the skin Rollers were not used in England: They were first introduced in this country by a Mr. [Hugh] Maxwell, of Philadelphia, about the year 1807, and soon after by him abandoned, not being able to make them work properly: they remained out of use for several years, until they were again introduced by Mr. [Daniel] Fanshaw [1789–1860], of New York, about 1815. They have never been considered so good as balls: being too heavy for the hand they are used behind the press, supported by two wooden cylinders; to one of these cylinders a crank is attached, by which the roller is distributed; and supplied with ink by a small hand roller, eight inches long, kept in the ink block for that purpose.

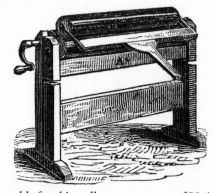

Fig. 19.13. *Cylinder inking table for skin rollers* – courtesy of University of Iowa Libraries

To Make a Skin Roller

Have a piece of wood turned perfectly true, about three and a half inches diameter, with an iron spindle at each end – the wood must be loaded with from 12 to 20 lbs. of lead, or other metal. A good thick blanket is then cut to the width required, one end tacked to the cylinder, and wound tightly round it about eight times, and fastened; the lining skin is then drawn over and nailed at both ends, the outer skin, being neatly stitched and wetted, covers the whole, and is drawn tight at both ends and nailed: it is then scraped dry with a ball knife, and ink put on ready for work.

Reading 19.19
Air-Inking Balls and Rollers
from *Improvements in Printing, Invented and Patented* by Major Bartłomiej Beniowski (1854, pp. 39–43).

> On the surface, Beniowski's arguments in favor of air balls and rollers appear to have some merit. His inking implements were light, durable, and unaffected by atmospheric conditions. In theory, they may have even worked, but I suspect that the concept was too radical at the time for most pressmen. He does not say what material was used, although it must have been some sort of elastic, perhaps rubber, since they could be inflated and did not have any seams.
>
> It is uncertain whether Beniowski ever manufactured these balls and rollers, although he states that he printed both editions of his book with them. Some say it was simply a scheme to raise money. According to W. Turner Berry and Edmond Poole in their *Annals of Printing* (1966, p. 240), "The handsome Major, who was a brilliant speaker and a master of the art of gullibility" raised money by subscription to finance his various printing inventions, which also included a failed system of logotypes for composition and a rotary press.

I [i.e., Beniowski] manufacture them of a water and air-tight envelope filled with compressed air. [**Fig. 19.14**, LEFT, represents an air-inking-ball; **Fig. 19.14**, RIGHT, represents an air-inking-roller.]

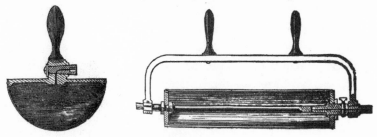

Fig. 19.14. LEFT, *Air-inking-ball;* RIGHT, *Air-inking-roller*– courtesy of University of Iowa Libraries

They claim superiority over those at present employed on the following grounds.

1. Being everlastingly elastic, and not affected by heat or moisture, one and the same roller is good for work at all seasons of the year, in all temperatures, and in all localities dry or moist. Hence the usual expenses in "rent" [see Reading 19.20 below] – about 24s. per roller per annum for recasting is spared.

2. Condensing the air, more or less, the hardness can be adjusted to the requirements of the work in hand; – letter-press, woodcuts, anastatic &c[.] – printing with black, red or any other colour. Whilst at present almost every kind of presswork requires a separate roller of a particular degree of hardness.

3. The labour and troubles at present incurred for protecting the inking rollers from atmospheric influences, when not in work, are spared.

4. The very great care, and hard labour of at least one hour's work per day of a skilful man, is at present required to clean the rollers, and bring them up to working order by various devices. Air rollers are ready for work at all times.

5. At present inking rollers get foul in the course of working; they become greasy, too soft or too hard, or you do not know what are their ailments; they require washing and brushing with water, lye, turpentine, spirits of wine &c. they actually demand being cajoled and humoured with the skill and undefinable tact of a physician in the presence of his hysteric customers.

6. The pressman often finds that he cannot produce good work and clear impressions, with all the care and attention he can bestow on the work; and this when his roller seems to be in condition, and no apparent cause can be assigned for the deficiency of quality. The roller is then said to be "sick" and the only remedy that has yet answered to remove this inconvenience, is to give the roller rest – to take another for the work in hand. Hence it is necessary to keep a stock of more rollers than are productively employed. This expense is spared by substituting air for compo.

7. In London and other large towns, the making of rollers constitute a separate trade. They are also sent into the country in boxes fitted for the purpose. But there are numerous situations in which it is not easy to obtain a regular supply of this necessary article and in such cases, printers must make them for themselves.

The making of compo-rollers requiring a great deal of skill and experience, not easily attained even when it engages exclusive attention, becomes doubly difficult when the printer, whose engagements are necessarily varied, must cast his own rollers. – Besides, in such cases the expenses for plant and utensils by far exceeds the usual price and rent of rollers. Hence all the innumerable places which are at a distance from the great lines of communication, must either incur great expenses, or forego having printing establishments deserving the name.

The exportation of inking rollers to distant colonies and foreign countries is of course an impossibility; – one might as well attempt daily providing Arctic adventurers or Australian diggers with fresh hot muffins from London Taverns.

With the substitution of air for compo, all these difficulties vanish.

The trade of MAKING inking rollers becomes MANUFACTURING in the strictest sense of the word. – The economical principles peculiar to factories in general become applicable to the manufacture of inking rollers. – One Metropolitan establishment conducted by superior and concentrated, because liberally remunerated, intelligence, may undertake to supply the most distant and secluded corners at home and abroad with an article cheap, efficient, durable.

8. If there were no other impediments in the way of Typography being admitted into private dwellings, and becoming a household convenience, the unmanageableness of the glue-and-treacle rollers, would be in itself sufficient to keep the divine art confined within the narrow and mysterious bound of printing-premises. –

I feel a particular pride in being able to announce that henceforth authors and others, will have the same easy command over inking-balls and inking-rollers as they already have over writing-pens and ink-boxes.

9. The air inking implements are much lighter than those at present in use. – A compo-roller of 24 inches weighs about 6 lbs.; an air-roller of similar dimensions weighs only 1 lb. 8 oz. A pair of usual balls weighs 5 lbs. ditto of air, only 1 lb. 8 oz. Such lightness must be considered an advantage, whether the inking is performed by hand or by machinery.

Besides, when the air is let out, they occupy very little room. This advantage, not to be despised under any circumstances, becomes really important in an article which has pretensions to distant markets.

10. A portion of the wear and tear of types is owing to the knocking, rubbing, pressing of the inking-balls and rollers. – Hence, working with implements almost as light and elastic as air itself, must be infinitely less hurtful to the type-face in general, and to their fine, sharp lines in particular.

Reading 19.20
Renting Rollers
from *The Art of Printing* by Thomas Curson Hansard Jr. (1851, pp. 118–119).

> Most printers had the tools and materials to cast rollers in their own shops; however, by mid-nineteenth-century, it was much more practical to rent rollers from a roller manufacturer. These rollers were cheaper and better than those that the pressman could make himself.
>
> Rollers were usually rented by the quarter, and the manufacturer replaced worn or damaged rollers at no extra cost. Even country printers were able to rent rollers, since suppliers went to great pains to accommodate their needs by shipping them in specially made boxes to insure their safe arrival.

There are in London, and probably in the larger provincial cities, parties who make an especial business of the manufacture of composition balls and rollers, which they supply to printers upon payment of a rent. The skill and experience of these persons enable them, as must be the case in every instance where a manufacture engages exclusive attention, to supply a much better and cheaper article than could be manufactured by any individual whose engagements are varied; consequently there are not many printers, either in town or country, who do not avail themselves of these opportunities. The rent is paid for each roller required, and by the quarter; that is to say, if a printer employs six presses, and consequently six rollers, he pays for six rollers, the manufacturer engaging to supply him with as many changes as he may require from their getting out of order or being injured; in fact, to keep him supplied with six rollers in good condition. The rent for a common press-roller is the moderate sum of six shillings per quarter; they are sent into the country in boxes fitted for the purpose. There are, of course, situations in which it is not easy to obtain a regular supply of the necessary article, and in this case the printer may very easily make them for himself; but the expense of the utensils is so great as to exceed the usual rent for years.

Reading 19.21
Some Notes on Rollers
from *Practical Printing* by John Southward (1882, pp. 388–389, 391–394, 397).

> Southward mentions that in large cities rollers are cast by specialized companies that both sell and rent out rollers, such as Harrild's in London. From the 1830s on, printers who wanted to cast their own rollers could buy ready-prepared composition, which made their work a little easier.
>
> He begins with an eight-point list that elaborates the characteristics of good roller composition and then proceeds to describe the process for making them. He suggests thinning thick composition with a little old ale. This was first mentioned by Crisp (1875, p. 113).

Southward includes detailed instructions on the correct way to pour the composition into the roller molds. The composition was poured against the core, also referred to as the *stock*, in order to keep the oil coating on the mold from mixing with the composition, since it will not adhere to the core if it is contaminated with oil. To make a good oil for the molds, he suggests suspending a twisted strip of lead in a bottle of olive oil for a month in the sun. Lard oils were also used as lubricants, as was sperm oil – which is no longer available commercially.

He gives two methods for drawing rollers out of tubular molds, both of which appear to be quite convoluted, as well as several methods for sealing the ends of the composition in order to keep it from pulling away from the core. Rollers were cast to accommodate both the atmospheric conditions and the type of work for which they were intended. Soft rollers were used for posters and newspaper work; hard ones for book and fine jobs.

Southward stored his rollers in a roller cabinet with holes in the lid so air could circulate freely throughout the cabinet. Rollers worked best when the temperature in the pressroom and the roller cabinet were the same. Storing rollers in a cool place also helped to keep them from mildewing.

In some of the large towns rollers are cast for the use of printers by firms who make that a speciality of their business. In London, for instance, a system was introduced by Mr. Harrild, by which rollers are renewed whenever necessary, on payment of a fixed sum per quarter. A similar arrangement is adopted by several other roller makers, and it is found very convenient to the printing trade. As, however, it is an essential part of every pressman's qualifications to know how to cast rollers, we present the following information on the subject....

56. It may be well to set out here the points which should characterize a good composition, when applied to a roller.

1. It should not shrink.
2. It should not become hard in cold weather, nor soft in hot weather.
3. It should retain its "suction," or "tack," or "lug."
4. It should preserve a good "face," and neither "skin" not "crack." ...
5. It should require washing only very seldom.
6. It should be capable of remelting readily.
7. It should be tough and durable, and stand wear and tear.
8. It should take up coloured ink readily, and give it off freely and without waste....

59. ... The composition, hot from the kettle, should be poured in very slowly upon the end of the stock, and in such a manner as to cause it to run down one side of the stock, allowing the air to escape freely up the other. The composition must not run down the inner surface of the mould, as that would be likely to take off the oil from the mould, and by flowing it against the core, would make it peel off when cast. The composition must be filled up to an inch more than the length of the roller....

60. *Drawing the Roller.* – This is the great difficulty when tubular moulds are used, and more rollers are destroyed in doing it than from any other cause. No one who had not actually witnessed it could imagine the tenacity with which a roller will "stick" to the tube. If the tube is too thin, it is in fact almost impossible to get the roller out....

The following are two simple and practical methods, which may suggest others.

Method No. 1. – Place the roller mould against an ordinary screw press (for pressing sheets), with a piece of wooden furniture or a mallet handle resting on the roller stock at one end, and the top of the press at the other. Hold the mould and furniture firmly, and get some one to screw the press down. The pressure thus brought to bear on the roller will cause it to move in the mould, and it may afterwards be easily forced out with a piece of wooden furniture.

Method No. 2. – Get a piece of wood a little longer than the roller stock, mortice into both ends pieces of hard wood a few inches high; through one cut a hole with a centre bit the size of the roller, in the other insert a screw – a bed screw will do. Place one end of the mould against the hole and apply the screw to the stock of the roller. A turn or two will start it; it can then be removed, without difficulty.

Roller stocks should always be kept well painted, to prevent the composition coming off in use.

61. *Trimming the Roller.* – As the composition extends over the ends of the stock, the roller requires to be trimmed. The spare stuff may be cut off in this way: Encircle the end with a piece of thin cord or fine wire, and pull each end of the cord or wire till the composition is cut through. Then dip the eighth of an inch of the ends into hot water. This will melt a little the composition, and not only give the ends a more finished appearance, but tend to prevent the stuff coming off the stock, by preventing water, ley, or oil from getting in between the composition and the wood, and making it peel at the ends.

Another way is to trim the ends with a sharp knife, bevelled towards the core. Then take a hot iron and run it around the ends of the composition, thus soldering it to the stock.

62. *General Hints.* – Good rollers cannot be cast except in perfect moulds.

Composition that is too thick may be thinned by the addition of a little old ale.

A good oil for use in the moulds is thus made: Put a pint of olive oil into a clean glass bottle; twist up a thin piece of lead into a spiral form (like a wood shaving, or a corkscrew) and suspend it in the oil by means of a string attached to the cork. Hang the oil thus prepared in the sunlight for one month, and at the end of that time the impurities will have settled at the bottom; then decant quite clear. This is the colourless oil used by gun and watch makers; it has the property of remaining pellucid. . . .

Some printers mix the oil for lubricating the mould with lampblack, as the latter serves to keep the oil well distributed. . . .

Much of the difficulty of drawing rollers arises from the kind of oil used for the mould. The common olive oil is perhaps the worst that can be selected, having a stronger chemical action on the metal than almost any other, which is the reason it cannot be used for the finer kinds of machinery. Sperm and lard oils are best for the purpose, being the least disposed to clog. The use of sperm oil will obviate much trouble and the loss of many rollers. . . .

63. After the roller is cast and trimmed, it should be put away for a few days. Every printing office ought to contain a roller cupboard, in which all kinds of rollers may be kept protected from sudden vicissitudes of temperature, as well as from dust floating in the air. The roller composition should not be allowed to come into contact with any substance whatever, and should be supported on bars running through the core of the stock. The roller cupboard should be the same temperature as the press room, hence it is best when the cupboard is fixed there. Sudden changes of temperature, as from a cold cellar to a warm press room, will soon injure them, and prevent them working a proper length of time. Air should be admitted to the rollers through small holes in the bottom or the lid, otherwise they will suffer from mildew. . . .

68. There are two general rules for the use of rollers, which must always be borne in mind:

1. A large poster or newspaper forme, or any large forme with old type, will require a *soft* roller, and one with much suction.
2. Book-work, woodcuts, or fine job work, require a *hard* roller, with a very smooth, elastic, and clinging surface.

Reading 19.22
The Care of Rollers
from *Practical Printing* by John Southward (1882, pp. 398–405).

> There was no consensus among manual writers regarding the care of rollers. Pressmen usually just followed the procedures that were currently in use in their printing houses. Southward offers a diverse, and sometimes conflicting, selection of methods for cleaning rollers.

69. Considering the great expense of rollers, every care should be taken to make them last as long as possible. With care, rollers may be made to last for months. After working they should be wiped down with a rag dipped in lye, and when all the ink is removed, well rinsed in cold water, or, in winter, tepid water. They should then be wiped with a clean dry sponge, so that no moisture remains on the face.

A little oil – neat's foot or sweet oil [olive oil] – smeared over them when not in use, will help to keep the face in good working order.

70. Some printers "smother" or "ink up" their rollers by covering them with a great quantity of old or dirty ink. This is a very bad plan; the "driers" often put into the ink cause the face of the rollers to harden and become stiff, for it is obvious that printing inks are made to dry, whether on paper or rollers.

The process of ink drying on the roller can be retarded by rubbing melted tallow, oily ink, or glycerine on the roller before it is put away. A kind of ink is made called "roller ink," which does not contain dryers, which is said to protect the roller from the effects of the atmosphere. But, as we have said, we do not believe in the utility of putting ink on rollers for this purpose at all.

If the roller has been inked up, it must be carefully scraped with a blunt knife before being used again. The "roller ink" may be kept for future use.

71. Some printers put their rollers away in a box containing damp sawdust, and slightly sponge them before using them again, claiming that when treated in this way the rollers last longer and do much better work than if ink were allowed to harden on them.

72. In several offices the rule is not to clean off rollers after they have been used, but before they are wanted again. After being used for a job, they are covered with very weak or oily ink, which is spread out on a board expressly kept for that purpose, on which all the rollers in the place are rubbed in the evening, and scraped off before beginning work in the morning. The scraped-off ink is put back in a place by itself.

The best knife to be used for this purpose is said to be one in a half-circle form, and not sharp.

Most rollers are spoiled in *washing*, a process to which we must direct the especial attention of the printer.

73. Clumsy workmen, when they want to wash a roller, first of all dash on a quantity of strong lye, and then commence rubbing it vigorously. Of course, this soon causes the ink to begin to dissolve, and with it the face. They then saturate the roller with water, give it a few wipes with their hands, and stand it up on one side, in the belief that they have finished the job.

The effects of this washing and wiping are, first of all, that drops of water are left on the ends and on the face of the roller, which not only loosen it from the stock, but "blister" its surface. Further, water left standing on a roller has a tendency to absorb and evaporate the best properties of the treacle in the composition, and in a short time the roller begins to crack and shrink.

74. There are several methods of cleansing a roller, each of which has its adherents, who consider it better than any other. We will repeat some of these methods.

Benzine is, by some, regarded as the best roller wash: first, because it cleans the roller much better than any other wash; because it does not cause the pressman to lose time in waiting for the rollers after being washed, as it evaporates almost immediately when used; third, it costs very little; and last, it does not deaden and cause coloured inks to spread, as oil is said to do. Lye, indeed, should never be used for fine coloured inks.

On the other hand, it is contended that benzine rots and cracks the face of the roller. It is replied to this that such does not occur when the benzine is properly used. It only rots the composition when allowed to remain on the roller after washing.

The mode of washing with this fluid would be as follows: Get a trough with rods stretched across it. These rods should be run through the core of the stock, and may be supported on the sides of the trough. Then, with a soft sponge or rag, apply the benzine, rubbing gently but firmly from the ends the full length of the roller; not, as many do, from the centre both ways, thereby washing the centre twice as much as the ends, and soon making the roller so hollow as to be worthless. After having thoroughly loosened the ink from the roller, with a sponge damped with clean water, wipe the benzine from the face of the roller, and finish by removing from the ends any drops of water or benzine that may have collected thereon. If the roller is small, stand it on one end and wash down the full length.*

75. This mode of washing a roller has come into vogue in some of the large offices, because it is quickly performed, and the roller can be used almost immediately. It is, therefore, undoubtedly a very convenient one; but whether it is the best for preserving the sensitive surface of the roller is another matter altogether. We fear it has a tendency to impart a parchment-like skin to the roller, that must materially affect the transfer of the ink to the forme surface when good work is required. If so, it is only a degree less objectionable than the old-fashioned lye, which eventually eats through the skin.

76. A plan not open to either of these objections is to wash all fresh rollers with oil. Even when the rollers can be no longer called fresh, this plan may be followed. After so washing them let them be thoroughly cleaned and rubbed with cotton waste, till the last particle of oil is removed. The process is not an agreeable one, but the dirtying of the hands is compensated by the protection and preservation of the roller. A little soap and water will remove the oil from the hands.

As the roller gets older, the naphtha or benzine wash may be tried; but care should be taken to finish up with clean water, and to use the rollers, not at once, but when in proper condition.

When rollers are really very hard, it may be admissible to wash them with lye; indeed, this is often done with great advantage. Water must be copiously used, and every trace of the lye washed away.

* Instead of benzine, naphtha may be used.

An eminent firm of roller makers says: – "Washing should at first be avoided, but when the lug [tack] becomes less sensitive, the rollers may be washed about an hour before they are required, using as little lye as possible, which should be well rinsed off without delay with cold water, as the effect of the alkaline salt on the composition is very injurious, hardening its surface, impairing its 'lug,' and ultimately destroying the ingredient that produces the peculiar qualities for which composition rollers are distinguished. *Hot* water should also be avoided, as it makes the rollers unfeeling, by depriving them of the saccharine substance which forms an important part of the composition."

77. Another way of cleansing a roller, and one which may be adopted if it is getting hard, is to let it be rolled in dust, which must be washed off with a piece of woollen cloth and clean water. This method is better than using lye, and preserves rollers from cracks much longer.

78. A readier way, also useful when the roller is new, is to scrape it, after it has been well covered with fresh lard. It must be rolled on a dry sheet of waste paper until it is perfectly clean, especially about the ends.

79. The principal *defects* of rollers are the following: –

1. They are too hard. – *Remedy*. If too hard from the beginning, they must be recast again, and less glue used. If from the effects of cold, warm them in front of a fire, turning them round all the time. If from being too old, recast them.
2. They have a skin over the face. – *Remedy*. Rub them with a damp sponge five or six minutes before they are wanted.
3. They are too soft. – *Remedy*. Hang them up again, or wash them once in spirits of turpentine.
4. They are too dirty, and cannot be properly cleaned in the ordinary way. – *Remedy*. Slightly warm the face before the fire, and put a little oil upon them while warming. Wipe the oil and hard ink off, and wash the face well with turpentine.
5. They are "greasy," and make friars. – *Remedy*. Rub them with a mixture of spirits of turpentine and water, or a little pearl-ash lye.

80. A "preservative" for rollers which have been clean washed with lye is thus compounded:

Corrosive sublimate	1 drachm
Fine table salt	2 ounces

Put them together in half a gallon of soft water, and let the mixture stand for twenty-four hours. The rollers may be sponged with the above twice a week.

Compounds for a similar purpose are the following: – In very hot weather a solution of powdered alum in cold spring water is very serviceable in sponging up rollers after the ink has been washed off them, and when they are hung up for the night or the dinner hour.

During hot weather they may also be placed in a damp blanket, wet sand, or soaked saw dust, but they must be properly cleaned previously. Stale beer is also used for "coaxing up" rollers.

A plan adopted in America, when rollers become somewhat dry and skin-like upon the surface from long use or from remaining out of use, is to revive them by damping them with a decoction made from once-used green tea leaves reboiled until the water assumes a greenish russet hue. This should be kept in a bottle, and is said to be much better than water for damping rollers, causing them to retain their faces longer.

81. *General Hints*. – More rollers are washed out than worn out.

A roller should never be put to press covered with dust or dirt of any kind.

Where sponging has been held to be necessary, see that the water has been properly removed before the ink is applied; for water remaining on the roller will cause it to tear, and prevent a perfect distribution of the ink.

For black inks, rollers should have a more adhesive face than for coloured inks. The hardness or softness of the roller will depend much upon the body of the ink, and even the quality of the paper to be printed on. Rollers used for coloured inks require a firmer face than those used for black. They should never be sponged just before going to press, as water deadens coloured inks, and causes many – especially vermilions – to precipitate on the forme. Where much coloured ink is used, a set of rollers should be kept exclusively for that purpose; not only because such inks require a tough, clinging face, but for the reason that a roller which is used for black cannot be washed sufficiently clean to prevent it from tinting reds and other lighter shades of colour.

If the colour is vermilion, chrome yellow, prussian blue, or contains a strong varnish or size, it should *never* be left on the roller. These inks are very quick driers.

The general effect of moisture is to *rot* the composition; while the air causes it to *shrink* and *crack*.

From the preceding it will be seen that the importance of washing a roller properly does not arise so much from the necessity of having it thoroughly cleansed, as from the way in which the process will affect the roller afterwards. Upon the mode of washing, in fact, will depend very much the extent of the usefulness of the roller, in preserving its suction, or, on the other hand, impairing or utterly destroying it.

Of the several ways of removing the ink, it may be said that each is good if done properly. The old plan of covering the roller with dust, and rubbing off the ink and dust together with a wet rag, had its recommendations. The use of lye may also be defended on the ground that it is cheap, convenient, and always at hand in solution, as it is used for washing type. Benzine, turpentine, and oil have their adherents, and good reasons are alleged for the use of each of them. But it should be remembered that whatever liquids are used, their strong natures render them injurious if they are allowed to remain too long on the face of the roller, which is essentially delicate. Hence, if any of these are used they must be applied very quickly, and when the ink is dissolved, rinsed off as soon as possible, before the roller can sustain injury.

In the different methods stress is laid on the importance, after rinsing, of wiping the roller dry with a sponge or cloth. The rinsing should be done with *clean* water and a *clean* sponge. Very often the same cloth or sponge that has been used to wash with is slightly squeezed and used in rinsing. This is only applying more lye or other chemical, only it is a little weaker, but still strong enough to do injury by destroying the suction, cracking the face, and shortening the term of usefulness of the roller. Similar bad effects ensue from only partially rinsing when benzine, turpentine, or oil is used. In each case clean sponging will prevent bad effects, and should by no means be neglected.

In the "Roller Guide" [1877], by Mr. [Charles] P. Stevens, of Boston, we find the following: – Never use lye upon new rollers. Very many rollers are often spoiled by inexperienced workmen, by washing them in lye when new. They will then wonder what is the matter with their roller, and blame the roller maker for what is their own fault. A sure way to detect the use of lye upon rollers when new, is by placing the thumbs of the hands lengthwise upon the surface of the roller, and pressing them apart, when the composition will readily split open, which cannot be done to new rollers fresh from the moulds. Rollers having received such doctoring, might as well at once be renewed with new composition, if the pressman would save further vexation and annoyance.

82. The results of neglect may be stated – indeed will soon be apparent – as follows: –

    1. A hard skin, with cracks. – Effects of lye.
    2. Slight irregular cracks, but less hardness of skin. – Effects of benzine and turpentine.
    3. Deadness of skin, with loss of suction. – Effects of oil.

Nearly all kinds of ink may be removed with lye, but heavy inks, both black and coloured, particularly when they have been allowed to harden on the roller, and when driers have been used, require benzine or turpentine.

83. In regard to the advantages of washing rollers after or before the work is done, much might be said on both sides. It is not always necessary, certainly, nor is it in many cases at all desirable in the interests of the rollers to wash them after the work is done, and to put them away cleaned. Perhaps the safest rule is never to wash them except when absolutely necessary, and then only in the careful manner enjoined. Every time a roller is washed it is injured as much as it would be by half a day's work. When washed and put away clean, the surface is exposed to the air, the drying effect of which must deprive it of some of its moisture, and in proportion as this is lost the term of its usefulness is shortened. It is obvious that to preserve the natural moisture in the face, and its softness, elasticity, and suction with it, the face should be protected as much as possible from the air.

When strong inks have been used, or inks in which driers have been mixed, it is then of course necessary to clean up before putting the roller away, or the ink will cake and become hard. But when ordinary or light inks have been used, the rollers may be put away without danger unwashed for as long as a week or ten days, or even two weeks, in ordinary temperate weather. Although standing in oil deprives them of their suction, the same effect does not ensue necessarily from their being covered with ink, as the oil in the ink is so held by its co-ingredients that it cannot be absorbed in any great quantity; that is to say, in ordinary inks. If the "roller ink" without driers is used, of course even this risk is reduced to a minimum. If the roller can be safely left covered, as here suggested, we have no hesitation in saying that its good quality of face will be preserved fully one-fourth longer than it will be by putting it away clean.

If rollers are kept clean without too much washing, and when it is really necessary to work them, they are washed if, in a proper manner; and if, further, new rollers are made as soon as those in use show signs of failing, any pressman may be able at any time to be confident of turning out a good job as far as the rollers are concerned.

Reading 19.23
Inking Frames
from *Typographia* by John Johnson (1824, vol. II, p. 557).

> The remaining readings in this chapter are devoted to *inking apparatus*, the generic term for a variety of manual and automatic *inking appliances* and *machines* that were used with handpresses. Unfortunately, manual writers themselves were not consistent when referring to them by name; even so, they can be divided into five distinct groups: (1) *inking tables* and *frames*, which consisted of a simple ink slab mounted on a table or frame; (2) *brayer inking tables*, such as the inking tables illustrated in **Fig. 19.17** on p. 569 and in **Fig 19.19** on p. 571; (3) *cylinder inking tables*, that charged the roller with ink, such as those shown in **Figs. 19.15, 19.16,** and **19.20** on pp. 567, 569, and 571 respectively; (4) *roller stands* that distributed the ink

onto a pair of rollers, which in turn, were manually guided over the form on rails, such as the one shown in **Fig. 19.21** on p. 572; and (5) *self-inking apparatus*, also known as *self-inking machines*, that were rigged up to handpresses and automatically inked the form whenever the rounce was turned. Two of them are illustrated in **Figs. 19.22** and **19.23** on pp. 574 and 575, respectively. Another self-inking machine attached to a Washington press is shown in **Fig. 20.1** on p. 577.

Inking frames – as Johnson refers to cylinder inking tables – were manually operated ink chargers with a *ductor*, or regulator, that allowed a predetermined amount of ink to adhere to the ink roller. **Fig. 19.15** illustrates a Cope cylinder inking table, which was also repeated in Johnson/Adams (1828, p. 314). Timperley (1838, p. 95) mentions other cylinder inking tables, saying, "many other descriptions of tables are in use: frames with mounted tops of marble, lead, or hard wood: those of the latter kind are in most general use throughout the kingdom."

These *Inking Frames* are made in the form here represented [in **Fig. 19.15**]; the whole is composed of iron, with the *Cylinder* turned off to the greatest exactness, under which is a steel edge that scrapes the ink off the *Cylinder* to the exact quantity required; this is regulated by means of *Counterpois Levers* that pass under the *Table*, on which is hung two weights, to be removed according to the quantity of ink required for the work; one end of these levers are to press against the *Ductor*, or *Regulator*. The *Ductor* and *Cylinder* are fitted together so close, that it will hold water; consequently there is not the least possibility of the ink escaping more than is wanted for the purpose required; the *Cylinder* has an ornamental iron cover, which is always kept on except when a fresh supply of ink is required: by which means all dirt and dust is kept both from the ink and *Cylinder*, the latter is moved by a small handle at one end: the *Table* is turned off in a lathe perfectly true, the same as in the presses.

Fig. 19.15. *Inking frame* (cylinder inking table)

Reading 19.24
Inking by Cylinders
from *Typographia* by Thomas Curson Hansard (1825, pp. 631–635).

The cylinder inking table – or *inking apparatus*, as Hansard refers to it – seems to have arrived in tandem with the roller itself. Johnson (1824) has an illustration of a Cope inking frame shown above in **Fig. 19.15** on p. 567 that is quite similar to the Applegath and Cowper inking apparatus shown below in **Fig. 19.16**. Savage (1822, pp. 78–79) was the first to describe it. The cylinder inking table was, in reality, nothing more than a fixed charging roller that, when brought into contact with a hand-held composition roller, transferred a line of ink onto the latter which was then distributed over the ink slab. The surface of this particular inking table was covered with lead. It is interesting to note how often lead sheeting is mentioned in printers' manuals. Because it was a cheap, easy-to-shape, water-proof material, it was used for both the lye and wetting troughs.

There does not appear to have been any precise control over the density of the film of ink that was deposited on the type during the rolling process. Hansard says that the roller passed over the type "once or oftener." Charging the roller by hand on the slab, however, gave the pressman more control over the quantity of ink that was picked up by the roller.

Throughout the nineteenth century, printers complained about the decline in the quality of printing papers. Apparently in the process of handling paper at the press, the paper generated a considerable amount of fuzz, referred to below as *flue*, which drifted in the air and eventually settled on the type, rollers, and ink slab. I am not quite sure why this happened unless they were printing on dry paper.

Benjamin Foster's inking stand – an early variation on the brayer inking table and shown in **Fig. 19.17** – has a narrow *stage*, or ledge, toward the back with spaces at each end for the ink and the muller. Foster's brayer has holes in the bottom through which the ink could flow as it was spread across the stage. This line of ink served as a fountain into which the roller was touched down in order to pick up fresh ink that was then distributed over the inking slab.

[The Applegath and Cowper inking apparatus (see **Fig. 19.16**)] consists of a trough for the ink – a cylinder to revolve in the trough – and the table to distribute upon – the whole of which is supported by a firm stand of cast-iron screwed to the floor. The frame is formed of two sides of cast-iron united by three bolts with nuts and screws. The ledges cast about the middle of the sides serve to hold a convenient shelf. The top is made with deal, which being screwed to the sides, is covered with sheet lead rendered perfectly level and smooth. To the upper back part of the sides of the frame are cast prolongations to receive the axles of the trough and cylinder. The receptacle for the ink, or trough, is formed chiefly of cast-iron; but it has a lip or edge of wrought plate-iron rivetted on the front, and ground very exact to the surface of the cylinder; and which is turned up at each end to work in grooves in the cylinder, in order to retain the ink. To the back of this trough are rivetted two pieces of iron upon a level with its pivots, which act as levers: and upon these levers are hung weights, which being placed at a greater or less distance from the trough, cause the ground edge before mentioned to press with greater or less force against the metal cylinder, and thus regulates the quantity of ink to be taken by the roller. The ink being in the trough, and the cylinder being revolved by means of the handle, it will acquire a fine even coat of colour[.] The hand-roller is then applied by the workman to the ink cylinder, from which contact it receives a single line of ink, and is then rolled backwards and forwards upon the table until the ink is thoroughly spread or distributed both upon the roller and table. He then conveys his roller to the forme, and passing it once or oftener upon and over the type, it will have communicated a coat of ink, of an equal consistency and colour throughout.

Fig. 19.16. *Applegath and Cowper inking apparatus* (cylinder inking table)

The material defect in the apparatus above described is, that the ink and entire surface of the cylinder and table must remain constantly exposed, during the whole time of work, to the flue and dirt arising in the press-room, which, from the nature of paper as now made, is known to be very considerable. The scraping of the cylinder against the edge of the trough occasions it to leave all the foul particles it may have collected, as well as what the roller may communicate of that which it gathers from the forme, along with the ink in the trough, which is all drawn together by the revolving motion of the cylinder, into a cylindric form also; and appears, when the latter is put in motion, to be a second black cylinder turned by the motion of the iron one. Thus all becomes mixed together until a considerable quantity of foul matter has accumulated in the trough, and it becomes necessary to clean out all the ink remaining, which is thus spoiled and wasted.

A more simple and cheap apparatus for this purpose was immediately got up by Mr. Foster, the inventor of the composition balls.

It is a stand [see **Fig. 19.17**] having its two legs and feet of cast-iron; and its top, upon which the ink is distributed, instead of lead, as in the former apparatus just described [see **Fig. 19.16**], is mahogany. Behind this, elevated about two inches, is the stage for taking the ink on to the roller. At either end of the stage is a recess for receiving the contrivance which contains the ink. This is similar in shape to the brayer formerly used; but turned hollow, with the handle and top to screw on; at the bottom are holes, and when ink is wanted on the stage, the workman, taking hold of this bottle-brayer, moves it, from one recess to the other, drawing it slowly along the stage. In this movement the ink, by its own gravity, will issue out from the holes at the bottom, and leave a portion on the stage, more or less, according to the rapidity or frequency of its transit.

Fig. 19.17. *Mr. Foster's inking apparatus* (brayer inking table)

Mr. [James] Arding soon improved upon Foster's apparatus, by making the ink-stage of cast-iron, with circular recesses; and the whole table more of a solid form; both makers now adopt the same pattern; but the bottle-brayer has not been found to answer, as the ink soon clogs up the holes, and the wood is liable to be split by the screw at the top; and an old servant of the press-room, the common brayer, has again been found the most effective for this purpose.

I have had several of these inking tables at work, and find a decided preference due to the last described. The mahogany surface seems more congenial to the temperament of the ink and roller, than either the lead or iron. The ink is taken better, and distributes better. A line of colour is taken as perfectly from the stage as from a cylinder, since the roller, being cylindrical, can only touch the ink in a line; and it is only giving the roller a portion of a revolution on the stage to make it take a greater quantity of colour if necessary. More of the flue and dirt, inseparable from the working of paper, is held by the wood than by the lead; and consequently, the roller keeps cleaner, and the forme works better. The table is easily washed by the lye-brush, and no further waste of ink is occasioned.

This apparatus has been further improved by substituting a box and cylinder for the stage and brayer. The advantage of which will be, that the quantity of ink on the cylinder to come in contact with the roller, is regulated by a pressure at the top, out of the body of the ink, instead of at the bottom against which the ink must rest.

The cylinder is of mahogany, and, as here shown [in **Fig. 19.18**], moves in a box or trough which contains the ink; and which has a lid moving on hinges coming nearly over the top of the cylinder. To the under edge of this top is nailed a slip of thick butt or sole leather. This, by its naturally elastic quality, will always press upon the cylinder according as the lid is more or less tightly screwed down by the thumb-screws shewn in the drawing. This leather will also intercept in its way any filth which may arise from the depôt [i.e., the fountain] of ink before it can reach the cylinder: and which, when accumulated, may, by unscrewing the lid and throwing it open, as in the upper figure, be instantly scraped away with one stroke of the knife; and no further waste of the ink incurred. It will be seen from the lower figure, that no part of the ink in this apparatus is exposed; and only a very small portion of the cylinder at the time of working.

Fig. 19.18. LEFT, *Arding's inking apparatus with the box lid open;* RIGHT, *Same with the lid closed*

Reading 19.25
Inking Appliances for the Handpress
from *Practical Printing* by John Southward (1882, pp. 383–384).

With the advent of the roller, an entirely new and different kind of inking surface was required. The ink block on the wooden press evolved into an inking table with a marble slab for use with the iron handpress. Its surface was at a convenient height for the inker and wide enough to charge the whole roller at once.

Southward discusses the brayer inking table and the cylinder inking table. Scaled-down versions of the latter, called *pedestal tables*, were used with small presses and when only a little color was needed in the same form with black.

44. *The Brayer Inking Table* [**Fig. 19.19**] may be made of iron or wood. It is so called because the ink is spread out upon it by a *brayer*, which is a rubber of wood or glass, and is flat at the bottom. This is sometimes called a *muller*.

Fig. 19.19. *Brayer inking table*

45. Where very large quantities of ink are required to be spread out on the table, an *ink slice* [**Fig. 19.4**, RIGHT, on p. 532] is sometimes used. It is made of iron, and shaped something like a gardener's hoe.

46. *The Cylinder Inking Table* [**Fig. 19.20**]. – The ink is contained in a receptacle called a fountain, one side of which is moveable, and can be adjusted by set screws at the back. This moveable side consists of an iron cylinder which is made to revolve by a handle at the side. The cylinder turns round in the ink, and receives at each revolution a certain amount of it. The inking roller is merely run up to the cylinder, until it gets a portion of ink, and there is no braying out required. The parts containing the ink are covered over with a lid to exclude dust. Taking ink is certainly a more cleanly operation when this kind of table is used, than when only the ordinary brayer is used.

Fig. 19.20. *Cylinder inking table*

Reading 19.26

Setting Up the Roller Stand

from *Typographia* by Thomas F. Adams (1837, pp. 280–282).

Even though Adams, here, and Gazlay, in Reading 20.7 on p. 584, are apparently discussing the same manually operated inking apparatus, I have included both of their descriptions in this book since each writer adds unique information about them. MacKellar mentioned and illustrated this same *roller stand* (**Fig. 19.21**) in every edition of his manual between 1878 and 1893. For distinctions between *charging* and *changing*, see my introductory note to Reading 1.5 on p. 23.

Fig. 19.21. *Hoe's improved inking apparatus* (roller stand) – from MacKellar (1878, 11th ed., p. 251)

The roller stand containing the distributing cylinder, should be regulated to the height of the press, bringing the shelf or bridge even with the corner irons, and of sufficient distance from the bed to allow it to run clear; the stand should then be firmly braced, as the constant turning of the rounce [Editor's note: Here the rounce refers to the handle on the distributing cylinder.] is very apt to loosen it, meanwhile being cautious to observe that the rounce in its revolutions does not come in contact with the frame of the tympan when up. The position of the distributing cylinder should be sufficiently high to allow the two composition rollers, at least one inch apart, to rest on its top without danger of touching the shelf or bridge below; we have found it advantageous to nail a narrow strip of sole leather on the face of the shelf, about a third from each end, which acting as bearers, cause the rollers to pass very smoothly over it.

The roller handle while in use should lie in an horizontal position, the back end being supported by an horizontal bar of wood or iron running parallel with the distributing cylinder. There should be a notch, or hook, about two inches from the end of the handle to catch on the wooden supporter, to prevent the rollers from jumping forward while distributing or changing. It is also necessary to have a back-board for the end of the roller to strike against in coming off the form, to prevent the rollers from falling backwards.

The ink-block is placed about five or six inches to the right of the roller handle, and about on a level with it; it is furnished with the ink slice, and a brayer, or small roller about four or five inches long, and of the same circumference with the large rollers, being cast in the same mould.

A few years since a great improvement was effected by having the ink-block made of cast iron, for the following reason: – it had been found necessary for the purpose of enabling the men to work the fine and stiff inks in cold weather, to have in the press room what was denominated a moveable ink-stand; this was a small square table, with an iron plate for the top, under which was a shelf to contain a lamp to warm the ink, and render it free to work; this was, of course, moved to the side of each press as wanted, but often proved a cumbrous article in a crowded room, when not wanted. The iron ink-block, as a complete substitute for the wooden one, with a little shelf underneath it, answered every purpose of the above described apparatus, with this additional advantage, it kept the ink cooler in hot weather.

Reading 19.27
Self-Inking Machines
from *Typographia* by Thomas Curson Hansard (1825, pp. 635–636, 682–683).

> Hansard describes below two self-inking machines: Thomas Parkin's and John Ruthven's – which were the first to be mentioned in a printers' manual – as well as Napier's self-inking Albion press (see Reading 3.37 on p. 156). For some reason, these automatic *self-inking machines* – or *self-inking apparatus*, as Hansard refers to them – did not catch on in England. Very little was said about them after Hansard, although in America, they continued to be used well into the 1880s.

An inking apparatus for the purpose of enabling one man to perform all the operations of press-work, was invented and patented by Mr. Thomas Parkin, in the year 1820. This was contrived, by frame-work, rollers, catgut-bands, colour-boxes, &c. to perform the complex operations of taking ink, distributing, and inking the forme, with the common composition-covered cylinder. The frame was fixed on the off-side of the press, and one pressman performed the whole of the work, by stretching his left arm across his forme at the same time that he lifted up his tympans with the right, drawing the cylinder once or twice over the forme by taking hold of the handle of the moving frame; next, retiring it back again, he proceeded on to throw up the frisket, and perform the other processes of press-work.

On the fixed frame of wood, is a square frame of iron, formed to slide to and fro upon guide-rollers; a narrow plate, or table, is fixed horizontally, on a plane with the forme, and receives the ink from a small roller, called by Mr. P. the furnishing roller; this is supplied with ink from two boxes, one being fixed at each end of the table; these boxes have the sides fronting the table open, except a covering of fine wire-gauze: the furnishing roller, by the same exertion of the pressman, traverses the table at right angles to the direction in which the inking frame moves, and striking against the porous face of the ink-box, receives a portion of the colour which exudes, the equal distribution of which upon the circumference of that roller, is effected by a number of small metallic rollers, fixed in its frame, and pressing on its upper quarter arc; the roller in its traverse along the table, leaves an equal surface of ink, which is then taken up by the contrary motion of the large cylinder, and thus imparted to the forme.

This invention, however ingenious in detail, was not found to answer its intended purpose. In the first place, it required a space on the off-side of a press which the situations of press-rooms would rarely afford; and, in addition to this inconvenience, the man had not sufficient command of the main roller to make the distribution and quantity of the ink suit the work; and as a final objection, and perhaps the greatest, it must have produced in the mind of every pressman it employed the unpleasant feeling that he was turning another out of work. I think I have as much perseverance as most men in any experiment of possible advantage, but my expectations from this machine were soon relinquished. . . .

Mr. Ruthven constructed a self-inking apparatus, to be attached to his press, which would not require any additional movements for the workman: a trough for the ink was placed at the left-hand end, across the press, with the usual application of the iron cylinder and composition rollers. The last, or inking roller, being fixed in a frame made to open like a pair of compasses by a connecting rod attached to the joint of the tympans, the raising of which would bring forward the roller over the forme. To render the distribution of the ink perfect a roller was constructed to accompany the last-mentioned one, having also a lateral movement while revolving; on bringing forward the platten and turning down the handle, a supply of ink would be taken and distributed on the rollers.

Reading 19.28
Spence's Self-Inking Machine
from the advertising appendix in *The Printer's Manual* by Arthur N. Sherman (1834, p. 87).

Sherman has an advertising appendix in his manual that mentions *Spence's Self-Inking Machine*. In this advertisement, William John Spence proclaims himself as the inventor of the original self-inking machine. His machine, when activated by the turning of the rounce, automatically charged the roller and inked the form. Apparently, Spence was not aware of the self-inking machines mentioned by Hansard in Readings 3.37 on p. 156 and 19.27 above.

Although not mentioned by name, in his dictionary under "Hand-Inker," Pasko (1894, pp. 252–253) is describing R. Hoe & Co.'s self-inking machine for the handpress: "A contrivance to enable the pressman on a hand-press to do his own inking. Originally two men were required to work at a press, one to lay on the sheet and print it, and the other to ink the form. After the iron press became common a boy took the place of one man at the rear [i.e., off side of the press], but about 1830 Samuel Fairlamb, of New York, invented an inking-machine, by which the press did its own inking, more power being necessary than before, the action being perfectly automatic and uniform. Other inventors modified and changed this appliance, but all alike had some method by which the pressman, in running out the bed, wound up a pulley, which caused the roller to pass over the form after the frisket was thrown up. There is no question that the work was better done than by an ordinary careless boy." Inking machines for handpresses proved to be more work than they saved; however, they were indispensable for steam-powered presses.

Fig. 19.22. *Hoe's patent hand press self-inking machine* – from Pasko (1894, p. 253)

Adams (1837, p. 321) commenting on automatic inking machines says, "About six years since a machine was introduced to supply the place of a boy in rolling the form, &c. which was acted upon by weights and springs wound up by the running in of the bed; this machine performed the various offices of rolling, taking ink, and distributing, but owing to its complicated construction, was very liable to get out of order. Within a few years, however, various improvements have been made upon them, and their construction much simplified, still they impose an additional labor on the pressman, who is unable to perform the same quantity of work with the machine that he was accustomed to do in the old way. Therefore we shall contend against any advantage being derived from the use of them, considering that what is gained in the wages of the boy is more than counterbalanced by the extra labor and consequent loss of speed."

Wm. John Spence; The original inventor of the SELF-INKING MACHINE [**Fig. 19.23**], as adapted and applied to the common hand press, respectfully informs the trade that he is the only true and valid patentee of the said machine, and that all others are imitations and infringements of the original, as has been tested in the suits of Fairlamb, *vs.* P. A. Sabbaton and W. J. Spence; and S. Wood & Sons, *vs.* Caleb Bartlett, proprietor of Fairlamb's patent.

The machines are now manufactured in an improved and superior style, and may be seen at the Methodist Book concern, and other offices in this city, where they will recommend themselves. . . . *New-York*, 1834.

Fig. 19.23. *Spence's self-inking machine* – courtesy of St. Bride Printing Library

Plate 24. Inking a form on a Washington press, late-19th century. (Courtesy of the Graphic Arts Collection, National Museum of American History, Smithsonian Institution.)

CHAPTER TWENTY

Inking

In Chapters 17 and 18, printing inks were discussed in considerable detail; and in Chapter 19, the implements and devices for inking forms were described. This chapter deals with the process of inking, that is, the transfer of ink to the type as well as other relevant printing surfaces, such as woodcuts and wood engravings, ornaments and decorations, and rules, by means of balls and rollers.

Inking was not, nor is it today, a particularly complex procedure. It is nothing more than a very routine and sometimes monotonous series of movements, albeit, a procedure that requires maximum attention and skill if uniform results are to be gained. In the simplest terms, the ink is removed from the slab onto an intermediary surface from which it is transferred to the face of the type. As mentioned in the last chapter, prior to the nineteenth century, all forms were inked with balls. The pressman who performed this task was called a *beater* because he literally beat the balls against the type.

Ink rollers were either hand-held or used in conjunction with inking apparatus. The latter are described in my introductory note to Reading 19.23 on pp. 566–567. The pressman who inked the form with rollers was called a *roller* or, when a lad took his place, a *roller boy*. Since the person who inked the form and the implement he used went by the same name – and the manual writer's meaning of the word roller may not always be clear immediately in some of the following readings – I have arbitrarily called him the *inker* in my introductory remarks to avoid confusion. As inking apparatus became more sophisticated, and the inking process became even more mechanized, both the inker and the roller boy were replaced by self-inking machines which were activated by the puller when he turned the handle of the rounce on the press. A Washington press with one of these self-inking machines is shown in **Fig. 20.1**.

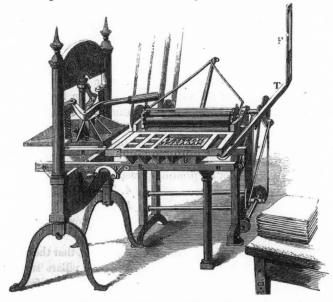

Fig. 20.1. *Washington press with a self-inking machine* – from Abbott (1855, p. 116), courtesy of Rochester Institute of Technology

Once the handpress was relegated to a secondary position in the printing office – that is, to pulling proofs and printing short runs – it is most likely that the inking process reverted once again to hand rolling. This method is preferred by most fine handpress printers today.

Quality control of the printed sheets was of the utmost concern to the master, whose reputation depended largely on the excellence of the work produced in his printing office. Responsibility for monitoring the printed sheets varied. Normally, when both puller and beater or inker were journeymen printers, the person inking scanned the sheets; however, when the form was inked by the roller boy, the puller checked them.

One of the most amazing non-truths to be found in a printers' manual comes from one of the most distinguished late-nineteenth-century printers, Charles Thomas Jacobi, who in his manual (1890, p. 170) says, "dampened papers requires more ink [than dry paper] and need not be so quick-drying, for the drying of the paper absorbs the ink." No other manual writer makes this claim and from my own experience, I can unequivocally say that printing on dampened paper uses only one-third the amount of ink needed for printing on dry paper.

The definitions of three technical terms will help the reader better understand some of the following procedures:

> *charging the ink roller*, priming the roller by picking up additional ink from the fountain;
> *changing the distributing cylinder or cylinders*, adding ink to the oscillating cylinders either manually or automatically;
> *distributing*, spreading ink out evenly on the ink slab or on the distributing cylinders.

Reading 20.1

Rubbing Out Ink

from *The Printer's Grammar* by Caleb Stower (1808, p. 354).

From Stower's description, it would appear that fresh ink was not put out every day, but added to the supply on the ink block only as it was needed. With such a lackadaisical system, it is little wonder that pressmen were constantly concerned about dried flakes of ink or other foreign particles getting into the ink and spoiling the work. All manual writers admonished pressmen to keep their ink clean and well worked up. This lazy practice was not just endemic to early printers; I remember seeing small proof presses in commercial print shops in the 1950s where the printers had let the ink accumulate on the ink plates and rollers for weeks on end before they cleaned them.

The process of inking began with the braying or rubbing out of the ink with a flat-bottomed wooden muller called a *brayer* like the one shown in **Fig. 19.4**, LEFT, on p. 532. By spreading the ink out in this manner, it was made more malleable, and became the source from which the beater replenished the ink on his balls.

Before the pressman goes to work, he rubs out his ink. If it has lain long on the ink-block, since it was last rubbed out, the surface of it is generally dried and hardened into a film or skin, for which reason he carefully takes this film quite off, before he disturbs the body of the ink; for should any, though ever so little of it, mingle with the ink, when the ball happens to take up the little particles of film, and delivers them again upon the face of the letter, they produce picks, print black, and deface the work; and if they get between the face of two or more letters, or the hollows of them, they will obliterate all they cover; and if they be pulled upon, and the pressman not careful to overlook his work, they may run through the whole heap. Having carefully skinned off the film, he brings forward a small quantity of ink near the edge of the block, which he rubs well with the brayer. Care should be observed not to brayer out much at a time; for if this be done, it will be impossible to preserve any degree of uniformity in taking ink.

Reading 20.2
Of Beating
from *The Printer's Grammar* by Caleb Stower (1808, pp. 355–356).

> Prior to the introduction of composition rollers, all forms were beaten with ink balls, one of which is shown in **Fig. 19.1** on p. 530. Beating, as its name implies, was a means of transferring ink from the balls to the printing surface while exerting a considerable amount of force on the type in the process. A pressman is beating the form with ink balls in **Plate 3** on p. 2. Rollers would later prove to be more efficient, but balls did have a few specific advantages since they were able to apply ink selectively over the form – increasing or decreasing the amount at will – and to follow the contours of the type which meant that slight variations in the height of the type were less noticeable than they would have been if the form had been inked with a roller. Ink balls are rarely used today except in museum-type reconstructions of historical printing offices where costumed pressmen give demonstrations on wooden presses, or occasionally, in libraries with bibliographical presses.
>
> Van Winkle (1818, pp. 182–183) notes: "Care should be taken that the ink does not accumulate on the side of the balls, which, by a little careless beating, causes monks. To prevent this the side of one ball must occasionally be distributed against the face of the other, alternately; for this purpose it is best to distribute *underhanded* as it is called."

Beating is an important part of a pressman's business, which, if not properly done, renders every other operation almost useless. A careful beater will never be found to take much ink at one time; but keep brayered out in the front of the ink-block a small quantity, that he might be certain of never receiving more than is necessary. The great art in beating is to preserve a uniformity of colour, which is easily performed by paying a proper attention to the taking of ink; this done regularly, and the form beat well over, the beater may be said to have done his duty.

All pressmen do not beat alike, but the method generally followed by good workmen is, the moment the tympans are lifted up, to lay the balls on the left hand near corner of the form, that he may the more readily carry them to the near right hand corner, while his companion is casting the sheet on the bank; if this opportunity be lost, it occasions delay, and in all probability leaves that corner untouched by the ball, and makes what is technically termed *a friar*.

In beating over the form, the elbows should be kept rather inward, and the ball stock handle inclining outward, in order that the balls may be perfectly upright; it will also enable him to go over the corner before mentioned with greater ease and certainty. This plan, if strictly followed, is unquestionably the most expeditious, as well as the least liable to defects, if common attention be observed by the beater. He begins, as already observed, at the right hand near corner, and goes up that side of the form and returns, and leaves off at the left hand near corner, taking care to make the form feel the force of the balls by beating hard and close. In the operation of beating the balls should be constantly turning round in the hands, as it keeps them in their proper shape, and thereby renders them more safe and pleasant to work with.

The balls should not go too far over the form, for they are liable to gather dust, and consequently throw picks on the form, which are not easily got rid of. These picks, and every other defect, it is the business of the beater to look carefully after, and to endeavour to mend and prevent. His companion can also, when taking off the sheets, give a slight glance over them; but the uniformity of the work will depend principally upon the beater. He will point out to the puller any defects in laying on the sheets on the tympan, or if he neglects to pull down the work with the force it requires.

Having thus gone twice upwards and downwards with the balls, beating close and strong, the form may then be considered sufficiently beaten; but if he beats the first sheet of a fresh form, or after a form has been lately washed and consequently damp, or makes a proof, he goes three, four, or five times upwards and downwards, for the letter will not take the ink without several beatings.

Reading 20.3
Hand Rolling
from *The Printers' Practical Every-Day-Book* by Thomas Shaw Houghton (1841, pp. 96–97).

Even though most nineteenth-century printers' manuals include directions for inking forms on a handpress with an inking apparatus, Houghton's manual is one of the few to give instructions for distributing the ink directly on the ink slab. Later, on p. 135 in his manual, he says, the inking apparatus is "also very important for the production of good work, because it is by this means only, that anything like regularity of colour can be preserved, without infinite care and labour. No employer, therefore, should be without one, unless, indeed, he is indifferent about his work."

The secret to good inking was consistency: a streak of ink was spread across the top of the brayer inking table. This streak, which was called the *fountain,* was the source from which the inker recharged his roller with fresh ink. By picking up an equal quantity of ink each time and distributing it evenly over the slab, he could, as Houghton suggests, conduct reliable tests to determine the number of sheets that could be printed with the same degree of uniformity before his roller had to be recharged at the fountain. Once the pattern had been established, he would continue to take up a little more ink off the slab for each impression he made in the predetermined group.

Houghton recommends using a small composition roller, or ink brayer, instead of the traditional wooden muller brayer. He also gives instructions for what to do when there is too much or too little ink on the slab. It was the inker's duty to check the quality of the inking.

[Rolling] also is an important part of press-work, for unless the colour of the sheets be kept regular, the work will still be indifferent, notwithstanding all the care and pains taken to make the impression even. But it is much easier than making ready, the principal thing to be observed being to take an equal quantity of ink and distribute it well, every certain number of sheets that is pulled. With a cylinder ink-table, nothing can be more easy or certain; the quantity of ink required each taking being easily adjusted to the greatest nicety, and liable to no alteration after it is adjusted. For those, however, who are compelled to do their work well without a cylinder ink-table, the best way is to use a small roller [ink brayer, shown in **Fig. 19.2**, RIGHT, on p. 530], instead of a [wooden] brayer. This will lay the ink along the off side of the ink-table much more regular than an ordinary brayer. Of course, the quantity of ink taken on the small roller, to be distributed out on the ink-table, must depend on the judgment and care of the person who rolls. Every thing being, as is supposed, in regular working order, the first thing to be noticed is the colour, whether it is too dark or too light. If it be much too dark, the ink should be taken off with a dry waste sheet; but if only about a shade or so, it may be worked off. The proper colour once obtained, observe particularly how many sheets the same uniform shade is preserved without taking ink, but with merely distributing the roller on the ink-table while each sheet is being pulled, and then take ink accordingly. Thus, if I find, on comparing the first sheet, which I conceive is a proper colour, with the fourth or fifth sheets pulled, and find the fourth as near the shade of the first as can be judged, and the shade of the fifth perceptibly lighter, I should conclude at once to take ink every four sheets. It is true, however, that if a greater quantity of ink is taken on the roller, when the four sheets are pulled, than there was on when the first sheet was rolled, a greater number of sheets than four must be rolled and pulled before the colour can again be what it was at first. But taking too much ink being amongst the things which must be avoided, it can hardly be necessary again to say that it should be taken off again with a waste sheet. As, however, a proper and regular colour can only be secured by taking ink in equal quantities regularly, it is essential that every workman should be careful in rubbing it out equally, whether with a brayer or small roller, and particular in taking a proper quantity. Failing to observe and attend to these suggestions, the sheets will exhibit almost every variety of colour; sometimes too black and at other times too gray, and scarcely ever six sheets alike. I am the more anxious to impress this fact upon the young workman, because nothing can compensate, in the appearance of work, for the want of care and attention in these particulars; in short, it is these that make up the art of rolling. The forme being rolled according to the principle I have endeavoured to explain, the sheet is laid on according to the tympan-sheet, and the work proceeds, the person who rolls taking care to cast his eye over every sheet that is pulled to detect picks.

Reading 20.4
Hand Rolling
from *Practical Printing* by John Southward (1882, pp. 444–445).

> Southward's instructions for hand rolling are similar to those given by Houghton in Reading 20.3 above, although Southward gives more specific directions for inking different types of work. He recommends taking up new ink from the slab for each sheet when rolling forms with large type or fine work, every two sheets for book work, and every three or four sheets for light work. In other words, with book work and light work the form is rolled multiple times before new ink is taken up on the roller. Southward says that the regularity or uniformity of the color is the responsibility of the puller. There does not seem to have been a fixed method for grasping the handles of the roller. The inker in **Plate 4** on p. 8 is holding the handles parallel to the bed, while the inkers in **Plates 13, 24,** and **27** on pp. 350, 576, and 632, respectively, are holding them perpendicular to the bed.
>
> When two pressmen were working the press – called *full press* – they would sometimes change places after a fixed number of tokens. Moxon (1683, p. 319) says, "Sometimes they agree to change every three *Tokens*, which is three Hours work, and sometimes every six *Tokens*; that they may both *Pull* and *Beat* a like number of *Tokens* in one day." Once inking apparatus were installed, inking and pulling became separate activities.

Rolling is equal in importance to any part of the pressman's duties, and if not performed properly all the care bestowed upon other operations is completely wasted.

A careful man will never take too much ink at one time, but keep brayed out a small quantity, that he may be certain of never taking more on the roller than is necessary.

The moment the tympan is up, the roller should be applied to the forme, beginning at the bottom and going on steadily to the top, then returning. The roller should not go beyond the type matter, or it will sink into the furniture and blacken the sheet, if unprotected there.

It is impossible to lay down a rule for taking ink. All depends on the nature of the particular job and the quality of the ink. A forme of large type might require the taking of ink for every sheet; some bookwork every two sheets; light formes three or four sheets. Very fine work, again, might require ink every sheet to keep the colour of each perfectly alike.

While the roller is taking ink, the pressman should employ the time looking over the heap, to detect any want of uniformity in the colour; to observe if any letters, quadrats, or furniture rise; that no letters are drawn out or battered; that the register be good, and the work free from picks.

When two men are working at press, one pulling and the other rolling, it is usual for them occasionally to "take turns," and alternate their occupation. Hence it is necessary for each to understand the whole routine.

Reading 20.5
Rolling with Inking Appliances
from *Typographia* by Thomas Curson Hansard (1825, pp. 589–590).

> Hansard's instructions necessitated the use of a brayer inking table, shown in **Fig. 19.17** on p. 569, or a cylinder inking table, shown in **Fig. 19.16** on p. 569. With both, once the roller had been charged, the ink still had to be distributed on the slab. It did not matter where the inker stood; the inking process always began on the side of the press closest to him. The rollers – which were the same length as the chases into which the forms were locked – were progressively moved back and forth across the whole form, spanning the matter on both sides of the short cross. Note that Hansard mentions making only one round trip.
>
> When not in use, the roller rested on the ink slab, which, with time, could flatten the roller. Modern two-handle rollers have *feet* on them, which hold the roller above the surface of the ink slab. Roll-up, or rolling-pin, rollers are usually placed in special racks, also called *cradles*, when not in use.

The application of the rollers will be guided by similar principles [i.e., those similar to beating]. Having either by turning the iron cylinder, working against the edge of the ink-trough, or by passing the brayer [Foster's muller, shown in **Fig. 19.17** on p. 569] conveying the ink along the elevated part of the ink-table, obtained a line of ink, the workman transfer so much as he deems necessary to the roller; and then, by repeatedly working it on the table, distributes the ink perfectly equal over the whole surface. At the moment the puller throws up the tympans, he moves the roller from off the table to the forme; and passing it from the near to the off side, and back again, replaces it on the table, and either repeats the operation of taking ink, or pays the necessary attention, at intervals, to the work on the bank.

Reading 20.6
Inking the Forme
from *Practical Printing* by John Southward (1900, vol. I, pp. 674-676, 689).

Even though these instructions came late in the century, they should be of particular interest to present-day handpress printers since Southward's method of inking is very similar to the one in use today. Depending on which inking apparatus the inker is using, he either brays out a line of ink at the top of the slab or he touches the roller against a charging cylinder that deposits a thin line of ink on the roller. Whichever way, the roller, as it revolves across the slab toward the front, leaves a series of thin parallel lines of ink at regular intervals on the slab. The process is repeated until a sufficient amount of ink has been laid down. Then the roller connects and smoothes out these lines of ink, distributing the ink evenly on the slab. Southward also offers solutions for reducing the amount of ink on the slab when too much has inadvertently been laid down. It is curious to note that even as late as 1900, over-inked or dirty forms were still being taken off the press to be cleaned, instead of cleaning them in the bed with a brush and benzine.

Southward's rolling technique is similar to that of earlier manual writers, although he does emphasize the need to ink lightly and to apply just enough pressure to the roller to cause the ink to transfer to the type. When Southward says to roll in "one direction and then in another," he means across the short cross and back. He says the inker is responsible for the uniformity of color and recommends that he keep a color reference sheet close by for comparison.

The direction of the lines in the bed of the press can also affect the inking. Cummins (1873, p. 7) gives the following advice to cylinder-press operators: "lock the form so that the lines of type will be parallel with the roller, as, if they run sideways, there is a great danger . . . of working the type off its feet." Forms are still locked up this way in most letterpress shops, although the modern practice on the handpress is to have the lines of type perpendicular to the roller. This permits the inker to make subtle changes in the amount of ink that is deposited on the type.

Take the can of ink and remove the lid. Then with a palette knife spread a little on the top of the ink table.* Let it be in a long streak, the full width of the table. Beware of taking too much; for present purposes try how little will be sufficient. Spread it out as thin as possible, avoiding clots. Take the roller in the right hand, and just touch the ink with it. It will take up a narrow streak of ink; the next thing to be accomplished is to get this nicely distributed all over the roller. Lay the roller down lightly on the table and draw it towards you. When you have got to the end of the table it will be found that the cylindrical shape has left a series of parallel streaks, while between them there is no ink whatever. Repeat, and some of the intervening spaces will have become filled up, provided the roller was not put down on exactly the same place. Do this over and over again, shifting the position and direction of the roller a little each time, and each time the coating on the table, as well as that on the roller, will be more complete and thinner. Go on, doing it quicker each time, till the whole is beautifully coated with a thin film of ink. This is called *distributing the ink*. It is a very important part of presswork, and pains should be taken to do it properly. Two cautions are necessary: –

Avoid having too much ink; it is easier to increase the quantity than to decrease it. The mode of increasing is, of course, to take a fresh supply. To decrease it, which is rendered necessary by the roller being "too black," there are two methods in vogue, apart from that of completely washing it. One is to scrape the roller with a knife and so to remove the superfluous ink. (Be very careful in doing so that you do not cut the roller.) The other is to lay a piece of strong clean paper on the ink table and distribute the ink on that, till it is nearly all off. The paper must be held with the left hand

* If a cylindrical inking table is used, some of these operations will be unnecessary.

at the upper end, or it will go round the roller and adhere to it. If strong paper be not used it will tear, and if there be any dirt on it, it will get mixed with the ink. This is called "sheeting the roller." The golden rule is to have too little ink rather than too much, and to go on taking a little more until the proper quantity is attained.

Secondly, be very careful not to let the roller "run into the ink" – *i.e.*, to run unintentionally into the streak of ink put down by the palette knife or brayer, or the roller will be "smothered," as it is expressively said. If not perceived, and the roller is applied to the type, there will be great blotches of ink in different places, perhaps filling it up and causing "monks," or black patches, in the impression. The forme may then have to be lifted, washed, dried, and again adjusted on the press.

Having got the ink table and the roller nicely and evenly coated with the ink, you may roll the forme. Do this lightly, yet with sufficient pressure to cause the type to take off some of the ink. Very likely the forme will not "take" the ink at first, but instead of getting more ink, briskly and repeatedly roll it over, even "dabbing" it in parts which repel the ink. Avoid inking the chase, furniture, or the press table; the roller should only touch the surface to be printed from. You should roll first in one direction and then in another.

Be careful that the suction of the roller does not draw out any of the types. If these lie on the surface unobserved, and the press is pulled, they will cause a "batter." ...

All the time when he is not engaged inking the forme or straightening the heap of paper, the pressman who is rolling should be distributing. That is one of the secrets of good presswork. It is the duty of this man to look after the due inking of the forme and to watch the colour – *i.e.*, to see that just the proper quantity of ink is applied each time. However, if the man at the forme observes that more or less ink is required he should immediately tell the other.

In most work it is well at the outset to select one sheet, and to keep that out as a standard by which to regulate the colour of the whole. The eye is very apt gradually to get accustomed to a pale colour, and when a late sheet is put beside an early one for comparison the difference is often very striking.

Reading 20.7
Putting on Ink and Rolling Forms
from *The Practical Printers' Assistant* by Theodore Gazlay (1836, pp. 109–112).

Gazlay has a notice in the advertising appendix of his manual for Rust's Patent Printing Presses that also mentions the availability of Rust's "patent cast iron hand inking frames." Since Rust's patents for the Washington press were later taken over by R. Hoe & Co., this inking apparatus is more than likely the predecessor of Hoe's roller stand, which was patented in 1847 and is illustrated in **Fig. 19.21** on p. 572.

Gazlay is describing a roller stand with a manually turned, oscillating steel or iron cylinder that distributes ink onto a pair of rollers set into a carriage called a *roller frame*. Once the rollers were sufficiently inked, the roller boy, holding onto a long handle, guided the roller frame across the type. *Running boards* or rails were placed in the bed next to the chase; they served as roller bearers, keeping the roller frame level as it passed over the form.

The roller boy brayed out the ink on a separate inking table set up next to the roller stand. A small brayer, which Gazlay calls a *hand-roller*, was used to charge the distribution cylinder with ink . Then the roller frame was drawn up to the distribution cylinder and held tightly against it until the rollers were sufficiently inked.

The distributing cylinder, for double rollers, is about seven or eight inches in diameter, placed in a frame behind the press, with a crank attached, by which the boy distributes the rollers with his left hand, while the right hand is employed in holding the handle of the roller-frame to its place while distributing, or in pushing the rollers over the form.

The distributing cylinder is placed about three inches beyond the bed of the press, the upper surface [of the distributing cylinder] about three inches higher than the upper surface of the bed. A strip of board, two or three inches wide, bevelled on the under side to cause it to fit close to the cylinder, and extending as near to the bed as possible without danger of rubbing, and as high as the corner irons of the bed, and two inches below the top of the cylinder, is attached to the frame of the cylinder. This is called the *running-board*, and its object is to pass the rollers smoothly on the form.

The roller-frame is made of iron, long enough to hold the rollers, with two slots in each end, four inches apart, to receive the journals of the cylinders; and a handle two feet long, at the end of which is a hook, to hold the rollers in their position while being distributed. The slots should be a little wider than the journals of the rollers, and an inch or two long, perpendicularly, to allow the rollers to play while distributing, and to prevent them from being lifted from the form while rolling by raising or depressing the handle.

When rollers are to be put up to a press, they should be put in the frame, and placed on the cylinder, each roller at precisely the same distance from the top, and the handle raised or depressed, until the rollers will distribute and change without coming in contact with the running-board: the handle should be made to recede or advance till the journals of the rollers are precisely in the centre of the slots. The handle of the frame may be firmly fastened in this position, by placing a shelf under the end of the handle to support it, with a block behind it to prevent its passing too far backwards, and an iron bar about a foot long in front, to hold the latch while distributing or changing.

The ink-block is placed immediately to the right [i.e., to the boy's left] of the handle of the roller frame, on a level with it, the front raised a little to cause the ink to remain in the back part of the block.

Putting on Ink and Rolling Forms

The ink is put on the rollers by a small composition *hand-roller* [shown in **Fig. 19.2**, RIGHT, on p. 530], from four to six inches long, which is distributed in the front part of the ink-block. Ink should always be put on the back roller, as it will then immediately distribute on the front roller: if it be put on the front roller it must, of course, revolve nearly around the whole cylinder before it arrives at the back roller, and much time will consequently be lost. A small quantity of ink should be taken on the hand-roller at once, which should be kept constantly distributed; if the form be large or close, or contains large type, a proportionate greater quantity should be kept distributed. When taking ink, one end of the hand-roller should be placed on the part of the back roller on which ink is required, and move diagonally across the roller, so that the ink will be taken off the whole surface of the hand-roller. If the hand-roller be moved across the large roller in one position, the ink will be taken from the hand-roller at the first revolution, and at the next there will be no more ink on that part of the hand-roller, and the color will consequently be uneven.

To prevent the ink from accumulating at any particular part of the rollers, the ink is put on by the hand-roller in different ways, as from *right to left, left to right, right and left, centre to ends,* or on any part of the roller that may require it. The rollers should be changed, by moving the handle of the frame to and fro while distributing, every time the ink is taken, to obviate the difficulty of taking ink precisely alike on all parts of the roller, and to keep the color perfectly even, as one part of the form sometimes requires more ink than another, and to prevent ink from accumulating between pages. Rollers should be changed both ways from the regular position, and distributed every time the form is rolled.

If the rollers be new and in good order, rolling over the form once will generally be found sufficient for ordinary work; as rollers when new are quite adhesive, the form must be rolled slowly, too much time would be consumed in rolling twice. But after the rollers have been in use some time, and have lost a part of their adhesive quality, it will be necessary to roll the form twice. The form should never be rolled very rapidly, or the rollers will jump and cause the form to fill up, and the color to be uneven.

For fine work a very small quantity of ink should be taken, and the form rolled several times, particularly if it should contain cuts.

Reading 20.8
Inking with the Roller Stand
from *The Printer's Manual* by Thomas Lynch (1859, pp. 158–159).

> Lynch gives instructions for good inking. From his description, he is probably using one of R. Hoe & Co.'s roller stands, which is shown in **Fig. 19.21** on p. 572. More details concerning its operation will be found in Readings 19.26 on p. 572 and 20.7 above.
>
> Lynch keeps the ink rubbed out thin and even on the inking table. Unlike Gazlay, he brays the ink directly onto the inking roller closest to the bed instead of applying it to the distributing cylinder. He takes fresh ink off the slab for each impression. When roller frames with two rollers are used, he recommends going over the form three or four times very slowly and uniformly. Less ink is deposited when the roller passes over the type quickly. An important reason for consistency in inking is to maintain the uniformity of color on facing pages, especially those that were printed in different forms.

In proceeding with the work, the rollers should be kept perfectly clean from dirt, particles of paper, or other extraneous matter.

The ink ought to be rubbed out thin and regular, on the block, so that, when first put on, it shall be diffused tolerably smooth on the surface of the rollers; this being more likely to produce good impressions. It is advisable, also, to keep rubbing the ink out on the block with the brayer, and to distribute the rollers as much as possible; because constant friction generates a slight amount of warmth, which is of advantage, especially when the weather is cold.

In taking ink, it should be put on the back roller; because it can be distributed faster, and with more ease, than if it were laid on the front roller and had to traverse the circumference of the cylinder before coming in contact with the other.

As uniformity of color is requisite for beauty in printing, the pressman should take ink for every impression, where the form is large; this may be thought troublesome, but there is no other way of keeping up the regularity of color which should pervade good work. There is nothing which looks worse, than to see two pages that face each other, the one of a full black, rather surcharged with ink, and the other deficient in quantity and of a gray color; yet this must happen, when, as is frequently the case, three or four sheets are printed between each time of taking ink.

Rolling, for fine work, should not by any means be slighted. The form ought to be gone over three or four times, when a pair of rollers are used. The motion should be slow and uniform; for, if they be made to go over one part of a form more quickly than another, that portion will receive less ink, and, consequently, the impression from it will be paler than that from the part which has been rolled more slowly.

The cylinder should be of cast-iron, or some other material upon which water would have no effect; for, if it be made of wood, its surface will, in a short time, become rough and uneven, on account of the water getting into its pores, when being washed.

Reading 20.9
Inking Forms with a Common Distributor
from *The Progressive Printer* by Samuel Whybrew (1882. pp. 22–23).

Whybrew was a champion of the handpress and argued for its continued use in small country offices. Despite the preponderance of printing machines, he also felt that handpresses could still fulfill an essential purpose in city offices.

The inking apparatus illustrated in **Fig. 20.2** is a double-cylinder distributor for a single ink roller, also known as a *common distributor*. It was probably the simplest of all inking appliances. An inking roller was placed in the well made by the two cylinders, which distributed the ink on the roller as the cylinders were turned. He also suggests occasionally flipping the ink roller from end to end – a procedure that is still practiced by handpress printers today. Because of the long handle attached to the roller, it can be assumed that the roller was guided across the form on running boards in the same manner described in Reading 20.7 on p. 584.

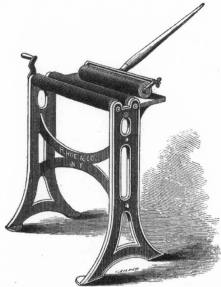

Fig. 20.2. *Common distributor* – from R. Hoe & Co.'s *Catalogue of Printing Presses* (1881, p. 29)

Whybrew recommends inking the form two or three times without exerting any pressure. While the puller was checking the sheets for color, the boy continued to distribute the ink on the cylinders.

The hand press has not yet been everywhere superceded by the more pretentious cylinder and steam engine, and until it has the apprentice must expect to follow in the wake of the thousands who before him have stood with inking pad or roller in hand performing that part of his duties which originally gave rise to the name of "devil." The hand press has not by any means outlived its usefulness, and the boy working in a small country office, diligently plying his brayer and roller, may find his counterpart in many large city offices where notwithstanding the busy hum of steam machinery is heard, the hand press is still considered an essential appointment.

Good press work cannot be accomplished unless the roller boy perform his part of the labor carefully. For newspaper work the ink should be spread very thin and evenly on the roller while resting on the cylinders; then turn the cylinders until the ink is thoroughly distributed. It is a good plan to reverse the roller, end for end, occasionally, to aid distribution. Having the roller ready, commence rolling the form a few inches from the edge, and then evenly across the form from end to end, two or three times. No pressure need be used in rolling; if the roller is in good condition, its own weight will be sufficient to bear it down well on the form. Should any type or metal be noticed adhering to the roller, the attention of the pressman should be called to it immediately. When not busy rolling the form the boy should be turning the cylinders, and as often as opportunity permits see that the ink on the slab is rolled thin enough for another application to the cylinders. The boy should be constantly on the watch for anything that may adhere to the roller – pieces of paper, dirt, flock, etc., and keep the roller free from all such foreign substances. When oiling the cylinders, care should be exercised that too much is not used, as it might flow on to the cylinders and cause trouble – three drops is generally sufficient. The pressman should indicate to the boy when insufficient or too much color is used.

Reading 20.10
Roller Bearers
from *The Practical Printers' Assistant* by Theodore Gazlay (1836, p. 112).

> Unlike ink balls, which were dabbers, rollers passed linearly over the whole width of the form from one side of the press to the other and back. Therefore, it was necessary to elevate the rollers – which were softer than rollers today – as they moved across the gaps between the pages of type in order to keep them from jolting against the type or dropping off into the gutters. Materials, such as cork, sole leather, etc., were frequently used for this purpose. Gazlay's primitive *bearers*, as they were called even then, were the precursors of modern roller bearers that are 18-point type-high brass rules.

It may be necessary to observe that the rollers must be prevented from sinking into the open places of the form, by bearers of cork, sole leather, or strips of pine, tacked to the furniture, between the pages, and where blank pages occur. Bearers should also be tacked on the furniture at the front and back side of the form, to raise the rollers on the plates or pages: the bearers should be about the thickness of a lead lower than the height of the page. If the rollers be not supported, they will sink into the open places between the pages, and when they rise, the weight of the rollers will come on the exposed sides or heads of the pages, and cause them to fill up. The necessity for using bearers may be avoided by obtaining furniture about two leads [about four points] lower than the height of the type.

Reading 20.11
Spring and Cork Bearers
from *The Printers' Practical Every Day Book* by Thomas Shaw Houghton (1875, pp. 117–118).

Spring bearers were probably already in use by the mid-1820s. In Johnson/Adams (1828, p. 313), Adams mentions placing a small steel spring about the thickness of a scaleboard on the crossbars to raise the roller as it moved across the form. Houghton first described them on p. 95 in the 1841 edition of his manual.

Houghton also refers to another type of roller bearer made of bottle corks, which he calls a *roller carrier*. Thin slivers of cork were glued with melted composition to the roller bearers in order to elevate them in troubled areas. This process functioned very much like the modern practice of selectively putting masking tape on the roller bearers. Jacobi (1890, p. 179) says, "Corks on the forme, placed judiciously, also prevent the roller from jumping or wiping on the extreme edges of the pages. It is a good plan to have these corks so arranged both on the near-side and off-side portions of the forme, in addition to being placed at the end of each space caused by the gutter or back margins, otherwise the roller will drop, in rolling across, between the line of pages, and deposit an objectionable excess of ink at the edge of the page." Cork bearers were also used as frisket bearers. See p. 404 in Reading 14.1.

Spring bearers, which are merely narrow strips of iron, a little bent in the middle and fastened across the forme to the furniture by means of spurs on the underside, to prevent the roller from throwing picks or filling up the head lines of the pages, are used with great advantage for most formes. Where they can be used, they undoubtedly should be, as every forme to which they are fastened will work clean much longer than without them.

Another sort of bearers or roller carriers for book formes are made of bottle-corks, cut to the proper height of the page from the chase, and fastened thereto with composition. The method is simple, efficacious, useful, and always at hand; and is generally liked and much practised amongst pressman. These bearers protect the type from filling up, prevent slurs, and bear the roller off the heads and corners of the pages. The method is this: – after cutting as many of these corks as required for the forme in hand to the proper thickness, a piece of waste composition is held to the flame of a gas-burner until melted, when it is rubbed on the cork until sufficient adheres to make it stick in the place on the chase or furniture for which it was cut. They are sometimes fastened also to the frisket in the same way, to fall between the grooves of the chase or gutter, to ease the impression or prevent a slur.

Reading 20.12
Preserving Rollers
from *The Printer's Manual* by Thomas Lynch (1859, pp. 173–174).

Being very temperamental, composition rollers required much more care than ink balls. They were especially unstable when subjected to dramatic changes in atmospheric conditions that could cause them to melt or harden. For more information about the care of rollers, see Reading 19.22 on p. 562. Fortunately, since many rollers today are made of rubber or synthetic materials, most of Lynch's concerns are no longer relevant.

Lynch notes that the forms and rollers were washed by the roller boys, not the pressmen, and that lye and water were still the solvents of choice. Occasionally turpentine was used on new rollers since water could weaken the fresh composition.

He also goes into some detail about storing rollers and the necessary changes that had to be made throughout the year in the roller cabinet due to atmospheric conditions. Lynch recommends giving rollers a coating of common ink that was later washed off with the centuries-old lye and water treatment.

The washing of the rollers is an operation very little attended to, by pressmen; though their preservation and good condition depend, almost entirely, on the care with which it is done. This, like the washing of forms, is usually entrusted to boys, who, if there be a number of rollers to be cleaned, frequently wash the whole with ley before any of them are rinsed with water and dried. This should never be done; because, if a roller be kept for a short time with either water or ley on its surface, the molasses will become dissolved, and the roller will lose its adhesiveness.

When it is necessary to wash a roller, it should be done as quickly as possible, by first loosening the ink with ley and a sponge, after which clean water must be thrown upon it till all the ink is removed. This being done, and the ley being rinsed out of the sponge, which should be squeezed as dry as possible, it should be rubbed over the surface and ends of the roller, so that it will absorb any water that may have been left on those parts.

When rollers are new, they should not be cleaned with ley, as it will have an injurious effect on them, although the utmost care may be taken in its application. The best method of proceeding, in such cases, is, to use either spirits of turpentine or coal oil to remove the ink; but, if neither of the above articles be at hand, new rollers may be cleaned by running them back and forth, a few times, over a dusty part of the floor which has previously been swept clear of all hard and large particles: the ink becoming absorbed by the dust, both of them can be removed, by using a sponge which has been slightly dampened.

The best method of keeping rollers in good condition is, to cover them at night, and when they are not likely to be wanted for some time, with a thick coating of common printing-ink; this keeps the air from coming in contact with the surface. When the roller is required for use, the superfluous ink may be taken off, by means of sized waste-paper, and the remainder can be washed off with ley and water.

If a roller become too hard, and the surface is clean, dampening it with clean water will restore it to a proper condition for working; but, instead of doing this, it is preferable to put it in a damp situation, where it will gradually absorb moisture. It will often be found that sponging a roller, while it is being used, will make it work as well as it would if it were washed. When this is done, the roller must be kept in constant motion, on the cylinder or stone, until all the particles of water are absorbed.

When a roller gets too soft, it should be placed where a current of dry air would act on its surface. This will evaporate the superabundant moisture which it contains, and cool the composition, if the room has been too warm. But a more expeditious and effective method is, to sponge it with spirits of turpentine, which will restore it to a proper condition sooner than any thing else.

When rollers are not in use, they should be kept in an air-tight box, so made that water could be put in or taken out of it, as occasion might require. With a box of this description, the rollers can always be kept in good order, by attending to the following directions: if the atmosphere be very damp, there should be no water left in the box, and the cover should be put down closely, so as to exclude the air; and, if the atmosphere be very dry, water should be put in the bottom of the box, the cover being as before; in the intermediate states of the atmosphere, the cover may be left more or less open, as circumstances require. [Southward, on p. 562 in Reading 19.22, also suggests adding damp sawdust to the box.]

Rollers should not be allowed to rest on the cylinder or stone for any length of time, as they will thereby become flattened, which will render them unfit for the uniform distribution of the ink; neither should they be exposed to the action of the rays of the sun, in summer, nor to the direct heat of a stove, in winter, as either will soften the composition so much as to cause it to run, and thus spoil the rollers.

Although rollers can generally be kept in good order, by attending to the foregoing directions, yet it will sometimes be found that, no matter what care be taken, the rollers will work badly. This can, generally, be obviated by allowing them to rest for an hour or two.

Reading 20.13
What the Germans Use to Clean Rollers
from *The Country Printer* by G. Krumbholz (1893, p. 27).

Many printers in the Midwest in the late-nineteenth century were of German descent, so it is not surprising to find that some of them were still influenced by printing practices that originated in their former homeland. I have included – perhaps with a bit of tongue-in-cheek – this curious little paragraph on solvents as an early attempt by nineteenth-century printers to be environmentally correct.

The Germans have resorted to the use of camphor oil for the purpose of cleaning rollers, type, wood cuts, machinery, etc. Essence of turpentine, petroleum and benzine have been abandoned for various reasons: First, because camphor oil is cheaper; secondly, because it is hygienic and purifies the atmosphere of the work-shop; thirdly, it is as efficacious and as prompt as the products hitherto employed; fourthly, it is not greasy, and therefore leaves no deposit.

Plate 25. Printing office with a Hopkinson improved Albion press, ca., 1849. (Source: *A History of Wonderful Inventions*, 1849, p. 66.)

CHAPTER TWENTY-ONE

Presswork

Presswork comprises the whole act of printing, beginning with making ready and making register, which are covered in Chapters 14 and 15, respectively, and inking the form, in Chapter 20; this chapter is devoted to the process of pulling the impression. The transition, in the early-nineteenth century, from the two-pull wooden press to the one-pull iron handpress was not as difficult for the pullers as it was for the beaters since the latter had to adjust to a completely new technology when they changed over from ink balls to composition rollers. The dynamics of the two presses may have varied in their pressure-applying mechanisms, but the preparation and operation of these presses remained basically the same for both. Within a few years, the printing machine surpassed the handpress as the printing apparatus of choice; even so, the two-pull wooden press was still in use in the 1830s for pulling proofs, as well as printing light work and short runs. Ironically, by the end of the century, its usurper, the iron handpress, was relegated to perform the same mundane chores that its predecessor had earlier in the century.

Positioned together on the near side of the press, the pressmen generally worked in pairs, one pulling, the other inking. It was only after the introduction of inking apparatus that the inker – or the roller boy – moved to the opposite side of the press, although it was still quite common to find them on the same side when the person inking manually charged his rollers on a brayer or cylinder inking table such as the one illustrated in **Plate 23** on p. 528.

There are two small and somewhat amusing decorative wood engravings in nineteenth-century printers' manuals that show the pressmen positioned on opposite sides of the handpress. Although fanciful, the *putti* are deployed in the same arrangement that the pressmen would have been in real life. One of these is to be found in Crisp, shown in **Fig. 21.1**; and the other in MacKellar, shown in **Fig. 21.2**. It is interesting to note that the toggle mechanism of the Washington press in the MacKellar engraving is mechanically incorrect. Here, as in several of the plates, the roller boy appears to be working at an awkward disadvantage due to his diminutive stature.

Fig. 21.1. *Printing putti* – from Crisp (1875, title page), courtesy of University of Iowa Libraries

Fig. 21.2. *Printing putti* – from MacKellar (1878, p.149)

As already mentioned on p. 9, I found only one illustration of pressmen working at a handpress in all of the pre-twentieth-century printers' manuals that I examined. I did, however, discover a number of woodcuts showing pressmen at their presses in secondary sources, such as books describing the art and history of the craft (see **Plate 20**, the frontispiece to Volume Two, and **Fig. 21.3** below) as well as woodcuts used by printers to embellish their bill heads or catalogs (see **Plate 13** on p. 350). Type founders also sold generic cuts for this purpose (see **Fig. 21.4** below).

Fig. 21.3. *Woodcut showing pressmen working at a Columbian press on the left and a bindery on the right* – from *The History of the Catnach Press* by Charles Hindley (1886, p. [vi])

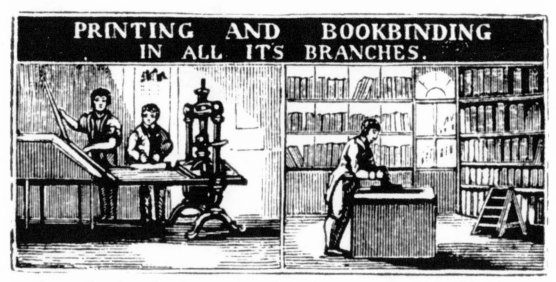

Fig. 21.4. *Generic woodcut showing pressmen working at an Albion press on the left and a bindery on the right* – from *Epitome of Specimens from the Foundry of V. & J. Figgins, Type Founders* (1845, cut No. 152 in the section headed "Polytyped Ornaments")

Reading 21.1
The Bank and Paper-Horse
from *The Printer's Grammar* by Caleb Stower (1808, p. 338).

Pressmen, who worked at both the two-pull wooden press and the one-pull iron hand-press, were able to ply their craft with very little additional equipment. Initially, they inked the forms with hand-held balls or rollers, although in many printing offices, these implements were later replaced by manual or automatic inking apparatus. The only other essential pieces of equipment that were needed in the pressroom were the "bank and paper-horse" – described below and illustrated in **Fig. 21.5** – and the lye trough – described in Reading 21.17 on p. 614 and illustrated in **Fig. 21.6** on p. 610.

In 1683, when Moxon published his manual, many pressmen were still using a flat bench for their paper (see **Plate 23** on p. 528). There are many pre-nineteenth-century depictions of pressmen working at wooden presses with the paper bench on either side of the press. When it was on the off side, it was usually placed parallel to the bed of the press. It was more convenient, however, to have it on the near side when handling larger sheets of paper. Moxon (1683, p. 298) set up his paper bench at a 75 degree angle to the tympan end of the bed. In the late-eighteenth century, Luckombe (1771, pp. 343–345) discusses the paper bank or bench without mentioning the horse, although on p. 499 in his manual, he specifically notes the horse in his list of technical terms.

Stower was the first to describe the bank and paper horse in detail. The uncovered, dampened paper, called the *heap*, was placed on the horse, a sloping, lectern-like platform positioned on the left end of the bank. As the printed sheets came off the press, they were stacked in a neat pile on the flat surface at the opposite end of the bank (see **Plate 25** on p. 592).

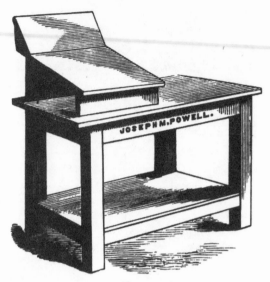

Fig. 21.5 *Bank and paper-horse* – from Southward (1882, p. 382)

The bank is a deal [fir or pine wood] table, three feet four inches long, twenty-two inches wide, and three feet high. About five inches from the bottom, a board is placed within two inches of the length and breadth of the bank, and fastened to the legs, which serves as a convenient shelf for pressmen to lay their worked-off heaps.

The paper-horse is also made of deal, two feet two inches long, and twenty inches wide, forming an angle of about forty-five degrees, six inches of the highest end of it rising nearly to a perpendicular. This horse receives the wet paper, and is placed on the bank near to the tympans.

Reading 21.2
Press-Work
from *American Encyclopædia of Printing* by J. Luther Ringwalt (1871, p. 366).

Stower (1808, p. 301) refers to "press-work" as the most important branch of the art of printing. Writing ten years later, Van Winkle (1818, p. 192) is still describing eighteenth-century presswork: "So much depends on the pressman, in wetting down, turning, and pressing his paper, in taking and distributing the ink on his balls, in keeping them in proper order, and in examining the sheets as they are pulled, that the press itself becomes, in fact, but a secondary consideration; hence the probability . . . when printers undoubtedly were men of more scientific knowledge, and more ambitious to be considered masters of their profession, greater inducements were held out to journeymen than at the present time."

In the reading below, Ringwalt comments on the fact that compositors are plentiful and pressmen, both on handpresses and printing machines, are scarce. This may have had to do with the increased demand for type that printing machines required, as well as a decline in the number of men needed to operate them. In reality, the pressman's duties were also less complex than the compositor's, which might account for the relatively small amount of space allotted to presswork in printers' manuals. Adams, in 1844, devoted only 46 pages to the subject out of a total of 287 pages; MacKellar, whose manual was widely read in America during the nineteenth century, devoted 58 pages out of 384 pages to presswork, including machine work.

It is a notable feature of the history of printing in this country [America], that a large proportion of those who have successfully prosecuted the art have been celebrated for their superior knowledge of, and attention to press-work. . . . It is too much the habit of apprentices to devote their attention exclusively to composition; and, as a consequence, compositors are always plenty and good pressmen comparatively scarce. All the money and labor spent in purchasing fonts of letter, and in setting up type correctly or elegantly, are well-nigh useless when bad press-work mars the products of the type-foundry and the composing-room. We have great faith in modern machinery, in improved presses, roller-composition, etc.; but no machinery and no chemical combinations will cover up the blunders or carelessness of a poor pressman. An expert in this branch of the typographic art will produce fine if not good work on any press, and give a presentable appearance to fearfully battered type; while a botch will produce comparatively imperfect effects with splendid type, good rollers, and the best press than can be made.

Reading 21.3
A Definition of Press-Work
from *Printing* by Charles Thomas Jacobi (1890, pp. 145–146).

> Jacobi notes that British printers who worked on handpresses were called *pressmen* in order to distinguish them from *machine minders* who worked on printing machines. This differentiation was never made in America, where all printers were called pressmen. Pressmen were generally not as well educated as compositors, although they still had to be intelligent and knowledgeable about their craft if they were to produce first-rate work.
>
> Even as late as the 1890s, the handpress was still preferred for certain types of printing. These included fine and color work, as well as short runs with complex makereadies – the tympans on handpresses were more accessible than those on printing machines. For this reason, William Morris was still able in 1891 to secure the services of professional handpress printers for his Kelmscott Press.
>
> Handpress work was harder and more physically demanding than machine work, which, though less arduous, was more boring. Jacobi notes that presswork was slow, averaging about 250 impressions per hour when two men worked the press; however, extra-fine work like Morris's could easily reduce that number to thirty or less impressions per hour. For more information about productivity on the handpress, see Reading 28.8 on p. 841.
>
> A few late-nineteenth-century manual writers made sentimental references to handpresses, such as Kelly (1894, pp. 4–8) who used the first five pages in his manual to praise the skills that could be learned at the handpress.

Press-work is generally understood to mean printing by hand by a flat or platen impression. The men who perform this part in the production of a book are called pressmen. Owing to the increase of mechanical means of printing, the old school of pressmen is fast dying out. Few lads are apprenticed to this department of the business nowadays, as the demand for hand labour is somewhat limited, the great improvements in machinery of various classes allowing of really good work being executed by machinery. The small platen machines, propelled by either foot or steam, have also very largely reduced in late years the amount of work done by the hand-presses even after the introduction of the larger printing machines. Notwithstanding this, certain classes of work must yet be done by the hand-press, and the exercise of a pressman's calling requires a deal of practice apart from the manual labour bestowed on the printing off. An ordinary press, with two men working at it, one rolling and the other pulling, is only capable of producing about two hundred and fifty impressions per hour, even when in full swing, and after all the making-ready has been finished. Small numbers and works in colours are the principal jobs relegated to this department. The preparatory stages in getting a forme ready to print are more accessible on the press, and a machine is paying best when running; hence the reason for small numbers with frequent making-ready going to the press-room. A pressman's educational qualifications are not always of the same standard as his fellow-worker the compositor, but it is requisite that be should be intelligent, and capable of exercising sound practical sense in the performance of his duties. These duties are only acquired in a proper manner by long experience. A good workman may always command constant employment.

Reading 21.4
General Remarks for Pressmen
from *The Printer's Companion* by Edward Grattan (1846, pp. 75–76).

> Pulling the bar of the handpress was a particularly strenuous and debilitating task. In addition to the generally unsanitary conditions found in many nineteenth-century workplaces – and the ever-present threat of alcoholism – pullers suffered from a number of diseases and deformities that could be directly traced to their occupation. These included back and kidney infirmities, and not surprisingly, an over-developed right shoulder from favoring that arm when pulling. Grattan lists seven rules to aid the pressman in performing his duties, including this one, which is one of my favorites: "Learn to make as few motions as possible."

[We] have only to observe: that the following rules, if attended to, will aid the pressman much in doing his work, and in winning him the good opinion of his employers:

1. Make out time, at least once a week, to take the works out of your press, and give them a thorough cleaning and oiling, keeping them always as clean and bright as you have found them.

2. Never attempt to work with bad rollers: more time will be lost in the endeavour than in casting a pair of new ones.

3. Never allow your boy to keep more ink on your ink block than he needs at the time, as it becomes dirty and thick, and will cause picks. Also have your ink block cleaned occasionally.

4. If your press slurs, never be satisfied till you have found out the reason: it generally proceeds from one of the following causes. The platen may rub against the drawer on the top or at the sides, in running in or out the bed. The tympan may not be screwed up sufficiently tight to prevent its working in the act of flying the frisket and putting the tympan down. The thumb piece of the frisket may be too long, so as to hit against the cheek of the press in running the bed in or out. The frisket, from being loose in the joints, from resting against a quoin when down, or from striking the furniture at some particular place, may move the sheet as it is lifted from the type; or the platen may stick to the drawer, in pulling, from dirt or in moist weather: a clean sheet of paper pasted on the drawer will obviate the last difficulty.

5. Always be sure that your points are screwed up tight, and that they make a clean, round point hole; that your chase is so quoined up that it cannot possibly move in any way; and if working stereotype plates, try each separately, to be satisfied that it is screwed tight on its block. If these

are attended to, and you lay your paper even on your bank in pulling the first side, keeping the edges moist by laying a damp cloth over each token as you pull it, you will never find any difficulty in making your register.

6. Learn to make as few motions as possible in pulling; keep your horse as high as you can work with it, and your heap as near your tympan as you can. Attention to these little matters save much time; and being obliged each pull to straighten yourself up as you put your sheet on the tympan, the motions will be found to be much more healthful.

7. Lastly, when fires are used in winter, particularly if they are in stoves and of stone coal, keep a kettle of clean water boiling, so as to have quite a steam in the room. This does away with the deleterious effects of the stone coal fire, gives an agreeable lightness and elasticity to the spirits, prevents those diseases of the throat and lungs so frequently brought on by the dry heat, and, moreover, makes it much less difficult to do good work during the cold weather.

Reading 21.5
An Introduction to Pulling
from *Typographia* by Thomas F. Adams (1837, pp. 278–279).

> Even though Adams was not the first manual writer to promote "modern press-work," his enthusiasm for it as presented below differs considerably from Houghton's dour pessimism in Reading 21.7 on p. 602. Adams felt that descriptions of presswork in earlier manuals were inadequate and obsolete since they were primarily limited to the two-pull press and ink balls. He stresses the new technology – exemplified by the iron handpress and rollers – and because of it, the availability of employment for industrious and careful pressmen.
>
> Adams may have seen the iron handpress, and its accompanying improvements, as an incentive to strive for a higher standard of professionalism in the industry, or perhaps he, too, was simply motivated by increased productivity and larger profits.

However laudable it may be to cultivate the art to perfection, it is to its common and more general application that we are to look for its great and beneficial effects upon the human intellect, and upon nations and societies of men. The Press is the great engine by which man is enabled to improve the faculties of his nature; – it is the preserver of the knowledge and acquirements of former generations, and the great barrier, when not perverted by the hand of power, against the debasement of the human mind, and the equalizing effects of despotism. [Editor's note: Adams has taken this paragraph verbatim from Stower (1808, p. 498).]

In former works upon this subject the directions to Pressmen have been found to be quite inadequate, being in a great measure confined to the two-pull Press, and to the minutiæ of balls, beating, &c. The various improvements in the art since those directions were written, have rendered them entirely obsolete, and it therefore devolves upon us to offer such new directions as will suffice to acquaint the new beginner with the peculiarities of modern press-work.

In the accomplishment of what we have here undertaken we shall strictly adhere to those rules which experience and observation have enabled us to select for our guidance, and which, we feel persuaded, are in accordance with the advanced state of this important branch of the art, a branch which is the very end and consummation of all the compositor's previous care and labor – a branch which, if in the least degree neglected, will cause all his taste and skill in composition, and the employer's expenses in beautiful type to be passed over disregarded.

Industrious and careful pressmen must stand high in the estimation of every master printer, yet it is to be lamented that so few endeavor to merit so desirable an appellation, and one so easily acquired by a little care and attention.

We shall now lay down a few directions, which, if properly attended to, will enable the pressman to execute his work in a manner that will do credit to himself and justice to his employer. [Editor's note: At this point, Adams continues with instructions for setting up the iron handpress and the roller inking stand.]

Reading 21.6
Of Pulling
from *Typographia* by Thomas Curson Hansard (1825, pp. 590–594).

Hansard – who repeats Stower (1808, pp. 356–362) – gives a very clear and detailed description of the puller's duties at the wooden press. At the same time, he adds some pertinent information about the iron handpress and rollers. All operations on a handpress were performed manually: the paper, sheet by sheet, was placed on the tympan; the form, inked with balls or rollers; the tympan/frisket assembly, lowered and raised; the bed, run in and out; and the bar, pulled home. Even so, the emphasis was always on economy of movement, keeping both hands occupied at the same time, taking the least number of steps until all the sheets in the heap were *worked off*, the pressman's term for *printed*. The printer in **Plate 17** on p. 400 illustrates the correct stance when pulling the bar.

One of the main differences between historical and modern practices is how the puller handled the printing paper. In this reading, the paper for the white-paper form was not pricked by the points until the first impression was made. It was merely laid on the tympan sheet – being held in place by either the suction created by the two dampened sheets of paper or by duck's bills. Jacobi (1890, p. 180) also mentions: "sticking pins in the tympan obliquely, two for the off-side and one for the foot. After the first side has been printed, these pins should be removed." Albeit, precise positioning was not critical since all four edges of the sheet were eventually trimmed off by the binder.

Note that the term *reiteration*, which means to *perfect* or *back up* the first side of a printed sheet, is spelled in various ways: Moxon uses *reteration*, and Hansard sometimes spells it *re-iteration*.

The puller lays on sheets, lays down the frisket and tympans, runs in and out the carriage, takes up the tympans and frisket, takes off the sheet, and lays it on the heap. All these operations are comprehended in the term pulling . . .

To take a sheet off the heap, the puller places his body almost straight before the near side of the tympan; but nimbly twists the upper part of his body a little backwards towards the heap, the better to see that he takes but one sheet off, which he loosens from the rest of the heap by drawing the back of the nail of his right thumb quickly over the bottom part of the heap (but in the reiteration, care should be observed to draw the thumb on the margin, or between the gutters, that the sheet may not smear or set off) and, receiving the near end of the sheet with his left-hand fingers and thumb, catches it with his right hand about two inches within the further edge of the sheet, near the upper corner, and about the length of his thumb below the near edge of the sheet, and brings it swiftly to the tympan, and at the same time twists his body again before the tympan, only moving his right foot a little from its first station forwards under the coffin-plank, or the table [bed of the wooden press]; and as the sheet is coming to the tympan (suppose it to be white-paper) he nimbly disposes the fingers of his right hand under the further edge of the sheet near the upper corner; and having the sheet thus in both his hands, lays the further side and two extreme corners of the sheet down even upon the further side and extreme further corners of the tympan sheet; but he is careful that the upper corner of the sheet be first laid even upon the upper corner of the tympan sheet that he may the sooner disengage his right hand. If, however, by a quick glance of his eye, he perceives the sides of the sheet lie uneven on the tympan sheet, with his left hand at the bottom corner of the sheet, he either draws it backwards, or pulls it forwards, as the sheet may lie higher or lower on the near corners of the tympan sheet, while his right hand, being disengaged, is removed to the back of the ear [thumb-piece] of the frisket, and with it gives it a light touch to bring it down upon the tympan, laying, at the same moment the tympan on the forme. He then, with his left hand, grasps the rounce, and with a moderate strength quickly gives its winch about one turn round;* but to regulate his running-in, he first makes a mark, as before observed, on the further rail of the tympan, to which mark he runs the carriage in, till he brings the mark in a range with the fore edge of the platten; and as it is running in, skips his hand to within an inch or two of the end of the bar, and then gently leans his body back, that his arm, as he pulls the bar towards him, may keep a straight posture; because in a pull it has then the greatest strength. He now puts his right foot upon the footstep, while his left hand holds fast by the rounce; as well to rest on the footstep and rounce, as to enable him to make a stronger pull; which will prove longer or shorter according to the strength put to it. Then disengaging his right hand again from the handle of the bar, he slips it to the bow of the bar, before the handle rebounds quite back to the cheek of the press; for should the bar by its forcible spring knock hard against the cheek of the press, it might not only shake some of its parts out of order, but subject the whole machine to injury; besides, the further the bar flies back, the more he is retarded in recovering it again. But yet he must let the bar fly so far back, as that the platten may clear the tympan; lest, when he runs in for his second pull, the face of the platten rub upon the tympan, and force the sheet upon the face of the letter, which slurs or doubles the impression, and destroys the sheet.

Having made the first pull, and the rounce still in his left hand, he turns it round again, till the carriage runs in so far as that the second mark of the rail of the tympan comes in a range with the further edge of the platten, as before[,] and then pulls his second pull, as he did his first, and slips his right hand again off the handle of the bar to the bow, guiding the bar expeditiously to its catch; and just as he has pulled his second pull, he gives a quick and strong pressure upon the rounce, to turn it back, and run the carriage out again: as soon as he has given this pressure, he disengages his left hand from the rounce, and claps the fingers of it towards the bottom of the tympan, to assist the right hand in lifting it up, and also to be ready to catch the bottom of the sheet when the frisket rises, which he conveys quick and gently to the catch; and while it is going up, he slips the thumb of his left hand under the near lower corner of the sheet, which, with the assistance of his two forefingers, he raises, and by so doing allows the right hand also to grasp it at the top, in the same manner, which lifts the sheet carefully and expeditiously off the points, and nimbly twisting about his body towards the paper bank, carries the sheet over the heap of white-paper to the bank, and lays it down upon a waste sheet or wrapper, put there for that purpose; but while it is coming over the white-paper heap, though he has the sheet between both his fore-fingers and thumbs, yet he holds it so loosely, that it may move between them as on two centres, as his body twists about from the side of the tympan towards the side of the paper bank.

* The description of this complicated motion, applies wholly to the two-pull presses.

Thus, both the pressman's hands at the same time are alternately engaged in different operations; for while his right hand is employed in one action, his left is busy about another; and these exercises are so suddenly varied, that they seem to slide into one another's position, beginning when the former is but half performed.

*Having thus pulled a sheet, and laid it down, he turns his body towards the tympan again, and, as he is turning, gives the next sheet on the white-paper heap a touch with the back of the nail of his right thumb, as before, to draw it a little over the hither edge of the heap, and lays it on the tympans, &c. as he did the first; and so successively every sheet, till the whole heap of white-paper be worked off.

As he comes to a token sheet [the two-hundred-and-fiftieth sheet], he undoubles it, and smooths out the crease with the back of the nails of his right hand, that the face of the letter may print upon smooth paper. And being printed off, he folds it again, as before, for a token sheet when he works the re-iteration.

Having worked off the white-paper of twelves, he places his right hand under the heap, and his left hand supporting the end near him, turns it over on the horse, with the printed side downwards: if octavo, he places his left hand under the heap, supporting the outside near end with his right hand, and turns it one end over the other; all turning of the paper for re-iteration is regulated by this principle, and called by the pressmen *twelves-ways*, or *octavo-ways*. In performing this operation, he takes from the heap so much at once as he can well govern, without disordering the evenness of the sides of the paper, viz. a token or more, and lays that upon the horse; then takes another lift, and so successively, till he has turned the whole [heap]. . . .

Having made register, he proceeds to work it off; but he somewhat varies his posture in laying on the sheet; for, as before, when he worked white-paper, he caught the sheet by the upper further corner with his right hand, he now, having taken up the sheet, catches it as near the further side of the further point hole as he can, with the ball of his right-hand thumb above the sheet, and the ball of his forefinger under the sheet, the readier to lay the point hole over its respective point; which having done, he slips his body a little backwards, and both his hands with it, his right hand towards the near point hole, with the back of the nails of his fingers to draw or stroke it over the point; and the fingers of his left hand, as they come from the further corner, nimbly slipping along the bottom edge of the sheet, till they come to the hither corner; and then with his fore-finger and thumb lays hold of it, in order to guide the point hole on that point also; then pulls that sheet, as before, as he did the white-paper, and so successively all the rest of the reiteration. The token sheets, as he meets with them, he does not fold down again, as he did the white-paper.

[Adams (1837, p 297) adds the following to the above: "When within a quire or so of the end of the heap, the warehouseman should be called, whose duty it is to count the paper, and if it falls short, he brings the pressman the number of dry sheets, which he turns into the heap from which the wet sheets are taken."]

Reading 21.7
Pulling
from *The Printers' Practical Every-Day-Book* by Thomas Shaw Houghton (1841, pp. 97–98).

From Houghton's disparaging remarks below, it would appear that the handpress printer's craft had truly fallen on hard times, and indeed, it probably had. The speed and ease of print-

---

* The description now becomes general for all handpresses.

ing machines made the pressman's job more and more obsolete until – as Houghton says – it was reduced to a mere "mechanical operation." Under such conditions, it is obvious that well-trained, conscientious pressmen would be difficult to find and to keep.

Being merely a mechanical operation, little need be said under this head. Putting on the sheet exactly according to the tympan-sheet, flying the frisket without moving the sheet, rolling in the press-carriage [bed], and pulling home the bar, is all that is required from the pressman who pulls, and is far inferior, in point of care and attention, to rolling. Of course, the press-carriage must be rolled out again, or the operation could not be repeated. The only care necessary in pulling is in keeping the sheets straight, in minding they do not slip, and in observing any pick whilst throwing off the sheet. At pulling, therefore, he is considered a good workman who can do these things certainly and expeditiously, and keeps his companion who rolls fully employed. This, however, must depend on the nature of the work, because [the] finer the work is [the] more care it will require, both in rolling and pulling. The only general rule, therefore, which can be given for doing press-work well and quick, whatever be the nature of the forme, is, first, to make sure that that portion of the operation which requires care cannot be mended, and then, second, to do the remaining portion, in which more than ordinary care is unnecessary, as quick as possible. For instance, a pressman acting upon this rule would make sure of the sheet being straight and exact to the tympan-sheet in putting it on, and then fly the frisket, roll in the carriage, pull the bar, &c., as quick as possible, and again make sure, in taking the sheet off the tympan, that there were no picks. It is to this system of working that first rate pressmen are indebted for their superiority and good name among their professional brethren. The forme being off, it is hardly necessary to count the heap, provided, of course, the token-sheets which mark every two hundred and fifty, be properly turned down when the paper was wet. When, therefore, a necessity exists for disregarding the token-sheets, the pressman himself must decide. The forme is now washed, and, unless ordered to stand, ready for distributing.

Reading 21.8
Ordinary Imperfections and Their Remedies
from *Practical Printing* by John Southward (1882, pp. 428–430).

> The puller and the inker were individually, or collectively, as the case may be, responsible for the quality of the printed image, with special attention given to uniformity of color. South-ward alerts pressmen about what to look for when inspecting their sheets and how to remedy the faults. In addition to the mechanical faults, which can easily be rectified at the press, many of the faults listed below are the results of improper or careless inking. These are also dealt with here since these types of defects will only become evident during the printing process.

This first proof must be very carefully examined, and its imperfections will afford a useful study to the young printer. We will refer to the most probable blemishes *seriatim* [point by point], and append the mode of remedying them.

The proof is crooked. – This shows that (*a*) The sheet was not properly laid to the pins; or (*b*) That the pins were too loose, and allowed the sheet to move when the tympan went down; or (*c*) That the pins were not properly placed. The manner of correcting these faults is obvious.

The proof is too pale. – Take more ink on the roller ... Be careful too much is not taken.

The proof is too black. – Take some ink off the roller by sheeting it . . . or if there be a corner of the ink table that has not received ink, distribute there, and the colour on the roller will be reduced.

The proof has light patches in some parts. – These are called "friars"; they are caused either by imperfect distribution of the ink on the table, or by insufficient rolling of the forme.

The proof has black patches in some parts. – These are "monks," caused also by improper distributing and rolling, but result from having too much ink. Distributing the roller well on the ink table may cure this evil.

Some of the letters do not print at all; only leave a blank impression. – They have missed rolling, most probably because the forme is damp. Observe whether the dampness proceeds from the forme or the table.

Some of the letters are "filled up," and print altogether black. – These are "picks"; they are caused by dirt on the forme or on the roller; in either case, perhaps, proceeding from dirt on the table. Get a pin, and carefully, without injuring the face of the type, pick out the bits of dirt, or rub the part with the brush made for this purpose called a "pick brush." If this is not effectual, the only remedy is to lift the forme and wash it over.

The letters print double. – This is caused by a "slur." It may be that the platen has been pulled down before the carriage stopped. But the defect may indicate a more serious evil. The platen may not be rigid; being hung too loosely. Ascertain if you can shake it or move it from side to side. It ought to be entirely free from lateral motion. Get a screw-key and try if the different screws connecting the platen with the piston are all equally tight. Do not screw one up more than another, or you will spoil the impression, but have everything tight and fast. The tympan may be loose. If so, tighten up the two screws which form the hinges and connect it with the carriage. This part of the press, too, should be entirely free from lateral movement.

The bottom lines are "smudged." – The platen has been brought down too soon, and rubbed over the lines as they have been moving on the press.

There are creases in the paper, and open ridges which have not been printed. – The paper has been badly laid, and been too baggy. Lay the next sheet flat and square and this will not occur again.

One half only of each letter prints; the type looks as if it had got on one side. – It has got off its feet, and if you examine it, instead of the top of the letters forming a straight line, they look as though they were the teeth of a saw. The only remedy is to unlock the forme and try to set them on their feet again, but this is exceedingly troublesome. Fortunately it is simply the result of carelessness in locking up, and thus can easily be prevented.

Now turn the paper on its back, and examine it in a good light; observing carefully the defects of impression.

The "pull" is very heavy; the letters seem disposed to run through the paper. – Take off some of the impression, by turning the impression screw or adjusting the wedge on the chill.

The impression is heavy in parts. – This may arise from a variety of causes. There may be dirt or paper underneath the forme; if so, lift it. There may be dirt on the tympan, and you will have to take off the tympan sheet. A very heavy ridge of unnecessary pressure shows that the blanket has got crumpled. Open the tympans and smooth it out.

The bottom of the forme has got too much impression and the top little or none, and *vice versá*. – This may arise from two causes. The platen may not have been properly hung, and is not parallel to the table. Get a spirit level and try it; any "hanging" at either side may be obviated by turning the screws of the piston. Or the carriage may have been run in too far, or not far enough. This defect often occurs on old presses. It can easily be discovered and by care easily remedied. For this and many other reasons, we advise the beginner to practise on a press in good working order, and with proper tympan and blankets. If the two latter have holes in them or are nearly worn out, they cause a variety of defects which can be remedied only after experience.

Some of the lines are heavily printed, and others only lightly. – The cause of this may be two-fold: All types are not the same height to paper, and types even of the same height, when new, get lower by use; the rubbing on the imposing stone reducing their altitude. The longer any kind of type is used the more worn, of course, it becomes, and this wear naturally reduces the height. This is the most common evil with which the pressman has to contend, and is the most difficult to obviate.

Reading 21.9
Off-Set and Slurring
from *Printing* by Charles Thomas Jacobi (1890, p. 182–183).

When freshly printed sheets were backed up, it was not uncommon for the ink on the first side of the sheet to set off onto the tympan sheet during the second impression. With time, the transferred ink would build up on the tympan sheet and eventually soil the back side of the sheet being perfected. Since most nineteenth-century handpress inks dried by absorption or oxidation, ink printed on dampened paper could not dry before the paper did.

Krumbholz (1893, p. 41) offers the following solution for drying the ink quickly: "To insure the rapid drying of ink on printed sheets, add a very small quantity of glycerine to the water with which the paper is dampened. This is especially advisable when posters are to be printed, as large letters will dry then in from fifteen to twenty minutes, while otherwise, or when no glycerine is added to the dampening water, several hours are required."

"Set-off sheets," also known as *slipsheets*, were pasted to the four corners of the tympan sheet. Unlike modern practices, they were not changed after each impression. Crisp (1875, p. 113) recommends saturating the setoff sheets with benzine. Any accumulation of ink could easily be cleaned off with a cloth doused with a little benzine. Krumbholz (ibid., p. 41) suggests rubbing lard oil on sheets of soft paper for setoff sheets since the oil will dry hard and not spoil the printed sheets. To combat this problem, present-day handpress printers often put a glycol drier in their inks or replace dampened set-off sheets after each impression.

It should be noted that Jacobi is not using the term "off-set" in its modern sense: the transfer of ink from one sheet to another in a pile of printed sheets, but as a synonym for *set off*.

Slurring, or the creation of a double image, was caused by the paper touching the inked type before the impression was made. This was easily resolved with frisket bearers or by tightening the tympan.

These are two . . . matters which should be watched for. The first is caused by the off-set of the ink of the first side in printing the second, if it has not had sufficient time to dry. To prevent this it is necessary to change occasionally the thin set-off sheets pasted by the four corners on the tympan. Oiled sheets are sometimes used for this purpose; home-made ones may be manufactured by washing them over with turpentine – this obviates the necessity of changing frequently. The following suggestions may also be of service:

Set-off Papers. – A paper saturated with benzine is as good as, or better, and much cleaner than oiled paper, to avoid a "set-off," when work has to be printed on both sides. Also a sheet of paper wet with glycerine and used as a tympan-sheet will prevent off-setting.

If not detected in time the set-off of ink will be transferred to the subsequent sheets in printing. Slurring, which gives the printed sheet a double or mackled appearance, is occasioned by the bagging of the sheet or sagging of the tympan or frisket, and may be remedied by slices of cork, or springs made of paper rolled up and fastened on the frisket between the pages on the part of the sheet at fault. Or it may be due to some mechanical defect in the platen, probably the platen bolts themselves requiring tightening up – under any circumstances the cause must be sought for, and the fault rectified.

Reading 21.10
Rules and Remedies for Pressmen
from *Typographia* by Thomas Curson Hansard (1825, pp. 605–608).

Most of these rules and remedies – in a slightly different form – can be traced back to Moxon (1683, pp. 333–345). They were repeated by Stower (1808, pp. 370–375), Johnson (1824, 534–535), and Hansard below. A little over a decade later, Adams (1837, pp. 297–300) adapted and updated them for the one-pull iron handpress and composition rollers. Some of his observations, in brackets, have been inserted into Hansard's text at the same point where they appear in Adams's text, which was taken from Johnson. Since the rules and remedies given here pertain to both the pressmen working as a team, the individual duties of the puller and inker are often so commingled or interdependent that the functions of pulling and inking cannot easily be separated.

Hansard also gives instructions for cleaning up at the end of the day and how to store unfinished work overnight. He uses the lye-and-water method for washing the form and ink balls, but does not, however, mention how to clean rollers. For information on washing rollers, see Reading 20.12 on p. 589.

One of Moxon's picturesque phrases (1683, p. 337), *naughty sheets* – which were the soiled or torn sheets mentioned on p. 607 below – seems to have gotten lost somewhere along the way before it reached Hansard.

About every three sheets a small quantity of ink should be taken,[*] and during the intervals in which the beater or roller is not employed in braying out or taking ink, he should be overlooking the heap in order to detect any want of uniformity in the colour; to observe if any letters, quadrats, or furniture rise; that no letters are drawn out, or battered; that the register be good, and the work free from picks: during this examination, the balls must be distributed as much as possible.

[Adams (1837, 297) rewrote the above paragraph: "About every five or six sheets a small quantity of ink should be taken; yet this will be subject to considerable variation from the nature of the individual work, and quality of the ink; a form of large type, or solid matter, will require the taking of ink more frequently, and a light form of small type less frequently; during the intervals in which the roller boy is not employed in brayering out or taking ink, he should be almost constantly engaged in distributing or changing his rollers. In taking ink, he should invariably take it on the back roller, as it will sooner be conveyed to the other roller, and consequently save time in distributing." – Editor's note: The roller boy is using a roller inking stand; therefore, he was not expected to check the sheets for uniformity of color.]

[*] This will be subject to considerable variation from the nature of the individual work, and quality of the ink; a forme of large type will require the taking of ink every sheet; some book-work, of heavy composition, every two sheets, light formes, three or four sheets; and again, very fine work, every sheet, in order to keep the colour perfectly alike of every sheet.

When, through carelessness, too much ink has been taken, it should be removed by laying a piece of clean waste paper on one of the balls, or on the roller, and distributing till the ink is reduced to the proper quantity.

If letters, quadrats, or furniture, rise up and black the paper, put them down with the bodkin, and lock the quarter up tighter.

If any letters are battered, the quarter they are in must be unlocked, and perfect ones put in by the compositor.

When [frisket] bearers become too thin by long working, they should be replaced by thicker ones.

When the forme gets out of register, which will often happen by the starting of the quoins which secure the chase, it must be immediately put in again, as there can scarcely be a greater defect in a book than a want of uniformity in this particular.

If picks, which are produced by bits of paper, skin, or film of ink and grease, or other filth, get into the forme, they are removed with the point of a pin or needle; but if the forme is much clogged with them, it should be well brushed over with clean lie, or taken off and washed in the lie trough: in the first case, before the pressman goes on again, it should be made perfectly dry by pulling a waste sheet or two, in order to suck up the water deposited in the cavities of the letter, in the latter it must stand some time to drain and dry before he again lays it on the press.

The puller should habituate himself to glance his eye over every sheet as he takes it off the tympan; this may be done without retarding his progress: by following this plan, he will be enabled to detect imperfections which may escape his companion.

In order to ensure uniformity in receiving ink from the block, care should be taken, when balls are used, to bray out at the edge of the block small quantities at a time. While this is doing, the balls must rest on the ball rack, with the right hand on the upper ball-stock handle.

[Adams (1837, p. 298) mentions rollers: "In order to insure perfect uniformity in the color, the roller-boy should be made to keep his ink well brayered out with the small roller, in proper quantities for the work in hand, and also to change his rollers well after taking ink, and at other times; the rollers are changed by moving the roller handle slowly to the right and left, while the crank is being turned briskly with the left hand."]

Torn or stained sheets, met with in the course of work, are thrown out and placed under the bank; but the pressman should be particularly careful to have them supplied by others from the warehouseman. Creases and wrinkles will frequently happen in the sheets, through careless wetting of the paper; these should be carefully removed, by smoothing them out with the back of the nails of the right hand.

In twelves, and other works at two-pull presses, where the platten pinches twice upon the centre pages, mackling or doubling the impression frequently happens; the following, among many others, are the causes of, and remedies for this evil.

It happens when the face of the platten and the inner tympan are both dirty, which occasions them to stick – they should always be kept perfectly clean.

Slack or rickety tympans will also cause doubling; and leaning the body against the carriage in reaching the bar, in presses without guide cramps, or where the cramps do not act with truth.

*The nut being loose in the head will also occasion this defect; the short bolts should be screwed up as tight as possible.

*If the platten be slack, or otherwise improperly tied up, this defect will always happen; also doubling will happen from the following causes, which must be remedied by the joiner and smith: viz.

* These paragraphs apply wholly to the joiners' presses.

* When the tenons of the head are so narrow as not to fill the mortises in the cheeks.

* The nut and garter so worn as not to admit the spindle to work close in them.

* The hose not working easy and steady in the shelves.

* The wheel on the spit not well justified, and its having too much play in the ear, which causes an unpleasant check.

The paper being rather too dry will also sometimes cause the impression to mackle.

Slurring and mackling will frequently happen when the tympans are carelessly and suddenly put on the forme: they should always be laid down easy, and the slur screw made proper use of. [Editor's note: The slur screw is an adjustable screw on the off side of the outer tympan placed near the tympan head band to elevate the tympan/frisket assembly when it is down in order to keep the paper off the inked type until the impression is made.]

Leaning against the carriage, as before mentioned, will also cause a slur.

If the platten rub against the rail of the tympan, it will inevitably cause a slur and mackle. This can easily be remedied by moving the tympan joints so as to clear the platten.

The ear of the frisket being so long as to cause it to rub against the cheek, always produces a slur: remedy – make it shorter.

Loose tympans will at all times slur the work; great care must therefore be observed in drawing them perfectly tight.

[Adams (1837, p. 299) notes: "In rolling the form, the pressman should see that the boy rolls it slowly, or the rollers will be apt to jump, which occasions a *friar*; to prevent the rollers from jumping or bounding, various experiments have been tried, as the most successful of which we would recommend bridges or springs made of thin steel, to reach across the gutters; these springs should taper off at the ends and have an oblong hole in each end, through which they may be tacked to the gutter sticks. In very open forms, it will perhaps be necessary to put bearers, or pieces of reglet where the blank pages occur at the end of the form, to prevent that end of the roller from falling down and leaving a friar at the opposite end. Of late year this difficulty has, in a great measure, been obviated by imposing the form in such manner as in most cases to bring the blank pages in the centre (see **Figs. 8.40** and **8.41** on p. 304. . . . This mode is peculiarly adapted for title pages and other light matter, as great advantages must arise from working such pages in the centre of the form."]

Independently of the above causes, slurring and mackling will sometimes happen from causes which baffle all art and patience to detect. It will be better in this case to tie as many cords as possible across the frisket, which will keep the sheet close to the tympan.

In the Stanhope presses it generally arises from the screw in the back plate becoming loose – the remedy is simple – screw it up again.

Before the pressman leaves his work, he covers his heap. He first turns down a sheet like a token sheet, where he leaves off, then puts a quantity of the worked off sheets on it, taking care to have the printed side upwards, that his companion, if he have any, on coming to work first in the morning, may not be deceived in taking it for the reiteration. Laying the blanket on the heap, after leaving off work, is a bad custom. If the paper be rather dry, it will be better to put wet wrappers on it. The blankets should always be kept as dry as possible, that they may not make the inner tympan damp and slack.

The pressman's next care should be to look after his balls. They should be well rubbed with a blanket soaked with lie, if they are inclined to be hard, that they may be in proper order for the next day's work. They must be left well covered up with the blankets; but if they are already sufficiently soft, they will not require rubbing, and what is termed a dry blanket will answer the purpose, viz.

* These paragraphs apply wholly to the joiners' presses.

one from which the water does not run. When the balls have been over-soaked, they should be left on the rack all night, with merely a piece of paper round them, as they will not bear the process of what is termed *capping* [wrapping in a urine-soaked blanket].

The pressman next observes whether his forme be clean; if so, he puts a sheet of waste paper between the tympan and frisket, and lays them down on the forme: if it be dirty, it must be rubbed over with clean lie. On his return to work in the morning, he takes care to wet the tympan, but not for very light work. If there should happen to be any pages in the forme particularly open, those parts of the tympan where they fall must not be wetted.

Reading 21.11
Wash for Formes
from *The Printers' Universal Book of Reference and Every-Hour Office Companion* by William Finch Crisp (1875, pp. 81–82).

> Crisp describes how to make printers' lye from potash and pearl ash – potassium carbonate. It should not be confused with the highly caustic lyes made from sodium or potassium hydroxide. He also emphasizes the need to rinse forms with clean water in order to remove all traces of the lye solution, which, if left on the type, could corrode it.
>
> There are a number of variant spellings of *lye* in pre-twentieth-century printers' manuals, including *ly, lie,* and *ley.*

There is a manufacture much in favour among the settlers in the dense forests of Canada and the American States, where it forms a considerable item in the annual profits derived by the farmer from his land. This is the manufacture of potash and pearlash, the process of which is very simple. The material from which potash is made is the more succulent branches of trees, and, in general, any kind of growing plant. All plants do not yield equal quantities of potash, but it is found to a greater or less extent in all, though there is little in the trunks and more solid branches, the leaves and twigs affording the chief supply. Nothing can be more simple than the manufacture of potash. A heap is made of the plants or branches of trees from which it is intended to obtain this salt. This heap is set on fire, and when burnt out, the ashes are put into a tub, or other vessel, having a false bottom, and a plug or tap between the false and real bottom. Into this tub the ashes remaining from the fire are put, a moderate quantity of water is then poured on the mass, and some quicklime stirred in. After standing for a few hours, the water will have taken up all the soluble salts, the insoluble matters will have settled down on the false bottom, and, by opening the plug, the clear water, containing the potash in solution, may be drawn off. This clear liquor is evaporated to dryness in iron pots. Finally, the residue which remains after the evaporation is fused, at a red heat, into compact masses, which are grey on the outside, and, when broken, pink within, and the manufacture is completed. Pearlash is made from potash, by calcining it on a reverberatory hearth; but as reverberatory furnaces are somewhat beyond the reach of the farmers, it is not worth while to go into the particulars of the process, which is, however, very simple. Potash, manufactured as we have described, is at once an article of commerce. It may, as we have already stated, be made from any succulent vegetable substance, even from the straw of wheat before earing, from fern, or from the stalks of our implacable enemies, the thistles. In using soda, there are two or three ways of mixing it to make it answer its purpose well; and, if properly made, it would be found the cheapest of any wash at present in use. The following is a method of making it, and the quantities: – Put six gallons of water in a washing copper (not having anything better), and make it boil. Then throw in one pound of unslacked lime and four pounds of common soda, which must be stirred for at least ten minutes, making it boil all the time. Then let it settle until it is cold, when it should be carefully dipped out, and it is fit for immediate use, leaving the dregs of the lime at the bottom of the copper. We would not advise any one to make a larger quantity, except their consumption required it. Perhaps half the above quantity would answer the purpose of many small printers. It should be kept covered in if possible. By this means you will get six gallons of good wash for a few pence, and no grit to injure the type, – which is a great consideration. Another system we would recommend to all printers, and that is, to well rinse their formes with clean water after washing: they cannot use too much, whether after washing with pearlash, soda, or any other substitute. The water will be found an excellent remedy to prevent the type corroding, especially if the forme is required to be kept standing for any length of time.

Reading 21.12
Washing the Form
from *The Printer's Manual* by Thomas Lynch (1859, pp. 165–166).

For some reason, which totally escapes me – unless it was for nothing more than economics and routine – book printers continued to use lye as a solvent to remove ink from the type throughout the nineteenth century. The whole form, naturally still locked up in the chase, was placed in the lye trough (**Fig. 21.6**). Using a special brush (**Fig. 21.7**), the type was then scrubbed with a solution of lye and water, and then rinsed off with clean water. Curiously, even though quick-drying solvents were used in job and news shops, it would appear that they were rarely employed for cleaning book forms. Lynch mentions below the one exception: spirits of turpentine, followed by alcohol to remove the oily residue, was used when the pressman needed to clean a form quickly, for instance, when the counters of the letters became filled with ink before the form was completely worked off. This method would also have been used for stop-press corrections.

Fig. 21.6. *Lye trough* – from Jacobi (1890, p. 182)

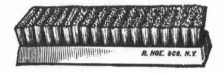

Fig. 21.7. *Lye brush* – from Ringwalt (1871, p. 288)

On the other hand, amateur printers were instructed by Holtzapffel (1846, p. 32) to clean their forms with turpentine. "If turpentine is used, it is only necessary either to pour a few drops on the type, or to dip the brush into a shallow vessel containing it, such as a plate, and then to apply the brush with moderate force to the entire surface of the type; this will immediately remove the ink, and the turpentine may be soaked up by dabbing and pressing a cloth upon the face of the type." Present-day handpress printers generally use naphtha to clean their type, although personally, I have always preferred benzine.

The ley used for the purpose of cleaning a form is, a solution of alkali in water; it ought to be made of the best pearlash. The usual proportion is, one pound of pearlash to a gallon of soft water; it should be stirred until the alkali is dissolved, which will soon take place. It is generally contained in a large jar, which should be kept covered, to prevent dirt and dust getting into the ley.

If hard water be used, it will require a greater amount of pearlash; as the acid in the water will combine with some of the alkali, to neutralize it; which, of course, will have the effect of making the ley weaker than if soft water, with which there is no such chemical combination, had been used.

Some printers use potash for cleaning the types; but, as it has a tendency to make the letters stick together, it should not be employed.

The [ley] brush should be nine or ten inches long, by three inches broad; and the hair should be at least two inches in length, of a soft texture, and set as closely together as possible. By not having a good brush, more types are destroyed, on account of its careless use in washing, than by almost any other process through which they are liable to be put. The reason for this is, that the washing is generally entrusted to boys, who scrub the faces of the types, instead of rubbing them just enough to leave the ink in such a condition that it could be separated from them by rinsing the form with water.

When a form is small, it may be rinsed by standing it on its edge in the trough and throwing water against the faces of the types; but, if it be over half a medium sheet, it should be laid flat in the trough. In either case, plenty of water should be used; for, a little care in this particular will always keep the types free from dirt.

Sometimes the counters of the letters become filled with ink before the working of the form is finished. In such cases, ley and water should not be used, as much time would be lost in drying the types. Spirits of turpentine and a soft brush will be found to take off the ink quickly, and the work can be proceeded with in a few minutes. When this article has been used, a few impressions must be made on waste paper, to remove the oil which remains on the types after the turpentine has evaporated; though, if alcohol be at hand, it will remove the oil more effectually.

Reading 21.13
Washing Formes
from *The Letter-Press Printer* by Joseph Gould (1876, p. 128, 147).

> In the last quarter of the nineteenth century, a number of manual writers described alternative solvents for washing forms. Gould recommends *benzoline* – another term for *benzine* – for cleaning areas in the form where the ink has clogged the type. He mentions a curious method for cleaning dried ink off the type by rolling the form with fresh ink, which, supposedly, would soften the dried ink.

Should the forme have "filled in" at all, brush over with a *little* benzoline, and pull a sheet or two of soft paper, previous to cleaning the roller and the slab....

After a forme has been worked off, it must be washed immediately. The duty of washing usually falls, in jobbing offices, on the person who has rolled for it, and in book offices upon the pressmen. In some large offices, however, the "washing" is done by the house, a person being appointed by the firm for that purpose. But, be the duty whose it may, the work should be done thoroughly: not the least ink or dirt must be left upon any part of the forme, chase, or furniture. After the whole has been well brushed over with ley, it must be rinsed, by dashing water over it, or by turning upon it a jet of water by means of a hose and rose [perforated nozzle].

If any forme has been allowed to remain unwashed until the ink has dried, it will be found best, before attempting to wash it, to roll it over with a roller well covered with common ink, and allow it to stand for an hour with the ink on it, when the forme may be cleaned properly; or use a little paraffin when the ink cannot be removed by ordinary means.

Type must be kept clean or work will be disfigured.

Reading 21.14
The Use of Benzine
from *Office Manual* by Theodore Low De Vinne (1883, pp. 45, 48).

In an era of gas burners for illumination and an environment where large quantities of paper were stored and processed, the possibility of fires in printing offices was an ever-present threat and a major concern to the masters. The introduction of benzine as a solvent only increased the chances for such disasters. It is perhaps apropos to note that the discoverer of benzine, Charles Bickford Mansfield (see my introductory note to Reading 19.12 on p. 550), died as a result of burns sustained while experimenting with it. Benzine, when handled properly, had many advantages over other solvents: it cleaned the type without leaving a greasy residue, dried quickly, and eliminated the mess and inconvenience of the lye trough since it could also be used to clean the form while it was still locked up in the bed of the press. Since benzine is carcinogenic, it is no longer used in the printing industry.

Recollect that many workmen have been burned to death by carelessness in handling benzine. Take care of your own life and think of the lives and property of others.

Benzine can be used only from the patent safety-can provided for the purpose.

The benzine-can must always be kept as far as possible from a light.

The cap of the can must never be unscrewed in the press-room and only in the yard when it is being filled.

The cap on the spout must be put on immediately after use. It must be done every time benzine is poured, even if it has to be done ten times in as many minutes.

Use all the benzine really needed, but recollect that too much is as great a blunder as too little.

Friction matches must not be used to light gas-burners. Nor will any person be permitted to take light from another burner with a piece of waste paper. When light is wanted, go to the foreman or his assistant, who will have the burner lighted with the lamp provided for the purpose.

Every pressman is requested to supervise the work of the boys who wash up, and to aid the office in the strict enforcement of these rules.

It is the duty of every man and boy – a duty he owes to the rights and lives of his fellow-workmen – to report at once to the foreman his knowledge of any misuse of benzine, or of any act which may endanger the office by fire.

The office does not wish to encourage meddling or tattling, but it considers every workman bound in honor, as in law, to report any act which imperils life and property. It will regard any one who stands cowardly or indifferently silent, while a risk of this kind is hazarded, as a party to the fault.

Reading 21.15
Cleaning Type
from *The Young Job Printer* by Sidney M. Weatherly (1889, p. 40).

> Weatherly notes that benzine was routinely used as a solvent for cleaning type in the composing room. Even so, in the last decade of the century, both MacKellar (1893, pp. 264–265) and Southward (1900, vol. II, pp. 649–650) were still instructing book printers to use a solution of lye and water to wash their forms.

If type would be preserved it must be kept perfectly clean and free from ink, when not in use. After pulling a proof from matter tied up on the stone or galley, or after taking a proof on the proof-press, the best thing to clean the metal with is benzine, rubbed on with a soft brush or rag.

There are in fact but two things used at present to clean type – benzine and concentrated lye diluted with water. The former is used in the composing-room before the type goes on the press and the latter after the form is run off.

If the diluted lye is too strong it will eat away the points [punctuation marks] and fine lines of the letters, and a similar result will happen if the lye, no matter how weak, is not rinsed off by clean water. If the lye is too strong it will not cleanse the ink from the type; it must be made just strong enough to feel greasy when rubbed between the finger and thumb, and the form must always be well rinsed with water after the lye has been applied with a soft brush. Nothing ruins type so quickly as neglecting to cleanse it.

Reading 21.16
Rags
from *The Practical Printer* by Henry Gold Bishop (1889, p. 120)

> Just as extra precautions had to be taken in printing offices where benzine was used, additional attention needed to be paid to the storage and disposal of soiled rags since they were also a potential fire hazard.

Rags should be supplied to the pressroom in sufficient quantities to provide for washing up properly and speedily, but, at the same time, should be well looked after, especially when they have become saturated with oil and benzine. If a printer wishes to have a fire he need only allow a pile of such dirty rags to lie in some corner until spontaneous combustion takes place, for which he will not have long to wait. Therefore, those who wish to prevent fires, and avoid the risk of having to answer for causing the death of some unfortunate persons, will take the precaution to have all dirty rags taken care of while in use and destroyed when done with.

Reading 21.17

The Lie-Trough

from *Typographia* by Thomas Curson Hansard (1825, pp. 594–596).

> The lye trough had been used for cleaning forms in printing houses for centuries. Moxon (1683) mentions it on pp. 12, 73–74, as well as illustrates one in plate 9 facing p. 67. The tray was attached to a horse by a pivot that allows it to tilt back and forth at will as the lye-and-water solution sluiced over the form, washing away the ink. A brush was also used to loosen any stubborn ink.

The forme being worked off, it becomes the pressman's duty to wash it clean and free from every particle of ink, not only for the cleanly working and well standing of the letter in the subsequent composing, but to save his own time in making ready when the same letter gets to press again; for if a pressman is at all remiss in this duty, either after working his formes, or pulling proofs, he will be at last obliged to do it, and wait the drying of the forme, before he can go on with his work in a fit and proper manner. Many an hour is lost from a pressman not bestowing a minute or two in thoroughly cleansing and rinsing his forme.

For this purpose, every printing office is provided with a lie-trough [**Fig. 21.6** on p. 610], suspended on a cross frame, and swinging by iron ears fixed something out of the precise centre, so as the gravity of the trough will cause it to fall in a slanting position.

This trough is lined with lead; the top front edge being guarded from the pitching of the formes by a plate of iron; and a moveable board is placed at the bottom upon which to rest the forme. The forme having been placed in a slanting position, on the further side of the bottom board, so as to cause the trough to swing over to the opposite side from which he stands, he takes hold of the rim of the chase by the key [a hook-shaped lever], or instrument for that purpose, and laying it gently down, sluices, by means of swinging the trough on its pivots, the *lie* (of which a sufficient quantity is always kept in the trough) two or three times to and fro, then taking the *lie-brush* [**Fig. 21.7** on p. 610], he well applies it to the whole forme, type, furniture and chase; and raising it to drain, he lifts the forme out of the trough into the sink, and then with clean water, rinses off the lie, and leaves the forme, in the appropriated place, to drain. With the completion of this process the pressman's responsibility for his forme ceases.

The *lie* is made of the strongest American pearl-ash. A large earthen jar is usually chosen for the purpose. The proportion is one pound of ash to a gallon of soft water; it should be stirred with a large stick till dissolved; the larger quantities in which it is made, and the longer it stands, the stronger it becomes. The jar should have a cover fixed on the head, with lock and key.

The lie-brush is made very large: the hairs close, fine, and long, in order not to injure the type, while sufficient force is applied to search every interstice of the letter, down to the spaces and quadrats, where the ink can have insinuated itself.

Reading 21.18

Printing on Parchment

from *The Printer's Manual* by Thomas Lynch (1859, p.153).

> From Johannes Gutenberg on, special copies of significant books were printed on vellum. In 1774, John Dunlop of Philadelphia printed the first book on vellum in the United States: *Observations on a Variety of Subjects, Literary, Moral, and Religious* by Jacob Duché.

Very little is said about printing on vellum in nineteenth-century manuals. Most printing on it was restricted to diplomas and deeds. Pasko (1894, p. 427) notes that "one out of four skins is spoiled upon the press."

When diplomas or deeds are to be printed on parchment, the harshness of the skins must be taken out, by putting them between damp sheets of paper, care being taken, at the same time, that the parchment does not become so wet as to destroy the polish on the surface.

Reading 21.19
Printing on Parchment
from *Harpel's Typograph* by Oscar Henry Harpel (1870, p. 234).

Harpel suggests rubbing the skins with benzine. When I was still printing in Italy, I used the same procedure, with equally good results, for degreasing vellum.

Printing on parchment is sometimes troublesome because of the animal fat that remains in the parchment. By rubbing the sheet over with a clean piece of cotton, dampened with purified benzine, previous to printing, a good impression can be had. But generally, if high grade ink is used, with little or no reduction by varnish, it will print parchment well.

Reading 21.20
Printing on Parchment
from *Practical Printing* by John Southward (1900, vol. I, p. 779)

Southward suggests interleaving skins with dampened paper, which is the method preferred by most handpress printers today.

According to [Jean Dumont's *Vade-mecum du typographe* (1891, p. 262)] the skins should be interleaved, skin by skin, with paper somewhat larger, which has been moderately damped. The paper must be good and homogeneous, and be evenly damped. The parchment will soon lose its stiffness, and as soon as it has it is fit for printing on. The damping does not require more than ten minutes, and it is very important that it does not continue longer than is necessary or the parchment will be discoloured. When printed, place each skin between sheets of dry paper and press between boards till dry.

Plate 26. Illustration by A. B. Frost of a printing office for W. H. Howells's short story, "The Country Printer," 1893. The artist has drawn a handpress in an acorn frame, although the pressure mechanism shown is inaccurate and would not have functioned properly. (Source: *Scribner's Magazine*, May 1893, p. 546, courtesy of St. Bride Printing Library.)

CHAPTER TWENTY-TWO
Printing Multiple Colors

Printing in two colors usually required more than double the amount of time needed to print one color since each color necessitated a separate press run. Color printing was primarily used for job work, such as broadsides, placards, and miscellaneous ephemera, although it was also used occasionally to add touches of color to book work, especially for title pages and tint blocks for illustrations.

By the 1820s in England, and the 1830s in America, there was a surge of interest in multicolor printing that extended well beyond the traditional use of red and black. Thus, by 1870, when Harpel printed and published *Harpel's Typograph*, an explosion of color was already to be found in all sorts of short-run job work. Harpel's book contains over 185 pages of specimens illustrating how printers could use colored inks to enhance their work. On p. 237 in his manual, he reminds pressmen, who were accustomed to printing only in black, that "A heavier impression and dwell than usual upon surfaces printed with colors is generally necessary, as such inks have peculiar bodies and do not take hold of paper so easily as black." Most late-nineteenth-century color printing was done on job presses.

There are three basic methods for printing multiple colors: (1) raised-type forms, (2) composite or disintegrated forms, (3) and separate or successive forms. All three methods were used by pre-twentieth-century handpress printers. The oldest is raised-type forms, which was utilized primarily for rubricating liturgical works and almanacs. Readings 22.1 through 22.3, beginning on p. 618, are variations on this method.

The second is composite forms and is described in Reading 22.5 on p. 621. With this method, all the colors were first inked separately, reassembled in the form, and then printed together in one impression.

The third is separate forms, or *skeletonising* as Southward calls it, and is described in Readings 22.7 and 22.8 on pp. 624 and 626, respectively. This is the procedure used by most present-day handpress printers, and the method that I preferred at my press in Italy.

A fourth method for printing multiple colors – which was not mentioned in nineteenth-century manuals – is called *work-and-twist*. It uses an imposition similar to the one shown in **Fig. 8.1** on p. 276, which was devised primarily for printing abstracts of title deeds of estates. In its modern application, the two colors are inked separately, one in each half of the form, and then an impression is pulled. The sheet of paper is next rotated 180 degrees, and the procedure is repeated, which, after the paper is cut, will result in two identical two-color leaves.

The first successful two-color printing machine was a single cylinder press made in England by [William] Conisbee in 1861. Prior to that, two-color work on machines required successive runs for each color. In America, the first two-cylinder press for color printing was made by Huber & Hodgman in the 1880s.

Reading 22.1
Of Printing Red, or Other Colours with Black
from *Mechanick Exercises* by Joseph Moxon (1683, pp. 328–330).

Moxon's instructions are for printing from raised type, a method that used the same form
for both colors, even though they were inked and worked off separately. Once the compositor had substituted quadrats for the red type, the black type was printed, after which the
compositor would underlay and replace the red type so the sheets could be worked off in the
second color. Although not specifically mentioned here by Moxon, the pressman was able to
vary the pull on the wooden press in order to compensate for the higher red type instead of
making changes in the packing. The fact that the form usually contained less type was
another reason for a lighter pull.

A note on scaboards: On p. 213 in his manual, Moxon uses the term *scaboards* to mean
thin strips of metal, and on p. 229, he uses a scaboard to divide the text from the marginal
notes. A problem arises, however, in his text below when he mentions a "thick" scaboard. I
have arbitrarily given it a thickness of three points, but perhaps it should be six points, the
same thickness as the reglets that Stower uses in Reading 22.2 below.

To further complicate the situation, on p. 29, Moxon notes that there were both "thick"
and "thin" *scabbords* – a variant spelling – and that they were available from "Iron-mongers."
In this context, they were used as furniture in order to justify the length of the pages, as well
as to register the form. He does not give any dimensions here for either the thick or the thin
"scabbords"; however, on p. 59, he says that they are equal to one half of a 6-point *nomparel*
(nonpareil) reglet, or three points. I think we can safely assume that he is placing pieces of
metal under the red type.

Finally, to confuse matters even more, the term *scabbard* was used in the nineteenth century to indicate a type of soft cardboard that was also known as *scaleboard*. When cut into
narrow strips, it was often used in making register, and could also have been used to underlay
raised type.

When *Red* and *Black* are to be printed upon the same Sheet, the *Press-man* first *Makes Register . . .*
and *Makes Ready* his *Form. . . .* Then having a new *Frisket Drawn . . .* He Prints upon his new *Frisket*
with *Black*. And having before a *Proof-sheet*, Printed *Black*, with the Words to be Printed *Red*
under-lined on that *Proof-sheet*; He takes off his *Frisket*, and lays it flat on a *Paper-board*, and with
a sharp-pointed Pen-knife neatly cuts out those words on the *Frisket*, and about half a Scaboard
[about 1½ points] *Margin* round about the words, that he finds under-lined on the *Proof-sheet*:
Then sets the *Frisket* by till he has wrought off his *Heap* with *Black*, and puts his common *Frisket*
on the *Joynts* of the *Tympan* again.

While the *Press-man* is *Cutting* the *Frisket*, the *Compositer* takes those *Words* out of the *Form*
that are *Under-lin'd* on the *Proof-sheet*, and in their place puts *Quadrats*, m-*Quadrats*, *Spaces*, &c.
to *Justifie* the *Lines* up again.

Then *Locking up* the *Form*, the *Press-man* Works off the *Heap* Black . . .

Having wrought off his *Heap* Black, he takes off the common *Frisket*, and puts on his new cut
Frisket: Then taking a piece of thick Scaboard [about three points] he cuts it into so many small
slips as there are *Whites* in the *Form* to be Printed with *Red*; These small slips he cuts exactly to the
length of the *Quadrats*, &c. the *Compositer* put in, and to the breadth of the *Body*; but rather a
small matter less than bigger, lest they bind at the bottom of the *Shank* of the *Letter*: for when the

Compositer takes out the *Quadrats*, &c. he put in before the *Form* was *Wrought off* Black, these slips of Scaboards the *Press-man* pricks on the Point of a *Bodkin* and puts them into their respective holes: And being loosen'd off the Point of the *Bodkin* with the blunt point of another *Bodkin*, are laid down flat on the *Press-stone*; These slips are called *Underlays* . . . Upon these *Underlays* the *Compositer* puts in again the *Words* or *Letters* he took out before the *Form* was *Wrought off Black*: So that these *Words* now stand higher than the other *Matter* of the *Form*, and therefore will Print when the other *Matter* will not. But yet for the more assurance that the other *Matter* Print not, the *New-cut Frisket* was prepar'd, which hinders any thing to Print but what Prints through the Holes cut in it; which Holes these *Underlaid Words* fall exactly through.

Having mingled the Red, or any other intended Colour with *Varnish* . . . he *Beats* the *Form* as with *Black*; and *Pulls* it very lightly, lest these *Underlaid Words* standing higher than the rest of the *Matter*, Print too *Hard*.

Reading 22.2
Printing Red, or Other Colours, with Black.
from *The Printer's Grammar* by Caleb Stower (1808, pp. 368–369).

Stower's instructions are similar to Moxon's, see Reading 22.1 above, with two exceptions: (1) Stower uses reglets to underlay the red type while the form is *face down* on a press blanket, and (2) he reverses Moxon's sequence by printing the red first, which, incidentally, would make it slightly more difficult to register the form for the second impression. I find it curious that the type was locked so loosely in the form that the pressman could push the type down with his fingers in order to insert the reglets. Also note that in Stower's time, the compositor was no longer required to make changes in the form once it was on the press.

Chalk marks were made on the stone or bed to register the position of the chase so that the latter could be replaced in its proper location after it was washed between runs. I find this practice somewhat haphazard, although it may have worked with great accuracy. I do not understand why they did not just fasten small pieces of scaleboard or reglets on the bed to serve as guides for the chase.

The practice of underlaying raised type with reglets comes from Luckombe (1771, p. 361). It is hard to imagine how pressmen were able to accurately cut 6-point reglets down to 12-point, or less, widths. Today, a printer would simply lay spaces end-to-end under the red type.

When preparing forms with large type, Stower keeps the form face up, and follows Moxon's method. He also briefly mentions using separate forms for each color when an extensive number of copies is required.

Separate balls were employed for black and red. Old parchment was often used for red balls that were made without stocks. In this case, they would have functioned more like dabbers than balls. Extra pairs of points were generally used with multicolor work to insure perfect register. There is more information about them in Readings 22.7 and 22.8 on pp. 624 and 626, respectively.

When red and black are to be printed on the same sheet, as in . . . almanacks, the form is made ready in the usual way, and a line traced all round the outside of the [chase] on the stone with chalk, or any thing that will accurately shew the exact situation in which the form must be placed after it has been taken off the press. The pressman then pulls a sheet in order to get those words or lines marked, which are to be worked red; while this is doing, he washes the form thoroughly, as the least dirt remaining on it, will destroy the beauty of the red. The form is then laid with its face downwards, on a letter-board covered with a press blanket. Those words marked to be red are then forced down, (which the soft and spongy nature of the blanket readily admits of), and nonpareil riglets nicely fitted into the vacancies, which raise the red lines and words all of an equal distance from the other matter. A sheet of paper is then pasted on the form, which keeps the nonpareil underlays in their proper places. The form is again laid on the press, observing the utmost care in placing it, agreeable to the marks before made on the stone. It must then be made perfectly fast to the corner irons, as it is highly important that it remain firm and immoveable during its stay on the press. The frisket (which is covered with parchment), is then put on, the form beat over with the red balls, and an impression made on it. The red words are then cut out with a sharp-pointed penknife, with so much nicety as not to admit the smallest soil on the paper from the other matter.

The red being finished, and the form washed, the compositor unlocks it, (which is best done on the imposing stone, as the pressman can easily lay it, agreeable to the marks made on the press), and draws out the red lines, and fills up the space with quadrats. When this is done, the pressman cuts out the frisket for the black.

An extra pair of points are used to prevent the black from falling on the red, which is termed *riding*.

When a very extensive number is to be printed, two forms are generally used, one for the red, and another for the black.

There is another method of placing the underlays, which is adopted for broadsides, &c. with large letter, and with perhaps only two or three lines of red in them. The red lines are taken out on the press stone, and the underlays put in with a bodkin, upon which these lines are placed, and the frisket cut out as before mentioned.

Balls having been once used for black, cannot be employed for any other color; and as printing with red, &c. is but rarely performed, the balls for that purpose should be made of old parchment, well soaked, which may be done in a few minutes. These balls are made without stocks, and of a small size. For almanacks, broadsides, &c. where a large number is printed, a new pair of balls are made in the usual way.

Reading 22.3
Printing Red with High Type
from *Typographia* by Thomas Curson Hansard (1825, p. 603).

> Hansard's method is similar in principle to both Moxon's and Stower's, but instead of underlaying the type to raise it for the red type as they do, he substitutes it with type that has been cast higher than the black type. Even though this would save some preparation time by not having to cut out the small underlay pieces, all of the red type would have to be set twice.

But the most effectual mode of printing in red and black from the same forme, has lately been invented by my father [Luke Hansard] for printing the returns made to the House of Commons of Charitable Donations. For this purpose he has a type cast, which, from its application, he has named *rubric*, the peculiarity of which is, its being cast with a longer shank, or body, so as to stand higher to paper by the square of its own body, than other type. The work being composed in the usual manner of common type, and the proofs having been read and sent out, such parts are marked by underscoring with red, as are to be worked red; when ready for press, such parts are taken out, and their places filled with quadrats. Then the parts so taken out are reset in rubric; and when the black has been worked, the quadrats are withdrawn, the rubric type inserted, and then worked in red.

Reading 22.4
Colour Printing
from *Typographia* by John Johnson (1824, vol. II, p. 533).

> To save time, pressmen usually mixed their own colored inks for small jobs, although Johnson suggests that colored inks were readily available from commercial sources as well. Note that composition balls are still being recommended here for color work.

The custom of printing broadsides, &c. with various coloured inks having become so very much into general use, has induced some of our ink makers to turn their attention to the manufacture of coloured inks; consequently the printers can now be supplied with that article without the delay and labour of making. Composition balls are also an additional advantage in the working of colours, from the easy manner in which the colours, except black, are removed off the balls; this may be done either by washing with a little lye, if hard, or scraping with soft varnish or spirits of turpentine, if soft.

Reading 22.5
Printing in Colours
from *The Printers' Practical Every-Day-Book* by Thomas Shaw Houghton (1841, pp. 98–104).

> By turning the individual letters into slugs or logotypes and imposing them in a composite form, Houghton was able to print large-format broadsides in multiple colors with only one pull of the bar. If made of wood, the letters were tacked to the reglets on either side of them; metal types were placed between reglets and tied with a thin cord that wound up the side of the reglet without overlapping. Houghton does not mention this, but it would be necessary to place a quad at each end of the line from which a color line or slug was removed; otherwise, the black type could not be inked without pieing the form. Houghton's method is somewhat reminiscent of the one that Lewis M. Allen describes in his *Printing with the Handpress* (1969, pp. 62–64). Allen, on the other hand, used Duco cement to create his slugs.
>
> Houghton gives an example of how to print a form in three colors using the composite method. It should be remembered that for each impression, the form had to be unlocked and relocked twice. The slugs are lifted out, inked between bearers with a brayer, and then returned to the form after it has been inked in black. Since the slugs were inked outside the form, it did not matter that they were slightly higher than the black type in the form – due to a thin piece of paper that was pasted to the bottom of the line. The difference in height would be compensated for in the makeready. With this method, the registration will always be perfect, even though the process is very slow.
>
> In the last paragraph below, Houghton describes a curious roller that was used for simultaneously inking more than one color, although it could only be used when the bar of

color ran across the whole form and the type was positioned at a right angle to the roller. The roller picked up ink from a series of ink slabs, one for each line of color. There was a narrow space between each slab to prevent the colors from blending together; therefore, each section of the roller had to be just wide enough to accommodate the adjacent lines that were to be inked in the same color. Another important consideration was to align the roller precisely with the lines of type before inking the form.

[Printing in colours, which], though much neglected, deserves the attention of every pressman. It is true that ingenious artists of the present day have exhibited much skill in illustrating works of history, &c., and have shown a wonderful genius in publications professedly connected with the fine arts; but as far as regards the average printing of the day, it is certainly neglected. This may be easily accounted for. To print in two colours occupies more than twice the time necessary to print in one; and it also requires more skill and ingenuity. These, unfortunately, must be paid for; and this pecuniary consideration is sufficient to banish from us this beautiful art. In the bustle and competition of the present day, time is money, and blue and gold, scarlet and green, give way to the equally useful but infinitely less beautiful uniformity of unredeemed black. To country printers, however, some knowledge of colour-printing must be of infinite advantage, as by a judicious use of colours, they may create an unlimited variety in job-work.

Except in the execution of works of a very high order, and the imitation of intricate and delicate patterns, printing in colours requires no addition to the ordinary accomplishment of printing, other than considerable ingenuity and a little practice in preparing the colours. The latter may, it is true, be purchased of the ink-maker prepared for use; but the charge for them is enormous, and they require constant replacement, whilst it is not possible to have on hand every variety of tint. By the purchase of the most simple materials from the oil shop, the ingenious printer has at his hand every colour that fancy can require, at the most moderate cost, without waste or delay. The appliances are few and cheap: – a muller, a marble slab, and a palette-knife; the materials, a can of printers' varnish, to be purchased of the ink-makers, which will keep any length of time, and the raw colours hereafter given, which may be purchased from time to time; care, however, being taken that they are of the best quality, or they will fade and turn rusty in a short time, and be a deformity instead of an ornament to the work. If necessity forces the use of painters' common varnish, about a quarter of a pound of soft soap should be added to every pound of colour, as this will keep the heavy bodied colours much longer suspended in the varnish, and consequently will not become so soon hard. . . .

. . . In fact, every pigment that painters can use can be used in printing, avoiding, as much as possible, all heavy colours. In truth, if the printer is desirous of imitating any particular colour, or of producing any particular tint, he cannot do better than consult the nearest artist in oil or water colours (oil in preference) or in default of that, the neighbouring house-painter. . . .

. . . When two or more colours are employed, and they are worked at as many different times, extreme nicety in the register and justification is required, in order that each colour may fall in its just place, without overlaying one colour with another. This would be very bad in any case, but most especially where the composition of colours would produce a third; as, for instance, if any part of a blue line should unfortunately fall upon a yellow, a green outline would be the result. The best way, however, to avoid this in posting bills, is to print all the colours at once, which is easily done without much if any loss of time. The way to do this may be illustrated by example.

Suppose the forme is to be worked, for instance, in black, red, and blue, and that it has been well washed and corrected, and again dry enough to go on with. The forme being fastened on the press-table, and made ready in the usual way, take out the lines to be worked red, and tack each letter, if possible, to the reglet on each side, that it can be easily lifted out at once. If this cannot be done, on account of the lines being in metal, tie up each with thin cord, and take care to begin to enclose each line, with the reglets, at the bottom of the shank of the type, and wrap it perfectly straight nearly the height of the reglet, so that it will lock up and lift like any other line. If this be done properly, there cannot be more than one thickness of cord in the whole height of the reglet on either side of the line, consequently, will not be liable to get off its feet. This done, paste a slip of paper on the bottom of the line, which will make it more compact while the forme is being worked. Should the line require overlaying, paste them also to the bottom as underlays. The red lines being now ready, proceed in the same way with the blue lines, and make them also as they will lift like so many lumps of metal or wood. Tightening now the remaining portion of the forme, by pressing the quoins up tightly with the fingers, roll it over with the black. If all the lines be properly justified, there will be no difficulty experienced from letters rising. Roll now, also, those lines, which have been taken out and made to lift easily, with their respective colours, replace them in their proper places in the forme, and again tighten all the quoins. The sheet being now pulled, is not only perfect, but is exact, which no other system can improve. This being done, the quoins are again slackened, the different lines taken out and rolled with their own colours, the forme on the press again rolled with black, the lines replaced, the forme quoined, and again pulled, which is continued, of course, till the forme is off. If an objection be raised to this system, on account of the apparent loss of time in taking out the lines every time the forme is pulled, it should be recollected, that in this there is only one making ready, while in working the colours separately there are three; that the frisket is only pasted and cut out once, instead of thrice; that there are no points used, and that the sheet is only once put on and once taken off the tympan; and that the sheet is only once pulled; whereas, by the other system, every sheet goes through the pressman's hands and is pulled three times! But even allowing that three colours may be worked, by underlaying the lines with nonpareil reglet, and each colour worked separately, in the same time, still the method which I have endeavoured to explain has a decided advantage, in the accuracy with which every coloured line falls in its proper place.

For those, however, who wish to work in different colours, Mr. Rider, of Liverpool, has invented a roller, which promises peculiar advantages. I have not seen it, but if what I understand be correct, with his roller, the various colours may be all rolled on the forme and worked at once. The plan is, to have as many boards or marble slabs as there are colours to be worked, each board or slab to have one colour and to be the width of the lines to be printed, blue, red, black, &c. The boards or slabs provided, each separated by a thin reglet and fastened on the ink-table, a portion of each colour may be put on each slab, in the order intended to be printed. This done, it will be necessary to put as many small rollers as there are colours on a roller-frame, sufficiently large to pass over the whole bill, from top to bottom, and [divide] each by a circular piece of tin, about the eighth of an inch larger than the circumference of the rollers. The roller rod also passing through these pieces of tin, which will project above the surface of the rollers, there will be no difficulty either in taking the different coloured inks together, or rolling them on the forme at once, inasmuch as the tin projections will fall between the slabs, and the lines in the forme, separated by the reglets. Of course, the projections must be always placed between the same slabs when distributing, and the same lines when inking the forme. If there be any objection to this plan of working all the colours at one time, it is, perhaps, the great number of various sized rollers, roller-frames, and inking-slabs that would be necessary to make it at all times available. For, certainly, it would not often happen that all the lines to be worked in different colours would be either in the same place or of the same depth. I think, however, if this objection could be removed, the plan would be excellent.

Reading 22.6
Printing in Colors
from *Typographia* by Thomas F. Adams (1844, p. 255).

> Adams points out that color work was not as common in America as it was in England. His remarks on color printing appear to have been taken, in greater part, from Houghton's in Reading 22.5 above.

The art of printing in colors has heretofore been almost entirely neglected in this country [America]; at least as far as relates to the embellishing works of ordinary excellence with vignettes, capitals, tail-pieces, and other devices of fancy, in beautiful tints, in the manner of the early typographers. This may very easily be accounted for. To print in two colors occupies more than twice the time necessary to print in one; and it also requires more skill and ingenuity. These, unfortunately, must be paid for; and this pecuniary consideration is sufficient to banish from our pages this lovely art. So did not our forefathers; *they* took pride in choosing the most tasteful designs, and most harmonious colors, to illuminate their productions, and beguile the reader into study by the illusive charms of gold, and blue, and crimson. Fortunately, either time was of little value, or the exclusive possession of the market enabled them to demand remunerating prices for the time thus well bestowed; but in the bustle and competition of our more mercantile days, time is money, and blue and gold, scarlet and green, give way to the equally useful but infinitely less beautiful uniformity of unredeemed black. . . .

[Editor's note: At this point, Adams goes on to repeat Stower's instructions here, although he substitutes rollers for ink balls. See Reading 22.2 on p. 619.]

Reading 22.7
Printing in Colours
from *The Letter-Press Printer* by Joseph Gould (1876, pp. 140–141).

> Even though Gould is specifically discussing printing multiple colors for job work on a handpress using a separate form for each color, many of the practices he describes here would also be applicable for book work. In addition, he includes information on the multiple-point-hole registration system which was used by most nineteenth-century pressmen to position the paper on the tympan when printing multiple colors. This system consisted of a thin metal strip with a single row of spurs aligned on it, one for each color to be printed. This strip was tacked to a piece of furniture in the form. During the first impression, the spurs – which were a little higher than the type, but low enough not to be crushed by the platen – pricked the paper. It should be noted that the spurs also had to be outside the range of the roller or they would damage it. After the first impression, the strip was removed and the paper was then put on regular points or paste points, using a fresh set of points and point holes for each color. Gould indicates that the point holes were pricked in the sides of the paper, not the top and bottom as Southward notes on p. 629 in Reading 22.8. Stephen O. Saxe has a portfolio of specimen leaves titled *Spécimen-album, gravure & fonderie de Charles Derriey*, which is undated, but published sometime between 1862 and 1877. The eight registration point holes are still extant at the top and bottom of a sheet printed in eight colors.

Broadsides were often printed without points; the paper was simply laid on the tympan. I imagine, however, that some sort of guides, whether pins or duck's bills, would have been used to keep the paper in place for the first impression and to register successive colors.

Another example of color printing from separate forms can be found in Ringwalt (1871, p. 105), who mentions *chromatic type*. These are multicolor letters, see **Fig. 22.1**, made of metal or wood, whose parts were precision cast or carved so that they would print in perfect register. When transparent inks were used, a third color could be obtained by overlapping the impressions.

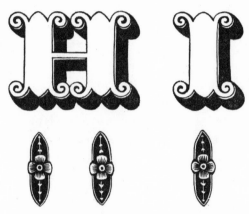

Fig. 22.1. *Chromatic type* – from Ringwalt (1871, p. 106)

The forme having been divided, if thoroughly clean, may be made ready in the usual manner. If a poster, circular, or card, the formes can be worked by "lay" only, points not being necessary. The sheets, however, must be laid with the greatest accuracy, and care taken that they do not move while the tympan is descending. But should the forme be very intricate, so far as the registering of the various colours is concerned, it will be the safest plan to use points. The points used in printing the first of a series of colour-formes are different from those used for book-work. They are made of thin sheet-iron, with spurs, which will stand, when the points are fixed on the forme, a little higher than the type, and are fixed on the furniture by small nails that are driven through holes made for the purpose. For a job to be worked in four colours, points with not less than three spurs must be used, so that there will be no occasion to use the same point-holes a second time. For a particularly fine job the points should be so placed that they may perforate the paper close to the edge of the margin, on each side of the forme, so that after the work is finished the perforated portion may be cut off, to remove the unsightly point-holes. After the first forme has been worked, the regular points, or paste-points, must be used, fresh point-holes being taken for each colour. In this way an accurate registering of the colours will be secured; but, should the same point-holes be used for a second colour, any damage they may have received in working the first will endanger perfect register.

Generally speaking, colours are more difficult to work than black; it is therefore of the utmost importance, in printing in colours, that the forme should be thoroughly inked, and that when extra colour is required it should be taken in as small quantities as is compatible with the job in hand, and distributed properly. To do colour-work in a satisfactory manner, and with the least expenditure of time, it is advisable to have rollers cast on purpose and kept for colour-work only. They must be a little hard – as hard as those used for the finest black inks – and have a smooth, tacky surface. Black rollers cleaned for a coloured job only cause annoyance, especially if they are cracked on the surface, for, after being in use a short time, they are almost certain to exert an injurious influence on the colour. . . .

As soon as one colour has been worked . . . scrape off all ink that has not been distributed, and put it back into its proper ink-tin. Oil and scrape rollers . . . and thoroughly clean the ink-slab. It is if the utmost importance that before commencing to print another colour the slab, rollers and everything about the forme should be perfectly clean.

If red or any other ink has been used that is difficult to remove, it will be found best to roll the forme with the oily roller, by which means the ink is softened and can be more readily cleaned off.

Reading 22.8
The Method of Colour Printing
from *Practical Printing* by John Southward (1882, pp. 523–530).

> Southward describes all three nineteenth-century methods of printing multiple colors. He is against the raised-type method because of the additional problems it causes with the packing. Citing Houghton's manual, Southward advocates composite forms only for very short runs. He does, however, go into considerable detail on how to print with separate or skeletonized forms.
>
> Since his instructions are for the handpress, he recommends using ink balls for color work, dismissing rollers as "most unsuitable." He also suggests pulling extra proofs of the whole form to be used later when registering successive forms.
>
> In sections 177 through 179, Southward's instructions for color printing are based on comments made by the Strasbourg color printer Henri Rodolphe Gustave Silbermann in *Traité de la typographie* by Henri Fournier (1870, pp. 393–398). Contrary to Southward's endorsement of ink balls, it should be noted that Silbermann mentions inking forms with rollers.
>
> Oldfield (1890, p. 89) offers the following solution for two-color work: "Stereotyping is sometimes resorted to for colour work. In this case two plates are cast, and the stereotyper, according to instructions, cuts away the lines required for one colour in one plate and the reverse in the other. Dissecting the forms for working from type is a long and tedious operation, apart from the amount of time required to secure register, so that stereotyping is usually found the cheapest."
>
> Even though lithography is not a letterpress technique, Southward mentions it in this reading since it was often used to print ground tints before the letterpress was added. Ground tints were more uniform in color and dried faster when printed by lithography.

172. Colour printing by the typographic process is done exactly in the same manner as plain printing in black. The forme is rolled and pulled in the ordinary way, and the mode of making ready, laying on the sheet, and taking off is in no way dissimilar.

It is obvious, however, that the difficulty in this kind of work consists in the inking of the forme with the several colours. The latter must be applied only to the particular lines which are to receive them, and all other portions of the forme must be carefully guarded against being coated with the ink. The common roller, as an inking instrument, is the most unsuitable that could be devised, and its chief recommendation for ordinary one-colour work, the ease with which it can be drawn along the entire face of the forme, is its chief disqualification when the ink has to be deposited locally and in patches.

173. There are several methods of obviating this difficulty. The first is that of "skeletonising" the forme. Let us suppose that it is a placard, and has to be printed in three colours, red, blue, and black. The forme is set up as though it were all to be printed in one colour; proofed, corrected, and carefully washed. It is then made into three forms, each of which contains all the lines to be printed in each one of the colours. Thus there is a red, a blue, and a black forme. The open spaces caused by the existence of lines of another colour are carefully made up with reglets and furniture.

If this plan is adopted the utmost care must be taken with the register. Each set of lines must fall exactly in their proper places. This involves two requirements. The formes must be accurately made up, and the sheet must be accurately laid on the tympan. If either is done imperfectly the appearance of the work will suffer.

It is advisable to pull a few blank sheets, without rolling over the entire forme. The indentations in the paper will sufficiently show the position of the lines. When each colour forme is made up it can be proved on one of these sheets, and if the coloured lines exactly coincide with the previously impressed lines, the accuracy of the making up of the forme will be shown....

174. The other method of colour printing is, instead of skeletonising the forme, to raise up the lines of one colour higher then the rest, which prevents the latter being printed. The principle is the same as the other, for one colour only is printed at one time. The roller is confined as much as possible to the lines which are to take its particular colour, but if others receive a portion of the ink, there is not much harm done.

This method, however, is not to be recommended. The inequality in the height of the forme is very inconvenient, and a proper pressure cannot always be got on such high lines.

175. There is a third method which may be described as that of disintegrating the forme each time an impression is worked. The various lines are lifted out, inked, and replaced, and the forme fastened up again, so that when the impression is pulled it is a complete one, and comprises all the colours intended to be used.

Houghton's work [see Reading 22.5 on p. 621] describes and recommends this method....

We cannot deny that in regard to register this method is unrivalled, but we doubt whether it is practically useful, except when the job is a very small number of impressions.

176. Lithography is very advantageously employed in conjunction with typography for colour printing, especially in working the ground tints. The latter would frequently, if printed on the letterpress, take a very long time to dry; but by doing it in lithography a clean, even tint may be obtained, which is dry almost as soon as it leaves the press.

There is great scope for the exercise of ingenuity in colour printing, and the intelligent workman is always able to effect new combinations and produce novel effects.

If solid ground-tint blocks of a light colour are used, words printed on them in a darker colour have the same effect as a two-colour line.

A shaded line – black and red, for example – may easily be produced with ordinary types. On a bright red ground tint print the first line in bright red, and then by printing the same letters in black laid slightly to the left of the red ones, as though falling on them, a black letter with a red shade on a light green ground tint may be produced.

Indeed, a good effect is often to be obtained by printing the lightest colour first from type a little larger than that used in the second working, which can then be laid so as to fall in the centre and leave the lighter or ground colour to show up all round the type worked last. Each colour should be allowed time to dry, and quick drying-inks be used.

177. *The French System of Colour Printing.* – The following remarks are by M. Silbermann . . .

It is always essential to avoid taking too much ink on the roller, as there is a great risk that the impression will be unequal and muddy. It is not the amount of ink which produces the darker shades, for they depend upon intensity of colour.

In general colour printing exacts great care, the least negligence in any part being easily seen in the result. The rollers require to be in good condition, and at each change either of colour or shade they should be carefully cleansed with spirits of turpentine or benzine. They should also, according to the colours used, be more or less elastic and more or less dry or fresh, practice being the guide in these cases.

178. *Plates for Block Printing.* – It is necessary that these should be made with great accuracy, and this is a serious drawback to most work of this kind, for mathematical exactitude is necessary, and the word almost must be banished from the mind of the operator. Wood is subject to the atmospheric changes; a storm or sudden alteration in temperature, the dampness or dryness of the printing-office, all affect the wood, and sometimes to a very considerable degree. A storm, followed by a sudden cooling of the atmosphere, may cause such an extension in a single night that the work already completed will not agree with that which is to follow; and we have known cases in which it has taken days of laborious experiments, by exposing the blocks to different degrees of temperature, to reduce them to their original dimensions.

It is better therefore to use plates in metal, and to make a stereotype from the original engraving to serve as a base for the blocks from which the colours are to be printed.

179. Paper can be used either sized or unsized, although the latter is preferable. In order to obtain good results, especially when the surfaces are large, the paper should be carefully smoothed upon a roller, and with plates of zinc. The impressions should always be dry, for the dampness destroys the brilliancy obtained by the glazing, and also causes shrinking.

It is, perhaps, unnecessary to add that the paper should be of good quality, equal in surface and perfect in colour – any defect in this respect neutralising the care taken in the impression.

180. *Register.* – This is the cornerstone upon which must rest all printing in colours, and it is this which gives typography an advantage over lithography. Thus the typographic impression is made by a stroke, dry and straight, while that by lithography is executed by a friction which stretches the paper by a movement more or less considerable, in proportion to its thickness and consistency.

To preserve this superiority, exactitude of register is one of the most important means, and numerous processes have been attempted, one of the best of which is to preserve for each impression a pair of special points.

For fine colour impressions the presses need to be in perfect condition, the tympans covered with silk, and not with either cotton or muslin, the blankets of thick and smooth satin, and everything in perfect unison. In a word, instrument and workman should be equal to the work to be produced, and all depends upon the care, intelligence, and practice of the latter and the perfection of the former.

Successive impressions seem essential to good work, the simultaneous impressions always leaving something to be desired. It is impossible to make the plates so perfect that no point of junction is visible, and in the next place this kind of impression requires as much time for the double or treble inking and the fitting together as is required for two or three successive impressions.

Colour printing is best done on the hand-press, for the reason that machines, by their own vibration, prevent perfect register, and seem serviceable only when worked so slowly that they have no advantage over the hand-press, especially when consideration is made for time required in cleaning when there is a change of colour.

Points. – The points used for fine colour work are different to those for common single-colour work. They are made of small pieces of thin sheet iron, each about 1½ in. long and ⅓ in. broad. To each of them are riveted three or four spurs, for working the colours in true register, and in each there are three holes for tacking them to the forme. The length of these spurs is such as to make them just or hardly as high as the surface of the type, and one set thus riveted forms a series. To the furniture of the first coloured forme only, two series of these points are tacked, one at the top and the other at the bottom of the forme, to fall at the extremity of the margin. Thus fixed, the tympan will fall upon the spurs and perforate the paper in the same direction as the impression is received from the forme. These perforations are the point-holes, by which each successive colour is made to fall, one after the other, in its proper place. The top series of these point-holes is represented thus .   .   . [Editor's note: The row of periods represent the point holes in the paper.]

For the second colour a pair of ordinary points is fixed to the tympan, and the first point-hole in each series is used to make this colour fall in register with the first. The second point-hole in each series is then employed to make the third colour fall, and so on with all the colours that are to be worked.

By this method a fresh pair of point-holes is reserved and used for each colour, and an excellence of register obtained which cannot be improved. After all the colours are thus worked, these point-holes are cut off the margin and the work finished.

181. *Hints and Cautions.* – Reference has already been made to the importance of the quality of the paper used in colour printing. Indeed, in printing in black the paper has a greater influence for good or evil than is commonly supposed. The ink should always be adapted to the paper. A brown tint in paper makes the ink look brown, and this fact should be taken into consideration and provided for.[*] Attention should also be paid to whether the paper is porous or glazed. If you press your tongue against it when porous it will immediately get soft from absorbing the moisture, and become semi-transparent. Porous paper is of course less transparent, and with a strong ink is more apt to be torn; it requires therefore thinner ink, and is generally printed from in a damp state, less ink being required.

Soft paper generally contains clay, sometimes as much as 30 to 40 per cent., which makes it brittle, and the powder is apt to fall off, and make fluff on the machine, ink-table, and rollers. The ink is then often accused of being unground, from the fluff sticking to it, and making it look rough and sandy.

Soft or engine-sized paper, from its absorbent nature, takes up ink rapidly, as in newspaper printing, where the impression is intended for immediate sale. In the case of tub-sized paper, which resists the action of the tongue, before-mentioned, dryer inks, specially prepared, require to be used, in order not to set off, as the ink is not absorbed and must therefore form a skin. Dryer inks, properly so called, require to be cleared up from type[,] tables and rollers each time the press stands, as the skin is apt to form, which may then either tear the rollers or come off in little pellets, filling up the type. This explains how some inks are said to dry on the paper and not elsewhere.

Clay in paper is detected by burning a portion of it and noticing the quantity and quality of the ash. In paper so adulterated the white ash nearly equals in bulk the original paper.

All ink, when opened, especially the thick and dryer inks, should be lifted from the top, keeping the surface as smooth as possible, otherwise the side portions will skin, and this mixing with

---

[*] Several of the above hints are taken from the "Special Instructions to Agents" of Messrs. Fleming and Co., the eminent ink manufacturers, of Leith.

the rest of the ink is apt to spoil the whole. All cans should be kept covered from the atmosphere, and all scrapings from table and boxes kept separate, for poster or coarse work. If water gets mixed with ink it will make it roll out badly, and work specky. Any skin formed should always be carefully removed to prevent its mixing with the undried ink.

Red inks made from vermilion cannot be used upon electro-plates of copper, on account of the formation of an amalgam and a sulphur, which destroys the brightness of the colour and eats away the block. The system of brass-facing casts is now adopted to obviate this evil, brass being unaffected by the substance of the ink; nickel facing has also been successfully introduced with the same object.

With the aid of a mitering machine and a few lengths of metal rules a great variety of borders may be obtained. An octagonal border may be locked in a circle. After one colour is printed it may be merely turned just one-eighth of a revolution, and again printed with another colour, thus producing a pretty and novel effect.

Instead of ground-blocks, a tint produced by putting together a number of pieces of border may be used with excellent effect. The border should be as new as possible, and not battered in any part, or it will not throw out the printing afterwards done upon it.

Reading 22.9
Blocks for Tinted Grounds
from *Printing* by Charles Thomas Jacobi (1890, pp. 103–105).

> Tint blocks were often used in decorative printing, primarily in combination with frames made up of rules and ornaments, as well as backgrounds for illustrations. Jacobi describes a number of ways to make and print tint blocks. He is one of the first manual writers to mention *celluloid* as a printing surface.

These may be made of various materials, such as brass, type-metal, box or other wood, celluloid, &c., and a printer in any great commercial centre is always able to satisfy his requirements almost at a moment's notice. A provincial printer may be seriously inconvenienced when one of his customers takes a fancy to colours. The way small German printers help themselves may, therefore, be read with advantage. They take a very smooth and even glazed board, such as is used in pressing and glazing the paper after printing, and cut two or three pieces out of it, a little larger than the desired tinted block. Similar pieces are cut out of common pasteboard, well sized and smooth, and the whole is then formed into a layer with best glue, and stuck, also with glue, on a solid wooden board – oak will suit best – so as to form a type-high block. This done, the block is put into a glazing press [standing press; see **Fig. 26.7** on p. 776], or into a letter-copying press [nipping press; see **Fig. 26.9** on p. 780], or you may simply put boards and heavy weights on it, just to let it dry under severe pressure, care being taken that the pasteboards are well united to each other and to the wooden block, as the result depends on this. When the wood and paper block is completely dry, the transfer may be made. The forme to which the tinted block is to fit is locked-up in a frame, as also is the block itself, the latter being disposed so as to fit in the composed matter as exactly as possible. Then this last one is lifted into the press or machine, and, after being well inked, one pull is made from it on to a sheet fixed on the tympan or cylinder. This done, the formes are changed, the block forme taking the place of the composition forme, after a sheet of thin pasteboard, of the thickness of common Bristol board, has been put on the bed of the press, to raise the block a little above the type height to give more effect to the pull. The tympan still bearing the impressed sheet, being now brought down and a pull taken, a negative copy of the contents of the forme will be obtained on the glazed-board block, the cutting of which may now be proceeded with. That operation is best effected with a thin penknife, or even with a small chisel, care being taken to cut in an outward slanting direction, so as to give the printing surface of the block a larger and stronger basis. When the cutting is finished, the block is ready for printing; but should the number of copies to be printed from it be large, it is better to give it first a coating of varnish. A coating of shellac, diluted in alcohol, applied twice, has proved most effective, and will stand the printing of a very large number of copies before any change is to be observed. In cleaning, lye must be avoided, and only a little petroleum or turpentine rubbed over with a smooth rag. When the tinted ground is to show a pattern, this may be obtained by sticking embossed paper on it, taking care to fill the indentations of the paper well with stiff glue, and to paste it thus on the block. When dry, it may be varnished and printed from as before stated.

Plate 27. Lithograph by P. Bineteau after Carl Schulin of a German printing office with a Stanhope press of the second construction, early-nineteenth century. The pressman and the inker are working on the same side of the press. Note that the inker is using a short roller, although the customary practice was to use rollers that were the same length as the bed. His ink source is an inking apparatus to the right of the press. Although unusual in the nineteenth century, this printing office also has its own type foundry shown on the right. The original lithograph is hand-colored. (Courtesy of the Gutenberg-Museum, Mainz.)

CHAPTER TWENTY-THREE

Printing in Gold, Bronzing, and Embossing

Although similar to printing selected segments of the text in multiple colors, as described in Chapter 22, printing in gold as well as bronzing and embossing were often referred to as *decorative* or *ornamental printing* since they were used primarily to embellish the letterpress. Despite the fact that manuscripts and early printed books occasionally had gold ornamentation added by hand, the first practical instructions for *printing in gold*, the generic term for *gold leafing*, did not appear in printers' manuals until the early 1840s. Most printers today prefer to use gold inks or stamping foils rather than bother with any of the more time-consuming procedures described below.

Johnson (1824, p. 547) has a brief footnote in his manual: "There is one instance of a Columbian Press . . . made for Mr. John Whittaker . . . for the express purpose of printing a most singularly splendid work in letters of gold, of the august Ceremonial of the Coronation [July 19, 1821] of his most gracious Majesty, George the Fourth." However, Johnson does not provide any specific information about the process.

Adams, in Reading 23.3 on p. 635, expands the definition of ornamental printing to include other decorative processes for enhancing the letterpress.

Reading 23.1
Of Printing with Gold and Silver
from *Mechanick Exercises* by Joseph Moxon (1683, pp. 331–333)

> Moxon's method of *printing* in gold and silver is actually a primitive form of *stamping* since the work is not done on the press. In his example, it would appear that Moxon is adding individual names to previously printed sheets of text. The names were set up in a composing stick, a practice similar to setting type in the hand pallet that bookbinders use for gold stamping. Then the type was inked with a special varnish, using small ink balls that were made especially for gold work. By turning the stick upside down, and with a little pressure applied by hand to the back of the stick, the pressman was able to impress the name on the paper, which was laid flat on a press blanket. I am assuming that he removed this blanket before he placed the gold leaf over the varnished image since he would need a hard surface under the sheet of paper in order to burnish the gold.

This Operation is seldom used but for Printing Names; and therefore rarely drest in a *Form* to the *Press*; but is usually Printed in the *Stick:* And then the *Composer Justifies* his *Stick* very *Hard,* as well that the *Letters* fall not out when the *Back* of the *Stick* is turned upwards, as that the strength of the *Hard Varnish* the *Face* of the *Letter* is *Beat* with, pulls not the *Letter* out of the *Stick.*

Therefore the *Press-man* makes two little *Balls,* by tying about an Handfull of Wooll in new clean Leather, and dabs one of his *Balls* upon the Hardest *Vanish* he has, and with the other

633

destributes his *Varnish* to a convenient Fatness . . . With one of these *Balls* he *Beats* the *Name*; and having his Paper *Wet,* he lays a single *Blanket* on the *Correcting-stone,* and his Paper on the *Blanket*; and with a *Riglet* fitted to the *stick,* he presses the *Letter* to keep it straight in *Line:* Then places the *Face* of the *Letter* exactly flat down upon the Paper, and with the force of both his Hands presses the *Letter* hard and even down upon the Paper, to receive an Impression: But he takes care not to wriggle the *Letter* in the *Stick* backwards or forwards, lest either the *Beard* Print, or the sides of the *Letter* be more or less besmeared with the *Varnish:* Because the Gold or Silver will stick to the least Sully that the *Varnish* may chance to make.

Then cutting his Gold or Silver to a size full big enough to cover the Printed *Name* or *Matter,* he lays his Gold or Silver on what was Printed, and with a little White Cotton gently presses the Gold or Silver upon the Printed *Matter,* and lets the Paper lye by a while; as well that it may dry, as the *Varnish* Harden, (which will quickly be) he with his Handkerchief gently wipes over the Printed *Matter.* So shall all the Gold or Silver that was toucht by the *Varnish,* stick to the *Varnish* on the Paper, and the other will wipe away.

If he lists [wishes] to Polish it, he uses a Tooth or the Ivory Handle of a Knife.

Reading 23.2
Printing and Bronzing in Gold
from *The Printers' Practical Every-Day-Book* by Thomas Shaw Houghton (1841, p. 105).

> Houghton's manual is the first to give actual instructions for printing and bronzing in gold. He describes both the gold leaf and the bronze powder processes, claiming that there is no "difficulty in printing in gold." Anyone who has tried either process may have reservations concerning this statement.
>
> Houghton adds a bit of pigment to his varnish, which in turn is added to the gold size, also known as *gold composition.* Ringwalt (1871, p. 185) gives the following description of gold composition: "A mixture of chrome and varnish." He neglects, however, to specify any quantities. Nor was I able to find a single recipe for it in any other manual. Houghton notes that the gold composition was thicker and more tenacious than regular ink varnishes. Today, genuine gold leaf is usually supplied in small booklets of twenty-five sheets, measuring about 3⅜ inches square.
>
> The type was rolled over in the same manner that it would have been for ordinary ink, and an impression pulled. The sheet was then removed from the tympan and the gold leaf was laid over and pressed against the image until it bonded with the varnish. Once the varnish was dry, the excess gold was brushed away. It is notable that none of the nineteenth-century manual writers mentioned burnishing the gold leaf at the press, although Jacobi, in his instructions on p. 644 in Reading 23.6, uses a press for burnishing bronze powders.
>
> Bronzing had been known in Germany since the 1750s; however, it was only in the nineteenth century that it was widely used for ornamental printing in England and America. Houghton's description of bronzing follows the same basic procedures as those for gold leaf except that the varnish is made thicker and the bronze powder is dusted or brushed over the wet image.

There is no difficulty in printing in gold; it is within the power of any typographer. The type is composed and made-ready at press as in the usual manner. A quantity of raw or burnt umber is mixed with printers' varnish, to the same consistency as it would be were it intended to be used as ink; but this mixture is then compounded with a considerable quantity of gold size, the same as that used by gilders and japanners [lacquerers]. The first mixture is necessary, because it has been found that the umber will not combine with the size. The type is then rolled with this compound, in the same manner that ordinary ink is applied, and the impression is taken upon the paper. Leaf-gold is then laid over it with a piece of wool, and pressed slightly upon it. When the varnish has had time to set, a piece of wool is rubbed roughly over the part printed, and the superfluous leaf is thereby removed, leaving the gold adhering to the varnish. The sharpness of the print will vary with the judgment of the printer in the quantity of sizing applied to the type; for if the press-work be bad, the print will be bad also. For inferior gold-printing, bronze powder is extensively used. For this the varnish is made very much thicker than for gold; the method of printing is the same; but after the impression has been given, the powder is brushed over the print, and will adhere thereto, whilst the superfluity may be easily removed.

Reading 23.3
Ornamental Printing
from *Typographia* by Thomas F. Adams (1844, p. 252–254).

In 1844, Adams added a new section to his manual that he called "Ornamental Printing," claiming that ornamental printing "sprung into existence . . . within the last twenty years." This term seems to have been unique to Adams, who continued to use it in all the remaining editions of his work. Other manual writers preferred to use Savage's term *decorative printing*, which comes from his ground-breaking book *Practical Hints on Decorative Printing* (1822).

Under "Ornamental Printing," Adams also includes card printing. Decorative cards were very popular in the nineteenth century and were often printed in a variety of exotic types in multiple colors, including gold and silver. Special presses were manufactured just for printing them. It should be noted that cards were normally printed individually; the printers cut large sheets of card stock down to the sizes they needed. Cards were also available in a variety of precut sizes. The earliest reference I have found to the modern practice of *ganging* – a method for printing multiple copies of an item from multiple settings that were locked together in a single form – is Southward's on p. 690 in Reading 24.12. Once printed, the sheets were cut into individual cards.

Adams expands on Houghton's instructions for gold printing and bronzing. Unlike Houghton, he does not recommend adding raw or burnt umber to the varnish. Bronzing was more frequently used since it was less than half the price of gold leaf.

One form of ornamental printing that Adams invented was called *polychromatic printing* for which he was granted a U.S. patent on September 17, 1844. He gives no details about the process in his manual other than noting that "any number of colors can be printed at one impression." This may have been similar to the composite-forms process described by Houghton on pp. 622–623 in Reading 22.5. Adams dropped it from the "Ornamental Printing" section beginning with the 1856 edition of his manual, although there still remained a one-sentence, non-existent reference to it on p. 255 in all subsequent editions.

I could not find any references to polychromatic printing in any of Savage's books even though Geoffrey Ashall Glaister notes in his *Encyclopedia of the Book* (1996, p. 387) that Savage used the term *polychromatic printing* for *chiaro scuro printing*. I do not believe that the two processes were the same. Adams is describing a process for printing multiple colors in one impression; Savage used a separate block and press run for each color.

Adams's method for *xylographic printing* is reminiscent of Victor Hammer's speculation on printing fifteenth-century two-color initials that appears in *Notes on the Two-Color Initials of Victor Hammer* (1966) by Carolyn Reading Hammer. The process consists of nested plates that are inked separately, reassembled, and printed with one impression. The basic difference here is that Adams removes the outer color plate for inking outside the form, while Hammer removes the inner. I believe Adams's system would be slightly more efficient to manage. Note, if the two-color block were to be printed together with the black text, both pieces of the block would have to be inked outside the form.

Under this general head, we will attempt to describe the various kinds of Ornamental Printing which have sprung into existence, as it were, within the last twenty years; and from our having been almost exclusively engaged in that branch of the art during the greater portion of that period, it will no doubt be expected of us to explain, for the benefit of the uninitiated, the result of our experience.

Card Printing has, perhaps, since the introduction of Enamelled or Polished Cards, made more rapid strides towards perfection than any other branch of the art; the fine absorbing quality of the Enamel, under proper management, producing the most beautiful results, in many cases scarcely discernable from copper-plate. A card, to be well printed, requires the same treatment as a wood engraving . . . at least so far as the making ready is concerned, and also in being worked without blankets, and with the finest ink. Having made a light impression on our tympan sheet, we place our pins so as to bring the impression as nearly as possible in the centre of the card, one pin at the lower side, and two at the off side, taking care that the head of the pin does not come in contact with the types. The pull should be exceedingly light until properly regulated, having at no time more than is actually necessary to bring up the *face* of the type. Composition Balls should be used for all small forms on the ordinary hand presses, where fine printing is required. . . . The printing of Cards has, however, been carried to such an extent of late, that they are now printed on small card machines at the rate of one, two, and even three thousand per hour; we have two of these machines in use, one capable of printing one thousand, and the other three thousand per hour. All prepared cards must be printed without wetting, and it is now very common to print all kinds dry.

Gold Printing, like most other novelties, has had its day, but is now more sparingly used; the process, even now, is not generally known by the profession, although within the power of all. The types are composed, and made ready at the press in the usual manner. A pot of gold size is then procured from the Ink maker, or Printers' Warehouse, with which the form is inked in the ordinary manner, and the impression taken upon the paper. The book of Leaf Gold having been previously cut, if for a large job, by merely taking off the back, if for a small one, by cutting it into pieces the size of the printed impression, which is done by pressing a straight edge across it, and cutting it through with the point of a sharp penknife, we proceed to laying on the gold in the following manner: we slightly wet the end of the fore finger of our right hand, and having placed the thumb of that hand on the pile of gold, we raise the edge of the paper with the fore finger sufficiently to dampen it with the moisture of that finger, then pressing the moistened edge of the paper on the gold, it will adhere sufficiently to enable us to lift gold and paper together, and place it on the impression, and so we proceed until it is entirely covered; we then gently pat the gold with the balls of the fingers, or any soft pliable substance, until it is set, when with a very soft hat brush, we brush off the superfluous gold, leaving a clear and beautiful impression of the subject in hand. The sharpness of the print will vary with the judgment of the printer in the quantity of sizing applied to the type; for if the press-work be bad, the print will be bad also.

Bronze Printing is more extensively used than gold printing, being attended usually with less than half the expense in the cost of the material; the method of printing is the same, except that instead of laying on the gold leaf, the impression is rubbed over with the bronze, by dipping a small block covered with a short fine fur into the powder, and brushing off the superfluous bronze with a soft brush, as in gold printing. Bronze can be procured of various colors, and when laid on with judgment, the effect is beautiful. The palest bronze is best.

Polychromatic Printing is a new mode of printing, by which any number of colors can be printed at one impression, with the usual rapidity, and for which we have applied for letters patent of the United States. Rights can be had by applying to us.

Xylographic Printing, signifies literally, printing from wooden blocks, but it is commonly applied to a species of Ornamental Bordering cut in type metal, the printing of which is from the surface, usually in colored inks. In 1827 we discovered a mode, which is practised to some extent, by which two colors can be printed at one impression; this is done by having two plates, the inner one blocked in the usual manner, the outer one moveable, and made to fit over it, resting on the same block.

Reading 23.4
Printing in Gold
from *The Printers' Universal Book of Reference and Every-Hour Office Companion* by William Finch Crisp (1875, pp. 86–89).

Crisp discusses another method for printing in gold called *bronzing*, which uses an imitation gold dust, whose main ingredient is copper. As Crisp points out, it was a tremendous health hazard since the powder routinely floated in the air and was inevitably inhaled by the workmen. Real gold and silver dusts were also used; however, they were very expensive compared to bronze powders.

Hansard Jr. (1841, p. 151) notes that during the printing of the special hand-bronzed issue of *The Sun*, a London newspaper, to commemorate the Coronation of Queen Victoria on June 28, 1838, "a very distressing disease arose, the hair became perfectly green, and the men were very seriously affected."

Crisp gives an interesting varnish recipe for gold leaf work that includes an ingredient not mentioned as such in any other printers' manual: *virgin wax*, which was probably nothing more than pure beeswax. This varnish was then mixed with a colored ink such as light chrome yellow or burnt umber.

Crisp also mentions using an imitation gold known as *Dutch metal* – or as he calls it *Fine Planier-Metal*, which was made at Fürth in Nuremberg. Dutch metal is an alloy of eleven parts copper to two parts zinc that has been rolled into thin sheets. Since both gold leaf and Dutch metal were laid on while the varnish was still wet, they had to be burnished in order to affix them properly to the paper.

Printing in gold can be done either by using the gold leaf or the gold dust. The imitation gold dust is generally known in the trade under the name of "bronze." A variety of colours may be had. There is white (which is made from silver leaf), pale yellow or gold coloured, orange-yellow, green, and red. No saving is effected by using the coarser kinds, as only the finer grains adhere to the impression; all the rest has to be thrown away. For the purpose of printing in gold, impressions should first be taken with ordinary printers' ink, after which the bronze dust should be immediately applied by means of a tuft of wadding. Some typographers apply the bronze with a large brush; but by this means a great deal of the dust mixes itself with the air, and is inhaled by the workmen, which is not without danger. The chief ingredient of this metal being copper, it forms verdigris, and is productive of colic and vomiting. The smoother the paper upon which the printing is done, the more brilliant will be the effect. If it is desirable to have very rich gilding, bronzes of various colours may be used. Care must be taken that the paper which is used for the bronzing process be perfectly dry. Porcelain paper is manufactured by applying several very thin and even coatings of a colour, consisting of Kremnitz white and a small quantity of glue and alum, to one surface of the paper. If the side of the paper which has been treated as above is laid upon a polished steel plate, and strong pressure put upon it in a copper-plate press, it receives that beautiful gloss which distinguishes it from all other satin and glazed papers. If this latter operation is delayed till after the gold bronze has been applied, it will much improve the appearance, especially if the card has passed several times between the rollers. These cards, previous to being printed on, should be slightly damped, which is best done by putting them for a few moments between wet sheets of paper. It is advisable to let the cards dry for a few days previous to their being rolled over. If this cannot be done, owing to pressure of time, the steel plate should, after each rolling, be well rubbed down to remove any possible stains, which might otherwise spoil the cards. The gloss may be made still more beautiful by wetting the cards, previous to pressing them, between damp sheets of paper, care being taken, at the same time, that the paper be not too wet, as it would otherwise cause the cards to adhere to the steel plate. As a matter of course, gold and silver dust may be used instead of common bronze, though the latter will be found good enough for all ordinary purposes, as that kind of work is but of rare occurrence which would warrant so large an outlay as the use of either of the former would entail. For printing in gold with leaf, the paper or card should be printed with a composition consisting of two parts of varnish of medium strength, one part virgin wax, and one part Venice turpentine. This must be mixed with the desired colour, more especially with one of such a shade as may resemble somewhat the colour of the gold, so as to hide any defects which might occur in the laying on of the gold. Light chrome yellow or burnt ochre gives a good and appropriate colour. After the impression is taken the gold leaf is laid on; if imitation gold is used, or "Dutch metal," as it is sometimes called, it may be laid on with the fingers; should it be found adhering to them, it is advisable to rub them with Spanish chalk. But if gold of fine quality is used a gilder's pallet is necessary, which consists of long badger's hairs fixed between two cards. These hairs should be slightly greased by passing them over one's cheek or head, which will facilitate the removal of the gold leaf from the book to the card or paper, upon which it should then be pressed by means of a cotton rag. To separate fine gold it should be laid on a leather covered cushion, which has been previously rubbed over with Spanish chalk, and then cut with a fine polished knife specially kept for that purpose. Generally speaking, the treatment of the fine gold requires a certain amount of dexterity, and it may be as well to notice the mode in which gilders and bookbinders perform similar operations. As for the imitation gold, the whole book may be cut through with a pair of shears. This gold being very cheap, it is not necessary to be as economical in its application as with the finer qualities. An essential point to the success of the operation is to procure gold leaf as thin as it can possibly be had, having taken care that all the leaves are of the same shade, since it often happens, particularly with the cheaper sorts, that some leaves are more or less yellow than others, which has a most damaging effect if used on one and the same object. The best and thinnest imitation gold is called "Fine Planier-Metal," and is largely manufactured at Fürth, in Nuremberg, Germany. Each packet contains ten books of 252 leaves, *i.e.*, 2,520 leaves; and it is calculated that a grain of the best metal will cover nearly sixty square inches. After the gold leaf has been applied to an impression, it should be laid between a sheet of paper, and gently rubbed over on the outside with the hand. This sheet, with the impression contained within it, must now be laid on the top of the next one, and then both should be brought under the rubber [burnisher], so that the gold may be fixed by means of pressure. If common metal is used, it is a good precautionary measure to have the impressions twice under the press. If there is time, copies should be allowed to dry for a few days; if not, they may be rolled immediately, care being taken to give only a very gentle pressure. In proportion to the coarseness of the gold used, the drawing to which it is applied should contain more massive and further separated lines; for this kind of gold does not affix itself easily to fine lines, and if the space between two lines be too narrow, the flannel is likely to remove the gold from the finer parts altogether. But if any description of fine gold is used, it may be applied with confidence to the finest drawings.

Reading 23.5
Printing in Gold
from *Practical Printing* by John Southward (1882, pp. 531–537).

> As always, Southward is an able compiler who draws very liberally from earlier manuals for his information. In his original text, he incorporates many of Crisp's observations from Reading 23.4 above, which I have deleted from Southward's text below.
>
> Even though lengthy, Southward gives a very informative account of how gold leaf is made. He also includes recipes for an adhesive varnish, which he calls *gold preparation*, although he does not give one for *gold size*, which is one of the former's main ingredients. Southward prefers a varnish without color and notes that its consistency needs to be altered for each new paper as well as for the type of gold to be used.
>
> In Section 188, Southward gives Frederick Noble's method for laying the gold leaf on the varnish. And later in Section 191, Southward describes a method for burnishing gold work between two sheets of plain paper under pressure. Another of his suggestions is to place the sheet with gold on a type-high board in the bed of a handpress, cover it with a soft blanket, and then pull the bar. Two other methods, which he does not mention, probably would have worked more efficiently: (1) putting the individual sheets, between their protective sheets, in a standing press and nipping them, and (2) running the sheets through a heated rolling press.
>
> Southward suggests using a zinc or wooden tray as a dusting bin into which the printed sheets were placed for bronzing. Even though he does not mention tilting the tray in order to allow the excess powder to fall away from the sheet of paper, it is only logical that he would have. By the 1870s, bronzing machines, like the one shown in **Fig. 23.2** on p. 644, were used to help meet the increased demand for gold work.

182. Printing in gold is very much more extensively practised in the present day than formerly, and has, in fact, become a regular adjunct of colour printing. It is not necessarily either a very difficult or a very expensive process, yet few ordinary pressmen can perform it with any degree of success.

This kind of work may be done in three ways: –

1. By using bronze powders.
2. By using gold leaf.
3. By using Dutch metal.

In regard to bronze powders, there is a variety of colours to be had, which are classified thus: –

Patent bronze powders, pale, deep, extra deep, and red gold; citron, orange, flesh, copper, orange copper, scarlet, crimson, purple, and green; white and silver composition. Hand-made bronzes: citron, orange, pale and deep gold; pale scarlet and crimson, brilliant pale and deep.

The prices of these powders vary according to the colours, ranging from 7s. 6d. to 50s. per pound. We would caution the printer, however, that no saving is effected by using the coarser kinds, as only the finer grains adhere to the impression – all the rest has to be thrown away. Very smooth and fine powders have a tendency to blacken the paper unless it is enamelled. Such powders, too, are not as brilliant as the coarser qualities. Hence, while fine powders are selected for the sake of economy rougher and brighter kinds are used when the job will permit of the extra expense.

The silver bronzes are of two kinds. One is made from real silver, and the other from white metal. The latter is bright when printed, but soon turns black. . . .

183. Gold leaf is called red finishing, extra deep, regular deep, lemon pale, white. There is also silver leaf in several descriptions, as well as aluminium leaf (chiefly for bookbinders).

Gold leaf is made in the following manner: The gold to be beaten into leaves or layers is prepared by melting in a plumbago [graphite] crucible, and then cast into ingots, forged, and passed between rollers until it assumes the shape of a long ribbon, and is as thin as ordinary writing-paper. Each of these ribbons is cut into a number of small pieces, and forged upon the anvil. These small square pieces weigh about 6 3-10ths grains [or 0.40824 gram] each, and are about the 760th part of an inch thick. They are next annealed, and interleaved with vellum about 4 in. square. About twenty vellum leaves are placed on the outside; the whole is then placed in a case of parchment, over which is drawn another similar case, so as to keep the packet tight and close on all sides. It is next laid on a smooth block of marble or metal, and the workman begins beating with a round-faced hammer weighing 16 lbs. The packet is turned over occasionally, and the beating continued until the gold is extended to nearly the size of the vellum leaves. The packet is then taken to pieces, and each piece of gold is divided into four, with a steel knife having a smooth but not very acute edge. These pieces are next interlaid with pieces of animal membrane, from the intestines of the ox, of the same dimensions and in the some manner as the vellum. The beating is continued, but with a hammer weighing only 12 lbs., till the gold is brought to the dimensions of the interleaved membrane. It is now again divided into four, by means of a piece of cane brought to a fine edge, the leaves being by this time so thin that any accidental moisture condensing on an iron blade would cause them to adhere to it. The leaves are next divided into three equal portions, and interleaved with membrane as before, and beaten with the finishing hammer, weighing only 10 lbs. The packets are now taken to pieces with the aid of a cane instrument and the breath, are placed flat on a leather cushion, and cut into squares one by one, by a small square frame of cane made the exact size, and are lastly laid in books of twenty-five leaves each, the paper of which is first smoothed and rubbed with red chalk to prevent the leaves adhering. By the weight and measure of the best gold leaf it is found that one grain can be made to cover 56¾ square inches, and from the specific gravity of the metal, together with the admeasurement, it follows that the leaf itself is a 282,000th of an inch thick.

184. *Dutch metal* is merely an imitation of the real gold leaf, and used as a cheap substitute for it. It is sold in bundles of 2,500 leaves each, at from 3s. to 5s. per bundle; but there are various qualities. No. 1 is the lowest grade, and No. 4 the best. The two higher qualities are the most useful for printing purposes.

185. Having described the materials for this description of work, we may explain how they are used. One general principle is applicable to the three kinds of metal. An impression of the forme must first be taken in adhesive varnish, and then the bronze, metal, or leaf must be applied. It is, therefore, a question of great importance to the gold printer how to secure an effective preparation of adhesive media for the materials with which he is working.

Any adhesive varnish which may be used for gold printing is called in the trade "gold preparation." Compounds of this kind may be made with or without body. They may consist of the adhesive medium pure and simple, such as melted gum, or long varnish and gold size, or this adhesive varnish may, for the purpose of increasing its strength, be modified by the addition of body colour, such as burnt umber, burnt sienna, or chrome. Where it is possible to use the adhesive varnish alone without the addition of body colour, it is best to do so. The primary qualification which a good gold preparation ought to possess should be a capacity for sticking. It should also work clean, as it is not the varnish or gold size in a gold preparation which fills up the forme and clogs the type, but the pigment mixed up with the varnish: the pigment or body should be avoided where possible. The paper used has much to do with the selection. A preparation without body may be admirably suited for printing on hard papers, while for softer paper it will sometimes sink into the fabric like water in a porous stone, leaving after awhile the bronze in a dry powder, which may be readily wiped from the surface of the sheet.

The object, then, is to get a material which shall possess the necessary density and toughness, combined with adhesiveness – one that is too thick to soak into the paper, and yet has a drying property sufficient to fix the metal or the dust.

The following are receipts for gold preparations: –

For printing on ordinary unenamelled printing paper, grind one ounce of burnt umber, or burnt sienna, in two ounces of extra strong varnish – technically known as "long varnish" on account of its elastic properties – and add one ounce of gold size.

For a hard-sized enamel surface, the long varnish and gold size alone may be used; but this cannot be adopted with safety for soft enamels.

For extremely soft papers, which require a preparation of extraordinary strength, long varnish may be ground in the very dense primitive chrome manufactured by Cory and Co., which stands up and dries glossy on the surface like gloss red.

186. Out of these preparations, the most suitable one for the job in hand must be selected. The pressman may be reminded that the compounds of burnt sienna and umber are pigments that dry up very rapidly, and soon cause the roller to lose its tackiness and freshness; hence frequent washing up is necessary.

The impression in gold preparation must now be sprinkled with the powder. This may be done in various ways. A tuft of cotton is often used. Some printers employ a hare's foot with the hair on, which is an instrument preferable to brushes and pencils, as it requires less bronze. The bronze, being really only copper reduced to an impalpable powder, is very injurious to those who work in it, and serious diseases will often result unless all possible precautions are taken to prevent the operator from inhaling the atoms which are dispersed through the air. In order to avoid these consequences, it is well to use frames about a yard square, with glass above and at the sides, so as to permit the workman to see his work. On the front face a longitudinal opening can be made, to allow the introduction of the sheet of paper and the arms of the operator. A bandage can also be worn across the mouth; and with such precautions workmen have followed the employment for years without suffering the least inconvenience.

In printing bronze work it is best to have a zinc or wooden tray in which to lay the sheets successively. The smoother the bottom, the more readily and completely the surplus bronze can be wiped up. A sheet of enamelled cardboard may be fastened to the bottom of a wooden tray; or, what is better, a sheet of glass of the proper dimensions.

Several excellently-designed bronzing machines [one of which is shown in **Fig. 23.2** on p. 644] have been introduced to the trade during the last few years, and are found to be very desirable acquisitions to a printing office, not only because they obviate the dangers and inconveniences of using loose bronze, but from the fact that they secure a considerable economy in the consumption of the material, and do the work at a higher speed than can be reached by hand. The bronze is contained in a receptacle something like the ink-duct of a printing machine, and is conveyed over the sheet by rollers covered with plush or felt. The sheet is placed on a traversing band and carried into the machine between the rollers, and discharged at the other end. The criterion of a machine of the kind is the completeness with which it works the gold into the impression; if faulty in this respect, the work is better done by hand.

187. For printing in *Gold Leaf*, the impression is first taken in a very strong preparation, one which seems perfectly flat and smooth on the paper. The substance known as "melted gum" is preferred by some gold printers, but the strongest lake or smooth chrome preparation may be used as a substitute. Others [e.g., Crisp on p. 638 in Reading 23.4] recommend a composition consisting of two parts of varnish of medium strength, one part virgin wax, and one part Venice turpentine. This must be mixed with the desired colour, more especially with one of such shade as may resemble somewhat the colour of the gold, so as to hide any defects which might occur in the laying on of the gold. Light chrome yellow or burnt ochre gives a good and appropriate colour.

188. The following is the most approved method of laying the gold leaf, as described by Noble in his work on "Colour Printing," [i.e., *The Principles and Practice of Colour Printing Stated and Explained* (1881)] ... "Take a piece of cardboard a pica less all round than the size of the leaf to be laid. Cut the edges of this round at the corners; then get a piece of very thick sealing wax, about an inch and a half long, and stick it in the middle of the card. Gently lift the paper of the gold leaf, and place the card, holding it by the wax handle, on the top of the leaf. If the gold be now gently blown over the edge of the card the leaf may be raised thereon and deposited in its proper place on the printed sheet." ...

190. For printing with *Dutch metal*, a soft and ductile quality should be selected, and the adhesive material should be strong enough, as the Dutch metal is liable to break away or peel off, especially at the edges of the work. The forme should have a hard impression all over, and the metal should be pressed into the impression with a large piece of cotton, until it adheres to every part of it. This is of prime importance.

191. After the gold has been thus applied, the impression should be laid between two sheets of paper, and rubbed over on the outside with the hand. The sheets with the impression contained within them must now be laid on the top of the next one, and then both should be brought under pressure, so that the gold may be completely fixed.

It is also a good plan, after the impression is pulled and the metal laid, to place the sheet on a flat board, type high, and lay on the top a soft blanket; then place the board and its sheet and blanket in a press and give a good pull, which will cause the metal to adhere perfectly.

Reading 23.6
Bronzing
from *Printing* by Charles Thomas Jacobi (1890, pp. 192–194).

Jacobi's method for bronzing follows the same procedures found in the previous three readings. He does, however, add some valuable new information about the process, such as burnishing the bronze by placing the bronze-dusted sheets back on the tympan – and after cleaning the type – working off the sheets a second time. This is similar to Jonathan Clark's process for printing with gold leaf that is mentioned in my *Printing on the Iron Handpress* (1998, pp. 323–324).

With the exception of Moxon, who mentions "having his Paper *Wet*" on p. 634 in Reading 23.1, none of the other manual writers specify whether the paper should be printed damp or dry. From my own experience, I find a slightly damp sheet the most effective for gold leafing.

Jacobi also recommends printing the bronze portion first to avoid the possibility that the bronze would also adhere to other still-wet inks on the same sheet. Krumbholz (1893, p. 36) offers another solution to this problem, "Powdered magnesia rubbed on a freshly printed job will allow of bronze being printed over a color without adhering to it."

Jacobi describes bronzing brushes, one of which is shown in **Fig. 23.1**. It has a screw on one end to regulate the flow of the powder. He also discusses a couple of mechanical methods for bronzing, such as the bronzing machine shown in **Fig. 23.2**.

Bronze work comes under the general head of colour work. The bronzes can be obtained of gold and silver. The part to be printed is rolled and pulled with an almost colourless varnish preparation, the bronze being applied with wadding, and the superfluous metal brushed off with the same piece. They should receive a further cleansing afterwards with a fresh piece of the material. The bronze portion of a forme should be printed first, as the bronze is likely to adhere to any part of a sheet in another colour if it has not had time to dry. This is the old way of performing the operation, and is satisfactory for small and occasional work.

Bronze brushes, [**Fig. 23.1**], have been made recently, with a receptacle to hold the powder, which is liberated as the brush passes over the required part. The proper amount can be regulated by the use of the screw at the end of the brush. This powder is injurious when inhaled to any extent, and a kind of respirator is necessary if much work has to be done, as the bronze flies about.

Fig. 23.1. *Bronze brush*

Mechanical appliances [one of which is shown in **Fig. 23.2**] have also been lately introduced, adapted for bronze work in large quantities. . . . The sheets are fed in at one end as in a rolling machine, and are turned out at the other end bronzed.

Fig. 23.2. *Bronzing machine*

Rolling is a decided improvement in bringing the bronze up, as it gets rid of the somewhat granulated appearance which bronze always gives as distinct from leaf printing. The last method [rolling] is not usually adopted in letterpress printing....

How to Improve Bronze Printing

Bronze work is very seldom thoroughly satisfactory. Its failure, as a rule, rests in the inability to fix it firmly on the paper. Of course rolling is the most reliable remedy, but if you do not happen to have a rolling machine, or the inclination to invest in one, adopt the following method: Work the forme with gold size and apply the bronze in the usual way; when the number required is completed, simply take all the rollers off the machine, clean the forme, but do not disturb it, and run the sheets through the machine again off the clean forme. The appearance of the work is greatly improved by this process.

Reading 23.7
Embossed Printing
from *The Printer's Manual* by Thomas Lynch (1859, p. 208).

> Embossing was often used in Victorian decorative printing, especially in conjunction with greeting cards that were often printed on lithographic presses. Occasionally, embossing was used to give the printed image a three-dimensional quality. Embossing could easily be grouped with what Adams referred to as *ornamental printing* since it was an extra procedure intended to give printed work an added visual impact.
>
> Lynch's instructions below are specifically for embossing on the iron handpress. There are two basic methods for embossing paper: (1) the hollowed out female die and (2) the three-dimensional sculptured female die. The first method requires a soft male die that pushes the paper slightly below the surface of the die. Even though the edges are rounded, the depth of the embossing is uniform over the whole image. The second method requires a sculptured male die that follows the contours of the sculptured female die. With this type of die, the depth of the embossing will vary, often resembling a bas-relief cameo. Embossing was added – always from the back side of the sheet – after the letterpress was worked off.
>
> Lynch describes the use of metal female dies combined with leather male dies. He also gives an alternative method for making the male dies from paper, a process somewhat similar to papier mâché.

This description of printing is done by using metalic dies, into the surface of which the lettering has been cut or punched.

The counter-die is made, by cutting a piece of thick smooth leather to the size of the die; the side which is to receive the impression must now be moistened, and being laid upon the surface of the die, a sufficient pressure must be given to it to make the leather go into all the cavities in the plate. The counter is then to be removed from the die and its edges trimmed so that both will be of the same size, after which the leather must be adjusted to its place on the face of the die, and its back covered with a thick mucilage, another impression must be made, so as to transfer the counter to the tympan. A thin sheet of gutta-percha [rubberlike gum] should now be warmed on one side, and laid upon the face of the plate, with the side which has been heated uppermost. An impression must again be made, by which the leather and the gutta-percha will become attached, the result being an elastic counter, which will retain sufficient firmness to throw up any part of the under surface of the card without breaking the parts at the edges of the letters.

When the job is a large size, such as a show-card, the counter-die may be made by pasting ten or twelve sheets of smooth paper together with mucilage, and while they are in a damp state, to press the die into the pulpy mass, and leave it dry before they are separated.

Reading 23.8
Embossing at the Letter Press
from *The Printers' Universal Book of Reference* by William Finch Crisp (1875, pp. 62–64).

Crisp fastens his female dies – which are the same thickness as stereotype plates – to an iron block the thickness of a stereotype mount. He then makes a male die – which he calls a "force" – from thick sheets of "gutta percha."

Crisp also describes a very time-consuming method of embossing large images on the handpress. He pastes a narrow one-inch strip of milled-board to the underside of the platen. To function properly, it needs to be centered and run perpendicular to the rails. The bed is advanced in one-inch increments under the strip of milled-board and the bar is pulled after each movement forward until the whole image has been embossed. The handpress is not ideally suited for most types of embossing since the process requires an enormous amount of pressure being applied to a very small area. An image requiring the effort described above would be more advantageously worked off on an embossing machine like the one shown in **Fig. 23.3**.

Fig. 23.3. *Embossing machine* – from Ringwalt (1871, p. 157)

By the new plan, a whole sheet of Royal [20 x 25 in.] may be embossed at a super-royal press as easily as possible. The process may be thus explained: get an iron plate, the thickness of an ordinary wood block used for mounting stereotype plates. It must be pierced with screwholes to allow the points to be fastened on in their places (the points for embossing are screwed on to the iron plate and made so as to be moveable to any place in a moment); fasten this plate to the bed of the press in the usual manner; then take the die, or dies, and level them by underlays in the usual manner of stereotype plates; paste a piece of rough brown paper to the bottom and cut it to the shape of the die; paste the bottom again and place it in the centre of the iron plate; run the press in to the centre and pull over, keeping the bar-handle over a few minutes; this done, let them alone till dry (about a quarter of an hour). Get some sheet gutta percha, about the thickness of four or five cards, and put it in some hot water; when soft, place it upon the die, putting a piece of brown paper over that to keep it from sticking to the tympan; run in and keep the pull over till the gutta percha is cold. The gutta percha thus prepared is called a "force." Wipe the die perfectly dry, trim up the force with a sharp penknife (it ought to be cut out as nearly as possible to the outside shape of the work – the same as children would cut out a picture), and, when this is done, paste the back of the force and again pull over, when the force will rise with the tympan. If the force is not perfect, hold a piece of lighted paper to the defective part till it becomes slightly warm; then, having with a camel's hair brush well greased the die with dry French chalk to keep the force from adhering to it, pull again, and repeat till the force is perfect. Now comes the part that has been kept so secret: If there is a large die, no power that any press ever had would bring off a sharp impression; but the desired result can be secured by simply pasting a strip of milled-board, say about one inch wide, underneath the platen, exactly in the centre and crosswise to the ribs. Then place the paper between the die and the force, carefully run the table of the press in until the piece of milled-board is exactly over the first inch of the die, pull, run in another inch, then pull again, and so on till the whole of the die has been pulled upon: the sheet is then embossed.

Reading 23.9
An Easy Way to Emboss
from *The Country Printer* by G. Krumbholz (1893, pp. 41–42).

> These instructions for embossing – even though intended for vertical-platen presses – could easily be adapted for iron handpresses. Krumbholz makes both the female and the male dies from a single piece of thick card stock. This method is appropriate only for very simple jobs consisting of a single embossed element. The male die is cut out of the card, leaving a hole that becomes the female die. The male die is then trimmed slightly all around so it can be pushed into the hole along with the paper. Like all other methods for embossing, the male die is fastened to the tympan.

Take a piece of six-ply card stock, with a smooth, white surface, just the size of the card to be embossed, and sketch the shape of the design with a pencil, afterward cutting out the design in one piece with a sharp knife; then trim the edge of the inside piece so that it will play freely through the outside piece. Paste the outside die firmly on the back of a wood letter large enough to hold it, and the inside die very lightly to the same letter, then lock up the letter and put it on the press; remove the rollers; make a good hard tympan, and, after thoroughly pasting the surface of the inside die, take an impression and hold the platen on the impression until the paste has time to dry. On opening the press the under die leaves the wood letter, on which it was lightly held, and adheres to the tympan, leaving the outside die attached to the wood letter on the bed of the press. Then set the gauges and feed in the cards. Printed lines may be embossed in the same manner after the printing is done.

Plate 28. Book composing room at *The State Gazette* Printing Establishment, ca. 1885. Note the tied-up pages of type waiting to be imposed on the table in the foreground. (Source: *The State Gazette* Printing Establishment, *Specimens of Printing Types*, [ca. 1885], p. 13, courtesy of Stephen O. Saxe.)

CHAPTER TWENTY-FOUR

Printing Wood Engravings and Other Relief Illustrations

Using woodcuts, Albrecht Pfister (ca. 1420–ca. 1470) printed the first illustrated book – *Der Acker-mann aus Böhmen* by Johannes von Saaz (ca. 1360–ca. 1414) – in Bamberg, Germany, around 1460. Ever since then relief (raised), intaglio (engraved or etched), and planographic (surface or flat) printing techniques have been used to illustrate books, although one only of these was usually predominant during any specific typographic period. Seventeenth- and eighteenth-century manual writers seldom mentioned illustration techniques, and when they did, their comments were brief, and most often restricted to relief illustrations, such as woodcuts or wood engravings that could be printed together with the type on a wooden press. Because of the pre-eminence of wood engravings in the nineteenth century, a substantial amount of practical information concerning them is available in most manuals of that period.

I think it would be helpful here if I elaborated on three nineteenth-century terms that are often used in connection with printing relief images. Early in the nineteenth century, the term *fine printing* (see Chapter 27) pertained primarily to the printing of wood engravings. Its later meaning of *typographic excellence* is a late-nineteenth-/early-twentieth-century concept. *Decorative printing* (see Reading 24.1 below) and *ornamental printing* (see Reading 23.3 on p. 635) referred to the printing of non-textual elements, such as illustrations, decorations, and large initial capitals, that were added to the typography in order to enhance or illuminate the page.

Instructions for printing wood engravings are usually found in a separate section devoted specifically to that subject, although they were often discussed in the section on "Fine Printing." Perhaps the most informative, as well as influential, early text on decorative printing was *Practical Hints on Decorative Printing* (1822) by William Savage. This text was freely adapted by most of the nineteenth-century manual writers who followed him.

In the nineteenth century, manual writers often used the terms *woodcut* and *wood engraving* interchangeably. Technically, a woodcut is a black-line image that is cut on the plank grain of a piece of soft wood; a wood engraving, on the other hand, is a white-line image that is engraved on the end grain of a single or laminated piece of hard wood. The generic term *cut* or *block* was used for both techniques, as well as for stereotype and electrotype plates that were made from them. These plates were fastened to wood or metal mounts to make them type-high for printing. Readings 24.2 through 24.12 beginning on p. 657 describe how to print woodcuts and wood engravings on a handpress.

Printing relief blocks necessitated a completely different approach to making ready. With type, the objective was uniformity of color and pressure (see Chapter 14). When making ready blocks, however, the pressman's duty was to *vary* the pressure in order to alter the density of color in specific areas of the image. This was done through a series of overlays, inlays, and underlays, for which progressive proofs were pulled on *dry* paper to avoid shrinkage. The overlays were used to regulate the density of color; the underlays and inlays, to level the blocks or plates in order to make them uniformly type-high. It is surprising how many makeready variations there were for what should have been a relatively simple and routine procedure.

Early nineteenth-century manual writers, such as Savage, Hansard, and Adams recommended inking the cuts with balls; later writers, such as Lynch, Southward, and Jacobi, favored rollers. They were, nevertheless, unanimous about using only the finest ink and smooth hard papers for the best prints.

The nineteenth century saw an explosion in relief illustration techniques, several of which are described in this chapter. Even so, illustrations printed directly from wood engravings, or indirectly from process blocks, continued to dominate book illustration throughout the century. In fact, most pre-twentieth-century printers' manuals are illustrated with wood engravings.

Before the 1830s, very little printing in color was done in England. *Chromo-lithography* – the nineteenth-century term for *color lithography* – was not used for book work until the 1840s. It should be noted here that there is a difference between *color* or *polychromatic printing* and *multicolor printing*. In the nineteenth century, the term *color printing* referred to illustrations that were printed from a series of separate blocks, one for each color; *multicolor printing* referred to letterpress texts that were printed in more than one color (see Chapter 22). The same inks were used for both types of printing.

In addition to book, job, and news work, there existed a flourishing trade in color prints throughout the nineteenth century. These prints ranged from expensive reproductions of paintings – or *imitations* as they were called – for art collectors, to cheap rustic pieces, often with humorous or sentimental subject matter, for the general populace. In the days before photolithography and the four-color process system there were very few methods for producing multicolor prints; four of them are described below:

1. The oldest, and perhaps the most convenient for the letterpress printer, was relief printing, which included woodcuts and wood engravings. If they were hand-colored with watercolors, they are technically referred to as *colored prints*.

2. It was only at the beginning of the nineteenth century that a separate block was used to print each color, shade, and tint. The resulting prints are generally called *color prints*, although print connoisseurs use the term *chromoxylograph* when identifying them. As already seen on p. 487 in my introductory note to Reading 17.2, William Savage used twenty-nine blocks and thirty colors to edition just one of his color prints.

3. Another technique, for which George Baxter (1804–1867) obtained a patent in 1835, was for printing multicolor illustrations by combining intaglio printing with relief printing. *Baxter prints*, as they were called, began with a master design, or *key print*, usually an aquatint, that was pulled from an engraved copper or steel plate on a rolling press. Then, using wood blocks or metal plates, the key print was overprinted with oil-base inks in a number of colors on a handpress. There is a complete lack of any practical information regarding this process in nineteenth-century printers' manuals, probably due to the exclusiveness of Baxter's patent; however, the procedures for adding the letterpress segments to the prints would have been the same as those for printing wood engravings in multiple colors as described in Reading 24.12 on p. 687.

Some of Baxter's editions were enormous: 300,000 prints. It is hard to imagine that quantities of this magnitude could possibly be produced efficiently on a handpress. Each block still had to be inked by hand and individually impressed on a sheet of paper that had to be kept damp – and in register – until the last color was printed. Even though the print illustrated in **Plate 8** on p. 192 is not one of Baxter's, it is a fine example of this technique.

4. Another method for adding color to prints was the *chromotype process*, described in Reading 24.13 on p. 698. It also consisted of a key block that was printed letterpress, and the colors were applied manually by means of stencils and brushes.

The use of photography in letterpress printing was slow to take hold, but once it did, it succeeded in eliminating most of the other relief illustration techniques by the end of the century. By then, even wood engravings were printed from linecuts made from reproduction proofs of the original blocks. Most of the gelatine processes – which were also photomechanical processes – were abandoned in favor of halftone plates.

The first book to use photography was *The Pencil of Nature* (1844) by William Henry Fox Talbot. In this instance, photographic prints were mounted directly on the pages of the book.

Not all of the new techniques survived, even though, at the time, they may have showed considerable potential. Many of these were *photomechanical processes*, perhaps more aptly named *photochemical processes* since they relied on chemicals as catalysts. To summarize these techniques, photography was first used to illustrate books in the 1840s; electrotypes were first introduced in the 1840s; collotypes, in the 1860s; color filters, in the 1870s; halftone plates, in the 1880s; and full-color separations, in the 1890s. None of these new processes, however, were able to completely supplant the popularity of the wood engraving; it continued to be the pre-eminent illustration technique throughout the century. Wood engravings became even more accessible in 1854 when photography was utilized to transfer the images to photo-sensitive wood blocks. This meant that the artist no longer needed to draw directly on the block; he could simply supply the printer with a pen-and-ink drawing on a piece of paper. It was also possible to transfer continuous-tone images, although they had to be converted first into line or dot patterns by the engraver (see Reading 24.16 on p. 704).

The quickest and easiest, as well as most economical, of all photomechanical processes involved etching a sensitized zinc plate in an acid bath. This process was used to make two types of plates: (1) linecuts or line engravings, which were made from black and white drawings, and (2) halftone plates or photoengravings, which were made from continuous-tone images such as photographs and wash drawings. For continuous-tone images, it was necessary to use a special screen that transformed the image into a dot pattern (see Reading 24.18 on p. 707).

For some reason, late-nineteenth-century manual writers had very little to say about full-color printing, perhaps because it was usually practiced as a separate trade that employed highly trained specialists. Southward (1900, vol. II, pp. 3–4) only devotes a few paragraphs to the art of "three-colour printing" without mentioning anything about its history or technical application. One of the few things he does say about the process is that the resulting color print is achieved with only three colors: magenta, yellow, and cyan. When black is added, it is called four-color process printing. The ability to separate colors mechanically by means of filters made full-color printing possible. This process should not be confused with color printing that is mentioned above and uses a series of individual flat colors.

Since intaglio and planographic printing – both non-letterpress techniques – were separate trades and generally done in workshops that specialized in editioning loose plates that were later tipped into books, I have not included them in this chapter. However, for readers who want to know more about them, Hansard has a short chapter in his manual (1825) devoted to copperplate printing (pp. 801–804) and a lengthy one on lithography (pp. 888–910). It should be remembered that lithography was still an emerging technique when Hansard first wrote about it. Perhaps he saw it as a potential adjunct to letterpress printing, which it did become later in the century.

Reading 24.1
Decorative Printing
from *Typographia* by Thomas Curson Hansard (1825, pp. 911–918).

Hansard discusses, at great length, some of William Savage's theories on printing wood engravings, taken from the latter's book *Practical Hints on Decorative Printing* (1822). Rather than quote directly from Savage, I have chosen to include Hansard's excerpts here together with his comments on them since he behaves in a manner that is completely unorthodox, as well as unbecoming, by doing something not to be found anywhere else in all the literature of nineteenth-century printers' manuals: he criticizes another printer's work in unbelievably vitriolic terms. Hansard dismisses Savage's theories on color printing as being "inutility," a sort of much ado about nothing.

Savage describes how to print relief blocks on a two-pull wooden press, as well as on a Stanhope, the same type of presses that Hansard probably would have had in his printing office. Savage includes two methods for printing illustrations from cuts for both book work and decorative printing, the second including color prints. The first method – *chiaroscuro*, the Italian term for light/dark – is a technique for imitating gouache, sepia, and India ink drawings that was first used during the Renaissance in Italy. The images were printed from a series of blocks in three or four shades of the same color. Hansard notes that Jean-Michel Papillon's book, *Traité historique et pratique de la gravure en bois* (1776), had a profound influence on Savage, and by extension, all nineteenth-century English-speaking printers.

The second method is a technique for reproducing multicolor pictures or color prints, which were printed from suites of blocks in various colors and tints. Hansard was adamantly opposed to employing this technique for color printing, going so far as to refer to one of Savage's prints – a print that required twenty-nine blocks – as a "monstrous abortion." Hansard's alternative was to print only the key block in letterpress and then to hand color the prints with watercolors. Today, most full-color work is produced by the four-color process.

By the 1820s, the majority of wood engravings were no longer printed from the original blocks. The blocks had always been unreliable: they warped, shrank, cracked, and were also subject to being smashed when too much pressure was applied. During the nineteenth century, there were several alternatives to wood blocks. Hansard mentions stereotyping; Crisp (1875, p. 60) notes that "in the present advanced condition of the art of electrotyping, by which process an exact *fac simile* can be taken, it is no longer necessary to use the original engraving."

As always, Hansard is very concerned about the appropriate paper for the presswork, even more so for wood engravings. He quotes from a letter that Michael Faraday – spelled *Farraday* by both Savage and Hansard – sent to Savage and published by him in his 1822 book. India paper was the preferred paper for relief prints; however, when book illustrations were printed on it, they were usually tipped into the book since India paper did not have the required strength for general book work.

Hansard offers his own solution for printing large multicolor capital letters. His method is somewhat different from the one Adams describes on p. 637 in Reading 23.3. Hansard made two identical stereotypes of the base design and then removed the color from each that was not to be printed. The plates, of course, still had to be printed separately.

Hansard, like most of the other writers in this chapter, emphasized the importance of having the pressman work closely with the engraver. He felt that the printer must also possess an artistic sensibility, which would enable him to better analyze the drawing in order to achieve the best results from it, and at the same time, be true to the engraver's intention.

This subject of fancy has been lately revived by the work of Mr. William Savage, a printer of acknowledged ingenuity and talent; but whose labours in this performance have been applied, I fear, more towards the honour of the art, than to his own emolument.

The principal view of Mr. Savage in compiling this work, appears to have been, to draw the attention of the British typographer to an art attempted many years ago, and which, most probably, was not then persevered in for the very same reason that will render futile the attempt to revive it in the present day, namely, its total inutility.

Mr. Savage divides the subject into two kinds of specimens; namely: – First, that of prints worked with different gradations of the same colour, which produces the effect of what is termed chiaro oscuro, or cameo. The first practiser of this method has been generally supposed to be Ugo da Carpa [i.e. Carpi, ca. 1480–1532], an Italian engraver of the sixteenth century, who, with other contemporaries, produced the effect of chiaro oscuro drawings, by means of two, three, or more, blocks of wood printed with different gradations of the shade of the same colour, upon the same paper....

Secondly, the printing a picture by suites of blocks, in various colours, "so as to give fac-similes of the productions of different masters, at a small expense, to serve as studies, or for the decoration of rooms, where, if framed and glazed, the eye should not be able to distinguish them from drawings." [Editor's note: Hansard is quoting Savage (1822, p. 16).] ...

It appears to me, that Mr. Savage may have first taken up his idea from the work...of *Papillon* ... upon the appearance of the first part of Mr. S.'s work, I was instantly struck with the resemblance of his first specimen of chiaro oscuro, to one of Papillon's executed precisely on the same principle.

To produce these effects, as many blocks, designed and fitted *en suite,* are employed, as are the tints or colours which the artist intends to produce. The first of these is termed the *blotch block,* which is used to print the first or lightest tint, out of which the extreme lights, or whites, only are cut, or excavated; the second block prints the next tint, and so on until the whole design is completed; the number of blocks being determined by the degree of finish intended to be given to the print.

In forming prints of multifarious colours, a similar routine takes place, the various blocks being traced from, and all matched to, each other, inked with the requisite colours in proper succession, and united and blended by the most skilful and patient workmanship, and by means of those *sheet* anchors of pressmanship called points, three, or even four of which are fixed (by what a printer calls, *paste-points*) upon the tympans, so as to act upon the margins of the print: thus, every block of which the suite consists will require separate beating, pointing, and pulling....

It appears, both from Papillon and Savage, that this mode of ornamental printing was practised by the earlier typographers: they both affirm the large ornamental capital letters of the Mentz [Mainz] Psalter (Faust [Fust] and Schoeffer, 1457) as well as the Bible and other books, to have been *printed* in *colours* with *suites* of *blocks.* The former asserting that there were three colours used, viz. red, blue, and purple, the latter contending for two only, viz. blue and red. I have had no opportunity of examining any one of these treasures of typography. The letter B [shown in **Fig. 24.1**] ... has been ... copied in fac-simile by several authors, and described by others; and I mean to give it in those two colours, both as an exemplification of the principle, and for the purpose of showing that it may be produced by a process certainly never yet called in aid of such a purpose, but which would save much time and expense of engraving suites of blocks; namely, stereotype; and, having one block only engraved, the rest may be effected by merely such hands as are on the ordinary establishment of a printing-office.

Fig. 24.1. *Letter B from the Mainz Psalter* – as illustrated in Hansard (1825, plate facing p. 913). NOTE: In Hansard, the letter is printed in red; the filigree, in blue. In Fust and Schöffer's Psalter the letter is printed in blue; the filigree, in red.

Mr. Savage, who examined a fine copy of this Psalter with the most anxious curiosity, says [on p. 50, "I] could not help admiring the great accuracy with which the workmanship was executed, in inserting a large capital letter into the surrounding ornamental part, where the exact shape is bounded by a fine line of a different colour, so near to each other, as to be separated by a space not more than the thickness of writing paper, and uniformly true in every instance;" but the general appearance of the work is heightened in beauty, by a more bright and delicate tint of each of those colours in other places written or painted in by hand, as well as some other emendations of even the black ink.

"It is a curious fact," says Mr. Savage [on pp. 6–7] "that under Fust [spelled Faust in Savage] and Gutenberg the process should be carried nearly to perfection; for some of the works they printed, both in the quality of the ink, and in the workmanship, are so excellent, that it would require all the skill of our best printers, even at the present day, to surpass them in all respects: and I do not hesitate to say, that in a few years after, the printers were actually superior to us in the use of red ink, both as to colour, and as to the inserting of a great number of single capital letters in their proper places in a sheet, with a degree of accuracy, and sharpness of impression, that I have never seen equalled in modern workmanship." . . .

Mr. Savage, in pursuing his plan of fully exemplifying the effect of ornamental printing, has given imitations of drawings in sæpia and Indian ink, in, from three blocks, increasing to nine – several head-pieces printed as cameos in different tints of the same colours; in heraldry, the arms of [George John Spencer, second] Earl Spencer [1758–1834] in heraldic colours; in imitation of coloured drawings, a combination of from two to twenty-nine blocks; three specimens in natural history, and three in sculpture; and others of various descriptions. The minutiæ of the process is explained, first, by tables of the coloured inks used in these prints, with definitions of their properties and necessary combinations, and general rules and cautions for the manual operation at the press: this, after the grand point, included in one technical term, the *making-ready,* is effected, is little more than would be dictated by the judgment of any clever, experienced, artist-like pressman. The operations of this method of printing the various colours used, and the succession of each block, to produce the required effect, appear fully explained in a "Succinct Description of the Illustrations" [beginning on p. 103], to which I must refer the curious inquirer: yet, still much, very much, must evidently be left to the taste and judgment of the printer who has leisure to make such experiments. No rule can be laid down for the exact order in which the various blocks of a suite are to be taken – the printer must not only be an artist in the limited acceptation of the term, but in the full extent of the term as applicable to the fine arts of designing, painting, and drawing, or he can never expect to produce the effect of either. It appears necessary, in the first place, to consider that the style of the drawing must be suited to the intended process: next to "analyze the drawing, for the purpose of ascertaining how many blocks it will require, and what parts of it will come into each, and to determine which block shall be first engraved" [Editor's note: Hansard incorporates his own words when quoting Savage on p, 60] – all this will require the united operations of the designer, engraver, and printer; and, in some of his pictures, Mr. Savage appears to have had the assistance of the two first-named artists [Fust and Schöffer], in an eminent degree. From his account of the difficulties he had to cope with, it is very plain that the practiser of this fancy must have no other business to divide his attention: the whole of the subjects, with one exception, were worked by himself, or his own family.

I think it unnecessary to proceed further with this subject, till some little consideration be given to that important question, by the solution of which the more or less general adoption of every art and science must be regulated; namely, CUI BONO? [to what end?] In posting-bills, lottery-puffs [lottery advertisements], titles of books, the printing in colours will be ornamental and decorative, but rather expensive; but for producing pictorial subjects "to serve as studies, or for the decorations of rooms, framed and glazed, not to be distinguished from drawings," [again from p. 16,] the *failure* is complete. Every head piece is managed by, first, working the type as a single leaf then by working three times more, for the three tints of the cameos. The picture illustrative of [William] Collins's "Ode of [*sic*] Mercy" [1746], which was intended as the *chef d'œuvre* of this decorative printing, is produced from twenty-nine blocks! thirty colours and tints to work one quarto leaf twenty-nine times over!! now, let the mind run over the probable cost to employ a journeyman capable of such work, and guess if something like the following may not be given as the probable result: –

29 blocks, making-ready, preparing colour, beating, and pulling, at least four times the time
　4　　of the operations of a forme of the work, quarto
────
116
　4　pages in a forme
────
464　times the cost of printing a page of fine type-work, exclusive of the expense of the designer, engraver, and box-wood. If for studies or pictures this expense could be borne, it is very plain that in book-decorations it is not likely to answer – if 500 fac-similes were wanted of the pic-

ture of Mercy, print it in outline, and the first artists in the country would be glad to colour them up to pattern for one fourth of the money, and produce something like a finished specimen.

I think this picture-print of "Mercy" a monstrous abortion – it is horrible – its only merit is in the patience and difficulty with which it was gestated and brought to parturition. I could wish, as Dr. [Samuel] Johnson said of the lady's piece of difficult music, it had been *impossible:* some other specimens in colours, where so much has not been aimed at, are so much the better; the less that has been attempted, the less is the failure.

In going regularly through the account of the Illustrations, we in time arrive at the finale of specimens of the printing art of Mr. Savage; and as if the climax of disappointment were still in store, after the failure of "Mercy" the list concludes with the "Cavern of Despair;" but what a surprise! what an unexpected reverse and relief to the sickened sensation, does this "Cavern of Despair" really prove! Is it accident or design? Is it meant as *stage effect?* In this picture the mind is refreshed by, and at last rests delighted upon, every excellence that wood-engraving and type-printing ever did or ever will effect. I cannot conceive superiority possible; to attempt any description of it would be folly, except saying, that it is in the true, legitimate mode of printing, one colour, a fine black: take all the other "Illustrations" away, cut out the whole portion of "Decorative Printing," and give me the remainder of the book, with the "Cavern of Despair" designed by [John] THURSTON [1774–1822], and engraved by [Robert] BRANSTON [1778–1827], and I will preserve it as one of the choicest specimens of typographic skill.

One specimen deserves to be mentioned with commendation for its splendid effect. This is described as an Ornamental Letter B, drawn and engraved by Branston; and executed to show that large ornamented letters might be introduced into books, printed at the type-press in colours, or with different shades of the same colour as cameos; and also to show the introduction of gold by means of the printing-press. This specimen has seven blocks, the lights are printed in gold – it would be rather a dear ornament, since it appears, that, in addition to the number of blocks, the peculiar skill of two typographic artists, besides Mr. Savage, was required to effect it.

Mr. Savage's work, upon the more ordinary operations of printing, contains a great deal of curious and interesting matter. His observations, as well as the extracts taken from Papillon, on the various woods proper for engravings, will be found valuable to the practisers of that art.

There is also, in this work, a valuable paper [i.e., letter, dated October 8, 1818] by Mr. Farraday [sic], of the Royal Institution of Great Britain, entitled "Chemical Analysis of French plate Paper, India yellow Paper, and India white Paper," the chemical details of which are well worth the attention of paper manufacturers[,] and the subsequent observations particularly interesting to those printers who are curious in the production of good impressions from wood engravings.

"I have no doubt myself" says Mr. Farraday [on pp. 82–83 in Savage (1822)], "that the superiority of the India paper is owing to the peculiar nature of the fibre used in its formation, and not to any particular process in the manufacture of it, or to the addition of any other substance. Indeed, as far as regards the making of it, I think it is inferior to our own; but it has a singular degree of ductility, even in the dry state, which far surpasses any thing I have observed in European paper: the slightest impression of the nail, or other hard body; the mark of a twist, or any form given to it by pressure, remain very perfectly after the force which produced them is removed; and by simple extention of the paper, or other means, these may be removed much more readily and completely than they can from a piece of English paper. Now, I presume that it is to this property, and which belongs to the peculiar fibre of which the paper is composed, that it owes its superiority: it permits the paper to mould itself according to all the inequalities of the surface against which it is pressed; and, consequently, entering and filling up more accurately the lines upon the copper-plate, it receives the ink from every place where it has been deposited, in a more perfect manner than any paper deficient in this quality can do. I endeavoured to convince myself of this, by scratching and cutting up a copper-plate with a steel point, and then covering one half with folded India paper, and the other with French plate paper, submitting the surface thus covered to pressure: I found, on removing it, that though both papers had been in precisely the same circumstances, there was an essential difference in the impressed form received by them: on the French plate paper I could only trace the elevations formed by the deeper lines on the copper-plate, but on the India paper every mark could be observed which the copper that it covered had received."

Mr. Farraday has confined his experiment and observations to the superiority of India paper for printing from copper-plates, but every reason which he has given applies with equal force to printing from wood. Many of the engravings in this work I would gladly have worked with the type, or as the next best mode, upon the same paper, but separate from the type; not finding this to equal my wishes I tried other samples said to be made of particular fabric suitable to such a purpose, and also a paper made from pure flax, so that no particle of cotton could have entered into the pulp; but they were all equally unsuccessful in competition with the India paper. I found it impossible to give at once the same intensity of colour to the black shades from the plane surface of the block, and the delicacy of the lighter shades from the engraved part, without, in the first instance, using such a body of ink, and considerable power of impression, as would fill up all the finer parts; and in the latter, by using the ink so sparingly and so light an impression as would not leave sufficient colour for the black parts. The India paper, on the contrary, by the flexibility of texture, and absorbent and congenial quality for fixing the ink, would take every light and shade with much less colour and pressure, and what is of infinite importance in printing, allow the ink to set, or dry, in less time than any other paper. A remarkable instance will be seen in this work in the print of Cogger's Press [see **Fig. 3.28** on p. 127], which has an extent of black ground, with clearness of the fine lines, and absence of all appearance of ink or oil on the reverse, that never could have been effected if European paper had been used. In fact, it went further, for owing to the qualities united of the paper and the ink (to say nothing of the workmanship) immediately as it was worked no ordinary pressure would cause it to set-off – and on the second day after, I had several copies hot-pressed to try the effect, without finding the colour either to spread or fade.

Reading 24.2
Overlaying Wood Engravings
from *Practical Hints on Decorative Printing* by William Savage (1822, pp. 36–39).

> When manual writers discuss *engravings* – unless the term is prefaced by *copper* or *steel* – the inference is always wood engravings. Savage was acknowledged as the foremost authority in the nineteenth century on how to print them. Even though the technology was continually in flux, he remained true to traditional practices, such as inking with balls and printing from the original wood blocks. His choice of press would appear to be his only major concession to the *new* advances in technology, recommending an iron platen because it produced a sharper and cleaner impression. He also advocates removing the soft blankets from between the tympans and replacing them with hard packing.
>
> One of Savage's cardinal rules for printing wood engravings is "neither the pressure nor the impression ought to be uniformly equal." With overlays, the printer can manipulate the varying degrees of light, middle tint, and shades. The pressure should only be on the surface

and the impression should not bite into the paper. Savage's basic instructions for making ready wood engravings would be followed well into the twentieth century. He discusses which papers are best for overlays and how to pare or tear them. In later years, these small overlays were called *overlay patches*, or simply *patches*.

Vignettes were frequently used in pre-twentieth-century books as head and tailpieces. Because of their irregular shapes, vignettes required special attention. Like the intaglio printer, the letterpress printer would remove any superfluous ink on the edges of his cut before pulling the bar. Sometimes a glob of roller composition was employed, although MacKellar (1866, p. 260) suggests using "a small roller without ink." Especially in vignette printing, type-high bearers were placed around the blocks to equalize the pressure of the platen on the form and to protect the edges of the block.

When an engraving on wood is printed, it also denotes the overlaying it, so as to produce an impression, which shall possess all the effect that the subject will admit of....

It must be evident, that when a clear sharp impression is wanted, that the pressure should be on the surface only, without penetrating into the interstices; of course, the tympan ought not to be very soft, neither should any blanket be used: the most perfect impression will be obtained, from new types or engravings in relief, when fine thick paper alone is used in the tympans; and even of this article I would not recommend many thicknesses.

The press stone and the platen ought to be perfect planes; and the platen should be so hung, that the surface of each should be parallel to the other. It will be found in practice that an iron platen is superiour to a wooden one, for producing a sharp clear impression, where fine work is wanted; for, by discarding woollen blankets, the pressure must be increased to obtain good impressions, which indents wood, and then requires so many overlays to make an uniform impression, that they produce nearly the same effect as blankets, and it becomes necessary to new face the surface frequently, which is attended with expense and loss of time....

... [When] an engraving is to be printed, neither the pressure nor the impression ought to be uniformly equal; if they be, the effect that is intended to be produced by the artist will fail; and instead of light, middle tint, and shade, an impression will be produced that possesses none of them in perfection; some parts being too hard and black, and other parts neither pressure nor colour enough, with obscurity and roughness; and without any of the mildness of the middle tint, which ought to pervade great part of an engraving, and on which the eye reposes after viewing the strong lights and the deep shades.

To produce the desired effect with engravings great nicety and patience are necessary in the pressman; for a single thickness of thin India paper is frequently required over very small parts, and the edges of it even pared down, where the engraving is fine: and I would advise that the overlay should never be cut at the edges; but, even where great delicacy of shape is not required, that it should be torn into the shape wanted, which reduces the edges, and makes the additional pressure blend with the surrounding parts.

In particular parts the impression will sometimes come up too full; it will then be necessary to add an additional tympan sheet, and cut those parts away from it, scraping the edges which come too hard: and scraping away half the thickness of a tympan sheet, in small parts that require to be a little lightened, will improve the impression.

Engravings that are in the vignette form require great care to keep the edges light and clear; and in general it is necessary to scrape away one or two thicknesses of paper, in order to lighten the impression and keep it clean; for the edges being irregular, and parts, such as small branches of trees, leaves, &c. straggling, for the purpose of giving freedom to the design, are subject to come too hard, and are liable to picks, which give great trouble to pressmen, and are difficult to be kept clear of, particularly with a wooden platen, which from wear has become uneven. In these cases high bearers, placed round the block, will be found advantageous, for the purpose of equallizing the pressure on the surface of the engraving; and they also protect the edges from the severity of the pull, which is always injurious to the delicacy of the external lines.

When great nicety of impression is required in a vignette, it will be found beneficial after the engraving is beat with ink, to take a small ball without ink, and beat the extremities lightly: this will not only take away any superfluity of ink, but will be the means of preventing picks, and give to the edges lightness and delicacy; particularly where distances are represented.

The pressman will find it an advantage, if it be necessary to do full justice to an engraving, to have a good impression from the engraver, and place it before him as a pattern; and then arrange the overlays and tympan sheets, till he produces a fac simile in effect. But, as I observed before, his best lesson will be when he can obtain the assistance of the artist at the press side, as by that means he will obtain more instruction of what is required than by any other method.

The light parts of a fine engraving require little pressure; but the depths should be overlaid, so as to produce a full and firm impression.

If a block be hollow on the surface, underlaying the hollow part will bring it up better than overlaying it. And if a block be too low, it is adviseable to underlay it, for the purpose of making it the proper height, in preference to making use of overlays; for they act in some measure as blankets, producing the lines thicker than the engraving, by being pressed into the interstices.

Reading 24.3
Printing Engravings on Wood
from *Typographia* by Thomas F. Adams (1844, pp. 251–252).

Because of the widespread use of wood engravings in illustrated books throughout the nineteenth century, printers' manuals usually included some information on how to print them. Unlike woodcuts – which were generally printed with soft packing and, like the type, exhibited a light indentation or bite in the paper – wood engravings required hard packing in order to get a sharp image and to minimize the bite. The art of printing wood engravings properly on the handpress, therefore, depended on the pressman's makeready skills – in other words, his ability to prepare precise and effective overlays and underlays.

Adams gives instructions for editioning a print from a single block, such as a book illustration or a broadside. His procedures closely follow those given by Savage in Reading 24.2 above. Adams begins by locking a small block into a small chase, which in turn, is locked into a larger chase. He proofs all of his blocks on thin sheets of India paper, and then, rather surprisingly, cuts the overlays out with a knife or scissors – two tools that were very much frowned upon by most other manual writers for this procedure. Each writer describes a slightly different way for attaching the overlay to the tympan. Adams first pastes his overlay to a loose tympan sheet, which he then aligns, face down, with the block. A little paste is put on the back of the tympan sheet before the tympan is lowered. By hand-rubbing the back of the tympan, the tympan sheet/overlay would adhere to the tympan in perfect register.

Timperley (1838, p. 97) notes that when "one form has wood cuts in it and the other none, it is best to work that form with wood cuts in last, in order to prevent them from setting off." Essentially, what he is saying here is that if woodcuts or wood engravings are printed first, a small amount of ink will be removed from the printed image during the backup process, which in turn, will disfigure the illustration by creating a *ghost impression* of the text visible, in reverse, on the back of the image.

Where a single block is to be worked in the centre of a large press, it should be imposed in a small job chase, and this chase again imposed in a larger one, to prevent the springing of the furniture. Bearers, letter-high, placed round the block, serve to equalize the impression, and protect the edges from the severity of the pull; they also render the subject more manageable, by enabling the pressman to add to, or diminish the pressure on particular parts, so as to produce the desired effect. The first pulls made after the block has been laid on the press, require a great deal of care, lest by too hard a pull, the delicate lines of the engraving should be crushed. . . .

The impression in an engraving on wood should not be uniformly equal; if it be, some parts will be too hard and black, and other parts have neither pressure nor color enough, with obscurity and roughness, and without any of the mildness of the middle tint, on which the eye seeks to repose after viewing the strong lights and deep shades.

To produce the desired effect, the pressman pulls a few impressions on soiled or damaged India paper, out of which he can cut overlays to the precise shape and size that are wanted, which he does with a penknife and a pair of small scissors, scraping the edges of the overlay in many cases, to cause the additional pressure to blend with the surrounding parts. The overlays being nicely cut, he lays them on the engraving precisely where he wishes them, and having slightly pasted that part of the tympan sheet, puts the tympan slowly down, and presses with his hand over the block sufficiently hard to cause the overlays to adhere to the tympan; this he repeats till his dark shades are sufficiently strong, and should the light parts then be too heavy, he proceeds to cut them out of the tympan sheet, and the sheets in the tympan if necessary; for in the printing of highly finished wood cuts, blankets should never be used, a couple of sheets of fine smooth paper being sufficient.

The pressman will find it an advantage to have a good impression from the engraver before him as a pattern, and then arrange the overlays, &c. until he produces a fac-simile in effect; but it would be still better for him, could he obtain the assistance of the artist at the press side.

It is indispensably necessary in the production of fine printing, of whatever kind, that the workman should be supplied with the finest ink, and a smooth hard paper, and that his rollers or balls, the latter being preferable for wood engravings, should be in the best order.

A fine engraving on wood should always be washed with Spirits of Wine [alcohol], and when out of use should invariably be kept with its face downward in a cool place. If an engraving warp, it may be straightened by laying the concave side on a few sheets of damp paper for a short time.

Reading 24.4
Wood Engravings
from *The Printer's Manual* by Thomas Lynch (1859, pp. 160–164).

Lynch expands on Savage's and Adams's instructions (see Readings 24.2 and 24.3 on pp. 657 and 659, respectively) for both making ready and printing wood engravings. The procedures Lynch describes below were already well-established by the 1850s, and with little change, they continued to be used far into the twentieth century.

Lynch emphasizes the delicacy and care that the printer must take when proofing blocks. He recommends starting with little or no pressure and gradually building up to the correct amount. He discusses the use of type-high bearers, but also notes that when they are not available, the old method of reglets or corks – mentioned in Moxon (1683, p. 293), Stower (1808. p. 350), and others – could be used.

In addition to parchment – the traditional tympan covering material – Lynch also mentions silk. He suggests taking the tympan off when pulling just a few proofs. In later years, the tympan/frisket assembly was discarded altogether when pulling proofs on the handpress. Many handpresses, with low platens, were manufactured in the first decades of the twentieth century specifically for pulling proofs of photoengravings.

To flatten warped wood blocks, Lynch, like most other manual writers, advocated placing them face-down on a few sheets of dampened paper where they were left for an hour or two with a weight on top.

When the workman puts the block on the press, he ought to be very gentle in the pull of the first impression, to prevent an accident, which has frequently occurred from thoughtlessness in this particular, by making the pull too hard, and crushing some of the lines; by avoiding this he will be safe, and can proportion the impression to the subject. The only correct manner of doing this is, to knock all the impression off, after which it should be put on, a little at a time, until the lightest part of the cut comes up with a proper degree of sharpness; then the heavier portions can be overlaid until the requisite amount of pressure is produced.

The pressman should examine, previous to pulling, that there be nothing, such as gauges or the like, on the tympan, which would strike on the block. Accidents of this kind sometimes happen, which either destroy the cut or else cause great trouble to the engraver, as well as loss of time and disappointment; beside these it entails a character of carelessness on the printer. . . .

[Lynch paraphrases Savage's instructions for preparing a single block. See Reading 24.2. on p. 657.]

The pressman will find it convenient to pull a few impressions, while he is making ready, on india-paper; for out of these he can cut overlays to the precise shape and size that is wanted, as he will find it frequently necessary to do in instances where great accuracy is required in overlaying particular portions; and in these instances he can not do well without a sharp penknife and a pair of good small scissors. . . .

Type-high bearers should be used, when printing an engraving or any other light job, to keep the impression from bearing harder on the edges than on the centre. They should be placed in such a position as not to be liable to get any ink on them during the time the form is being worked. If they can not be used, pieces of reglet or cork, pasted on the frisket, and taking a bearing on the furniture, must be substituted; but the high bearers are to be preferred, when they can be adopted, because they equalize the pressure on the surface of the engraving, and protect the edges from the severity of the pull, which is always injurious to the delicacy of the external lines. They also render the subject more manageable, by enabling the pressman to add to, or take from, the pressure on particular parts, so as to produce the desired effect. . . .

If the extremities be engraved much lighter than the central parts, underlays should be pasted on the middle of the block, which will give a firmer impression to those central parts of the subject. It would save trouble to cause the block to be a little rounded on the face, as it would give facility in obtaining a good impression.

When highly-finished engravings are worked separately cloth, or any other soft substance, should never be used for blankets, as the impression will sink into it; two or three thicknesses of smooth hard paper, or even a piece glazed pasteboard, placed in the tympan, is better.

The silk or parchment, which is next the engraving, should be stretched tightly, and it should be thin and uniform of texture, so as to enable the pressman to obtain an impression from the surface of the engraving only.

The rollers should be in the best condition for this kind of work; and the pressman should be very particular, in taking ink, that but little be put on at a time, and that it be thoroughly distributed before the rolling is done, or else he will not obtain a clear and uniform impression.

Should a wood-cut be left on the bed of the press or on the stone, for any length of time, it is apt to become warped. When this happens, a very good method of restoring it to its original shape is, to lay it, face downward, upon the imposing-stone, with a few thicknesses of damp paper under it, and to place a flat weight of some kind upon it; and, in the course of an hour or two, the block will be restored to its former position. This method is preferable to wetting the block with water, which is often practiced; for the latter swells the fine lines of the engraving, and consequently affects the impression. To retain the appearance, as it comes from the hand of the artist, the block should never be wet with water; and, for this reason, when wood-cuts and types are worked together, the engravings should be taken out before the form is washed. [Editor's note: MacKellar (1866, p. 261), suggests another method, "To prevent warping during the dinner-hour or the night, turn the tympan down upon the form, run the carriage in, and, pulling the bar-handle home, fasten it so that it will remain in this position during the interim."]

When a few proofs only are wanted from an engraving, good impressions may be obtained, with very little trouble, by taking the tympan off, and using three or four thicknesses of paper between the face of the engraving and the platen.

Ley should never be used to clean a wood-engraving. It will be found, in practice, that spirits of turpentine take off the ink quicker, and affect the wood less, than any other article used; and the facility with which the block is again brought into a working state more than compensates for the trifling expense incurred, as nothing more is required than to wipe the surface dry, and to pull two or three impressions on waste paper.

Reading 24.5
Overlaying Cuts
from *Harpel's Typograph* by Oscar Henry Harpel (1870, pp. 238–239)

Harpel discusses the engraver's proof and its importance as a guide to faithfully reproducing the artist's vision. The engraver usually pulled his proof by burnishing the back side of the paper, and with skill, he was able to manipulate the density of color in any given area by increasing or decreasing the pressure on the burnisher. The pressman, on the other hand, could only try to simulate these effects with overlays.

If the overlay paper is too thick and the patches are cut out with a sharp tool, a stair-step effect will be visible in the printed image where the patches overlap. This can be avoided by scraping or rubbing the edges of the patches. Once the overlay was finished, it was placed between the tympans, which also helped to ease the transition between the layers of patches. All overlays needed to be checked periodically and retouched when necessary. Fine tissue was used for minor touch ups.

Another writer, Cummins (1873, p. 23) prefers "to take two or three impressions on three different thicknesses of paper, as thin, medium, and thick, using the thin as the ground, and cutting out the lightest parts in that. I find these afford a sufficient variety for every degree of shade or solidity."

Harpel also mentions a non-traditional method for preparing overlays using "three-, four-, and even five-ply photograph-mount card-board." It is difficult to say exactly how thick these overlays were, but they appear to be excessively bulky to me. This method was used for long runs and was obviously not as subtle as plain paper overlays. When using this procedure, the makeready process was reversed. The darkest areas were brought up first and then the lighter areas cut away.

Harpel also recommends using benzine for washing blocks. I suspect that he is referring to metal plates since benzine could both dry out and harm wood blocks.

The popular opinion of a wood engraving, or its copper or type-metal representative, is inseparable from its treatment by the pressman. If the cut is badly printed, the verdict is – "It is a poor cut;" while a carefully overlaid and well-printed cut is termed "A good piece of engraving." But the criticism may be totally incorrect in either case; for that which is condemned may be intrinsically a beautiful and meritorious work of art, while that which is praised may be nothing of the kind beyond what the printer has wrought for it.

As far as practicable, the printer's and engraver's arts should be accommodated to each other, and we are glad to observe that a disposition to do this is becoming more common than formerly.

The *engraver's proof* is generally considered to exhibit the standard of effect the engraving is capable of producing. Using the best of ink carefully laid on the block, and paper manufactured expressly for the purpose of proving his work, the engraver skilfully "brings out," by means of his smooth ivory burnisher, the strongest effects, treating more gently the middle tones, giving a proper degree of finish and delicacy to the fading tints, and treating the lights and mere tracery that expresses distance, etc., with a view to preserve that harmonious yet natural effect so pleasing to the critical eye, and, at the same time, making visible the thought or thing to be expressed definitely and according to the artist's intention.

In first-class printing from wood-cuts, the engraver's proof may be quite equalled, and sometimes surpassed, in many features. . . .

Aside from the quality of the paper or ink, one of the chief processes by which effect from cuts is reached, is by what is termed "overlaying;" and to do this well is not the least accomplishment of the thorough pressman.

The first step toward overlaying is to take a clean and well-defined impression of the engraving upon a sheet of paper that is moderately sized and calendered, but not too hard. Upon this impression he builds or pastes "*overlays*" of exact cuttings – made from other impressions on other papers of various thicknesses – of the dark parts, the middle tones, tints, and whatever requires stronger relief than the ordinary flat impression would produce. The precise lines of the object to be overlaid must be carefully followed in making these cuttings, and a small, keen-bladed knife alone should be used. Delicate outlines requiring but little impression, when they appear too strong, are to be cut out or "reduced" one, two, or more thicknesses of the tympaning.

After the various important parts of a cut are overlaid according to the relative degrees of strength and blending desired, it sometimes becomes necessary to scrape or rub down the edges of overlays, so as to prevent the marks that might otherwise be made from the edges being too abrupt.

When the overlaying, reducing, and scraping processes are completed on the detached sheet, it must be fixed with great precision over another impression of the cut taken upon one of the under [i.e., inner] tympan-sheets of the press. After careful examination to see that no overlays have been doubled over or displaced, have two or more outer tympan-sheets over all, and get an impression to ascertain if the proper effect is produced; and, if not, add to or reduce the overlaying until it is correct. This will require good judgment, and some idea of the proper amount of light and shade due to the subject. Sometimes a cutting of fine tissue paper will be sufficient to produce a clear, smooth effect where it is lacking; and in portions where the subject appears too heavy or harsh, the removal of a very little overlaying will often make it right.

The minor parts of an engraving, if they be well cut, require but little attention after the main features are thoroughly attended to.

While we would advocate complete overlaying in every case of any importance, we cannot gainsay the fact that even partial overlaying – say that of the dark effects of a picture – is better than none at all; and almost every cut that is sent to press can be improved by even a little attention to this particular.

Another method of preparation to print cuts is to use three-, four-, and even five-ply photo-graph-mount card-board, and to cut away the lights and fainter tints of a picture, allowing the stronger portion of it to stand, or, in other words, reversing the operation of overlaying or build-ing up. This is principally employed for newspaper illustrations and large cuts, upon which long runs of presswork are to be made. The photograph-card will last longer than paper overlaying, but we do not think it produces so delicate an effect.

Overlays require more or less attention during the printing of a form of cuts, and sometimes need to be repaired or renewed....

Wood-cuts must never be washed with lye. Benzine or camphene only should be used.

Reading 24.6
Bringing-Up Woodcuts at Press
from *The Printers' Universal Book of Reference and Every-Hour Office Companion,* by William Finch Crisp (1875, pp. 56–57, 59–62).

Even though Savage (1822) went into a great deal of detail in his book about printing wood engravings in multiple colors, very few manual writers prior to the last decades of the nine-teenth century, mentioned color printing in their manuals. Procedures for editioning wood engravings were generally limited to single blocks printed in black. Crisp repeats Savage's instructions for single-block printing, although he replaces the original wood blocks with electrotypes (see Reading 25.11 on p. 758).

Crisp recommends using the handpress for printing fine woodcuts and wood engrav-ings. His tympans were covered with muslin for common work; parchment, for fine.

The engraver was given the luxury of having to produce only one perfect reference copy of his design which the pressman was expected to reproduce with the same subtle effects of the original at the rate of 250 to 500 copies an hour. The latter figure works out to be about one copy every seven *seconds*, a speed that is hard to imagine even possible on the handpress. On the other hand, popular pictorials – which had their beginnings in the 1840s – printed over 100,000 copies on cylinder presses weekly. These pictorials were profusely illustrated with wood engravings printed from electrotypes.

As the method of printing engravings on wood, here described, applies to what is termed fine printing, it may be as well in the outset to define what is meant by this expression, in its application to this subject. Fine printing is the art of obtaining impressions from an engraving on wood [Editor's note: Crisp is paraphrasing Savage (1822, p. 19)] – of the surface and the surface only – so as to produce the effect which the artist intended, in the highest state of perfection. There is a material difference in the manner of obtaining impressions. Those from an engraving on wood are produced by coating the surface of the lines with ink by passing a composition roller over it, and then, with the paper upon it, submitting it to pressure between two parallel plane surfaces, or by a cylinder rolling over it. In other words, by the agency of a bed-and-platten or a cylinder printing press. We speak now of careful hand-press work, and the printing of an engraving unaccompanied by letterpress. After putting a block on the press, the workman ought to be very gentle in the pull for the first impression, to prevent an accident – which has many times occurred from thoughtlessness in this particular, by making the pull too hard, and crushing some of the lines. By avoiding this indiscretion he will be safe, and can proportion his pull to the subject. He should also examine, previous to pulling, that there be nothing on the block – no pins that he may have for his tympan sheet, or any needle with which he may have been taking out a pick. Such accidents have caused great trouble to the engraver, as well as loss of time and disappointment, besides entailing a character for carelessness on the printer. . . . A few thicknesses of stoutish, hard, smooth paper, in lieu of them, between the tympans, is much better; indeed, sometimes a piece of glazed pasteboard is used to great advantage. The parchment covers must be in good condition, tightly stretched, and of uniform thickness, so as to enable the pressman to obtain an impression as nearly as possible from the surface only of the engraved lines. Muslin covers may answer very well for ordinary jobs, but the fine printer that once uses parchment will be very loath to fall back on muslin. A large woodcut left on the press all night is very apt to warp. When this happens, a good method to restore it to its original flatness is to lay it on its face upon the imposing stone, with a few thicknesses of damp paper underneath it, and to place the flat side of a planer upon it, and four or five octavo pages of tied up letter: in the course of a few hours the block will be restored to its original flatness. However, in the present advanced condition of the art of electrotyping, by which process an exact *fac simile* can be taken, it is no longer necessary to use the original engraving, and electro-types are not liable to warp. Whenever it may be necessary to make up, impose, and send to press a series of wood engravings with a type forme, after being worked, the forme should be laid up and the cuts taken out before washing. If you want to preserve the original perfection of fine wood engravings you must keep lye and water away from them. When only a few proofs are wanted from an engraving, good impressions may be obtained with but little trouble on dry India paper, with about six thicknesses of the same sort of paper laid over it, and pulled without a tympan. This observation applies to small cuts, and those of a moderate size. If proofs are wanted from larger ones, it will be found advantageous to put the India paper for a few minutes into a heap of damp paper. You may ask, very reasonably, "What shall we wash wood-cuts with, if lye is repudiated?" The best method we have found in practice, is to wipe the ink off with a piece of woollen cloth, damped with camphene or spirits of turpentine; and if it should get foul in working, to clean it with either of these fluids with a softish brush. It will be found in practice that either of these fluids will take off the ink quicker, and affect the wood less, than any other article used; and the facility with which the block is again brought into a working state more than compensates for the trifling additional expense incurred, as nothing more is required than to wipe the surface dry, and to pull two or three impressions on dry waste paper. The engravers always show an impression when the block is taken home to their employer; and this impression is taken in a manner – where the subject is not of a large size – such as to produce a superior effect to what a printer can with a press, when he has a number to do, which are generally worked in a forme with types, and his price so low for printing as not to enable him to do justice to the subjects. The engraver's proof is obtained by means of a burnisher, with one thickness of paper in addition to that printed on, so that he can examine each part to bring it up where it is required, and leave the others as delicate as he pleases. He thus obtains an impression from the surface only, perfect in all its parts, with the best ink that can be procured: this is a very tedious operation, hours sometimes being consumed to produce one impression, while the pressman is expected to produce like effects at the rate of two hundred and fifty, or even five hundred copies an hour. Papillon, in his work on Engraving on Wood, published in 1766, complains of a plan nearly similar being adopted by the French engravers, with which he finds great fault. The following is a translation of the passage: – "Some engravers on wood have the knack of fabricating the proofs of their engravings far more delicately, and in a more flattering manner than they really ought to be; and this is the means they make use of – They first take off two or three, in order to adjust one of them to their fancy, and which they think will favour their imposition; having selected it, they only beat anew the parts of the block charged with shades and the deeper strokes, and in such a manner that the lighter ones, distances, &c., being only lightly covered with ink, in as far as not being touched in the new beating, they retain no more than what was left by the preceding impression; the result is that the new proof comes off extremely delicate in those places, and appears pleasing to the eye; but when this block is printed in conjunction with letterpress, the impressions then appear in their natural state, and totally different from that which they presented on delivery of the work. The strokes are of one equal tint, hard, and devoid of softness, and the distances are often less delicate than the foregrounds [....]" The pressman will find this an advantage, if it be necessary, to do full justice to an engraving, to have a good impression from the engraver, and place it before him as a pattern, and then arrange the overlays, &c., till he produces the same effect; but the most valuable lesson will be when he can obtain the artist at the press side, to direct him in making ready the cut; and we would advise him by no means to be impatient at the tediousness of the operation, as he will obtain more information how to produce a fine impression by this than by any other means. It will also instruct him how to meet the wishes of the draughtsman and the engraver with regard to effect, in a way superior to any other; and will, with care and attention, ultimately lead him to excellence in printing engravings on wood. So far, notwithstanding the vast improvements in printing machines, we must admit that the finest woodcut printing is still done upon the hand press; but when you come to our mammoth pictorials, issued by the hundred thousand weekly, machines are absolutely indispensable, both on account of the size of the forme and number of impressions. Fine woodcut printing, however (such as is produced in the Christmas annuals), will continue to be done by hand, until still greater improvements are made in our steam printing machines.

Reading 24.7
Cut Work at Press
from *Practical Printing* by John Southward (1882, pp. 451–453).

> In this reading, taken from the first edition of his manual, Southward gives clear and precise instructions for printing cuts from the original wood blocks. I find this a bit strange since electrotypes had already been in use for more than half a century before his manual was published. In reality, his procedures are an amalgamation of those set forth by earlier writers.

I suspect that even though these instructions date from the beginning of the nineteenth century, they must have still been widely practiced in printing offices in the 1880s.

Southward prepares his overlay off press. He attaches the overlay patches to a loose tympan sheet using a pin-registration system, in which he pricks the overlay at a precise point in the image and then aligns it with the same point in the image printed on the tympan sheet. I find it curious that Southward places his overlays on the front of the tympan instead of burying them between the tympans.

Southward offers two solutions for dealing with blocks that are too high: (1) planing the bottom and (2) reducing the packing in the tympans. The latter would, however, create another problem since the block would be higher than the type; and if printed together, the block would bear ink and pressure off the adjacent type.

We now approach the most difficult of all the different branches of press-work. The proper "bringing up" of cuts demands patience, judgment, and an artistic faculty, which is very difficult to describe. Some men seem incapable of doing this kind of work, and equally incapable of appreciating it when it is done. There are others – and fortunately they form a large proportion of the trade – who are quite able to do the work, but who have had no opportunity of practising it, for want of the necessary knowledge of the principles involved. It is for these we write, and to penetrate the mystery with which it has very foolishly been surrounded. Week by week there is a greater demand for men who, to their other acquirements, add that of being able to make ready a fine wood-cut; and when found they are always well paid. As illustrations become more popular this demand will increase, and there is no reason why a very interesting, profitable, and useful art should be placed for selfish motives beyond the attainment of any competent pressman.

Pre-supposing, then, that we are addressing those who are fully acquainted with the branches which have already engaged attention, our directions may be given in a more concise form than would otherwise be advisable.

123. The following are the different stages of the process, which must follow in the order here laid down; –

1. Take out the cuts, and pull three careful proofs of each. Let these proofs be taken on fine paper, of a good yielding surface. Highly sized or calendered paper is not suitable for the purpose.

2. Replace the cuts in the forme, and bring them up exactly type-high, by judicious underlaying. This is done as follows: –

To ascertain how much they are too low, lay one or more cards or scale-boards on the face of the wood-cut, and by means of a straight edge, or by feeling with the fingers of the right hand, it will be known whether the intended underlay be exactly even with the face of the letter. If it be not, other underlays must be added, and their effect tested, until all is on an exact level.

When the underlay has been made even, or level, unlock the quarter in which it is situated, and take the wood-cut out of the forme. Fit a scaleboard, or card, or whatever is necessary, to the bottom of it, and place it thus raised in the forme. To make additionally sure, lock up the forme again, pull a waste sheet upon it, to make it sink as low as it will go, and then notice whether it is a proper height. Add or take away in the same manner until a clear and perfect impression can be obtained.

If the wood-cut is too high it must be planed low at the bottom; or a few sheets may be introduced in the tympans and cut away on the part that bears on the wood-cut, until the general impression is even. Blocks are now so well cut by the makers of engravers' appliances that this difficulty will seldom occur.

It is desirable that the heaviest of the underlays should be exactly under the solid effects of the various engravings. Let this underlaying be done carefully, and with precision.

3. Take an impression on a sheet "of its own," on which to attach the overlays when ready.

4. Cut out carefully, with a sharp scraper, one of each of these proofs, leaving little but the heavy lines and solid effects of the subject, taking care to cut slantingly – that is, the edges must be bevelled off.

5. Take the second proof of each, and cut out in like manner all the light effects, and here and there such of the heavier as judgment shows to be expedient, shaving the overlay in all such places gradually from the heavy to the lighter parts.

6. This done, take the third proof of each, and cut out the light effects only, using discretion in shaving off partially such portions as appear desirable or proper.

7. Next paste slightly, very slightly, the *second* cutting, and place it line for line exactly over the *third* cutting; then in like manner the *first* cutting over the *second*. [Editor's note: In this procedure, Southward is aligning the printed images.]

8. Having treated all the engravings in the same way, scrutinise them critically, and scrape or shave off such portions as are likely to create an abrupt impression, or prevent the lights and shades from gradually working into each other, and your overlays are ready.

9. Next, carefully, but very slightly, paste them only enough to stick. Note particularly two parts of the engravings near the extremities, and run a pin through each, taking care to find the same points on the tympan-sheet, and then fasten them.
The importance of extreme care in pasting the overlays line for line over each other needs no comment. The lines out of place will completely spoil the effect of the engraving.

10. Now very carefully apply the sheet to the forme, getting the lines of the proof and those of the engraving exactly over each other. Paste a little at the corners, but not over a block; pull, and the sheet will adhere to the tympan. The overlays thus placed in position, take a sheet of tissue paper the size of the forme, paste two of the edges, above and below the make-ready, and so cover the whole for its protection.

11. Next take a proof of the forme, from which proof you will probably find that the necessities of your engravings have partially taken off the impression from the adjoining text. This you remedy with tissue overlays in the proper places; and perhaps you also discover some portion of the cuts could also be improved with an additional overlay of tissue, or your scraper can be employed to advantage.

You may now begin to work off the forme, but if after pulling a score or so of sheets you find that the engraving can still be improved by the scraper or more overlays, by all means do so.

Reading 24.8
On the Cutting of the Overlay
from *A Practical Treatise upon Modern Printing Machinery and Letterpress Printing* by Frederick John Farlow Wilson and Douglas Grey (1888, pp. 336–341).

Wilson and Grey are describing the preparation of overlays for printing electrotypes of wood engravings on cylinder presses. It should, however, be noted that the makeready process for both wood blocks and metal plates was the same for all nineteenth-century presses.

The authors include a diagram, shown in **Fig. 24.2**, that explains their theory of gradations in the density of color to be found in printed wood engravings. Their instructions do not substantially differ from those given by earlier writers, although one of the pluses in this reading is its accompanying set of step-by-step progressive proofs for an overlay, shown in **Figs. 24. 3** through **24.7**. Because of the expense of printing on machine presses, overlays were usually prepared off press – on a handpress – and then transferred to the cylinder press. Wilson and Grey recommend peeling or scraping away thin layers of paper from the heavy base sheet – the thickest piece of paper in their overlay. For the rest of the overlay, they use patches of thin paper.

They also discuss the preparation of metal plates to be printed with text, noting some of the intrinsic problems that occur in book work when the two are printed together. As always, simplicity is the key word for overlays. Each additional layer will alter the pressure on adjacent areas, sometimes necessitating the expansion of the overlay into the text area.

It must be admitted that complete success is largely dependent upon the engraving itself. Some engravings are cut in sharp, distinct lines, bold and effective, while others are close, and consequently shallow. In one case the labour is comparatively slight, a level impression often yielding fairly satisfactory results, while in the other the work is materially increased, and the ultimate effect often unsatisfactory.

Since the proper making of overlays takes some little time, it is advisable to have them prepared prior to laying the forme on machine, so as to save unnecessary delay. Impressions should be pulled at hand-press from the blocks or plates to be printed from. It is perhaps unadvisable to take the pulls from a wood block for this purpose, if it is to be subsequently electrotyped for machine, as the plates are frequently of slightly different size from the original, owing to the uneven contraction of wax in the moulding. Added to this, blocks will frequently warp, and sometimes split when under pressure.

The thickness of paper used must be to some extent regulated by the system of making ready to be adopted – with or without a blanket. It is patent that the effect will be much more apparent when the overlay comes into direct contact with the cut – *i.e.,* with only the thin cylinder-sheet intervening – than when a thick woollen blanket is employed. Really delicate effects can rarely be produced in the latter case, as the blanket is apt to interfere with the true definitions of sharp lights and shades.

Presuming we are cutting an overlay for a cylinder hard-packed, the electro should be laid upon an iron bed in the press and (say) five impressions be pulled. It will be found sometimes necessary to slightly underlay the cut to obtain a perfectly level impression. The pulling of pieces for overlaying is very often looked upon as a very unimportant matter; but if ordinary care is not exercised, the work of the cutter will be materially increased. One of these pieces should be printed on tolerably thick plate paper, hard paper being used for the remainder. The ink must be stiff, and care must be taken that the plate is well and thoroughly rolled, so that the impression may be as perfect as possible. Avoid the use of too much ink, or some of the half-tints will be too dark. If this is not attended to, it is apt to create an uncertainty in the manipulation, and render constant reference to the India proof necessary. Before commencing to cut out, allow the impressions to become thoroughly dry.

The object of an overlay is not to equalise the impression, but to intensify the pressure upon the dark parts or solids, that they may be firm and bright, and to lessen the impression upon the lighter shades, in order to give them that degree of delicacy and cleanliness that would be altogether wanting if the pressure exerted were uniform. Supposing an engraving to possess prominent solids, together with graduated tints, were the impression sufficient to give the necessary depth to the blacks, the tints would appear dirty and harsh, and almost perforate the paper, owing to the distinct and sharp lines. On the other hand, if the pressure were regulated to suit the tints, the solids would appear rotten. This can be easily understood, when we consider that the fine lines are sharp and piercing, and sometimes necessitate the use of a bearer to prevent the paper being forced down on either side of the thin line, while the solids in themselves are capable of resisting a considerable pressure without injury.

Before giving examples, we may say that generally an engraving possesses five different gradations, or tones of colour – the extreme solid, the semi-solid, the half-tint and the open-line work, and finally the lightest tints.

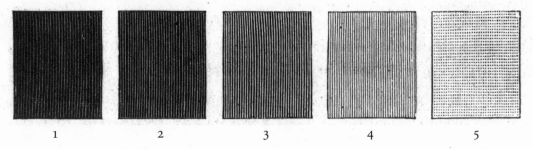

Fig. 24.2. *Gradations of colour.* Figs. 24.2 through 24.7 courtesy of University of Iowa Libraries. KEY: 1, extreme solid; 2, semi-solid; 3, half-tint; 4, open-line; and 5, lightest tints. NOTE: The key numbers have been reset.

The above [figure] will give a general idea of what is meant, it being understood that the example has been cut, not as a sample of engraving work, but rather of colour.

First procure the India proof of the engraving. This is, or should be, perfect. It is the engraver's impression of his own work; and as it is often passed by the artist who made the drawing, we may assume it to be the standard of excellence. It is perhaps as well to bear in mind, however, that the means used in its production are very different to those employed by the printer. Superfine ink and paper are used, and by the aid of a burnisher, and by "wiping," effects are frequently produced which it is impossible to equal by mechanical means. However, it is far better to have a super-excellent proof – with effects exaggerated – than to be left to our own idea as to how a cut should appear. It must be the aim of the overlay-cutter, by so adjusting the impression, to follow as clearly as possible the general "go" of the India proof.

The pulls being perfectly dry, take the impression printed upon the thickest piece of paper, and cut out the "whites," or those portions upon which there is absolutely no work. The high lights, or palest tints, should be peeled. Run the knife lightly round the parts adjacent to the middle lights, and carefully peel or scrape a layer of paper away. In no case should the paper be cut sharp down. It is advisable to pare the edges, otherwise the distinction in the impression may be too sudden or marked. After this has been done, take one of the pulls on thin paper and cut out the solids, or blackest parts, and with very thin paste place the pieces *exactly* in position on the first pull. The third impression must be more general, containing the tints marked 1, 2, and 3 – in fact, embracing all the forcible parts, cutting out the lighter tints, 4 and 5. From the fourth or last impression only the lightest tones should be cut out (5). Rarely are five pieces used, as the last would require to have the high lights omitted; and if, when the overlay is finally placed in position, it is found that the lightest tints suffer, a piece over the entire cut will generally effect what is required.

Fig. 24.3. *First pull (the foundation for the overlay)*

Fig. 24.4. *First cutting*

Fig. 24.5. *Second cutting*

Fig. 24.6. *Third cutting*

Fig. 24.7. *Effect of the complete overlay*

It must be remembered that the cutting of an overlay is not merely a mechanical operation. Unfortunately, it is frequently looked upon as such. Although every machine-minder should be capable of bringing up a cut in an artistic manner, we are afraid that such is not always the case. To turn a sheet to the light and determine where a patch is required to equalise impression is a very different matter from ascertaining if the appearance of a cut answers the expectation of the artist, engraver, or, in fact, the critical public. The quality of printing, at the present time, is advancing rapidly, and the "general reader" is able to discriminate between honest and careless printing, especially in the case of "pictures."

If really good printing be required, the overlays should never be scamped [performed in a careless manner], otherwise endless trouble will be the result; for when an impression is pulled, it will be found thoroughly unsatisfactory, and another overlay will have to be put up, thicker than should be necessary, to remedy in some measure the defects consequent upon the first being improperly done. This, of course, affects the general impression, as the additional thick overlay bears the pressure off the letterpress immediately adjoining. Then commences a plentiful distribution of patches on the parts affected – resulting generally, in the long run, in loss of time and unsound making-ready....

Overlays should be as thin as is consistent with securing the desired result. If the impression on the various tints has been so adjusted as to produce an artistic effect, it becomes simply a matter of dead impression, which may be dealt with by placing a piece of paper over the whole. In dealing with the high lights, care must be taken that the pressure is not excessive, as, in addition to the result being extremely harsh, the fine tints will become thickened – battered, in fact. In this case the cut is ruined. Again, over-anxiety to give the solids their full value must not tempt the operator to indiscriminately overload those parts with pressure, as in this case, also, the electro will be forced down by the heavy impression, and the very object of the machine-minder be defeated, as the surface of the plate will be pressed so low that the inkers will be unable to deposit the necessary quantity of ink.

As little work should be put into an overlay as possible. If it is overdone in the first instance, successive pieces have to be put up, and the probability of a successful print is very remote. As before stated, if the letterpress impression is satisfactory, and it is found desirable to patch the overlay, the pressure of the pages in close proximity is likely to be borne off, necessitating the placing of pieces on those parts affected. So it will be readily understood that this process may go on indefinitely, and at the same time yield a very unsatisfactory result in the end. It is not a question of the amount of actual work in the preparation of overlays, but of how the work is done. A man with fairly artistic taste will prepare an overlay which will "tell," in one-third of the time that another will occupy. We are free to admit that the latter may work very much harder and more anxiously; but the value of efforts is judged by final results, not by the amount of labour those results have entailed.

Reading 24.9
Printing Woodcuts
from *Printing* by Charles Thomas Jacobi (1890, pp. 183–188).

> Jacobi, whose manual is profusely illustrated, notes that the wood engravings in it were printed from electrotypes. He also refers to wood engravings as "woodcuts." His instructions are for the single-block process.
>
> An important addition to this reading is his mention of *process blocks*, in this case, metal plates made by any mechanical process, such as stereotypes, electrotypes, and photo blocks (see Reading 24.16 on p. 704). The last of these was also cast and should not be confused with photoengravings or halftone plates, both of which were etched by acid.
>
> Curiously, Jacobi under-inks his overlay proofs. He recommends using a heavy paper for the base sheet and two thin sheets of paper for the patches, adding two more patches, if necessary, for very fine work. Even though he inks with a roller, he mentions beating the cuts with the roller in order to add more ink to specific areas. In many ways, this is reminiscent of beating the blocks with balls.

The art of *woodcut printing* is capable of a large amount of treatment. To bring out the degrees of light and shade of an illustration which has much work in it is a task which requires a great deal of experience; in fact, the workman should possess some artistic qualification to appreciate and to give effect to the artist's design. To print a block correctly, the system of overlaying must be adopted. This is performed in a similar way to ordinary making-ready, but of course requires much more judgment and practice. In the first place, though the woodcuts themselves are not always used, a good electrotype taken direct from the original block, provided it has not been printed from, is almost equal to the wood-block; in the case of an accident on press to the electro, the cut can be easily duplicated by the same process.

Woodcuts, too, are very apt to get warped, and the joints, though bolted, are liable to open through a variety of causes, such as washing over or rapid changes in the weather. Under any circumstances, when illustrations are printed from woodcuts, they should be cleaned with turpentine and wiped carefully with a rag – water must by no means be used; if left on the press for any length of time, they should be run underneath the platen with the tympan first turned down. Sometimes it is well to pull the bar over and fasten it with a slight pull on. In the event of the cuts warping or twisting, a good plan is to lay them face downwards on something damp and run them in under the press, leaving them overnight with a small amount of pull on.

In preparing an *overlay,* the engraver's proof should be obtained, or, in the case of process blocks, the original drawing, as these very greatly assist the workman in bringing out the details, and at the same time give prominence to the parts required. It is quite possible to give two different effects to any cut by the system of overlaying, if the meaning of the picture cannot he readily grasped; therefore it is very advisable to work by some proof or copy in cutting out. The same amount of delicacy cannot be always realized in printing as in an engraver's proof. Perhaps the latter is taken singly, with a very special ink, and burnished up by hand to give the necessary difference in light and shade – even the excess of ink, in light tints, sometimes being partly wiped off. However, the india proof should be emulated as far as practicable in the making-ready.

The work in a cut, assuming it is landscape, may consist of three degrees as regards depth, *i.e.,* solids, light tints, and medium – the foreground usually being the more solid, and the background the lighter work, the intermediate part forming the medium shade. This is a general rule, but objects in the background have sometimes to be brought forward by means of overlaying, and the reverse applies to the foreground, when it is requisite to cut away. Distance must be allowed for in looking at a picture; this can be increased or decreased in a very great measure by perseverance in the art of overlaying. It is an important thing, too, that rottenness of impression should not be mistaken for light tints, as frequently in cutting away the workman is liable to take too much. All the work must be there, and, as before said, there is a distinction to be drawn between lightness and rottenness or broken lines. If the artist or engraver desired the latter, he would not go to the trouble of cutting work which is not to appear. Let your work be sharp and sound, even if very light. This is a great feature in woodcut printing. In cutting away lights skiver or peel away your thickness of paper, and do not make a straight deep cut. Vignette work is particularly difficult in this respect, and these remarks chiefly apply to this kind of work.

Cutting Overlays

To commence with the overlay: pull three or four good sound flat impressions, with not too much ink, on a hard kind of paper – cream wove is preferable, say about 24 lb. large post; do not use a laid paper by any chance. This done, they should be put aside to dry. Four is an advisable number to pull in case of accident, but three only will be really required for most cuts. The object now is to blend the three impressions into one overlay, by cutting away certain parts of each and pasting together. Let your paste be good and strong, but of a thin consistency, otherwise the delicacy of your work will be impaired. Take one of the pulls, and treat this as your number one, or foundation for the whole. In this one all the light tints may be carefully cut out – not abruptly, but in a gradatory manner – by using your knife in a slanting direction, and consulting the engraver's proof for differences of light and shade. When this has been done thoroughly, the second pull can be adapted for the solids, by cutting these parts out very clearly and sharply; the edges of these need not be cut out so slopingly, but great care must be taken in pasting these pieces on, that they fit exactly on the corresponding portion of the first impression cut out, because, if they shift by any means, the whole labour expended on the overlay is wasted. If the paste is not sufficiently tenacious, the pieces are likely to move in printing, and the result may be disastrous to the appearance of your cut. Number three of the pulls may be treated thus: cut away the light parts, and retain the solids and medium. In cutting out the last part of this pull the medium parts should be softened down in the cut by slanting your knife. To obviate hardness on the edges of your cut, the overlay, when all has been pasted together, may be rubbed down slightly, or even skivered. These three thicknesses will be sufficient for most cuts; difficult cuts may have four, if there is a broad difference between the depths of shade comprised in the illustration. Before putting the overlays on, if the cuts are printed with type, the blocks should be underlaid so as to bring them up to a slightly higher level than the type. In fastening the overlays up, after the remainder of the making-ready has been performed, great care must be taken that they are pasted down in their exact position. When they have been fixed, and a trial sheet has been pulled, they can be further humoured and touched up. All overlays should be preserved, packed up, and labelled, because in the case of reprints much valuable time and expense are saved by keeping them.

Process blocks are generally of a more sketchy nature, though lately some marvellous specimens of photo blocks as regards fineness and details of work have been produced. Special papers are even more necessary for these than for woodcuts, owing to the little depth in the face of the blocks, and dry super-calendered papers are the most suitable for their proper production. Very frequently more effect is got out of a flat pull, supposing it has been first roughly levelled, than by an elaborate overlay. A sharp and hard impression, with a suitable paper and good ink, is required. In printing these the original drawing, from which the block is made, is a good guide in making-ready. As dry paper is used for these process cuts, a good drying ink, to work clean, is necessary. For woodcuts the same kind of paper is used, but plate paper, or woodcut (semi-plate) paper, is perhaps more frequently in demand for this class of work. Papers are also now made termed "art papers." These have a prepared surface, apparently obtained by enamelling, and are well adapted for some classes of work.

Printing Heavy Cuts

In press-work it is necessary to beat the cuts with the roller in order to impart the necessary amount of ink. It requires some skill to perform this properly if the blocks are placed in the midst of type. On machine, exceptionally heavy cuts are sometimes made a separate and distinct working.

Examples of Cut Printing

For the sake of comparison we give here two illustrations. [**Fig. 24.8**] is simply a flat pull without any making-ready whatever, and [**Fig. 24.9**] is printed with an overlay of three pieces cut out and pasted together. These prints are taken from two separate electrotypes of the same wood-block. If these different impressions are carefully studied, the result of overlaying will be seen. The exact details of each overlay cannot be shown in print – at least, not in any cut with a fair amount of work. The difference between two prints, one overlaid and the other not, is sufficiently marked to give some idea of effect.

Fig. 24.8. *Flat pull without make-ready* – from Jacobi (1890, plate following p. 188)

Fig. 24.9. *Pull with make-ready* – from Jacobi (1890, plate preceding p. 189)

A competent person who has an appreciation of pictorial effect can get much better results out of a woodcut or process block than one who is not gifted with some amount of taste, though the latter may labour at it, and spend considerably more time over it.

Let it then be remembered that the last specimen here given has been executed simply with three thicknesses in overlaying, a little subsequent finishing being applied when placed in position. Some cuts of more elaborate nature as regards light and shade may take four or even five, but three are sufficient for an average cut. Moreover, it is best to avoid so many distinct and separate pieces, as the impression of any great thickness on the surface of the cut has a damaging, or at least depreciating, effect on the block itself after any large number has been struck off.

Rolling of the paper, both before and after printing, improves the appearance of illustrations, but the paper need not be glazed in the first instance if it has already a good surface.

Reading 24.10
Substitutes for Cut Out Overlays
from *Practical Printing* by John Southward (1900, vol. I, pp. 703–704)

As the reader has seen, preparing overlays for cuts was very time-consuming and demanding; therefore, it should come as no surprise that printers tried to find shortcuts to eliminate the centuries-old practice of paper overlays. Southward describes three of these solutions, which I have included here more as a curiosity than as legitimate overlay procedures.

All three of these roundabout processes required a lengthy period for drying, so I do not see how any time was actually saved. None of these procedures could possibly be faster than Jacobi's simple three-piece overlay described in Reading 24.9 above.

Of late years experiments have been made, chiefly in the United States, with a view to finding substitutes for the ordinary overlays so as to enable pressmen to begin printing off earlier than is now possible. The new methods are known as the Gelatine relief process, the Plastic process, and the Emery-flour process. None of them have come into general use, but the modern printer ought to know what they are.

The following descriptions are condensed from an article by Mr. [William] J. Kelly which appeared recently in the *American Pressman*.

Gelatine relief is obtained by the application of a pasty liquid, made of one ounce of white shellac dissolved in two ounces of methylated spirits of wine, which may be reduced to proper consistency by the addition of two ounces of naphtha. Two days is necessary to effect dissolution of the shellac. The manner of applying this gelatine is with a soft hair brush. It is employed to build up the stronger lines shown in an engraving or broken lines of type. In the hands of an accomplished workman speed and fair results are obtainable. It is specialty adapted for short editions of ordinary work.

The Plastic process has not been received with much favour. The materials employed in making the composition vary; some using the ordinary embossing compounds, some powdered shellac, others fullers' clay, etc., with suitable adhesive solvents and adhesives. An impression of the engraving is taken in the composition so formed, after which it is hardened by careful baking, and, after being trimmed of all surplus portions, is applied to the tympan in the usual overlay manner. It has this advantage over those to be named hereafter, that it can be amended by taking from and adding to portions of an illustration where such treatment may become necessary. In addition to this, the toning of vignetted edgings is one of its best features, as the plastic mould furnishes good facilities for cutting down and scraping away edges that show too strongly on the printed sample. The plastic composition is thinly and evenly laid on sheets of thin manila paper, and the face of the engraving oiled to permit of the material lifting smoothly from the engraved plate after pressure on the press.

The Emery-flour process or "Beck Process" involves the use of powdered emery, shellac, and quick-drying adhesive ink or sizing. The cut is rolled up with ink into which a fairly strong varnish has been worked. A sufficient quantity of ink is used to bring out the subject of the engraving, four or more impressions are struck off, and these are separately and carefully covered over with the powdered material and then left to dry, care being taken that the powder is not rubbed off or scratched on the face before being thoroughly dry. Usually, four sheets of paper are necessary for one overlay; these are trimmed at the corners of the several sheets, and then fastened together so as to register over each other in a perfect manner; after this preparation the overlay is applied to the tympan in the same way as a cut-out overlay. The solids or strong tones naturally take up more ink than the high-lights, and thereby accumulate a greater quantity of the powdered material, and thus build up varying degrees of strength in the overlay. This process of overlaying cuts has its chief advantage in speed, but only in certain cases. It cannot be properly adapted for vignetting, nor for the better class of illustrated work, nor indeed for fine mechanical detail; because if any part of the proofs taken from the engraving (made for receiving the powdered covering) has not been rightly secured, or from any cause the powder becomes disengaged from the proof sheets (overlay sheets) either before or after being fastened on to the press, there will necessarily occur defects in the overlay and in the printed product. In other words, the printed work will appear "scabby" in spots – particularly so in half-tone illustrations.

Reading 24.11
How Coloured Pictures Are Produced by the Letterpress Process
from *Practical Printing* by John Southward (1900, vol. II, pp. 95–102, 104–115)

Southward's description below is the first major contribution to printing illustrations in color since Savage's book, which was published in 1822. Southward did not even mention color printing in the 1882 edition of his book; in fact, in that edition, he devoted only six pages to the whole subject of printing blocks. On the other hand, in the 1900 edition, his comments on color printing are so extensive that I have divided them into two readings. In this one, he explains how the various blocks are made, proofed, and overlaid; in the next, he tells how to print them.

When making register, instead of moving the blocks, Southward shifts the metal plates on the mounts, which he does by prying up and repositioning the plates. It is sometimes hard to accept the fact that Southward actually worked in a commercial printing office where he would have witnessed printers at work. Some of his methods are so convoluted that common sense alone would tell the pressman to avoid them.

He discusses the pros and cons of printing the key block, usually the black or darkest image, first or last. Even though it is easier to print the key block first, he prefers – and I concur – to print it last with the printing sequence going from the lightest to the darkest color. When printed first, the key block loses some of its sharpness.

Regarding paste points, Jacobi (1890, p. 191) is a little more precise than Southward: the paste points are "pushed through the tympan from inside [back, using the holes made by the strip of spurs], and pasted over on the back with paper to prevent shifting."

Unlike Jacobi on p. 675 in Reading 24.9, when Southward mentions *process blocks*, he is referring only to photoengraved blocks made from black and white drawings that have been photographically transferred to zinc plates and then etched. By the 1890s, photography was also utilized for enlarging and reducing images. Prior to its use, a pantographic machine would have been employed to resize images on the blocks.

When coloured pictures are produced by wood engraving the key block is drawn on wood from the original design and cut by a competent engraver. Then transfers are taken from this key block and set-offs taken and transferred on to as many plain pieces of boxwood as there are to be workings in colour. The artist, with the original design before him, makes up his mind what each colour shall do for the perfect production of the picture. Taking, for instance, the yellow block first, he paints into the key everything he wishes to be produced in the yellow block. Some parts of it will be left absolutely solid, while the other parts which are intended to be more or less toned down will be indicated by an attenuated wash of the same colour. The engraver having these indications to go by, supplemented probably by verbal instructions from the artist, cuts the block. The half and quarter tones are obtained by skilful tinting and cross-hatching. Much of the best colour work done in Germany was in former years produced in this way; but the vast improvement which has recently been made in the production of process blocks is rapidly causing this method to be superseded.

There is a great deal of analogy between the two systems; for while the effects in one are produced by skilful engraving, those in the other are obtained by skilful etching; but in both cases the same high qualities of technical and artistic culture are necessary to get the best results.

In process work the original key is drawn by the artist on a piece of cardboard in black and white. This is then photographed, and a zinc block made therefrom. Before the plate is etched a black stipple is added from a tint-plate. When the key blocks are made impressions are pulled therefrom, and the artist colours them up according to his own idea of what is fitting, and these coloured keys form the originals from which the artist-etchers do their work. Transfers from the key block are taken and set off on (say) four zinc plates, and what was done by the engraver on the wood block has to be done in a different manner by the fine etcher upon the zinc plate. The gradations of tone which are obtained in one case by skilful tinting and cross-hatching are in the case of the zinc plates obtained by a careful sequence of baths, which enables the artist to so etch his plate that he may obtain, in the aggregate, a result which shall as nearly as possible perfectly represent the picture.

Proving

The complete set of blocks being in our hands for the purposes of proving or printing, a variety of considerations offer themselves as to the best method of performing this function. The primary consideration is to settle whether the key shall be printed first or last – there is much to be said for both sides of the question. If you elect to print the key first, and you have long numbers to do at machine, you spare yourself many anxieties with respect to the register, and this is especially true if you are not absolutely certain of the character of your labour. Much colour printing is done during the night by supplementary hands, and in an imperfect light. In cases like this it is a distinct advantage to print the key first. On the other hand, something of the force and sharpness which the key is intended to give is lost by printing the key first. If, therefore, we are quite sure of the character and competency of our labour, and the conditions are otherwise favourable, it is perhaps best to print the key last.

When the proving is done with the key first, the whole process is much simpler than when the key is printed last. The key plate is fastened to a mounting board, laid on the bed of a press, and impressions are taken from it on enamelled paper just like any ordinary forme of woodcuts; only, for the purposes of register, it is necessary to fix in the board four points for the registration of the colour plates which would follow, *i.e.*, one point for each colour forme. [Editor's note: Southward fails to mention that two boards, or strips, of points are necessary – one for each end of the form.] There is another thing which must be borne in mind in printing the key first. Inasmuch as the subsequent colours are all more or less transparent, the black ink in which the key is printed should contain plenty of driers, and the printed copies of the key should be allowed to become bone dry before the colours are put on.

When the key is printed last, the yellow working is printed first, followed by the flesh, then the red, the blue coming next, and the black last. The yellow being the first working, it becomes necessary to fix firmly four points in the yellow working for the registration of the four subsequent colours; but inasmuch as the second working is a pale flesh, and the yellow does not offer an infallible guide to the register, it is desirable to put the key on second; register it to the yellow, and pull a few register sheets as a guide to prevent any possible risk of bad registration; and it is this complication which renders it undesirable to print the key last. It must be understood that the key, in this case, is only put on tentatively to prevent any mistake in the register.

With these cursory allusions to the method of printing the key last, we now return to the mode of printing the key first, and propose to carry it through in all its details. The making ready of the black would be dealt with in the ordinary way, namely, the plate would be carefully underlaid, and overlays cut with equal care, so that the black parts of the engraving become firm and brilliant and the light parts soft and delicate. This done, the black may be printed off. This should be perfectly dry before the yellow working is put on.

When there is a suggestion of a water-colour wash in the foregrounds and in the sky tints, the effect is primarily due to the finely-etched grain of the plate; and, secondarily, to extreme care exercised in softening the edges in the making ready.

In preparing the yellow plate for printing, an impression would be pulled for underlaying upon thick plate paper, that is to say, paper which would be about 45 lb. demy. In this sheet the light parts on the edges would be cut away to reduce the pressure, and the solid parts forced by the addition of paper somewhat thinner than the sheet we have pulled. The impression upon this sheet, now dealt with, is pasted under the plate, the printer taking great care to get his underlay in accurate coincidence with the work. He would now pull another sheet, and if necessary treat that in the same way. So far as the underlaying goes, the operation should now be complete. Generally speaking, one thick sheet carefully treated should be sufficient, and hardly ever more than two.

The underlaying being definitely finished, the plate may be fixed on the board by means of eight ordinary ⅜-inch tacks, two at each corner of the plate. The next process is to make the register. This is done as follows: The printer takes an impression of his black key and finds two places in it at each corner of the sheet which agree with corresponding parts in the yellow plate. These parts may be a scarf or a button. If, for example, there should be a couple of uniforms in the plate with yellow buttons fitting into the key, the printer will cut out in the impression of the key forme he is now dealing with those parts where the yellow buttons should print. Having done this he will lay the sheet face downward upon the yellow plate, and by means of the holes which he has cut in the key sheet he will find the exact position that the yellow plate should bear to the key plate. This done, the next thing to do is to slightly damp the tympan with some diluted paste, to put the tympan carefully down and take an impression. This will cause the sheet which is on the yellow plate to adhere to the tympan. The next process will be to fix the register points thereon. The printer may make use for this purpose of a pair of the ordinary paste points sold by all printers' brokers at about 1s. per pair, or if he is economically inclined he will find a very excellent substitute in a couple of ordinary drawing pins [thumbtacks].

Having selected in the key impression now on his tympan the holes he proposes to use, he should have by him a stick of Prout's elastic glue and fix his points to the tympan by that means, having of course in the first instance placed the spurs of the points through the holes he has elected to use. This done, he is almost ready to take an impression of his yellow forme in yellow ink for the purpose of register; but before doing this there is one precaution he must not omit to take. It will be remembered that the yellow plate is tacked down on a mounting board. If he were to pull a sheet with the points on his tympan as they now are, they would simply become fixed in the board, would be pulled from the tympan, and all his labour would be thrown away. Therefore, before pulling his first register sheet he must devise some means by which this does not occur. The usual method is this: He takes a little ink (red or yellow) on the top of his palette knife and touches the tips of the points on his tympan with it. Then he gently lowers the tympan until the points with the coloured ink on touch the board. This indicates to him exactly where the points will fall on the board. Then he will get a punch, or, in the absence of a punch, a large nail, and make two holes in the board at the places indicated by the coloured ink. When his first sheet is pulled the spurs of the points will fall in these holes, and he may proceed to make his register with perfect safety.

Before pulling a sheet for register the printer should get up upon his slab the yellow ink he proposes to use for the yellow working. This may be made with No. 2 chrome reduced with thin or middle varnish, or it may be made with yellow lake, which is a perfectly transparent colour, and a small portion of No. 3 chrome. It must be borne in mind that all yellows made with chrome are more or less opaque, and their transparency when in tint with varnish depends upon the amount of varnish which is used to reduce the body colour of which the chrome colour is made. Yellow lake, on the other hand, is a transparent pigment in itself, and where a black key is printed first it is perhaps better to use a yellow made of this colour.

Having settled the tone and strength of the colour to be used, the next important thing to be done is to see that the slab and roller are absolutely clean; if this is not done very carefully there will be no purity in the yellow, and consequently no brightness in the picture; for not only do we depend upon the cleanliness of the slab and roller to give us pure yellow tones, but the yellow enters into the composition of the greens, which are caused by mingling with portions of the blue plate. The yellow is not unfrequently used as a basis for the strong red which is used in many subjects. For instance, when a vermilion tone is required inclining more to bright scarlet than crimson, the artist would arrange that the yellow should form an underprint upon which the solid vermilion or lake should print. Hence it is of primary importance that the utmost cleanliness should be exercised in the preparation of everything appertaining to the yellow forme. If the roller which it is intended to use should have been used for any darker colour, it must be washed frequently in turps until every particle of the dark colour has been got rid of. It is, however, infinitely better for the colour printer to keep one or two rollers especially for light tints; and, as these are nearly always transparent tints, they require very fresh rollers made with the old composition, which may be well sponged when necessary, or they may be firm patent rollers, which are naturally fresh and require no sponging.

Bearing all these facts in mind, and having made our ink of yellow lake and No. 3 chrome, we pull a sheet for register. If very great care has been taken, as it ought to have been done, in taking a sheet upon the tympan, the register should come as nearly as possible right; but if any alteration should be needed, the printer may make it in one of two ways, *i.e.*, he may shift the points on his tympan and thus twist the sheet round, so that the yellow falls accurately into the key, or he may leave his points intact and shift the plate upon his board. The latter method is, in the writer's opinion, the most preferable. The way this is done is as follows: When it is necessary to slew or twist a plate round, the tacks which hold the plate at the corners are loosened by prising [prying] with a small chisel, the plate is then gently tapped with the hammer in the direction it is necessary to force it, and thus, after one or two essays, the register is finally made.

If the underlaying has been skilfully performed, not much should be left to be done on or inside the tympan, but what little there is to do should be done with great care and judgment. Practically, the printer should only have to get rid of the hard edges, so that the light tones in the foreground and on the edges of the sky are so softened that they go off to nothing. The quickest, and probably the best way of doing this is to pull an impression upon the thick plate paper we have already mentioned; shave all the edges off by means of a sharp knife or some fine sandpaper; stick the sheet upon the tympan, and the making ready is finished.

Everything that has been written with respect to the preparation of the yellow plate applies to the flesh, red, and blue, which colours are printed in the order given. Each of these will print solid in some places, and in lines more or less close in others, till in places there will be but occasional touches, the intermediate varieties of strength being obtained by the graduated etching of the plates. Each, too, will in places over-print the preceding colours to produce fresh colours or variations of tone. Thus the flesh tint on the black stipple and the yellow will give a copper hue; it will also in places warm the yellow chrome where it over-prints that working alone, the degree being determined by the solidity of the two plates at the points of over-printing. The red will deepen the flesh tints, give orange of varying shades where it over-prints the yellow, and brown of varying intensity where it over-prints the black.

The blue, besides performing its natural function as a blue, has often to perform those generally done by a grey; but it is only by skilful blending of blue, flesh, and yellow that the artist can dispense with a grey working. In judicious conjunction with the flesh, it gives beautiful varieties of purplish-grey; by over-printing the half-tone in the flesh it forms a very pale purple. Several shades of green are obtained by causing it to over-print portions of the yellow plate; while a rich purple is produced by the key in solid and stipple over-printed in great strength by both red and blue. . . .

Preparation of Original Blocks

There is no subject of greater importance to the colour printer than the skilful and accurate preparation of blocks intended to be used as originals, from which multiples are to be taken by the electrotyping or any other process. Any time spent in the minute elaboration of original blocks is so much saved in all the subsequent processes. So well is this fact understood and acted upon in all large establishments, that no original in the remotest degree defective, either in point of engraving or of register, is ever suffered to be used; and there is no doubt that this is true policy, and in the end a wise economy.

The substances usually used for the production of originals are brass, zinc, wood, and soft metal. All these are used for engraving upon; but, in addition, the zinc is used in producing plates which are bitten out by means of acids. Taking all things into consideration, there is little doubt that brass is the material which gives the best results. When a set of colour blocks is once engraved upon brass and approved, they always afterwards remain in the same condition; they never vary in size, they never warp, shrink, or expand; they are not susceptible to atmospheric influences; or, at all events, this is so slight as to be practically inappreciable. These qualities are priceless when dealing with original colour blocks intended for high-class work, where it is a *sine quâ non* that the register must be absolutely true.

When original register blocks are engraved upon wood, they require as much care as delicate babies. If you have just proved a set and found them all right, and then by any chance happen to place one of them in a damp place or on a damp sheet of paper, it immediately begins to swell larger; a very short time will suffice to increase a wood block 3 x 4 a thick lead all round. If this is not discovered before the blocks are electrotyped, the whole fabric of the design is marred through the electros not registering; and even if it be discovered, it is a troublesome matter to get the block to its proper size. It must be put into a warm place, shrunk back, and re-proved until it fits again.

None of these things ever happen with brass, or indeed with any metal originals. On brass the very finest and most delicate work may be cut with the most satisfactory results. Of course, register blocks frequently are cut on wood; but those who elect to have their original blocks done on this material have to put up with many inconveniences from which brass ones would be free. When large original blocks are required for show-card or tablet work, zinc and soft metal are frequently used. Neither of those substances affords a first-rate printing surface. The zinc affects some colours prejudicially, and the surface of the soft metal interferes with the purity of any tint inks which may be used in printing from it. Therefore, when colour blocks are cut upon either zinc or soft metal, they should be used exclusively as originals from which electrotypes should be taken; and where it is required to print vermilion red from the latter, they should be silver-faced, or the chemical action which takes place between the copper and the vermilion causes the latter to turn black.

Registering

The Management of Points. – When a set of colour blocks is received by the printer they require to be proved. In the first place, it is only necessary to prove the blocks for register. A very convenient and effective way of doing this is to register all the blocks separately into the key. This may be done in the following manner: Take the key or outline block and lock it up in the middle of a chase; if the set of blocks is in six workings, you will require a pair of points of five spurs each (these are usually soldered into small plates of brass or copper), which may be fixed to the furniture at a convenient distance from the block, or may be fastened inside the tympan by means of compo, gum, or paste – the latter is, in the writer's opinion, the better plan, because by adopting this system the holes are made from the back of the sheet, which therefore renders the pointing of the subsequent workings easier and more certain.

The Use of Points. – In all colour printing the exact adjustment of the points is a matter which requires the careful and intelligent attention of the pressman or machine minder. When a mistake has been made, either through carelessness or ignorance, on this matter, the consequences are simply disastrous; it is ten chances to one that the paper used for the first working will be spoiled. A fruitful cause of mischief with the points is the practice which prevails with some inexperienced or careless workmen of fastening points to unprotected pieces of furniture with which the first working is locked up.

For example: we may have to print a couple of octavo blocks in several workings; the first working of these may be imposed in a chase with a piece of double-broad separating the pages. The pressman may thoughtlessly screw or fix his first working points in the middle of this piece of double-broad, and thus run the risk of spoiling his work if the piece of furniture should shift during the progress of the printing.

First working points, whenever it is possible to prevent it, should never be fixed to the surrounding furniture, but to the wood itself upon which the block or blocks are mounted. If there be no other means of securing the points except by fastening them to the furniture, the latter should be so wedged and secured in the chase that its shifting would be an impossibility. When, however, we elect to fix our first working points within the tympan, instead of to the forme, we get rid of many of the dangers incident to the latter method of procedure. If the points are once firmly gummed, glued, or pasted inside the tympan, the only thing that can affect the register prejudicially is the shifting of the forme itself; and as this cannot happen if it be properly secured, any failure in the registration can only take place through gross ignorance or gross carelessness on the part of the operative. It must be remembered that first working points in colour work are simply marks, which should always be at the same relative distance from any part of the first working. The moment this condition is changed, the most essential necessity of good register is wanting, and we soon find ourselves in a labyrinth from which it is by no means easy to extricate ourselves in safety.

There are certain well-defined conditions which it should be the object of the colour printer to attain in regard to first-working points. The system that offers the most absolute security is that in which the first points are secured to the block itself; when this is done, the risk of shifting is reduced to a minimum. Thus, if we have a forme consisting of four octavo electro plates which are intended to form the first working of a subject in several colours, the most certain way of dealing with them is to have them mounted, with the proper margin between them, upon one board, with the first working points fixed thereto. The adoption of this method minimises the risk, and is a good one to adopt in large establishments where the quality of the labour is unequal, and dependence cannot always be placed on the individual intelligence and care of all the workmen.

The only objection which can be urged against it with any force is that the holes are made in the front of the sheet instead of from the back; consequently, when the second and other workings come to be printed there is a burr at the back of the sheet, which necessitates greater care in pointing than would be necessary if the holes were made from the back. However, when the points for the first working are fixed to the board itself upon which the plates are mounted, it is scarcely possible for an accident to happen. It does not matter, so far as the register is concerned, if the forme becomes loose and shifts about the table of the press or machine; for the points, being fixed to the board upon which the plates are mounted, shift with the latter and are consequently always at the same relative distance from any part of the plates. The only thing which can possibly cause mischief would be the shifting of the points or plates upon the board, and this can scarcely happen if they are screwed down as they should be. Even if the tympan became loose and shifted backwards and forwards laterally, no harm would accrue to the registration of the subsequent workings, so long as the points and plates on the board were still secure, because the point-holes would still be made at the same distance from any part of the printing surface.

If, however, the points are placed within the tympan, so that the holes may be made from the back of the sheet, very serious mischief would result to the after registration if the tympan became loose so as to allow lateral play. This would not, of course, happen with a competent, careful man, because he would be sure to look to the security of his tympan before starting. When points for first workings are placed within the tympan and the latter shifts, the effect is just the same as if points were fastened to furniture surrounding the forme and the latter moved about during the printing – there would be an ever-varying distance between the points and the plates.

In the establishment of Thos. De la Rue & Co. the system adopted during the writer's time was that of fastening the points to the iron plate upon which the electrotypes were mounted; and the latter were screwed to solid iron plates and the points were also fixed thereto. Consequently, no mishap ever occurred through the shifting of the points. Therefore, when the work is intended to be printed at machine, this system may always be adopted as the best, because in machine work the pointing of the subsequent workings is invariably done from the front of the sheet, which is the side on which the holes are perforated. In presswork this is different; the holes are there made (when the points are placed in the forme) on the front of the sheet, but the pointing is done from the back, and the objection of the burr remains. This objection is removed when the points are fastened within the tympan, but care must be taken that the forme and tympan are absolutely secure. Having stated the advantages and disadvantages incident to both these systems, we must leave the reader to judge for himself which he elects to use.

Proving the Blocks

Reverting to the set of blocks which we have to prove: we first of all propose to take the outline or key block and make that – for the purpose of testing the register in this preliminary proving – the first working. This block should be locked up in a chase and firmly secured all round; it is not, as a rule, sufficient to lock it up simply at the tail or side – it should be fastened beyond the possibility of shifting. Then, having levelled it, the points should be fastened within the tympan by new compo or strong paste. The points sold by the printers' brokers are generally soldered into a plate of brass, which is usually somewhat thicker than a thick lead, and are designed for the purpose of being screwed to the mounting board or furniture. This plate of brass is consequently too thick for the purpose we have in view, *viz.*, to paste inside the tympan. Therefore, when it is desired to use points in this way they should be made specially for the purpose, and the spurs should be soldered into thin strips of copper not thicker in substance than a thin lead.

Assuming that points of the right sort have been obtained, they should be pasted on the spur side and pressed through the back part of the front tympan; a piece of stout, tough paper should be pasted over the back of the copper strip to which the points are soldered, and when this is dry the points may be considered secure. It will be further necessary to fix two narrow thin strips of cork to that part of the mounting board or furniture upon which the points will fall, so that when an impression is taken the descent of the platen will cause the spurs, falling on the strips of cork, to punch a series of clean holes, free from burr, in the back of the sheet.

The points being properly secured, and a careful examination of the tympan made, so as to ascertain that it is perfectly tight without the least play, we next turn our attention to the frisket, which should have been carefully pasted so that it dries flat and free from wrinkles. When the frisket has been cut out, a sufficient number of register sheets should be pulled for the registration of the five other workings to come. As we shall require two sheets of each working in absolutely dead register – so far as the blocks will allow – for the use of the engraver, it will be necessary to pull about twenty-five sheets from the key block. When this is done, the latter may be lifted, the first working points removed from the inside of the tympan, and the second working laid on.

It will be remembered that the purpose of this preliminary registering is merely to test the register, so that no bringing up – beyond merely levelling the block – is necessary. It should also be stated that the key block should be pulled in black or any other dark colour, while it is not material what colours are used for the other workings, so long as they afford a strong contrast to that which is used for printing the key. We may therefore print the other workings in a light blue, pink, or green, as may be most convenient. Having levelled the second working, it will be necessary, before locking it up, to place a few thin leads and thin cards around it, in case the block requires shifting. When this is done, the block may be locked up, a tympan sheet laid, and the points fixed for the registration of the second working.

The tympan sheet may be laid in either of the following ways: you may lay a white tympan sheet and pull this on the forme after the forme has been rolled and the ink pulled off, thus giving a faint impression of the block thereon, and then take one of the impressions of the key block and find two points in it into which the second working registers. Place a couple of straight pins through these, and pin the sheet to parts which coincide with them in the impression on the tympan sheet: this will afford a guide for the fixing of the second working points. If it be intended to use paste points, they should be pasted at the back and the spurs passed through the two holes intended to be used (which are of course shown in the impression of the outline pinned to the tympan sheet), and thus fastened to the parchment; or if the ordinary screw points are used, fastened by the point screws. The other method of laying the tympan sheet is to take an impression of the outline and cut out two small pieces into which corresponding parts of the second working print; this sheet is then laid upon the forme so that the parts which print into the key show through the holes which have been cut in the sheet. The tympan is then slightly damped and the sheet taken up, and the points are then fastened as in the other case.

A fresh frisket should be pasted for each working. When the frisket has been cut out, a sheet of the outline should be taken and pulled for register. If the tympan sheet has been laid and the points adjusted with care, the second working should not be far out of register. If the block is found on the first impression not to be quite in register, the forme must be unlocked and the block shifted until it absolutely fits so far as it is capable of doing. A set of colour blocks – no matter how carefully they may have been cut – very rarely fit at a first proving, and the purpose of this proving is to show the engraver those parts which need correction. When all the blocks have been treated in this way, an impression of each, accurately registered to the key block, is sent to the engraver, and when the corrections are made they are returned to the printer to prove for colour and effect.

Multiplying the Blocks

When original blocks have arrived at this condition, they have reached the stage at which it usually becomes necessary to electrotype them, for except for bookwork plates which contain no cuts stereotyping may be considered almost obsolete.

Stereotyping

When colour blocks are to be subject only to one working, the stereotyping process is in many instances unobjectionable. If, for instance, we desire to produce multiples of a show-card block which has been cut in one working, where there is consequently no register to make, stereotypes (except for delicate tints) are almost as good as electrotypes. For delicate tints the surface of the stereotype metal is not so good as that given by copper electrotypes. Stereotypes are wholly unsuitable for colour blocks when the subject to be printed is in more than one working, because they shrink so unequally in cooling that they always vary more or less in size; therefore no dependence can be placed on the registration when stereotypes are used.

Sometimes stereos are *faced* with copper, brass, or silver. This copper or brass facing is a distinct process, differing from that of electrotyping, as the latter is understood in the printing business. In the former process the plates themselves are placed in the battery until a thin film of metal is deposited on their surface; in the latter process the matrix, whether of wax, gutta-percha, or lead, is placed in the battery and the metal precipitated into it. A stereotype which has been copper-faced and a copper electrotype present externally the same appearance; but in the first case, unless the copper-facing has been particularly well done, it is liable to peel off in a skin during the rolling of the forme.

Qualities of Good Electrotypes

The chief qualities which a good electrotype should possess are that the copper skin should be very hard; that this and the backing metal should be perfectly homogeneous, and that it should be in every particular – especially in point of size – an exact reproduction of the original block. The hardness of the copper skin depends upon the quality of the metal used, while its homogeneousness is in a great measure governed by the rapidity with which the copper deposit is made. If the deposit is allowed to be made too rapidly, there is want of cohesion in the particles, and a brittle electrotype is the result. At Messrs. De la Rue & Co.'s the originals are frequently allowed to remain in the battery for from three to seven days; the growth of the copper skin is slow, but the result is a plate almost as hard and sharp as if it were cut in brass.

There are few colour printers who have not at one time or another experienced disappointment at the faulty registration of their electrotypes. Of course this has nothing at all to do with the electrotyping process, if the original blocks themselves do not fit; but it not unfrequently happens that the original blocks register accurately, although the electros taken from them do not, and it is to this point that we wish to direct particular attention.

Wax is the material commonly used to form the matrices in electrotyping colour blocks. This substance is more or less affected by atmospheric conditions. In a very cold temperature it shrinks, in cooling, more than it does in a warmer atmosphere. If, therefore, we have a set of blocks in six printings, and three of them are moulded on one day and three on another, it is a mere chance if the whole register accurately. The difference in the temperature will probably cause a difference in the size, and this difference will be marked in the same ratio as the variation in the temperature at the time of the respective mouldings. The practical inference to be drawn from these facts is that the whole of the original blocks of any one subject should be sent to the electrotyper together, and these should be moulded at one and the same time.

The Mounting of Blocks

In printing from electrotypes the material to be used in mounting them is an important consideration. There is no doubt that the very best substance for the purpose is an iron plate. When wood is used for heavy work requiring much impression, the fibre of the wood becomes compressed and the impression yields. Machine minders who have had to do with cut work, where the solid parts of the engraving have been heavily overlaid, often find the wood upon which the electrotype has been mounted sunk as much as a thick lead. When this is liable to happen, the impression cannot be firm and solid. It is therefore important to choose a material which shall be as unyielding as possible. Mahogany is generally used; walnut-wood is preferable to it, but iron is the best of all.

Reproduction by Photography

Multiples of register blocks may be made by means of photography, in increased or diminished size. Thus, for example, a set of blocks six inches by four may, by this process, be accurately reproduced three by two or twelve by eight inches. It must, however, be borne in mind that where the electros are increased in size any defects the original blocks may possess are magnified, while the converse of this is true if the electros taken from them are diminished.

A Substitute for Silver-Facing

There is one other observation to make before quitting this subject. In our remarks on colours it has been stated that when it is required to print vermilion red from electrotypes they should be silver-faced. This is an expensive process, and the writer therefore offers the following suggestion as a substitute, which may be applied with success in a great many cases. The object in view in silver-facing electrotypes is to prevent the chemical action of the copper from disorganising the vermilion, thus making it print a dirty brown instead of a bright red. It follows therefore that if we can give the electrotype a coating of something which shall prevent the chemical action from taking place, it will answer the same purpose as the silver-facing. The substitute we suggest is not suitable for very long numbers or for fine engravings, but for solid tablets [white-letter blocks], for show cards, or for any short number, say 500 or 1,000 pulls, where the forme is of such a character that it does not require much washing up, it will be found an admirable substitute for the costly silver-facing.

Suppose we have the first working of a show card to print in vermilion from a copper electrotype. Instead of having this silver-faced, take one ounce of Winstone's gold size, and grind up with it a quarter of an ounce of the "lake brilliant" of Cornelissen. Roll the electrotype with this preparation and allow it to remain for twelve hours, by which time it will be as hard as stone, and the vermilion red may he printed from the plate without the smallest diminution in its brilliancy.

Storage of Plates

When out of use electrotypes should be kept in a dry place, and the surface of the plates oiled, to prevent verdigris. When electrotypes become clogged with hard, dry ink, which the pick-brush and turps fail to remove, they may be cleaned and made equal to new in five minutes by covering their surface with a little creosote, and afterwards brushing the face out with turps.

Reading 24.12
Printing from the Blocks
from *Practical Printing* by John Southward (1900, vol. II, pp. 116–139)

This is a continuation of the previous reading. Southward now describes how to print color blocks on an Albion press. Even though long runs were usually printed on cylinder presses, the handpress was preferred for short runs and fine work. It offered the pressman more immediate control over his work since he was able to examine each print as it came off the press. Curiously, Southward is the only manual writer to recommend using blankets in the tympan when printing wood engravings.

As late as the end of the nineteenth century, pressmen were still preoccupied with their rollers, which continued to be adversely effected by atmospheric changes. These men not only had to contend with colored inks of varying body weights, but also with a wide range of printing papers. Nor was it unusual for a job to be printed on two different papers, each requiring a separate overlay. In theory, subtle changes in the density of the color were best achieved when the overlays were buried between the tympans, and the parchment was separated from the inked surface by nothing more than the tympan sheet and the printing paper. The objective was to print the blocks with the same flatness and softness that was found in lithographic printing.

Electrotype plates were screwed to wood or iron mounts. Southward describes the practice of underlaying, or, in this case, more accurately, *inlaying* – which was first discussed on p. 428 in Reading 14.18. Inlaying is a system for putting the underlay between the metal plate and the mount instead of under the block. This was only done for very fine work since it was very labor intensive, requiring that the plate be unscrewed and reattached for each modification. Curiously, none of the manual writers mentioned gluing the plates to the mounts. Perhaps the available adhesives were not sufficiently strong to bond metal to wood. Today, of course, there are double-stick tape and magnetic bases.

In this reading, Southward gives, as an example, step-by-step directions for printing an illustration of a flower in six or seven colors. Since the colors were not mechanically separated, he needed a separate block for each individual color, which included three pinks and two greens.

Our blocks being now in order we are to prepare to print from them, and the question arises whether we shall use a machine or a hand press. For long numbers there can be but one answer: a machine is imperative unless price be no object, and for comparatively short numbers a treadle platen may be used. But where the very best work is required or where the numbers are sufficiently short to admit of it, the hand press is to be preferred. We say the best work is done at the hand press because, as we have already pointed out, the best inks are those made with the stiffest varnish, and very stiff coloured inks cannot be relied on to work with at machine, and again each impression is under the immediate control of the pressman, who can influence it by his personality in a way that cannot be done at machine. We will therefore first consider the working off of a colour job at press.

In the writer's opinion the Albion press is far the best for all purposes, and we shall assume that it is a press of this kind which is to be used. We shall take for granted that the reader has a thorough acquaintance with its working parts and with all that has been stated in [Chapters 3 and 4] as to the essentials for good work, and that if such a thing as a crease or buckle or slur should occur he will, by the instruction already given him, know what steps to take to remedy it. Assuming, then, that the press has been properly cleaned and scrutinised, that it is quite rigid and free from even the suspicion of a shake, it is ready to receive the first forme. Before laying this on in order to make it ready, however, it will be appropriate to state at this point the sequence of the various processes which enter into the preparation of colour formes for printing. These are as follows: –

1. The forme has to be underlaid.
2. The points have to be fixed in their proper place.
3. The register is to be made.
4. The bringing up is to be done.
5. The roller is to be chosen and the colour matched.

The Impression: Hard or Soft Packing

As colour blocks vary very much in the area they present for printing, that is an element which must be borne in mind in determining the sort of impression they shall be worked with. Some formes would be very heavy and nearly solid all over; others might be very light and only contain a few dashes of colour here and there. It is obvious that the sort of impression which would be suitable for the solid, heavy forme would be unsuitable for the light, open one. In the first case, it might be necessary to put a blanket inside the tympan; while in the latter a thin card would possibly be the best thing with which to work the job. The question as to whether it is better to use a hard or a soft impression is not one that can be settled dogmatically in favour of either one or the other of these systems; it must be determined by the character of the particular forme to be dealt with.

There is also another circumstance which will influence our judgment in deciding whether the impression shall be a hard or a soft one, and that is the nature of the material to be printed upon. Sometimes the colour printer may have to deal with a very hard, unyielding card, not too smooth on the surface; while at another he may have to use a smooth, soft, well-glazed paper, and this may happen on the same forme.

Suppose, for example, that we have a show card to print, of which the first working is a solid white letter block, from which half the number is to be printed on a thick, hard card and half on smooth, soft paper. In making ready this forme for the cards, it would probably be necessary to use a blanket inside the tympan with a thick overlay – the whites being cut out – behind the blanket, so that the blanket itself and not the overlay comes next the card, with only the parchment of the tympan intervening. This would give us the best chance of forcing the hard card into the surface of the plate, thus producing a solid, firm impression. The thick overlay behind the blanket would further assist us, and the very toughness of the card itself would prevent the impression dipping into those parts of the block which have been cut away. When, however, we come to print the soft, thin paper, the conditions are wholly changed, and a modification must be made in the character of the impression. If we pull an impression on the paper, we shall find that the softness of the blanket will force the paper into whites, thus causing a want of sharpness in the outline; whilst the bulging of the paper would be liable to interfere with the registration of the next working. In a case like this, the impression should be made harder, the blanket may be removed, and a dozen sheets of the thin double crown used in most offices substituted. If the dip still continues and the impression is not perfectly flat, the overlay may be put on the tympan which is next the forme. If this sort of hard impression had been used for the cards, it would have been extremely difficult to have got the forme solid, and then only with great power and a possible risk of breaking the press.

The general deduction to be drawn from the foregoing is, that when the block or forme to be dealt with is nearly solid all over, with few whites therein, and a card exceeding the thickness of a four-sheet board is to be printed from it, it would always be right to put a blanket in the tympan. If we had to print a perfectly solid flat tint a blanket would be the best thing with which to work it, whether paper or card were used in printing from it, the only disadvantage arising from a blanket impression being the dip which would occur round the edges, and which would have to be controlled by a thick overlay cut to the exact size of the plate. When it is deemed expedient to use a blanket for colour blocks, it should not be a thick one. A piece of fine white Saxony wool cloth is the most suitable, or, at all events, it should not be thicker than the description known in the trade as fine Napier [cloth].

The cases, however, in which it is desirable to make use of a blanket impression are comparatively rare, and may be said to be confined to very solid formes which are printed on hard cardboard. In dealing with ordinary formes printed on paper, or thin, smooth card, thin double crown will generally answer every purpose, and the number of sheets suitable for putting inside the tympan must be governed by the open or solid character of the forme to be treated. If the forme be a very light, open one, a few sheets only, say eight or ten, of thin double crown would be sufficient. If, on the contrary, it is a full solid one, twenty-five to thirty may not be found too many. There are, however, instances in which the impression given by the limited number of sheets we have just named may be found too soft.

Besides dealing with formes of blocks of various degrees of openness, the colour printer has frequently to print a border of a single line either in gold or colour. In such cases, in order to ensure great sharpness and flatness in the impression, it may be necessary to discard paper inside the tympan altogether and use a glazeboard or thin ivory card. Sometimes title pages in expensive books are printed in red and black, the brass rule border and a few of the salient lines being in red. In this and similar cases it would be best to use a thin card inside the tympan, because the hard impression, by preventing all "dipping," would give us the best chance of producing a sharp, clean impression. Again, supposing we have a forme of solid borders to be printed in gold, the gold line being about a nonpareil wide; in this and analogous cases the object of the printer is to get his impression as firm and as flat as possible. Paper, therefore, or any other soft material, inside his tympan would cause the impression to dip at the edges; so that a card would be the best thing with which to work it. The colour printer, in determining the character of his impression, should do so with the endeavour to emulate the firmness, flatness, and softness of lithography.

Making Up the Forme

We left the press prepared to receive the forme, which for our present purpose may be supposed to be of a simple and elementary character. For the sake of illustration, we will assume that 4,000 small show cards are required, and that it has been determined to print them four-set [ganged in fours], either mounted upon a foolscap mounting board, or mounted separately and imposed in a chase; it must be further assumed that the show card is in two workings, of which one, the first, will be a solid white letter block, while the second working will consist of the shading only to print round this lettering.

In some offices a set of this description would be made up in the composing room, but it is frequently expected in colour houses that the pressman shall be competent to make up his own blocks. Assuming that the latter is the case, he would first procure a foolscap chase, put one of his blocks in each quarto, and place the necessary furniture and quoins around them. Then, having procured a sheet of the card intended to be used, he would have to consider, before making his blocks up, the question where his first working points should be placed.

It may be that the cards are sent in trimmed, so that if the blocks were made up out and out [without trim margins], one cut in the middle each way would give the exact margin. In this case the points would have to be placed *exactly* in the middle of the gutters, either at the top and bottom or on the short cross, so that when the cards were cut up the knife would divide the holes made by the points. This might not be objectionable for common work, but it undoubtedly would be for work of a high character, in which case an additional thick lead should be placed in each of the gutters, which would give a nonpareil extra for the points to fall into, so that they might be cut out altogether when the cards were cut up. It would, however, be a mistake to give the pressman cardboards to print cut to the exact size; there should always be sufficient space left beyond the limit of the margin necessary for the card itself, for the points to print on. When this is so, the pressman would only need to get the exact size it is intended to cut the card to, make up and carefully straightedge his forme to this, and fix his points beyond the limit of the outside margin of the card. Thus, in the forme we are dealing with, if half an inch margin were required round each card, an inch of space would of course be left in the gutters, while another inch should be left on the outside; half an inch for the margin of the card, and half an inch for the point-holes, which would be cut off. In making up his forme the pressman must therefore be guided by his point-holes and their relation to the boards he may have to print. Assuming that he had satisfied himself in this respect, he would now turn his attention to adjusting his impression, with the view of underlaying the forme.

Making Ready

In underlaying block formes which have to be printed on cardboard, this part of the making ready should be done with great thoroughness. The object we have in view in underlaying our blocks is two-fold – it is not necessary merely as a means of levelling the impression, because this might be done, however improperly, by overlaying; but it is essentially important that the blocks should be made perfectly level by underlaying, because if this is not done the blocks of which the forme consists vary in height, and thus prevent the effective rolling of the forme. The amount of underlaying which electro blocks require depends greatly upon the even thickness of the mounting boards and the plates themselves. Some electrotypers merely turn the backs of the plates, while others plane them; the latter is the method which gives the most satisfactory results.

Before pulling a sheet for the purpose of underlaying, the reader may be reminded that we are now dealing with four white-letter blocks mounted separately, and fastened to the board by means of screws. Having inked our roller – any colour will do for the purpose of making ready – we roll the forme and pull a sheet for the purpose of testing the impression. The sheet thus pulled should be examined on the back. If there be too little pressure, the impression on the back of the sheet will be scarcely visible except in those parts of the plates which are unequally thick. If, on the contrary, there be too much, the thick parts of the plates may print so strongly as to nearly burst the paper. The intelligent pressman would, in adjusting the necessary pressure, take the mean of these two effects; but in underlaying plates it should always be borne in mind that it is much easier to bring up a low part by underlaying than it is to reduce a hard one. If, for example, one corner of a plate prints very strongly, and another corner lightly, you have only a choice of two things in levelling it, *i.e.*, you must scrape away the bottom of the plate where the heavy impression occurs, or you must bring up the light part of the plate to the impression of the heavy part, and, in practice, the latter is the easier method. Therefore, in assessing the amount of pressure with which we will begin to make ready the forme, we must be mainly guided by those parts which print the strongest – the pressure should be sufficient to make these print fairly well, and the light parts should be brought up to them.

The impression being adjusted, a sheet of rather stout paper should be chosen – about a 30 lb. demy would do – and another impression pulled. This sheet should be pasted or pinned in the margin to a board slanted at such an angle that when the light falls on the sheet it brings out all defects of the impression. The pressman is now ready to level the sheet; but before he begins he must settle in his mind whether he shall place his underlays at the bottom of the mounting boards, or unscrew the plates and paste his underlays [technically, *inlays*] to the back of the plates themselves. In determining this question the pressman would probably receive his cue from the employer or overseer, for if the job were one which the exigencies of a cutting trade required to be done quickly without much regard to quality, he would undoubtedly elect to underlay the blocks without removing the plates; but if, on the contrary, careful work of high character were required the proper way would be to unscrew the plates and underlay them.

It may, however, be not amiss here to briefly sketch the difference in treatment between high-class and low-class work of this character; for in these days of keen competition the competent operative should be capable of grappling with both.

Quick Mode. – Supposing, then, quantity and not quality to be the desideratum, the pressman would obtain thick brown paper or thin wrapper; and, glancing at the sheet before him, his trained eye would take in at once the inequalities of the impression. Bearing in mind the fact that the underlay he is making is to go underneath the board, he would take no notice of local defects in individual plates, but confine himself to the endeavour to make every plate relatively equal in impression. Perhaps on the first sheet he may have to place three thicknesses – to use an expressive word known to block printers – of wrapper under one of the blocks; two under another, possibly leaving out a hard printing corner in each; the third block may only require a piece of wrapper on one side; and the fourth may be sufficiently level to be let alone. Having thus rapidly gone over the sheet on the back, which should not occupy longer than ten or fifteen minutes, the pressman turns the sheet over on its face, and proceeds to cut the pages up close to the printed boundary line of each block.

Beginning with the left hand top corner, he cuts out the underlaid impression of this block and places it, face downwards, on the corresponding block in the forme; then, having dealt with the other pages in a similar way, he unlocks the forme all round, takes each block out separately to prevent mistakes, and pastes the underlay, printed side outwards, to the bottom of the block.

The blocks in each quarto should now be tightened by pressing the quoins with the thumb, a sheet of waste laid on the forme and the platen pulled down on it several times to get the blocks firmly on their feet. When this is done the forme should be again rolled, and another impression pulled. Possibly, if the first sheet has been underlaid with great judgment, the blocks may all be equally level; if not, the second sheet must be treated in exactly the same way as the first: this will probably be found sufficient, although in extreme cases a third one may prove necessary. The underlaying may now be considered completed.

The pressman would next pull a sheet for overlaying, so as to correct any local failing of the impression in individual plates. In doing this he should choose a thinner paper than that used for underlaying; say, a 20 lb. demy. Having pulled the sheet he should, before he begins to bring it up, lay his tympan sheet. This should be cut to the size of the card he has to print, folded into 4to, damped all over with a sponge, and pasted on the damp side all round the edges. The sheet is then laid on the forme, so that the crease exactly divides the margin. The tympan is next let down and pulled very slightly, just sufficient to cause the damp sheet to adhere to it, and is then raised, and the bottom part of the tympan sheet pulled away from the parchment and pressed perfectly smooth with the hand, so as to exclude all air. The top half being treated in the same manner, it may be left to dry – which it should do quite flat – pending the bringing up of the sheet which has been already pulled. In printing white-letter blocks care must be taken not to pull a damp tympan sheet too soon after it is laid, or the wording will be embossed on the damp parchment, thus causing the impression to dip when the cards come to be printed.

Proceeding with the bringing up of the sheet, the pressman again has recourse to the slanting board. Examining his sheet on the back, he might, if the local defects were very strongly marked, bring this sheet up in the same way as he has done the sheets already treated; but the bringing up of white-letter tablets is not like bringing up so many pages of type. If, therefore, the underlaying has been effectively done, he may have some difficulty in discerning the weak parts of the impression when examined from the back part of the sheet. When a doubt of this sort enters his mind he should at once turn the sheet over on its face and bring it up by filling in the light parts with a paper equal to a 12 lb. or 14 lb. demy: the weakest parts of the impression will probably require three thicknesses of this to make them level.

When brought up, the sheet should be pasted to the inner tympan, so that the sheets or blanket with which the job is worked intervene between it and the forme. This is done so that the effect of the pieces used in levelling the sheet may be less abrupt than it would be if the sheet were fastened to the parchment which is next the forme. The sheet would of course be fixed in its proper position in relation to the forme by means of pin-holes made through the back of the tympan, in the method fully described [on p. 629 in Reading 22.8]; but it is necessary to mention that before pulling a sheet for bringing up "over," a sheet of white paper may be pasted on the inside of the inner tympan. When this is done there is never any difficulty in finding the pin-holes; while if it is not done, it is always a troublesome and frequently a doubtful matter to find them in the parchment itself.

By this time, also, the tympan sheet should have dried hard and flat, and the making ready may be considered sufficiently complete to justify the printer in pulling a card in the colour intended to be used in printing the job. The preparation of a forme of this character – after the blocks are made up – should not occupy more than an hour and a half or two hours.

It will be noted that in this method of treatment there is no attempt at elaboration; no overlay has been cut out – the forme has been simply levelled by two or three sheets placed underneath and one over.

Better Mode. – We will now proceed to notice the other and, it must be admitted, better method of treatment.

Going back to the point where the pressman has pulled his first sheet for underlaying, he provides himself with some thinner paper than he would use for underlaying the blocks – some of the 30 lb. demy he has pulled his sheet on would do very well. He levels the sheet on the back in the way he did in the first instance, but less heavily and with more care. Should any of the plates be extra thick in parts, thus causing the impression to be very hard, these parts may be reduced by filing with a flat, rough file, or, if this be not at hand, a piece of broken glass may be used as a substitute. Having pasted the underlays to the bottom of the plates, taking care that the paste is not put on too thickly, the plates should be carefully placed over the screw-holes, the impression pulled down and another sheet pulled. This second sheet should be thinner than that first used, which will enable the printer to see more distinctly the impression on the back, and the local defects may also be further corrected by pasting small pieces of paper on to those parts of the face of the impression which print very lightly. This second sheet should, in the majority of cases, be found sufficient; but before screwing the plates down the printer will do well to take one of the cards intended to be used for the job, roll his forme, lay a sheet of paper on the plates, place this card on the top of it, and thus pull the sheet; first taking off some pressure, to allow for the thickness of the card.

The impression thus pulled will enable him, to form an accurate idea of the condition of the impression in relation to the card upon which he has to print. This sheet should be examined, and any defects it exhibits should be corrected by pasting pieces of thin paper to any parts of the plates which still present appearances of weakness in the impression; and this process of pulling a sheet with a card on the top should be repeated until the impression is thoroughly sound and firm all over. When this point is reached the plates may be screwed down.

This system of underlaying necessarily occupies more time than that first described, but it is very much more thorough – especially so if the blocks are mounted all on one board; for in that case they are always in the same relative position, and in case of a reprint, if the overlay is preserved, the forme is practically ready to be worked off. There is another advantage which the system of underlaying the plates has over that of underlaying the blocks: the underlays are always secure and never get knocked off or lost, as is frequently the case when they are pasted to the bottom of the mounting boards.

Following up the process of making ready with the same thoroughness with which it has been initiated, the pressman takes another sheet of the 30 lb. demy, and, rolling his forme, takes an impression. Before raising his tympan he pierces two holes in the margin through the back of the tympan and the sheet on the forme; then he pulls another sheet on the same paper, but does not make the holes through it as in the first instance. This last sheet is intended to form the overlay, while the first one is to be used to paste the other on it. The next step is to make the overlay.

The objects to be aimed at in printing white-letter tablets [i.e., white-letter blocks] are, so far as the bringing-up is concerned, very simple. The tablet should be perfectly firm and solid all over, so that it will print full and deep in colour without an excessive quantity of ink, while the curves and outlines of the letters should be sharp, clean, and free from dip or burr. We shall be assisted in obtaining these results by a carefully cut-out overlay. The pressman should therefore have the sheet pulled for the purpose, and cut out the white parts of all the wording, leaving nothing but the skeleton of the tablet in each of the four cases. These should then be pasted to the sheet with the pin-holes in it and fixed in proper position, by means of two pins, to the parchment which is next the forme.

If the tympan sheet has been laid, as it should have been, before the overlay was cut out, it will now be perfectly dry, and all that remains to be done is to get three pins, one to stick at the bottom of the tympan sheet, and the two others in the offside edge, so as to support the card on the tympan.

If the frisket is now cut out, the preparation of the forme has reached the stage at which the pressman must think of the choice of a roller, the thorough cleaning up of his forme and slab, and the preparation of the colour in which the forme is to be worked. Before doing this and committing himself to the printing of the cards, he may not unprofitably review mentally what he has already done, by asking himself firstly – Is the margin correct? Are the points in their proper position, is their perforation complete, and are they perfectly secure? Is the tympan quite tight, and are there any "bites" in the frisket? If these questions can be answered satisfactorily, he may safely proceed to the next step in the process.

The forme we have just dealt with may be accepted as a type of all tablet work at press, so far as relates to the making ready.

Choice of a Roller

We have now to consider the choice of a roller and the preparation of the ink . . . The sort of roller required is suggested by the forme itself. In the first place, we do not require so good a roller as we should if we were dealing with a forme of solid woodcuts, containing masses of light and shade and much fine engraving. It will be noted that the tablet forme contains no fine engraving – there is scarcely anything in it to keep clear and prevent filling up. A roller, therefore, which is well matured and very firm would be the best for the purpose we have in view; one about a fortnight old, and inclining more to hardness than to softness, would answer the purpose best. In dealing with solid cuts, or with solid tablets printed in black, the objects aimed at generally are to get the maximum of depth and intensity with the minimum of ink, and this result is obtained by using a good dense black, and rolling the forme thoroughly well.

Although this is sufficient for subjects printed in black, it would, in the writer's opinion, be a mistake to apply the same principle to solid subjects printed in colour. It should be borne in mind that black ink is the densest we have, and that the thinnest possible covering is sufficient to blot out the paper. This is not sufficient in solid tablet work printed in colours, the densest of which are less opaque than black; while some of the paler tones would look quite washed out and impoverished if the forme were only kept just full enough to conceal the paper. If this reasoning is correct, it follows, therefore, that tablet work should always be kept full, and this is especially the case with those colours which are themselves remarkable for possessing little body, such, for instance, as the purples made from aniline. There is of course a limit to the quantity of ink proper to be kept on a forme of this description, and when this limit is exceeded, it is at once shown by the absence of sharpness in the outline of the letters.

For white-letter tablet formes, which do not contain any fine engraving, a well-matured roller, free from damp, may generally be chosen. If the tablet contains any fine work, a newer and softer roller must be chosen, with the view of keeping the fine work in the engraving clean. Some colours require rollers which would be wholly unsuitable for others. For instance, browns made from sienna and umber require fresh, new rollers, because these pigments dry so rapidly that the rollers used quickly "go off" and become dry on the surface. Vermilion, on the contrary, requires a very dry roller, no matter what sort of work it may be used for. Chinese blue and carmine require fresh, good rollers, and so do the green lakes. In printing rule work, care should be taken that the rollers are not too damp, or the work will be wiped.

Managing the Ink and Rollers

In dealing with large solid formes, especially if stiff ink be used, in the winter time it is frequently a matter of great difficulty to get into work, both at press and machine. Nor is the difficulty of working very large blocks confined to the cold weather. It is true that automatic brakes have been applied to some of the machines used for this kind of work, which have the effect of easing the cylinder over the impression, thus pulling the sheet gently from the forme. But if it is desired to print the ink at its fullest strength from the largest formes, the machines and presses should be fitted with apparatus for imparting heat, when all difficulties of this sort vanish.

This softening of the colour by means of heat is in every way preferable to reducing the ink with thin varnish or lowering oil, which impoverishes it. It is not at all times possible to avail ourselves of heat, no matter how desirable it may be to make use of it. For example, we may have got fairly into work with a solid forme containing some fine work, printed in a bright light blue (made with ultramarine and white), and for which we should require a tolerably good roller. Assuming that we leave this all right on a Saturday, and that a severe frost occurs between Saturday and Monday morning, we should probably find that the roller had become so hard as to be useless, and that the ink had become set and putty-like from the action of the cold. In the absence of appliances to furnish heat to the slab, it would be necessary, in a case like this, to reduce the ink with a small quantity of thin varnish, and regrind it with this, at the same time adding a small quantity of pure ultramarine ink to compensate for the diminution in body caused by adding the thin varnish.

It sometimes happens during a continuance of wet weather that all the rollers in an office become very damp. A most effective way of dealing with rollers in this condition is to wash them in turps, and wrap them up in blankets which have been made warm. When rollers become very hard and skinny in cold weather, they may be washed in hot water, which will soften them and give them a new face.

In country or small offices, where the supply of rollers is small and the choice limited, and where, therefore, it is not always possible to get a roller to suit the ink, the latter may be modified to suit the roller. Thus, if the rollers are hard and not sharp, some strong varnish may be added to the ink with advantage; while if the rollers are fresh and damp, and do not take up the ink at its normal strength, this treatment must be reversed and thin varnish added. New, soft rollers are, as a rule, not suitable for gold preparations, except in the case of preparations made from sienna or umber, for which fresh rollers are best; because these pigments dry so quickly that unless the roller used be very fresh, it soon goes off.

Assuming that the first working of the show-card forme we have been discussing is to be printed in four different colours, *viz.*, light blue, light green, light purple, and gloss red, a reference to previous pages would tell us that the basis of the light colours would be white ink, of which we have already treated, that is to say, it would consist of flake white ground stiff in middle varnish. A small quantity of either ultramarine or Chinese blue should be added to the white, according to the tone of blue required, the ultramarine looking best, by daylight, and the Chinese best by artificial light. For the green, a small quantity of deep blue-green lake should be added to the white; but if a light green of a yellow tone is wanted, the white must be discarded altogether, and the colour made of lemon chrome and a little Chinese blue, or with the palest shade of drop green lake. The purple must be made with white ink and purple lake, while the gloss red may be made with lake brilliant ground in thick middle varnish. This colour will not be absorbed into the card, but will gloss as it dries.

The main things to be aimed at in tablet work are to get the colours as solid and rich as possible. The richness depends upon the amount of body in the ink, and the solidity depends upon perfect making ready and the thorough clearing of the forme at each impression. If the ink does not clear the forme, it is shown by the "motley" appearance of the printing. Should this happen, it must be controlled by the addition of a little soap or strong varnish.

Making Ready the Second Forme

Turning to the second working, which would be printed in black, and would only consist of the black shading to the lettering, it is only necessary to observe that the blocks would be registered in the way already described in detail, but it will be necessary to change the sheets or blanket we may have inside the tympan, and substitute therefor a thin card and a few sheets of thin paper. This is done with the view of preventing the dipping of those parts of the shades where they come to a point. These should be all carefully cut away in the making ready, and, if time be not an objection, the work would be all the better if an overlay were cut out for them.

Overlays

The preparation of overlays for block colour printing, no less than for black cut work, is an important factor in faithfully reproducing the effect obtained by the artist in his original drawing; only in the case of subjects treated in colour the matter is obviously more complicated than it is in ordinary black cut work, where the printer has but to imitate the effect produced and exhibited by the engraver's india proof. In doing this he has to deal only with one block, in which are contained all the effects of light, shade, and perspective which are produced by gradations of tone in the engraving. In coloured subjects, although the same principles apply generally, yet they are so far modified that many tones of colour enter into the composition and are used in working up the general effect of the picture.

In black cut work the printer has always the cumulative result of his labour before him. In coloured subjects the effect is built up by a succession of impressions in various colours, upon the careful treatment of each of which the ultimate result depends. In black cut work, where the printer has the engraver's india proof to guide him, he may correct his treatment of the making ready as he goes on, because he may compare the strength of every part of his impression with the proof before him; while in colour work he must judge of the strength or weakness of his making ready, not only by the appearance of the impression before him, but by the modifications which will be effected when the subsequent workings are printed. A little deviation from truth in the strength of a colour, or undue hardness in the impression of any of the workings, may be sufficient to distort the perspective and damage the final effect when all the colours are put in.

The method of preparing overlays for colour printing does not materially differ from that adopted in ordinary cut work; the outline block, or last printing, in most colour subjects is in fact a cut which contains all the work in a reduced or skeleton form, as if it were to be printed in one colour.

A well-printed engraving, when thoroughly made ready, should be perfectly flat; there should be no part of it dipping; the light parts should be so softened off that they just print and no more, while the solids should be made absolutely firm. It should be borne in mind that every line in an engraving is intended to print at its exact strength. Therefore, on the one hand, the lights should not be softened so much that they are broken or "rotten," as it is technically termed; nor, on the other hand, should the impression be left so hard that any line prints thicker than is shown in the block itself. In colour blocks where the subject is divided into many colours there must necessarily be large spaces of white in the various blocks; and if proper care be not taken both in the adjustment of the impression and the preparation of the overlays these whites are liable to dip to such an extent as to cause the registration to be faulty.

In order to avoid this, and get the impression as flat as possible, colour formes should be made ready with a very light impression. Then, as the solids are gradually overlaid, they have the effect of bearing off and throwing back the lights, so that it is only necessary generally to cut these away at the edges where any symptoms of dipping are apparent.

In dealing with colour blocks to be worked on dry rolled paper, as is nearly always the case, it is best to paste the extreme solids first on to the sheet, so that the general and intermediate overlays which are pasted on afterwards intervene between them and the forme and so soften their effect.

It is a good plan, in bringing up colour blocks, to use black ink in the process of making ready, because good bookwork black prints better, as a rule, than do most coloured inks. Therefore, if the making ready appears perfect in an impression pulled in black, any imperfection shown when its own colour is used may be safely attributed to the imperfect furnishing of the ink.

The cardinal rule to be observed in the preparation of colour blocks is to avoid all hardness in the impression; it is only by attention to this that the chromo-typographer can hope to compete with his formidable rival, the lithographer. Every succeeding tone of colour should be made to blend with the preceding one, and this result is attained by skilful treatment in the making ready, as well as by a complete agreement of the tones of colour used.

We will endeavour to illustrate this by a few examples. If we take a woodcut engraved to print in one colour – say, for example, of a rose, in which all the work is in the block – we get a more or less faithful reproduction of the form of the flower when the block has been properly overlaid and brought up. If, however, it be intended to produce the same thing in colour, at least two, and possibly three pink blocks would be necessary for the effective bringing out of the flower; while a pale yellow and two green blocks would be required for the reproduction of the leaves and stems. What is given in the first place solely by gradations of tone in the engraving is in the case we are now discussing produced by graduated tones of colour, printing one on the top of the other. In order to produce a true and artistic effect, two things are necessary – first, that the colours themselves should be appropriate in strength and tone, and, secondly, that the making ready should be of the exact strength to cause these tones to blend without undue hardness.

In a set of blocks of this character the yellow working would be a solid flat block (possibly containing a few lights), embracing all the leaves and stems, and in this instance all that the printer need do is to get his impression very firm without the least dipping round the edges. A block of this sort should be made ready as flat as if it were lithographed.

The preparation of the overlay would be very simple, and would consist of only one thickness of paper, because there would be no variety of tone in the engraving for the printer to bring out. He would simply have to pull two pieces of paper, of which the first would be pricked to go inside the tympan, while the second would be used to make the overlay. This would have to be cut close round the edge of every part of the impression and pasted – taking care that the paste is put on very thinly – exactly on to the impression of the first sheet, which would then be placed inside the tympan.

It is of course a matter of extreme importance that the overlay should exactly coincide with the block. If an overlay is not on the block properly, the impression at once shows where it is off, and it must be shifted until it fits the block exactly. On pulling another sheet it should be found that the impression is fairly sound, and that the effect of the overlay has removed most, if not all, of the dips round the edges. If it has not, another sheet should be pulled, and treated in the same manner; only in the second instance it will not be necessary to use such thick paper as was required in the first case.

A couple of sheets thus overlaid should be sufficient for the bringing up of a block of this character; but if any of the edges still dip, they must be cut away in another sheet until the impression is perfectly flat. A good way to test the completeness of the making ready is to pull an impression in black ink on the paper intended to be used. If the block is quite solid and well covered with a fair quantity of ink only, and it shows no signs of dipping round the edges when examined on the back, the bringing up may be considered done.

The second working would be the first tone of green. This would cover up the whole of the stems and all the leaves, except those parts where the full lights were left in the engraving. In making an overlay for a block of this description, where we have only to make sure that those parts which are graduated in the engraving are sufficiently soft, it will not be necessary to use more than two thicknesses of thin paper.

On pulling an impression of this green working it would be found to print almost entirely over the yellow block, except where it would be cut away in the leaves on either side of the central fibre to create the lights, and it is to this point in work of this character that the printer should direct his attention. These lights would start from the solid parts of the green block at the base of the leaves, and would gradually widen until the yellow first working was allowed to burst through it.

Now, if these and similar effects in colour blocks are not properly treated in the making ready, the whole effect is spoiled. Every succeeding tone of colour put in by block after block should be an imitation, as far as possible, of the effect which would be produced by the brush in painting. In the green block we are dealing with, the effect obtained in painting by a number of lines softening off to nothing is imitated by similar lines cut in the block; but if these are left too hard in the impression no artistic effect is produced. And all that has been observed respecting the first green block is equally true respecting the second, which would be of a deeper tone than the first, but there would be no abrupt contrast in the colours. This block would be softened off at the edges in the engraving, so that the tone of one colour gradually merged into that of the preceding one. This, however, is never the case unless the overlaying is skilfully treated.

Two tones of colour like these should so blend with each other that the line which separates the blocks should not be visible. If the impression of the second green block were left hard on the edges, the result of the engraver's art would be thrown away, because, instead of a soft blending of the colours, we should get a hard line and a strong contrast between them. In all those cases, therefore, where tones of colour fall on and merge into each other, the preparation of the overlays should be an imitation of the preparation of the blocks. Where the blocks are softened off in the engraving by means of fine lines starting from a solid and toning down to nothing, the overlays should be similarly treated, and should be cut or scraped away on the slant to give a gradual increase or diminution of the impression.

Reading 24.13
Chromotype-Printing
from *The Printer's Manual* by Thomas Lynch (1859, pp. 207–208).

Lynch describes a stencil technique that was used for adding color to letterpress images. This same technique was used in the fifteenth century to add color to playing cards, and on occasion, to book illustrations. In later centuries, stencils were also used to color intaglio and planographic prints. Lynch is using *chromotype printing* to apply color to railroad maps, as well as borders to large broadsides. He calls this latter application *illuminated printing*. Since I have not come across this term in any other printers' manual, it may be unique to him.

This type of printing required no more than a stencil for each color, a variety of brushes, some fine-grained sponges, and water-base colors. Lynch also describes how to prepare the colors.

Being a very slow hand process, chromotype printing had limited commercial relevance. During the last decade of the nineteenth and the first two of the twentieth century, it was most often used for art prints and illustrations in deluxe editions. Today, this process is better known by its French name *pochoir*. The best manual on the subject is *Traité d'enluminure d'arte au pochoir* (1925) by Jean Saudé.

This kind of work, although generally called by the above name, is not printing, in the strict sense of the word; because, part of it only is done at the printing-press, the remainder being finished by the use of stencils and water-colors. Chromotype-printing is employed to put in the colors of the maps in such jobs as the large cards printed for railroad-companies, and for coloring parts of the borders of large cards. The latter kind of work is called illuminated-printing.

The stencil is formed by pulling an impression of the job on a card, and cutting out the parts intended for one of the colors; a new stencil being cut for each of them. The colors must be laid on with a fine-grained sponge or soft camel-hair brush.

Any color which can be used for maps may be applied to this purpose. The following will answer very well:

Red. – Steep ground brazil-wood in vinegar, and add a small quantity of alum.

Steep cochineal in water, strain it, and add a sufficient amount of gum-arabic to keep it from depositing.

Dissolve litmus in water and add spirits of wine.

Yellow. – Dissolve gamboge in water; or, steep french-berries in water, strain the liquor and add gum-arabic.

Blue. – Dissolve prussian-blue in water and add some gum-arabic.

To a solution of litmus add distilled vinegar.

Green. – Dissolve verdigris or sap-green in water and add gum-arabic.

A solution of litmus may be rendered green by adding a small quantity of any of the alkalies to it.

Ox-gall can be added, to brighten any of these colors.

Reading 24.14
Collotype Prints
from *Photo-Engraving, Photo-Litho and Collotype* by W. T. Wilkinson (1890, pp. 113–114, 121–128).

Collotype – as it is generally called in England and America – is just one of several processes employing a swelled-gelatine plate. The process was invented in 1854 by a Frenchman, Alphonse Louis Poitevin (1819–1882). *Phototype*, as he called it, was not introduced into England, however, until 1865 when a pair of Frenchmen, Cyprien Marie Tessie du Motay (1819–1880) and Charles Raphael M. de Marechal took out a British patent for it. Within a short time, there were dozens of similar processes on the market, among them *lichtdruck* (relief printing by light), *albertype, artotype, ink photo,* and *heliotype.* The prints could be editioned on either hand or rolling presses.

Toward the end of the nineteenth century, it became more of an art technique than a letterpress process. Very little was written about the collotype process in the majority of nineteenth-century printers' manuals – one reason was that the making of gelatine plates was considered a separate trade. In addition to Wilkinson's book, there were several other noteworthy texts on the subject, such as *Collotype and Photo-Lithography* (1889) by Julius Schnauss and *Practical Guide to Photographic and Photomechanical Printing* (1887) by William Kinnimond Burton. One of the best twentieth-century manuals on the subject is *The Practice of Collotype* (1935) by Thomas A. Wilson.

I have focused on Wilkinson's instructions for printing collotypes on an Albion press. On pp. 114–120 in his manual, he discusses "Preparing the Collotype Plate" and "Sensitive Collotype Mixture." On p. 117, he describes coating the plate with a solution of stale beer and syrupy silicate of soda, a procedure that is repeated below.

In the processes of Photo-Zincography and Photo-[Lithography], the original must be a drawing or engraving in line, dot, or stipple, but in Collotype, negatives from nature can be used, and prints made at press or machine in ink, the smooth half-tones being represented in the same degree of gradation as in an ordinary silver photograph.

Collotype prints are made from a thin film of bichromated gelatine dried upon a plate of thick glass, exposed to light under a negative from nature, the film of gelatine taking ink from the roller exactly in proportion to the amount of action of the light during such exposure.

Negatives for Collotype must be of the very best quality, soft, without flatness, brilliant, without hardness, possessing full gradations of tone from the deepest shadow to the highest light; negatives that are hard and under-exposed, or flat and dirty, are quite useless for Collotype.

Negatives for Collotype may be made either by the wet collodion or by the gelatine dry plate process, the wet process being best when film negatives are required, that being the best form of negative for printing from upon the Collotype plate, contact being so easily obtained between the whole of the negative and the Collotype plate; that not being the case with negatives upon the ordinary dry plates of commerce, they being as a rule far from flat, and either break in the printing frame, or give a blurred image.

Negatives for Collotype must be reversed, and if made with a reversing mirror behind the lens, either by the wet or dry process, patent plate glass should be used to make them upon, or may be made without the mirror, and then stripped and (in the case of a wet collodion plate) made into a flexible film, or, (if a dry plate) taken from its original plate, and transferred to a sheet of patent plate glass.

Negatives for Collotype that are too valuable to run the risk of stripping must be reproduced; a carbon transparency being first made, the reversed negative being made from this, by contact upon an ordinary dry plate.

If the gelatine dry process be used, the new celluloid films will be found very good indeed, being flexible, contact is easily obtained in the printing frame. . . .

Presses &c. for Collotype

For the production of prints from the collotype plate, a press, a leather lithographic roller, a typographic roller of glue and treacle, inking slab, ink, thin lithographic varnish, sponge, damping rag, mask frames, parchment paper, gold size, and a good sample of paper upon which to pull the proof are required.

The press used may be a typographic press of the form called Albion, an ordinary Lithographic press, or a special press made for collographic printing, of which there are several in the market.

If an Albion press is used, the platen should be lowered so that the requisite printing pressure can be obtained without the use of an inordinate amount of backing. To use an Albion press a piece of thick plate glass is first put on the bed with a sheet of white blotting paper underneath, upon this sheet of glass is placed another sheet of wet blotting paper, the collotype plate being placed upon this, the wet blotting paper holding the plate firm, and forming a couch for the collotype plate. . . .

Whichever form of press be used, the operation of printing from the plate will be just the same so that each operator can adopt that press which is handiest to him.

To obtain clean margins in a collotype print the plate must be masked, as it is impossible to get a clean margin without doing so.

There are various methods of masking, but the best way is to use an iron frame, made to fit over the collotype plate, this frame being covered with a sheet of thin parchment paper, the edges of paper being gummed or pasted round the iron frame, the paper wetted, and when dry it will be like a drum head, a coat of gold size painted upon the underside of parchment paper will, when dry, give a mask that with care will last a 1000 impressions. For a plate 13 by 10, the mask frame should be made of quarter inch iron rod, inside measurement of frame being 13¼ by 10¼, the inside corners to be square, the outside corners, either round or square, at least three of these frames should be provided for each press, so that in case of an accident to the mask, another one can be got ready in a few minutes, instead of delaying the work till the pasted paper and gold size are dry.

The rollers are very important and must be of the very [best], the leather roller which is used first, must be a best French skin, of the quality known to lithographers as a nap or chalk roller, *i.e.,* the grain of leather must be outside. A new roller must be properly prepared before use, and that will take from three to six weeks to accomplish, and when in good order it must be very carefully kept. . . . The beginner is strongly advised to buy his first roller ready for use, which can be done at an advance of about ³⁄₆ or ⁵⁄- upon the list price of a new roller. The best sizes of rollers are 10 inches and 12 inches long. With the rollers a pair of leather handles are requisite.

The second roller may also be of leather, but in this case a different kind of roller is required, *viz*: a colour roller in which the grain of leather is outside, these rollers require no preparation, beyond being kept clean, and free from ink when not in use.

The general form of second roller however, is a typographic roller of glue and treacle cast in seamless mould, and may be purchased from any Lithographic or Letterpress dealer.

The inking slabs (two) may be thin lithographic stones, or sheets of zinc screwed upon wood blocks, the size of these slabs should be at least 18 inches by 15 inches, so as to have plenty of room for rolling up the ink.

The ink must be the best quality lithographic ink, the black ink being known as best chalk ink; for making coloured inks, brown, sepia, red, and blue, are mixed in various proportions, to get the effect desired.

The ink as received is far too stiff to use and will require deluting with thin lithographic varnish, the ink and varnish being mixed either with a stone muller, or a strong palette knife.

The paper upon which the collotype prints are made must be of the best quality, with a smooth surface, a good enamel paper giving the richest prints, closely followed by Dickinson's Art Printing Paper, or a good plate paper. . . .

Printing from the Collotype Plate

To prepare the collotype plate for the press it is first soaked in cold water for an hour, the back is then cleaned from any clots of gelatine that may have flowed over the edges during coating, the plate is then wiped with a soft sponge and dabbed with a damp soft rag, placed upon a levelling stand, and the surface covered with the so called etcher composed of –

Glycerine	5 ounces.
Water	10 ounces.
Oxgall	10 drops.

This is allowed to act for half an hour, during which time the press must be prepared, the nap roller scraped, the ink mixed, the second roller washed with turpentine, the slabs cleaned down with turpentine and a rag, and the printing paper cut to size; the mask frame should have been covered some time previously, and the gold size be quite dry.

All being ready the glycerine mixture is removed from the plate with a sponge, the plate placed upon the bed of press, the film dabbed with a soft cloth until the surface is dry, it is then rolled up with the leather roller, slowly and with plenty of pressure, when if all operations previously have been carefully attended to, the shadows will first take ink, followed by the middle half-tones, the rolling being continued slowly and carefully until the picture is evenly inked with perhaps more than the proper proportion of ink upon the shadows, and little or none upon the high lights; now take the second roller charged with ink a little thinner, (*i.e.* mixed with more thin varnish) and roll over the plate using a quicker motion, and less pressure, the result of which will be, that the surplus ink upon the shadows will be removed, and the lights will receive their due proportion, the image being more harmonious throughout. A mask is now laid over the plate in such a manner that the iron frame encircles the plate, the top being flush with the surface of plate, the image can be seen through the goldsized parchment paper, and a slight pressure of the finger upon the margin of print, will leave an impression of the picture upon the mask, which is now lifted away. Now roll up the picture again, first using the leather roller, then the second roller as before.

The mask is now placed upon a spare sheet of glass in the same position that it occupied upon the inked up plate, and after carefully measuring the mask upon the surface, two lines at right angles to each other, by which the paper must be laid so as to get the collotype image in its proper position upon the sheet of paper to be used. This being done, the paper upon which the image is impressed is cut away, using a straight edge and a sharp knife to get a good edge, and cutting the aperture about a sixteenth of an inch larger all round than the actual size of picture, so that the mask will not cut into the margin too close up to the picture.

The mask is now placed over the inked up plate, and the opening will show the image, whilst the margin of plate will be covered by the parchment paper between the opening and the frame.

Lay the printing paper upon the mask, putting the edges, against the lines marked for the lay upon the printing paper put a sheet or two of blotting paper, lower the tympan, run the bed of the press under the platen … then carefully feel for the amount of pressure and if correct pull through, then return the bed, lift the tympan, remove the print and examine, if the ink has come away in patches the pressure has been too light, and more must be given for the next impression, a heavy pressure must not be used, or the plate will be sure to smash.

Should the print be very weak and flat, the ink is perhaps too thin, and must be mixed with fresh ink from the tin. Ink for collotype printing must have very little varnish with it, in fact only just sufficient to allow the ink to be spread upon the roller.

If the film has not been sufficiently soaked, the picture will also be flat, but in this case the margin will take as much ink as the shadows, in this case sprinkle a little turpentine over the plate; then deluge with water and wipe clean with a soft rag, cover the film with the etching solution of glycerine and water, and allow from half an hour to an hour to soak in, then wipe off and ink up again, do not waste the glycerine solution as it improves with use.

Sometimes after long etching and with very stiff ink, the image remains without high lights, in this case wash out with turpentine as before, wipe surface dry, then wash over quickly with –

Glycerine	5 ounces.
Water	20 ounces.
Cyanide of potassium	10 grains.

And as quickly wash off with a sponge saturated with water.

After a drastic course of this kind the plate may refuse to take ink at all, in which case remove from the press, and let the film dry again, then etch for half an hour, and ink up. The cause of this refusal is simply on account of the cyanide having softened the gelatine, the film has absorbed too much water, and consequently it cannot take ink, the drying down gets rid of the water, and restores the film to its normal state.

When any particular portions of the picture are wanted lighter than the rest, the plate should be wiped dry, and those portions painted over with the etcher, leaving it to soak in, for say fifteen minutes, then cover the whole film for ten minutes, wipe dry and roll up.

After each print is made, the mask is removed, the plate damped with the etching solution, by means of a sponge, then wiped or dabbed off with a soft damp rag, before again inking up.

Different tints of ink can be made by mixing several colours together, but it will be far better to buy the tints from the dealers, as it will then be mixed so much better than can be done by hand.

These preliminary stages of a collotype plate are very important, as if not properly carried out the subsequent operations will only be lost time, the old films must be thoroughly removed and the surface well re-ground, the silicate of soda and beer must be well filtered and sufficiently stale before use; if the mixture of beer and silicate after standing a few hours (after mixing) precipitates in a flocculent mass, the silicate is not good, and a fresh sample should be obtained; the beer and silicate should be kept at least six hours before using.

Instead of beer albumen may be used, the whites of five eggs, mixed with ten ounces of water, well beaten up, then add two ounces of silicate of soda, and keep six hours before use.

The plan of using a substratum of bichromated albumen, or gelatine, is not recommended as it is troublesome and tedious, and demands the use of a tank of hot water in which to soak the plate before coating with the sensitive gelatine solution, else the collotype film will peel off under the roller.

Reading 24.15

Printing Collotypes in Color

from *American Dictionary of Printing and Bookmaking* by Wesley Washington Pasko (1894, p. 102)

From the 1840s on, chromo-lithography played a major role in book illustration. A decade later, with the advent of photomechanical processes, photography was also used to transfer images to zinc lithographic plates. In the 1860s, the same process was adapted for making gelatine plates for single-color collotypes.

Even though many color prints were still being produced by letterpress, the discovery of color photography in 1861 by James Clerk Maxwell (1831–1879) and the introduction of color filters in the 1870s made it possible to print collotypes in multiple colors. Pasko restricts his entry on collotypes to printing them in color. The process for making the plates would have been the same regardless of the number of colors (see Reading 24.14 above). It is interesting to note that a piece of colored glass was used to filter out one color from another. Even after the invention of the full-color separation process in 1890, collotypes printed from relief plates rarely took advantage of this new technique.

Regarding production runs of collotypes, Philip Gaskell in his *A New Introduction to Bibliography* (1974, p. 271) says, "1,500 impressions from a single plate could be printed on a hand press at the rate of 200–300 a day."

This is a method of preparing a process plate by gelatine, in its basis like the albertype or heliotype. [Josef] Albert [1825–1886], [Edward] Bierstadt [1824–1906], [Albert] Frisch [d. 1818] and others have succeeded in producing very beautiful pictures in colors by preparing several gelatine plates, each plate bearing particular parts of the picture and being used for printing the appropriate colored ink. As many as seven different plates are employed successively in producing the picture. There are different methods in use for preparing the several plates. One plan is to make a separate negative for each color. This is accomplished by interposing a suitable screen of colored glass or colored liquid between the object and the photographic plate in the camera. For example, a screen which shuts out all colors except blue will permit only the blue portions of the picture to be photographed on the negative, and a gelatine plate from this negative may be used for printing with blue ink. In a similar way another screen will furnish a negative and plate for the red portions of the picture, and so on. Another plan is to prepare the gelatine plates from one and the same negative by stopping out all of the picture except that of one color.

Reading 24.16
Photo-Engraving Using the Swelled-Gelatine Process
from *The American Printer* by Thomas MacKellar (1885, pp. 39–40).

When MacKellar uses the term "photo-engraving," he is not referring to a *halftone*, but to a photomechanical process that was used to transfer a line image to a gelatine plate by means of a photographic negative. The principle is the same as collotype except that the gelatine plate, in this case, was not used as a printing surface, but as a mold to create a relief cast in plaster or wax that would be used to make a stereotype plate.

First, the image was photographed at twice the required size. With pen and ink, the artist recreated the image in thin lines and stippled dots directly on the photograph, which was used only as a pattern. Next, the photograph was bleached, leaving only the pen-and-ink drawing, after which, a photograph of the drawing – reduced to its finished size – was taken. The negative was placed on top of a sensitized gelatine plate and exposed. The parts that came into contact with light were hardened. When the gelatine was soaked in water, the soft areas – the whites not hardened by the light – would swell. The gelatine plate could also be washed in warm water, which would dissolve the soft parts, leaving the hardened parts standing in relief. The gelatine plate was then used to make an electrotype. MacKellar refers to this as the "wash-out," or "photo-electrotype" process.

MacKellar mentions Joseph Nicéphore Niépce (1765–1833), whose early experiments with photography began in 1813. Niépce also produced the first photographic image in 1822. His research made photomechanical processes possible.

Photo-engravings are produced by means of photography. It is a fact worthy of note that experiments in photographic engraving gave rise to photography itself. The aim of Nicéphore Niepce, when he began his researches in 1813, was not only to fix the image obtained by the camera obscura on a plate of metal, but to convert this plate into an engraving which could be used on a printing-press; but his early death prevented his perfecting the process to which he had devoted much time and study. From that time experimenting has been continued by others, and the result is the production of a number of different processes of photo-engraving. The most popular of these is known as the swelled gelatine process, though the plate is somewhat inferior in point of depth, and must be handled by the engraver with considerable skill.

This method of engraving has an advantage over wood-engraving in the matter of cheapness; but it has countervailing disadvantages, and there are very many subjects in which wood engraving surpasses all methods of process engraving.

To reproduce a drawing for printing purposes, the picture should be formed of clean, sharp, and very black lines or dots on perfectly white paper. Flat tints and washed or blurred shadows cannot be photo-engraved, unless they are first translated into lines or stipple. Where an engraving is to represent a piece of machinery or portrait, for example, a photograph of the object is taken twice the size the plate is to be when finished. The photograph, or silver print, as it is technically called, on which the drawing is to be made, is not toned, but simply fixed in a fresh fixing bath, and then thoroughly washed and dried. It is now ready for the artist, who, with pen and suitable ink, draws directly on the silver print, making in delicate lines and dots the lights and shadows of the photograph. After the drawing is complete the photograph is bleached, by pouring upon it an alcoholic solution of bi-chloride of mercury, leaving the ink lines of the artist on clean white paper. The advantage of this method of drawing is at once apparent. The artist has the advantage of working directly on and over the enlarged photograph of a person, machine, landscape, or building, thus securing a perfect likeness of the object.

After the drawing is finished it is sent to the gallery, where a negative is taken of it, reducing it generally one-half. The importance of this part of the process can hardly be over-estimated, for on the sharpness and opacity of the negative depends the perfection of the subsequent electrotype. The focus of the camera is adjusted with a microscope upon a fibre of paper laid upon the drawing. The sensitive plate is then exposed to the drawing for a few moments, when it is taken into the dark room and developed, after which it is treated chemically until the part representing the white portions of the picture becomes perfectly opaque, while those parts representing the black lines in the drawing remain as clear as the glass itself. This negative is then sent to the gelatine room. All the light entering this room passes through yellow screens, so that, although it is well lighted, it is photographically dark, as yellow light has no effect upon the sensitive gelatine. In this room the gelatine is dissolved, made sensitive, poured on large lights of plate-glass, and chilled by being placed in a gelatine refrigerator for a few moments, when it is taken out and placed in the gelatine drying-box, where a current of dry air is constantly passing over it. When dry, it is sensitive to white light, and is ready for exposure under the negative. The necessary exposure varies from one to thirty minutes in direct sunlight.

On removing the gelatine from the negative, the picture is plainly seen, every dot and line on the negative having been duplicated upon the gelatine by the action of light, which renders the parts so acted upon insoluble, while the portions of gelatine protected by the opacity of the negative from the action of light remain perfectly soluble, and may be swelled up by immersion in cold water, so as to form a mould for a relief cast in plaster or wax, or may be washed away with warm water, so as to leave the insoluble portions raised and in relief. The former method is known as the "swelled-gelatine" process, and the latter as the "wash-out" or photo-electrotype process. The casts from swelled gelatine are reproduced in metal by the stereotype process, and the washed-out reliefs are electrotyped. Each method has peculiar advantages for certain classes of work.

Reading 24.17
Process Blocks
from *A Practical Manual of Typography and Reference Book for Printers* by Arthur Oldfield (1890, pp. 145–146).

> *Process blocks* is the generic term for mechanically produced blocks. These blocks replaced much of the work that would have been done on wood. In this reading, Oldfield is describing an early type of linecut called "zinco-blocks" or "zincotypes." For process blocks, the image was drawn on a piece of lithographic transfer paper and then conveyed to a zinc plate by means of a rolling press. The plate was eventually placed in a series of acid baths. Great care had to be taken in order to keep the acid from underbiting the image. Before each bath, the raised portions of the image would be protected from further contact with the acid by a coat of shellac varnish. A similar process had been attempted earlier by William Blake (1757–1827) when he used relief-etched plates for his *Songs of Innocence* (1789).
>
> Oldfield mentions *Zincography, or Process Block-making* by Josef Böch. He is actually referring to the English editions of Böch's *Die Zinkographie in der Buchdruckerkunst* (1885) that were published in the late 1880s under the title *Zincography, a Practical Guide to the Art as Practiced in Connection with Letterpress Printing.* Böch's is not a photomechanical process, although in later years, a photographic negative replaced the lithographic transfer paper on which the original drawings were made.
>
> To add to the confusion, the term *zincography* was also used for another very different printing process, lithography. As its popularity increased, lithographic printers sought faster and cheaper methods for creating images. From its inception, Bavarian stone had been used; however, during the 1850s, it was discovered that images could be transferred to zinc plates and printed on lithographic presses.

The art of producing raised surface blocks for letterpress printing from zinc is termed Zincography. The process is not difficult, and the expense for plant, &c., trifling. Hence this process has been made to replace much of the work hitherto done by the wood-engraver. We will endeavour briefly to explain in what the process consists, our information being derived from the excellent handbook on "Zincography, or Process Blockmaking," in which work the whole process is much more fully explained, as well as illustrated. This handbook forms one of the manuals comprised in "Wyman's Technical Series."

The materials required are as follow: – Etching-box, which must be so arranged that it can be given a rocking motion, either by hand or mechanically; a litho. transfer press; a washing-trough; hot plate; various brushes and etching tools; five rollers, litho., – three leather-covered, one cloth, and one velvet-covered.

The drawing or print must first be obtained on a specially-prepared paper, ordinary litho. retransfer paper will do. The drawing should be made with ordinary litho. writing ink, or ordinary printing ink, thinned down. The sheet of transfer containing the drawing upon it is placed between damp sheets of paper, and, when sufficiently moist, is taken and placed, drawing side downwards, on a prepared zinc plate, a few sheets of paper placed on the top, and a glazed board; and the whole is then put through the press, at first with light, and then with gradually increasing pressure. The drawing should be examined several times, and damped with a wet sponge. When sufficiently pressed, the plate is immersed in water for a short time, when the paper may be taken away, the composition washed off, and the design will be found transferred to the zinc plate.

The plate next requires rolling up, preparatory to etching; the design is first washed, and the hard roller used with hard resisting ink. It is dried, and then dusted with powdered resin.

The plate is then immersed in a bath composed of 60 parts of water and 20 of nitric acid, and rocked for a quarter of an hour, then it is taken out, rinsed, and dried, and rolled up again, and all places, which are not required to be acted upon by the acid are stopped out with shellac varnish. The plate is again immersed in the acid bath for some minutes, and then taken out, rolled up, and heated so as to cause the ink to run down the sides. This is done to prevent the acid from eating away the foundation of the design.

The plate undergoes this treatment for the two last immersions; the cloth-covered and velvet-covered rollers are used in rolling up, and softer ink, so as to go down the sides of the design, and only allow the acid to act in making the whites deeper. The lines in a design should be wide at the bottom. After the requisite etching has been done, the plate is dried, trimmed, and mounted.

The zinc plate, before being transferred upon, should be thoroughly cleaned. It should also have the surface roughened by being immersed in a weak acid bath.

This brief outline is sufficient to give some idea of the principles of the process, but the student or printer who may wish to master the art of Process Block-making should not fail to procure the manual on "Zincography, or Process Block-making," by Josef Bock; for, as the *Printers' Register* pointed out a short time ago, "Mr. Bock's book enables any one of ordinary capacity to make zinco-blocks effectively, readily, and economically."

Reading 24.18
Printing from Half-Tone Process Blocks
from *Practical Printer* by John Southward (1900, vol. I, pp. 762–768, 770–771)

> The halftone plate – which was invented by Frederick Eugene Ives (1856–1937) of Philadelphia in the 1880s – was primarily used for news work; however, by the end of the century, it too had made significant inroads as a viable illustration technique for book work. Southward explains the whole process from making the plate through printing it. Today, halftone plates are seldom printed on handpresses.
>
> The procedures for making halftones were the same as those for linecuts, the only difference being the intervention of a screen during photography for converting a continuous-tone image into small dots of various sizes. Since printers were able to print directly from the resulting plates – and new plates could easily be made from the original artwork – there was no need to make stereotypes or electrotypes from them.
>
> It is curious to note that even though MacKellar used a halftone portrait of himself as the frontispiece to the 1893 edition of his manual (see **Fig. 24.10**), he did not mention the process in any edition of his *The American Printer*.

Fig. 24.10. *Halftone portrait of MacKellar* – from MacKellar (1893, frontispiece)

Proofs at the handpress were taken without a tympan, which accounts for the lack of tympans on some nineteenth-century handpresses. The inked block was centered on the bed, a sheet of proof paper was placed on top of it, followed by two or three more sheets of paper and a piece of hard-glazed cardboard, which served as the packing. Vignettes were proofed either face down or face up depending on the nature of the cut. For cuts with soft edges, four or five sheets of well-glazed paper were laid down on the bed, covered by the proof paper. The inked block was then placed face down on these. Southward does not mention placing any packing between the block and the platen. Vignettes with hard edges were proofed like full-image bordered blocks.

Printers did not always agree about how to make ready these halftone blocks. Some treated them no differently than wood engravings – underlaying and overlaying them. The best printers, however, used only underlays.

Linecuts and halftone plates were usually made by specialists. Bishop includes a tipped-in leaf for the Lux Engraving Co. of Boston. The recto (**Fig. 24.11**) shows an example of their work, a halftone portrait of a young woman; the verso (**Fig. 24.12**) describes the company's services.

Fig. 24.11. *Half-tone* – from Bishop (1891, facing p. 152). **Figs. 24.11** and **24.12** courtesy of University of Iowa Libraries.

Fig. 24.12. *Advertisement for Lux Engraving Co.* – from Bishop (1891, facing p. 153)

Southward describes the history and process of halftone engravings. Commercial arc lights, which had been used since the 1840s, gave platemakers more control over the exposure. Even though these plates had shallow bites, the whole surface, including the white areas, was covered with a dot pattern which prevented the paper from sinking into the whites. An enlargement of these dots in **Fig. 24.13** shows the range of comparative sizes. Since the image was on the surface, these blocks required less makeready than wood engravings.

Before giving instruction in printing from half-tone process blocks it will be well to state very briefly how these blocks are made, for unless their nature be fully comprehended by the pressman he cannot perform his work with them with intelligence, and they now form a portion of the printer's plant almost as important as his types, for their cheapness and rapid production have caused them largely to supersede woodcuts, and to permit of illustrations which otherwise would be impossible.

Half-tone process blocks are the result of an invention of Herr [Georg] Meisenbach [1841–1912] of Munich, made about the year 1882. What but for his process would be an ordinary photographic negative is broken up into dots of varying magnitude, and a print from this dotted or stippled negative is obtained upon a smooth surface of zinc or copper, which is afterwards etched with an acid, the white parts being eaten away and the various sized dots being left. It is these which receive the printing ink and give the impression.

The breaking up of the picture is performed by putting in the camera just before the sensitised plate, which is to become the negative, a glass screen ruled with crossed lines. Such screens have now been brought to great perfection, mainly by [Max and Louis] Levy of Philadelphia, and the best cost large sums of money. The lines number from 55 to 200 to the inch – those for newspaper work ranging from 60 to 85, those for the finest art work ranging from 160 upwards, and those for ordinary work ranging from 120 to 135. Obviously the more the lines the finer the dots will be and the more perfect the picture, but correspondingly the more difficult will be the printing.

The following is a short description of the making of a half-tone block: The drawing, photograph, or other picture is placed on a vertical screen, and then by means of a camera and powerful arc-lights it is photographed through one of the ruled screens mentioned, a stippled negative being the result. Then a polished plate of zinc is evenly covered with a sensitising solution and dried, and after the negative has been developed and fixed in a dark room, the plate is put under the negative in a photographer's printing frame and exposed to the rays of a powerful arc-light. Over-printing is guarded against by watching the effect of the light on sensitised paper, placed close to the negative. The printing being accomplished, the plate is rolled with transfer ink and turpentine, and then developed with water, the parts of film on the plate not acted on by light being removed by gentle rubbing with cotton wool. An artist now retouches the negative plate if any part is defective, and the plate is then put in a bath of nitric acid, which etches it, biting away all parts not covered by the film. The plate, having been sufficiently etched, is now handed to a printer, who, with a hand press, pulls a proof from it. If any part seems to require amendment it is operated upon by a skilled engraver with his graving tools, and in any case he cuts out parts which should show up white. The plate is then passed to a router who, with a fast revolving drill, cuts away all parts not intended to show, and this done it is mounted or fixed on a block of hard wood so as to be type high. It is now ready for the printer, and on examining it with a magnifying glass it will be seen that where in the drawing the parts are blackest the dots are so large and close together that they run into one another, and that where the light parts in the drawing appear the dots are fine and far apart, the varying size and spaces between the dots giving the gradations in tone.[*]

The annexed illustration [**Fig. 24.13**] shows a small part of a half-tone block greatly magnified. The difference in the size of the dots and the way in which the largest dots run into one another will be observed, and the effect can be estimated by looking at the illustration from a considerable distance.

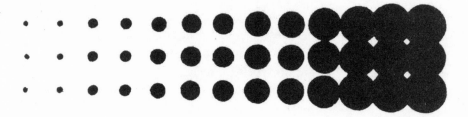

Fig. 24.13. *Magnified half-tone dot pattern*

As the dots are produced by very fine points of metal, the white parts being eaten away with acid, it sometimes happens that in taking electrotypes of the original blocks the wax in the mould gets under the dots during pressure and some of these get torn away when the mould is removed. Hence electrotypes of half-tone blocks are often not so satisfactory as those of engravings, and the best work is done from the original blocks.

For the printer to do full justice to half-tone blocks requires (1) a high-class press or machine in perfect condition, which will give a quite even and rigid impression; (2) soft-sized paper of a high grade, with a beautifully finished face; if double-surfaced or enamelled so much the better, but the enamel should be dull, and should not have been brushed so as to be made to glisten; (3) the finest ink, whether black or coloured, stiff yet soft and velvety; (4) hard, well-seasoned rollers, of the glycerine type, accurately cast, and with unimpaired surfaces; (5) the most ample distribution; (6) the most thorough inking, with just the right quantity of ink; (7) a very hard-packed

---

[*] The reader who wants detailed instruction in the making of these blocks is referred to such books as *The Half-tone Process* [1896], by Julius Verfasser, and *Half-tone on the American Basis* [1896], by William [i.e., Wilhelm] Cronenberg, both published by Percy Lund & Co. at 2s.

tympan, platen or cylinder, as the case may be, in perfectly even condition; and (8) just the right make-ready.

On the subject of the make-ready opinions differ. It is of course universally admitted that blocks or plates must be evenly type high and rigidly mounted, but whether they should be under-laid or overlaid or both is a matter of discussion. Most printers underlay with hard paper, if neces-sary, to obtain a perfectly level surface, and then overlay to get the proper gradations of tone; yet there are some, and among them men who have produced strikingly beautiful work, who insist that all the making ready should be in the underlay, no overlay being used. When overlays are made they should be very thin, made with hard paper, and carefully graduated at the edges; they may run to three or even four thicknesses, and of course they must be fixed up very securely and very accurately.

Taking Proofs of Half-tone Process Blocks

Mr. Noble, junior, who had a great experience with some of the first makers of process blocks in London, described in the *Printers' Register* his methods of proving the blocks. After stating his preference for an Albion press with a satin tympan and discussing the necessity for a perfectly rigid and even mounting surface, whether of board or iron, he declares his decided preference for fine paper with an extra coat of enamel, and continues: "Important as the paper undoubtedly is, it would not be of much utility if a cheap and unsuitable ink were used. Here the best the market can produce will no doubt be found to be the most economical in the long run. A hard ink, not far removed from litho ink in body, and which when used gives a rich, velvety black and dries rich and velvety, is what is wanted. Of course there are blocks where a bright ink would be out of place, notably those made from chalk drawings, which should be proofed in a greyish ink, and, by the way, very little of it used. Line blocks as a rule should also be proofed in this ink, as greyness improves them. But these exceptions are not many, and the proofer, if he has any artistic knowl-edge at all, and is given a chance of seeing the original, will readily discriminate. To manipulate this hard ink, see that you have got the right rollers. Do not attempt to use the ordinary printer's varieties, as they will not do at all; they are too soft and 'fresh' when new; and even when they are, say, a twelvemonth old, and are sufficiently dry and tough, a damp wet day is enough to render them utterly useless; for few things have a greater capacity for absorbing moisture than a patent roller. Now, gelatine is quite unaffected by changes in the atmosphere, and is of the right consis-tency; that is to say, it is hard without being glassy, and, in our opinion, is the best known substance for these rollers.

"With the press level, and the ink and paper what they should be, the proofer's task should be an easy one. In the case of most of the ordinary square blocks, his second impression should be his finished proof, though of course vignettes are not included among these – they take longer and require more skill. Let us now suppose we have to proof a few blocks of a varied char-acter, and see how they are to be done. We take an unmounted half-tone about 6 by 8. Before inking it up, we touch it over with a dry brush – this removes dust and metal chips and helps to keep the roller clean. Having rolled it up and placed it in the centre of the mounting board, we lay a piece of proofing paper on the top, and then two or three sheets more paper, with a piece of hard glazed cardboard, and take the impression. With this impression we see what is required in the way of underlay, which we supply, and then clean the plate with turps, dry it well and care-fully remove all pieces of fluff and rag. Then pull again, and this time, if it has been rolled up intelligently and the weight of the impression accurately judged, the proof should be as good a one as can be got from the plate. We next deal with a mounted vignette about 6 by 5. [Wiping] off our mounting board and seeing that the bed of the press is clean and smooth, we lay upon it from four to five sheets of well-glazed paper, and on these the paper, enamelled side up, for our first impression. Then, having inked up our block, we lay it face downwards upon the paper and pull it upside down. By this method an extremely hard impression is obtained that gives the unprotected edges of the vignetted block no chance to dip. Our pull shows that the edges print hard, while the solids in the centre require a deal more pressure to make them print firmly. To remedy this we underlay it in much the same way as ordinarily, but with this difference, that the underlay must in this case be what we may call an exaggerated one; that is to say, one must patch up the solids and throw away the edges to about three times the extent that would be required were the block to be pulled face upwards in the ordinary manner. A little practice is no doubt required in 'feeling' the impression, as in this case a very little difference one way or the other will spoil the proof. But when the necessary skill has been acquired, this method affords the means of obtaining good proofs in a very short space of time. All vignettes, however, are not susceptible of this treatment, as sometimes parts that require a good deal of impression are in too close proximity to soft edges that require hardly any. These have to be pulled face upwards and the edges made soft by a little rough overlaying on the tympan. This can be well done with two sheets. In the first, cut away the edges to the extent of a nonpareil, and in the second tear the edges roughly round; while to obviate any suddenness, place a few sheets of tissue paper next the block when the proof is pulled. A little billiard chalk placed on the edges after the block has been rolled up will also assist in obtaining a quick proof of a vignette. This may not sound legitimate, but there are tricks in every trade."

Proofs obtained in this way can be had in fifteen to twenty minutes....

Half-tones in Colours

It is now very common to print half-tone blocks in coloured inks, but to our mind none do them justice so well as black, except perhaps the various photo-browns. Maroons and dark greens give good effects, but bright, light colours should be eschewed, and whatever inks are used they should be free working, as most of those compounded with lakes are, and of the best and finest description. Ochres and other earth pigments must be avoided, for they fill up the fine work in the blocks. Ultramarine too always works thick, and therefore when blue is wanted, one composed of cobalt or cyanide of iron is to be chosen....

[Line Blocks]

Line blocks are produced photographically from line drawings, in the same way as process blocks are made, only in this case no breaking up into stipple is required, and consequently no lined screens are introduced into the camera. The lines in these blocks are solid, and the blocks themselves are dealt with by the printer like coarse wood engravings. These blocks can be printed on low-grade papers, and do not require a calendered surface. They are therefore eminently suited to newspaper printing...

The Keeping of Process Blocks

Most half-tone blocks are made of zinc, and as this metal rusts with the application of the least moisture, it is necessary to keep them in a dry place and to handle them with care, for the ordinary perspiration of the hand is sufficient to impair them if it be not wiped off. For the rust eats into the metal, and the fine work gets destroyed. Mr. Wood Smith and Mr. Martin drew attention to this in the *Printers' Register*, and recommended that when such blocks were to be put away for a considerable time they should first be coated with either shellac or bees' wax, which would prevent moisture attacking the surface. This can be removed by heating and the subsequent application of methylated spirit or turpentine. A sufficiently good and more simple method is to cover the surface of each plate with a layer of pure vaseline. The plates are then laid face to face, with some thick wrappers or papers between, and sent to store. Where, however, the blocks are frequently used, by far the best plan is to have them nickel-faced; the cost of this will be saved in a very short time.

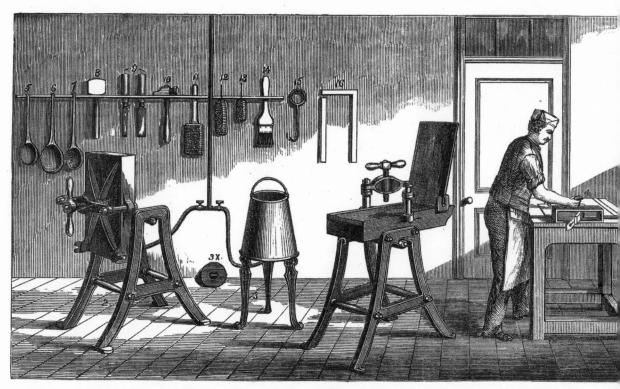

Plate 29. Nicholson Stereotype Foundry, 1872. This engraving shows the articles required to make stereotype plates and their locations in the foundry. They are described in Reading 25.10 on p. 749. (Source: Thomas Nicholson, *Instructions for the Successsful Manipulation of the New and Improved "Nicholson" Stereotyping Apparatus*, 1872.)

CHAPTER TWENTY-FIVE

Stereotype and Electrotype Printing

The stereotype process as perfected by Charles, third Earl Stanhope about 1803 – even though not new – was, along with the handpress, just one of the major mechanical innovations that Stanhope introduced to the printing industry early in the nineteenth century. Southward (1882, pp. 551–552) gives an account of the origin of the word *stereotype,* which was first used by Firmin Didot (1764–1836) in 1795, "Stereotype is a word compounded from two Greek words – *stereos* fixed, and *typos* form; stereotype printing being the art of taking impressions from a fixed immoveable forme, and is thus distinguished from typography, in which impressions are taken from mobile or moveable types." There are three basic processes for making stereotype molds, or *matrices* as they were sometimes called: (1) plaster, (2) clay, and (3) paper; the last process included *papier-mâché* and *flong* molds.

As early as 1725, William Ged (1690–1749) began experimenting with a method to cast type-metal plates from plaster molds. In the 1780s, another plaster process, similar to Ged's, was invented and patented by Alexander Tilloch (1758–1825) and Andrew Foulis [d. 1829], the younger, who later sold their patent to Lord Stanhope around 1800. In 1802, Stanhope engaged a printer by the name of Andrew Wilson to help him develop the process; and in 1803, they established a stereotype foundry and printing office in London to cast and print the plates.

Throughout the nineteenth century, numerous other inventions were implemented that improved the stereotype process. In 1829, Jean-Baptiste Genoux (d. 1835) of Lyons took out a patent for his plaster, clay, and papier-mâché processes; the first British patent for the papier-mâché process was granted in 1839 to Moses Poole. In 1861, James Dellagana received a patent for his "mangle" press, which was used to mold flong into stereotype matrices.

Stereotyping is not a substitute for typefounding or typesetting since the text must first be composed either by hand or machine. Only after the text had been set, could the molds be made, using one of the three processes mentioned above. These molds were used for casting plates in type metal. Early advocates of stereotype printing claimed that works printed from stereotype plates were almost indistinguishable from those printed from the original type or wood engravings – a point that is debatable today. Undeniably, stereotype printing did have certain advantages: there was a great saving on the wear and tear of the type; future editions could be printed from the same plates, which eliminated the need to keep type standing; and plates were not subject to any new errors that might occur during the resetting of the text for reprints.

Stereotype printing was a revolutionary concept. Many printers worried that it would put compositors out of work. Some complained that it was more cumbersome than convenient. From the beginning, printers and booksellers alike feared that stereotyping would be used for forgeries and the printing of unauthorized editions. Printers have always been reluctant to break with tradition. For the same reason, in the late-twentieth century, they resisted the use of polymer plates.

I have not gone into much detail about the various stereotype processes in my introductory notes to the readings since the manual writers themselves provide a great deal of technical information about them. On the other hand, I have included only one reading on electrotype plates, which were not generally made by the printer, but by commercial electrotypers who delivered the plates to the printer ready for the press. Electrotype plates were made from electrical deposits of metal on the lead type, a process that required expensive and complex equipment.

Composing machines, which were perfected in the 1880s, somewhat diminished the demand for stereotype and electrotype plates, although plates were made from both Linotype and Monotype settings for certain types of work. The stereotype papier-mâché process was used well into the 1950s for casting curved plates for cylinder presses. When I was a book designer at Alfred A. Knopf in the late 1960s, books were still being printed letterpress from both stereotype and electrotype plates at the Kingsport Press and Haddon Craftsmen, two of the leading trade-book printers in the United States at the time.

Reading 25.1
On Stereotype Printing
from *The Printer's Grammar* by Caleb Stower (1808, pp. 484–490).

Stower was the first to mention stereotyping from plaster molds in a printers' manual. I have included only the part of his text that relates to Andrew Wilson and Lord Stanhope's improvements in the art, which were based on the patent Stanhope purchased around 1800 from Alexander Tilloch and Andrew Foulis, the younger. Stower tries to be objective, saying below, "That we may state the case *fairly*, we shall here lay before our readers the arguments for and against the introduction of this art in the printing business."

He prefaces his arguments by reprinting an unattributed, negative article on stereotyping from *The Monthly Magazine* for April 1807, vol. 23, p. 264. Wilson's rebuttal appeared in the next issue of the same publication (May 1807, pp. 372–373), and was quoted extensively by Stower in the reading below. Wilson sets forth all of the advantages of stereotype printing: among them, the plates were completely free of errors, assuming that the original setting was correct, and twice the number of impressions could be pulled from stereotype plates than from movable type.

Stower concludes by giving five of his own arguments against the stereotype process, of which, in the third, he says that "The printer in stereotype must use higher-priced presses [i.e., iron handpresses] than are now commonly used." He did not believe that the wooden presses had enough strength to pull good impressions from stereotype plates. It should also be noted that printing done on the Stanhope press was charged for at a higher rate than the same work printed on the wooden press.

He mentions that the presses of the Universities of Cambridge and Oxford had adopted stereotyping for prayer books and Bibles around 1804. The process was especially well-suited for small books that sold in large numbers and required few, if any, changes with each new reprinting. All the same, in 1807, London booksellers did not feel that the extra expense of casting solid pages was warranted. For them, it was cheaper to keep type standing.

Some years after Mr. [Tilloch] had given up the prosecution of this invention, Mr. Wilson, a respectable master printer, engaged with Earl Stanhope for the purpose of bringing it to perfection, and eventually to establish it in this country. Earl Stanhope, it appears, received his first instructions in this art from Mr. Tilloch, and had afterwards the personal attendance of Mr. Foulis for many months at his seat at Chevening, where his Lordship was initiated in the practical part of the operation.

After two years of incessant application, Mr. Wilson announced to his friends "that the genius and perseverance of Earl Stanhope had overcome every difficulty; and that accordingly, the various processes of the stereotype art had been so admirably contrived, combining the most beautiful simplicity with the most desirable economy, – the *ne plus ultra* of perfection with that of cheapness."

Many insurmountable difficulties, we are persuaded, attend the adoption of this invention, for *every* department of the printing business. It must be confined to books of standard reputation and extensive sale, and to such as cannot be subject to any alterations. The saving of case-work appears to be the principal advantage in stereotyping; the gain, therefore, on works printed with any letter larger than [long primer (10-point)], must be trifling. In heavy works only, set in pearl [5-point], nonpareil [6-point] or brevier [8-point], will this advantage be felt.

That we may state the case *fairly,* we shall here lay before our readers the arguments for and against the introduction of this art in the printing business.

The following paragraph appeared in the Monthly Magazine for April, 1807.

"Stereotype printing has not been adopted by the booksellers of London, because it does not appear that more than twenty or thirty works would warrant the expense of being cast in solid pages; consequently the cost of the preliminary arrangements would greatly exceed the advantages to be attained. On a calculation, it has appeared to be less expensive to keep certain works standing in moveable types, in which successive editions can be improved to any degree than to provide the means for casting the same works in solid pages, which afterwards admits of little or no revision. As the extra expense of stereotyping is in all works equal to the expense of seven hundred and fifty copies, it is obvious that this art is not applicable to new books, the sale of which cannot be ascertained. Although these considerations have induced the publishers of London not to prefer this art in their respective businesses, yet it has been adopted by the Universities of Cambridge and Oxford; and from the former some very beautiful editions of Common Prayer Books [i.e., *The Book of Common Prayer* (1805, 1808)] have issued to the public; probably the art of stereotyping applies with greater advantage to staple works of such great and constant sale, as prayer-books and bibles, than to any other."

In the next number of that work [*The Monthly Magazine* for May 1807], Mr. [Wilson] made the following remarks in contradiction to the above statement.

"In this statement there are several mistakes, calculated to mislead the public mind. It is due from me, not to the *booksellers of London,* particularly, but to the Booksellers and to the PRINTERS too, of England, Scotland, and Ireland, to the Masters of public schools and private seminaries, to the Governors of Institutions for the gratuitous circulation of books, to all persons interested in the faithful and economical education of youth of both sexes, and in general to the whole literary world, – it is due from me to bring forward something more than bare assertion upon the present occasion; to state what really are the advantages peculiar to stereotype printing, which I presume I am rather better qualified to do than are those persons who know nothing of the subject. The advantages arising from an application of the stereotype invention to the manufacture of books, are not confined to any particular department of the printing business. In every department of expenditure they are as self-evident as profitable, and need only to to [*sic*] be mentioned to be well understood. In the first place, the *wear of moveable* types, in stereotyping, does not exceed [5] per cent. of the heavy expense incurred by the old method of printing. – 2dly. The expenditure upon *composition* and *reading* is nearly the same by both methods, for a first edition: but this great expense must be *repeated* for *every* succeeding edition from moveable types; whereas, by the stereotype plan it *ceases for ever.* – 3dly. The expense of *stereotype plates,* when I am employed to cast them, is not [20] per cent. of that of moveable type pages. – 4thly. The expenditure upon *paper* and *press-work* is the same by both methods; but it is not incurred at the same time. The old method requires an advance of capital for a consumption of four years; whereas, by stereotype, half a year's stock is more than sufficient. It follows, therefore, that [12½] per cent. of the capital hitherto employed in paper and press-work is fully adequate to meet an equal extent of sale. – 5thly. A fire-proof room will hold stereotype plates of works, of which the dead stock in printed paper would require a warehouse twenty times the size; and thus *warehouse-rent* and *insurance* are saved; with the additional advantage, in case of accident by fire, that the stereotype plates may be instantly put to press, instead of going through the tedious operations of moveable type printing; and thus no loss will be sustained from the works being out of print. – 6thly. In stereotype, every page of the most extensive work has a separate plate; all the pages, therefore, of the said work, must be equally new and beautiful. By the old method, the types of each sheet are distributed, and with them the succeeding sheets are composed; so that, although the first few sheets of a volume may be well printed, the last part of the same volume, in consequence of the types being in a gradual state of wear as the work proceeds, will appear to be executed in a very inferior manner. – 7thly. The stereotype art possesses a *security* against *error,* which must stamp every work so printed with a superiority of character that no book from moveable types ever can attain. What an important consideration it is, that the inaccuracies of language, the incorrectness of orthography, the blunders in punctuation, and the accidental mistakes that are continually occurring in the printing of works by moveable types, and to which every new edition superadds its own particular share of error, – what a gratifying security it is, that all descriptions of error are not only completely cured by the stereotype invention, but that the certainty of the stereotype plates remaining correct, may be almost as fully relied on as if the possibility of error did not at all exist! – If these observations be just with reference to the printing of English books, how forcibly must they be felt when applied to the other languages generally taught in this country! – how much more forcibly when applied to those languages which are the native dialects of the most ignorant classes throughout the United Kingdom, but which are as little understood as they are generally spoken! – 8thly. Stereotype plates admit of alteration; and it will be found that they will yield at least twice the number of impressions that moveable types are capable of producing. – Lastly. All the preceding advantages may be perpetuated, by the facility with which stereotype plates are cast from stereotype plates.

"Such is a general outline of the present state of the stereotype invention; and such are the obvious advantages arising from it to learning and to ignorance, – to every state and condition of civilized life. From the whole it results, that a saving of [25] to [40] per cent. will accrue to the public in the prices of all books of standard reputation and sale, which, I believe, are pretty accurately ascertained to comprehend THREE FOURTHS of all the *book* printing of England, Scotland, and Ireland. It is fair to conclude, therefore, that the sales, both at home and abroad, will be considerably increased, and that the duties on paper will be proportionally productive; so that the public will be benefited in a twofold way by a general adoption and encouragement of the stereotype art. With this view, I think the period is now arrived when I ought to announce to all the respectable classes before mentioned, particularly to printers and booksellers, that I am fully prepared to enable them to participate in the advantages to be derived from the stereotype art, in any way that may be most conducive to their particular interests, either individually or collectively."

We shall now state the arguments generally advanced in opposition to the practice of this invention.

In the first place the expense of the composition of every page, (it being imposed separately, and two proofs, at least, taken from it before it can be in a proper state to undergo the process of making a plate from it), must be considerably greater than in the common mode.

Secondly. In a first edition the bookseller has not only to pay for the higher-priced composition, but must be at the great expense of the stereotyping, which, in metal, independent of the charge for workmanship, is equal in weight to one fourth of the same work set up in moveable types.

Thirdly. The printer in stereotype must use higher-priced presses than are now commonly used, and must consequently increase his charge per ream; for hitherto all stereotype works have been printed at the Stanhope press, and at these presses it has not been done at the *common price.*

Fourthly. The shape and manner of the first edition *must* be continued, or the first expense must be again incurred; for no deviation as to plan or size can possibly take place, nor any advantage be reaped from the future improvements in the shape of types.

Fifthly. The bookseller has, *at present,* the certainty, or nearly the certainty, of detecting, particularly in town, any unjust advantage which might be taken of him, in point of number, by those with whom he entrusts his works: that important security will be wholly done away by plate-printing. He must also be subject to the loss sustained by the damage of plates, (a highly probable circumstance), together with fraud by the *"facility with which stereotype plates are cast from stereo-type plates."*

We shall not now enter into any particulars upon this last, which we conceive, most important objection to stereotyping; it is however an objection that will not lose weight by examination, and may be well worth the attention of those who are hesitating whether the OLD PRACTICE or the NEW is the *safest.*

Reading 25.2
On Stereotype
from *Typographia* by John Johnson (1824, vol. II, pp. 657–658).

Johnson mentions stereotyping together with steam and manually operated printing machines as commendable advances in printing technology, although he believes that all three of these contributed to the rapid decline in the quality of printing in the two decades prior to the publication of his manual. He was a staunch supporter of the iron handpress for superior work, and was also concerned that stereotyping would take work away from skilled compositors. Even though stereotype printing had been in existence for about twenty years, Johnson indicates that it was not universally accepted or practiced. He repeats the same arguments against stereotype printing held by Stower on pp. 718–719 in Reading 25.1.

Johnson gives a short history of the invention taken mostly from *An Essay on the Origin and Progress of Stereotype Printing* (1820) by Thomas Hodgson. This book was used by most nineteenth-century manual writers as their primary source on stereotyping. Johnson also includes a short account of the invention of the plaster process, but he does not describe how the molds were made or how the plates were cast.

Being now arrived at the period when we are called upon to perform a most serious and important part of our duty, and it is with a degree of pain that we find ourselves reluctantly compelled to advert to it: we allude to the very peculiar and most extraordinary transactions which have taken place in the profession (particularly within the last twenty years) since the partial introduction of the *Stereotype* process; and, latterly, that of *Steam and Hand Machines* for the purpose of printing, instead of following the old, sure, and beaten track, by means of Presses, which are, unquestionably infinitely superior in every point of view: and we boldly assert, that there are presses now in use, as far superior to the machines, as is the meridian sun's bright rays, when placed in competition with the murky clouds of night; which assertion we doubt not we shall most satisfactorily establish (in the opinion of all candid and unbiased minds) before we have concluded this brief article.

It appears that the invention of Stereotype, like that of Printing, is somewhat involved in mystery . . . but, with respect to the former, we conceive that its author is not worth the pains of our tracing; and more particularly when we reflect, that so many of our brethren who well deserve (from their ability) a comfortable subsistence, and who ought to be enabled (from their profession,) to move in a respectable sphere of life, are now, through this process, reduced to a very humble pittance, thereby bringing the first Art in the world down to a level with the lowest; and, at one season of the year, nearly one half of the valuable body of men alluded to may be considered as totally destitute of employ, on account of the standard works, which was the summer's stock work, having been Stereotyped.

We find that William Ged, a goldsmith of Scotland, from the suggestion of a friend (a printer) left his business in 1725, and turned his attention to this subject; having spent all his property in experiments, he engaged with a person to advance him money, who did not fulfil his engagements; he afterwards entered into a contract with two others, named [William] Fenner and [John] James, who obtained the patent for the University of Cambridge, which was made out in the name of Fenner; they soon after disagreed, when Ged was turned out: on the death of Fenner, the University refused to renew the patent to his widow. The new Patentee was ordered to resort to the old process of printing; and we find that all the plates of the Bible and Common Prayer were sent to the Chiswell Street Foundry, and there melted down in the presence of a confidential agent appointed by the University. Ged died in poverty soon after, and his companions failed in realizing their fancied expectations; thus ended Stereotype at this period, in the total failure of all concerned. Experiments were afterwards made upon it by several others, but not continued: about 1804, it was again revived by the late Earl Stanhope,[*] assisted by Mr. A. Wilson, a printer, who turned his whole attention that way, and entered very extensively into it: His Lordship's idea was, that Stereotype editions should be sold very cheap; but we find that the first Stereotype works were charged full as high, or higher, than by the regular mode.

Reading 25.3
The Process of Stereotyping
from *Typographia* by Thomas Curson Hansard (1825, pp. 846–870, 920).

> Hansard's comments on stereotype printing are of special interest since he had in his possession Lord Stanhope's original manuscript on the plaster process for making stereotypes and was able to refer directly to it. Even though Hansard does not give the date of this manuscript, it can reasonably be assumed that it was written sometime around 1803. The technology of stereotype printing had gone through several changes in the twenty-year interim

---

[*] Mr. Tilloch and Mr. Foulis, of Glasgow brought Stereotype to a degree of perfection, without knowing, as they state, of the discovery by Ged; and for which they took out patents both for England and Scotland; but it appears that they made no use of them. It is said that the late Earl Stanhope received his first instruction from Mr. Tilloch, which was completed by Mr. Foulis: Mr. T. observes (in a brief account of the Stereotype process,) that it would benefit both pressmen and compositors; with respect to the former, we well know that they ever detested it; and, as to the latter, it could only be of service to them, if Mr. T. could prove that men are better off without employment than with it: which, he says, he could support if he had sufficient space: in truth, we never consider a man's simple *ipsi dixit* [statement] worthy of notice, unless it is borne out by something like sound argument.

between Stanhope and Hansard, thereby giving Hansard an opportunity to add his own observations on these advancements. In the reading below, whenever the material in brackets is part of Hansard's original text I have mentioned this in a footnote. Even as he was writing his manual, Hansard continued to upgrade his foundry, adding a note on p. 920 toward the end of his manual, in which he describes some of these improvements.

Hansard quotes from a pamphlet titled *The Method of Founding Stereotype, as Practiced by Charles Brightly, of Bungay, Suffolk* (1809). Brightly had been engaged in stereotype printing for several years before he printed and published this work. I am not sure where Hansard found these three paragraphs since neither Rees (1819) nor Hodgson (1820) included these passages in their books, and Hansard admits on pp. 837–838 in his manual that he did not have access to Brightly's pamphlet. Brightly discusses the proper type and spacing materials needed for stereotype casting, as well as the thickness of the plates. The pages were locked up in separate chases, which Brightly then took to his stereotyper for casting.

In the beginning, stereotype was not intended for long runs, but short runs of reprints. It was also a means of making expensive type in small quantities last longer. Another advantage included its capability for making duplicate plates of a single-leaf prospectus that could be printed together in a single form. Wood engravings and ornaments were routinely cast from plaster molds.

By the end of the nineteenth century, the casting process was very much improved and simplified (see Section 14 on p. 755 in Reading 25.10). Paper prevailed over plaster and clay molds, although plaster molds were still preferred for casting wood engravings.

In an effort to prove that stereotype printing saved money, Hansard also reprints, in his manual on pp. 838–841, several tables of calculations from Hodgson (1820, pp. 170–175). Even so, Hansard was not completely convinced that Hodgson's figures were based on actual costs.

"The first object of attention," says Mr. Brightly, "in this department, is the form of the type most convenient for casting plates. In new founts, the letter-founder should be directed to leave the body of the letter square from the foot to the shoulder; the leads and spaces corresponding in height with the shoulder of the letter; so that, when standing together in a page, the whole may form one solid mass, with no other cavities than what are formed by the face of the letter. The composition of which the moulds are to be made, when applied to such pages, having no interstices to enter, and being indented only by the face of the letter, may be easily separated: but if cavities be left in the page, the mould will unavoidably break, and injure the impression.

"The quadrats should be cast rather lower than the shoulder of the letter, about one-third of the depth of Pica. Otherwise the plate, which corresponds with the page, will be inconvenient to work at press: for where the whites are considerable, and the quadrats nearly the height of the letter, it is difficult to prevent the fouling of the paper. But if the quadrats be cast lower, this inconvenience will be avoided; and the cavities formed by these quadrats being large and shallow, there will be little difficulty in separating the moulds from the pages. If the composition break in those cavities, which sometimes happens, it is of little consequence, as it does not affect the face of the letter; and the metal may be afterwards reduced where it stands up too high. As the thickness of the plate, however, must, in some measure, be regulated by the position of the quadrats, care should be taken not to have them sunk too low, or the plate, when cast, will have holes in the places where the quadrats stood.

"Each work should be provided with four, five, or six small chases, according to the nature of it, so as to lock a quarto page, or two octavos or smaller ones. Previous to its being delivered to the founder, the compositor's work must be carefully examined to see that every correction has been made; that it has been imposed with the brasses or leads on each side, to form the flanch of the plate by which it is to be fastened to the block or raiser; that it has a thick lead at head and foot to protect the head and signature lines; that it has been locked up perfectly square, and very tight; or the effect which is commonly termed suction, will occasion the mould to draw up even the whole page; that it has been accurately planed down, washed well with lye, and rinsed with clean water after the pulling of the last proof; and the moulder must take care that it be perfectly dry, as the least moisture will prevent the due effect of oiling, and the mould will certainly break; particularly if it touch any damp reglet or furniture."

I am now arrived at that part of my work at which the Stanhope Manuscript will be introduced, with such observations of my own as may show any variation in practice which experience and convenience may have suggested since his lordship's time.

"Stereotype Imposing Furniture. – The stereotype imposing furniture for a page consists of an iron frame, an iron side-stick and foot-stick, an iron head, and two, three, or four iron quoins, with four bevelled brasses, to give a slope to the edges of the stereotype plate. Chases are made of different sizes and shapes, suited to folio, quarto, octavo, &c. But the thickness of all chases and furniture should be strictly conformable to a given height; for upon their truth in that respect depends the perfection of the thickness of a stereotype plate.

"It being taken for granted that types are, what they ought to be, all of the same height, my object, in constructing this new imposing furniture was, to obtain a uniform level around the page, without which, the stereotype plates must vary in respect to thickness, exactly to the degree of imperfection which belongs to the furniture. It is, therefore, essential, in the first place, that the imposing chase and its apparatus be made correct in these respects; and, in the second place, that in the stereotype workman's hands, they be made to lie fairly upon the moulding table; for, though the furniture may be well made, yet, if there be any want of cleanness in this part of the operation, or such inattention as to allow any part of the furniture to stand higher up than its true level, an inequality in the thickness of the stereotype plate will take place from that cause.

"I adopted the use of metal furniture all round the page, in the persuasion that it was better calculated to preserve the page in its proper shape, than if wooden furniture were made use of." – *Stanhope Manuscript.*

Observation I
I have preserved Lord Stanhope's description of his apparatus in this instance, as I shall in others, for the satisfaction of those who have already adopted, or may choose to be informed concerning his elaborate and expensive mode. The necessity of being more economical has simplified the stereotyping apparatus in this, as well as in many other parts. My foundry was erected upon the principle of having every thing as effective, but at as little expense, as possible; and after having given Lord Stanhope's (perhaps more perfect) mode, I shall submit that which I find practically good, and, withal, much less expensive.

Such very nice preparation of the furniture and chases is by no means necessary. Common cast-iron job-chases, and wood furniture, cut a little higher or thicker than ordinary, is all I find called for in this particular. But this is owing to an improvement and simplification of the moulding-frame, which will be hereafter described. Any variation in the thickness of the plates is corrected by the lathe, which must, at all events, be resorted to; as it will be impossible to meet with every plate of one uniform substance in the most expensive and best mode of casting. Bevelling off the side brasses or leads will also be wrong, as there would then be a difficulty in getting the chops of the chuck of the lathe to take good hold; and by a plane and block, of simple contrivance, the bevil is quickly made as the final process of preparing the plate.

"*The Gypsum.* – Gypsum, or plaster of Paris, the well-known material of which statuaries form their figures, models, moulds, &c. serves for making moulds for the stereotype plates, when mixed up with water, in the manner detailed [on pp. 726–727 below] under the Section descriptive of the moulding process.

"It is necessary to attend to several circumstances, in order to have it in a good state for stereotyping. Previously to being burnt, in order to prepare it for making the moulds, it should be broken into pieces, none of which should exceed the size of a hen's egg. When broken, it is put into the upper oven, in pans which are supported at a distance of three inches from the bottom of the oven, in order that the pans may not be unequally heated by resting on the bottom; and, calculating from the time when the heat is capable of keeping tin in fusion, it will be found that three hours burning will prepare enough of gypsum for ten or a dozen moulds; if more gypsum is wanted to be prepared, a longer time for burning may be allowed, or an increased heat given to the oven; but to lengthen the time of burning is preferable, as thereby the gypsum is more equally prepared from the outer surface of its masses to their cores. Care should be taken neither to burn the gypsum too much, too little, nor unequally. If it receive too much burning, it will, when mixed with the usual proportion of water, look too thin, have a gritty appearance, and exceed the proper time which it should take in becoming firm enough to be detached from the types. If it be under-burnt, it will be found to set too rapidly, not affording time sufficient to dab the page, while thin enough for that purpose; and will be adhering so firmly to the shaking tool, at the time when it is to be cleaned, as scarcely to be detachable from it. It will also, in the under-burnt state, be very injurious to the dabbing brush, by clogging it with gypsum nearly to the points of the hair; and to cleanse it from clogged gypsum tends very much to tear it in pieces. Well-burnt gypsum possesses the characteristics of steering clear of both these extremes. It allows a very adequate time for shaking; has the appearance of fine thick cream when poured upon the types; allows good time for dabbing the page well; is still thin in the dabbing brush and shaking tool, when the workman, after dabbing, sets about cleaning them; and it is only when gypsum is in this well-burnt state, that reliance can be placed upon the moulds being secure against cracking when immersed in the metal-pit.

"If gypsum be burnt unequally, that may arise either from the pieces being too large, so that their outer surfaces may be quite done though their cores be very far from having received enough of heat; or though the pieces of gypsum be of a proper size, if too great heat be applied, by which the outer surface may be over-burnt, and the inner under-burnt. Gypsum, in this state, is not so easily detected at the time of moulding, for it then has very much the appearance of being well-burnt, probably, from the extremes counterbalancing each other; but it is mortifying to the workman to find, that when moulds, made of such gypsum, are immersed in the type-metal, they are almost invariably spoilt by cracking.

"After the gypsum is thus prepared by burning, it is to be pulverized very finely, and sifted through a sieve not having less than 40 meshes in an inch. For pulverizing the gypsum, I have contrived an apparatus, which acts in resemblance to the grinding of flour in a flour-mill. I inclose the sieve for sifting under a table, to prevent the fine particles from being lost by flying off, and also to keep every thing else near it free from being covered with it." – *Stanhope Manuscript.*

Observation II

In the metropolis, where plaster of Paris can be had ready prepared, this direction for its manufacture will not be of much utility; but it contains, at the same time, so many excellent cautions, pointing out remedies in the course of process, that it cannot fail of being acceptable in every foundry. Three sorts of plaster are prepared by the statuaries: the second degree of fineness is that chiefly used for moulding from type. It must be kept perfectly dry, and free as possible from air. Even in this state it will often require to be baked in the oven before mixing.

The foundry will not require any great space or expense for casting the compositor's work of one office; but must, of course, be proportionate to the concern intended to be carried on. "A room sixteen or eighteen feet square will be sufficient to forward as many pages as can be set up by fifteen or twenty compositors; and it should be well ventilated to prevent the fumes of the metal from injuring the workmen." Thus, if circumstances admit of it, the melting-pits should be set in the space of a large chimney-opening, with the flues ascending three or four feet up the chimney on each side, leaving a large vent in the centre, and by having a door or window on the opposite and each other side of the room, such a current of air may be gained over the melting-pit as will effectually carry away the noxious vapour and heat up the chimney, and leave the foundry as clear from either as any room in the printing-office. Such is the plan I have adopted, which will be clearly understood by the following sketch[see **Fig 25.5**]: –

A trough for speedily cooling the casting-pots and metal should be so placed as to be equally contiguous to the circuit of the crane and to the melting-pit. The other conveniences and apparatus necessary are as follow: – a moulding-table or bench, with pieces of perfectly level marble, or stone, or cast iron, with turned plane surfaces, about eighteen inches or two feet square, to contain three or four of the chases, in order to form the moulds from the pages – another common wood bench or table; with some shelves to lay plates, moulds, tools, &c. upon; which may be placed wherever the workman pleases. The material fixtures are, the melting-pit and its furnace; the oven and its furnace; and the crane; the pit being set so far projecting into the room as to allow of the tackle of the crane being suspended ever its centre. If a second oven could be added, for heating the pots in which the mould is inclosed, before the immersion into the metal-pit, it would be a great convenience. The crane may be made of either wood or iron; but it must be so arranged as to swing over the centre of the pit, as well as of the cooling-trough.

These erections being completed, the stereotyping process commences with the moulding, which I shall describe from the Stanhope Manuscript.

"The work of the stereotype manufacturer begins at that part of the compositor's business when the pages are finally corrected, and made ready for press; at which stage, instead of [being imposed, read, and]* going directly to press, in order to print off the number of copies wanted, the pages are delivered to the stereotype workman, who proceeds in the following manner: –

"1st. Not reposing implicitly upon the compositor for putting into his hands the pages in a state sufficiently clean and dry for stereotyping, the stereotype workman examines them in these respects; as he is well aware that either of these causes would prevent the mould from being good; especially the circumstance of the types being wet or damp; for, in such cases, the purpose of oiling the types [as explained beneath, in the 3rd article of this section]* would be defeated.

"2ndly. When the stereotyper has ascertained that the types of a page are clean and dry, he places the said page upon one of the moulding tables. Previously to laying a page down upon a moulding table, care is taken to have it clean, and completely free from any thing which might

* [Editor's note: Hansard's brackets.]

hinder the page from lying quite flat. Any small gritty particles, lying upon the moulding table, would push up the types they might happen to get under; and on that account, if a plate is cast from a mould taken from such a page, it must either be entirely rejected, or the letters which stand above the proper level of the page must be cut out, and the plate repaired in the manner detailed beneath [on p. 734]. If, on the other hand, there be any thing on the moulding table to prevent the imposing chase and its furniture from lying flat, one of the following bad effects might take place, viz. 1st, supposing the page to be planed over, and forced a little lower than any part of the chase or furniture, then the plate cast from a mould taken in such case, would be of unequal thickness; 2ndly, supposing the chase, its furniture, and the types, to be relatively correct, yet, if there be any vacancy between them and the moulding table, some particular types might be pushed down by the operation of dabbing, and, consequently, being low in the plate, would either render that plate useless, or require it to be repaired in the way just alluded to.

"3rdly. Oiling the types is absolutely necessary; for, unless this be done, the gypsum will adhere very firmly to them; the mould will break in attempting to detach it from the types; the types will be filled up with the gypsum; it will be found exceedingly difficult to clean them; and, in cleaning, they will run great risk of injury. The application of the oil is a security against all this mischief; and, at the same time, it is laid on in so small a quantity as not to prevent, in any sensible degree, the mould receiving the perfect form of the types. The oiling of the types being resorted to for no other purpose than preventing the adhesion of the gypsum, the thinner it is applied, the better; and, with this view, sweet oil, or drippings of sweet oil, mixed with an equal quantity of spirits of turpentine, to render it very fluid, has been found most perfect and convenient for use. The brushes used for applying the oil to the types, are of that sort which painters call sash brushes; but large ones, and which are ground at the points, are picked out; they are chosen large, that they may oil the types quickly and thoroughly; and the grinding imparts to them these double properties; 1st, softness, whereby little or no injury is caused to the types in the operation of oiling; 2ndly, fineness to the points of the bristles, by which fine points the oil is applied to the minutest hollows of the types. Very little oil should be used; it is only necessary to take care that no part of the page is omitted to be oiled. Besides drawing the brush along and across the page, it should, for further certainty, be dabbed both perpendicularly and in a sloping direction. Observe that the oil and brushes just spoken of are for the types only; and that other oil, and other brushes, are made use of for the moulding-frames, as follows:

"When the types are oiled, the brush that was used for that purpose is hung up over the vessel which contains the oil.

"4thly. The lower and upper moulding-frames. The lower one is cut flat, both on the upper and under side, and is gauged throughout to an equal thickness. It has two steady pins, one at each end, which fit into the ears at the ends of the imposing chase, and serve as guides to raise the mould without any irregular motion. The separation of the mould from the types is effected by gently turning, alternately, each of the three screws, which are buried within the thickness of the frame, when it is lying upon the chase, and has the upper frame upon it. These screws have no heads, their threads being cut their whole length – there is a notch in each for the screw-driver to turn them; they have each a small round hole in the centre; and the screw-driver has a corresponding point, to keep it from rubbing against, and thereby injuring the screw threads which are in the frame. The lower moulding-frame determines the thickness, the length, and the breadth of the mould, as the mould is actually formed within it. The sides of the moulding-frame slope inwards, at an angle of [   ] degrees; [Editor's note: Stanhope left blank spaces here and below for the number of degrees.] and consequently, when the frame is raised by the turning of the three screws, the mould is lifted from the page at the same time. The upper moulding-frame is only cut flat on one side, to make it lie close upon the lower one. The dimensions of the upper frame are the same as the lower, and its sides are also formed to the like angle of [   ] degrees; but its slope is outward, as the widest side of its opening is put to correspond with the widest side of the opening of the lower frame. The upper frame is only made use of to avoid the scattering and loss of gypsum by dabbing, and is therefore removed as soon as the gypsum acquires such a consistency as to enable the work-man to proceed to the smoothing of the back of the mould. The moulding-frames are oiled with drippings of sweet oil, without any mixture of turpentine, and the oil is applied upon them with a hard unground sash-brush. As it is of considerable consequence that the mould should fall easily out of the moulding-frame, its inner sides should be particularly well oiled; this is not so essen-tially necessary upon other parts of it." – *Stanhope Manuscript.*

Observation III

I have before alluded [on p. 722] to an alteration in the moulding-frame which varies it from the foregoing description. That which I have adopted is shewn in the engraving [**Fig. 25.5** on p. 735]. It must be somewhat larger than the pages it is to be used for, so as to admit about a quarter of an inch margin of mould all round. It is of cast-iron (a pattern in wood, must, of course, be first made to cast from) about three-quarters of an inch square, bevelled on the inside, and having circular projections at each corner, drilled and tapped to receive screw-pins to serve as feet. As this frame determines, not only the strength of the mould, but the substance and regular thickness of the plate to be cast; it is of the utmost importance that the greatest accuracy should be observed in its construction. To effect this, I have mine turned on both sides by the same machinery which is used for turning entire surfaces of cast-iron. The legs, as said before, screw into the circular projections at the corners. They have each a groove to receive the turn-screw. Upon the right management of these legs depends every thing most important in this part of the stereotyping progress. First, they must be turned and set so that the frame will stand perfectly parallel with the moulding-table, at any given distance. Secondly, that distance must be so arranged as to give, in the result, the chosen degree of thickness to the plates, which is regulated by this means alone – the higher the frame is elevated, by turning the screw legs out, the thinner will be the plate – the lower it is dropped, by screwing the legs further in, the thicker the plate.

But even this nicety of apparatus may be dispensed with if the wood furniture be made of such a thickness that the moulding-frame, when lying upon the furniture, will give the proper thickness for the mould and plate. In this case no screws, or legs, or turning are necessary. If the wood pattern be truly made, and the iron-casting be flat and perfect, every requisite is acquired. I, at first, went to the expense necessary for the arrangement above described, but have, for some time, wholly laid aside the legs and screws.

"5thly. Concerning the quantities and the proportions of gypsum and water, which are mixed up for moulding, it is proper to observe that these should be as uniformly the same as possible; for, though deviations may not seem at first to be of any material import, because the gypsum sets sufficiently firm with different proportions of water; yet, as it is found, that on account of such differences, there arise variations in the dimensions of the stereotype-plates, this cannot but be viewed as a cogent reason for circumspection. One object with printers who devote their attention to the execution of fine printing is, to have the lines of one page fall immediately on the back of the lines of the other page. Without stopping to ascertain whether this is requisite or not, it may just be remarked, that the stereotype art interposes no obstacle to the attainment of this object, when care is taken to mix up the gypsum and water uniformly in the same proportions. As the best burnt gypsum mixes up most conveniently in the proportion of seven parts of water to nine parts of gypsum, copper cups are made for measuring these proportions, formed upon that calculation. Thus, say that the cup for measuring the gypsum is made to contain nine gills [36 fluid ounces]; then the cup for measuring the water is made to contain seven gills. Now, each of these cups being subdivided by distinct marks, into halves, quarters, and eighths, the proportion is preserved in any quantity which is going to be mixed, either by filling each cup, or measuring, by each, at the half, the quarter, or any given number of eighths.

"6thly. The shaking tool now comes to be used. According to the degree of burning which the gypsum has received, the shaking will require to be continued a shorter or a longer space of time; if underburnt, it will allow too little time for shaking and for dabbing; if overburnt, the mixture will look thin; assume a gritty appearance, and will take a long time to set. But when, avoiding these two extremes, the gypsum has received the proper degree of burning, the shaking of the gypsum and water may be continued half a minute, and yet sufficient time will afterwards remain for dabbing before it sets. The shaking is performed quickly, the left hand being under the shaking tool, and the right hand upon its cover; and, with a view to effect the perfect mixture of the gypsum and water, the regularity of current in the shaking tool is interrupted by a few momentary stops in the course of shaking." – *Stanhope Manuscript.*

Observation IV

"The shaking tool" is not an expression quite to my mind. The "mixing-pot" would be more appropriate. Mine is made of copper, with a lid to sink inside instead of going outside of the pot. The copper-smiths call it a salve-pot.

The dabbing brushes I have made in the manner of the patent penetrating hair brushes.

"7thly. The gypsum is not poured all at once upon the page; but, at first, only as much of it as will cover the page very thinly. This is done with a double view, both of much consequence; first, the air confined in the hollow parts of the types, which, if not expelled by dabbing, would occasion dots in the stereotype plate, has a more free passage through the thin body of gypsum, than it would have, if the whole of the gypsum were poured on at once; and, secondly, the gypsum is not so much scattered about as it would be, if the dabbing were to take place through the whole body of the gypsum that is to form the mould.

"8thly. Dabbing is adopted solely for the purpose of extricating the confined air; the brush is held perpendicularly, so as to touch with the whole of it at once; and the dabbing is continued as long as the thin state of the gypsum will allow. The hair of the dabbing brush is only about three eighths of an inch long, made thus short, to give the hairs sufficient strength to reach into the fine hollows and divisions between the types.

"9thly. As soon as the workman has finished the dabbing, and poured upon the page the gypsum which he had left in the shaking tool, he must clean out the gypsum adhering to the inside of the shaking tool, by putting clean water into it two or three different times, and agitating it violently. The dabbing brush must also be immediately attended to, else the gypsum would set in so firm a body between the hair, as greatly to injure the brush, if cleaned in that state. The dabbing brush is cleaned by rubbing it with the hand, either when immersed in water, or when held under water running from a cock.

"10thly. The pallet knife is a very useful tool; it serves to collect any loose gypsum, and to return it for use to the back of the mould; it serves to give a general level to the back of the mould, when the gypsum lies thicker on some places than on others; and it likewise serves to clean the imposing chase and moulding-frames from any adhering gypsum and oil, after they have been used.

"11thly. *The straight edge.* – By means of this tool, a flat back is given to the gypsum mould. Its flat edge is made a little hollow, and serves to give a preparatory flatness to the back, leaving it a little too high, that a thin body of gypsum may be cut off by the knife-edge of the tool, when the gypsum is well set, and cuts firmly. If the cutting-edge of this tool be not kept truly straight, a different thickness in different parts of the same plate might be the consequence; for instance, suppose the back of the mould to be cut hollow towards the middle, then the stereotype-plate would prove thickest in that place; because the pressure of the metal is such as to force the back of the mould strongly against the cover of the casting-pot, and the mould will bend somewhat to this pressure, or break.

"12thly. In adverting to the time necessary for the setting of the gypsum, it is to be observed, that unless the proper degree of burning, which the gypsum requires, be scrupulously bestowed, the time of setting will vary; but if the gypsum has been properly burnt, it will be found to have acquired great firmness, and may be detached from the types, at ten minutes after the gypsum and water have been mixed together. A good way of examining the firmness of the gypsum, is to put the point of the pallet knife a little way into the mould, and observe the resistance it makes to the spring of the knife. This method will always be found a sure guide, and probably the best, for the workman to proceed to.

"13thly. The raising or separating the mould from the page is accomplished in a neat and correct manner, by means of two steady pins at the end of the moulding-frame, fitting into the ears of the imposing chase, and of three screws, which are sunk within the thickness of the moulding-frame. The screws are turned alternately; and, at first, neither of them is turned more than one eighth part of a round, increasing by degrees, so as to raise the mould perpendicularly, and separate the whole surface of it from the types at the same time. The beauty and perfection of a plate are much promoted by carefully raising the mould from the types; as this care prevents the gypsum from breaking in the quadrat lines, or between rule lines; and, generally speaking, in the fine interstices between the types, where the mould, from being fine, is consequently weak. A good workman, who oils the pages well, and carefully raises the mould, will have very little disfiguring of plates from the breaking in of the gypsum." – *Stanhope Manuscript.*

Observation V

This mode of raising the mould is found too slow and complicated. It also depends upon the peculiar correspondence of the moulding-frame with the chases and furniture already proposed to be dispensed with in Observation I. The mode now adopted in this operation is the application of two levers, as chisels, or irons with claws, which the workman uses by resting the ends upon the chase, and elevating the centre against the edge of the frame, which he, at the same time, keeps steady, to move the mould as directly upwards as possible, with the finger and thumb of each hand. This raising of the mould certainly requires much care and dexterity, which, if not nicely performed, will occasion parts of the composition to be left on the face of the letter.

The furniture, also, must be so contrived that the legs of the frame may rest upon the table, either outside or inside the chase, with the centre of the page as near the centre of the frame as it can conveniently be brought.

"14thly. The mould being raised from the page, the workman places the moulding-frame, with the mould in it, and the face of the mould upwards, upon a plane piece of wood prepared for the purpose, there being fixed upon this piece of wood two thin slips of metal, upon which the moulding-frame is supported, and thereby leaving a vacancy all along under the mould. Having so placed the moulding-frame, the workman puts one hand upon it to hold it steady, and gives one, two, or more smart blows with a mallet under the projecting ear of the frame, which blows cause the mould to fall out of the frame upon the flat piece of wood. As the oiling of the moulding-frame is on purpose to prevent the gypsum from adhering firmly to it, if the oiling be imperfectly performed, there is great risk of the mould being broken, or at least partially cracked, by adhering more in some places than in others, and by too many blows of the mallet being required to detach it from the moulding frame." – *Stanhope Manuscript.*

Observation VI

There is no occasion for these preparations of wood and metal upon which to lay the frame to knock out the mould. The workman will turn the frame on his hand, resting it, perhaps, against his breast, and will detach the mould with two or three blows of his hammer, receiving it upon his left hand; then laying down his hammer, he will take the frame in his right hand, and having disposed of that, he has both hands at liberty to manage his mould.

"15thly. The mould now only requires a little degree of dressing, to make it fit for being put into the oven to be dried, and afterwards cast. This dressing is confined solely to the removing of any high parts of gypsum upon the edges which surround the face of the mould, and which high parts can only arise from a want of truth in the imposing furniture, or from an injury which it may have received. These high places are cut off by the pallet knife, the workman taking care not to cut away any gypsum from the outer part of the edges, which part of the mould, from the nature of the furniture, must always be correctly taken. If furniture has been used, which does not of itself form gits to the mould, for the admission of the metal, the workman may easily cut gits[*] [**Fig. 25.1**] at each end, with the pallet knife, of this shape."

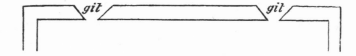

Fig.25.1. *Gits*

"16thly. The mould being now completed, it may either be immediately put into the oven, or laid aside till wanted for that purpose. If it be laid aside, the precaution of placing it upon a flat surface is necessary, to avoid any warping of the moulds. I have used a thick marble slab, made truly flat; and, the moulds, as taken, are piled upon each other, with their faces downward to prevent their getting dust, or any thing else which might prove injurious to their faces." – *Stanhope Manuscript.*

Observation VII

The Oven for baking the Moulds. – It is much to be regretted that the Stanhope Manuscript has left this article in a very defective state. It contains bare references to the laboratory at Chevening, and to drawings which his lordship intended to have made of this as well as of every other part of the apparatus: but as the references would have been totally useless without the drawings to which they apply, I have therefore omitted them. Neither the size, nor shape proper for the oven is prescribed. If made on purpose, perhaps two feet long, eighteen inches high, and thirteen inches deep, would answer every common routine of work for the foundry so far described. It may be divided by two shelves into three compartments – the undermost about four-and-a-half inches,

* This should be "*geat*, the hole through which the metal runs into the mould."...

for heating the casting-pots previous to immersion – the middle one eight inches, for quarto-sized moulds – the upper one five-and-half inches, for smaller work[.] Drying-racks must also be provided, similar to toast-racks, made of stout wire to hold the moulds upright in the oven.

"The number of moulds to be put in at once must, of course, be regulated according to the total number to be cast within a given time. Six or eight will get dry enough for casting by an hour's heating; and it is convenient that the moulds nearest the sides of the oven are somewhat sooner ready for casting than the moulds placed towards the middle of the rack. As the heat of the ovens is regulated by keeping it so as to melt tin in the upper one, that must be referred to frequently, on purpose to be safe in not getting these too hot, which should be avoided, for this additional reason, that moulds bend if exposed to too great heat. The stereotype workman may soon be able to know, by the colour of the moulds, when they are fit for casting; for, at that time, their type surface puts on the brown appearance of toasted bread.

"At the time when the moulds are put into the oven, it is the stereotype workman's business, also, to light the fire under the type metal pit, in order that the metal may be in its proper state for casting, as soon as the moulds are sufficiently dry, which, as we have observed before, will be in about an hour's time. The metal must be brought to such a heat as to light a piece of brown paper when held in it, and, consequently, kept at this heat during the whole time of casting. If the metal be not sufficiently hot, the plates cast in it will be deficient in that sharpness wherein consists the principal beauty of a stereotype plate; attention to the fires, therefore, both of the ovens and of the metal-pit is at this time very requisite." – *Stanhope Manuscript.*

Observation VIII
The Process of Casting now commences, the chief apparatus for which is – first, the casting-pot to contain the mould; secondly, its floating plate; thirdly, its cover; also the nippers; a contrivance to fasten down the cover by a screw, which can be so fixed as not to be immersed along with the box into the fluid metal, and which may be easily disengaged for succeeding boxes, while the first are gradually cooling; and, fourthly, a pair of hooks, or shackles, or a rack and pinion to be attached to the crane, which may be quickly fixed or unfixed without the workman being in danger of burning his hands.

The casting-pot must be of a size proportioned to the plates which are to be cast in it; for, if it be large enough, although no exact fit is necessary, yet much excess of size will be attended with inconvenience. Its shape is clearly shown in the engraving [**Fig. 25.2**]. It is required to be of cast-iron, and to be made with four ears, or hollow square projections – two for the nippers, and two for the shackles. The cover is cast, also, with a rabbet to fit, but cut off at the four angles to admit the metal; and having a projecting piece in the centre, upon which acts the screw of the nippers. The floating plate [**Fig. 25.3**, MIDDLE], also of cast-iron, fits to the bottom of the pot. The nippers are distinctly shown . . .[in **Fig. 25.3**, LEFT]. They have a hook or claw at each extremity to fit into the ear of the box; and a strong screw in the middle, with an eye at top, which, when put to use, is screwed on to the projecting top-piece of the lid, and has a hinge on one side, allowing it to be opened for being fixed, and for adapting it to various-sized pots. These two articles, last described, are separately shown over the moulding-frame [**Fig. 25.3**, RIGHT]. The face of the floating plate, and inside face of the lid, are turned with the greatest possible accuracy; for upon these depends the approach towards a true level of the back of the stereotype plate, as well as its equal thickness. The crane and shackles are for the purpose of swinging by a perfectly horizontal motion the casting-pot and mould into the liquid metal. The shackles are plainly shown in the drawing as fixed to operate.

At the extremity of each arm is a kind of finger and thumb projection; the finger catching into the ear of the pot, while the thumb catches on the lid. A turn of the nut-handle upon the transverse bolt, near the top, fixes them in an instant; and the whole, as represented, is ready for immersion into the metal-pit. The mould having been previously placed in the pot face downwards on the floating plate, the whole is then suspended by the crane, which turns over the metal-pit, and lowered very gradually into the liquid, and there kept steady by the contrivance of a lever and weight resting upon the top of the shackle, or the same purpose may be effected by a rack and pinion fixed to the crane. The metal will then enter the box at the corners of the lid, causing a bubbling noise by the expulsion of the air, and by its gravity insinuating itself beneath the floating plate, which, being specifically lighter than type metal, the buoyant powers of the latter cause the plate and mould to float, so that the back of the mould is pressed against the lid of the pot, and the ledges of the gypsum mould are brought in contact with the floating plate, the metal, at the same time, insinuating itself by the geats into the part of the mould containing the type *en creux* [sunken]; nothing remaining between the face of the floating plate and the inner face of the lid but the mould and the stereotyped plate. When the bubbling noise, above-mentioned, ceases, the pot is supposed to be completely filled; and if the metal has been at a proper degree of heat, which should be tried by the test before-mentioned, it will be ready to be taken out. Having remained immersed from six to ten minutes, it is drawn out by the crane with great care and steadiness, and swung carefully to the cooling-trough, into which it is gently lowered, and rested upon a stone or brick, or wet sand, so as to just touch the water, in order that the metal under the floating plate, at the bottom of the pot, may first begin cooling. The cooling is a most essential part of the process. Lord Stanhope, and with great reason, considered that it demanded the most minute attention; yet, in present practice, the shape of the casting-pot is much simplified from that which he recommends.

Fig. 25.2. *Casting-pot*

Fig. 25.3. LEFT, *Nippers;* MIDDLE, *Floating plate;* RIGHT, *Moulding-frame*

"The shape of the pot itself, having both ends considerably enlarged, is prescribed by what is found to take place in this method of casting; for it is essential, that as the metal shrinks in cooling, a provision be made to afford a supply thereof uniformly; which is accomplished, by causing the stereotype plate to begin to set in the middle, and proceed progressively to each end. Heads of metal are therefore provided at each end for this purpose; and to be certain of having the metal longest in a fluid state, exactly opposite to the gits by which it flows into the mould, the pot is besides made to descend at the ends, thereby forming a sort of feet, and by the mass of metal securing a delay in the cooling of each end. In co-operation, and to attain perfect effect in this principle, the cover of the casting-pot is made hollow, so that the middle of it is an inch and a quarter lower than its ends; and it is only three sixteenths of an inch thick in substance over the back of the mould. This is truly a grand principle in the stereotype art, which ought, in no case, to be departed from; and which imperiously prescribes to the pot and its cover the shapes I have given them." – *Stanhope Manuscript.*

Observation IX

In casting small plates, which are usually cast by two at a time, this precaution of the hollow lid is not necessary; but for large octavos and quartos it cannot be dispensed with. In the act of cooling, the metal will contract, and for the first two or three minutes very rapidly. To supply for this effect, the workman will, perhaps, five or six times, take some metal in a ladle kept for the purpose, which he will pour in at the angles of the pot till he finds it set, and not capable of admitting more. The nature of the process is this – the metal having become expanded beyond its natural capacity by the application of powerful heat, contracts again as it cools, or recovers its natural temperature. It will have a tendency to cool first in those parts which are most exposed to the air, and which are consequently the corners of the plates; or, in those parts where the lid is of least substance to retain the heat. Hence, if the lid be thickest at the centre, it retains its heat there longer than at the thinner extremities; and the metal is thus kept fluid in the centre after it is set at the corners: consequently, the contraction, which would take place there last of all, could not be counteracted by the filling in at the corners, and the middle part of the plate must, in such case, remain defective. To remedy this, the hollow, recommended by Lord Stanhope, is absolutely necessary. Accordingly, I have the lids of my quarto pots cast or turned hollow like a saucer, till, at the very centre, not more than a quarter of an inch in thickness is left; across which hollow I lay a bar of iron, upon which the point of the nippers rests. The engraving [**Fig. 25.4**] will make this perfectly clear. The hollow, when drawn out of the melting-pit, will contain some metal, which must be cleared off with a knife or any simple implement, and replaced by wet sand. This hollow in the lid I find completely reverses the process of cooling above described, so that I have no plates defective in the centres. Even if more rapidity of cooling be necessary, I obtain it by laying a little wet sand or gypsum in the hollow, which may also be done, if thought necessary, round the projecting part of the smaller lids.

Fig. 25.4. *Melting-pot with hollow in lid*

The cooling-trough may be shortly described, although it must be evident that no determinate shape is necessary. It should, however, be sufficient in length to hold two or three pots – of depth sufficient to contain water enough to cool the pots, without the water becoming too hot. A long stone, about as wide as the bottom of the pots, should be elevated by bricks, so as to be within three inches of the top of the trough. The water must be barely level with the stone; and must be kept to that height, as it exhausts by evaporation, by a supply from the cistern.

The shackle having been disengaged and applied to another box, which had been in the mean time prepared with another mould, by the time the second or third box is in the trough, the nippers of the first may also be disengaged.

"If casting-pots are to be used a second or third time on the same day, the plates should be taken out of such pots, without waiting till they are very cold, as, by retaining some of their heat, they will be the sooner hot enough for next time of casting. To get the plate out, the nippers are first disengaged, and then the cover taken off; after which, the bottom of the pot is turned upwards, upon a very strong table [or block]*, above which it is lifted about 8 or 10 inches, and let fall from this height, and by repeating this several times, the mass contained in it is separated from the pot. The four corners of the type metal are then knocked off with a hammer, and the metal which surrounds the sides of the mould is forced away, after which separation, the mould, plate, and floating plate are easily got at. The floating plate is returned into the pot, its cover is put on, and it is again placed in the oven to heat; what gypsum can be readily detached from the stereotype plate, is taken away from it, and the plate is put into the water-trough to soften the remaining gypsum that it may be easily brushed off. The bristles of the brush used for this purpose should be no stronger than what is necessary to reach well to the depth of the beard of the letters; and the brushing should be effected with the plate either under water or held under a running cock; for an abundant supply of water contributes greatly to the plate being quickly and well cleaned.

"The operation of stereotyping is now completed; and when, by a proof of the stereotype plate, it is found to be faultless, the types of such page are returned to the compositor for distribution and further use." – *Stanhope Manuscript* [.]

Observation X

It will now be clearly understood, that upon, first, the truly plane surface of the floating plate; secondly, the equal thickness of the mould, by the accuracy of the moulding-frame; thirdly, the perfectly plane surface of the inside of the lid; fourthly, the perfect pressure of the nippers and shackles; and fifthly, the steadiness of the motion of the crane and pullies, will depend the degree of accuracy, and even substance, of the stereotype plate. The whole apparatus must float both in the air and the metal, and be rested in the trough perfectly parallel and horizontal. The mass of metal which has accumulated under, and will be attached to the floating plate, may be disengaged by a smart blow with a mallet. It will be proper to reserve this superfluous metal for the next melting, as throwing it immediately into the pit will cool the mass.

Notwithstanding the utmost care, and every possible success, still the plate will be found imperfect in a greater or lesser degree by dirt, or dross, or small globules of metal getting into the eye of the a, e, &c. it is, therefore, now turned over to *the picker,* who must possess the sharp eye and fine tools of an engraver to do his business effectually. Such minute, but serious, defects may be thus easily removed, as well as larger impurities occasioned by the mould not having been perfectly discharged out of the white-lines, space-lines, quadrats, or other lower parts. Some trimming will also be necessary, by means of planes, adapted to the purpose, about the ends and sides of the plate, particularly bevelling the flanch by means of which the plate is attached with brass

* [Editor's note: Hansard's brackets.]

slips or claws, or screws, or some similar contrivance, to the block which raises it to the height of type. Faulty, or wrong, letters or words can be repaired by punching out the part, and squaring with proper files so as to admit the letters to be inserted, which being brought to a level with the face of the plate, and the stem cut off to a level with the back of the plate, with a little solder and a hot iron, they may be secured and made as firm as the other parts of the plate. In some cases it may even be requisite to cut off a portion of the plate, and to substitute another part, which, having been previously cast, is joined on to the other by the soldering process. It has also been found a matter of great uncertainty, whether the plates, even with the most perfect apparatus, are all cast of equal thickness, and, consequently, a complete foundry must be provided with machinery for turning and dressing the backs of the plates. This is generally effected by a turning lathe, having an accurately turned chuck-plate fixed to the mandrel, with universal chucks or chops to embrace the plate, and a slide-tool, with carriage and cutter so accurately adjusted, that when the lathe is put in motion by the foot, the turning the handle of the slide-tool may cause the cutter to traverse longitudinally from the circumference to the centre of the chuck and back again, till, by the revolution of the plate upon the mandrel, against the point of the cutting-tool, a perfectly level and true surface is obtained in concentric circles upon the back of the stereotype plate. An apparatus of this sort will cost from fifty to one hundred guineas.

Many other tools will be found either necessary or convenient, concerning which, nothing but experience and circumstances can lay down rules; for instance, files, chisels, accurate straightedges, lathe with circular saw, fine punches, piercers, a small press for proving the plates; tubs for the dross, waste plaster, &c. brushes; cloths with which to handle the hot boxes, metal, plates, &c. to enumerate and describe which would be an endless trouble; and to purchase them for the use of the foundry alone, no inconsiderable expense.

Making the metal. – The metal used for casting stereotype plates is as various in its mixture as the judgment and views of the operator. The considerations, however, by which he must be guided are these: If it be too hard the plates will be more liable to damage by the failure of delicate strokes in the face of the letters, which cannot be so easily rectified as where such defects happen to fusil types. If, on the contrary, it be too soft, the want of durability is a self-apparent consequence. Type metal is, in general, for the reason just stated, too hard; if used, it must, therefore, be lowered. But it is not to the interest of a printer to use type-metal, that is, old type, since in exchange for new type he will obtain a far greater value for it than it will cost him to prepare his own metal. If the metal is purposely compounded from the simple ingredients, one founder gives the proportions (but which do not appear very *precisely* defined) of from five to eight parts of lead to one of regulus, and one-fiftieth of block-tin. If genuine regulus, or unmixed with lead, can be obtained (but which is hard to be done), 1 cwt. [abbreviation for hundredweight] regulus to 6 cwt. lead; or, in fractional numbers, $1/7$ regulus, and $6/7$ lead, will make a metal of excellent quality. . . . The lead most preferable for this purpose is that usually denominated Tea-lead; or that which comes from China as the lining of tea-chests. This varies in price according to the market price of ordinary lead. . . . This lead is very pure in itself, and is also enriched by a considerable quantity of very fine solder used for the numerous joinings. This must be first melted down and carefully skimmed of all ashes arising from the paper and dross, which will rise sufficiently to purify it by bringing the mass to a light crimson heat. Let it then be run into pigs, for which purpose I use casting-pots; and weighing each pig carefully, mark its weight, and put it into store till the metal is to be made.

The *making the metal* is a process requiring much attention and labour. The regulus, to assist its more ready fusion in the previously fused lead, must be first broken into very small pieces. A smart blow with a hammer while lying in the hand or on the floor will separate it readily the way of the grain. The metal while in the state of fusion must be constantly attended to, and stirred until the regulus and lead become intimately blended. The dross will require to be cleared off by throwing on small portions of oil or grease after the grosser parts have been skimmed off. Even these skimmings and ashes will contain considerable quantities of metal, and must, therefore, be laid aside for subsequent refining. The metal may then either be left in the pit to be re-melted for dipping, or run into pigs for store. Repeated fusion impoverishes the metal, so that if much residue be left in the pit after a day's casting, or if plates are melted down to be again cast into plates, the metal must be restored by an addition of new metal or of regulus. By way of assay either when making the new metal, or at any other time when you wish to ascertain its quality, you may run a ladle full into a mould roughly made of clay, or gypsum, or any other convenient substance, or even on a flat stone, so as to let it be of a moderate thickness; and letting it get cold, break it by a smart blow against the edge of the moulding-stone or table; if it breaks sharp, without bending, and shows a face perfectly uniform, and but the first degree towards sparkling, it will be good metal; if it appears too sharp, having your pigs of soft lead in store, the remedy is at hand. It is impossible by description alone to make any one acquainted with the precise hue necessary to be acquired; but the darker it is, the less rich is the metal.

It will readily occur to any one that the processes just described must be the most disagreeable and injurious to the workman, of any part of his business in the foundry. The running down of the tea-lead is particularly offensive; and the final mixture of the regulus the most injurious to his health. But this may be entirely avoided by judiciously planning the foundry: namely, by securing a draught of air from the other sides of the room to a flue nearly over the melting-pit, by which means the entire effluvia are forced *from* the workman to escape into the funnel of the chimney, and thence into the open air. In my little experimental foundry, a representation of which is here given [**Fig. 25.5**], I have so well succeeded by leaving a portion of the large chimney between the smaller flues of the two furnaces, just at the back of the pit, open, with a window opening at each side, as to keep the place always wholesome, pleasant and cool. In fact, any one may be in my foundry during the worst parts of the process, without any inconvenience or injurious effects.

Fig. 25.5. *Hansard's experimental stereotype foundry*

I must, however, confess, that I have found in this, as in many other branches of trade, that where considerable discretion and practical skill are requisite, and where a manufactory is established for one particular business, it is far better, and cheaper to purchase the relative articles ready made, than to attempt the embracing of every branch under one concern. This observation will apply very closely to that of smelting and compounding of metals; requiring furnaces and apparatus of far greater power than are requisite for stereotyping; besides that, the process, from the stench and danger of fire, ought never to be carried on in the midst of a populous neighbourhood. I am, moreover, well convinced, and again repeat, that even independent of the latter, and certainly important consideration, I have the metal ready made, to any required strength, much cheaper than it would cost me by being made at home. Mr. Mason, of Cornwall-road, Surry, has paid great attention to this branch of manufacture; and I have from him the metal, in pigs, ready for the foundry, made from foreign regulus and tea-lead, at about 40s. per cwt.; and my dross and sweepings refined for 14s. per cwt. on the product, which could not very well be done in a foundry at any expense.

It may be necessary here to observe, that I by no means intend to assume that either the foundry or the apparatus, as here shown and described, are in exact conformity with other stereotype foundries; or have any pretensions to superiority. But it is, altogether, what I find effectual for the intended purpose; and calculated to produce plates equal to any, and superior to most that have come into my hands. I converted a spare kitchen into a foundry, chiefly for experiment, and that I might be perfectly competent to say, that no part of this work has been written without a practical knowledge of every branch of the profession treated of. I had some standing work by me which I could practise upon, although with every inconvenience of low spaces, quadrats and leads. If I succeeded I might keep the plates and release my type: and if I found it agreeable to pursue the art still further, I might make my foundry a permanent addition to my business and undertake work in this branch, for my own connexions, rather than let it go elsewhere. . . .

[Editor's note: Hansard adds the following addendum to his comments on his foundry.] Since [the above] was written, and the view engraved [see **Fig. 25.5**], I have had occasion to remove that foundry, and erect another upon a larger scale. The only part of the apparatus essentially different from that here described, is the mode of lowering the melting-pot into the pit. This is by means of an apparatus containing a rack and pinion, attached to the crane, in lieu of the rope and shackles, by which the pot is lowered and kept at any chosen position; as also a method of fixing and unfixing the claws without the process of unscrewing.

Reading 25.4
The Clay Process
from *Typographia* by Thomas Curson Hansard (1825, pp. 880–882).

Very little has been written about the clay process for making molds for stereotype plates. It does not seem to have acquired as much of a following as the plaster or the various paper processes did. Hansard describes a clay process invented by Marc Isambard Brunel (1769–1849), although he does not give any particulars about it or when it was first introduced. We know that another clay process was patented in 1829 by Jean-Baptiste Genoux of Lyons.

Clay was used to make curved plates for newspapers printed on cylinder presses. It was also used to make duplicate plates so the work could be printed on two presses at once.

The latest invention brought forward in this art, in England, is that of Mr. Brunel, of Chelsea. His object, which is expedition in the process, was, at the time, solely adapted to the view of stereotyping daily newspapers, in order to set two or more printing machines to work instead of one; or to apply the columns of a newspaper to a cylindrical press, instead of an horizontal machine, and thus increase the rapidity of the produce. The invention consists, first, in a new mode of taking the moulds; and secondly, in a new mode of attaining the stereotype plate from such moulds. His process is, by pressing on the type the material which is to form the mould; for which purpose he proposes to make a composition of seven parts pipe-clay, twelve parts chalk or burnt clay, very finely powdered, and one part starch, making twenty equal parts in bulk, not weight. These ingredients, being incorporated with water and made into a paste, about the consistency of stiff putty, are to be spread over a steel plate, somewhat larger than the stereotype plate proposed to be cast; which steel plate is to be about the thickness of a saw-blade. The types being secured in a chase or galley, and the clay spread upon the thin plate of steel, as above described, a skin of parchment is then spread over the composition, and several thicknesses of thin calico (stretched in a light frame) over the types. The plate of steel, connected to the galley of types by hinges, is then, with its layer of clay, covered with the skin of wet parchment, turned over upon the types, and pressed or rubbed with sufficient force to spread or distribute the clay into the general form of the intended stereotype plate. The use of the skin of wet parchment and the coverings of calico is, to prevent immediate contact between the clay and the types while the clay is spreading or disposing itself over the mould-plate. After the general form of the proposed cast is thus produced, the coverings of parchment and calico are then removed, and two thin sheets of paper substituted in their place between the clay and the types. The process of turning the mould-plate with the clay on the types is again repeated, and the whole passed under a rolling press, by which the impression of the types is rendered more distinct. The two sheets of paper are then removed, and the type slightly brushed over with oil, the mould-plate is again turned down, and the last or finishing impression given to the mould: the clay and the types being this time brought into immediate contact, the impression of the mould is perfected. The flexibility of the mould-plate greatly facilitates the operation, and the thinner the mould-plate is rendered, the better. The mould-plate is placed in a tray of proper dimensions to form the plate, having an edge or rim about one inch high, the bottom of which tray is full of holes, for the purpose of admitting water to cool the mould when the hot metal is poured in to produce the cast. The metal to be used for the stereotype plate may be the same as usual; but when expedition is required, the well-known alloy of bismuth ten pounds, lead six pounds, and tin four pounds, may be used by heating it to about 400°. The mould-plate being laid in the tray, with the face upwards, a plate of cast-iron is placed upon it, raised, by adjusting screws, so as to regulate the required thickness of the stereotype plate about to be cast, and render it perfectly parallel. Things being thus disposed, the whole is to be heated to about 200° before the fused metal is introduced to the mould. When this is done, the metal is poured out, having insinuated itself into the mould and filled it up to the regulating plate; cold water is injected by a flexible pipe from a reservoir into the tray, which, coming in contact with the mould, cools the cast immediately. The superfluous edges of the cast are then broken off, the composition of clay, &c. washed from the stereotype cast, and the new-formed plate may be then considered as fit to be printed from.

As it is requisite to have a great pressure upon the metal when the finest casts are made, it is proposed, under such circumstances, to place the tray with the mould, &c. heated as above, in a chamber which can be closed with a lid and luted so as to be air-tight; this chamber containing the mould may be exhausted, and then the fluid metal introduced by means of a tunnel and stop-cock to the mould, which fluid metal, when it has perfectly insinuated itself into the mould, may be acted upon or pressed by condensed air admitted into the chamber from a condenser attached thereto. In this situation cold water can also be injected into the tray for the purpose of cooling the cast as before described.

Reading 25.5
Working the Plates
from *Typographia* by Thomas Curson Hansard (1825, pp. 884–887).

Hansard continues his discourse on stereotype printing by describing the preparation of the stereotype plates for press. After the type-metal plates were cast, they had to be mounted in order to make them type-high for printing. There were several kinds of mounts: iron, cement, wood, and type metal. He begins by explaining how Stanhope mounted his plates on iron blocks with screws. The plates could easily be replaced after each form was printed.

Hansard had devised a system for casting a *riser*, also called a *raiser*, onto the plate using Roman cement in a type-high form. With this system, the plate and the mount were permanently bound to each other. Another method, popular with printers for short press runs, was nailing the plates to wood blocks with brads.

Hansard invented and patented an apparatus for mounting stereotype plates on type-metal blocks. I have omitted his account of this invention in favor of the following description of it that appeared in Savage's dictionary (1841, p. 704): "The Risers are made of Type Metal, or with any other metal or substance, cast in a Type-founder's mould, having somewhat the form of what are called Quotations. I take the usual standard for Printer's admeasurement, and cast them quadrilateral to four Pica m's; then longer ones as parallelograms, four by eight, four by twelve, four by sixteen, and smaller ones, four by two, four by one, and four by a half; in height they are about three-fourths of an inch, or sufficient to raise the Plate to the usual height, or somewhat higher than common Type; these being cast and dressed perfectly true, in body and height, may be easily combined to form the size of any page necessary, with the certainty of having a uniform plain surface for all the plates, however numerous; they are cast as hollow cubes, the larger combinations, having divisions to give sufficient support to every square against any pressure which can be brought upon them.

"The Holdfasts or Claws are formed of Brass or other hard metal, accurately adjusted in thickness to a Brevier [8 points], or any other body chosen, with a projecting Bevil at the top. They may be of various lengths, as to 4, 8, 16, 24, or more or less, Pica m's, the elongated parts of the larger ones being to the height of ordinary Reglet, having the Holdflast or Claw in the centre, or towards each end. They may be opened, or pierced, as well to make them lighter, as to cause them by pressing and indenting into the furniture of the forme, to be less liable to be drawn out: the height of the Claw is about seven-eighths of an inch, or sufficient for the projecting bevil of about one-eighth of an inch to lay upon the flanch of the plate when resting on the Risers."

The stereotype plates being completed by the hands of the picker, the next consideration will be the working them at press. It is first necessary to raise them, by some mechanical means, to the same height as type, which is effected by various methods. Lord Stanhope says, "It became necessary, in the progress of the art, to devise a method of fixing the plates upon the press with facility, and to enable the workmen to enlarge or diminish the margins as wanted. It is true, that former stereotypographers could not proceed without attending in some degree to this point. But they were content with the clumsy shift of nailing the plates upon blocks of wood; a method evidently very ill calculated for general use, when the art became more perfect, as the plates would unavoidably be exposed to great injury by the irregular warping of the wood. I have contrived iron blocks, which are cut to such a thickness, that a plate and a block together are exactly type height. There is an overhanging ledge upon each side of the block, the whole length of it, and cut to fit the sloping sides of the plate. One of these ledges is fixed; the other moveable, to admit of putting in and taking out the plate. In the moveable ledge there are three screws, by which the plate is held very flat and firmly. Different margins, to the different sizes of paper, are made by placing the blocks at a greater or less distance from each other." – *Stanhope Manuscript.*

Another mode has been practised, by laying the plate face downwards on the stone, and surrounding it with four straight pieces of iron of the exact height of moveable types, so as to form a mould precisely of the shape of the page, which being filled with a quantity of Roman cement, mixed to a proper consistence, the excess of the cement being struck off correctly level with the iron frame, it is obvious that the plate and cement together will form a plate similar to a page of moveable type. If there were no other objection it is evident, that the room requisite to deposit the pages of a work upon this plan would be an insurmountable one.

Another method of mounting stereotype pages is by nailing them to a board of the proper height. But the more mechanical method upon this principle is a plate of iron, with sliding ledges, for each page – a plan which has been adopted by some whose work lies chiefly in stereotype.

But neither of these methods is applicable to the convenience of a printing-office for general business. The expense of the first is very great, as every metal block must be turned in a lathe to procure a truly plane surface; and then it must be fitted up with the ledges and screws. The cheaper substitute has been blocks of wood, with brass ledges; but even these are expensive, and extremely liable, although made ever so fine in the first instance, to become afterwards defective; like the metal blocks, too, they can only serve for the same size of page for which they were originally made: and as the lowest expense of the cheapest of these contrivances is from ten to fifteen shillings a block, a printer must work many reams of paper before be can be repaid his expenses.

These considerations induced me to invent an apparatus for raising stereotype plates . . . [Editor's note: See quotation from Savage in my introductory note on p. 738.]

To Prepare Plates for Working
Form, with the raisers, the requisite number of pages for the forme or sheet, by the various combinations, and any difference that may be wanting in length or breadth make up by reglet, leads, or scale-board; then lay on the plates; and at the side of each, place such holdfasts as may, from the size of the plate, be deemed sufficient for proper fastening; after which, proceed to make margin or dress the formes, and lock up in the usual mode.

To Change the Plates
When worked, unlock the forme; slide off the done-with plate; replace by a new one; lock up again; and if the plates have been all cast truly to one gauge in thickness, width, and length, you will have, throughout the whole work, exact and uniform register, and equal impression. When

the work is completed, the same raisers and holdfasts, by admitting of every necessary variety of combination, may be formed into any other sized pages for any other sized plates.

The cost of these raisers, sufficient for a sheet, is not so much as for a sheet of the ordinary metal blocks; and the advantage which results is, that an office is at once provided with a stock sufficient to keep two presses constantly going of any sized work, without any additional expense: for if they have been used, for instance, for pages of octavo, a few minutes time will serve to convert them into pages of duodecimo – of octo-decimo, &c. – having a few over of each size to enable the various measures and lengths to be accommodated: and the metal is, at all times, worth a considerable portion of the original cost.

Reading 25.6
The Moulding-Frame
from *The Printer* (1833, pp. 81–82)

> I have included this short reading on the "moulding-frame" that is shown in **Fig. 25.6** because it best illustrates the arrangement of the various elements when they are locked into the apparatus. The molding frame in **Fig. 25.3**, RIGHT, on p. 731 is empty.

The first operation is that of taking a *mould* from each page of moveable types. The pages are not arranged as they would be combined in a sheet, and wedged up together in one iron frame or chase, but each page is put in a separate chase. It is essential that the face of the types should be perfectly clean and dry, and that no particle of dirt or other substance should attach to the bottom of the types, so as to prevent them from being completely level upon the surface. The page is now placed upon the lower part of a *moulding-frame*, represented in [**Fig. 25.6**].

The upper part of the frame is somewhat larger than the page, and the margin of the mould thus formed determines the thickness of the plate.

Fig. 25.6. *Moulding-frame* – courtesy of Rochester Institute of Technology

Reading 25.7
Making Up Stereotype Forms
from *The Practical Printers' Assistant* by Theodore Gazlay (1836, pp. 31–33).

The pages of movable type, from which stereotype molds were made, were imposed individually in small chases. Working with type-metal plates involved certain additional procedures that were not required when working with set matter. One of these considerations was that stereotype plates needed to be mounted before they could be printed.

Gazlay imposes the unmounted blocks first, locking them up securely in chases without crossbars, although the pressman still had to allow enough space for the point spurs. Then, the plates were attached to the blocks by hooks or screws – following the same general rules for imposing pages of type. The heads of the plates were aligned flush with the tops of the blocks, and the margins were adjusted by inserting furniture. Since stereotype forms were lighter than those with type, they were usually not locked up as tightly as the latter.

Stereotype blocks are generally imposed in chases without cross-bars: the margins, particularly between small blocks, are seldom wide enough to admit a cross-bar; and as the forms are light, much force in locking up is not required, and the chases are strong enough without them. Cast-iron chases, without any bars, are most convenient.

The blocks should be laid on the imposing stone, or a board, in the same position that the pages would be for the same form, with the hook of the block that holds the plate towards the outer edge of the sheet, and the screw in the back margin; the next block should be reversed, which will leave the screws of the blocks facing each other in the back, and the hooks facing each other in the outer fold of the sheet: the same order must be followed throughout the form. The blocks are laid in this manner for convenience in screwing and unscrewing the plate, as the screws are brought more closely together by this method, than they would be if the blocks were all laid one way.

After the blocks are placed in the proper position, the plates may be placed upon them, according to the schemes of imposition; the head of the plate should be placed even with the top of the block. The plates should be screwed on firmly, but not so tightly as to batter the sides of the plates with the hook.

To make the margins, fold a dry sheet . . . in 8vo, 12mo, &c., or as it is intended to print the form, and lay a plate on the outer leaf of the folded sheet, about two pica m's nearer the back than the outer edge of the sheet, (if a large page with large margins,) and one pica m nearer the back than the outer edge; if a small page, such as twenty-fours, thirty-twos, forty-eights, &c., leave the same distance from the top of the paper to the head-line of the plate, as there is between the plate and the back of the sheet; leaving the surplus margin at the bottom of the page. Mark the outline of the page with a pencil, and prick through the folds with a bodkin all around the page; or cut the size of the page clear out with a knife; this sheet, when opened, will show the correct positions in which the pages should stand when printed, and of course, the correct size of the margins. The plate being laid even with the block at the top, of course the furniture for the head margin must be exactly as wide as the space between the dotted lines at the top. The furniture at the side and bottom of the blocks will be less than the space between the dotted lines, owing to the block being wider and longer than the plate. The margins may be adjusted by placing the dotted lines on the edges of the plates, and putting in the furniture required to keep them in that position. After the margin is obtained for one quarter of the form, of course the balance of the form must be precisely similar. After the furniture is all inserted, place the open sheet on the form, and ascertain whether the plates stand in the correct positions.

The paper when wet, will stretch sufficiently to make up for the unevenness of size; the two pica m's in the off-cut or outer fold, are sufficient allowance for the unevenness in cutting the sheet; and the stitching in the back will take up as much paper as it will be necessary to trim off the outer edge, to make the leaves smooth: and the pages of the book[,] if properly bound, will stand at precisely equal distances from the back, the outer edge, and the top, leaving as much surplus margin at the bottom of the page as is necessary to make the book of handsome shape, and for convenience when holding.

Locking Up and Registering Stereotype Forms

Stereotype forms should not be locked up very tightly, or the blocks will spring. After they are placed on the press, the quoins should only be sufficiently tight to hold the blocks to their places.

The sides of a stereotype form must first be registered with the points; and the majority of the heads will come in register: if all the heads should not come in, they may be moved up or down on the block, until complete register is obtained. The side register will, if the points are not moved, remain good through the whole edition, it being only necessary to register the heads, when a new form is laid on; and a little pains in laying on the plates, if they are head-planed evenly, will generally enable a pressman to place them in good register. When it is necessary to move the plates, they should be unscrewed, and moved with the hand. Plates are frequently battered by being knocked up and down on the blocks with a stick, when screwed on tightly.

If the blocks be not exactly true, or the catches be sprung, leads may be inserted between the blocks, or narrow strips of pasteboard inserted between the plate and the catch at the back of the block.

Reading 25.8
Working Plates
from *The Printer's Companion* by Edward Grattan (1846, p. 77).

> The first form of stereotype plates was generally delivered to the pressman locked up and ready to print. Thereafter, the pressman was responsible for imposing the remaining signatures himself.
>
> Grattan underlaid his mounted plates in order to level them, very much as he would have done with wood engravings. I suspect, however, that he is actually inlaying the plates since once the blocks were locked in place, it is very unlikely that he would have unlocked the form again for each small adjustment. Grattan, like all other manual writers on the subject, reminds pressmen that "The fewer the overlays on the plates the better."

Only the first form of plates is imposed for the pressman, he being required to impose the remaining signatures of the work himself. He has therefore to free his plates from the blocks, when worked off, and to impose others.

When the pressman has laid his plates, screwed them up, and examined them so as to satisfy himself they will not move, he next makes his impression. This is done by underlaying such parts of each plate as may be light, with paper sufficiently thick to bring it up, and by cutting out such places as are too heavy from the sheet on the drawer. The fewer the overlays on plates the better; and if your press is a good one, there is scarcely ever need of more than the one thickness.

The register of plates is made by moving them a little on the block, and inserting a small piece of card or a space between the catch and the plate. A plate is frequently injured by allowing one of the movable catches of the block to slide under instead of grasping it, as it is screwed up, and then pulling upon it: frequently also, by allowing one of the spaces used in making register to get under the plate.

If pressmen would only once adopt the plan of washing plates carefully after using them, they would soon find their profit in it; but we are sorry to say that this is the only part of the business that seems to be generally neglected: and yet, if there is any thing whatever, in which it may be considered allowable for one workman to keep an eye on another, it is in this particular; for no one knows who is going to get the dirty plates for the next edition.

Reading 25.9
Stereotyping
from *The Letter-Press Printer* by Joseph Gould (1881, pp. 150–157).

Gould discusses the *flong process* – a variation on the papier-mâché method – for making molds for stereotype plates. He notes that flong was a "comparatively recent invention." The papier mâché process had been in use since 1829, but flong was not introduced to English printers until 1861. It was the most practical of all the materials for making molds and was also available commercially in a ready-made form. One of the greatest advantages of the flong process was that the molds were reusable for multiple castings. By Gould's time, printers were casting eight pages or more at once for small forms.

In the late-nineteenth century, printers became more and more dependent on stereotype printing to increase production. Gould describes a simple method that could be used in small printing houses that had only an occasional need for stereotype plates. He recommends easy-to-use, inexpensive equipment, similar to the casting boxes shown in **Figs. 25.7** and **25.8** on pp. 755 and 756, respectively.

He describes how to mount the plates. With wood blocks, he uses brads or flat tacks on either side of the plate corners. He also mentions "mechanical contrivances" but says that for most purposes, "wood blocks are the handiest and cheapest."

Stereotyping is a process whereby a matrix of a type forme is made in either plaster or paper, and a cast in type-metal taken therefrom, which presents a true fac-simile of the face of the forme in every detail; and if properly done, the work produced by the cast when printed from cannot be distinguished from that printed by the type itself.

The process – especially the paper-machie, as it is sometimes called – is comparatively a recent invention; but it has been found of such an immense benefit to printers that it has gradually spread till it is now found in every department – in news-work, book-work, and jobbing. Although it is carried on in most large towns exclusively as a separate branch of the trade, supporting its own workmen, who follow that branch alone, it has been found so indispensable that most newspapers, with large circulations, have been compelled to introduce it with their web-feeder machines; all extensive book-houses also have their "foundry," and even many jobbing offices, having joined issue, have their own "stereo-apparatus," and do their own work.

The manipulations required in the process are simple; and under favourable circumstances it is not difficult to succeed in executing excellent work; but I am acquainted with several printers who have failed in their attempts to master the details of the art so far as to produce workable results, and who, in consequence, are led to believe that the business can only be successfully carried on even in a small way by those who have served an apprenticeship to it.

I believe those who have already tried and failed, and those who understand nothing whatever of the process, will find in the following remarks instructions that, if faithfully followed, will enable them to accomplish everything required in the art of stereotyping, and to work out all its details in a satisfactory manner, and produce good stereotypes of ordinary work without a failure.

It is not easy to enumerate the benefit stereotyping confers upon all those who adopt it, but the small jobbing printer who has his "apparatus" is enabled to execute orders which, under ordinary circumstances, he would have found it impossible to undertake. He finds that one machine with stereo can turn out the work of at least two machines without stereo; and that his small founts of type are rendered by its aid nearly as efficient as large ones. In fact he finds his stereo-apparatus is both machines and type to him.

Stereotyping, as here pourtrayed, must not be understood as embracing the whole routine as practised by the Stereotyper proper, with his elaborate foundry, complete in all its details; but as practised by the printer, with his "stereo. apparatus," complete only as far as necessity compels; but still sufficiently so to meet the requirements of such as only occasionally need to bring it into use. However, the process as here described – so far as manufacturing flong, beating-in and making the matrix, drying, melting, casting, trimming, and other minor operations – will serve to illustrate the manipulations in use with the "foundry" as well as with the "apparatus."

I will, in the first place, describe my own appliances, so that I may be the better understood. They consist of a royal folio casting-box, which also serves the purposes of hot drying plate, and is supplied with gas-jets underneath for heating; melting pot, with atmospheric gas burner; imposing surface; shooting-bench and plane, for trimming the edges of the plates; beating, dusting, oiling, and pasting brushes; ladles, skimmer, chisels, punches, hammer, mallet, brads, &c., which, with flong, stereo-composition, and metal, makes the "foundry" complete and in working order, so far as the necessities of the small printer are concerned.

When intending to stereotype, in the first place lift out the melting-pot, light the atmospheric gas-burner from the top, and replace the pot; then light the jets underneath the casting-box, putting down the upper plate, as this will enable both the upper and lower plates to be heated at the same time, and so facilitate the drying of the matrix.

The Flong

Now make your flong, which is done in the following manner: Paste a sheet of good, soft, thick blotting-paper evenly all over, lay a sheet of fine smooth tissue-paper on it, and pat it down thoroughly, or roll it with a desk roller; then thinly paste the tissue paper, being careful not to damage it in so doing, and add another sheet, patting it down or rolling it as before; turn over and paste the blotting, and cover it with another sheet of blotting paper. Stereo-paste – or as it is called, "composition" – must be used.

The Stereo Composition

The stereo paste should be made of three ounces of glue, four ounces of Paris white, and eight ounces of flour. Melt the glue; mix the whiting till thoroughly smooth in water, and do the same with the flour, making both about the consistency of cream; then incorporate the mixtures of whiting and flour, and boil thoroughly; and lastly pour in the melted glue gradually, stirring well the whole time. Add a couple of table-spoonfulls of carbolic acid to prevent fermentation.

Nearly every stereotyper has his own method of making this paste, and each considers his the best. But the paste and flong described here are most excellent, and answer the purpose they are intended for admirably.

To Make the Matrix

Lay the forme (which must be "dressed" with type-high furniture) on the imposing surface, pour a little oil into the palm of the hand and lightly rub it over the surface of the oiling brush, and then brush over the face of the forme well, being particular to slightly oil the whole surface, or the flong will adhere to any part that may be missed, and spoil the matrix. Now dust a little French chalk over the tissue surface of the flong with a dusting-box, spreading it with the long-haired brush, and lay it tissue side down on the forme. Have a square piece of calico ready, which dip in clean water, squeeze well on taking it out, and place it evenly over the back of the flong. Take the long-handled beating brush and commence beating gently on the calico. This operation must be performed with great care to prevent beating the type through the tissue, for if this should be done it is probable when the metal is poured in it will penetrate underneath the tissue and spoil the matrix. Beat in (if the forme is small, say quarto demy) for about ten minutes, evenly over the whole surface, turning the forme round or walking round it, so that the whole may receive the same amount of beating, continuing until the impression of the type can be plainly seen on the back. Then raise a corner of the matrix – being careful not to lift it off the forme – and examine to see if it has become of sufficient depth; and examine other parts in the same manner. If any part appears too shallow beat over that portion until a sufficient depth is attained. During the whole of the beating-in operation bring the brush down squarely and flatly on the calico which covers the back of the flong. Having obtained sufficient depth, paste a sheet of wrapper-paper, place it on the flong, and beat it well into the matrix without using the calico; then, if the page contains any whites, cut pieces of thick card or old matrix about half the size of the whites, paste the pieces slightly, and put them into the middle of each open space – this is done to prevent the metal when poured in forcing the matrix flat again, and thus allowing no more depth in the whites than other parts. Having packed all the open spaces properly, paste another sheet of wrapper-paper, place it over the whole, and pat it gently on with the hand or brush, and the matrix is ready for baking.

In using ready-made flong, first soak it in water. If made of hard, thick wrapper-paper it will take no harm by being left in the water for an hour or two; in fact I have made good matrices with some that had been in water all night. The softer descriptions can be used after passing two or three times through warm water or after being in cold water a quarter of an hour. The ready-made flong being prepared with tissue ready for use, simply requires the water blotting off it, after having been soaked, by laying a sheet of blotting on it and rubbing it over with the hand, and then dusting with French chalk; after which proceed exactly as already described. But as ready-made flong is sold by several makers, each make varying considerably in the softness of the material it is manufactured from, it will be found that experience will be needed in its use to ensure unvarying success; and that the various descriptions require somewhat different treatment.

Drying and Baking the Matrix

Lift the upper plate, or lid, of the casting-box, place the forme on the lower plate, being careful that the matrix or packing be not shifted, put a thick blanket over the matrix, lower the upper-plate, and screw it down moderately tight, the pressure being regulated to suit the size of the form – heavier for larger than for smaller formes. If too tightly squeezed, however, the type may be made low by the pressure, or the stereo-composition forced through the tissue, therefore due care must be exercised, to avoid damaging the type or matrix. Allow the forme to remain in the casting-press about ten minutes, to harden it a little; then unscrew and raise the plate, take off the blanket, and allow the matrix to dry for about the same time; then raise the matrix carefully off the face of the type, tap up the quoins, which the heat will have slackened, all round, and lift the forme. Now lay the matrix on the hot plate, placing stereo-furniture on the edges (clear of the face of the cast), and allow it to remain till dry – perhaps it may require about half-an-hour, unless the plate is very hot; after that trim the edges, and it will be ready to cast.

If the matrix should not be thoroughly dry before pouring in the metal, although it may not be entirely ruined, it is probable the weight of the metal will cause the damp matrix to yield in the open parts, a plate cast from it, therefore, would be deficient in depth; it is important in consequence that the matrix be thoroughly "baked," it will then resist the weight of the molten metal and produce a cast of proper depth.

Casting

First paste a piece of brown paper at the edge – this must be an inch or so wider than the matrix, and long enough to allow one end to hang out of the top of the casting-box, when the matrix is in position – and well fasten it to one edge of the matrix; I usually fasten it to the imprint edge [i.e., the edge closest to the mouth of the apparatus]. Place the matrix in the centre of the casting-box, and the gauges in position, on the edges of each side and bottom of the matrix, cover the whole with a sheet of brown paper, also large enough to come a few inches beyond the mouth of the casting box, let down the upper plate carefully, so as not to move the gauges; screw up tightly, take out the pin – or release the catch, as the case may be – that secures the box in its horizontal position, and then tilt it up. With the skimmer remove all dross, &c., from the surface of the metal; then take sufficient metal in the ladle to cast the plate and allow a few inches to spare; test the heat by dipping a piece of paper into the metal, and if the heat turns it of a light-salmon or straw colour it is ready to pour. Pour in a quick, steady stream of metal, avoiding splashing; allow about one minute for the metal to "set," bring the casting-box to its horizontal position, raise the lid, lift off the plate, with matrix attached, place it on imposing-surface, matrix side uppermost; pat the back of the matrix (if it does not lift at once), and raise it with the greatest care if it adheres to any part of the plate. If metal be good, matrix dry, and these instructions properly followed, you will have a good workable plate, which now will only need dressing. Nick the plate along with a chisel, a pica or so from the imprint, and, taking it in the hand, give it a smart tap against the edge of the imposing-surface where it has been nicked, and the "tang" will break off.

Should it be found impossible to remove the matrix from the plate by ordinary means, put both into water; the matrix of course will be spoilt, but the plate may be good.

Trimming

Trim the edges of the plate at the shooting-bench, holding it sufficiently slant to give the edges the required bevel, or if no bevel is needed it may be laid flat; and plane all sides close up to the face of the cast. If any open part of the plate should appear to be too shallow – through careless making and "deepening" the matrix – hollow out the parts which may be liable to "black" with a chisel or gouge.

Mounting

After trimming the plate properly at all edges, punch holes with the small-ended punch through it near the corners, choosing a hollow part for each punch-hole, or if there are no hollows of sufficient depth, counter-sink the punch-holes a little with a drill (which may be fastened in a chisel-handle), so that the heads of whatever are used to fasten the plates to the blocks shall stand well below the surface of the plate. If several casts are to be mounted, measure in the same manner as in book-work to find the proper space to be allowed between each page, and mark the mounting-block, by running a pencil along the edges of the plates, where each page must be fixed. Drive in brads, and strike them well into the plates with the broad ended punch, to prevent their blacking; and, if properly mounted, the stereotypes are ready for machine or press. When solid pages with borders are stereotyped it is often difficult to find an opening for a brad; when stereotypes of such pages are to be mounted always make a good bevel when trimming the plates, they can then be held on the mounting-boards by driving in common tin-tacks so that their heads may catch the bevels on every side. For mounting purposes there are several appliances, stereo-furniture with catches, stereo-beds, and other mechanical contrivances; but for the general jobbing-printer and for such as do only a limited quantity of book-work, the wood blocks are handiest and cheapest. Mahogany is preferable to any other wood that I am acquainted with, but common deal is extensively used, especially for mounting single pages; and up to crown or demy, if properly clamped, deal answers fairly well. When mounted on mahogany, brads or tacks will hold the plates well; but when using the softer wood, half-inch screws keep a firmer hold, and are consequently more to be relied upon.

Stereo-Metal

I think it will not be out of place to say a few words about the metal used for stereotyping; as unsuitable metal is a fruitful source of failure. For some time before I published the "Compositor's Guide" [1878] I had been practicing stereotyping, and had been successful to a very encouraging degree, always being able to obtain at least a passable plate. The metal I had then on hand, however, having been all used just at the time I wished to stereotype the "Compositor's Guide," I was obliged to use up a large quantity of broken leads and other refuse that had been accumulating for years. That something was far from right with that metal I have no doubt; for I had failure after failure – some of the formes I took at least a dozen matrices of, and cast over twenty times, before obtaining a passable plate; and even after all the labour expended upon them, I found, on putting the plates to press, some of them ought to have been recast. Soon after finishing the stereotyping of the "Guide," I found myself compelled to send to a firm for a new supply of stereo-metal. The metal arrived in due course, and I found on using it all failures vanished – every cast was a perfect and sharp plate, and all successful. This I considered was attributable to the effect of good metal, and helped to prove the metal that had been immediately before in use was bad. Lately I have been troubled in the same manner, but in a lesser degree; I therefore wrote for professional stereotyper's opinion on the subject. I was ordered to "flux with grease and resin," and they had "no doubt I would find all right." I did what I was ordered to do, and found a cure for that description of metal at least. It was old type, in which had been melted about two pounds to tea-lead to five or six of type-metal.

When obliged to stereotype with an inferior description of metal I find I can obtain the best results by making a matrix of moderate depth – just deep enough to print properly – having casting-box, gauges, and matrix very hot, the metal about the usual temperature, and pouring in as quickly as possible. It is a great saving of time and temper, however, to send to some respectable firm and obtain proper metal for stereotyping.

Causes and Failure

Failure not unfrequently occurs even when the amateur stereotyper has taken – as he imagines – the utmost pains to ensure success. In some cases the failures have been so complete and persistent that the apparatus has been sold for what it would fetch, and an impression obtained that none but the professional stereotyper could accomplish respectable work. Bad metal is sometimes the cause of ill-success, but the most fruitful cause is not allowing the matrix to become thoroughly dry before attempting to cast. The casting-box being too cool is often the only impediment in the way of securing a good plate. The matrix may be beaten till some parts burst, which will allow the metal to penetrate beneath the tissue. Although this does not always spoil the cast, it often ruins the matrix. Metal too hot is another cause of failure. In stereotyping, bear in mind that the matrix must be dry, the casting-box, gauges, &c., hot, the metal of a moderate temperature; and, having a good matrix and good metal, if the foregoing instructions have been properly attended to success may confidently be expected.

Remarks

In casting a sheet or two of small pages – such as the "Compositor's Guide" – it is advisable to cast them in sections of a sheet or half-sheet, eight pages in each, with the proper furniture between the pages. It saves a great deal of time, and the plates are much more easily mounted, and the pages are better to register than if cast singly.

When intending to cast a section of a forme containing a number of pages, an extra lead or two will be required in the furniture, to allow for the shrinking of the plates in cooling.

If the tissue surface of the matrix has been burst in beating-in, the matrix may be made serviceable by pasting slips of tissue over the broken parts, and smoothing it well down with the end of the finger, rubbing on French chalk at the same time.

If a matrix has been torn in lifting off a plate when cast, and more plates are required, the same remedy will often repair the mould sufficiently to allow of more casts being taken. If the tissue on any part has been raised, smooth it down before attempting to take another cast.

Before attempting to take a matrix from any very open job – such as table-work, &c. – cut up an old matrix, and lay pieces in the open spaces, to bear up the flong, and beat in very gently and with the greatest care over the open parts. The pieces of old matrix in the hollows must not stand too high, or the casts will have to be deepened to prevent blacking.

If any wood-cuts or wood lines are in a page which requires stereotyping, after making a matrix in the usual manner, place the forme and matrix in the casting-box, which must only be warm, and allow them to remain a few hours. After that the matrix may be very carefully lifted, dried slowly, with type-high furniture laid round it to keep it flat; after which apply the usual heat to expel all moisture.

If it is desired to take a cast from an old matrice, lay it on the hot plate for a short time before doing so, or it will probably be found to have gathered too much moisture to allow of a cast being taken.

When pouring metal into the casting-box, stand well to one side, away from the mouth. Should the matrix be damp the metal may fly.

On putting cold metal, or cold ladles into the molten metal, stand clear, for the same reason[.]

Reading 25.10
Stereotyping
from *Practical Printing* by John Southward (1882, pp. 552–568).

Even though there were numerous commercial stereotype foundries, many large printing offices maintained their own. Southward also recommends that printers in small offices make their own stereotypes, especially for those offices with a limited amount of type. The stereotype process is simple and the equipment was relatively inexpensive. He notes, "Any intelligent youth can be taught to practice stereotyping." His instructions are directed primarily to stereo-typers working in these small in-house foundries. He frequently refers to Thomas Nicholson, whose book *Instructions for the Successful Manipulation of the New and Improved "Nicholson" Stereotyping Apparatus* (1872) had a profound influence on Southward's methods for making stereotype plates. Nicholson's stereotype foundry is illustrated in **Plate 29** on p. 714.

Southward mentions, in passing, three methods for making molds: clay, plaster, and paper, although he does not provide any information about the clay process. In the reading below, I have omitted his section on the plaster process since it is similar to those described in Readings 25.1 through 25.3 beginning on p. 716. Southward is most enthusiastic about the flong process and gives four reasons why he prefers it above the others: (1) it is rapid, (2) multiple castings can be made from the same mold, (3) the molds can be stored for future use, and (4) it is the simplest. He concedes, however, that the plaster process produces sharper images and is better for wood engravings.

1. . . . No large printing-office now dispenses with stereotyping, but we would just say that few small offices can afford to do without it. It is in the latter class of offices, indeed, that its advantages are most obvious. Where the stock of type is small, such a simple and cheap method of increasing it is most important. It does away with the necessity of keeping many standing formes. It reduces the wear and tear of type. It increases the productiveness of a limited stock of machinery or presses. It dispenses with labour, and saves room; and in fact economises time, money, and mate-rial to an extent which would hardly be credited by those who have not experienced it.

The art is simple, and the apparatus comparatively inexpensive. Any intelligent youth can be taught to practise stereotyping, and an entire foundry, with all necessary utensils, may be pur-chased for considerably less than twenty pounds. The following instructions will have reference to such an outfit; as we have not space to describe the operations of large stereotype foundries.

2. The two essential parts of stereotyping are – 1st, making the mould or matrix; 2nd, the plate or cast. The latter is always formed of an alloy, which may here be said, generally, to be somewhat similar to ordinary type-metal.

3. There are three materials from which the mould may be formed – viz., clay, plaster of Paris, and paper; and these divide stereotyping into "the clay process" [see Reading 25.4 on p. 736], "the plaster process" [see Reading 25.3 on p. 720], and "the paper process" [described in Reading 25.9 on p. 743 and in this reading]. The system of forming a plate by deposition in an electric battery

is also a kind of stereotype, but as it is known as electrotyping, and practised as a separate art [see Reading 25.11 on p. 758] . . .

The paper process is unquestionably the simplest of the three processes named, and we will begin with it.

4. *Materials required.* – The following is a list of materials required for casting small plates – say up to royal folio. For larger sizes several more elaborate utensils are desirable.

Melting Furnace. – (No. 3 in engraving [here and below, see Plate 29 on p. 714]. . . .) The use of this is to melt the metal required to form the cast. Any stout iron pot, with a flange to rest on the furnace, will do for a melting-pot. The fumes from type-metal are very prejudicial to health, and should therefore be carried away by means of a flue, or chimney, placed over the melting-pot.

The makers of the portable stereotyping foundries have introduced specially contrived gas furnaces for this purpose, which are exceedingly convenient. They are heated by an "atmospheric" burner attached to a piece of flexible india-rubber tubing, which is connected with the gas-pipe. They are thus easily put aside when not wanted, and the heat is quickly got up when necessary, without the dirt and trouble of coals. Another advantage is that the insurance companies do not levy any increased rate on account of these appliances. The furnace is double, one part holding the metal, and forming the pot, or crucible, and the other forming a hot-air chamber when the gas-jet inside it is ignited. A sufficient quantity of metal can be got ready for use in about thirty minutes. The pot is provided with a moveable lid (3 x) to keep out dirt and dust when not in use.

The Drying and Casting Press. – This apparatus (No. 2 in the engraving) is the most important feature of the paper process. The mould is formed of a composite kind of damp paper (papier mâché), and requires to be dried before it can be cast from. The press consists of a flat planed iron surface. Attached to one end by hinges is a lid, which is raised and lowered like the tympan of a printing press. At two sides of the bed are two upright pillars, and between them a moveable plate into which a screw works, being actuated by two handles. When these handles are turned the screw descends, like that of a copying press, and exerts any required pressure upon whatever may be below. In short, this screw, together with the lid of the press, will squeeze, on the platen principle, any forme laid on the bed underneath. The screw piece, or head of the press, is made to move laterally, so as to be out of the way of the lid when turned down or raised up. Underneath the press there is a gas-burner to heat it, this burner being connected by a flexible gas-pipe with the ordinary gas supply of the apartment.

The bed of the press stands on four iron supports, but it is attached to them only on an axle, and can be changed from the vertical to a horizontal position. A pin, fixed in one side of the stand, keeps the table in a horizontal position when necessary. The object of setting it upright is to pour down into it the molten metal when casting.

Ladles. – (See Nos. 5 and 6 in the engraving.) These are of the ordinary kind used by founders. Two of them will, at least, be required, one having a bowl four inches, and one about two inches in diameter. They are used for transferring the molten metal from the melting-pot to the casting-box, or press.

The Skimmer. – (No. 7 in the engraving.) A ladle with a perforated bowl. It is used for removing impurities or foreign matter from the melting-pot while the metal is being melted.

The Mallet. – (No. 8 in the engraving.) Shaped like an ordinary carpenter's mallet, and with a squarer head than that used by the printer.

Chisels. – (No. 9 in the engraving.) Two of these are required, one being a half-inch broad, and one an inch broad. They are used, with the mallet, for trimming the plates.

The Hammer. – (No. 10 in the engraving.) Which calls for no special remark.

Beating Brush. – (No. 11 in the engraving.) A strong hair brush with a handle, used for beating the paper pulp into the interstices of the type. It should be about five inches long, and two and a half broad, and have a handle about seven or eight inches in length.

Oil Brush. – (No. 12 in the engraving.) A small brush used for oiling the face of the forme previous to taking the mould, and for preventing the paper adhering to the forme.

Chalk Brush. – (No. 13 in the engraving.) For removing the superfluous chalk from the surface of the paper mould.

Paste Brush. – (No. 14 in the engraving.) For pasting together the sheets of paper which are to form the mould.

Casting Gauges. – (No. 16 in the engraving.) They serve to regulate the thickness or height of the plate by keeping the lid and the table of the casting-box at the proper distance apart.

Plane and Shooting Board. – (No. 4 in the engraving.) This is used for planing the backs of the plates, and for bevelling their edges if necessary. It should be set up on a strong bench. A circular saw arranged in the side of the latter is a very useful addition.

A *Hook,* for lifting the lid off the melting-pot (No. 15 in the engraving).

These are all the special apparatus that are required; but several materials and appliances generally found in a printing-office must be brought into use. For instance, a small imposing surface must be arranged so as to stand near to the casting-press and the melting-pot.

The plates are cast from a papier mâché matrix called a *flanc,* or as it is phonetically written in this country, "flong."*

This flong is formed by uniting several sheets of paper by means of a particular kind of paste.

5. *To make the Paste.* – Take 1 lb. good wheaten flour, 9 oz. white starch, 1 dessertspoonful of powdered alum. Mix up smoothly with a sufficient quantity of cold water for the purpose, and boil it in the usual manner for making bookbinders' paste. When it is required for use, mix intimately with it an almost equal quantity of pulverised whiting.

Prepared paste or "stereotype composition" may be had from the printers' brokers. This plan of preparing it was introduced by Mr. T. Nicholson, who has issued a little book [*Instructions for the Successful Manipulation of the New and Improved "Nicholson" Stereotyping Apparatus* (1872)] on this kind of stereotyping, to which we will be indebted for some of the following instructions. Nicholson's composition is specially prepared for the process, and is claimed to be of an imperishable nature, retaining its requisite properties for any length of time. It is always ready for use, there being no fermentation, and it is said to produce a sharpness on the face of the plates quite equal to the type, and, with care, almost any number of casts may be taken from one matrix.

The mode of using Nicholson's composition is to take 1½ lb. of it, add 1 lb. of whiting and one pint of hot water. This mixture when cold should appear in substance like very thin bookbinders' paste.

6. *To make the Flong.* – Lay down upon a smooth iron or stone surface a piece of stout brown paper. Paste the surface of this over equally with the paste already mentioned. Lay a sheet of good blotting paper upon the pasted surface, and press it down with the hand. Paste this over, and then put

---

* For the sake of future typographical antiquarians to whom the derivation and origin of this word might cause considerable difficulty, we may say that the paper process altogether was invented by the French, and first introduced here by Messrs. Dellagana, an eminent firm of stereotypers. When young, Mr. [James] Dellagana was in the habit, with his fellow-workmen, of frequenting a *café* in Paris, where they often partook of a kind of pastry called *flanc,* an edible much like in appearance the oat-cake of our northern counties, but thicker, and made in layers like the "flong" of the paper process. For want of a better word the workmen, when they were inducted into the mysteries of the new mode of stereotyping, used the well-known and suggestive name *flanc,* and it was then brought over here, where it has been acclimatised as "flong."

another sheet of blotting paper on; smooth well, paste this over; then place a sheet of good tissue paper or copying paper upon the blotting paper. Press it well down again, paste over again, lay another sheet of tissue on the last, and smooth the whole carefully. Some stereotypers pass a small steel roller over the flong to better incorporate it together, and give it greater firmness.

Flong may, like the paste, be had ready prepared; or it may be made with Nicholson's paste in the following manner: Paste a sheet of thick blotting paper evenly with the prepared composition and lay upon it a sheet of tissue. Turn the sheet and paste the blotting paper again, and lay upon it a sheet of thin demy paper. Turn again and paste the tissue side, and lay down a second tissue. Paste again and lay down a third tissue. This flong must not be immersed in *hot* water; with this exception it may be treated according to paragraph 11 *post* [below].

Having the flong prepared, we are now ready to begin casting. If one of the portable foundries such as Nicholson's is used, the gas jet under the drying and casting press should be lighted. The lid should be put down so that it may be warmed to an equal temperature with the rest of the press. This is necessary in order that the mould may be properly dried.

The gas burner in the furnace or melting-pot should also be lighted. In using Nicholson's furnace "when lighting the gas in the furnace the gas should in all cases be turned full on, and the light applied inside, from the top, by lifting out the metal pot. Should there be an insufficiency of pressure the gas is liable to ignite at the bottom where the gas and atmosphere enter the burner, in which case the metal will not become fusible. The metal pot will become covered with a thick coating of gas black, and a suffocating smell will arise from the gas. If lighted properly the gas flame will be of a bluish colour, and the heat will be so intense that 100 lbs. of metal will be ready for use in half an hour."

7. *Stereo Metal.* – Take six pounds of lead, and one pound of antimony. The antimony is a white metal, and so brittle as to be easily pulverised. When heated to redness it melts; at a higher heat it evaporates. It should be broken into very small pieces, and thrown on the top of the lead when it is at a red heat.

8. The simplest mode of making stereotype metal is to melt old type, and to every 14 lbs. add about 6 lbs. of grocer's tea-chest lead. To prevent any smoke arising from the melting of tea-chest lead, it is necessary to melt it over an ordinary fireplace for the purpose of cleansing it, which can be done by throwing in a small piece of tallow about the size of a nut. Then stir it briskly with the ladle, when the impurities will rise to the surface, and can then be skimmed off.

Care must be taken in the mixing of lead and type-metal, that there are no pieces of zinc in it. The least portion of zinc will spoil the whole of the other metal that is mixed with it.

Zinc is of a bluish-white colour; its hue is intermediate between that of lead and tin. It takes about 80 degrees more heat than lead does to bring it into fusion. Should any metal float on the top of the lead, do not try to mix it, but immediately take it off with the ladle.

Another test of zinc in the type-metal is obtained by plunging a red-hot poker into the metal when it is at the heat that it would scorch a piece of paper black. If the metal does not adhere to the poker it is free from zinc; if, on the contrary, metallic patches appear upon it, zinc is present.

The proper heat for casting is when the metal will turn a piece of white paper straw colour. If it makes it black, it is too hot. The mould, being paper, cannot sustain an intense heat.

9. *General Hints.* – The careless pasting of the blotting and tissue papers is a fruitful cause of failure in stereotyping. Great care should be taken with this preliminary operation, as bad flong will endanger the success of all that follows.

The imposing surface on which the forme will be laid, while the mould is being beaten into it, should be firmly fixed up, so as to prevent any vibration during the beating.

The iron plane should be so contrived as to prevent friction against the side of the plate, which would warm it, and perhaps distort its shape.

Where a number of plates are wanted, a saw and planing bench is almost indispensable. It should include a circular saw – 6 in. diameter is a useful size – an imposing surface, and a plane and shooting bench. It should have a moveable gauge or guide. The best article of the kind will have a steel spindle running on steel centres for the saw, a band and treadle to actuate it. The top should be capable of being lifted off, while the saw is being adjusted. The plane should be fixed at the right hand side, and have a receptacle underneath for catching the shavings of metal. The circular saw should be placed at the left side. Underneath the surface a couple of strong drawers may be fitted up.

10. Having compounded the flong for taking the mould, and got the metal hot, and ready for making the cast, the next thing to do is *to prepare the forme.*

Place the forme on the small imposing surface and unlock it. It must be prepared for moulding from by being surrounded on all sides with metal furniture or clumps, type-high, and about a pica or two thick.

Metal type-high furniture is much superior to wood, and should always be used when possible. If you have a small stock of metal furniture in lengths – which may be had from the printers' brokers – cut four pieces sufficient in length to go entirely round the forme, and enclose it as in a border. This furniture is bevelled or "chamfered" on one of the top sides, and the bevelled portion should be against the forme, and so as to leave about a nonpareil [six points] of "white" or open space between the face of the furniture and that of the type.

If you have not a supply of this furniture it is easy to make one. With most of the portable apparatus are sent out type-high gauges, which may be adjusted to the proper thickness, and the furniture cast with them as directed in the following paragraphs in the case of type plates. Of course you will not use any mould.

If the forme to be cast consists of eight or more pages, a little extra care must be taken in preparing it. Take out the furniture in the margins, and instead of it insert a piece of *double bevelled* type-high furniture between the pages. There will thus be a distinct break between each page, consisting of two channels or whites, caused by the double bevel of the furniture, and the furniture itself. In this way you will not only get a guide for the true and square dressing up of the plates, but an opportunity for separating those of the respective pages by merely knocking them, at the point where they are intended to be separated, against the edge of the imposing surface.

The side and footsticks are, of course, placed *outside* the furniture. Next tighten the forme a little with the finger. See that it is perfectly clean, that there are no spaces standing up, no leads or rules riding, and that the quads, &c., are all even and secure. If the forme is perfect, lock it up in the usual way, taking great care not to bow or bend it.

Ascertain next that the forme will lift with safety, that no quads or letters "dance" or become loose. Then slacken the quoins, so that they are not too tight to be moved with the fingers.

Next, *oil the forme.* This is done with the brush provided for the purpose. The plan recommended by Mr. Nicholson is to pour a little oil into the palm of the left hand, and to rub the brush evenly into it. Apply the brush and the oil it contains only to the face of the forme, but let the latter have a complete, though slight, coating of the oil. Either sweet oil or olive oil may be used; the latter is preferable.

Again lock up the forme tightly, and in such a way that it is perfectly square and level on the face, and has no leads, spaces, letters, or quads out of their places. It may be planed down, as a further precaution.

11. *Making the Mould.* – Cut a piece of flong and two pieces of soft but stout wrapping or sugar paper to the size of the forme, including the type-high furniture. Immerse [this] piece of flong in hot water, in a similar manner to that for damping paper for printing. Do this three or four times, and each time immediately place it face downwards on a sheet of blotting paper to absorb the superfluous water. Whilst in this position, paste the two pieces of wrapper with ordinary bookbinders' paste, as evenly as possible, and lay them aside. Mr. Nicholson says that for open work it is well to mix an equal proportion of whiting to that of paste. It will facilitate the drying and give body to the matrix.

It is a good plan, after damping the flong, to lay it face downwards on a sheet of dry blotting paper, on an even surface, and to roll it evenly with an ordinary office [roller]. This will take out a great amount of water, facilitate the drying, and strengthen the matrix.

For open work, it is well to mix an equal proportion of whiting to that of paste. This will facilitate the drying, and give body to the matrix.

Now, keeping the forme on the imposing surface, place the flong on it with the tissue paper side, to which the composition has been applied, next the type. Over it spread a piece of damp linen, and, with the beating brush, begin to beat the flong into the type. Take care to beat lightly on those parts of the forme which are open. Continue beating until the paper has well penetrated the forme, and sufficiently to give the required depth to the cast. This is a matter of experience and practice, but the knowledge when to leave off is soon acquired.

Next add one of the pieces of wrapper, already pasted, and beat it into the flong, having removed the piece of damp linen. Great care must be taken to effect a perfect union of the flong and the wrapper, and to exclude any air bubbles that may have got in between them.

If there are any white or very open spaces in the forme, it is advisable to fill them up with a little softened pipe-clay. Or a piece of thin millboard may be cut out and pasted upon the forme, so as to project a great primer [eighteen points] above the face of the type.

Next lay the *second* wrapper, already pasted, on the back of that just finished. Again beat, somewhat lightly, and use similar precautions against the entrance of the air. The moulding is now finished.

The whole process of making the mould should not occupy more than five or ten minutes.

Some stereotypers vary the process already described, but in minor details only. After the flong has been applied to the forme, they exert a gentle pressure on it, by giving a slight pull at a printer's or a bookbinder's press; and the larger stereo apparatus have a special press contrived for this purpose. The object of this pressure is to fix the mould in its place. The precaution must be taken of laying a sheet of paper upon the back of the mould to prevent it from adhering to the platen of the press.

Instead of the damp linen previously spoken of, a piece of stout calico may be taken, and soaked in water. The superfluous moisture should be wrung out, and the calico, doubled, laid on the back of the mould.

Any large stiff-haired brush will do for beating, if it has a long handle. The beating over the fabric which covers the mould should be regularly and evenly done. The face of the brush must be brought down perfectly flat.

To ascertain if the impression is sufficiently deep, one corner of the mould may be carefully lifted from the forme. If the required depth has not been reached, replace the mould gently, and beat a little longer.

If there are extensive depressions in the forme, as in title pages, labels, and forms, a few fragments of an old mould may be cut out and pasted on such spots before affixing the sheet of brown paper.

12. *Drying the Mould.* – As already stated, we are now describing the use of the portable stereo foundries. All that is necessary, therefore, is to show how the drying can be done without the aid of a furnace, such as is used in large stereotyping establishments.

Lift up the lid of the drying and casting press, and place the forme on the centre of the surface, between the two upright pillars. Spread a piece of thick machine blanket over the forme, and immediately cover the whole with the lid, and screw it tightly down with the lever, say a little more than can be done with one hand. Let it remain in the press about ten minutes, then raise the lid, which will allow the confined steam to evaporate, and let the lid remain so about two minutes, to allow the matrix to dry thoroughly. Then remove the forme back to the imposing surface, and take off the mould.

13. *Trimming the Mould.* – It will be found that the metal furniture round the forme has left its impression, which looks like a frame round the type. The removal of the superfluous flong beyond this is called trimming the mould.

Trim the mould with a pair of shears, flush with the outside of the impression of the furniture. The latter is to serve as a resting-place for the casting gauge. Should any projection appear at the point where the metal is joined at the corners, &c., be particular to hammer it down quite flat. Paste a piece of stout brown paper on one edge of the mould. It should be of the same width as the mould and about four inches in length, and be brought up to the indentation left by the type-high furniture on the top edge of the mould.

When this is dry, dust the face of the mould well with powdered French chalk, applied by means of a soft brush. Then remove the superfluous chalk with the chalk brush. If you have not a chalk brush, turn the matrix face downwards and strike the back smartly with a cane, to cause the superfluous chalk to leave it. The mould is now ready for casting from.

14. *Casting the Plate.* – Place the mould on the bed of the drying and casting press, face upwards, and as near the centre of the two uprights as possible. Lay the pica gauges on the margin of the mould. Place another sheet of thoroughly dry smooth brown paper on the mould, to project the same distance as the one pasted on the matrix [as shown in **Fig. 25.7**].

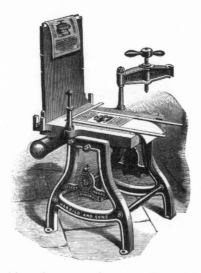

Fig. 25.7. *Casting box, mould, and gauges* – from Southward (1900, vol. II, p. 248)

The paper that was pasted to the mould will be found to protrude several inches from the mouth of the drying and casting press. The paper last mentioned should also project to a similar extent.

Put down the lid of the casting press, and screw it down tightly by means of the weighted handle at the top. Take out the small pin attached to the side of the iron framework, and very gently alter the position of the press from the horizontal to the upright. It is now ready for pouring the metal on to the matrix [as shown in **Fig. 25.8**].

Fig. 25.8. *Casting the plate* – from Southward (1900, vol. II, p. 249)

The metal must be poured between the two projecting sheets of paper.

Previous to pouring the metal into the casting press its heat should be tested. Fold a piece of writing paper and insert it in the metal. Should the paper quickly turn a lemon colour it is ready for pouring. In all cases carefully remove the scum from the surface of the metal pot, in order to take into the ladle bright metal only. Take especial care that all the metal is perfectly dry and free from water. You may drop a piece of Russian or other tallow into the pot, in order to flux the metal, and skim off the impurities and dross, which arise to the surface, with a perforated skimmer. Warm the ladle before putting it into the metal.

Pour the metal gently and steadily into the casting press until it is full, or nearly so. Then restore the press to its former horizontal position and fix it with the pin as it was before.

Now unscrew the lid, and the cast will be seen. Turn the cast over on its back, and raise the mould gently, by working the forefinger of each hand gently along underneath the edge of the mould – being careful not to put too much strain on any particular part.

Sometimes, especially if there has been any paste or dirt on the face of the mould, it will not come off the plate. Plunging both into cold water may save the plate, but it will destroy the mould.

15. After the plate is cast it must be trimmed. The superfluous metal, called the "pour," must be taken off with a saw. The edges must be bevelled with the plane, and the back planed with another plane. If the forme is one of eight pages it should be separated from the superfluous pour with a saw or a mallet and chisel, and planed evenly all round, leaving about a pica margin from the matter for bevelling the edges, if required.

When the plates are cast type-high they are "cored" by placing a core or thick metal plate in the box above the matrix.

A scarifier and graver are necessary to remove any superfluous metal adhering to the plates. They are then to be pulled and the imperfections carefully noted. The proof is sent with the plate to the "pickers," who remedy those defects that are marked.

The preceding directions will, it is hoped, enable any one to cast an ordinary plate in one of the portable foundries which are now so much in use. They also exemplify the general principles of the process, and are equally applicable to the large machinery employed in extensive stereotyping establishments. A short account of the latter may, however, be of service.

16. The stereotype furnace is about two feet square. It is in shape like an ordinary household washing copper, the melting-pot occupying the place of the copper. The front is of iron, and provided with a small door, through which the coals are supplied. Bars underneath and a small hearth allow of the removal of the cinders.

Extending about twelve feet laterally from the furnace, and on a level with its top, is the iron "surface." It is hollow, and forms part of the flue of the furnace. It is supported by one or more piers of brick.

At the extremity farthest from the furnace there is a screw press.

The forme is dried by being placed on this surface, and various degrees of heat can be applied according as the forme is placed nearer to or more distant from the furnace end. After moulding, the forme and matrix are placed under the press for awhile, then allowed to dry on a warmer part, with a metal plate on to keep the mould down, while another forme is placed under the press, and so on.

The casting press is called a "casting register." It is placed on an axle on an upright stand. The construction is similar to that already described.

A complete foundry for general work consists of the furnace – with surface, press, drying chamber, flange and metal pot; the casting register; the moulding table and iron roller; the planing slab and planes; and the planing machine. . . .

18. In regard to the comparative advantages and disadvantages of the paper and plaster methods, it may be stated that: –

a. The paper process is by far the most rapid; which is of great importance in newspaper and hurried work.

b. By the paper process a series of plates may be cast from one matrix; in the plaster process, on the contrary, the matrix is destroyed when casting a plate, by releasing the shell or cast. Hence the paper process is the most useful when a number of casts are required from a job to be worked together on the machine.

c. The paper matrices may be preserved for future use, and can be packed and sent any distance at any time.

d. The paper process is the simplest, and can be practised, as we have seen, on a very small scale.

e. The plaster process, on the other hand, has the advantage over the paper process of giving finer and sharper casts, thus rendering it preferable for stereotyping woodcuts; but electrotyping has now nearly superseded both methods.

Reading 25.11
Electrotyping
from *The American Printer* Thomas MacKellar (1866, p. 22).

By the 1860s, electrotyping, which had been first introduced in the 1840s, became the preferred process for making metal plates, although stereotyping was still used for modest editions and wood engravings since it cost less than electrotyping. One advantage of this process was that the whole form could be electrotyped at once.

MacKellar was the first to include a section on electrotyping in a printers' manual, although earlier, Lynch (1859, p. 164) had mentioned it in passing, saying, "Stereotype- and electrotype-cuts can be treated in the same way as wood-engravings, as far as making ready and overlaying is concerned; but as a stereotype copy is never equal to the original, it is not worth the trouble to overlay a cut of this kind. On the other hand, an electrotype, when correctly made, being an exact facsimile, it should be worked with the same care as if it were a wood-cut.

"On account of the cheapness and durability of electrotypes, they should always be used in preference to the originals; because, if an accident should occur, the plate can be renewed at a small expense, and it obviates the necessity of keeping water from the cut, as it can be washed in the same manner as ordinary type."

Savage (1841, pp. 249–261), who also mentioned the term *electrotype* in his long article on "Galvanism," describes the electrotype process in great detail. In this same article, he includes an illustration of a page printed from an electrotype plate that had been made from a page of type originally set in Diamond (4½-point) type.

Ringwalt (1871, p. 152) defines electrotyping as "The art of separating the metals from their solutions and depositing them in solid form, by means of the electric current, excited by the Voltaic battery, so as to manufacture, by the process, copies of engravings, or forms of type, from which impressions can be taken by the methods usually employed in letterpress printing."

Electrotypes were generally made by commercial electrotypers. In his article on "Electrotypying," Pasko (1894, p. 166) notes: "There are now about six hundred journeymen electrotypers in the city of New York and about thirty-five offices. This is about a quarter of the whole number in the United States." He includes many illustrations on the mechanics of the process in the same article on pp. 157–166.

Victor Strauss, in his *The Printing Industry* (1967, p. 228), sums up the popularity of electrotypes when he says they "are the elite of duplicate relief image carriers because they combine the highest quality, greatest precision, and exceptionally long press life."

Lately, stereotyping has measurably given way to the application of galvanism named Electrotyping, and may be superseded by it, though the former is better for moderate editions.

The pages being made ready and laid in a press, a pan of prepared wax, warmed, is placed over the pages and pressed down to the counter of the types. The mould is carefully dusted with plumbago, to give it a metallic surface, and is then suspended in the battery. On this, in a few hours, is deposited a thin shell of copper, which, after being coated with tin solder, is backed up with metal to the usual thickness of a stereotype plate. This method of electrostereotyping is desirable for Bibles and other works of which immense editions are required. Wood-cuts are usually electrotyped, as a stereotype mould cannot be drawn unless the woodcut has been previously coated with gum, which thickens the lines and injures the effect of the engraving.

The same care in preparing the pages for electrotyping must be observed as for stereotyping. For stereotyping, high slugs are placed only at the top and foot of the page; but, for electrotyping, they must be set around on all sides, and the bevelled flange must be made by side-planing.

Plate 30. Paper warehouse at *The State Gazette* Printing Establishment, ca. 1885. (Source: *The State Gazette* Printing Establishment, *Specimens of Printing Types*, [ca. 1885], p. 8, courtesy of Stephen O. Saxe.)

CHAPTER TWENTY-SIX

The Warehouse

Traditionally, printers' manuals separated the operation of the warehouse from the other departments in the printing office. A description of warehouse personnel and their duties has already been described in Readings 2.21 through 2.23 beginning on p. 68. In this chapter, the emphasis will be on paper handling before and after printing.

Apart from storing and distributing paper, the main activity of the warehouse was drying and pressing printed sheets, a chore that was very time-consuming since each process often required up to twelve hours to complete. This meant that a whole day was lost between the time the sheet was printed at the press and when it was ready to be gathered in the warehouse. It was not unusual for a large printing office in the nineteenth century to have between 75,000 and 100,000 wet sheets to dry out each week.

Nineteenth-century printers customarily delivered books in gathered and folded sheets to the client – the author, bookseller, or publisher – or directly to the binder. A few large printing offices had in-house binderies; but because of the rapid expansion of specialized trades in the printing industry during this period, the general practice was to send the books out in quires or ungathered signatures. As Philip Gaskell notes in his *A New Introduction to Bibliography* (1974, pp. 232–233), "In the early nineteenth century printers still normally delivered their work in the form of quires, with individual books ready gathered, so that the binder did not have to gather but only to fold the sheets for each book. . . . Then books began to be delivered from the printers in ungathered heaps of separate signatures, just as they came from the printing machines, so that the binder gathered as well as folded the sheets." Despite his assertion, manual writers, throughout the nineteenth century, continued to give instructions for gathering and folding sheets in the warehouse. In addition, by the 1860s, printers had access to a number of labor-saving mechanical devices to help them process the work more rapidly and efficiently.

Reading 26.1

The Warehouse

from *Practical Printing* by John Southward (1900, vol. II, pp. 203–205)

> Southward discusses the operation of the printing warehouse. A paper warehouse, ca. 1885, is illustrated in **Plate 30** on p. 760. Among other things, it served as a clearinghouse for both white and printed paper, which was the single most costly item in the printing budget and remained so until late in the century when the cost of labor surpassed that of paper. Since the paper was often supplied by the client, every sheet had to be scrupulously accounted for; therefore, it was essential that the flow of paper through the warehouse was strictly controlled. This was accomplished by means of an elaborate system of checks and balances which Southward describes below.

After the paper has been printed . . . it is sent to another department of the printing-office, and operated upon by a distinct class of operatives. This department is called the Warehouse, whose operations now have to be described.

In the warehouse the printed sheets are counted, and, where those operations are required, dried and pressed. They may also, according to circumstances, be folded, collated, cut up, again counted, parcelled, and delivered to the customer, unless they are to be stored. They may, on the other hand, require to be immediately bound up, in which case they go to the binding-rooms. In the warehouse, too, are kept the various kinds of paper and card which may be wanted by the pressmen. It should therefore be well provided with proper racks, cupboards, and pigeon-holes, and everything in it should be kept in an orderly and methodical manner. . . .

Entering the Work. – It is a rule in the warehouse neither to receive nor to part with even the smallest quantity of paper without proper written authority. Even when this authority is received it must be filed, and whatever is done in accordance with it must be duly recorded in the several warehouse-books. The warehouseman must be ready at any time to state accurately how much white paper and how many copies of any given printed sheet he has in stock. It is obvious that it is only by a proper system of bookkeeping, rigorously carried out, that this end can be accomplished. In large offices the bookkeeping is done by the warehouse clerk, and the direction of the hands employed alone occupies the principal warehouseman.

White Paper. – This sort of paper . . . includes all kinds of stock not actually printed. It will be brought in from the stationers, together with a delivery-note stating the number of reams, bundles, or reels that ought to be sent. The delivery-note is compared with the material, the parcels-book of the carter signed, and some of the hands arrange the parcels in a convenient place in piles. Then the quantities are entered into the stock-book, and the paper can be opened and stored.

At the appointed time the warehouseman receives from the foreman of the machine or press department a note requiring the delivery of a certain quantity of paper. This must be attended to, and a receipt obtained for the quantity of the paper that is given up, which receipt will be filed or passed on to the clerk to be entered in the stock-book. While the warehouseman is debited with all paper received, he is, of course, credited with what he delivers to be printed. Great care should be taken not to run short of paper for any job whose recurrence is known beforehand, such as the ordinary issues of a periodical, carelessness in this respect being regarded as a most serious offence. When the number of copies of a periodical is understood, the manager is supposed to confide in the warehouseman that he always has sufficient paper in stock, both for the edition and any probable extra demand that may arise; and if he has not enough paper, that he will at once acquaint the proper person of the fact.

Reading 26.2
The Warehouse Department
from *Typographia* by Thomas Curson Hansard (1825, pp. 763–777).

> On pp. 13–14 in Reading 1.2, Hansard described the procedures for dampening and drying paper in the printing office. In this reading, he supplies us with an excellent description of how paper was packaged and managed in the nineteenth century, as well as important information about edition sizes.
>
> Paper was ordered in *perfect* or *imperfect* reams. A perfect ream consisted of 516 sheets of good paper; an imperfect ream, 480, of which the first and last twenty-four sheets were seconds. If imperfect reams were used, the warehouseman would simply mix the seconds with

good sheets when giving out paper for a signature in the middle of the book, effectively burying the defective sheets where they would be less noticeable.

Since paper was expensive, every effort was made to reduce waste. Hansard recommends using 106 sheets for a short run of 100 backed-up copies. That leaves only six percent for proofing, register, and waste, which, by any standard, is meager. At my press in Italy, we always increased the number of sheets by twenty percent for backed-up forms, and another ten percent for each additional color.

When the pressman came upon a bad, soiled, or torn sheet – or a sheet that was spoiled in the printing process – he would request a replacement sheet from the warehouseman in order to keep the number of copies in the edition uniform. The discarded sheets would be doubled over and left in the heap since they might be needed later to make up additional books if the warehouse boys ran out of good sheets.

Throughout the handpress period, wet paper was hung up on poles to dry just as it had been in the fifteenth century (see **Plates 4** and **6** on pp. 8 and 100, respectively). Hansard follows the procedures set down by Stower (1808, pp. 402–417) and Johnson (1824, pp. 560, 565–571), although he occasionally elaborates on their texts in order to bring them in line with current practices. Moxon (1683) has a pair of plates, shown in **Figs. 26.1** and **26.2**, of workmen handling printed sheets of paper. His is the only pre-twentieth-century printers' manual to illustrate this process.

It is sometimes hard to imagine the amount of weight that the wet paper exerted upon the poles. A *lift*, the term used to define a single batch of paper, could have between six and twenty-four sheets, although Hansard says that seventeen was normal. The number of sheets taken up in a lift also depended on the thickness and the size of the sheet, as well as how soon it was needed elsewhere. In **Fig. 26.2**, the paper handler is placing two lifts at a time on the poles; Hansard, on the other hand, recommends taking up multiple lifts, by staggering them on the peel. In both cases, they will overlap the previous lift as they are placed on the poles. Well into the twentieth century, Jacobi (1919, pp. 350–356) was still instructing printers to use this traditional method for drying wet paper.

Fig. 26.1. *Taking up printed sheets with a peel* – from Moxon (1683, plate 31, in the section of plates following p. 394). **Figs. 26.1** and **26.2** courtesy of Rochester Institute of Technology.

Fig. 26.2. *Hanging up printed sheets to dry* – from Moxon (1683, plate 32, in the section of plates following p. 394)

There are numerous references in printers' manuals to dust and filth in printing offices; so it is not surprising to learn that the dry sheets – which were taken down in reverse order – had to be brushed off before they could be further processed. As was the custom in the 1820s, Hansard proceeds directly to gathering and folding once the sheets were dry. The gathered and folded books were then placed in a standing press and pressed. Later nineteenth-century manual writers, such as Adams in Reading 26.5 on p. 775, recommended pressing the dried sheets individually before they were gathered and folded.

Books were gathered by placing stacks of signatures in their proper sequence with the signature on the warehouse boy's left as he faced the bench or table. He picked up one sheet at a time from each stack, moving along the table from the lowest signature to the highest.

The term *collating* is sometimes misused to mean *gathering*. Collating is actually the process of verifying that all the sheets for each copy in the edition are accounted for, placed in their proper sequence, and correctly oriented.

The last step was to fold the gatherings, alternating the folds as they were stacked. The warehouseman then counted out the number of copies that had been ordered and proceeded to press them. Once they were pressed, the books were tied into bundles for delivery or storage.

Of Giving or Setting Out Paper for the Press

A bundle of paper contains two reams – a ream of paper, *perfected*, consists of 516 sheets, or twenty-one quires and a half, twenty-four sheets to each quire. If not perfected, twenty quires to the ream, of which the two outside quires are called *corded* or *cassé*, as they are generally rubbed by the cording of the ream. These quires are by the paper-maker made up of torn, wrinkled, stained, and damaged sheets; not that the whole quire always consists of such sheets, some good or passable being generally found in looking them over. But the general custom now is, for booksellers and authors to send in their paper *perfect*. When, however, it is sent in imperfect, it is the warehouse-man's business to lay by the two outside quires, to cull them when most convenient, and to add the quires to make the bundle perfect. What he afterwards selects as passable of the sheets in the outside quires, he must take care to dispose of so that they may neither be at the beginning nor end, but about the middle of the volume; or to have them used wholly for jobs or proof paper; for they are seldom so perfect as the inside quires.

It is the general custom to print of every work what is termed an *even* number, either 250, 500, 750, 1000, &c. These quantities are set out for the wetter in *tokens*: viz. for 250 (sheets) one token, containing 10 quires 18 sheets; for 500, two tokens, one 11 quires, and the other 10 quires and a half; for 750, three tokens, two of them 11 quires each, and the other 10 quires 6 sheets; and for 1000, four tokens, three of them 11 quires each, and the other 10 quires. If a work is printed in half-sheets, it, of course, requires only half the above quantities.

As it will sometimes happen that other numbers different from the above are printed, it may be necessary to give some hints to warehouse-men on this head [subject]. In giving out fractions of a ream of paper for short numbers, some loss will necessarily arise in the division of the over-plus. The twenty-one quires and a half of twenty-four sheets each, making 516 sheets, is ample allowance, (if the paper has been honestly supplied) for the overplus books expected by the booksellers, and for waste, in numbers amounting to 500. But since the tympan-sheets and regis-ter-sheets are equally used for either small or large numbers, an overplus proportionate to the above will seldom be found sufficient for numbers under 500. Hence, when paper is given out for smaller fractional numbers, an additional allowance must be made; or it will be difficult to make up even the proper number; since, according to this rule, the proportion of the sixteen sheets overplus in a ream, divided among ten sheets of 100 number each, would be only about three sheets; for 50 number, about a sheet and a half: whereas, in every case, one sheet for tympan, one or two for register, and as many more for incidents and accidents, would be absolutely necessary. Where strict attention is paid to the press-work, the men will be rather encouraged to throw out, and have paper to replace any they may discover in progress of work to be bad sheets, as soiled, torn, or spoiled in working; a work of even to the extent of 1000 number will seldom pass through an office, in which the exact proportion of the paper by reams will last out to the end of the reckoning. Indeed, so well are the most respectable booksellers convinced of the impolicy of being particular in this respect, that I have found them ever willing to grant any reasonable allowance. If they were not so, the consequences would be obvious upon reckoning the overplus books and waste. The printer, with regard to the paper account, as, indeed, in many other cir-cumstances over which he has no control, is made the scape-goat of the sins of others. The paper is made up at the mill, passes through the lands of the stationer's men to be made *perfect*, and gets into the printer's warehouse-book upon an assumption, not bearing a doubt, that every ream contains 516 sheets! It is next to impossible for him to count the paper except by reams and quires; but instances frequently occur where an expert warehouseman, feeling out a very light quire, on counting it finds only eighteen or twenty sheets, and often an outside or cassé quire, which will be only nominally a quire; such instances are sufficient to clear a printer's conscience if, after due care has been taken, he cannot make up to the uttermost copy what he may wish and his employers may expect. Generally speaking, in numbers from 1000 to 2000, one over copy in each hundred is the least that should be made up – in larger numbers more, in proportion, may be expected.

It would be difficult to form any positive and invariable rule for the quantity to be given out for short numbers, as it must depend, in some degree, upon the quality of the paper. The more expensive papers, on which, generally, short numbers or fine copies are printed, must be given out more sparingly than common paper; and the tympan and register sheets be supplied by a more common sort, to cut to the size of the finer.

For numbers up to 150, on ordinary paper, six sheets over will, generally speaking, be necessary. Thus, I should order for

25 number	1 quire	7 sheets
50	2	8
75	3	9
100	4	10
150	6	12
200	8	14
250	10	18

But if these fractions were added to even numbers, I should give out scarcely any overplus. Thus, a 250 has, in the share of the overplus of a perfect ream, by giving out 10 quires 18 sheets, got eight sheets over; therefore, for

275 I should only add	1 quire	2 sheets	
300	2	3	
400	4	6	and so on:

the warehouse-man always bearing in mind to reckon for each 25, so many quires of 24 sheets, and the same number of sheets in the first instance, and then to add the necessary overplus.

In giving out paper for what are termed *jobs*, a little further observation will be necessary. It has been usual to give tables for this purpose, and the Printer's Grammar [Editor's note: Hansard is actually referring here to *Typographia* by John Johnson (1824, vol. II, pp. [561]–[564]), not Stower (1808).] gave a very elaborate one, showing the quantity of paper to be given out for any job from 25 to 5000; and from two on a sheet to 128; but it was totally useless: it never could be acted upon: the calculation was made upon quires of 25 sheets, which never are found in a book or job office; so that if the directions of this table were followed in a case, for instance, where it gave the quantity as 11 quires, without attending to the above circumstance, the work would be found 11 sheets deficient.

The only way I have ever found practicable, has been, to try by division how many sheets are requisite for the purpose; for example, a job (label or any thing else) 750 number, 32 on a sheet, will require 24 sheets, which will give an overplus of 18. If this is not thought sufficient, a remnant or sheet more must be given out, calculating that where a sheet has to be cut into many parts, some further allowance must be made for accidents.

The overplus sheets being partly allowed for tympan-sheets, register-sheets, and other incidents; such as bad sheets, faults committed in beating, pulling, bad register, &c.; in any of these casualties the pressman doubles the sheet in the middle, and lays it across the heap as waste: for in case that sheet should run short of its proper number, the gatherer may chuse out the best of them to make good the deficiency. In setting out the paper, the warehouse-man lays each token with the folded side, or back part, one way, and the other token with the folded, or back side, the other way, that the wetter may distinguish the different tokens. When this is done, he writes a label, and puts it into the bundle, thus, [Joseph] *Guy's Spelling, Nov. 7* – or whatever may be the title of the book, that the pressman, when he takes up the heap, may not take the wrong one by mistake; and by this label, he can at all times ascertain how long the paper has been wet, and thereby know the state it is in for working.

Of Hanging Up Paper to Dry

When the paper is worked off, the warehouse-man takes the heap and carries it to the room where poles are fixed for the purpose of hanging the sheets upon to dry, and this most generally is the appropriation of every room in a printing-office that has sufficient height for the paper, when hanging on the poles, to be out of danger from the workmen's lights. He lays the heap down on a stool, or table, of a convenient height, then takes the handle of the peel [see **Fig. 26.4** on p. 773] in one hand, and lays the top part down upon the heap, so that the upper edge may reach near the middle of the sheet; and, with the other hand, he doubles over so much of the printed paper as he thinks sufficient to hang up at one lift; which should be about seventeen sheets, as near as he can guess; or, if he has pole-room to hang them on, twelve, and down to six, according as he can allow time for drying. Some warehouse-men, to forward their work, will hang up a quire or more at a lift, which, through its thickness, keeps wet a long while, where it bears heavy on the pole; besides it often draws out turpentine from the wood, which leaves a yellow stain upon the paper. But supposing the poles well-seasoned, and not likely to stain, still it is hazardous, and ought on no account to be allowed. Some kinds of paper [are] much more liable to mildew than others, and particularly that part which rests on the pole, as it retains the water longer than the sides, which having the advantage of the air circulating between, get dry first.

Having thus doubled the first lift on the peel, he shifts the peel with his right hand, two or three inches towards the left, and then taking an equal quantity for another lift doubles that on the peel; and continues so doing till he has got as many lifts as the peel will carry; then he raises it, holding it aslant, that the shorter fold of the sheets may open from the peel, in order to convey them over the pole; and inserting one end of the peel so as to take all the lifts but one, he raises them so as to slide easily so far as to leave the next lift lapping about one inch over the first; proceeding in the same manner till he has disposed of all the lifts he carried up by that loading of the peel. He then, at his table, reloads, and proceeds as before. It will sometimes be necessary, where the end of a pole is exposed to any strong current of air, as a window, &c. to *lock* the last lift. This is done by folding a lift two or three times so as to concentrate its weight in a small compass, and hanging this over the last lift near the window it will generally prevent the air taking the sheets off the poles.

Of Taking Down the Sheets When Dry
When the sheets are sufficiently dry, the warehouse-man takes his peel and brush, and with the peel begins with the last lift hung up, on account of the wrapper being with that lift; and continues to proceed to the other, in the reverse order to that of hanging them up, successively taking them down and brushing them, till he has finished the whole; taking care that he lays the single signature of each lift one over the other; if this is not done, it will occasion considerable trouble to turn them when they are to be collated.

There is also another way of taking the sheets down from the poles, which is, by laying the flat side of the peel against the edge of that lift which hangs over the other books, and pushing the peel forward, forcing them to slide, one doubling over the other, and so finishing the business with more expedition. But this method cannot be recommended, because the dust, which flies about while the sheets are hanging, must lodge on them, and by pushing them forward, is rubbed in, instead of being brushed off.

Of Putting By the Sheets, or Signatures, When Taken Down
When the heaps are taken down, the warehouse-man removes them to the warehouse, knocks [jogs, aligns] them up, and puts them by in that part of the room where they will be most out of his way, till he has a sufficient number of signatures to form a gathering. But two or three sheets of each signature should be put by, in case the author, bookseller, or master, should want a copy of the work, or a specimen of as many sheets as are finished, before they are gathered. If this has not been

done, and clean sheets should be wanted, he would then be obliged to lift every signature to get a sheet out of each, which will occasion a great loss of time, this may easily be prevented by reserving a few sheets as they are worked off.

Either the bookseller or author should be supplied, from time to time, with one copy of each sheet when printed, if from manuscript, in order to secure a copy from which to reprint in case of the calamity of fire. When he lays down the gathering, if such sheets have not been wanted, they are easily returned to their respective signatures.

Of Laying Down a Gathering

To lay down a gathering, is to place the several heaps, with their signatures following each other, upon benches or forms of a proper height, beginning with the first signature of the body of the work, and laying it upwards, which is sometimes marked A, but in general B, placing it on the left end of the gathering-board with the length of the sheet before him, and the single signature (A or B) next him. He then follows with C, D, &c. laying them close to each other in the same position as the first, till he has laid down a sufficient number of sheets, which is commonly from B to M, unless the volume consists only of fourteen or fifteen sheets; in that case he may as well lay down the whole at once, rather than make two gatherings of them; he will then save himself the trouble of booking them: but where a volume runs through two or three alphabets, several gatherings must be made. In such cases, eleven or twelve sheets in a gathering is quite enough. The title, with signatures a, b, c., cancels [cancellans, replacement signatures], &c. if any, should be left till the last, and placed at the end of the gathering, so that, when folded, they may be found withinside.

Should the impression of each signature be so large as to cause the heaps, when laid down, to be too high for the boys, he must lay the gathering by bundles. Where pamphlets and small books are done, containing three or four sheets, they should be laid down three or four times, to the full length of the gathering-board.

Of Gathering

This is the proper work of the warehouse boys, all working together: the art required in gathering chiefly consists in not taking up more than one sheet at a time, and following each other in rapid succession. They begin at the left-hand of the row; laying the left arm across the first heap, taking a sharp-pointed bodkin or needle in the right-hand, and with the sharp end of it, just touching the right-hand corner of the sheet, and raising the hand, lift up that corner, which is immediately received in the left, and is conveyed to the next heap, being particularly careful to place it even over the other, that there may not be much trouble in the process which is to follow; taking the second in the like manner as the first, and going to a third, fourth, &c. to the end; and then proceeding to *knock the gathering up;* viz. to make the sheets lie exactly even over each other; which is done in the following manner: a table being provided for this purpose, or one end of the gathering-board left clear, on which is placed a wrapper, they take the ends of the sheets between the thumb and fingers of each hand, and grasping them loosely, hold them upright, with the long side or edge on the surface of the table, then lifting them up about four inches high, they let them drop quickly through their hands, and catch them up again several times until they are quite even; for by these repeated jerks, those sheets which were above the rest are driven downwards, and those that were lower, upwards, and forcing the hands forward at the time of their falling causes them to be even at the sides; when they become exactly even, they lay them on a wrapper, and proceed gathering on as before, knocking them up, and placing them on the heap just gathered, with the single signature of each gathering lying successively one upon the other, still going on in the same manner, till they are piled to a convenient height. The pile is then covered with a wrapper, to keep the dust from soiling the top sheet, and thus accumulating, pile after pile, till the whole is finished. But, while gathering, attention must be paid in looking over the sheets, lest any should be torn, dirty, &c. and if any are found of that description they must be doubled up and put at the bottom of the heap they belong to.

The most general, and perhaps the most expeditious mode, is to use neither bodkin nor needle, but damp the end of the thumb with the tip of the tongue, and by this means lift up the sheets; but great care must be taken that the fingers are perfectly clean, or a number of sheets will be spoiled.

When the gatherers have worked till one of the sheets is deficient (for it would be an extraordinary circumstance for them to be just equal), they double up the odd sheets upon one another, cover them up with wrappers, and then put them by till collated.

Of Collating Books

The warehouse-man takes some of the books which have been gathered, and puts them on a table or gathering-board, with the single signature before him, at his right-hand, and his left-arm across the heap; he then, with a sharp-pointed bodkin or needle, lightly pricks up the corner of the first sheet of the single signature, viz. A, or B, and with the thumb of his left-hand catches it up, and nimbly shifts it between the two fore-fingers of the same hand, that he may be ready with his thumb to do the same to a second, &c. for if he does not thus secure the sheets between his fingers, on receiving the next, the latter sheet would immediately fall back, and obstruct his view of the following signature. The collator cannot be too attentive in observing whether the gathering be true; that is, free from having two sheets of one signature; sheets turned the wrong way, or left out in the gathering, &c. and if he finds a sheet wanting or damaged, he may supply the defect from the heaps on the gathering-board, as it is the best and the most expeditious mode for the warehouse-man to go on with the collating at the same time the gathering boys are proceeding with the gathering. If duplicates have been gathered, he draws the overplus sheets from the rest, and lays them aside till he has collated the pile, after which he distributes them to their respective signatures.

Having collated a gathering, he lays it on his left, with a wrapper underneath, to keep the board from soiling the sheet; he then collates another, and puts that on the one just laid down, not even, but rather across it, that when he begins to fold, he may with ease distinguish each division, proceeding in the same manner till he has thoroughly examined the pile. Others again do not lay the gatherings down separately; but, when one is done, put the collated corner from them, and draw the next near them, and so proceed, moving each gathering backwards and forwards as they collate them; and when they have got a sufficient handful, turn them over, and keep going on as before, till the pile is finished. This way, if properly attended to, is the best, as it expedites the work, and answers the same end.

Of Folding

Having collated the heap, or pile of gathered books, he proceeds to folding, which is performed in the following manner. The gatherings being on one side of him, he takes down one of the books from the rest, knocks it up on the board or table, and then keeps the single signature of the first sheet with its face downwards to the table, so that when he doubles it up, the last sheet will be folded inwards, and the first outwards. The manner of knocking the book up having been already described, a repetition of it here is needless; so, supposing the sheets exactly even one over the other, he lays the gathering flat on the table, and having hold of the ends, or sides, in his hands, doubles the right-hand hold over to the left; but before be relieves the end of the book from his right hand, he nimbly shifts it to his left, between the two fore-fingers of that hand, and then releases the other end from out of the right; by having it in that position, that is, with his fore-finger between the two folds, he can (though not doubled quite even) shift it which way he thinks proper, without discommoding any of the sheets.

It being now doubled up, and the edges placed exactly even over each other, he rubs the palm of his right-hand hard on the fold or back part of the book, that it may remain close together. When this is done, he lays it on the wrapper near him, and works, on as before, observing to fold them as the work requires; viz. if twelves, in the long cross; and if folio, quarto, octavo, sixteens, eighteens, or twenty-fours, in the short cross.

Folding books is an important concern, and ought to be particularly attended to by the printer, because, if they are unevenly folded, the dust, by long standing, will work in, and soil those sheets that come out further than the rest, so that, when bound, they will have on the margin a border of dust, unless the binder cuts very deep, which must be allowed to deface the beauty of a volume. On the other hand, if the binder is nice in his work, and will not suffer a bad sheet to appear in it, he sends word that it is wanting, and it is very rarely that he sends back the damaged sheet, which impoverishes the waste, and is likewise an additional disgrace to the warehouseman for his negligence in not properly collating the books; and should it happen to be the sheet which is short in the gathering, a book must thereby be rendered imperfect, none of that signature being left to make good the deficiency. It is necessary here to observe, that though books seem apparently uneven, it is not always owing to the folder's negligence; therefore, before blame can properly be attached to him, the books should be examined; because, though the quality of the paper has been attended to by the purchaser, yet perhaps nicety respecting the size may not have been so much regarded by him, so that some of the sheets in a volume, or gathering, are frequently found to differ, half an inch in size, particularly since the introduction of machine-made papers.

In some paper the sheets run equal enough as to size, but are not square; and if, in such cases, folios, quartos, octavos, or sixteens were to be folded with the two bottom corners even together, they would be extremely uneven; therefore the best that can be done, when it so happens that the sheets run in this unsquare manner, is to knock them up well, and fold them so that they may at least be brought even at the middle of their outer margins; then the outer margin of each side will share the defect alike.

When sheets are flimsy, which is sometimes the case, the more the folder knocks them up the worse they are, for the knocking them up only batters their edges, instead of bringing them even; therefore, before they are folded, the uneven sheets must be pulled even, and then gently knocked up.

Of Counting Out and Pressing of Books

Having folded a parcel, or the whole of the gathered books, the warehouse-man proceeds to count them out into proper quantities, according to the thickness of the gathering: if very thick, only five; if thin, ten, fifteen, twenty, or twenty-five, nay, sometimes fifty, according to their thickness, and observes to keep the same number in the count of each different gathering throughout the work. He then lays them flat on the table, and gives them a blow or two with the palm of his hand on the folded or back side, to make them lie close; after which he gently knocks them up even, and puts them in the standing press [**Fig. 26.3**], if empty; if not, in a convenient place, on a wrapper, or waste sheet, till the press is disengaged, with the fold or back side of the first parcel one way, and the second quantity of books with the folded side or back the other way, continuing, in the same manner, to put them on one after the other, till the press will permit no more in height. He then proceeds to pile up, range [row] by range, till full, observing that each range contains an equal quantity of books, and stands in a right parallel, so that when they are screwed down they may all receive an equal pressure; the reason why he is particular in reversing the edges of each portion is, that if he did not, it would be impossible to pile them up straight with their backs to lie all one way: for, in printing, if the matter does not run close and even alike, but, on the contrary, some pages are loose and open, and others close, the open pages receiving a deeper impression than the close, make that part of the sheet swell, while the remaining ones lie closer; therefore, were a number of books to be piled, before pressing, with their backs one way, they would be raised up at one end, and consequently would soon slide down; which inconvenience is remedied by reversing them; for, turning the thick end on the thin, they are brought to lie level; besides which, their number then can the more readily be told.

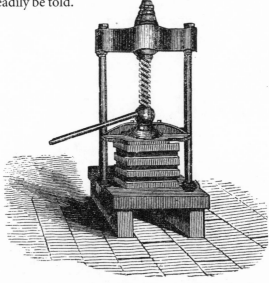

Fig. 26.3. *Screw standing press* – from *The History of Printing* (1862, p. 195), courtesy of Bridwell Library

The press being full, the warehouse-man takes the short pin belonging to it, and screws it down as low as he can, after which he takes a strong iron bar, about five or six feet in length, and with it works the screw of the press round with all his force as tight as he possibly can, then calling for the assistance of others in the warehouse, the pressure is finally completed, and the books remain in it from 12 to 24 hours. Where an hydraulic press is used, the screwing-down process is of course changed for the pumping. The pressure acquired is so great in these presses, that they may be charged and discharged three or four times in the day. He then takes them out of the press, and piles them up against the sides of the room, or in stalls, if the house is so fitted up, covering them neatly and closely with a wrapper under and over, so that the dust may not easily penetrate. A label is then attached to the pile, on which is expressed the title of the book, and how many the parcel contains. Should the impression be more than the press will admit of at once, it is filled up again in the like form as before, and so continued till the whole is completed.

If the impression is not very large, and will make only a few bundles, or is expected to remain some time under the charge of the warehouse-man, he ties them up into bundles, laying a wrapper under and over each, and having written the title and the number of books in the bundle on the upper wrapper, he puts them aside in the store room, or some convenient part of the warehouse, that he may have free access to deliver them out according to order. As soon as the books are finished, he acquaints the author or bookseller that the whole of the impression is ready for delivery.

Of Making Up the Waste

After the books have been collated and folded, and the duplicate sheets that were drawn out distributed, he takes the last signature first, and shaking the spoiled or doubled-up sheets out, if any, from between the others, he lays the overplus clean sheets flat on the table, with the single signature towards him, and opens the doubled or spoiled sheets, and places them on the former with the signature the same way. This done, he turns them over; knocks them even; folds them; and puts them near him, with the single signature upwards. He then takes the sheets that lie next to the signature he has just folded, and does the same to that, placing it on the other, and continuing till he has finished the whole; after which, he presses and ties them up together, and writes on the bundle the title of the book; also which sheet is deficient. They are then put in a proper place, whence they may be easily taken when wanted. But it must be observed, if there should be, amongst the sheets distributed, any of the signature that was short, he gathers again, till that, or some other sheet is deficient, collating and folding them, and putting them with the other books.

Of Booking the Different Gatherings

When a volume runs through several alphabets, it must consequently make more than one gathering; therefore to put the different gatherings together in regular succession to make a complete volume, the warehouse-man takes as many counts of the first gathering as he can conveniently carry, and lays them on the place where they are intended to be booked. He then lays a wrapper on the gathering-board, and takes the first count of reversed parcel, which he places on it, with the single signature upwards; a second quantity is then laid down in the same way, with their backs one on the other, and placed so that the end of one of the parcels may project outwards, while the end of the other is turned inwards: thus he continues piling them in this distinct manner, till he has got them sufficiently high. After this is done, the second gathering is placed by the side of the first, with their outer margin against the backs of that gathering, and piled up in the same manner, till it contains the same number of gatherings as the first parcel.

If a book makes more than two gatherings, they are laid down one after the other, as before observed. The utility of laying down each count, so that they may project a little over each other, will be readily perceived; for should he take two gatherings of one sort, or let one slip from his fingers unperceived (which is not improbable where there is a number of gatherings in a volume) on their being placed in this manner, he quickly discovers his error by their not running equal at the end of every count. If he does not lay them in this manner, a mistake of this sort will not be detected till he comes to the bottom of each gathering; and then to rectify the error will be attended with much trouble. When he has laid down some of each gathering, he proceeds to book them, which is done by taking one from each parcel, beginning with the first; he then knocks them even, and places them on a wrapper, reversing each book. They are afterwards tied up in bundles, or piled away in a convenient part of the warehouse, with a wrapper under and over, and a label in each pile. If some odd gatherings are left (which is highly probable), they are then added to the bundle of waste, and a memorandum made of it on the upper wrapper.

Reading 26.3
Hanging Up Paper
from *The Printer* (1833, pp. 56–57).

> The instructions given by the author of *The Printer* are similar to those given by Hansard in Reading 26.2 above; however, there are some notable differences. In this reading, the wet

paper is taken up in lifts consisting of two to three or eight to ten sheets, numbers that are substantially less than those specified by Hansard. Drying paper was not considered difficult work. It was done by lads between the ages of fifteen and eighteen, although they did have to be physically strong since the heaps of printed sheets – which could weigh as much as seventy pounds or more – had to be carried from one operation to the next.

When the printing operation is completed the paper is still moist, and, as well as the ink now impressed on it, requires to be thoroughly dried. For this purpose the warehouse-rooms are provided with poles arranged parallel to each other at some distance below the ceilings. When the heap of wet printed paper is brought from the press or machine, it is delivered to the hanger-up, who is furnished with a wooden peel [as shown in **Fig. 26.4.**] The width of the top is about two feet, the length of the handle is proportioned to the height of the room. The top, which is very thin, is laid flat on the heap, and a certain number of sheets, depending on the substance and state of the paper, and the speed with which they are required to be dried, varying from two or three to eight or ten, are lapped over the top of the peel. It is then moved sideways a few inches, and another portion is lapped over, till the peel is full. With this instrument the sheets are easily transferred to the poles, but are distributed so that merely the edges of the sheets overlay each other. The whole then hangs till thoroughly dry, when the hanger-up takes them down again with his peel, and places each sheet in a separate heap, till he has enough of any one work to form a gathering, or till it is otherwise needed. Lads from fifteen to eighteen are employed in this work, which requires care in the arrangement, and much attention to cleanliness, for if the sheets are soiled by being hung on dirty poles, or through any other cause, they become unfit for use, and occasion a most serious loss. If, also, through carelessness in the arrangement, different sheets or different works are mixed together, the separation is a work of much difficulty, and creates a great deal of useless labour. The occupation is clean and healthy, and is not laborious, though it requires more strength than the preceding divisions, as the heaps, as they come from the press, and after they are taken down, when they have to be stowed away, weigh from forty to sixty or seventy pounds or more, and require dexterity in the handling, so as not to rub and deface them.

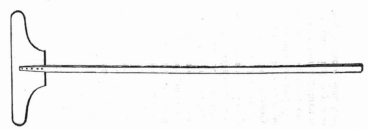

Fig. 26.4. *Peel* – courtesy of Rochester Institute of Technology

Reading 26.4
Drying the Sheets
from *Practical Printing* by John Southward (1882, pp. 583–585).

Southward describes how sheets were dried in the 1880s. Even though poles were still being used for book work, this method was discouraged after the 1840s when printing offices were illuminated by gaslights. Their presence was always a potential source of fire hazard. There were, however, alternative methods, such as the drying rack shown in **Fig. 26.5**. It was used primarily for job work. One advantage of a drying rack was its mobility. It could be placed next to the press so that the sheets could be laid directly on the trays as they were printed, thus saving a few extra steps in both the pressroom and the warehouse.

Dampened paper should never be laid directly on the wooden framework of the drying tray without a piece of waste paper intervening between the wood and the printed sheet. Today, when wooden racks are used for drying paper, a piece of nylon netting is usually stretched over and stapled to the tray in order to keep the sheet fully suspended and off the wood.

Woodcuts were best dried in cold air by spreading them out on drying racks. Other types of printing were dried by hot air or steam pipes when available. At my press in Italy, we had drying frames that were suspended from the ceiling. These frames were strung, at one-inch intervals, with nylon fishing line and clothespins that left enough room to clip two sheets of paper together on each line. This method was later abandoned in favor of placing the dampened sheets overnight between thin pulpboards, a procedure that removed the moisture and flattened the sheet at the same time.

Southward also discusses the best ways to test inks for dryness, as well as procedures for quickly drying down inks with "calcined magnesia," also known as *magnesium carbonate*.

In very small offices, cords or lines are strung across the press-room: hence the phrase, "on the line." The paper is laid upon them by means of the "peel," a strip of wood to which a cross piece is attached [see **Fig. 26.4** on p. 773]. It is a prominent feature in engravings of old offices [see **Plate 3** on p. 2]. A better plan is to erect poles or rods near the ceiling of the warehouse. After hanging the sheets up in parcels of a quire or so, they are left to dry by the ordinary evaporation of the moisture. This plan is open to three serious objections. It is dangerous, as the gaslights, often placed underneath, are liable to ignite the sheets, and perhaps set fire to the whole building. The plan is also defective from the tendency there is of the dust of the room discolouring the paper, particularly over the fold, or the "break," more especially as this exposure must be maintained for a considerable time. The plan also detracts from the orderly and methodical appearance which should always be exhibited in the warehouse.

The very finest kind of woodcut work can, however, only be dried properly in cold air. The process is slow and tedious, and involves much space. The best plan is to lay out the sheets in twos or threes upon trays. If there are very heavy cuts, the set-off sheets ought to be left in, as they come from the machine.

The best way of drying sheets, where it is practicable, is to use hot air or steam pipes. A room with stone or brick flooring, and bare walls, is the most suitable, as with the greatest care there is always the danger of fire breaking out.

The best arrangement that we have seen is one [for a drying rack, see **Fig. 26.5**] which may be described as a series of domestic clothes-horses standing nearly close together. Their front edges are wider than the rest of the frames, and approach each other quite closely, so that when all are in position the side of the series forms a complete partition. By making them run in grooves one horse [tray] may be withdrawn at a time, and the sheets moved and replaced, the rest of them, meanwhile, not being exposed to as much cold air as if a wide door had to be opened. In such a room the work should be hung in quantities of about half a quire, although sometimes smaller and sometimes larger lots are better. The temperature of this room may be about 125 degrees, but this is a matter influenced by the character of the work, and one which experience alone can settle.

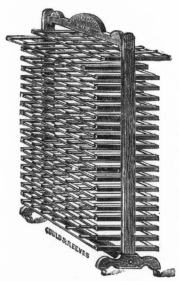

Fig. 26.5. *Drying rack* – from Southward (1900, vol. II, p. 206)

Some kinds of paper dry much more readily than others, and in regard to printing ink there is always danger that while it appears on the surface to be dry and "set," it may be more or less wet beneath. If a smear results from the finger being slightly rubbed over it, of course the sheets must be kept hung up for some time longer, but it is better to test one of them by laying over it a piece of printing paper, and rubbing the back of that with a paper-knife. If, when removed, there is no set-off, it may be taken for granted that the sheets are ready to be pressed or sent out, as the case may be. . . .

If it be necessary to dry a few printed sheets immediately, for any sudden emergency, such as completing the sheets of a volume, calcined magnesia may be dusted over them, which will not sensibly affect the colour of the ink, and yet remove or absorb so much of it as remains above the surface of the paper. A pad of cotton wool is preferably employed, and the ink may then be rubbed over, as in applying bronze powders. Powdered French chalk is also useful, but it makes the paper very slippery.

Very fine work, when received from the printing-office, is generally examined, sheet by sheet, to ascertain whether there are any finger-marks or smears on the margin. Such may be removed by the use of stale bread, india-rubber, or an ink-eraser [knife with a scraping blade]; but fine glass or sand paper is also occasionally resorted to.

Reading 26.5
Of Filling In and Pressing Sheets
from *Typographia* by Thomas F. Adams (1837, pp. 346–347).

> Adams was the first manual writer to advocate individually pressing dry sheets before gathering them. He was very critical of the English practice of pressing the books after they had been gathered and folded. When Johnson's section "Of Counting Out and Pressing of Books" (1824, pp. 569–570) – which was taken almost verbatim from Stower (1808, pp. 413–415), and later repeated by Hansard on p. 770 in Reading 26.2. – was reprinted in Johnson/Adams (1828, p. 290), Adams adds the following footnote: "This is the only method that Mr. Johnson has laid

down for pressing books – we are not, however, disposed to believe that it is the only one practiced by the London printers, as their works are generally well pressed, which could not be the
case if they followed the above directions only. The method generally practiced in the printing
houses in this country [America], is to place every sheet (before it is folded) separately between
smooth pasteboards, and let them remain in the standing press twenty-four hours."

The bookbinder's wooden or standing press, shown here in **Fig. 26. 6**, would not have
had sufficient power for pressing sheets between pasteboards. Adams's method required the
use of a very strong standing press, like the all-metal improved press shown in **Fig. 26.7**, to
press the sheets properly.

Fig. 26.6. *Pressing books* – from Moxon (1683, plate 33, in the section of plates following p. 394,
courtesy of Rochester Institute of Technology

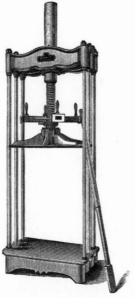

Fig. 26.7. *All-metal improved standing press* – from MacKellar (1878, p. 297)

Adams was also the first manual writer to mention females working in a printing office. He mentions that they were employed in the warehouse to interleave printed sheets with pasteboards. We know from other sources that later in the century women also worked in composing rooms (see Reading 2.4 on p. 44).

When the sheets are taken down, the warehouseman removes them to the warehouse, where they are filled in between smooth pasteboards made for the purpose. This operation is generally performed by boys or girls, who, after a little practice become exceedingly expert at it. We shall endeavor to be somewhat minute in our description of this operation, as it seems to have been entirely overlooked by former writers on this subject; we will suppose the pasteboards to have sheets between them which will be the case after they have been once used. The warehouse being provided with long tables or benches, secured to the wall, and a sufficient number of moveable tables about the size of the largest paper; the warehouseman places one of the small tables endwise against the long one, forming a right angle, and upon which to lay the pressed sheets, as they come out of the boards, the boy then takes his stand at the right side of the table, with the dry unpressed sheets at his right hand, and the pasteboards at his left somewhat elevated, leaving sufficient space before him, to fill in the sheets, he then proceeds as follows: – He first moistens the thumb of his right hand, and reaches across to the pasteboards at his left, drawing one off with his thumb, and placing it before him; he then catches a sheet of the dry paper also with his right hand, and places it as near the centre of the pasteboard as possible, then twisting his body nimbly round to the left, he slides the pressed sheet from the pile of pasteboards, to the table at his left side, and in resuming his former position, again draws off a pasteboard with his thumb, and so on, till the gross or bundle is filled. It is then laid aside, and another bundle filled and laid across the former, taking care always to keep the bundles separated, until they are put in press, when they are separated by smooth boards made of cherry or other hard wood. The bundles being all filled in, the warehouseman then proceeds to fill up the standing press, putting in one bundle at a time, and placing a pressing board between them; there should also be a stout plank introduced between the top board and the platen. In case the press should not hold quite as much as we would wish, more may sometimes be added by unscrewing the press, after it has been once screwed down, which so compresses the bundles, that one or two more may often be admitted. The press is then finally screwed down as tight as possible, and should remain so for at least twelve hours, when it should be entirely emptied before the sheets are taken out of the boards. In all these operations care should be taken to keep the sides of the piles or heaps perfectly even.

Reading 26.6
Pressing Jobs
from *The Printer's Companion* by Edward Grattan (1846, p. 107).

For reasons that are not clear to me, Grattan is opposed to using pasteboards for pressing printed sheets. Perhaps he is objecting to the glazed surface that the boards could impart to the paper under pressure. Instead of pasteboards, he recommends using heavy paper, interleaving it with both dry and wet sheets as they come off the press. His instructions for pressing dampened paper are similar to the pulpboard method that I describe on p. 355 in *Printing on the Iron Handpress* (1998).

The practice of pressing jobs in boards is one of the most ruinous that can be adopted in a job office: none should ever be pressed in them which are not perfectly dry. Every printer should supply himself with about a thousand sheets of the very heaviest kind of printing paper, of each size he may require, as medium, folio post, and foolscap, and should press his jobs in them. A job on dry paper may then be pressed the moment it is worked, without injury to it or anything else, as whatever ink sets off should not be on the job, and will not injure the sheets, as it drys into them almost immediately.

When it is desired to press a job perfectly smooth, which has been worked on wet paper, press it in sheets as soon as it comes from the press; then dry it, and press it again in boards. This will give it a most beautiful appearance.

Sheets used for pressing wet paper should be dried before they are used again.

Reading 26.7
Pressing the Sheets
from *The Printer's Manual* by Thomas Lynch (1859, pp. 166–168).

Lynch gives very detailed instructions for hanging the paper up to dry. He also gives the exact dimensions for the poles and offers some solutions for the inevitable problems of dust and weather. Paper hung on poles usually required at least ten to twelve hours for the ink to set and the paper to dry out completely.

Like Adams on p. 777 in Reading 26.5, Lynch also advocates pressing the sheets individually between pasteboards in a standing press for ten to twelve hours. When a glossy, or glazed, appearance was desired, the sheets were placed between two sheets of zinc and run through a rolling press, similar to the ones shown in **Fig. 26.8** below and in **Plate 21** on p. 484.

He also describes a method for hot pressing, a procedure in which the wet sheets were placed between heated, sheet-iron pressing boards, or plates, and pressed in a hydraulic press. This procedure was often done by outside specialists.

Fig. 26.8. *Rolling press* – from Ringwalt (1871, p. 123)

The paper being all printed, it must be exposed to the atmosphere a sufficient length of time to let the ink set firmly in the paper, before it is put in the standing-press.

The poles, upon which the sheets are placed to dry, should be two and a half inches wide, and made of one-inch white-pine. They should be placed across the room, about fourteen inches from the ceiling and nine or ten inches apart, resting at each end on a piece of wood fastened to the walls of the room, in notches to retain them in their situations. They should be kept clean, and, if they have not had paper hung on them for some time, the dust must be brushed off before they are again used. As the weight of the paper would have a tendency to bend the poles, they should be turned over, as occasion may require, to keep them straight.

The number of sheets put, in one place, on the poles, must be regulated by circumstances. If the work be in a hurry, or the poles be not in a favorable situation for drying, or the weather be rainy and the air charged with moisture, no more than three or four should be hung in a place; but, if the situation be favorable for drying, and the weather be warm, eight or ten sheets may be put in each place.

If the sheets be allowed to remain on the poles ten or twelve hours, it will, in most cases, be found sufficient, for the purpose of setting the ink or drying the paper.

They are now ready to be put in the standing-press. This is done by laying up a press-board, and putting on a paste-board and one of the sheets of the work to be pressed, alternately, until all the sheets of paper are in the paste-boards. The pile must then be taken, fifty at a time, and placed in the centre of the standing-press, with a press-board between each lift. The press must next be screwed down tightly, and suffered to remain in that condition ten or twelve hours; when it will be found that the sheets are as smooth as they were before being run through the press.

When highly-glazed paper is printed, the ink is liable to be transferred from the sheets to the paste-boards. In such cases sheets of common printing-paper should be put between them.

If it be wished to give the surface of the print a glossy appearance, instead of proceeding according to the above method, each sheet of paper should be put between two sheets of zinc, to the number of twenty-five, and run forward and back, three or four times, between iron rollers similar to those of a copper-plate press. This will be found to give jobs done in gold and silver a brilliancy which can not be obtained by the former mode of pressing.

Still another way is, to put the sheets of printed paper between sheet-iron pressing-boards, which have been heated previously; and then the whole is subjected to the power of a hydraulic press.

Although the last method mentioned is the best, it can not come into general use, on account of the expense and tediousness of the process. When, therefore, work is to be pressed in a manner superior to that which can be done by the common standing-press, the sheets of zinc and roller-press can be used with advantage.

Reading 26.8
Pressing Paper
from *Practical Printing* by John Southward (1882, p. 586).

> Prior to the adoption of hard packing in the nineteenth century, handpress printers were seldom concerned with the depth of the bite of the type in the paper – which was caused by soft packing – since the indentation would be minimized during the pressing process. However, from the 1850s until the end of the century, one of the chief goals in pressing paper was to give the sheet a flat, smooth, glossy appearance that was completely devoid of any evidence of a bite.
>
> Today, except for full-color illustrated books, glossy inks and glazed papers are seldom used when printing trade books.

When the paper is thoroughly dry, it is ready to be pressed, or smoothed, and freed from the indentations caused by the pressure of the types. It is usually held to be desirable that these should be removed, and that a perfectly level, polished surface should be given to the paper. In America, the acme of the printer's art is supposed to be reached when every trace of the pressure of the types has been removed, and the sheets present the smooth and glossy appearance of polished ivory. Amateurs of fine printing in France – the home of bibliophilism – on the other hand, rather prefer to see the effect of the pressure, and do not admire the high glaze so much valued elsewhere.

Reading 26.9
Cold Pressing
from *Practical Printing* by John Southward (1882, pp. 586–589).

> Southward describes the equipment and accessories used for cold pressing paper. Among them, he mentions a nipping press (**Fig. 26.9**), a standing press (**Fig. 26.7** on p. 776), the Athol press (**Fig. 26.10**), and the Boomer press (**Fig. 26.12**). The Athol press is a genuine Victorian curiosity. Its arms, or grips – the mechanism that lowers the platen – were cast in the shape of legs, bent at the knees and clad in boots.
>
> The invention of the hydraulic press (**Fig. 26.11**) by Joseph Bramah (1748–1814) in 1795 revolutionized the way paper was pressed in the warehouse. Initially, it was used by paper-makers, but by the early nineteenth century, it made its way into printing offices and binderies. The hydraulic press worked on a completely different mechanical principle than the screw press. In fact, it eliminated the screw altogether, instead relying on water pressure that forced the base plate up toward the fixed top plate; thereby, exerting pressure on the paper between the two plates. It was phenomenally effective, accomplishing in two hours the same amount of work that the screw press required twenty-four hours to do. There is also an illustration of a hydraulic press in **Fig. 4.17** on p. 185.
>
> Hansard gives a lengthy description of this press, including its dimensions and capabilities, as well as other pertinent technical data in his manual (1825, pp. 224–226).

11. The earliest system adopted was to beat the printed sheets with a heavy hammer – a tedious and laborious process, and one requiring great dexterity. After this there was introduced the screw press. The smallest and most elementary appliance of the kind is called the "Nipping Press." It consists of a frame with cross-piece, into which a screw is wormed, to the end of it being attached a platen. The paper is placed underneath this, and the action of the screw bringing down the platen causes the necessary pressure. This machine is, of course, only suitable for small jobs, and it is made up to about twenty-four inches in length.

Fig. 26.9. *Nipping press* – from Jacobi (1890, p. 260)

12. The screw, or standing press, is a development of the last-named. The sheets are placed either singly or in lots of three or four between "glazed boards." This process involves the handling of the sheets twice – first, in laying them between the boards and putting them in the press, allowing them to remain a number of hours to obtain the desired surface and finish; second, the removing of the sheets from the press and taking them out of the boards.

13. The glazed boards are made in various sizes and thicknesses. They are somewhat costly, but only the best ought to be used, as they are more economical than the thin descriptions. For "filling in" the boards two boys or girls are employed. One stands before the pile of paper, another on his left before the pile of boards. One lays down a board, the other instantly deposits on it a sheet, immediately after which the first lays down another board, and so on, till the whole of the paper is between boards. The heap is then taken to the press and placed on the bottom or bed. The arm – a long lever – is then placed in the slot left for it, and by thus turning the screw the whole is pressed. The piece answering to the platen of a printing press is called the "follower;" the space between that and the bed is called the "daylight." Some screw presses are actuated by a three-limbed appliance like the three legs in the arms of the Isle of Man, and are called "Athol presses." [See **Fig. 26.10.**]

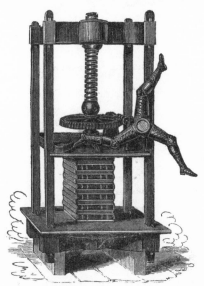

Fig. 26.10. *Athol press* – from *Bibliopegia* by John Andrew Arnett (1835, facing p. 168)

The warehouseman should be very particular to ensure that the work is thoroughly dry before it is put into the press. If this be neglected, there will be a set-off on the glazed boards, which will reappear on a subsequent lot of sheets being set in.

14. The deficiency of the screw or standing press consists in the fact that it is impossible to get sufficient pressure from it for certain kinds of work. Hence there was invented the "hydraulic press," which is sometimes called after its originator, Bramah the engineer. It depends upon the principle that a pressure exerted on the surface of a liquid is transmitted undiminished to all parts of the mass and in all directions. We must omit details of construction, but the following are the essential parts of the machine: Into the cavity of a strong metal cylinder a piston passes, but watertight through the top. A tube leads from the cylinder to a force-pump, and by means of this water is drawn from the tank into a cavity, so as to force the piston upwards. The piston supports a table, on which is placed the paper to be pressed, and the rising of the table presses the mass against a strong crosshead, fastened to the side pillars of the press. The power of the press is calculated in the

following manner: Suppose that the pump has only one-thousandth of the area of the piston, and that by means of its lever-handles the piston of the pump is pressed down with a force of 500 pounds, the piston of the barrel will rise with a force of one thousand times 500 pounds, or more than 200 tons. The rise, however, is slow in proportion to the power.

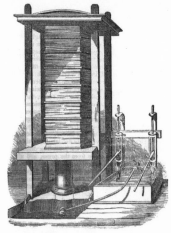

Fig. 26.11. *Bramah's hydraulic press* – from *The Printer* (1833, p. 58), courtesy of Rochester Institute of Technology

The enormous multiplying power given by this machine has been employed for many years in the printer's warehouse, presses suitable for printers being made of various sizes up to quadruple demy, which can be pumped up by steam or hand power. It is found advantageous, when a number of presses are used in an office, to employ steam. An eccentric should be fixed to the shafting. Any number of presses may be supplied by a single pipe, by having a joint at each press fitted with a screw valve, which can be opened or shut at will.

15. The *Boomer Press* [**Fig. 26.12**] is a comparatively recent invention. The principle by which its enormous power is accumulated is by a combination of four levers working upon toggle joints, through which passes a right and left-hand screw. The rotation of the screw causes the two joints to approach or diverge, according to the direction of such rotation, with a perfectly uniform motion.

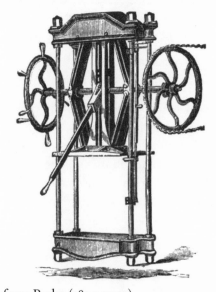

Fig. 26.12. *Boomer press* – from Pasko (1894, p. 55)

This press possesses several advantages over both the ordinary screw and the hydraulic presses. The pressure once applied, cannot yield, so that the material is in no way released, and can therefore receive a finish in less time than when under hydraulic pressure. The construction is simple and not liable to get out of order. The power accumulates with every turn of the screw, the movement of the platen or "follower" being rapid at the commencement of the pressing, gradually diminishing in speed as the power increases and the material under pressure becomes the most dense. The movement of the follower can be regulated with nicety, being continuous in action, not intermittent, as with the hydraulic. The press is specially adapted for smoothing damp sheets and pressing printed sheets between glazed boards. It often does as much work in two hours as in the screw press would require twenty-four hours.

Reading 26.10
Hot-Pressing Paper
from *Practical Printing* by John Southward (1882, pp. 590–596).

Hot pressing was considered by many to be superior to cold pressing. Even though the printed sheets were usually turned over to professional hot pressers by the 1880s, Southward describes how hot pressing could be done in the printing office. First, the individual sheets were interleaved with glazed boards. Then, a heated plate was placed below and above each batch, as well as additional plates about every 130 glazed boards. The workmen had to work very fast since the plates were prone to cooling off quickly. Because of the tremendous amount of pressure required, this type of hot pressing could only be done in a hydraulic press.

Southward recommends baking the glazed boards to harden any ink that may have been transferred to them during the pressing process. On the other hand, Crisp (1874, pp. 120–121) offers a completely different solution for cleaning glazed boards: "When the boards are much soiled with ink, take a clean dry duster [dust cloth] and rub them well on both sides till a polish is put upon them; when they are extra dirty a little turpentine may be applied on a piece of flannel before rubbing with a duster. Coarse ream wrappers, rolled into a ball, may also be used as rubbers [erasers] for the above purpose. Some printers only screw the boards down with or without a sheet of clean paper between them."

The Gill Hot-Rolling Machine (**Fig. 26.14** on p. 786) was another method for hot pressing paper. One of its innovations was the elimination of the glazed boards. It was used for both drying and pressing sheets in one operation. The process is somewhat reminiscent of Baskerville's, in which he placed the dampened paper between heated copper plates and ran them through a rolling press. Daniel Berkeley Updike referred to this procedure in his *Printing Types* (1922, vol. II, p. 108), "In printing a book, Baskerville had ready a succession of hot copper plates, and between such plates each wet sheet was inserted as it left the press – something no eighteenth century printer had up to that time attempted. The high finish of these hot-pressed sheets – the 'gloss' of his paper – compared with that on modern papers, does not seem to us very noticeable. His contemporaries, however, thought otherwise, and the Abbé de Fontenai, in a notice of Baskerville, describes it as 'so glossy and of such a perfect polish that one would suppose the paper made of silk rather than of linen.'" The Gill machine was also used to calender paper in order to make it thinner.

Southward's smudging and burnishing tests to determine if the sheets were ready to be pressed are still used today.

17. Hot-pressing, as a process for finishing sheets by removing the indentations of the printing, and imparting smoothness and glossiness to the paper, is very much superior to cold-pressing. There is also the special advantage connected with its use, that the work is done in considerably less time – a matter occasionally of the highest importance.

On the other hand, unless hot-pressing is properly done, it may spoil instead of improve the appearance of the sheets subjected to it, especially by browning the ink, making it spread, and by causing set-off. Very few printers indeed know how to do it efficiently, and the ordinary text-books of printing give no directions that are practically useful. In the Metropolis, the two or three firms that make a special business of it decline to afford information to others as to its *modus operandi,* while very jealously guarding their own plant from the inspection of outsiders. The following details may be depended upon, as representing the best methods adopted by the professional hot-pressers.

18. *The Press.* – The press that has given the best results hitherto is the hydraulic press [see **Fig. 26.11** on p. 782], described in [Readings 26.9 on p. 780]; though there would seem little reason why the Boomer press [see **Fig. 26.12** on p. 782] should not perform the work equally well. The ordinary screw press, however, is not powerful enough. The chief disadvantage of the hydraulic press is that it "gives" after impression is put on. This, however, only occurs with what is called "spongy" work; that is, soft piles or "stacks" of paper whose compressibility is greater than usual. When the stacks are put in "solid," the pressure is maintained. On a good hydraulic press the average pressure may be about 200 tons.

19. *Arrangement of the Press.* – On the bed of the press about twenty glaze boards, or "cards," or "skins," as they are usually termed, are first of all laid down to form a firm foundation. Then there is laid on them a heated iron plate, about ½ or ¾ inch thick. Above that comes the stack, consisting of sheets of the paper alternated or "sandwiched" with glazed boards. About 130 glazed boards form a stack. Above them again comes another hot plate, and then, according to the available space, other stacks, a heated plate; twenty or thirty cards being laid on the top of all. The "follower" is now nearly reached, and the action of the pump and piston below the bed forces the latter up, and causes the impression. This filling of the press is called "building up," and it has to be done with the greatest rapidity, otherwise the plates would get cold.

20. *Heating the Plates.* – This is done in a specially contrived oven, with a damper at the top, which is opened for the admission of cold air if the plates have become too hot; or, in technical language, are "over-baked." To know whether the plates are hot enough, the workman applies his finger, covered with a little saliva, in the same way as tailors are accustomed to test the temperature of their irons. If the saliva is at once evaporated, the plate is hot enough.

21. *Building up.* – The whole of the stacks must be put in the press together, to prevent the plates becoming too cold. They are kept in the press from eight to twelve hours: in the former case it would be called an "eight-hour press," in the latter a "twelve-hour press."

22. *The Boards.* – Unless the work is very common, one sheet only is put between each board. The boards should not be too thick; if they are, much of the force of the impression is lost. As is well known, the boards are expensive, but practically they may be said to never wear out. This may seem remarkable, but it is quite true; plenty of boards are now in use in houses doing this kind of work regularly that are thirty and forty years old. Constant wear is apt to make them broken and ragged at the edges; but this is a different thing to wearing them out, to which it would be thought they were especially susceptible.

23. *Cleaning the Boards.* – In the printing-office the operation of cleaning the glazed boards is regarded as being quite as necessary as it is found to be tedious. Yet in a regular hot-presser's establishment the boards are never cleaned at all. Whenever it is thought that there is danger of set-off, the boards are simply "baked," or exposed in the oven for heating the plates, to a moderate heat. The effect of this seems to be to indurate the board with printing ink, which, even with the finest work, never sets off. This has been a trade secret hitherto, and one that has been jealously guarded. Now that those who use the hot-pressing process are in possession of it, the saving that may in this way be effected will no doubt be appreciated. Boards that have been in use a dozen years have the appearance of black polished ebony, through the successive "bakings" and the ink thus ingrained into them; but that no set-off is thereby caused is simply a matter of practical experience. Sometimes they are baked twice, but this is after exceptionally heavy and "wet" ink has been passed through them.

Care should be taken to have the boards well filled up, as if they are unevenly packed, or all the paper is not placed in the centre over the ram, there is great danger of breaking the press.

24. *When Sheets may be Pressed.* – The two methods of ascertaining whether the sheets have been sufficiently dried as to allow them to go into the boards already referred to, apply to hot-pressing. The sheets may be slightly rubbed with the finger, and if there is a smear resulting they are not yet fit. Or a piece of paper may be applied to a portion and rubbed with a paper-knife; if there is any ink adhering to the white paper, in the shape of set-off, the print is too wet.

25. *Filling in.* – The boards may be filled in with sheets in the way already referred to under the subject of Cold Pressing [in Section 13 on p. 781 in Reading 26.9]. There is, however, a much more rapid plan, adopted in the large hot-pressing establishments, which may be here described. The boards are emptied of their last jobs and filled in with new work simultaneously. The workman stands with a pile of printed sheets at his left hand, a pile of boards at his right hand, and a vacant space in the middle. He "fans out" the boards, and does the same to the sheets, so that they may the more readily be picked up. Of course the sheets are fanned towards the right by the use of the left hand, the direction of the fanning of the others being opposite. Now, with his right hand, he takes a board and places it in the space between the piles of sheets and boards. Then, with his left hand, he takes a sheet and places it in the centre of the board. Then, with the right hand, he places another board on the sheet; afterwards another sheet, and so on to the end, or until a stack of about 150 boards has been reached. By careful practice, remarkable rapidity and precision may be attained in this operation.

Let us now suppose that we have on the left hand a pile of work that has to go into the press, and on the right a stack that has just come out of the press, consisting of boards and sheets. Taking out each sheet singly, lift the board with the right hand, and place it on the right-hand side of the stack. In the same way, with the left hand, take the sheet off the stack, and place it on the left of the stack, and so on. In the result the boards will, of course, be empty again.

The method used when two boys are employed, is that one is always emptying a stack of pressed work while the other is always filling in the boards. The following diagram [**Fig. 26.13**] of the arrangement of the table or bench may explain this: –

1. Pile of impressed sheets to go into boards.
2. Stack of boards and sheets to go into the press.
3. Stack of boards and sheets taken out of the press.
4. Pile of sheets taken out of No. 3.

Fig. 26.13. *Arrangement of the stacks for filling in*

While one boy is taking the sheet from No. 3 and placing it on 4, the other picks up the board and lays it down on 2. Meanwhile, a sheet from 1 has been transferred to 2, and a board belonging to 3 released through the pressed sheet it contained going to 4. This board is laid on 2, while another sheet is being lifted off 3, and another board made available.

26. *The Gill Hot-Rolling Machine* [see **Fig. 26.14**]. – The speciality of this machine is that by means of it work may be finished directly after it is taken from the machine, the drying and pressing or "rolling" the sheet being done at one operation.

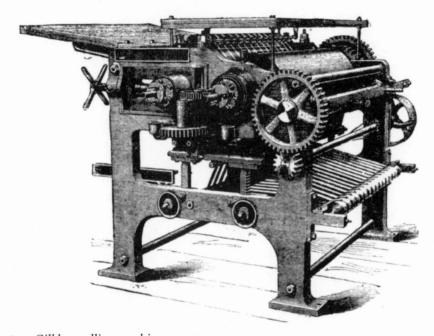

Fig. 26.14. *Gill hot-rolling machine*

The machine consists of two polished steel cylinders, through the centre of which a small steam-pipe passes. At the upper end is a feeding-board, on which the work is laid, and at the other end, under the cylinder, is a delivery arrangement somewhat like the flyers of a printing machine. The machine can be set up by any engineer, as all the parts are carefully marked. . . .

If the rolls are too hot, the Gill machine will render black ink slightly brown. This result is also met within ordinary hot-pressing if the plates are too hot. It is advisable not to roll immediately after printing, as the machine in such case necessarily takes some of the colour off. If the ink is allowed to set, there is no tendency of the kind. With a little experience and care any workman will be able to roll all sorts of work satisfactorily.

The machines will roll anything, from a trade card to a quadruple demy sheet, with cuts or otherwise. As much as 200 reams of double-crown and demy sized sheets have been rolled on a 33-inch machine in an ordinary week. The machines are shown to have saved one London firm alone £500 a year, comparing the cost of rolling with that of drying and pressing.

Reading 26.11
Paper Cutters
from *Printing* by Charles Thomas Jacobi (1890, pp. 258, 261, 263).

Paper cutters, or *guillotines* as they were also called, were first introduced into printing offices in the late 1830s. In addition to the two English cutters shown in **Figs. 26.18** and **26.19**, I have appended illustrations of three nineteenth-century American cutters. The first is the Gage paper cutter, which was manufactured by S. C. Forsaith in New Hampshire. As shown in **Fig. 26.15**, it is an excellent example of an early, primitive paper cutter.

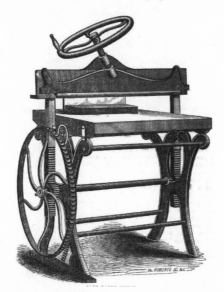

Fig. 26.15. *Gage paper cutter* – from Ringwalt (1871, p. 179)

The second, shown in **Fig. 26.16**, is the Minerva, a more sophisticated paper cutter made by Curtis and Mitchell in Boston. It was known for its great power and accuracy, as well as its effectiveness in making a clean, smooth, and true cut – important attributes for any paper cutter.

Fig. 26.16. *Minerva paper cutter* – from Ringwalt (1871, p. 306)

The third – which can still be found in modern print shops – is the Challenge paper cutter, shown in **Fig. 26.17**. Its unique feature is the lever bar that brings the cutting blade down across the paper diagonally. Today, the Challenge Machinery Co. manufactures massive electronic guillotines.

Fig. 26.17. *Challenge paper cutter* – from Pasko (1894, p. 91)

In connection with the warehouse certain mechanical appliances are necessary. Presses for cold pressing – the power for which is generally obtained by hydraulic pressure; rolling machines both for hot or cold methods; and cutting machines for paper. . . .

Hot pressing is as a rule undertaken by people outside, and is generally performed by a hydraulic press, hot plates being inserted at frequent intervals. The impression is taken out more easily by this method, and a better finish usually given by the heat employed. The sheets are placed between glazed boards as in cold pressing. This process is well adapted for cut work owing to its thoroughness in pressing and finish without an excess of glaze, which is given by hot rolling. . . .

Cold rolling may also be performed by the last-mentioned machines, but for any great quantity the older kind of machine is advised. Less surface is imparted by this last process, and if cuts have to be printed on a paper which has not a good surface, cold rolling is resorted to – as also after the work is printed. If cuts are printed on one side only, as for separate plates, the paper need only be rolled on one side. To do this it is customary to send two sheets through the machine at one time, back to back, the outside of the two sheets only being glazed and the inner sides retaining somewhat the old surface. This plan prevents the paper being made too thin. There are two methods of rolling, viz., plate, and that performed simply by running the work between the bare rollers, without anything in the shape of boards, sheets, or plates. In rolling printed work great care should be taken to prevent offset of ink. The hot-rolling apparatus has an automatic arrangement for cleaning the rollers when in use. For cold rolling the best way is to first have the printed work thoroughly dried, or it will assuredly be spoiled.

Cutting machines form an important feature in the warehouse department, and the selection of a machine offered by well-known firms is advised. Various machines are before the trade, but those on the guillotine principle are the best. Some give a straight and direct cut, others a diagonal, and there is also a self-clamping arrangement used. Furnival's machine, [**Fig. 26.18**], is one of this class, embodying all the latest improvements, and thus effecting a great saving of time in cutting large quantities.

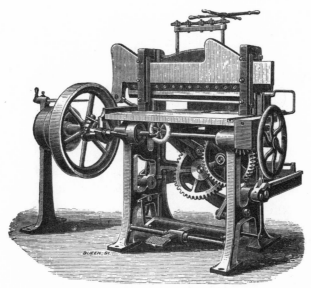

Fig. 26.18. *Furnival's machine*

For the cutting of small jobs a *spring guide* is used, which allows of the work being pushed to the front for the cut – the width of the platen preventing this in the ordinary machine.

A *card-cutting machine*, [**Fig. 26.19**], is likewise useful in this department.

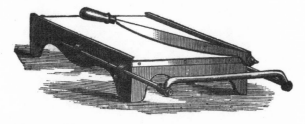

Fig. 26.19. *Card cutting machine*

Reading 26.12
Preparing Books for the Bindery
from *Practical Printing* by John Southward (1882, pp. 597–601).

Southward guides the warehouse personnel through the basic procedures for preparing books for the binder. These procedures include hand or machine folding, collating, gathering, and finally, counting out the required number of copies to fill the order. By the 1870s, manually operated folding machines, such as the one shown in **Fig. 26.22** on p. 793, were often found in printing offices that specialized in book and news work.

Rotary gathering machines, like Howe's shown in **Fig. 26.21**, were very effective labor-saving devices since the operator was able to remain in a fixed position as the signatures moved past her. These machines were more likely to be found in commercial binderies than in printing office warehouses.

27. *Folding.* – If the sheets in hand consist of bookwork, they are now ready for folding. This is done either by hand or machine.

Machine-folding requires no directions. The sheets are fed into the apparatus as in a printing machine, receive their folds from the mechanism inside, and are delivered at the bottom, all that is necessary being to remove them whenever the pile has become sufficiently large. Some machines register by points as in printing, in others the work is merely fed up to gauges. The alteration of the apparatus for two, three, or more folds is done according to the directions for use supplied by each manufacturer, which are applicable only to his particular machine; hence it is unnecessary to reprint them here. Care should be enjoined upon the operator, usually a young woman, that her hands are clean, and that the sheets be as little handled as possible, lest smears be caused.

28. Hand-folding is an operation requiring both precision and dexterity, qualities of a somewhat diverse character. The operator must fully understand the object and uses of signatures [in Reading 8.4 on p. 286]. There is a different method adopted for each form of sheet, the quarto, octavo, twelvemo, and the rest, each requiring special treatment. The general system, however, may be gathered from the following account of the folding of an *octavo* sheet: –

Take a pile of about a ream and lay them out flat on the folding-board. If any of the sheets are irregularly piled up they must be brought to lie exactly on the top of each other by being knocked-up, which will be described hereafter. It is most essential for proper folding that the pile should be perfectly straight and square.

Now turn it so that the *inner* forme is uppermost – that is, the side containing the second page of the sheet. The principal signature will be underneath; but the secondary signature, such as B 2 of sheet B, will be exposed to view, and be on the extreme right hand. The order of the *printed* pages [see **Fig. 26.20**, LEFT] will now be as follows: –

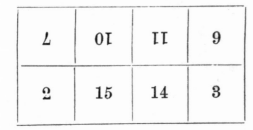 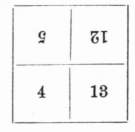 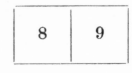

Fig. 26.20. LEFT, *Sheet of octavo with the printed pages of the inner form facing up;* MIDDLE, *Sheet of octavo after the first fold with four pages from the outer form facing up;* RIGHT, *Sheet of octavo after the second fold with the inner most pages facing up*

At the foot of 3 will be the second signature. Now fold the half of the sheet containing pages 3 and 14 entirely over the other half, and stroke down the line of the fold. It may be that the off-margins of pages 2 and 3 are not exactly equal, but that must be disregarded, and the pages of the print themselves made to fall exactly over each other. The following pages [see **Fig. 26.20**, MIDDLE] will now be uppermost: –

Bring that half of the sheet containing 5 and 12 over, upon the top of 4 and 13, and stroke the fold [see **Fig. 26.20**, RIGHT]. Now there is presented only pages [8 and 9.]

Fold 9 over 8, and page 16 will be exposed, the folding being now finished. With the left hand remove the sheet to the left side, and commence folding the next.

The right hand should be used for turning the sheet and stroking down. The adjustment of the pages, or making them register, is done with the left hand immediately before stroking. The sheets ought to be well flattened, or they will give subsequent trouble, and it is advisable to have large pieces of wood on the folding-table to keep the pile straight.

29. *Knocking-up* is a simple operation, yet somewhat difficult to describe verbally. Its object is to get the sheets lying exactly on the top of each other, in an even pile – in non-technical language, making all the edges coincide. Take up twenty or more, loosely between the two hands; place them on edge, lift the lot up and bring down smartly on the board; by which the bottoms of all will be made regular and even. Then, without disturbing their position in that direction, turn round the lot and bring the other edge against the table. This will probably bring the whole pile right; if not, it must be turned again until all the refractory sheets have assumed their proper places.

30. Although properly appertaining to Bookbinding, the two operations of *Gathering* and *Collating* may be briefly described.

The several sheets of a volume having been folded, and otherwise finished, have now to be brought together in due order and sequence. Each signature is laid out in a pile on the board of the warehouse, and the gatherer begins with taking a sheet of the first signature, then one of the second, third, and so on till all have been exhausted. It does not always happen that the stock of printed sheets "runs level" – there will generally be a few more of some sheets than others. The actual number of books is, of course, the number of complete sets of sheets that can be gathered. All sheets remaining are designated as waste.

31. *Howe's Rotary Gatherer* is an arrangement for economising space and labour [the mechanics of which is illustrated in **Fig. 26.21**]. The various piles of printed sheets, arranged in order according to signatures, are placed on a circular revolving table. The person gathering has merely to stand still in his place, and each pile will be successively presented to him. He takes one sheet from each, and places it on a fixed table at his side. Two or more persons may simultaneously gather at one machine, as the piles will pass each of them in succession.

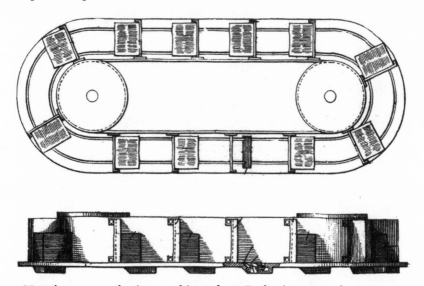

Fig. 26.21. *Howe's rotary gathering machine* – from Pasko (1894, p. 55)

32. *Collating* is simply examining each set of sheets to ascertain whether it includes one copy, and only one, of each signature, and that all the sheets comprised in it are in proper order. The operator takes up the lot by one corner in his left hand, by which means the sheets are slightly separated and the signatures exposed. He runs his eye over them, and instantaneously detects any inaccuracy.

33. *Counting*... is one of the most frequent operations in the warehouse, and it is of the greatest advantage to be able to do it properly – that is, methodically, rapidly, and accurately. The process is very simple, yet difficult to describe; and the best way to learn it is to watch some experienced hand. A sufficient quantity of sheets – which practice alone can indicate – are taken in the right hand; then, by a dexterous turn of the wrist, they are separated fan-wise, so that the edges of each are distinctly seen. The left hand is laid on the top corner, a certain number of sheets are counted by a glance of the eye, and the left thumb introduced. The hand is now advanced so as to keep this portion a little back, while another portion is counted and the thumb introduced, and so on. The rapidity with which this is done by an expert seems marvellous to the inexperienced. The thumb seems mechanically to travel through the successive portions, and there appears to be no mental calculation at all on the part of the operator. The only directions we need give on this subject are, not to attempt to count by too many numbers – five being the most convenient portion – and that the workman should accustom himself always to count by the same number.

34. *Cutting* is done by hand and by machine. By hand the process is quite simple, and, indeed, understood by nearly every one. To do the work really well, however, requires care and practice. The paper must be carefully folded down and smoothed with the paper-knife; a proper cutting-knife well sharpened must be used, and the cut given firmly and continuously; otherwise the paper will be "saw-edged," and require to be trimmed.

Cutting at the machine is also a simple operation, requiring little instruction. The ordinary guillotine cutting machine [see **Figs. 26.15** through **26.18** beginning on p. 787] has a table on which the paper is laid. The pile is then pressed back so as to come under the knife, being kept in position and supported at its back by a kind of clamp, worked by a handle underneath the table. It serves also to ensure a square shape to the paper. The clamp is then brought down by the gearing provided for the purpose, and finally the handle is turned and the knife descends. When it has made the cut, the wheel is stopped, and the handle re-ascends automatically. Some machines are self-clamping, and require less attention than others. The process, indeed, may be learned in a few minutes by watching a practised hand.

Finally the sheets are parcelled up and warehoused, or sent away to the customer. The contents of each parcel should be legibly written upon it, and it must be carefully tied up with string. If it is to be kept in the establishment it should be removed to a suitable, cleanly, and accessible place, where it can be obtained when required with the least amount of trouble.

Reading 26.13
Folding Machines
from *The American Printer* by Thomas MacKellar (1878, 11th ed., p. 249).

> The book folding machine, shown in **Fig. 26.22**, is manually operated. The paper handler, in this case, a woman, aligned the sheet on the bed of the machine by means of gauges. Next, she brought the creasing blade down, which, in turn, forced the paper through an aperture in the table. The sheet was then caught by a pair of rollers that pressed and carried it through to the delivery board.

Fig. 26.22. *Book-folding machine*

Book and Newspaper Folders are entitled to a high rank among modern labour-saving machines. For newspapers of large circulation and in book establishments they have become indispensable. The finest books may be folded by them with accuracy, speed, and economy; and periodicals can be folded, pasted, and covered at about one-fourth the cost of hand-folding alone; while the daily folio newspaper can be folded in two, three, or four folds as fast as the machine press can print; or an eight-page daily or weekly can be folded three or four times, and all the pages pasted together at the back fold, and the head margin trimmed. All these processes are successfully accomplished by the various machines made by Chambers, Brother & Co. of Philadelphia. The engraving given [in **Fig. 26.22** above] represents a book-folding machine.

Plate 31. Printing office of the *Rocky Mountain News*, ca. 1860. The pressmen and compositors appear to be working under rather dangerous conditions considering the number of weapons that are strewn about the workplace. (Courtesy of the Colorado Historical Society.)

CHAPTER TWENTY-SEVEN

Fine Printing

In addition to the usual sections on imposing, making ready, and printing, many nineteenth-century printers' manuals – beginning with Stower (1808, pp. 490–498) – included a section on "Fine Printing" or "Fine Presswork," in which the writers were able to voice their opinions regarding the aesthetics of their craft. Even though Johnson (1824, pp. 645–648) was writing in England sixteen years after Stower, and Adams (1837, pp. 301–306) in America almost thirty years after the publication of Stower's manual, their arguments are very similar, since they repeated Stower's observations almost verbatim. All three writers lament the sad state of printing in general, and their national presses in particular.

When defining the art of fine printing, the iron handpress was always central to their arguments. Despite great technological advances in the printing industry during the second half of the eighteenth century and the first two decades of the nineteenth, they express their obvious disappointment in the lack of exacting craftsmanship on the handpress. In their eyes, the primary villain was the printing machine, which produced a proliferation of fast and impersonal work. In response to this trend for cheap printing, they used these sections on fine printing to stimulate an interest among printers and clients alike for a higher standard of excellence in the trade.

John Baskerville, who represented the transition from the old style to the new, was held up as a printing innovator, as well as their mentor. Curiously, toward the end of the nineteenth century, Baskerville's prestige was in decline; so much so that Ringwalt (1871, p. 170) was able to say without blushing, "Mechanical excellence in an art so largely mechanical as printing is, must inevitably progress towards perfection with the succeeding ages, and the best letter-press of the nineteenth century is, beyond dispute, far superior even to the highest efforts and the most loudly-vaunted triumphs of Baskerville or Bodoni."

Reading 27.1
Fine Printing
from *The Printer's Grammar* by Caleb Stower (1808, pp. 490–498).

> Stower's comments below were to have a profound influence on many of the manual writers in the first half of the nineteenth century – in particular, Johnson (1824) and Hansard (1825) in England and Adams (1837) in America. In most cases, these writers appropriated Stower's text, adding new bits of information as technological advances presented themselves.
>
> Stower notes that the quality of printing in England, which had fallen into a serious decline in the first half of the eighteenth century, was beginning to show signs of improvement in the early nineteenth, due, in part, to the singular accomplishments of the maverick printer, John Baskerville in the 1750s. Even so, Stower felt that superior workmanship could only be found on the Continent. One reason for this disparity was attributed to cli-

mate: England was damper, more subject to variations in temperature. Any sudden change in atmospheric conditions could adversely effect the properties of the paper, rollers, and ink. But the real problem in England was a lack of professional training. Many pressmen were not even able to distinguish between common and fine work, a very subjective topic that continued to trouble printers throughout the nineteenth century.

Stower's manual was written specifically for the letterpress printer, and so it is quite understandable that he would emphasize the convenience of being able to print wood engravings together with type – contrary to copperplate engravings that had to be printed elsewhere on rolling presses. He goes into considerable detail when describing the strengths and weaknesses of these two techniques, noting that wood engravings should not try to imitate copperplate engravings, and vice versa. On the positive side, he notes that it was possible to print large areas of solid black with wood engravings; however, on the negative side, they required complex makereadies, which were not necessary when pulling copperplates.

Finding good paper seems to have been the bane of their existence for nineteenth-century English and American printers. The introduction of cotton rag and bleaches weaken the fibers in the paper, causing it to be less receptive to the stiff inks that were used in fine printing. Even though chlorine was invented in 1774, the first English patent for bleaching paper was not taken out until 1792. Stower believed that French paper was superior to English paper, and despite the fact that India paper was generally not strong enough for book work, he considered it the best paper for editioning wood engravings.

Although commercial inks were readily available in the first decade of the nineteenth century, Stower indicates that a few printers continued to make their own inks for fine printing. He also praised the numerous mechanical advances that had been made in the printing industry during this period, such as the iron handpress and stereotype printing.

Beginning with Moxon (1683, pp. 307, 389–390), the terms *setoff* and *offset* were used interchangeably. By the end of the nineteenth century, however, there was a clear distinction between them. Technically, setoff is the transfer of wet ink from the back side of a sheet of paper to the tympan or the slipsheet during the backup process; offset is the transfer of wet ink from one sheet to another when stacked.

It must be as gratifying to those who are particularly interested in the advancement of the liberal arts, as to those who contemplate them with a patriotic regard, to behold the present state of British Typography. Many years ago Baskerville gave the first impulse to improvement, which has since continued to increase through almost every part of the kingdom. The printers on the Continent for a considerable period of time took the lead in beauty of workmanship; and indeed, from several circumstances which will be mentioned hereafter, the path was easier for them to tread than it could be for us, as some of the impediments which retarded our early improvement, cannot be easily removed or overcome. The works of several foreign printers are celebrated throughout the lettered nations of the world; and it must be satisfactory to reflect, that their names can now be met by some of our own countrymen. By those only who have attempted to bring the art to perfection is the difficulty of its attainment truly appreciated; – they best can estimate the labour who have toiled in the pursuit.

Fine printing has lately been attempted by so many persons, that there seems to be as much discrimination necessary in judging of a well printed book, as there is in forming an opinion of the production of the pencil or the engraver. Some printers imagine, if they make their pages sufficiently black, that the end is gained; others, if they are pale and clear; so that each has a style peculiar to himself.

Real perfection is however unalterable, as far as relates to the duty of the printer, and however we may differ in our opinion respecting the fanciful display of our pages, or the form that constitutes beauty in our type, there is an effect which cannot be dispensed with. The great endeavour of many printers, who have aimed at improvement, has been to produce a sharpness of impression and fulness of colour, corresponding with that which is so easily attainable at the copper-plate press; but however eagerly such an effect may be sought after, an absolute match will never be produced, though it may be very nearly approximated. In seeking after the effect which belongs to another art, we are neglectful of the excellences which are characteristic of our own, nor have we occasion to lament our failure in the pursuit, when we consider how much ours is capable of performing. With proper materials, properly employed, the impression from the printing press will exhibit its peculiar character; and the fine relief and clear outline which it will produce, is more to be prized than that of an art to which it may bear some relationship.

Those who have had opportunities of inspecting the early productions of the press, will naturally conclude that in course of time this art became retrograde; for there are yet in existence works of the fifteenth and beginning of the sixteenth century, which, whether we examine them for the difficulty of their execution at case or at press, will bear a near comparison with any that are now produced. Few of the mechanic arts seem, on their first invention, to have made such rapid approaches to perfection as the art of printing; this may be accounted for by the early estimate of its value to society and the cause of literature, and by the unexampled patronage it obtained as being the gate to knowledge and to fame.

The improvements which have taken place in all the arts connected with letter-press printing have given a powerful stimulus to the exertions of the printers of this country. As engraving on copper and on wood was cultivated, it became absolutely necessary that the typography, which was a frequent companion, should not, by its common and imperfect appearance, abate that satisfaction which was sought to be communicated. That the powers of wood-engraving, an art most intimately connected with our own, are limited, is easily demonstrable; yet its importance is by no means unworthy of regard. Were we not to attempt to force it beyond its capabilities, its general advantages would be more apparent and more sought after. A capricious taste has been produced in consequence of several first-rate artists putting their genius to the stretch, that their works might vie with copper-plate, and some have produced very wonderful specimens. But, however curious these productions may appear, and however nearly they may attain their end, they will be found, on a comparison with copper, to be very unlike. This difference will always exist; it is a consequence of their different methods of working; their powers are as various as the effects produced are dissimilar, and we are as much disappointed in examining a wood engraving, in hopes of finding the softness of flesh and delicacy of skin, which is produced by a good artist upon copper, as we are disappointed in not meeting with that broad, deep shade, and strength of contrast, which the engraver on wood may always exhibit. The great point seems to be to discriminate properly what is the real province and usefulness of an art, and not, by overstraining its powers, to raise expectations which it cannot gratify, and which, while our eyes are directed beyond what it can perform, leave it unregarded, and suffer the art and the artist to sink together.

No kind of engraving is better calculated to preserve the real outline and proportion of the designer, than that of which we are now speaking: this will be easily credited when it is stated, that he generally makes the drawing with pencil upon the block, and the duty of the engraver is with the greatest exactness to leave those lines standing by cutting away the interstices. Thus, as the most unfinished etchings on copper, of the ancient masters, are more valuable than any imitation of them by a second hand, the powers of the engraver on wood can always be depended upon for giving, as far as the drawing and proportions are concerned, a faithful transcript of the performances of the designer.

It may be necessary here to remark, that the difficulties attending the printing of wood-engravings are very considerable, and that, however the designer and the engraver may labour, should the printer not be a judge of the effect intended to be brought out, and know well how to manage his block, all their labour will be fruitless. This observation applies more particularly to the finer kinds of engraving, but in some degree to all. In this department of the art much depends upon the quality and colour of the ink, no public vender of that article having yet, as far as the writer hereof has seen, succeeded in producing a kind that will give satisfaction to real judges of beauty and effect.

It has been before stated, that the printers on the Continent (those of Parma [e.g., Giambattista Bodoni (1740–1813)] and Paris [e.g., François Ambroise Didot (1730–1804)] in particular), have it in their power to produce finer specimens of printing than can be done by us. One of these advantages arises from the nature of their climate, which is not subject to the variations of temperature we daily experience, and which acts powerfully upon the oil of which our ink is composed, disposing it at one hour to spread equally over the balls, and at another rendering it so glutinous and stiff, as to tear the surface of the paper, and defy the efforts of the pressman, without a great increase of heat in the place where he is working; and even should he raise the temperature ever so high, if the frost be intense, his endeavours will he fruitless. It is a curious fact, that heat will not entirely counteract the effects of a freezing atmosphere upon some kinds of printing ink.

But the chief obstacle to the production of fine printing, or indeed to any printing above the very commonest standard, arises from the practice which has been lately adopted, of using cotton rag, in the manufacture of fine paper, and the application of the oxygenated muriatic acid for the purpose of obtaining dispatch and delicacy of colour, and producing a paper in appearance good, from an inferior staple. Nothing can be more perplexing to a printer, nor more detrimental to his labours, than what is called *bleached* paper; for although it may be thick and seem strong in the ream, no sooner does the water penetrate through it, than it loses its adhesive quality, and becomes so loose and soft as scarcely to bear handling, and in working sinks down into the letter, leaving a part of its substance behind after every impression, until it so clogs the type, that the work is often rendered scarcely legible. Nor is it less exceptionable in point of durability, as it must moulder away in a little time with the common use that popular works generally undergo. The very best paper that is produced in this country, is not so well calculated for printing upon as that manufactured in France; there is a toughness, accompanied with a softness of texture, in French paper, which is much superior to ours. But of all paper, that which is made in India is superior for taking clear impressions from wood blocks, and for producing a sharp impression from a letter-press form; it cannot, however, be recommended for strength or durability. . . .

With respect to the colour of printing ink, a difference of opinion certainly exists; one kind being admired for its glaring effect, and another for its softened richness and warmth; the latter, though in fact of as deep a colour as the former, is yet so tempered, as not to injure or fatigue the eye, becoming more agreeable the more it is examined. A few printers who have cultivated the art, now manufacture their own ink: indeed that which has hitherto been sold by the usual makers, possesses very few of the requisites necessary for fine printing.

Some directions may be expected for assisting the printer in producing fine specimens; but everyone who has attempted improvement has some peculiarities which are not in common practice; therefore all that can be done is to give a slight sketch of the general method.

The Press best calculated for this, or indeed for any other kind of printing, is that lately invented by [Charles, third] Earl Stanhope, and originally made by Mr. [Robert] Walker. The perfect plane in the table and plattin has long been a desideratum, which is in this machine completely supplied. The public at large, and the printers in particular, are much indebted to this patriotic nobleman for his invention, and the only circumstance to be regretted is the great expense of its purchase which precludes its general use; but this evil, it is to be hoped, will yet be remedied, as it is a great impediment to the benefits designed by his Lordship to have been conferred upon the art.

The Paper to be wet in such a manner as to retain its firmness, yet be sufficiently soft to apply closely to the surface of the letter, and take up all the ink.

The Ink is left to the judgment of the printer as to colour and quality.

The Balls, on which so much depend, ought to be particularly attended to; the skin to be trodden until it adheres to the foot, and not to be nailed on the stock until it will imbibe the ink freely, without the application of heat.

The Tympans to be continued in a state of tension, by changing the blanket and the slip-sheet as they become damp.

The Blanket must be of fine broad cloth or kerseymere, and only one to be used.

When printing large letter, the surface of which requires to be well filled with ink, a sheet of tissue paper, or common paper damped, is often laid between every impression, to prevent the sheets from setting off on the back of each other.

The foregoing observations are chiefly the result of the practical experience of the writer, and are communicated to the public at the earnest request of the editor of this work. He wishes it to be recollected, that they were drawn up amid the hurry of business, and that he was not applied to until the press was nearly at a stand for this part of the work.

But however laudable it may be to cultivate the art to perfection, it is to its common and more general application that we are to look for its great and beneficial effects upon the human intellect, and upon nations and societies of men. The Press is the great engine by which man is enabled to improve the faculties of his nature; – it is the preserver of the knowledge and acquirements of former generations, and the great barrier, when not perverted by the hand of power, against the debasement of the human mind, and the equalizing effects of despotism.

Reading 27.2
Fine Presswork
from *A Dictionary of the Art of Printing* by William Savage (1841, pp. 222–223).

> Savage in this reading and Stower in Reading 27.1 above, were the most frequently quoted nineteenth-century manual writers on the subject of fine printing and fine presswork. Their observations were repeated, with little modification, throughout the century by those who followed them.
>
> With the exception of the first two paragraphs below, Savage drew upon his earlier work, *Practical Hints on Decorative Printing* (1822, p. 19) when compiling this entry for his dictionary. Even though Savage includes printing from type in his description of fine presswork, his primary focus in this text is the printing of wood engravings, stating that "Fine Presswork is the art of printing perfect impressions from the surface of engravings in relief."

As will be seen on p. 848 in Reading 28.8, the price of printing depended largely on the amount of attention that had to be given to the work, as well as to the quality of the materials.

[Fine presswork] is the technical term for presswork of superior quality; it is in some measure indefinite, for, as presswork is paid a certain price for a given number, and the price advances according to the time and care bestowed on it, that for which the lowest price is paid is termed common work, and after the price has advanced about one half in addition, it is styled fine work; although it may advance gradually to six times the lowest price, or more, it is still called fine work.

In aiming at excellence in printing, it will be found that Presswork deserves particular consideration, as a part on which the beauty of a book so much depends.

It will be necessary, in the first instance, to endeavour to define more particularly what is meant by the term Fine Presswork, for except this be understood, we shall come to no satisfactory conclusion, as workmen vary in their opinions respecting it, and frequently produce sheets of different shades of colour in the same volume, when it is done at different presses, and all under the name of the finest work; and when the same person either actually prints the whole, or superintends it, the work will be executed according to his criterion, without any fixed rule whereby to decide; thus one man shall produce the finest work, according to his opinion, of a pale grey colour, while another will produce it so black and surcharged with colour, that if the ink be not of a very good quality, it will not only smear, but the paper at the edges of the letters, nay, even the whole page, will be tinged with the oil which separates from the colouring matter of the ink, to the entire destruction of all beauty of workmanship.

Fine Presswork is the art of printing perfect impressions from the surface of engravings in relief.

By obtaining perfect impressions, I would be understood that the subject transferred to paper should be an impression from the surface and the surface only of the engraved lines, of such a tone as to produce all the effect of which the subject is capable, without either superfluity or deficiency of colour.

Reading 27.3
On Fine Printing
from *Typographia* by John Johnson (1824, vol. II, pp. 645–648).

Notwithstanding all the technological advances in the art of printing that were attributed to Baskerville in the 1750s, Johnson regrets that the craft, as practiced on the iron handpress, had regressed irreversibly by the 1820s. The inks were weak; the papers, debased; the typefaces, gross – just to name a few of the dilemmas that confronted Johnson and his fellow printers.

Johnson repeats most of what Stower says in Reading 27.1 on p. 795, although Johnson's text reflects the several transformations that had occurred in the printing industry since Stower's manual was published: (1) the labor force had changed with the introduction of out-door apprentices – independent lads who no longer lived under the master's roof; (2) the stereotype process, which altered practices in both the composing and pressrooms; and (3) printing machines, which were capable of turning out larger numbers of work in less time and at cheaper prices.

Johnson also adds new information to Stower's text on the art of printing wood engravings, one of the hallmarks of fine printing. He notes that there has been an extraordinary increase in the demand for wood engravings "in the last twelve months," a demand, perhaps, influenced by Savage's *Practical Hints on Decorative Printing* (1822), which was the first print-ers' manual devoted primarily to the printing of wood engravings.

Skin balls were rarely used after 1815, having been supplanted in that year by composi-tion balls. By Johnson's time, some printing offices had abandoned balls altogether. Even though he speaks out against using rollers for fine printing, believing that only ink balls were capable of producing fine work, Johnson does concede that rollers are better suited for cer-tain types of wood engravings and for forms with heavy type. He also mentions that the manufacture of ink had improved due to increased competition. Unlike Stower, he does not say anything about printers making their own inks for fine printing.

In the reading below, I have omitted many of Johnson's comments that were taken directly from Stower's text. They will be found in their entirety in Reading 27.1 on p. 795.

We are grieved to find, on entering upon this subject, that we are deprived of the power (by the con-duct of the majority of the Profession) of complimenting our brethren for the advance which they have made in the improvement of our Art. About twenty years back [ca. 1804] we were highly grati-fied with many of the productions of that day, and we then lived in hopes (from the spirit of emu-lation which was then abroad), that we should find the printers of the British Metropolis still per-severing in the laudable career in which they had embarked, until they should have attained the grand summit of perfection. It was boasted, formerly, that the press of this country had arrived at a degree of excellence equal to that of any portion of the globe: but, alas! we must now say, that, lat-terly, the Art has made a retrograde, instead of a progressive movement. We can fancy that we hear our readers calling upon us to account for this falling off in the Profession; this we shall briefly do: the first blow was the disputes with the men, which ended in that ruinous system, the general intro-duction of out-door Apprentices: the second was the revival of the Stereotype process: and, lastly, the baneful effects of the Steam and Hand Machines, which have created such competition for low prices, that it is completely out of the power (except in a few instances) of the fair tradesman, and those who wish to improve the Art, to pursue that career by which alone a lasting fame can ever be attained. Notwithstanding what we have here advanced, there are a few individuals to whom our praise is justly due, for their steadily persevering in the course of improvement: this they have been enabled to do by uniformly adhering to the usual practice of the Profession.

The first step towards improvement was ventured (many years ago [ca. 1750]) by Mr. Baskerville, since which, others have made further advances towards perfection: but it is to be regretted, that uncontrollable causes preclude us from partaking of those benefits, which are so essentially necessary in the production of Fine Printing . . . [Editor's note: At this point, Johnson repeats Stower's comments on the effects of climate on printing.] It is not the ink alone that is thus affected, but also the skin and composition balls, and likewise the rollers, which are so out of order at certain times, that it is utterly impossible for the pressman to produce even passable common work, much less that of a superior kind: of these evils the public are little aware, but they are severely felt both by the employer and the men. . . . It is well known to the Profession, that the best paper produced in this country is very inferior to that manufactured in France; the latter is very tough, and at the same time possesses a softness of texture which is well adapted for taking off fine impressions, and is far superior (in every point of view) to any description of paper which we can boast: but even this (great as are its advantages for Fine Printing) is far eclipsed by that which is manufactured in China, most particularly for wood engravings, although we cannot recommend it for strength or durability. . . .

The art of Engraving on Wood, which is so closely connected with printing, also kept pace with it in improvement; and it is highly creditable to those gentlemen who have thus persevered in the advancement of the Art. We are of opinion, that the persons who formerly stated that a capricious taste was produced (from the attempts of the first-rate artists to rival copper) will now think otherwise, after viewing the most extraordinary productions which have appeared during the last twelve years: it was also asserted, that softness and delicacy could not be produced from them at the press; but in this their expectations have been disappointed, and we trust that we shall still witness much greater efforts towards perfection in this curious branch of Art, and that the printers will not be behind hand in executing their part, to the satisfaction of the admirers of Art, and all real judges. . . .

There has been a most extraordinary demand for engravings on wood within the last twelve months, but we are sorry to observe, that by far the greater portion are of an inferior class, which reflect no credit on the eminent artists under whose names they are sent forth.

A difference of opinion exists respecting the colour of printing ink; some admire the glaring effect of a dark black, while others prefer the softened richness and warmth of a deep mellow tone, which is always pleasing to behold, without in the least being fatiguing to the sight. Ink-making being formerly confined to one or two persons, they troubled themselves little about improvement, until others started up, since which it must be acknowledged, very superior inks have been manufactured; and we humbly hope they will persevere in their career of improvement. The printer must exercise his judgment respecting the colour and the quality of the Ink. . . . [Editor's note: At this point, Johnson repeats Stower's requisites for producing fine printing. I have only included Johnson's comments on "Balls" since he adds new information about them not found in Stower.]

The Balls, on which so much depend, ought to be particularly attended to: those made with skins are now rarely used, they were supplanted by those of the composition, which are infinitely superior in every point of view; even the last-mentioned have been generally laid aside, and have given place to the Rollers, very many offices not having a single Ball in them. With respect to the Rollers, our ideas still remain the same, having pronounced (long before we had seen them in action) that they would not execute the work equal to the Balls: this opinion time has fully verified: we are ready to admit their excellence for heavy forms and the general run of work, but not for fine work, or wood engravings, for neither of which are they so well adapted as the Balls; as to the last, they are totally unfit to produce any impressions worthy of notice.

Reading 27.4
Fine Printing
from *Typographia* by Thomas Curson Hansard (1825, pp. 610–614, 616–618).

Like Johnson in Reading 27.3 above, Hansard also relied heavily on Stower's text in Reading 27.1 on p. 795. Again, in order to minimize repetitions, I have omitted several sections from Hansard's text that were taken directly from Stower's.

Hansard elaborates on the difference between common and fine work. He discusses the work of several printers who were active in the first quarter of the nineteenth century. Three of these – Thomas Rickaby (d. 1802), Charles Whittingham (1795–1876), and Charles Corrall – also produced a series of fine editions of miniature or pocket books. To illustrate the problems facing fine printers during this period, Hansard notes that Millar Ritchie had to do all of his own inking with balls because he could not find journeymen who were willing to give the necessary care and attention that his projects demanded.

Hansard mentions the changing fashions in typefaces. Printers gradually shifted from old-style faces, which consisted of thin meager-faced letters, such as early Caslon, to modern faces, which consisted of heavy square-faced letters with hairline serifs, such as Bodoni and Didot. Hansard attacked the popular use of fat-faced types for book work. The most egregious of these were from the type founder Robert Thorne (1754–1820), whose faces were originally intended for job work.

Baskerville succeeded in producing a type of superior elegance, and an ink which gave peculiar lustre to impressions from his type. The novel and unusual excellence which his works presented gave a stimulus to the exertions, and drew forth the emulation, of many of our countrymen. The first who started in this novel course was Mr. Millar Ritchie, a native of Scotland. . . . An edition of the classics, in royal octavo, consisting of the works of Sallust, Pliny, Tacitus, Q. Curtius, Cæsar, and Livy, was the work upon which this leading attempt at superior printing was made . . . This work was also the means of first introducing Mr. Whatman's yellow wove royal paper. The next work was a quarto bible, in two volumes, upon the same paper, and two unique copies upon India paper, printed on one side only. . . .

Another work executed by Ritchie, with uncommon splendour and expense, was "Memoirs of the Count de Grammont" [by Anthony Hamilton (ca. 1646–1720)], a small page, upon quarto, 1500 copies small paper, 500 on Whatman's wove royal, one copy on vellum, and three copies having this diminutive quarto page worked in the centre of a whole sheet of the royal paper.

On his first diverging from the beaten track, Mr. Ritchie encountered considerable difficulties. The paper-maker, Mr. Whatman, and the ink-maker, Mr. Blackwell, contributed, most successfully, all their skill to his laudable design, but the want of journeymen to enter into the spirit of the undertaking with that extraordinary exertion of care and ingenuity which it indispensably required, was a difficulty the most discouraging, which he had long to contend with, and never wholly conquered; men he could get who by bodily strength would pull down the press, and give the impression, but the giving the colour required a skill and patience so far exceeding what pressmen had any idea of in this country, that Mr. Ritchie found himself obliged to manage the balls and beat every sheet of those works with his own hands. He had men to pull, but every other part was effected by his own personal labour. . . .

It will hence be evident that Mr. Ritchie, notwithstanding all his perseverance and skill in fine printing, had not the art of getting independence by his labours: he failed in business, and was succeeded in his efforts by Mr. [William] Bulmer: Mr. [Thomas] Bensley and Mr. [John] M'Creery followed, and from the presses of those gentlemen have issued some of the finest specimens of typography which this or any other country has produced.* Emulation is a powerful principle in our nature, and the success which has attended their exertions, contributed in a great degree to give a new tone and character to the profession. The first efforts at fine printing tended to any thing but a general improvement in press-work.

Every thing that was not paid for as "fine work" was "common work;" and by the pressmen, who, at the time alluded to were more masters of the trade than their employers, it was

---

* It will not be thought foreign to the subject to observe here, that about this period Mr. [John] Bell, in publishing his British Theatre [1776–1778], first set the fashion, which soon became general, of discarding the long f.

treated accordingly, perhaps for the sake of making the contrast the greater. Subsequent events, arising from the conduct of the workmen, together with the general introduction of the Stanhope and other improved presses, as well as machinery, having placed the choice of their workmen once more in the power of the masters, the general style of printing has become much improved.

Printing in very small type, below Brevier [8-point], has been pursued to a great degree of excellence but by very few printers. Mr. Rickaby,[*] the predecessor of the author of this work, was among the first who turned his attention to the beautifully minute. An annual work, of the pocket-book class, called "Peacock's Polite Repository" [various editions between 1800–1873], and a pocket dictionary, called "Peacock's Johnson," were among the best efforts of his ingenuity. Mr. Charles Whittingham, in small editions of the "Common Prayer" [i.e., *The Book of Common Prayer* (1812)], was eminently successful; but the "Diamond Bible" and "Prayer Book," by Mr. Corrall, in the beauty of eye-straining minuteness, surpassed all others, and took the lead of future efforts.

The great improvements in type-founding have proved an additional spur to the printer; and fine printing has of late been attempted by so many professors of the art, and so numerous and variable are the specimens they have produced, that a discrimination as minute as that which is required in forming an opinion of those of the pencil and the burin, seems necessary in judging of what is really superior in typography. Some printers imagine, if they do but make their pages sufficiently black, that the end is gained; others, if they are pale and clear; so that each exhibits a style peculiar to his own fancy. In typography, as in the fine arts, it is difficult to specify and investigate the qualities which constitute excellence and beauty; yet to an accurate observer, the productions of the several typographical artists vary as much as the figures of Flaxman, Chantry, or Canova, from the rude efforts of a rustic stone mason. Real excellence does not, however, depend upon so unfixed a principle; and, therefore, it would be difficult to point out every particular which it is necessary to combine, in order to accomplish that which may rank as a *chef-d'œuvre* in the art; yet to understand when it is effected is not so intricate; for when any one who has acquired a correct taste, sees a beautifully uniform type imparted to the paper, displaying all its proportions with a just degree of lustre and harmony, his conceptions of typographic beauty become satisfied, and the more he looks the more he admires. . . .

The improvements which have taken place in all the arts connected with letter-press printing have acted, no doubt, powerfully in stimulating the printers of this country to that extraordinary exertion by which such fine specimens of typographic beauty are now so frequently produced. As engraving on copper and on wood progressively improved, it became necessary that the typography which accompanied them should not, by a coarse and common appearance, serve but to disgrace that which it should rival, and abridge the gratification which might be reasonably expected from a union of the arts. . . . [Editor's note: At this point, Hansard paraphrases Stower's comparison on the difference of copperplate engraving and wood engraving.]

Taste, which is continually changing, has made strange revolutions in the form of our printing types; we no longer use the thin and meagre-faced letter of the Elzevirs, Baskerville, [William] Martin [d. 1815], &c. with which our works were formerly printed. That there was ample room for

---

[*] "Mr. Thomas Rickaby, of Peterborough Court, Fleet Street, died August 21st, 1802, Æt. [at the age of] 49. He printed The British Critic, and was, in many other respects, a printer of eminence." – [John Nichols, *Literary Anecdotes of the Eighteen Century . . .* vol. iii, p. 737].

improvement is sufficiently manifest, but the rage unfortunately ran into the opposite extreme, and nothing was considered handsome but that which exhibited as broad a surface as the dimensions of the body of the type would admit, in many instances forcing the letters so close together, that the word appeared an indistinct mass of black, not to be read with facility. This proved a short-lived fashion, and of benefit to no one, except the ink-maker. Another extravagance has been daily increasing upon us, from the desire of the letter-founders that their types shall stand well in line, and which is certainly a great perfection: in order to render this object more apparent, the horizontal line at the top and bottom of the letter, where it occurs, is carried so far out, on each side of the stalk, as to give the page somewhat the appearance of being ruled. Nor can the present general squareness of form and grossness of face be considered as removing any defect. The disadvantages attending such letter are manifold. Owing to the delicacy of the top and bottom lines, it will not last so long as that of the old fashion, the slightest use destroying these lines, and at the same time the newness of its appearance; besides, by exhibiting a much larger surface to the pressman, to be covered with ink, more beating is required, and a heavier pull, a duty which we rarely find men, striving in the ordinary course of business to make the best use of their time, willing to bestow, nor can we expect it, without increase of pay; and without this care, the effect produced is worse than that of letter from the old matrices. The public taste will, it is to be hoped, in time settle between the two extremes, and when that shall take place, we shall have the pleasure of seeing strength, grace, and lightness, exhibited on the same page.

This has, in fact, since the above was written, been the case. Most of the eminent booksellers now object to the use of the fat-faced type; and founders of the highest repute are vying in the production of letter with a face elegantly proportionate, and formed for durability and profit to the printer. The introduction of fat-faced types into book-work has been severely reprobated by many as well as the author of this work: yet, it must be admitted, that when cut with taste and ability, when quite new, when used in printing open and thick-leaded works, as poetry, &c., and when carefully worked, at twice or thrice the expense of common work, an effect brilliant and ornamental is produced; though not very congenial, perhaps, to the eyes of those who buy books to *read* them. The disrepute into which letter of this cut has fallen has probably arisen from the negligence, inattention, and want of taste with regard to shape and symmetry with which they were cut when first introduced. It has been already said, that in typography, as in the fine arts, it is difficult to investigate and specify the qualities which constitute beauty: but fatness seems to have been considered by the letter-founders as an adequate substitute for all such qualities.

At one period, in imitation probably of the celebrated [Firmin] Didot, a practice prevailed of cutting the ceriphs [serifs] and fine strokes of types to an excessive degree of sharpness. This, though it gave to fine work and early impressions a neatness and finish resembling copperplate, was very detrimental, as these sharp edges would not stand for any length of time the action of the press, but either broke off or were blunted, so that the fount soon acquired the appearance of age and long service.

But these extravagant fancies have had their day, and the shape of type is subsiding to a happy medium, likely to become a standard between the awkward stiffness of the Elzevir and Baskerville, and the outrageous kind of face only adapted for placards, posting-bills, invitations to the wheel of Fortune, and job-printing in general; and for which purposes it appears so appropriate as to induce a probable supposition that its use will be permanent in that class of printing.

Fashion and Fancy commonly frolic from one extreme to another. . . . To the razor-edged fine lines and ceriphs of type just observed upon, a reverse has succeeded, called "Antique," or "Egyptian," the property of which is, that the strokes which form the letters are all of one uniform thickness! – After this, who would have thought that further extravagance could have been conceived? It remains, however, to be stated, that the ingenuity of one founder has contrived a type in which the natural shape is reversed, by turning all the ceriphs and fine strokes into fats, and the fats into leans. – Oh! sacred shades of Moxon and Van Dijke [i.e., Christoffel Van Dijk (1605–1670)], of Baskerville and Bodoni! what would ye have said of the typographic *monstrosities* here exhibited [see **Fig. 27.1**], which Fashion in our age has produced? And those who follow, as many years hence as you have preceded us, to what age or beings will they ascribe the marks here exhibited as a specimen?

Modern Antique, or *Two line English of 1824.*
ENGLISH ITALIAN FOR 1824.

Fig. 27.1. *Typographic monstrosities* – from Hansard (1825, p. 619)

From such *whimsicalities* as these, after-times may fall into many a whimsical illusion; and it is not impossible but *unique antique typographiques* imprinted in "London's City," may be sold to the best bidder as genuine Egyptian relics of antediluvian origin, and form a choice portion of the treasures in the museums of the virtuosi!!

Reading 27.5
On Fine Printing
from *Typographia* by Thomas F. Adams (1837, pp. 302, 306).

Adams continued in the Stower tradition when he adapted Johnson's *Typographia* (1824) for an abridged American edition in 1828. Subsequently, when Adams issued his first manual under his own name, he again drew extensively from the above-mentioned sources. The major difference between Johnson and Adams is the latter's preference for rollers over balls for inking. Throughout his career, Adams was a champion of technological advancements in the printing industry.

Curiously, Adams claims that the work done by British printers is far better than that done by American printers – both Stower on p. 797 in Reading 27.1 and Johnson on p. 801 in Reading 27.3 believed that the work of English printers was "retrograde."

[Works] printed in this country are less valued than those from the English press, whose works are printed on paper of a fine fabric made mostly of linen rags, and sufficiently strong to bear a fine ink; while in this country the pressman is obliged to accommodate the ink to the softness of his paper, which will seldom bear any thing above the lowest priced book ink....

The paper to be wet in such a manner as to retain its firmness, yet to be sufficiently soft to apply closely to the surface of the letter, and take up all the ink; if too wet it will be impossible to produce a clear or black impression.

The rollers, on which so much depend, ought to be particularly attended to....

The tympans should always be kept in a state of tension, by changing or drying the blanket, and removing the slip sheets, as they become damp.

Reading 27.6
Fine Hand-Presswork
from *The American Printer* by Thomas MacKellar (1866, pp. 253–258).

Unlike Johnson (1824) and Adams (1837) – whose source was Stower (1808) – MacKellar adapted his section on fine presswork from Savage (1841), after eliminating all of Savage's references to wooden presses and ink balls. MacKellar, like Savage, mentions substituting duck's bills for pins to hold the paper in place on the tympan while the white-paper form was being printed. Pins were not mentioned in printers' manuals until the 1840s, although they must have been in general use for some time before then.

MacKellar laments that American printing was inferior to British printing. It is hard to tell whether he is just repeating Adams's remarks on p. 806 in Reading 27.5, or if he was independently making this statement based on his own observations.

MacKellar discusses rollers and paper, as well as iron handpresses and tympans, recommending that the latter be covered with silk. He says that the best paper is moderately sized and made from linen rags without any additives, such as cotton rags or bleaches. He still mentions hanging up wet printed sheets on poles to dry.

Emphasizing the importance of inking, MacKellar describes in great detail the characteristics of good ink for fine printing – one of Savage's areas of expertise. Hard packing, which had by the 1860s become synonymous in America with fine printing, helped to contribute to the uniformity of color throughout.

Fine presswork is the art of printing perfect impressions from the surface of type or engravings in relief: that is, the subject transferred to paper should be an impression from the surface, and the surface only, of the types or engraved lines, of such a tone as to produce all the effect of which the subject is capable, without either superfluity or deficiency of colour.

The press ought to be in the best condition; otherwise it will be impossible to get an equal impression without much trouble and loss of time. The joints of the tympan should not have any play, or the correctness of the register will be affected, and slurs and doubles be caused.

The parchments on the tympans should be thin, and of a uniform thickness, and stretched on the tympans so as not to be flaccid. On account of its thinness, smoothness, and uniformity, silk is probably preferable.

The face of the platen ought to be a true plane, and parallel to the press-stone, or table.

The advantage of having a good press is unavailing for the production of fine work if the types are much worn; for it is impossible to produce a sharp, clear impression when the type is worn and the fine lines are rounded by much use. In consequence of this roundness of the letter, it is necessary to use a thick blanket in the tympan to bring up the type; thus producing a gross and irregular impression of more than the surface.

Ink for fine work should be characterized by the following peculiarities: –

> Intenseness of colour.
> Impalpability.
> Covering the surface perfectly of the type or engraving.
> Quitting the surface of the type or engraving when the paper is pressed on it, and adhering to the paper.
> Not smearing after it is printed.
> Complete retention of colour.

Ink ought to be reduced to an impalpable smoothness, either in a mill or on a stone with a muller. This is essential, as the process gives it the next quality, – that of completely yet very thinly covering the surface of the type or the lines of the engraving, and insuring an even and perfect appearance to the impression on the paper. Another important requisite is, that the ink shall not only cover the surface of the lines on the paper printed, but that it shall also quit the face of the type or engraving and leave it quite clean when the paper is impressed on it, and attach itself to the paper, so as to give a perfect impression of the subject represented, without the colour of the paper appearing through the ink; and that this peculiarity of quitting the type or engraving and becoming attached to the paper shall continue the same through any number of impressions, without any accumulation of ink on the surface printed from. After having obtained these results, and when the printing is as perfect as it can be made by workmanship, something more is requisite, – viz.: that the ink shall not smear on being slightly rubbed, and that it shall retain its colour and appearance without spreading at the edges or tinging the paper.

The rollers should be in good condition; otherwise the pressman may exert his skill in vain, with a great loss of time and waste of paper.

The quality of the paper is of great consequence in fine printing; but it is frequently overlooked by the printer's employers, who are apt to pay more attention to a showy appearance and a low price than to quality.

The best paper for printing on is that which is made of fine linen rags and moderately sized, without the use of acids in bleaching, and without being adulterated with cotton rags: this paper takes water kindly, is easily got into good condition, receives a good impression, is durable, preserves its colour, and does not act upon the ink.

The use of cotton rags, the introduction of gypsum into the manufacture of fine and other papers, the application of acids and bleaching powders to improve the colour and produce apparently good paper from an inferior staple, – these form the grand hinderances to the American printer in his efforts to equal or excel foreign productions. Hence it is that works printed in this country are less valued than those from the English press, which are printed on paper of a fine fabric, made mostly of linen rags, and sufficiently strong to bear a fine ink.

A pressman should, as a matter of course, be well acquainted with the entire routine of presswork; in addition to which, to form his judgment, he should examine the most splendid productions of the press, and study them as patterns of workmanship.

In making ready, it must be evident that, when a clear, sharp impression is wanted, the pressure should be on the surface only. Of course the tympan ought not to be very soft, neither should a woollen blanket be used: the most perfect impression will be obtained when fine thick paper alone is placed in the tympans; and even of this article but few thicknesses should be employed.

After an impression is printed, the pressman examines if it be uniform throughout; if it be, – which is very rarely the case, – he goes on with the work; if not, he proceeds to overlay, in order to produce regularity of pressure and of colour over the whole form. Wherever the impression is weak he pastes a bit of thin, smooth paper, of the size and shape of the imperfect part, on the tympan-sheet; he then pulls another impression, to examine the effect of his overlays, and continues to add to them where wanted, till the pressure of the platen is the same in every part and the impression is of a uniform shade of colour.

If the impression come off too strong in parts, or at the edges or corners of the pages or on the head-lines, it will be necessary to cut away the tympan-sheet in those parts, and, if that does not ease the pressure sufficiently, to cut away the same parts from one or more of the sheets that are within the tympans.

It is generally preferable to overlay on a sheet of stout smooth paper inside the tympan, particularly where the same press does the whole or great part of a work; this sheet is cut to fit the interior of the tympan, so as not to slip about, and has overlays pasted on it where wanted, to bring up the impression till it is very nearly equal. In all succeeding sheets it saves the pressman a great deal of time, as he will be certain that when he pulls a sheet of another form of the same work it will be nearly right, and he will only have to place thin overlays on occasional parts to make the impression perfect.

It is necessary, where short pages occur in a form, to have bearers to protect their bottom lines and the edges of the adjoining pages. These may be of double pica reglet pasted on the frisket, so as to bear on some part of the furniture or chase; but bearers made to the height of the types are better, when they can be used.

It happens occasionally that the tympan causes the paper to touch the form partially on being turned down, and occasions slurs. This may occur from the parchment being slack or the paper being thin and soft. To prevent this inconvenience, it is customary to roll up a piece of thick paper and paste it on the frisket adjoining the part. Many pressmen prefer pieces of cork cut to about the thickness of double pica, and pasted on the frisket.

In working the white paper, instead of pins stuck into the tympan, to prevent the paper slipping, a duck's bill (a tongue cut in a piece of stout paper) is frequently used: it is pasted to the tympan at the bottom of the tympan-sheet, and the tongue projects in front of it; indeed, the tympan-sheet appears to rest in it. The bottom of each sheet is placed behind this tongue, which supports it while the tympan is turned down.

The rollers should be kept clean, but should not be too moist, as this will prevent the ink from distributing equally over them, and from covering evenly the surface of the types or engraving; nor should they be too dry, as in that case they will not dispose of the ink smoothly enough to produce a fine impression, neither will they retain particles of dirt on their surface, but will part with them to the form, thus causing picks.

The ink ought to be rubbed out thinly and equally on the ink-block, so that when it is taken it may be diffused smoothly over the surface of the rollers. It is advisable to keep rubbing the ink out on the block with the brayer, and to distribute the roller almost constantly; the continual friction produces a small degree of warmth, which is of advantage, particularly in cold weather.

As uniformity of colour is requisite for beauty in printing, where the form is large the pressman should take ink for every impression: this may be thought troublesome, but it is advantageous in producing regularity of colour. It is unpleasant to see in a fine book two pages that face each other differing in colour, – the one a full black, surcharged with ink, the other deficient in quantity and of a gray colour; yet this must happen when, as is frequently the case, three or four sheets are printed with one taking of ink.

In fine books, particularly where the paper is large and heavy and the type large, set-off sheets are used to interleave the whole impression while working: these remain till the printed paper is taken down from the poles by the warehouseman. These set-off sheets are put in when the white paper is working, and moved from one heap to the other during the working of the reiteration. They prevent the ink from setting off from one sheet to another while they are newly printed, from the weight of the paper.

To secure uniformity of impression, the pull should be so adjusted in the first instance as to give a proper degree of pressure on the form when the bar is pulled home; then, checking the bar, it should be allowed to rest in that position during a short pause.

It will be perceived that, to produce presswork of a highly superior character, great expense and much time are required; and that it is requisite to have a good press in good condition; to have new types, or types whose faces are not rounded by wear; to have good rollers in good condition; that the ink should be strong, of a full black colour, that will not fade nor stain the paper, and ground so fine as to be impalpable; the paper should be of the best quality, made of linen rags, and not bleached by means of acids or bleaching powders, which have a tendency to decompose the ink; the rolling should be carefully and well done; the face of the type should be completely covered with ink, without any superfluity, so as to produce a full colour; and the pull should be so regulated as to have a slow and great pressure, and to pause at its maximum in order to fix the ink firmly upon the paper. These particulars observed, with nothing but paper in the tympans, perfect impressions of the face alone of the type will be obtained, and a splendid book will be produced in the best style of printing.

Reading 27.7
Excellence in Workmanship
from *Harpel's Typograph* by Oscar Henry Harpel (1870, p. 3).

> Harpel approaches the subject of excellence in workmanship from an aesthetic point of view. The aim of his manual was to inspire printers to produce more imaginative work by giving them examples of fine printing that they could copy or adapt in their own printing offices. For him, it was all a matter of taste and elegance, and, of course, good craftsmanship. He believed – as customers became more discerning – that printers would have to refine their skills and take advantage of new developments in the typographic arts if they wanted to be competitive in the marketplace.

The abundant supply of excellent and beautiful typographic appliances of every description now presented to the choice of the Printer, and the cultivated tastes and often exacting caprices of his patrons, render it not only comparatively easy but very necessary for him to attain to excellence in workmanship. If he would reap the rewards of profit and honor, he must be prepared to meet the varied demands of popular patronage with intelligence, taste, and skill, as well as be constantly alert to the best practical effects, if not the extreme possibilities, of his craft.

It cannot be denied that refined taste and elegance in his productions give the printer a hold upon public consideration and support that the most laborious and obliging incapacity – with even better advantages in other respects – would fail to retain for any considerable period. It is from lack of ability or carelessness in arrangement that bungling workmen are compelled to accept the offal of patronage, while the good craftsman culls the best of it, and distances his weaker rival in the advance to financial success. For this reason, if for no other, all engaged in the business of printing should take advantage of every avenue leading to better information and practice in its accomplishment, if they would reach the higher results of this progressive art.

Plate 32. Outdoor printing office of *The Kingston Shaft*, 1886. This was the first daily newspaper in New Mexico. It is not quite clear why the press was set up outdoors. It would appear that the equipment is not just waiting to be moved indoors since the young man is printing on the job press on the right. Aside from the weather, the dust alone would have made it impossible to print well. (Photo by J. C. Burge, courtesy of the Museum of New Mexico, MNM No. 14691.)

CHAPTER TWENTY-EIGHT

The Business of Printing

My main purpose in this chapter is to shed a little light on the byzantine system of economics that prevailed throughout the printing industry in the nineteenth century. It is somewhat difficult for me to discuss or even to make any generalizations about the business practices of this period since I have limited my sources primarily to the manuals themselves, which, for this subject, were more often than not vague or incomplete. The fact that English and American printers used different methods to calculate their costs, as well as two very diverse currencies, further complicates the situation. In addition, I have elected not to attempt to give monetary equivalents or current values of these costs. If my figures do not always add up, the fault may be attributed to the disparities within the texts themselves.

Printing has always been a very competitive business, as well as a precarious and potentially ruinous activity. At best, it offered few opportunities for great financial rewards. From the beginning, it was the sort of business that required an enormous outlay of *risk* capital – to use one of today's buzz words. It is, therefore, quite ironic that the first printer of note, Johannes Gutenberg, should have fallen victim to under-capitalization. He was forced into bankruptcy by Johann Fust, who foreclosed on his loans to Gutenberg in 1455.

The handful of nineteenth-century printers' manuals that preceded Stower's *Printer's Grammar* (1808) were often referred to in the trade as *ready reference guides*. Unlike Stower's manual, these guides were not intended to train novice printers, but to provide experienced journeymen with useful information about such things as tables of signatures and imposition schemes. One feature common to all of them were the "Scales of Prices" which helped master printers determine what to charge their clients for various types of work. The first two printers' manuals to be specifically designated as *price books* were both published in 1814. They were *The Printer's Job Price-Book* by Philip Rose and John Evans, which contained eighty-one tables of the master printer's charges to the public, and Stower's *The Printer's Price-Book*, which also included over 300 pages of typographic specimens. Later in the century, in 1869 and again in 1871, De Vinne issued his own price lists, the first of their kind to be published in America. I have deliberately selected readings from the latter edition since it arrived on the scene at a time when printers were more conscientiously referring to such lists when making their estimates.

When nineteenth-century manual writers mentioned the "business of printing," they were essentially referring to the following four aspects: (1) setting up an office; (2) dealing with customers; (3) costs for materials, such as type, ink, and paper, and labor, which included composition and presswork; and (4) estimates, which were based in theory on the Scales of Prices. These are also the main topics covered in this chapter.

The rapid growth of the printing industry in America was summed up by Ringwalt (1871, p. 427): "On the 1st of June 1860, the book, job, and newspaper establishments, returned from 36 States and Territories, numbered 1666. They employed an aggregate capital of $19,622,318, and 20,159 persons, including 2333 females, at an annual cost of $7,588,096, and paid for materials the sum of $12,844,288. The total value of the product was $31,063,898, an increase of $19,477,349, or

168 per cent. over the value of the same industry in 1850." Later, on p. 429 in the same article, he notes that the American book trade did an estimated $16,000,000 worth of business in 1856, of which the four largest contributors were: the cities of New York, $6,000,000; Philadelphia, $3,400,000; Boston, $2,500,000; and Cincinnati, $1,300,000.

By comparison, in 1926, the American manual writer Ralph W. Polk notes on p. 13 in his *The Practice of Printing*: "The census reports rank printing as the sixth industry of this country with respect to the value of its product, although in some other respects it is entitled to be classed as the third great industry, and in some, even as the second in rank." He goes on to give the following statistics: capital investment of over $1,000,000,000, employing more than 450,000 printers, whose annual salaries are approximately $560,000,000.

Reading 28.1
Advice to Those Who Intend Commencing Business
from *The Printers' Assistant* by William Mason (1814, p. 27).

Traditionally, printers came up through the ranks. Master printers – the owners of the printing offices – usually achieved their positions through inheritance, mergers, and marriage; however, early in the nineteenth century, enterprising young men, who may, or may not, have completed their indentured apprenticeships, began to open their own printing establishments. Mason's manual is one of the first to give this new breed of entrepreneurs sound advice on how to set up and conduct a printing business. Being familiar with prices and the quality of materials was also an essential prerequisite for succeeding in the printing trade, which by implication, meant that the young man probably would have had some previous training in a printing office.

Mason, like all of the authors in this chapter, emphasizes the need to do good work, deliver it on time, and be fiscally responsible. Printing was basically a "cash-and-carry" business. He warns against extending credit to clients, although in most cases, the printer would be operating his own business on credit from his suppliers.

He advises purchasing materials at sales where a printer could save as much as thirty percent. Other writers, such as Harpel on p. 818 in Reading 28.3, tried to discourage the young printer from this practice. New type could also be purchased for cash with a 7½ percent discount. When buying type, Mason recommends having it all cast at the same time and delivered in one consignment. In addition, he urges the printer to always have the terms of the sale and the credit agreement specified in writing. For presses, he suggests getting a written agreement from the manufacturer that grants the printer the right to return the press after six months – without any costs or expenses – if the press does not meet his expectations.

In commencing business, it is essentially requisite to possess a general knowledge of the prices and quality of materials, that you may not be imposed on; for many characters, tho' upright in every other respect, think it no wrong to cheat *in the way of business*; and as most young beginners are destitute of the above knowledge, a few lines on this head [subject] appear a desideratum in this small work.

To those who are not in haste to begin, I would advise them to purchase at sales, taking a person with them acquainted with the price and quality of materials; as, in consequence of so many continually taking place, a saving of thirty per cent. may actually be made. But if, on the contrary, you wish to have every thing new, first obtain specimen books from the different founders, for your choice of type; where, for ready money, you will be allowed 7½ per cent. Be particular in agreeing for the whole to be delivered by a fixed date, and to have it all at one delivery, otherwise they will send directly what they have *by them,* to secure the order, and you may wait their pleasure for the remainder. And give strict instructions that they do not send you *more than you have ordered,* as is a common case; for if it is only, 50 lbs. in each fount on the average, it will swell your account so much, as, perhaps, to embarrass you. Always have the term of credit specified in writing on the bill of parcels, as tradesmen are generally suspicious of young beginners, and if they think you are not doing well, will *pounce* upon you immediately, in order to secure themselves, tho' a long term of credit may have been verbally agreed upon.

With respect to purchasing new [wooden] presses, always have an agreement in writing that, if not approved of by you at the expiration of six months, that they shall be taken back without any costs or expences whatever; and the same with respect to all joiners' materials, as they are frequently made of green wood, and after two or three months are not worth house-room.

Be not too eager in obtaining an extensive business [i.e., a business based on extending credit to clients], as it is so difficult to obtain payment, even of those who have it in their power. If you agree to do work for a certain price, be particular in having a fixed date for payment, and that interest be paid for after time.

Never accept a bill of exchange *unless for value received,* as those who are necessitated to ask for *accommodation bills,* as they are termed, seldom have it in their power to take them up when due.

Reading 28.2
The Printing Business in America
from *The Printers' Guide* by Cornelius S. Van Winkle (1818, pp. x–xi).

William Caxton [ca. 1421–1491] established the first printing press in England at Westminster in 1476. Printing was, therefore, well entrenched in England by the time it reached Colonial America, where the first press was set up in Cambridge, Massachusetts, in 1638. It was not until 1693, however, that William Bradford [1663–1752] established the first press in New York City. New York would eventually displace Philadelphia and then Boston as the center of the printing industry in America.

Van Winkle's manual (1818) was the first to be written by an American – the honor of the first manual to be printed in America, however, goes to *The Printer's Manual: An Abridgment of Stower's Grammar* (1817) by Caleb Stower; which was printed in Boston. Even though influenced by existing British manuals, Van Winkle's work reflects a typical American attitude toward independence and equality in the workplace. His goal, aside from instructing printers, was to impress upon his readers the viability of careers in the printing trades. In 1818, Van Winkle notes that there were about fifty printing offices in New York City, employing 500 hands. The practices in New York City reflected the state of the art and growth of the industry throughout the country.

Referring to Stower (1808, pp. 1–33) who devoted thirty-three pages to the "history of printing," of which fifteen pertained to the "introduction of the art into England," Van Winkle decided against including any comments on the history of the art; instead, he recommended *The History of Printing in America* (1810) by Isaiah Thomas, to his readers.

It may be the opinion of some, that we ought to have given, in imitation of Mr. Stower, a history of printing; at least, of its introduction into America, and of its subsequent progress in the United States. But as we have no data from which to give an account of the present state of printing, nor of its late improvements in this country, we must content ourselves with referring those who seek for information on this subject, to Thomas's History of Printing, which is brought down to the commencement of the revolution.

By comparing the state of printing at the above period, with the state of it at the present time, in the city of New-York, we shall have a tolerably correct criterion by which to ascertain its progressive improvement in the United States; for we think we shall not exceed the truth when we say, that printing has increased in the same, or nearly the same ratio throughout the whole country. And here we are led to digress, in order to remark, that the extent, and the importance to the nation, of this branch of domestic industry has never, we are fully persuaded, been properly estimated. Mr. Thomas gives an account of only twenty-two printing establishments in the city of New-York, from the first introduction of the art into this colony, in the year 1693, down to the year 1775, embracing a period of eighty-two years; and at present there are established in this city about fifty printing offices, employing nearly five hundred hands constantly.

The number of individuals engaged in, and who derive their support, directly and indirectly, from the business of printing in this country, far exceeds all calculations hitherto made. We have no means at present to make an estimate, with any degree of accuracy; but unless we are anticipated by some one more competent than ourselves, we shall, to the best of our ability, give it at some future, and, perhaps, not distant period.

Reading 28.3
General Business Management
from *Harpel's Typograph* by Oscar Henry Harpel (1870, pp. 241–244).

Unlike so many other trades, printing could only be practiced after a considerable outlay of capital had been made. There were presses, type, ink, and paper to be purchased, and labor to be compensated for, which, by comparison, was the cheapest component in the estimate. All master printers paid, more or less, the same amount for all of these commodities and services; the only real difference was the quality of the work they produced. We can see this today by comparing an example of printing – which is not bad – from one of Kinko's nationwide copy centers with one from The Stinehour Press in Lunenburg, Vermont. Superficially, they may resemble each other, but even from a casual examination of the two, it will be evident that Stinehour's printing is far superior in quality to that of Kinko's. It is simply a matter of the degree of skills that the workmen possess and the quality of the materials. This dissimilarity between ordinary and fine work was just as evident in the nineteenth century.

Harpel laments the fact that almost anyone in the 1870s could set up a printing office. Even so, he offers a lot of valuable advice to novice printers. He includes a detailed list of the "do's and don't's," among them the need for careful estimates and cash payments, as well as lessons in diplomacy with customers. Now and then, he adds a couple of catch phrases, such as "neatness and dispatch" and "time is money" in order to spur the young man on toward his goal of operating a successful printing business. Another of Harpel's simple pieces of advice – one that printers today would normally take for granted: keep regular business hours.

According to Harpel, the majority of printers, even as late as the 1870s, did not have a standard for estimating labor, consumption of materials, wear, waste, and other necessary expenses that were often not factored into the estimate. They did, however, have scales of prices at their disposal, but these only covered the base costs, and generally did not include all the little extras. The practice of prospective clients "getting bids" – estimates from several printers – seems to have come into existence in the printing industry about this time. With competition fierce, it was always a temptation to cut prices, ignoring the true value of one's work, a habit that could lead to financial ruin.

Scarcely any other branch of skilled industry, involving as much capital and intelligence for its proper prosecution as the general printing business, has such contradictory and widely varying charges for its products. Proprietors of offices and those who have them in charge, having, in a majority of cases, adopted no standard whereby to estimate labor, consumption of material, wear, waste, and other necessary expenses, seem to transact their affairs in this particular by a system of guesswork, or some other hap-hazard principle, which has caused the idea to exist in the minds of many persons who employ printers frequently, that the profits of the craft are so exorbitant that the smallest sum a piece of work can be had for, (often without regard to quality it is true), is ample remuneration for the amount of work done.

The foolish, not to say reckless, greed of incompetent parties, who will have business at any price or risk, is mainly accountable for the inadequate prices that rule for many kinds of printing; while those who can do better things, but have placed themselves in competition with the suicidal disposition to underbid, – so rife among certain wretched printers, – have the satisfaction, if such it is, of knowing they will be the real sufferers, *ad finem* [in the end].

That many persons engaged in printing are fairly intentioned, but culpably ignorant concerning the true value of their own work, – laboring on industriously for years with little or no advance in their worldly circumstances, – is literally true. Undecisive of character, although possibly capable as workmen, they underrate themselves, and constantly yield to the representations of interested parties, who make it their business to get the most labor for the least money, and who have, by a practice of "getting bids," made printing almost a beggarly vocation in many quarters; besides which, the too ready disposition to reduce the prices of work, etc. below, rather than increase them up to, a fair valuation, seems to become, as time progresses, more and more the rule among printers themselves. . . .

Many of the evils that attend the prosecution of type and press-work arise from the want of a good system of apprenticeship, now almost totally ignored throughout our country. A lad or young man of any age is permitted to enter an office in some capacity, uncontrolled by any *legal* regulation bearing upon the generally verbal agreement made between the parties, After serving what he deems a sufficient time in his case, or until he feels disposed to quit, whether capable as a workman or not, the youth starts forth, joins a "*Union*," and, presto! he must rank, so far as wages are concerned at least, with the really good workman who has served a full and faithful term of *indentured* apprenticeship, during which he has become excellent and expert in his calling.

Again: chance or opportunity may place the inferior printer in charge or possession of an office of greater or lesser resources, where, knowing his incapacity to compete squarely with his betters, his resource is to compel patronage by doing miserable work for undiscriminating customers at the poorest prices, and thereby often causing his abler competitor to take less than what he knows is just compensation for his work, or leave his facilities unemployed.

The following rules for business management have been found correct, both from observation and practice, and we cannot urge them too strongly upon the attention of every one who conducts a printing concern with something more than a mere pittance in view:

Do not go beyond your capital in purchasing material, and never purchase what is not likely to be of immediate use, no matter how cheap it is.

Avoid buying odds and ends of second-hand printing material about which you know little or nothing.

Insist upon order, and the careful usage of the implements, etc., whether the office is your own or otherwise.

Have regular hours for opening and closing business, and require all your workmen to observe them.

Preserve a carefully considered, just, and fixed system for estimating work according to its quality, keeping in view the probable consumption and waste of all material, wear and tear of implements, superintendence, and other expenses, no matter how trivial they may seem; for the least cost can be computed by an average per centage.

Having determined what amount of money a piece of work is really worth, including a positive and not suppositious profit, make that the price, and do not deviate from it.

Be courteous and willing to accommodate all reasonable demands, but be decisive in your transactions. A host of errors results from a vascillating disposition.

Be prompt, making no promises that you may not reasonably expect to fulfil; and fill your orders according to your promises. In hurried times do not put aside one customer because a later one is urgent, unless the first one has allowed ample time wherein you may accommodate the last one also; for, though you may have gained a new patron by the measure, you will he apt to lose the former one if he be disappointed by not getting his work when promised.

When customers want good work done at less than it is fairly worth, reason with them calmly; and, if they will not be convinced, but make assertions in regard to the prices charged by others that seem unreasonable, or seem disposed to go elsewhere, do not go into a tirade against your competitors. Neither would we have you yield, knowing you are adopting a wrong; but simply declare you cannot do business at such rates and realize a fair profit.

Have a clear understanding with a patron before what he desires is done, what the price for it will be, – approximately, but large enough if it cannot he determined at once, – so that there will be no disagreeable compromise to make after the work is rendered and to be settled for.

Lost valuable time occasioned by the customer, such as extra work, alterations, etc., should be charged. Too little regard for these items causes sad leaks in the profits of an office. A price is given, based upon the ordinary contingencies of a piece of work; but the party for whom it is to be done proves capricious, and demands frequent changes, proofs, etc., although the first piece of work may be performed neatly and well. It is but just, then, that he should pay for it. Where no guide is given or any style indicated, or where there has been no previous understanding concerning such waste of time, its cost should be stated immediately before it is made, so as to make it optional with the patron to have it done or not.

Careful estimates, cast-ups, and the like, requiring time and experience to make, should be charged for, unless the work is guaranteed to the office, in which case it should go with the estimate for general superintendence.

The *cash system* should be closely adhered to, and strangers, without any exception, on account of appearance or address, required to pay in advance, or to leave a sufficient deposit to prevent absolute loss.

Workpeople should be paid *in full* every pay-day; but it would be well to have an understanding with them concerning the time they are to give an employer, and the employer them, notice of separation for any cause. As an earnest, on the part if the accepted workman, it should be made a part of the business contract that he leave in his employer's hands a certain sum weekly to be forfeited in case of his non-compliance with the agreement. An equivalent, whereby to bind the employer, might also be made by a written agreement or stipulation properly witnessed. This would prevent the sudden departures and discharges that usually occur in the most improper seasons.

While it is always right to be amiable and pleasant with those who patronize an establishment, their familiarity with workmen during working hours should not be permitted; and informing them of matters in hand not necessary for them to know, had better be left unsaid. Loungers [idlers] should be repelled by the simple information, politely but pointedly told, that your affairs require your personal attention, and that it retards the workmen to converse with them. This will generally suffice without giving offence.

Do not suppose, if orders are plenty and customers easily managed during busy seasons, that dull times will not come and patrons be exacting or hard to please. It is during business lulls that many are tempted to work below what they can afford to do, and to yield advantages that are pretty sure to remain advantages *to the customer* in future transactions.

Never retain an unprofitable workman unless you can afford the expense, or it is done out of charity. One who receives more than he yields becomes a burden, and should not be needlessly encouraged.

Have no more workmen than your materials and implements will keep comfortably employed without waste of time. It is often a false idea that the more people there are about a concern, the more business is being done.

In the type department, it should be the rule to distribute forms as fast as they are released from the press, unless there is a prospect of their being used again within a reasonable length of time. But, unless there is an arrangement made with a customer to keep type standing for him, its being kept in form should be solely for the benefit of the office.

Make it incumbent upon compositors to send forms to press thoroughly justified, revised, and leveled, leaving nothing for the pressman to do but make it ready on the press and print it. Also insist upon the forms being returned from the pressroom as soon as they are off, thoroughly washed and free from attachments that are no longer useful, such as underlays, etc.

Do not be lured into purchasing everything new that emanates from the foundries. Obtain what you really need *when* you need it, and then select what you deem the most appropriate and best for your purpose. Much of the embarrassment that occurs among employing printers comes from the disposition to increase their stock of types, etc. with the latest productions, whether their incomes warrant it or not. It will require a pretty considerable business and large profits to permit the purchase of the temptations that our friends the type-founders spread before our eyes so constantly. But, we repeat, beware of indulging in novelties too often.

If your business is good, do not be niggardly with such supplies as hasten forward your transactions. Let there be enough sticks, chases, leads, slugs, metal furniture, small tools, etc., to permit workmen to keep at work and not wait upon each other. But this does not imply that unnecessary quantities should be got merely for transient convenience. As fast as an article of general supply is released, it should be placed in a position for immediate use again, and not have to be searched for when needed.

Avoid practising or encouraging the prevalent disposition among customers to have, and workmen to do, what may be termed *useless composition* – that is, having several justifications of as many styles of letters in one line, when one, or at most two, kinds of letters would look neater and better, and require less expenditure of time and labor. Elaborate border and flourish work, and curving type lines and rules into a bad imitation of engraving, may be ranked with this kind of composition, which, unless it is amply paid for, becomes a nuisance and a positive bar to the profitable prosecution of a job. At the same time we advocate the most elegant and *artistic* effects that can be produced, *if it is paid for*. Otherwise adhere to the rules of "neatness and dispatch," permitting nothing to be done that is not well done; but, at the same time, let it be done without unnecessary waste of time; for in nothing is the fact that "time is money" more pronounced than in the printing business.

Reading 28.4
The Business of Printing
from *American Dictionary of Printing and Bookmaking* by Wesley Washington Pasko (1894, pp. 463–464).

> Pasko notes that in order to be successful, the printer should be a hands-on manager. The more knowledgeable the printer, the more precise his estimates will be. He also discusses the percentage of profit a printer could expect from his efforts, noting that the markup for profit should not be less than 15 percent. This is considerably less than the 30 percent markup Hansard mentions on p. 841 in Reading 28.7.

It is a necessity in the management of a printing-office that every item of cost shall be known and estimated. Nothing is too small and insignificant for this purpose. Labor and materials used are never omitted by any employer, but a multitude of little expenses are. At the end of each year all of the expenses for whatever purpose should be added together, including a fair amount for the services of the proprietor or proprietors, and the receipts should also be taken. The latter may be unduly low from losses, or they may be small because collections have not been made. In the former case the business should not be adjudged to have been unsuccessful simply because one or two failures have occurred. When an inquiry has been made with diligence as to the standing of a customer, and the best authorities have replied that he is worthy of credit, the printer is not to be severely blamed because in some cases of this kind the information is worthless. If, however, he has more to collect at the end of one year, in proportion to the volume of business done, than at the end of the preceding year it shows wrong management. The amount outstanding never ought to exceed two months' receipts. The expenses of all kinds, including deterioration, placed in conjunction with the sums which ought to be drawn out by the proprietor, should be reckoned and then an allowance made for profit, including interest on the capital with which the business is conducted. This allowance for profit ought not to be less than 15 per cent., and the least possible sum upon which business can be conducted would be 10 per cent. Thus, if a printing-office has $20,000 capital and does $40,000 worth of work its expenses of all kinds ought not to be over $35,000. The uncertainty and variableness of the occupation demand an average return at least as high as this in order to make up for losses in some years and the constant need of renovation and improvement. Every employing printer should make himself familiar with paper and ink, knowing what they cost and how they can be used. He should also familiarize himself with the exact performance of his presses, so that he may not be misled in estimating. Every little detail must be watched, and nothing taken for granted. If the printing-office is not large the proofs in page form should be looked over by him more or less, and he should always see proofs of title-pages and important matters. It is important to know how the work is progressing, and what are the capacities of the older and more valuable workmen. Nothing should ever be decided from caprice, but according to rule. Rules, however, as to misconduct can frequently be made too severe, and it is wiser sometimes to overlook a fault than to punish it. As a rule the foremen are held responsible for their men, and must not be interfered with. Yet this government should be under the control of the house.

Branch printing-offices, generally speaking, are unprofitable. To render the trade remunerative the master's eye should be upon the work, and this cannot be done in two places at once. There can be no objection, however, to offices for the collection and delivery of work. Opinions among printers are divided as to the expediency of employing canvassers. They are tempted to cut down prices in order to get work, and there is, therefore, a double expense on all jobs thus procured, first for commissions and second on reduced prices. When canvassers are thus employed 10 per cent. is the usual amount paid, 15 being the highest. The canvasser does not receive his commission until the work is paid for.

Reading 28.5
Hints on Taking Orders
from *The Printer's Price-List* by Theodore Low De Vinne (1871, pp. 402–417)

De Vinne is one of the most articulate and informative of all nineteenth-century manual writers. He had an encyclopedic mind and a typographic sensibility that was unequaled by any other manual writer in nineteenth-century America. De Vinne systematically provides the printer with advice on every aspect of the printing business, as well as all the necessary tools to estimate jobs accurately.

This particular reading is one of the longest in this book; however, I feel that it is an essential document because it gives the modern reader a true and clear sense of what was involved in the business of printing in the last three decades of the nineteenth century. For the most part, De Vinne is addressing professionals, experienced master printers with hands-on management skills. His aim is to make their businesses more efficient as well as more profitable. Many of the practices he describes below were still in effect in commercial printing offices as late as the 1950s.

He begins with "Receiving Copy," a reminder to us that before typewriters and computer floppy disks, all copy was set from either manuscript leaves written by hand in ink or, in the case of reprints, from pages of previously printed text. When accepting copy from the client, he advocates: "Take down all directions in writing. Trust nothing to memory."

The major part of his book consists of tables of prices, which, if used properly, could mean the difference between profit and loss. Even with hundreds of examples, very few jobs, unless they are exact reprints, will be alike. He reminds printers about all the little "hidden" costs and expenses in the printing office, such as solvents, postage, and waste paper that must be factored into their estimates. He notes that accurate estimates can only be based on the actual time it takes to complete a job. Like all of the other authors in this chapter, De Vinne was opposed to extending credit to clients. His dictum was "Cash should be the rule; credit, the exception."

De Vinne points out that printing became more and more specialized toward the end of the century. Book, job, and news work were usually separate trades and done on presses designed specifically for them. Even though I have placed an emphasis in this book on the handpress, I have also included some of De Vinne's comments on job printing since it was an integral aspect of nineteenth-century printing, and on occasion, made use of the handpress for certain types of work. Job work is defined as any kind of printing not specifically covered by book or news work. In the mid-fifteenth century, even Gutenberg, who printed papal indulgences, was engaged in job work; as were Fust and Schöffer when they printed a poster for Diether of Isenburg (ca. 1421–1482, Archbishop of Mainz. Savage (1841, p. 428) defined a job as "Any thing which printed does not exceed a sheet." Five years later in America, Grattan (1846, pp. 94-108) included a section dedicated specifically to job printing. By mid-century, job printing had become a separate specialization, although many book offices and newspapers had job departments attached to them. One of the things that helped to establish this specialization in job work was a series of new vertical-platen presses, such as those introduced by Stephen P. Ruggles (1808–1880) in the 1840s and George P. Gordon (1810–1878) in the 1850s.

De Vinne touches on a subject that conjured up for me some unpleasant memories from the past. He says, "make bids for large contracts with caution. . . . Consider well the costs of doing the work." In the late seventies, a German affiliate of American Express offered me a half million dollars to print two limited editions for them. While working on the budget, I soon realized that I would need forty hand binders just to complete each edition by the deadline; at the time, I was having trouble finding just *one* good hand binder. Needless to say, I had to turn the offer down.

De Vinne has a note on what types of work not to accept, such as scurrilous or defamatory works – printers, after all, were just as legally responsible for what they printed as their clients were. He comments – just as today – that printers are frequently asked to do gratis printing for charities. His attitude was, if so inclined, to make a generous cash contribution, and to charge for all work at the regular rate.

De Vinne's manual is the first that I am aware of to mention printing salesmen, also called *canvassers*. He alerts the printer to certain problems that may arise when salesmen make too many concessions in order to gain an order.

Throughout this reading, De Vinne refers his readers to various price lists that are used to calculate printing costs.

Receiving Copy

Persuade your customer to furnish his own copy, written in ink. Avoid writing it for him. If it must be done by you, notify him distinctly that he is responsible for its supposed accuracy as to names, dates, places, and figures. The office can be responsible only for the orthography of ordinary words – not at all for uncertain proper names or figures.

Never take in a small order without reading the copy critically. If it is obscurely written, re-write it in the customer's presence, and make clear every obscure point. Let there be no ambiguity between the capitals I and J, or between T, Y, and S in proper names, or in figures.

It is not practicable to read over copy for a large piece of composition, but it should not go to the compositor until it has been fairly examined. See that the leaves are properly numbered, and that the compositor will have no difficulty in keeping the connection. If the manuscript is bad, or is too bulky to be re-written, persuade him to have it copied. Advise him that the expense of re-writing the copy will be much less than the probable alterations of type, and that the time spent in making a clean copy, so far from hindering, will really speed and cheapen the work. Inform him that although a compositor may be able to read very bad manuscript, or to put in order badly digested copy, that such extra work cannot be done at the price of legible copy. Somebody must pay for all delay occasioned by negligence or obscurity.

If possible, obtain all the copy before you commence work, and get all the directions. It is not always practicable to do this, but the attempt should never be relaxed. The customer should be reminded that when copy is given out in fragments, there is always a great loss of time in doing the work, as well as an impaired feeling of responsibility concerning it – not only in regard to the time of performance, but even in regard to its accuracy and neatness. The knowledge of the fact that the customer has more copy to bring in, that his directions are still incomplete, and that he will probably alter or disarrange the existing plan of the work, is injurious to both foreman and compositor. The work is not and cannot be undertaken earnestly, for there is a sense of divided responsibility.

Take down all directions in writing. Trust nothing to memory. Attach these written directions to the copy, and let them always accompany the work, in every stage of its progress. See also that they are fully entered on the order book.

Unsatisfactory display work is largely caused by bad preparation of copy. It is the fashion to censure the compositor for this imperfection in work; when most of it rightfully belongs to the author or to the office. To avoid this fault, it will be found economical for most offices to prepare and re-write job copy before giving it out, marking out definitely the size and style of the work, the width of the measure, the size of border, the relative prominence of displayed type and every other matter that could guide the compositor. The preparation of copy in such style will save much useless labor. An able foreman who pursues this method can do much really fine work even with imperfect workmen.

Obtaining Directions

Obtaining directions is a difficult task. Few persons know how to give an order for printing. Most customers are ignorant of the names, qualities and appropriateness of papers, types or bindings, and can not give explicit directions. Many of them have very indistinct notions as to what they really want in both size and style. To obtain the proper directions, it will at the outset be necessary to exhibit specimens of work, which may be used for the purpose of suggesting the needed directions.

Even with this aid, it will be necessary to ask questions in order to ascertain the customer's wants. The number, the style, the paper, the color, and in fact nearly every practical direction can be had only by questioning. But much discretion must be used in this matter. Never try to alter or even to direct a customer's choice unless specially requested. Never persuade him to take any style of work or quality of paper for which he manifests no preference. Point out the advantages or disadvantages of each, fairly and fully, but only in the way of information, and not in such a manner as to produce the impression that you are trying to direct him. If he orders an expensive piece of work, do not tell him it is expensive, but tell him only the price. Let him make his own decision.

Persuade him not to pick out favorite styles of type for display lines. Show him, but with discretion, both his and your own inability to determine the proper length of lines, or their fitness in contrast. But while you avoid receiving minute directions concerning every line, be careful to get specific general directions as to the style of work wanted. Find out whether the display is to be in bold and black-faced type, or in light and open type, or in quaint or grotesque type – whether the arrangement is to be simple or complex, etc. From these general directions, accompanied by a specimen pattern, it will be much more easy for a compositor to show a satisfactory proof than it would from more minute directions.

Different Methods of Taking Work

Two methods may be used in taking orders of composition. 1. To guarantee satisfaction to the customer in the style of composition. This involves the taking of one or more proofs and the making of as many alterations as are ordered. It is the usual course on all small orders like those for cards and billheads. But it is hazardous. Such orders should always be priced at the highest rates to cover the probable expense of alterations, which are certain to be troublesome, in many cases exceeding the price obtained for the work. 2. To fix a price for the composition of the work, and to charge extra for all alterations of whatever nature, other than typographical or mechanical errors. This is the usage by which all Book and Pamphlet work and all large Job work is done.

The use of these two systems in the same office, and often on work for the same customer, makes trouble. Erroneous opinions are formed by customers concerning their rights and the printer's duties. Some think it is their right to alter a piece of composition indefinitely, without extra charge. To obviate disagreement, there should be a fair understanding with the customer concerning alterations. He should be informed that for the agreed price only a certain amount of time should be spent on his work. If the work is fairly done, the office has completed its duty. All extra work ordered by the customer for its improvement, should be charged specifically. If this explanation is made before the work is commenced, all contention may be prevented. . . .

Responsibility for Alterations

To rightfully claim an extra price for alterations, the office must from the first follow all the customer's directions. If they are impossible of execution, as is sometimes the case, he should be advised of it at once, and new directions should be had. But if the directions are possible of execution, they should be obeyed. The fact that they are inconsistent with a compositor's notions of good taste is quite immaterial. The customer has a right to have his work done in any style he chooses, whether it is tasteful or absurd. The compositor has no right to alter his directions. Nor is it judicious to accept his notions of display or method with a grudging assent. When a customer gives positive directions, evidently knowing clearly what he wants, the printer should heartily endeavor to aid him in carrying out his views, as far as he can, even if they are contrary to all accepted rules. Advice and opinion on such matters should be given only when they are asked, or are evidently acceptable. The compositor's notions of display or of good taste are quite as often incorrect as those of the customer. The workmen's traditional rules concerning the contrast of sizes and faces, and the balancing of long and short lines, useful as they may be in some cases, are absolutely erroneous in others. When specific directions have not been given, the office should see that the composition is done in workmanlike fashion. It should not only be accurate, but should show sufficient evidences of good taste to satisfy the reasonable requirements of a reasonable customer. The first proof of the average job compositor will seldom meet even this modest requisition. This is not the customer's fault. The office should not evade its responsibility. The customer is entitled to fair work, and the office, for its reputation, should not abate the standard of workmanship. The faulty piece of composition should be put in workmanlike shape, no matter what it costs. It is only after this has been done that the improvements ordered by the customer can be charged.

Few customers have a proper notion of the time consumed in making alterations. The amount is always surprising, and is often a matter of dispute. Of this the customer should be forewarned. It will be found judicious to mark on every new proof the time spent in correcting the last proof. No better check against capricious alterations could be devised.

How to Make Special Estimates

You may be asked for an estimate for work that is not priced in this book. To do this properly, you should be acquainted with the prices of all leading articles. You should know the value of all ordinary papers, not only by the ream, but by the 1000 in ordinary fractions; you should know the time spent upon and the prices asked for the ordinary numbers of all leading kinds of work. This will require study. Much may be learned from this book, but much more can be learned by observation and reflection. For trivial orders, like cards, billheads, handbills, etc., you should be able to furnish prompt answers to all common inquiries. The promptness of an answer does much toward impressing one with the justice of the price. To hesitate or boggle, to ponder and calculate, does not impress a new customer favorably. Where he sees uncertainty in knowledge, he infers unreliability in price. But if you are not sure of the accuracy of your knowledge, never give the price till you are sure. You will have to run the risk of the imputation of ignorance. For long and complex estimates, ask time for consideration. Avoid making such estimates in the presence of the customer, or at any time when you are likely to be disturbed. Analyze the work carefully; compare the prices for each item with the prices of this book. Where you have exact knowledge of cost of work, use the knowledge confidently and boldly; where you have not, defer to existing usage so far as you are informed. Do not be above asking advice or information where you know you need it. In so complex a business as this a novice should not be ashamed to confess ignorance of many matters. If you do not, you will certainly suffer more from its detection than you could from its confession.

Your manner has much to do with the impression that is produced. Prices are often thought too high by reason of the timid and apologetic manner in which they are asked. This timidity and a too confident boldness are equally to be avoided.

It is not difficult to make estimates, even of complex work, if you commence properly. Keep this rule before you: Do but one thing at a time. Each item of cost must be fairly examined. For every ordinary job of printed work, you will have to compute the value of Composition, Paper, and Presswork. For more complex work, you will have to compute items like Electrotyping, Binding, Engraving, etc. In all cases, each item must be separately computed. Begin with paper, as the basis. You will have learned from the customer what quality is wanted. You have next to find the proper size and price. This is a matter for which no special directions can be given. The most useful knowledge about paper can be gained only by handling it, and using it. Ascertain what fraction of a sheet, or how many sheets, each copy will require. Pay no attention whatever, at this stage of the work, to the number of forms, if it is a pamphlet, or to the number of impressions, if it is a job in colors, or if printed on both sides. . . . This knowledge cannot aid you here. It will rather confuse you. All you have to know for this purpose is, how many sheets or what fraction of a sheet one copy will require. When you get this fact, the calculation is simple. If two or more kinds of paper are used, make special calculation for each.

You next proceed to compute the value of composition. If the work is open display, or of irregular form, it must be rated by time; if it is plain common matter, it should be rated by the thousand ems. If you are not a practical printer, or are not thoroughly conversant with the rules and usages of the trade, so that you can discriminate intelligently, take advice. Never make a price because the work appears to you to be no greater than that of other or similar work, with the price of which you are familiar. Know to a certainty that it is no greater before you hazard a binding price. Most serious mistakes are often made by estimates based on a supposed analogy. Read carefully the general prices for book and job composition and compare them with the special prices that may be elsewhere given. In many cases these prices are variable, as must be the case with time work. For the fixing of this time work, consult a compositor or printer if he can be had, but do not accept his estimate implicitly. It will probably be too little. Experience will teach you that the work that a compositor thinks may be done in ten hours will, in most cases, take twelve hours. In your estimate of time allow, if you think it expedient, for probable alterations or delays, for which it may be injudicious to make special charge. If electrotyping is needed to cheapen the work, or for other reasons, ascertain how many plates can be used to advantage. In duplicating plates for a handbill or a check you can make so many plates that the bill for presswork will be trivial. This should be avoided. . . . You will also have to decide whether plates should be blocked, or not. . . . Of the relative advantages of each method you must decide. Here, too, you may need advice.

Your next step is to compute the presswork. Upon small orders of ordinary work like handbills and labels, when printed from one form and in one color, the prices have already been made under the proper headings. If two or more plates are used for the purpose of cheapening presswork, you must calculate the number of impressions. For example: 20,000 copies of a handbill, medium 8°, from one plate will make 20,000 impressions, for which the price would be $1.00 per 1000 impressions; from two plates there would be but 10,000 impressions, for which the price is $1.50 per 1000 impressions, for the edition is smaller and the sheet is larger; from four plates there would be but 5000 impressions, for which the price is $2.00 per 1000 impressions. . . . If the work is to be printed on both sides, in the same color, you should estimate for presswork by one impression, in all cases where it can be done with advantage. If the form is very large, if paper or press of double size cannot be had, or if the number of copies is quite small, it will be more economical to print the matter on the back by a separate impression. Upon large orders, it is the usage to print work in large sheets, for it is both quicker and cheaper. In computing the value of presswork done in this manner on both sides, be careful to put down correctly the number of impressions that will be required. The caution is needed, for errors are frequently made at this point. Recollect, where both face and back are imposed together, that every impression makes one copy; if the job is set up or stereotyped twice, one impression makes two copies, etc. Forget, if possible, all about the number of plates (or the number of pages in the form), and think only of the number of copies that one impression will make. Divide the total number of copies wanted by the number of copies that are made by one impression. This will give you the entire number of impressions. Caution is needed here also. You must remember that the value of presswork increases with the size of the sheet.

For ordinary work in two plain colors, like plain black and red, combined prices have been made in the printed tables. For red and blue, or red and gold, and for all other colors, the separate prices should be used for each color respectively. If color is required in any quantity, and you can obtain advice from an expert about the probable quantity, you should ask it. . . . If the job makes more than one form, as in a pamphlet, and the forms are of uniform size, you will only have to determine the price of presswork for one form to use it as a unit for all the others. . . .

There is a method of computing presswork from paper largely practiced on book work, for which it is useful, which is here mentioned only to be avoided. For Book work, in which full-sized sheets only are used, it is customary to rate four tokens to the ream. The reams of paper being known, one has but to multiply the number of reams by the figure four to ascertain the entire number of tokens. But for Job work, in which it is customary to print from half, third and quarter sheets, on forms of one and two or more duplicates, and often in sections of different size, such a method of calculating presswork is impracticable if not impossible. It is certain to lead to error.

These four items of Paper, Composition, Electrotyping and Presswork are those that give most trouble in calculation. Ruling, Binding, Engraving, Lithography, Paging, Gilding, and many other processes are needed to complete some kinds of work. Each of these should be examined in turn, and priced by the aid of the tables here given, and such other information as may be had from practical workmen.

Keep Estimates

Keep a Record of every estimate, not only of the gross amount, but of the value allotted on each item. You will need it for reference on estimates of other work. If your estimate is accepted, it will be an instructive study to compare the actual cost of the work, after it has been done, with its estimated cost. There is no method by which you so readily acquire a knowledge of the real value of work.

Never give a detailed estimate to a customer. It is not your duty, nor is it good policy to expose your methods. The customer bargains only for a result, and not for methods of accomplishing that result. He may take no exceptions to the sum total; he probably will except to one or more items. That little knowledge, which is so dangerous a thing, is never more so than when used by a customer who knows a little about paper, and a little about printing. You will have to waste much time in trying to explain matters to one who from the nature of the case has not sufficient knowledge to appreciate your explanation. His knowledge of the items will certainly be used to your disadvantage. The customer will buy the paper, and will probably get that which is unsuitable, or he will undertake to do the binding, and the result may be that you will have to complete his unfinished work at needless cost. By all means, refuse detailed estimates.

Never make estimates for work you cannot do, or choose not to do. Do not allow yourself to be made a tool of. It is a common practice with some tradesmen, when dissatisfied with one printer's bill, to go to another printer for a new estimate, giving the erroneous impression that the work for which estimate is wanted is about to be ordered, and is to be an exact reprint of the copy. The fact that the first printer has spent many hours in capricious alterations and experiments is suppressed. The new estimate for a reprint work is made without allowance for time spent in alteration, and is consequently lower, and the first printer is unjustly accused of excessive charges. In this way many enmities are made, and fair prices are lowered. If you have reason to suspect such a state of affairs, decline an estimate altogether, until you have the request of both parties. It is not fair to price another printer's work from partial representations of the case. In all cases where estimate is given to unknown parties, on reprint work, give it in this form: "For an exact reprint," so much; "For work from manuscript copy, with alterations, etc.," a much higher price.

About Prices

Where it is possible to make a price before the customer leaves, do so. Never let him go away with erroneous notions about the cost, if it is possible to correct them. It is better to lose the work altogether, than to have a wrangle over it when done.

Let there be a fair understanding as to price, time, proofs, alterations, etc. If the customer is not satisfied with your conditions, when the necessity for them has been fairly and courteously explained, and he offers his copy grudgingly and reluctantly, decline his order. It is best to have no dealings with any one who thinks he is not receiving a fair equivalent.

Whatever your prices may be, you will frequently be told that they are too high, that they are more than those of your competitors. This statement, reduced to first principles, really means that the customer does not want to pay so much money. It may affect, but it should not altogether control your price. The statement may or may not be true, for a customer's knowledge of general prices must be partial and imperfect. That which is true of one item in your bill may be untrue of another. You may charge more for paper and less for presswork, more for composition and less for electrotyping or binding. If your prices are based as they should be on actual cost, as well as in deference to prevailing usage, do not alter them until you are convinced that they cannot be maintained. But this decision should not be made on the instant. In so important a matter, take proper time for inquiring into the facts of the case and give them proper consideration. If they are higher than the prices of other fair rivals, and you can afford to make a reduction, you may choose to do so. If you cannot afford to do it; if your prices are just and reasonable, and if you are well convinced that a reduction is a positive loss, stand by your first price. You may lose custom [business], and probably will. Every tradesman must. You cannot reasonably hope to secure the custom of every person who asks for your prices or gets an estimate, or who has been in the habit of dealing with you. The withdrawal of custom does not necessarily imply dissatisfaction. A lower price usually secures the sale of ordinary merchandise, when two or more are in competition, but it will not secure it in an order for printed work. Personal preference or other accidental circumstances are often more influential than low prices.

It may be that your prices are higher than those of other printers, and, it is presumed, for necessary reasons. Inform your objector that printing is like other merchandise, like iron or flour or cloth, some qualities of which are worth twice as much as others. Yet while worth twice as much, the difference in appearance to an inexpert is often barely noticeable. Tell him that the comparison of competing prices, for work yet to be done, is not a fair comparison. The workmanship and material of one printer may be worth more than that of another, as he would readily admit on examination, and that the higher priced may yield the least profit and be worth the most money. Assure him, as you probably can, that your price is no more than is just for good workmanship and material, for speed, care and the intelligent supervision of competent workmen, and responsibility for errors and accidents, which can seldom be the conditions under which the cheapest work is done. Tell him, that to carry on the printing business in a proper manner, satisfactory both to the customer and to the proprietor, it is necessary to pursue a liberal policy; that low prices cannot give all the customer needs; that prices are not everything. The printer whose prices are lowest must, of necessity, be chary [cautious] of every expense in time or material. New or modern faces of type, tasteful composition, clear and bright presswork, promptness in the execution of orders, and general attendance to his varied interests, are rather more important, in many, if not in most cases, than low prices. Those who have the most printing to do, find out sooner or later that a printer who is just to himself can afford to be liberal to them in his method of doing work. He may charge more for his work, but he will probably do it both quicker and better. With some persons, these observations will have influence; with others they will not.

Do not make prices unusually high, even where they can be had. It is impolitic as well as unjust. All the profit that can be had by too high prices, is more than offset by the damaging reputation that will be earned.

If you have agreed with a customer to do a piece of work at a certain price, and subsequently find that it will cost more than you expected, stand by your bargain, and accept the loss. Neither try to cheapen the work, nor to get an extra allowance, nor yet make any complaint. Be content with notifying the customer what your price will be for future orders of the same kind.

If you do work badly, and wish to avoid its total loss, make a liberal reduction in the charge. Do not wait to be told of it, nor justify it, nor higgle about it. You will make better terms by voluntary concession, than by contention.

Be careful in altering prices by percentage, especially in making a reduced price. If paper is sold at an advance of 25 per cent. on cost, it requires a reduction of but 20 per cent. from this selling price to restore it to the first cost: ($4.00 + 25 per cent. = $5.00. $5.00 − 20 per cent. = $4.00.) The frequency of this error should be considered as a sufficient excuse for the re-statement of so simple a rule of arithmetic.

When you are requested to give a price for a very large quantity of work, it will be prudent to give at the same time price for a small quantity. The reason for difference in price between large and small quantities is but imperfectly understood by the public, and you will be expected to print a small number at the price of a large number, unless you make distinct prices for each at the outset.

Competition

"If my neighbor offers to do work for my customers at less than my prices, what shall I do to retain my work?" This is a most difficult question to answer. If the neighbor is considered a fair rival, and there is reason to believe that the offer has been made by mistake or thoughtlessness, assume that it is so, and see and remonstrate with him in a friendly manner. To assume, without positive knowledge, that your rival is maliciously injuring you, and to defame him therefor, is the surest way to perpetuate the evil from which you suffer. If remonstrance will not answer, strive to retain the work by superior execution or accommodation. But hesitate long before dropping too rashly to his lowest offer. Of the many persons who make lower offers, few are able to do the work properly. There may be reason to believe that the work will ultimately come back at your price. If you have done your work satisfactorily, your customer will probably find that what he may gain in price, he loses in time, in accommodation, or in the quality of workmanship.

Make bids for large contracts with caution. Do not be blinded by the amount of work or money. Consider well the cost of doing the work.

In no case, take work at cost, or at a pittance above cost. Such action will not defeat a certain class of competitors. Prices could not be named that would be low enough; there will always be some, who will make them still lower. To put prices down to cost, or below cost, to meet the competition of unscrupulous competitors, is to invite bankruptcy.

Avoid Over-Estimates

In making special prices for new work, be careful not to over-estimate the performance of men or machines. This is a common error. You may be able to do with your own hands one-half more work than is done by most workmen, but you are selling their labor, not your own, and your prices must be based on their performance. Even if you do the work yourself, you should not need the reminder that you are clearly entitled to all the advantages of superior skill. If you have good executive abilities, you can employ them when you have abundance of work to much better advantage in planning and directing labor, than in working with your own hands. It is possible for you to increase the average product of an office, by intelligent direction and by personal supervision, but there is a point of performance beyond which the average workman cannot pass. Your prices must be based on the actual, and not upon an ideal, performance. On good book work, the average performance of twenty men will not much exceed 5000 ems [a typographic measurement equal to the square of the type size]; on newspaper, or other common work, it will not be more than 6000 ems per day. Any estimate of cost based on a higher product will be found deceptive. You should apply the same rule to the performance of a job compositor, or of a machine press. The average performance of a large cylinder press, on ordinary job work, taking large and small forms and long and short editions together, will not exceed 5000 impressions per day in a busy season. If the average of an entire year is taken, in which dull seasons and lost time are included, it will be rather less than 3000 impressions per day. These are not speculations. They are demonstrable facts. This is the experience of the great majority of printers, and it will probably be your experience.

It is well to have a generous self-confidence, but it is well also to consider that there are able men in the business beside yourself. You will probably make a grave mistake if you think that you can do more work within a given limit of time, at less expense, and with greater profit, than your competitors. You may surpass them in some points, but not in all. If you base your prices on an impracticable standard of performance, your labor and ability will be wasted. If your older competitors, who are probably printers of intelligence and ability, and are enjoying the benefit of accumulated capital and experience, refuse, under stringent inducements, to put prices below a certain standard, it is unwise for you to try the experiment.

Concerning Some Customers

To take in orders in a manner satisfactory to the customer and profitable to the office, requires much discretion. It is probably unnecessary to remind a salesman that politeness and attention to the customer's wishes are of the first importance. It is to be presumed that every salesman must know that surliness or indifference is neither good manners nor good policy. But while a willingness to oblige should be apparent, it should not lead one to damaging concessions that will make the work utterly unprofitable. This is a common error with salesmen who are more anxious to secure custom than to make profit on work. It is largely in the power of a salesman to make work cheap or expensive, light or troublesome. The dissatisfaction that is sometimes evinced by customers over their work when finished, is often caused not so much by workmanship that is bad, as by workmanship that is disappointing, and which has been occasioned solely by the inability of the office to redeem the rash promises of the salesman. It is natural for a customer to desire all the advantages he can get. He certainly will ask for them if he imagines they will be conceded. You will have requests for the special purchase of new type, for extra or unusual composition, for many proofs, for clean press-proofs, for a guaranteed satisfaction in the work, for the privilege of keeping the type standing, and for unusual accommodation in many ways, all of which involve serious extra expense and trouble, and none of which are properly included in any ordinary price for work. No absolute rule can be laid down for the guidance of a salesman, in answer to all these applications. Some may be conceded, and some must be declined. Every special case must have its special judgment. The salesman should oblige the customer, if he can do so without positive loss. Failing to do this, he should convince him with pleasantry that his request is unreasonable and unusual. He must see that the customer does not form any improper notions of his own rights or of the printer's duty. All this requires much patience, much politeness, and much tact.

Great latitude should be allowed for the peculiarities of any customer who responds to his obligations, and pays for all his work. It is not wise to hedge him up with rules or restrictions, or to thwart his wishes. But the customer who expects his work to be done at the lowest ordinary rates, who is unable to give specific directions, or alters them capriciously, and who insists on seeing repeated proofs, and on making alterations at pleasure, should be reminded by the salesman that the ordinary rate does not cover his experiments with type. This caution is especially needed by those whose willingness to oblige renders them peculiarly liable to needless exactions. There are men who will take hours in giving directions about the most trivial matters – who are never sure they are right, who are continually recalling copy to make a correction or addition – who do not know at the outset what they want, and who find it out only after repeated experiments by the compositor – who want from two to six proofs from every form – who must examine all the specimen books, and must have all the new type – who keep proof out for days and weeks, and who are generally so fussy, meddlesome and exacting that they damage all plans and break up all system. When an office finds itself imprudently committed to satisfy such a customer, it should keep its obligation, and satisfy him at any cost or at any trouble. And it should be done cheerfully as well as courteously, at probably a still greater expenditure of patience. But the customer should be notified of the cost of the labor he has imposed. Nor should the lesson be forgotten. No subsequent order should be accepted from the same person without a distinct acknowledgment of his entire responsibility for the expense of all alterations, extra proofs or extra work.

You will sometimes be asked by vindictive persons to print scurrilous or defamatory circulars. In all other cases where you have to decline work, do it courteously. In this case, take higher ground. Make no apologies or explanations, but refuse flatly. By the common law, the printer is implicated with the author in the publishing of a libel. Apart from the moral obligation every good citizen has, to refrain from fomenting strife in which he is not interested, it is specially foolish policy for him, upon so small an inducement, to render himself liable to a criminal prosecution.

Avoid taking an order from any one who bears the reputation of a trickster or a sharper, or whose business is palpably that of defrauding the public, even where it may be done in a manner not strictly illegal. It is unsafe for a fair trader to have any dealings with a known rogue, even where he protects himself with every possible precaution.

To a customer, never depreciate rivals in business. You may have both reason and provocation, but as a matter of policy, such criticisms are in bad taste. It rarely ever leaves a good impression. You may find it necessary to criticise his work. Avoid it as far as possible. If you have to do it, let it be done with entire absence of any feeling of animosity or prejudice.

About Credit

When work is offered by an entire stranger, without settled or known place of business, prepayment should be requested. This is a delicate duty, but it may be done courteously, and without giving offence. An honest and reasonable customer will readily see the necessity of the rule, and will as readily comply with it. If the necessary precaution is omitted, the office must look for many losses.

Credit is frequently requested. This is an application that no clerk has a right to entertain, even from persons of known responsibility. In all cases such a request should be referred to the proprietor or manager for his decision. It is a matter in which there is much conflicting local usage, and for which no positive rules can be given. There are cases in which credit is beneficial to both parties, but upon most applications it should be declined. The apparent value of printed work, and the disposition to pay for it, is never greater than it is on its first receipt. It will be found judicious to avoid all running accounts, and to secure at least monthly settlements with all customers. Cash should be the rule; credit, the exception.

To persons of an enthusiastic and a speculative temperament, printing promises great advantages in the prosecution of business. Their proclivity to run in debt should not be encouraged by any printer. If the applicant has not the money to hazard in an advertising experiment, it is more than probable that he never will earn it. There are certain kinds of printing for which credit should never be given. All kinds of election work, the publishing of a newspaper or a book, or the establishment of an invention or patent medicine, are as full of hazard as any form of gambling. The party intending to reap the reward should take the sole risk, and should be prepared from the outset to pay the loss.

Probably no class of tradesmen suffer more severely from the failure of adventurers than printers. A thrifty printer, who wishes to maintain his own credit, must be inexorable in refusing credit to all new and unendorsed publishing enterprises. Work should stop when pay stops. Cases will occur where the application of such a rigorous rule will appear both harsh and injudicious. But it is the experience of all old printers, that it is much the wiser course to lose an apparently valuable customer and profitable work, rather than take risk with him. To break friendly business relations on grounds of distrust with an estimable man is always an unpleasant duty, and one that will require some nerve on the part of a young printer, especially if the customer is already somewhat in debt, and refusal to trust him further is probably equivalent to a certain loss of the indebtedness that has been already incurred. This disagreeable task can be materially lightened by advising the customer before the work is accepted, that under no circumstances can there be any credit; that a failure to make weekly payments from any cause whatever will stop the work. A customer who declines to accede to such arrangement is not desirable.

When credit is given, it should be given with a limit as to amount, but fully and heartily in form.

Orders are frequently given for election printing, and for the printed work of societies and of incorporated companies by irresponsible persons, without sufficient authority. Where there is the slightest reason to doubt this authority, and the acceptance of the debt by the person or society to whom the work is ordered to be charged, decline the work until a satisfactory order is produced. Pay no attention to evasive or conditional promises. Accept no equivocation or division of responsibility. If the person ordering will not advance the money, and the person who is expected to pay the bill will not give a positive order, decline the work as positively. Insist on a settlement of the question of responsibility before any work is done. This course is sure to give dissatisfaction – perhaps to make an enemy – but it is the only safe course for a prudent man to follow.

Printers are constantly importuned to furnish printing and advertising without charge to charitable associations. Charity is a matter of personal duty or inclination, for which advisory remarks are unnecessary; but the idea that a printer's work costs little or nothing should be stoutly opposed. Gratuitous printing, or the furnishing of printing at nominal prices, is more of an injury to the trade than to the printer. It is the wiser course to contribute liberally in money to all deserving charities, but to insist on full payment at regular rates for all work done. That which costs nothing is usually estimated as nothing.

About Management

To do work efficiently and economically, the first point is to get control of the work. This control, until first proof is shown, should be absolute and undivided. Whatever agreement may have been made with the customer concerning the type, the method of work, or time of performance, should be carried out to the letter, at any cost. But no agreement should be made allowing the customer the right to personally overlook work in progress. The right of the customer to alter or correct should be exercised only when he sees proof.

Most Job work is wanted in great haste, and most customers have unreasonable expectations concerning the time that will be required for doing it. It is to the mutual interest of both office and customer, to have printed work done quickly. But there are limits to the performance of both men and presses. Hurried work that overrides previous orders, that compels the lifting of forms from press, or the doing of work at night, is always unprofitable. When work is offered by a stranger to be done in so short a time that it will disarrange all existing plans, and will certainly delay work to the disappointment of other customers, refuse it at any price.

Be punctual with all customers. To do this[,] much discretion is needed. The work that one thinks may be done in two hours, often takes three. Some allowance must be made for accidents or detentions. Allow for these, and make promises accordingly. To oblige a customer, it is frequently to the interest of an office to tax its resources severely, to do some work at great sacrifices or even at positive loss. The willingness to oblige a customer is not always accompanied with a corresponding ability. He who good naturedly promises more than he can perform is much more likely to offend by his failure, than by his decided but courteous refusal. In no branch of business is order and method of more importance than in a Job office. If you allow the last customer to be served first, or let his importunity overrule your better judgment, you will throw your office in confusion, and will earn neither reward nor thanks.

Aim to have all work well done. Pay as much attention proportionably to a little card as to a fine book – to an unimportant as to an important customer. Show, not at all by words or professions, (avoid that by all means), but very clearly by performance, that you intend to give a fair equivalent for your price.

Take Receipts for work delivered, as well as for wood cuts and all other property of value. This may sometimes appear to be a very unnecessary formality, but you will find it extremely difficult to prove a delivery without a receipt.

Look closely after your work. It is not enough for you to hand copy over to a foreman, and give up all care over it. You should keep yourself constantly informed about its progress, and be ready to aid it wherever it is lagging.

If you find it judicious to make stereotype plates, or to do engraving on wood for any work, and do them without order from the customer, the risk of profit or loss is yours. If you do not charge for them specifically in the bill, the plates or engravings are yours, and cannot be claimed or removed by the customer. The right of use may be exclusively his, but the right of possession is your own. This is the settled usage of lithographers. It has been found quite effectual in preventing transfers of work.

It is not judicious to take all work that is offered, even at a fair price. When one has to spend much more than the profit to be derived from a work in purchasing sorts for that work, it should be declined. It is clearly impracticable for any printer to hope to excel in all departments. The tendency of the trade now is to the developement of certain branches, which, if not practiced exclusively, are cultivated with great success as specialties. It is much better for the trade at large, as well as for the individual member, that there should be these special departments. Books, Posters, Show Cards, Railroad work, and many other branches are done better and cheaper for the public, and more profitably to the printer, when they are practised as specialties by a few printers, than when they are done in little quantities by all printers. Whoever undertakes to do every variety of work, must be prepared to mortgage all his profits, for years to come. Nor will any amount of personal activity prevent him from being surpassed by those who confine themselves to specialties.

Do not strive to get more work than you can do to advantage. To get more and more work appears to be the great object of many printers. It is a common belief that the amount of profit is always in proportion to the amount of business done. There is no greater delusion. To do work profitably, even at the highest ruling prices, the material, the capital, and the personal supervision of the proprietor must be in even ratio with the business. The personal supervision is probably the most essential. Much of this supervision of an office can be done only by the proprietor in person. It cannot be bought for money. Any attempt to evade this condition will be disastrous. When an office is crowded with more work than can be safely done with its capital of types, presses, and money, or when this work is too much for the control of the manager, it must be doing its work at cost or at a loss. The haste, with its consequent neglect and error and waste, must be more pernicious than the lowest prices. It is possible for a printer of but ordinary ability to prosper on a small business, while an abler man will fail in attempting to do an amount of work beyond his means.

Directions about the practical management of a printing office do not come within the scope of a book that is intended to treat of prices only. It may not be considered as overstepping the limit, to allude to one method of management which has a direct bearing on prices. There is a method of management that seems to be profitable, the end of which is ruinous. To work an office up to its highest capacity, with an insufficient number of workmen who are constantly spurred up to diligence; to neglect distribution of material, until the office is a chaos of pi; to refuse to purchase leads, or reglet or quadrats, or labor-saving material, or new type, so long as it is avoidable; to slight work by haste or neglect; to foist such work on customers against their protest; to disregard their requests for attention to little matters – all these are conducive to an increased performance of work. One may take work at low prices, with such methods, and still make business pay – for one year – perhaps for two or three. But no longer. For by this time the office is used up, and the customers are dispersed.

About Numbers

Take special pains to give full numbers on all work. Be very exacting with all workmen who are neglectful in this matter, for they are tampering with your reputation. Two or three copies short on an order for one thousand copies is no trifle in the damaging effect it is likely to produce. Dishonesty may not be inferred, but the most lenient critic will say you are careless, and a reputation for carelessness is especially bad for a printer. If a customer leaves you because your prices are too high, you may not regret it. You may be sure you are right. If he leaves you for bad workmanship, you may excuse yourself on the ground that the fault was an accident or a misfortune. But if he leaves you for a short count, it is a mortification for which there is no relief. Never allow a ream to be rated as five hundred. Even when you print work by the ream, notify your customer distinctly that to a certain amount the risk of waste is his. Never give a short or a stationer's quire, so called, in making up an order for cheap blank books, without explaining the usage. In all cases let the customer know precisely what he may expect, and see that be gets it.

Commissions

A discount of five to ten per cent. may be allowed to any house in business that guarantees the responsibility of, and acts as broker for, a third party at a distance. Such commission is fairly earned when such broker gives positive orders, attends to the correspondence, oversees work, reads proof, and pays bills. But no person, ignorant of the details of the business, who has to go to the printer to get information as to how the work in hand can be judiciously done, and who consumes more time, and is more troublesome every way in making explanations and requisitions, than would the customer direct – no journeyman printer out of work, nor any other person in any kindred business, who does no more than introduce a customer – has any right to discount or commission. Such persons have done nothing to earn it. It is unjust for the printer to pay it out of his profits; it is unjust to charge the expense indirectly to the customer. Nor is it to the interest of the trade to aid in making a class of middle-men who do it a positive injury.

Stationers' Work

When a stationer of experience and intelligence offers work in proper manner and in large quantities, relieving the printer from the trouble of listening to the tedious explanation of the customer, when he buys the paper, has it ruled, when he attends to many of the petty details that make printing expensive, he is entitled to a reduction on these prices. The discount granted varies with the style as well as the quantity of work. On some work, but five per cent. is allowed; on other kinds, ten per cent. Those who do most work for stationers make special prices therefor. The usage is variable. Many large firms make no exceptions in favor of stationers, but adhere inflexibly to one price for every class of custom.

Reading 28.6
Prices for Press Work
from *The Printers' Guide* by Cornelius S. Van Winkle (1818, p. 213, 221–222).

Even though the prices for presswork were standardized, there were – in addition to the usual variations due to paper and type sizes – several other factors that could alter these prices. There were always *little* extra charges that had to be added to the estimate; for example, "Three cents extra to be paid on forms containing wood engravings."

Three different methods were used to calculate the costs of presswork. Prior to the nineteenth century, the first and only method was to charge all work by the *token* or *hour*. Technically, a token consisted of 250 sheets, which was also equivalent to the number of impressions that two pressmen were *expected* to print in an hour, although in practice this was not always the case. This method of reckoning becomes slightly fuzzy when one realizes that it actually takes four chargeable hours to print 250 backed-up sheets since two pressmen, the puller and the inker, were required to operate the press in order to print the sheet on both sides. The second method was based on the thousand-sheet ream, and the third, by the hour. For the last, tables were drawn up which specified the hourly rate for every conceivable type of work based on the size of the paper and the type.

A quick look at the increases in pressmen's wages throughout the century reveals some interesting statistics. Van Winkle mentions that New York City pressmen on newspapers – the lowest paid pressmen in the trade – made between $8.00 and $10.00 per week in 1818. It is curious to note that the Boston printer Adams (1837, p. 372) says that "No Pressman to work for less than $8 per week – six days of ten hours each to constitute a week." Does this mean that pressmen in Boston in 1837 were sometimes being paid less than those in New York in 1818? I do not know, but it would appear that the weekly rates did not seem to fluctuate much in the intervening nineteen years. However, by 1871, De Vinne, another New York City printer, says that the rate had risen to $20.00 a week, and in the 1890s, Pasko (1894, p. 574) was still quoting the pressmen's rate at $20.00 per week.

In the table below, Van Winkle gives the prices for presswork. If the master printer charged his client $ .56¼ for printing a token of medium paper from Brevier type (8-point), his profit would be, after he paid each of his two pressmen $ .13 an hour, just over 50 percent of the total charge. This seems to be the standard markup in the first quarter of the century.

The following prices included labor and are the prices agreed upon by the master printers of New York City at a meeting held on September 18, 1815.

PRESS WORK.*

Medium paper [18¼ x 22⅞ in.], or less size, on Brevier or larger type, per token,	$0.56¼
On Minion [7-point],	0.62½
On Nonpareil [6-point], and all less,	0.75
Royal paper [19⅝ x 24¼ in.], on Brevier or larger type,	0.68¾
On Minion,	0.75
On Nonpareil, and all less,	0.87½

* These prices are calculated for an edition not exceeding two thousand copies, or eight tokens on a form. For each token exceeding eight on a form, on type larger than Minion, 6¼ cents advance; if on Minion, 12½ cents; on Nonpareil, 18¾ cents; if on type less than Nonpareil, 25 cents.

When a form contains one or more wood engravings, an addition of 6¼ cents per token to be charged.

Rule work must be charged one price and a half.

Pressing sheets, single, one dollar per 1000; double, 75 cents.

The credit on Book Work shall not exceed four months, nor shall more than seven per cent. be deducted from the face of the bill for cash. . . .

Press Work

1. Book work, done on Brevier or larger type, on medium or smaller paper, 33 cents per token; on smaller type, 35 cents. Royal paper, on Brevier or larger type, 35 cents per token; on smaller type, 37½ cents per token. Super-royal paper [19⅞ x 27½ in.], on Brevier or larger type, 36 cents per token; on smaller type, 39 cents per token.

2. A token of paper, if on book work, to consist of no more than ten quires and a half; and if on a daily paper, no more than ten. For covering Tympans, 37½ cents each; Tympan and Drawer to be considered as two.

3. Jobs, folio, quarto, &c. to be paid 33 cents per token.

4. Cards, if 100 or under, 30 cents; for each additional pack, if not more than five, 12½ cents if over five, 10 cents.

5. Broadsides, on Bourgeois [9-point] or larger type, 45 cents; on smaller type, 50 cents per token.

6. Three cents extra to be paid on forms containing wood engravings.

7. No journeyman working at press on a morning daily paper, shall receive a less sum than 10 dollars for his weekly services; nor those on an evening paper, a less sum than 9 dollars. If the quantity of work should exceed eight tokens per day, the whole to be charged, if on a morning paper, at the rate of 45 cents per token; if an evening paper, 40 cents per token. Daily papers not exceeding six tokens per day, if a morning paper, 9 dollars per week, if an evening paper, 8 dollars per week.

8. All works done on parchment to be settled between the employer and employed.

9. Working down a new press to be settled between the employer and employed.

10. If at any time a pressman should be obliged to lift his form, before it is worked off, he shall be allowed 33 cents for the same.

11. A pressman shall receive for teaching an apprentice press work, for the first three months, 5 cents per token, and for the three months following, 3 cents per token.

Reading 28.7
Of the Charge of the Master Printer to His Client
from *Typographia* by Thomas Curson Hansard (1825, pp. 791–797).

The scales of prices generally represented the printer's out-of-pocket expenditures, although Hansard also gives the marked-up price – the one he charged his client. His markup on presswork was also more than double as demonstrated in the Table of Pressman's Charge per Hour on p. 840.

Of all the early manual writers, Hansard was the most open-minded, and perhaps even the most progressive of his age. He was willing to try almost anything that would increase his output and profits. He was also against trade secrets – a quality that immediately endeared him to me – and was very altruistic about sharing many of his practices with other printers, practices that the latter would have been hesitant to reveal with anyone else.

For many years at my press in Italy, I used a schedule of costs for pricing my work that I had devised myself. I described this method in an article titled "The Economics of Printing Limited Editions," which appeared on pp. 134–137 in *Fine Print*, 1987, vol. 13, no. 3. Even though I was unaware of it at the time, my system was very similar to the one Hansard illustrates in the Table of Estimate Profit and Loss on p. 841.

Hansard reminds his readers that the printer, when pricing work, needs to take into consideration the "great expenses of fitting up a printing-office." The increase in the cost of type – its average value – is shown in the Table of Comparative Price of Compositor's Wages on p. 839. It had gone up from 1s. 7½d. a pound for the period 1763–1792 to 3s. 2d. for the period 1816–1822.

The Scales and Rules that Hansard used were agreed upon at a general meeting of master printers that was held at Stationers' Hall on February 8, 1810. The Stationers' Company was the governing body of the printing industry in Great Britain, having received its first charter from Queen Mary [i.e., Mary I (1516–1558)] in 1556. Under these scales, compositors were paid by the piece. In England the unit of measure was 1000 letters, although the actual unit was ens [a typographic measurement equal to one-half the square of the type size], not letters, which were considerably thinner than ens. The *piecework payment* – as this method was called –was 4½d. per 1000 ens in 1785; by 1801, it had risen to 7½d. In America, piecework was based on 1000 ems.

Though the cost of materials had increased 100 percent, wages and other charges only increased 50 percent. In the 1820s, the greater proportion of the cost of presswork was the expense of labor.

Even though the scales of prices were used for estimates, there were always exceptions. Hansard mentions two books – the first, *The History of England* (1806) by David Hume (1711–1776), which was published by Robert Bowyer; and the second, a Bible (1800), which was published by Thomas Macklin. Both were printed by Thomas Bensley. Hansard gives these as examples of extra fine work, for which only three tokens per day could be printed if the quality of the presswork was to be maintained. That is just over one-third of the amount of work that was normally done at a press.

The foregoing statement of the wages paid by the master to the journeymen for their labour, naturally leads to the consideration of the mode usually adopted by the master of making his charge to the bookseller, author, or other employer, in order to repay his outlay of materials, wages, and other expenses, and obtain a profit for his labour and capital employed. Although I may expect to be able to make myself understood, as far as regards any general rule, to the members of the profession, yet to effect this as any certain guide to others, even in the bulk of a whole volume, would totally fail of being effectual; since it is a rare occurrence for any two works to be of precisely the same value in wages. Mr. [Stower] compiled, in 1813, "The Printer's Price Book," [1814] in which, with considerable labour and ingenuity, he has given 326 pages of various dimensions, type, pages, &c. &c. and 86 pages of tables of the prices per sheet. Yet I never found a single instance where some variation in width, length, proportion of various type, number, extras, or something or other varying in combination, did not take place to render an entirely new calculation necessary; and, I will venture to assert, that if any master printer in London was to look over his books, he would not find two works in fifty which were so exactly fellows, that they would, in every respect, be of the same expense to him, and, consequently, charge to his employer.

Hitherto, in all treatises on the practice of our Art, this subject seems to have been studiously avoided: in the education also of printers, and in the conducting the business, it has seemed a mystery into which no one was to be initiated till he actually became a master, and then he was to gain his information as well as he could when he had no one to instruct him. The consequences have been such as might have been easily foreseen. The young adventurer has launched into business for himself without any impression being made upon his mind of the vast expenses for outgoings in the concern; his ideas have been dazzled by the *great profit!* which he hears is charged upon the composition and press-work, but which (as will be shown presently) is but a small portion of the master's expenses; he judges that the way to establish a connexion at first setting out, before, perhaps, he has any family to provide for, is by being satisfied with less profit; he offers to work much under the price that the established masters have charged, obtains employ by low estimates, and soon finds himself possessed of less disposable income, than would be obtained by a respectable journeyman.

Now, I see no necessity for all this mystery; and I do hope, that by plainly laying down what my experience has taught me to believe an equitable mode of charging, founded upon the usage of the respectable members of the trade, and giving also some reasons to substantiate it, to promote a certain degree of stability in those who have yet to begin life, and to convince such of our employers as may condescend to give these pages a consideration, that our profits are not such as will bear any diminution, if they wish ample justice to be done to their work, and that we should retain that rank in society which is the surest pledge for a regard to literary and moral character.

The mode of making the charge of Composition and Reading is, first having fixed, by the Scale and Rules hereinbefore given [Editor's note: Hansard is referring to pp. 786–787 in his manual where he gives the scale for compositors which was established in April 1816.], the proper pay for the composition, to add one fourth of that charge for the reading, and then add to that total one half of its amount to cover the various expenses and yield a profit. The exception to this rule is when the smaller kind of type is used; the Type-founder's charge arising rapidly from four shillings per pound (the price of Brevier) to seven, eight, and fourteen (the prices of Nonpareil, Pearl [5-point], and Diamond [4½-point]), the printer increases his addition to the labour-price in nearly the same proportion, to meet the additional expenditure of materials.

The next article of a Compositor's charge is Corrections; which . . . is the most onerous part of the business to both journeyman, master, and employer. The former, who are paid by the hour, about the same as for per thousand composing, find that it throws them out of the regular quick habit of composing, and deadens the nice sensibility of feel of the tips of the fingers, so essential to the Compositors' business – the master, from the delay it occasions in the process of a work, the destruction of his type and materials by the use of the bodkin, the proof-paper used, Reader's time occupied, and boys to carry proofs out, and fetch them back again. This work is always valued, and I think very inadequately, by doubling, without any charge for reading, the Compositor's charge, and therefore amounts to one shilling per hour, per man, for whatever time the proofs may take: extra for occasional table matter, small type more than may be paid for in the notes, peculiar characters, Greek, Hebrew, &c. is valued by the same rule.

In calculations of Table Work all the brass rule, actually cut up for the work, is charged at prime cost, the cuttings and old brass going for the profit. So of any peculiar sorts cut or cast purposely for a work, if not likely to be again useful as the necessary stock of a printing-office: of course, in a second edition of the same work, this extra expense does not recur. Postage and coach charges are just re-charged what they cost.

Out of these charges, in addition to the actual cost of workmanship, is to be paid the great expense of fitting up a printing-office in the first instance: then the vast expense of type, with its certain and speedy deterioration till condemned to the metal-pot; then furniture, another perishable article; proof paper; fire and light; rent, taxes, and repairs; capital sunk, or paid for in the shape of interest, to give the accustomed trade-credit; all of which amount to so considerable a sum in the aggregate, that I very much doubt, were it possible to analyse the value of material employed and expenses attendant upon each individual work and job, whether any profit whatever, above common interest for the capital employed would accrue upon this branch of his business upon the great majority of works passing through the house of a London printer; but it has been handed down to us from ancient times as the established criterion of our charge for Case-work.

It may have been possible, in the early ages of typography, to have made a nearer approximation towards a fair quota of expense attendant upon each separate work; the type was of a fashion, and the metal of a quality, formed for much longer endurance than what we get in this age; the eye of the Bookseller and Reader were satisfied if they got a clear legible impression of good old English characters, and a fount of letter arrived to a fair old age before any objection was made to its use for repeated editions of the same work; till, in some old established printing offices, the type was of an age "time out of mind" of either master or man. I need not add, how different, in every respect, is the case now; few works are expected to be re-printed in the type which was employed on the previous edition, and a comparison of the prices of type for the same periods as has been given in the Table of comparative price of Compositor's wages [below], by which the master's price was equally regulated, will show that his recompence for that great outgoing of his concern, has by no means kept pace with his outlay, the former showing an advance of about 50 per cent, the following very little short of 100 per cent: –

		Thus, from 1763 to 1792.		Same Founts in 1816–1822.	
		s.	d.	s.	d.
Pica [12-point]		1	0 per lb.	2	6 per lb.
Small Pica [11-point]		1	2	2	8
Long Primer [10-point]		1	6	3	0
Bourgeois		2	0	3	8
Brevier		2	6	4	0
	5)	8	2	5) 15	10
Average		1	7½	3	2

Thus, the amount of wages paid, forming the ground-work of the charges made, seems to be the fairest mode which can be adopted, because any advance in the former would proportionably elevate the latter; but if that was right in former days, to cover the expense of what may be called the raw material, it must be a much worse trade now, when the material has borne an advance of 100 per cent, and wages and charges only 50 – add to which (and it is no slight consideration) that from the increased price of paper, the more expensive type of Long Primer, Bourgeois, and Brevier is called for in a three-fold proportion.

For press-work, a greater proportion is laid upon the sum paid to the workmen for expenses and profit, in order to compensate, not only for his wages, the expense of wear and tear of presses, parchments, blankets, oil, proof-paper, balls, rollers, and the endless variety of utensils called for in mechanical operations, but the INK also. This was formerly calculated by taking the exact sum paid for the working of the first 1,000 into the same calculation as the composition and reading, and then adding (as it was called) the thirds* upon the whole; about 1810, it was, from the vast increase of expenses, judged necessary to abandon this mode, and charge the whole impression as ream-work, by the scale following; viz.

Pressman's Charge per Hour, or Token, or Half Ream perfect, being 4½ d.	*or per Ream 3s. 0d.*	*The Charge to Employer. is per Ream 7s. 0d.*
5	3 4	8 0
5½	3 8	9 0
6	4 0	10 0
6½	4 4	11 0
7	4 8	12 0
7½	5 0	13 0
8	5 4	14 0
8½	5 8	15 0
9	6 0	16 0

Thus increasing the charge to the employer for every ½d. per token paid the journeymen, 1s. per ream; which, as the greater the wages paid, so much more, either in quantity or value, will be the ink used, the time of the press occupied, proof-paper destroyed, &c. appears as rational a mode as could be devised.

For works of a superb description, it is necessary to pay a vast increase upon the above scale; 1s., 1s. 3d., 1s. 6d. per token are frequently paid for working with the finest descriptions of ink, greatest care, interleaving every sheet with common paper, and other niceties; the finest works are done on establishment, per week, and limited to doing only so much per day; thus, those grand works of British typography, Bowyer's England, and Macklin's Bible were limited to about three tokens per day, and three or more hours were expended in making ready a single forme.

In this branch of his business, as well as the former, the master printer is paid much less, by comparison with former times, for his work in proportion to his increased expenses. Blackwell's ink, at the period before alluded to, was 1s. 3d. per lb., now we can use nothing for good book-work under 2s. 6d.

The best presses were made by [James] Arding [& Son, printers' joiners and wooden press makers] for eighteen or twenty pounds each, now we are thought unfit for good work with presses that cost less than from seventy to eighty guineas [Editor's note: A guinea equals one pound plus one shilling]. Then pressmen could be trusted to do their work properly with only the general superintendence of the master or overseer; now we must keep a foreman at high wages to attend to the press-room only. Then we had long numbers and easy work to keep a press going for days together; now all our long numbers go to cormorant [omnivorous] machines.

The following calculation of a printer's profits [in the Table below] was given by an eminent printer [J. L. C. (i.e., John Lewis Cox)] to the Select Committee of the House of Commons on Printing and Stationary . . . [on] 30th July, 1822 . . .

---

* I have heard that some have agreed to revert to the old mode; but I am convinced, from the most minute calculation, by weighing the ink used for reams of various works, the value of the rental on the cost, with wear and repairs of the machine, the expenses of balls or rollers, oil, parchments, blankets, set-off paper, wetting and drying, warehouse-work, &c. &c. &c.; that adding "the thirds" to the first 1,000, does not pay expenses, much less yield profit to live by.

"ESTIMATE PROFIT and Loss on Printing 500 Copies of an Octavo Volume.

Total charges for printing 500 copies of an Octavo Volume,
consisting of 26 sheets (or 416 pages) at 39s. per sheet   £ 50 14 0

CALCULATE – Case-work   0 16 0 ⎫
                    Reading   0   4 0 ⎭ 1 0 0
                        Add Profit and Loss   0 10 0
                                                                    1 10 0
                    Press-work, 1 Ream   0   9 0

                                Per Sheet   £ 1 19 0

ANALYSIS –   Paid Compositors   0 16 0 ⎫
               Reading and Overseers   0   4 0 ⎭ 1 0 0
                    Add 50 per cent   0 10 0   to cover cost and wear and tear of
TYPES, and other materials used for the work; rent, taxes, and other incidental expenses, interest
and capital employed, and profit.

Charged for one ream Press-work, 9s.; viz.
    Paid 2 Pressmen, 4 hours each, at 5½ d.   0   3   8
    Warehouse-work*   0   0 11

                                               0   4   7
    Add difference   0   4   5 To cover cost of INK, wear and tear of
presses, rent, taxes, &c. as above.
Charge for Profit and Loss: – At Case   0 10   0
                            Press   0   4   5

                                               0 14   5 per sheet, which, on 26 sheets, amounts to
£ 18 14 10. Of this sum not more than one third can be reckoned as actual profit, which is £ 6 5.
on the 500 volumes (= 3d. each), and gives about 12 per cent on the total charge.

J. L. C."

Reading 28.8
Prices for Presswork
from *The Printers' Price List* by Theodore Low De Vinne (1871, pp. 69–79)

De Vinne discusses the cost of printing on all types of presses. Even though most job work
was done on vertical-platen and cylinder presses, he also includes valuable price information
on handpress work. I have included some of his figures for machine work as a comparison
for handpress work. One of the greatest problems with job work was its diversity of formats.
Each job usually required a unique imposition and makeready.

He mentions that piecework – for the pressman, this was the token – went out of fashion
with the handpress. Most labor by the 1870s was paid an hourly rate per week, which was based

---

* Taking-in and stowing the paper, wetting down the paper; hanging-up after printed off, for drying; taking-down,
smoothing, and pressing; laying on the gathering-boards; gathering, collating, and putting into portions for delivery to
the bookseller or binder, &c.   L. H. [Luke Hansard]

on the estimated time that it took to perform certain tasks. He includes a table of "Weekly Expenses of a Double Medium Cylinder Press" on p. 847 below. Many of these expenses would also have been applicable when figuring out the weekly expenses for a handpress, such as higher prices for hurried or night work. Needless to say, the handpress was the slowest of all the presses in a printing office; however, they were also more efficient than the faster presses for certain types of work, especially short runs and extra fine work. Curiously, it cost about the same per day to operate a handpress as it did a Gordon vertical-platen press, even though the handpress produced fewer sheets per hour. Pressmen usually worked at only one type of press.

At the beginning of the nineteenth century, printers were still working twelve hours a day, six days a week. By the 1870s, the work week consisted of sixty hours – 7:00 a.m. to 6:00 p.m., and both compositors and pressmen seem to have been paid around $20.00 per week regardless of the type of composition they were setting or the kind of press they were operating. By 1900, the work week was reduced to fifty-five hours.

Book Work and Job Work are the two principal branches. Newspaper and Wood-Cut Work are common to both. Color Work and Card Work are more practiced in Job offices.

Book Presswork is done almost exclusively on Adams Presses; Job work and Newspaper work on Cylinders; Wood-cut and Fine Color work on all presses, but with many the Hand Press is preferred; Card work is done on small Card and Machine Presses.

Skill in handling these presses is acquired only by long practice. As a pressman usually works at but one kind of press, each branch of the business may be considered as almost a distinct trade. An excellent Cylinder pressman is usually found incompetent when he supplies the place of an Adams pressman, and both of them are often incapable, or at least inefficient, when they attempt Fine Cut or Color work on a Hand Press.

The Expenses of a Press Room

To do work properly and economically, it is necessary to have many kinds of presses, and, in a large office, different classes of pressmen. The cost of these presses, the expense of running them, and their performances, are very unequal. Before hazarding any observations on the prices of Presswork, it will be proper to state the ordinary expenses of a press room, which will to some extent prepare the reader for the irregularities of prices.

The Size and Value of the Press. An ordinary Card Press, of bed 3 x 5 or 5 x 9 inches, costs from $150 to $250, according to patent. The larger Adams, and the Drum Cylinder Presses that are used in Job work, cost from $3000 to $6000. Double Cylinders and Perfecting Presses cost more. Between these extremes are many intermediate sizes at corresponding prices. Viewed only as an investment of money, and without regarding their expenses while running, the interest on money invested is unequal. It costs more to own and hold the larger press; all work done on it must be at higher price than on the small press.

The Cost of Labor. Piece work went out of fashion with the Hand Press. All the labor of a press room is paid for on time, irrespective of the performance of the workman. All estimates of cost must be based on probable time.

A Card Press, or small Machine Press, is usually managed by a boy, who makes ready his form, furnishes power, feeds, and perfects his work without assistance. A novice is paid rather less than $1 per day; but when really fine work is wanted, an expert must be had, who is paid from $2 to $3 per day, and sometimes more.

Hand, Cylinder, and Adams pressmen are usually paid $20 per week, but the rate is not so absolutely fixed as it is for compositors. Inexpert workmen are often paid $15 to $18, and superior workmen $22 to $25. Some who are specially active, as well as skillful, receive still higher wages.

A large press of any kind requires many servitors. The Feeder, who lays the sheets, receives from $6 to $9 per week, according to ability. For fine Book work or Color work, requiring accurate register, two Feeders or Pointers are needed on the reiteration, who double the expense of feeding.

On some presses, a Fly-boy at $3 or $4 per week is needed. For the finest Wood-cut and Color work on Cylinders, it is necessary to employ a boy to interleave the sheets as they are delivered from the fly, to prevent set-off. Such work requires the undivided care of the pressman. He can run and oversee but one press. The cost of labor alone for a press employed on such work is often more than $8 per day.

The Feeders, Pointers, Fly-boys, and Interleavers, are attached to one press. But in every large job and book office many workmen are employed who are attached to no particular press, but who work for all, in cutting, wetting, packing, and dry-pressing the sheets, in making rollers, in caring for plates, or in general supervision. The general Foreman of the room, or Head Pressman, is paid from $25 to $40 per week, according to his ability and value of service. The Warehouseman, who wets-down and dry-presses the work, is paid from $12 to $15 per week, and the wages of each of his Press Boys are about $4 per week. The Cutter's wages are about the same as the Warehouseman's. The Porter is paid from $9 to $12 per week.

The cost of labor on a large press, which requires so much attendance, increases almost in proportion to its increase of size. But there are many other working expenses besides that of labor.

Steam Power is an item of cost that will vary with the number of presses. In a large press room, where the expense is divided among many presses, it may be less than 40 cents per day for each press; in a small office of but one or two presses, it may be $3 per day, or more. When power is hired, $3 @ [to] $4 per week is the usual rate for one-horse power, and a double medium Cylinder or Adams is usually rated as requiring one-horse power. Sixty cents per day per press would be a low general average.

Room Rent, Light, Fuel and Water are items not often considered. The space occupied by a large press is not great, but the finishing of the presswork by Dry-pressing requires much room. Hydraulic presses, with their appurtenances of drying poles, or steam-heated drying rooms, and laying and folding tables, sometimes require half the space of the entire press room. Where rent and taxes are cheap, this is of little amount; in crowded cities, where rents, gas light, fuel and water taxes are high, these expenses have influence on prices.

Materials Consumed. These are Lubricating Oil, Rubber Cloth, Muslin, Flannel, Pasteboard and Paper for make-ready material, Turpentine, Ley, Benzine, and other cleansers, and small sundries. The quantities used of each will depend upon the nature of the work. Ordinary Newspaper work, and the commonest kind of Job work do not require many rollers nor cleansers. The expense for all materials combined will not exceed, and perhaps not equal, $50 per year, on the largest press. For fine Book and Job work, and Colored work on large presses, for which a new impression surface is wanted with every form, and for which there is frequent washing-up of rollers, the cost of these materials may exceed $100 per year.

Rollers. For plain black News, or common Book work, a gang of four double medium Rollers, made from glue and molasses, will cost about $10, and can be made to last about four weeks, perhaps longer, if carefully handled. The same rollers, employed on fine Wood-cut and Color work, are usually condemned after two weeks' service.* The cost of ordinary Rollers for a large press will range from $60 to $150 per year.

Ink. Of all the varied expenses of the press room, that of Ink is most irregular and most deceptive.

On common Book and Newspaper work, and ordinary Job work, the value of the Black Ink used is so trivial that it is rightly considered as but one of the contingent expenses of presswork – an item too small to appear in a bill, or even to be computed in making a statement of cost. On fine Illustrated work, for which Black Ink at $2 to $5 per pound is required, the value of Ink used is too large to be overlooked. In many varieties of Job work, the value of the Ink is as great, and some-times more than twice as great, as all the labor of presswork. . . . In the present inquiry concerning expenses, it will be sufficient to state that the average consumption of the Black Ink for which no special charge is made, including that which is unavoidably wasted as well as that which is used, is about $7 per week for such Job work as is usually done upon a fully-employed Double Medium Cylinder Press. Smaller presses on the same class of work will use and waste Ink in a similar pro-portion. On Small Card and Machine Presses, the value of the Black Ink used may not reach $1.50 per week. But where there are many changes of color and quality, the value of Ink wasted will be twice this sum.

Repairs. With the most careful workmen, accidents are not only possible, but unavoidable. An annual allowance of 3½ per cent. on the cost of the press should be considered as a low estimate for this expense or loss.

Depreciation. The durability of a press depends upon its construction, and upon the care it receives. No exact time can be assigned as the life of any press. Sooner or later it will be worn out, and every day's use will make it, theoretically at least, less valuable. It is a rule with owners of swift-running machinery to rate its annual depreciation at 10 per cent. For a well-made and carefully handled press, the rate is too high. For common presses, as commonly used, the rate is just. In making a true estimate of profit and loss, this allowance for an annual depreciation at the rate of 10 per cent. should be applied to all machinery.[†]

The Expense of a Press

The foregoing observations will give a notion of the regular expenses of a press room. The expense of running a representative press for one week on a variety of ordinary work, should be the basis upon which an estimate of the cost of presswork should be based. A Double Medium Cylinder is probably the fairest representative press that could be offered, being better adapted for various kinds and sizes of work than any other.

---

*The frequent washing-up required for fine and colored work is destructive to the roller. It is necessary to condemn it as soon as any cracks or abrasions appear on the surface. The Patent Rollers of [L.] Francis & [F.W.] Loutrel are more expensive, but they are more durable, and ultimately much more economical. [Editor's note: These rollers were made of glue, glycerine, and castor oil.]

† The probability that the press will be much reduced in value, even if in fair condition, at the end of ten years, through the competition of superior inventions, is a contingency that must be considered and anticipated. The Washington press superseded the Ramage; the Tufts and Treadwell supplanted for a time the Washington; the Adams virtually abol-ished them all, as book presses. The Drum Cylinder, for large work, is now the deserved favorite in all job offices; but no one dare say that within five years some new press will not be made that will supersede the Drum Cylinder as effectually as the Type-revolving Ten Cylinder or Bullock Press has superseded the old fashioned Double Cylinder.

WEEKLY EXPENSES OF A DOUBLE MEDIUM CYLINDER
Press and connections valued at $3,000.

Pressman, at established wages	$20.00
Feeder, with partial employment of Pointer	9.00
Rollers, of ordinary quality	2.00
Rubber, Blankets, Wasted Paper, and Make-ready Material	1.00
Oil for press and counter-shaft, etc	.50
Ley, Benzine, and Cleansers	.75
Ink, ordinary quality Black, average used and wasted	7.00
Cost of Dry-pressing sheets (about one-fourth the work done)	3.00
Steam Power	3.00
Room Rent, Light, Fuel, and Taxes	3.00
Interest on money invested and Insurance	2.50
Probable Repairs, averaged through the year	2.00
Depreciation by Wear, apart from Repairs	3.00
Sundry Expenses	2.75
Total, ($10 per day)	$60.00

This analysis of expenses will be found applicable to the largest number of offices. With some, Labor will cost less; with others, Power will cost more. It will be found, however, that a great saving in one item is usually off-set by increased cost in another. As an average, the analysis is barely just. In most small offices, where miscellaneous work is done at greater disadvantage than in a large office, there will be an increased expense for Ink, Dry-pressing, and Steam-power. If Labor is injudiciously cheapened, there will be at least a double proportion for Repairs and Depreciation. In a very large office, where a nice organization of Labor can be effected, and where special branches are practised, expenses may be somewhat less.

Expenses will fluctuate with the quality of work done. If an extra boy in required to point or to inlay sheets; if two or three presses have to bear the whole expense of the steam power; if much fine or colored work is done, requiring a frequent renewal of rollers and use of expensive Inks, and waste of make-ready material; if pressmen are employed at $25 or $30 per week, the expenses will reach $13 per day. Again, if a pressman runs two presses; if work is not pointed, interleaved, or dry-pressed; if cheaper ink is used; if the expense of steam-power is divided among a dozen or more presses – the running expenses may be but $7 per day. But many of these expenses are unalterable by any economy in management, being the same whether much or little work is done.

It is a common mistake with novices to consider only or chiefly the item of Labor in their estimate of the daily expense of a press. Other expenses are considered as too trivial for account. By this table, these are the per-centages of expense:

Labor	.48
Rollers, Ink, Cleansers, etc.	.19
Repairs, Depreciation, Insurance	.15
Dry-pressing	.06
Steam-power	.05
Rent and other sundries	.07

Thirty dollars per week is not the highest cost of Labor; but, even at this rate, the general expenses of this press are as much as the special expense of Labor.

If Labor were reduced one-half, or to $15 per week, the general expenses could not be reduced in proportion. Some items would be increased. At $15 per week for Labor, the general expenses would be more then double the cost of Labor.

By the methods used in making up the previous statement, it appears that these are the expenses of Presses of various sizes:

Small Card Press. If run by a boy, on common work and on long editions, the expense may be rated at $3 per day. If run by an expert, on good or fine work, the expense will be from $4 to $5 per day. The average expense should be assumed at $4 per day. . . .

Hand Press. The daily expense of a super-royal Hand Press, with a self-inker, on cheap work, with boy workman, should be rated at $4 per day. With roller-boy, $5 per day. For fine work, with skilled pressman, the expense will very from $6 to $8. The general average should be $6 per day. . . .

The Performance of Presses

The Performance of a Press depends upon its construction, its size, its power, its management, the quality of paper and ink used, and the care given to the work.

The Hand Press is the slowest of all presses. Platen Machine Presses are much quicker. Cylinder Presses are the fastest.

A small press is always quicker than a large one of same kind. With increasing size and cost there is invariably a decreasing performance.

Dry paper on Cylinders may be handled and printed with rapidity. Wet, thin, and large sheets are handled and fed to disadvantage.

Stiff Black Ink and Colored Inks can be used only at slower speed than is usual with ordinary Black. The frequent washing-up required to maintain purity of color is always a serious hindrance.

Making-ready is the great hindrance. A form may take a half-hour, an hour, five hours, a day, two or three days. There is no rule by which a proper allowance of time can be computed. It is at the option of the employer. In all cases, the allotment of time is but a choice of evils. A small form can be made-ready roughly on rubber-cloth in half an hour or less; but the value of time saved is lost, on a long edition, by increased wear of type. If the same form is neatly made-ready on hard card-board, it may take from three to five hours. The quality of workmanship is improved, and wear of type is saved, but much time is lost. In allowing time for making-ready a form, the first question to be decided is, the quality of the work; the next, whether it is judicious to sacrifice time or type.

The Edition, or number of copies printed will greatly influence the product of the press. If a form can be made ready in one hour, and then be printed at the average rate of 800 per hour, the day's performance will be 7,200 impressions; but if five such forms are made-ready, requiring five hours, the day's performance would be rated at 4000. But it will seldom reach 4000. On a short edition, it is rarely practicable to get the speed of the long edition. Little stoppages have to be made for the adjustment of some defect, and these stoppages seriously reduce the performance. . . .

One of the greatest hindrances is the dissimilar nature of the forms, and the irregular manner in which they have to be printed. A book form may be followed by a large poster, and this may be followed by a ruled blank-book heading, and this, perhaps, by a sheet of checks in a different color of ink, and this by a card in many colors. To do this work properly, for each form there must be a change of ink, a special washing-up of rollers, and perhaps a change of backing on the cylinder, in addition to all the usual detail of making-ready. The time spent in changing color and impression surface is often twice as great as that spent in the actual presswork of the form. In a small office, in which two or three presses have to do all the work, the time lost in getting a press ready is much greater than in a large office, where special presses are appropriated for different classes of work. But no office, however large or well organized, is exempt. In all, it is a great hindrance, which must be allowed for in an estimate of performance.

Average Daily Performance of Presses

On editions of irregular numbers, with a small allowance of time for making-ready.

The estimates of the following table are for miscellaneous work, done in the usual manner, with little making-ready, and under the favorable conditions of a busy season. It is supposed that the presses are at work full ten hours; that feeders and pressmen are expert and diligent; that paper, rollers, steam power, ink, etc., are in perfect order, and that there are no detentions or accidents.

These estimates are applicable only to a press when in full employment.

Make Ready Time. Hours.	Style of Press.	Number of Forms.		Time of Press-work. Hours.	Rate per Hour when at Work.	Daily Perform-ance. Impress.
	CARD PRESS.					
1	One Form of	7500	impressions	9	833	7500
4	Four Forms of	1000		6	666	4000
6	Eight Forms of	250		4	500	2000
	SMALL MACHINE PRESS.					
1	One Form of	6000	impressions	9	666	6000
5	Five Forms of	500		5	500	2500
8	Eight Forms of	100		2	400	800
	HAND PRESS.					
1	One Form of	1500	impressions	9	156	1500
4	Four Forms of	250		6	166	1000
	MEDIUM CYLINDER.					
1	One Form of	7500	impressions	9	833	7500
5	Five Forms of	750		5	750	3750
7	Eight Forms of	250		3	666	2000
	DOUBLE MEDIUM CYLINDER.					
2	One Form of	5000	impressions	8	666	5000
5	Three Forms of	1000		5	600	3000
7	Six Forms of	250		3	500	1500
	MAMMOTH CYLINDER.					
3	One Form of	4000	impressions	7	570	4000
5	Two Forms of	1250		5	500	2500
7	Four Forms of	250		3	333	1000

The allotment of impressions to forms is not fanciful. The proportions are those of actual practice. In every Job office, small editions are always in excess.

In the previous table, the highest performance of any press, averaged for three days, is 18 tokens[*]; the lowest is 3 tokens. The general daily average is about 12½ tokens per press. Small as this average may appear, it is, as will be further shown, really in excess of the usual performance. There are not many Job offices in which this average can be maintained.

[*] In this and in all other places where the word Token is used, it should be understood as 250 impressions, or any fraction thereof.

These estimates of performance and cost are made on the hypothesis that each press is fully employed. But presses are not always fully employed. There is no Job office that can keep even a card press constantly occupied with work. There are dull seasons, common to all offices, in which many presses are idle for many days. Some presses are idle in busy seasons for want of appropriate and profitable work. They are often idle from delays and accidents that cannot be foreseen or prevented by the best management. There will be losses of time through bad ink and bad rollers, bad paper and bad workmen. There will be absence of workmen and non-arrival of material. There will be damages to plates and types and accidents to presses. An abatement of twelve per cent. for all losses from these causes will be accepted as most reasonable, but this abatement will reduce the average performance of the presses to about Eleven tokens per day.* But there will be no corresponding reduction in the expenses. During protracted dullness of business, workmen may be suspended, and unnecessary extra expense for labor may be avoided. But it is not always judicious to do this even when workmen are but partially employed. Whoever undertakes to do work, must have the men to do it.

This daily performance of Eleven tokens should be accepted as the true average product of machine presses throughout the country, when they are employed on miscellaneous Job work.

With these results concerning the expenses of presswork, and the average performance of presses, certain definite conclusions may be reached as to the cost of the work.

Cost of Presswork,

With small allowance of time for making-ready, and for ordinary black ink only. Applicable only to presses when in full daily employment. See [the following Table, which lists De Vinne's prices only for the Gordon Press and the Hand Press].

Number of Impressions.	Cheap Work.	Ord' Work.	Fair Work.
GORDON PRESS.			
Per Day.	$4.00	$5.00	$6.00
100 impressions	.45	.57	.65
250	.50	.63	.75
500	.70	.87	1.05
1000	1.00	1.25	1.50
5000, per 1000	.80	1.00	1.20
HAND PRESS.			
Per Day.	$4.00	$6.00	$8.00
100 impressions	.80	1.20	1.60
250	1.00	1.50	2.00
500	1.80	2.40	3.60
1000	3.00	4.50	6.00
5000, per 1000	2.50	3.75	5.00

* The average daily performance of a large press room of this city [New York], made up from the abstract of an entire year's business, was but Eleven tokens per press. The presses were: 12 Cylinder, 2 Gordon, 2 Card, and 2 Hand Presses. The total yearly performance was 60,611 tokens. The business was active, and was more uniform throughout the year than is usual. The smallest monthly performance was 3382 tokens; the largest, 7109 tokens. The work was strict Job work, of great variety, of all sizes, and at all prices from $1 to $20 per 1000 impressions. The highest performance of any one press in one day of 10 hours was 16,250 impressions. The largest edition was 90,000 impressions, but there were many forms ranging from 25,000 to 50,000 impressions. The greatest number of forms were of 1000 impressions or less. Most of the presses were in steady service every day, but during the dull season were not worked to their full capacity. Few of

When more than one hour is allowed for making-ready on a small press, or more than two for a large press, or when the value of ink consumed is more than ten per cent. of the cost of work, these estimates will be found too low.

These estimates of cost are only for forms appropriate to the size of the press.

The cost of one hundred or of a single token, on cheap work, is rarely ever less than one-tenth the cost of a full day's work; the cost of a single token on a large press, is about one-fifth that of the day's work.

The cost of large quantities should be somewhat less than the rates assigned for 5000 impressions.

When a single specialty in Job work, like that of Cards, or of Newspapers, or Labels, or Posters, is exclusively practised, the cost of work should be less, but will not be, unless labor is well organized.

The Cost of Presswork may be apparently reduced by cheapening labor or by increasing speed. Either plan is of doubtful ultimate economy. If one pressman attempts to run too many presses, on short editions, the presses must do less work than when they are efficiently manned. Work done in haste must be of inferior quality. Type or stereotype plates not fairly made-ready, will be needlessly damaged. If run by unskilled men or by boys, at lower price, the presses will be neglected. There is no large machinery that requires care, cleanliness, and nice adjustment in greater degree than a cylinder press. If presses are pushed up beyond a proper speed, they will be injured. Between neglect and injurious speed, the presses will be soon unfitted for fine work. The extra losses by Repairs and Depreciation will more than off-set all saving made by cheaper labor. To this should be added the actual cash losses produced by bad workmanship, as well as the damages to business reputation that necessarily follow. Five presses properly manned and cared for, and run at a moderate speed, will, in two years, do more and better work, at less cost, than seven presses inefficiently manned, and run at violent or improper speed.

Prices of Presswork

Special Prices, per thousand or per token, for ordinary Presswork, will be found in the following pages [Editor's note: De Vinne includes 311 pages of tables of prices for every type of work.], classified under appropriate headings. The prices given for one hundred or one token are the usual current prices, and as such they have to be inserted. It will be found, however, by comparing them with the tables of Cost of Presswork [in the table on p. 848 above] . . . that they rarely ever exceed cost, and in some cases are less than cost.

PRESSWORK BY THE HOUR

Card Press	$ .50
Gordon Press	.75
Hand Press	.75
Cap Cylinder	1.00
Medium Cylinder	1.25
Double Medium Cylinder	1.50
Double Royal Cylinder	1.75
Mammoth Cylinder	2.00

them stood idle for many days together. Most of the work was done on large presses, and was fairly made-ready and well printed. Slighting of the work would not have raised the average performance to 13 tokens per day. If all the work of the Hand Presses had been excluded, the daily performance of the Steam Presses would not have reached 12 tokens. It appears from a statement in the Printers' Circular, of January, 1870, that the daily average performance of seven small machine presses, during a period of fourteen weeks, was but a fraction over 10 tokens.

These are prices for ordinary work, for the services of ordinary workmen, and for the use of common Black Ink only. Fine work, requiring extra or expensive labor, or use of Colored Inks of any kind, must be at higher rates.

When a contract is made for the use of a press for many days, on common work, lower rates per day may be accepted. Time contracts are unusual. Most work is done by the thousand, or by the token, the printer taking upon himself the loss or gain occasioned by differences in performance from average estimates. The rates per hour should be used chiefly to test the value of the work.

Hurried Work should always command extra price. If a form is lifted from press to give place to one in greater haste, or if a press is kept waiting for a form, all the time lost by detention or by the re-making-ready, should be specifically charged.

Night Work cannot be priced to satisfaction. For the work of a hand press or treadle press at night, one-half more than the price of day work would be ample; for the work of one cylinder press, run by steam, double day rates will prove insufficient. The best plan is, to compute actual cost and add what may seem just. In most cases, the cost will be about double day rates. Night work is unprofitable, and should be avoided.

The Quality of Ink used should control the price of Presswork. A fine Black Ink is of stiffer body than a cheap ink. It is distributed more slowly, and the press upon which it is used has to run at slower speed. As the performance is less, the price of the work should be greater, even if the fine ink and cheap ink cost the same.

All changes of color on the same form should be at extra price. The waste of labor, ink, and benzine, in cleaning up a card press cannot be rated less than 25 cents; the cleaning of rollers and fountain on a small cylinder seldom costs less than $1.00. A single token in any color that requires special washing-up should on large forms be about double price.

Extra price is required for colored work, not only on account of the greater cost of the ink, but for the greater labor it imposes. The difference in value between Blue Ink and Black Ink on 1000 Checks would be covered by 25 cents; the difference in time of performance is seldom covered by $1.00. On cheap colors and light-faced or open forms, an advance of one-third or one-half over the price of black may be a reasonable rate; but when color is used in quantity, double price is often insufficient.

On ordinary presswork, in Black ink, ten per cent. of the cost of work may be allowed as the proper proportion for the value of the ink, for which no specific charge should be made. All excess should be at extra price, and may be charged specifically.

The Size of the Form should, to some degree, determine the price of the Presswork. Every increased size is printed at increasing expense. On common work, in Black Ink, not many graduations of price are needed . . . [An example of which may be seen] in the table of Handbills, on page 217 [in his manual], in which but five sets of prices are made for sheets from 6 x 9 to 24 x 38 inches. On Fine Work, like Cards, fifteen graduations of price are needed between sizes 1½ x 2¾ and 22 x 28 inches. . . . These graduations of price, although arbitrary for a few cases, are imperatively required for most work. The distinctions in price between small and large forms, are carefully observed in England and France.

The Shape of the Paper also determines the price of the Presswork. Most sheets are oblong, in the proportion of two to three, in which shape they are quite manageable, as this is the usual shape of the bed of the press. But when the sheet is square, it compels the use of a large press, and should be done at the price of the larger sheet. When the sheet is long and narrow, in the proportion of one to three, or one to four, as in the case of a theatre bill, it is more difficult to feed and fly, and the press has to be run at slower speed. When the sheet is disproportionately large for the form, or requires a constant shifting of the form, or the alteration of the feed-guides, as is the case with a bank-check, cost is materially enhanced. Double the ordinary price is often insufficient....

The Nature of the Form. An ordinary Book or Newspaper form, in which the types are of one body, or very nearly so, gives but little trouble to the pressman in making-ready. Such a form is properly rated in the cheapest class of presswork. But any form that calls for an irregular apportionment of ink, or for great strength of impression on one portion and great delicacy on another, makes extra labor for the pressman, and should be at extra price. Forms full of brass rule, or with fine wood-cuts, or with mixed large and small type, or of irregular shape, always require extra time in making-ready. Other forms of bold type, or tints, that may require but little time in making-ready, often require a still greater expenditure of time in interleaving, to prevent the set-off of the ink.

Reading 28.9
Prices for Labor in New York City
from *The Printers' Price List* by Theodore Low De Vinne (1871, p. 424)

De Vinne mentions that a few compositors were still being paid by the piece rate, while others were paid a fixed rate per week. When piecework was paid, it was by the 1000 ems, the dollar amount depending on the size of the type; for example, 1000 ems of pica (12-point) type set from reprint copy was paid at a rate of $ .90 per 1000 ems. The fixed rate of $20.00 per week was based on the Scale of April 1869.

BOOK COMPOSITORS

Manager of a large office	$30 @[to]
Foreman of a large office	25 @ 30
small	22 @ 25
Assistant Foreman	22 @ 25
Proof reader, critical, first class	30 @ 35
superior	22 @ 25
ordinary, 1st proof	20
Maker-up (3 cents per 1000) or	20 @ 22
Stone-man	20 @ 22
Distributor (12 cents per 1000) or	15 @ 20
Boys or Apprentices, 1st year	3 @ 4
2d year	4 @ 5
3d year	5 @ 7
4th year	7 @ 10
Copy Holders, according to age and ability	5 @ 10
Messenger Boys	3 @ 4
Porter	9 @ 12
Overrunning	25 cents per 1000 ems
Compositor*...	

Indentured apprentices are almost unknown in New York City. Boys who learn the trade commence as messengers or occasional copy-holders, and are promoted according to their ability.

* [Editor's note: Compositors were paid by the 1000 ems, or a weekly rate of $20.]

In some offices they are paid two-thirds the piece rates given to men; in others, at a fixed rate per week, which is variable.

Girls who undertake to learn the trade are also unequally paid. In some offices they receive nothing for the first two weeks, or, if they are dull, nothing for the first month. All they earn is given to the compositor who instructs them. At the end of the fortnight or month they are paid about 40 cents per 1000 ems. In other offices they are paid $3.00 per week for the first six or eight weeks, and after that at the rate of 40 cents per 1000 ems. When sufficiently expert they are, in some offices, paid the same rate as men. The more common rate is 45 cents per 1000 ems. For leaded reprint, some offices allow but 40 cents per 1000 ems.

BOOK OR JOB PRESSROOM

Manager of a large room	$35	@	
Foreman of a large room	25	@	35
Read Pressman, or Assistant	25	@	30
Cutter of Wood-cut Overlays	15	@	30
Superior Maker-ready	22	@	24
Cylinder Pressman, superior	22	@	25
ordinary	18	@	20
inferior	14	@	16
Adams Pressman, superior	22	@	24
ordinary	20	@	22
inferior	15	@	18
Hand Pressman, ordinary			18
inferior			12
Gordon Pressman, superior	14	@	18
inferior	8	@	10
Feeder, boy, first six months	4	@	5
fair workman	5	@	6
good	7	@	8
Feeder and Pointer	8	@	12
Boy learning the trade,* 1st year			9
2d year	10	@	11
3d year	12	@	14
4th year	15	@	17
Errand Boys, or Helpers	4	@	6
Sheet Boys	3.50	@	5
Paper Cutter and Label Trim'er	15	@	18
Sheet man, supervising pressing	15	@	18
Plate man, caring for stereotype plates	15	@	18
Porter	10	@	13

* This pay of $9 per week is never given to a complete novice. It is supposed that the boy learning has been employed as feeder for at least two years, and as errand boy or sheet boy for at least one year before he is put to feeding.

Girl feeders on Adams presses give their first two weeks of service gratuitously. When considered expert, they are paid $7 per week, which is the uniform price.

Reading 28.10

Prices for Printing Equipment

from *The Printers' Price List* by Theodore Low De Vinne (1871, pp. 438–439)

I think it might be of some interest to modern readers to see a few comparative prices for handpresses in the nineteenth century. Stower (1808, pp. 514–517) has a list of articles used in the printing business along with their prices, including five printing presses: (1) common-size, £ 31 10 0; (2) foolscap, £ 21 00 0; (3) Stanhope made by Robert Walker, £ 73 10 0; (4) Stanhope made by Shield & Co., £ 63 00 0; and (5) Brook's, £ 42 00 0. As can be seen from these figures, cast-iron presses cost more than double their wooden counterparts.

A Washington and a Smith press, both with a 19 x 24-inch platen, were listed by Gazlay (1836, p. 132) at $240. In 1871, De Vinne, in the table on p. 853, lists the same presses at $250. Gazlay lists the same models with a 24 x 38-inch platen at $275; De Vinne, at $335. It would seem that in the thirty-five-year interim, the price of handpresses did not really increase very much. In 1969, I purchased a Hoe Washington for $500 from Joseph Low, later selling it in 1988 for $5,000. This price was, of course, based on its rarity and provenance, not its intrinsic value.

On October 22, 2001, a Stansbury press sold for $9,200 through the online auction Web site eBay. In 1845, when this press was new, it probably cost around $145. More recently, on May 18, 2002, Paul Aken acquired a beautiful Columbian press, ca. 1830s, from the same auction Web site for $9,312.

In the tables below, De Vinne also gives prices for three types of inking apparatus: the patent self-inking machine, illustrated in **Fig. 19.22** on p. 574; the improved inking apparatus, in **Fig. 19.21** on p. 572; and the common distributor, in **Fig. 20.2** on p. 587.

WASHINGTON AND SMITH HAND PRINTING PRESS. . . . R. HOE & CO.

Platen.	Bed.	Price.
14½ x 19½ inch	18 x 24 inch.	$210
19 x 25	22½ x 29½	250
22½ x 28	26 x 32½	275
21 x 30	24½ x 34½	290
22 x 32½	25½ x 37	305
23 x 35	26½ x 39½	320
24 x 37	27½ x 41½	335
25 x 39	28½ x 43½	350
26 x 41½	29½ x 46	365
27 x 43	30½ x 47½	425
34½ x 43½	38½ x 48	500
Extra, if with frame in pieces		20

Above price includes two pairs of Points, one Screw Wrench, one Brayer, One Slice, and extra Frisket. Boxing and Carting, or setting-up in New York, $7.50. . . .

NEW PATENT SELF-INKING MACHINE. . . . R. HOE & CO.

To Work by the Action of the Press.

Foolscap	$100
Medium	110
Super Royal	120
Nos. 1 and 2	130
Nos. 3 and 4	140
Nos. 5 and 6	150
No. 7	160

IMPROVED INKING APPARATUS. . . . R. HOE & CO.

With Vibrating Cylinder, Railway and Carriage, to Work by Hand.

Foolscap	with 1 Ink Roller	$35.00
	with 2 Ink Rollers	37.50
Medium	with 1 Ink Roller	37.50
	with 2 Ink Rollers	40.00
Super Royal	with 1 Ink Roller	40.00
	with 2 Ink Rollers	42.50
Nos. 1 and 2	with 1 Ink Roller	42.50
Nos. 1 and 2	with 2 Ink Rollers	45.00
Nos. 3 and 4	with 1 Ink Roller	45.00
Nos. 3 and 4	with 2 Ink Rollers	47.50
Nos. 5 and 6	with 1 Ink Roller	47.50
Nos. 5 and 6	with 2 Ink Rollers	50.00
No. 7	with 1 Ink Roller	50.00
No. 7	with 2 Ink Rollers	55.00

DISTRIBUTORS

With Stand and Frame, Complete.

Medium	$20.00
Super Royal	22.50
Nos. 1 and 2	25.00
Nos. 3 and 4	27.50
Nos. 5 and 6	30.00
No. 7	35.00

Appendices

Appendix I

Concordance of Citations from *Mechanick Exercises* (1683) by Joseph Moxon

Due to the rarity of Moxon's manual, Asa Peavy, at the San Francisco Public Library, has compiled the following concordance in order to give readers an opportunity to have firsthand access to Moxon's text in a readily available twentieth-century reprint.

Page numbers			Subject
Rummonds[1]	Moxon[2]	Davis & Carter[3]	
10	9–10	15–18	setting up a printing house
29	12	18	lye and rincing troughs
42	7	12	printing-house personnel
46	269–270	252	pressman's trade
47	373	338	definition of devil
51	362	329	horse (pressman)
101	37	45	wooden presses
101	37–70	45–77	Blaeu press and its parts
169	37–70	45–77	assembling a wooden press
199	302	277	tympan paste
199	54–55	63–64	Moxon's tympan
201	301–303	277–278	covering tympans
212	162–196	162–190	type founding
241	358	324–325	game of jeffing
262	212	204	visorium
275	232	223	imposing
401	291	269	underlays
424	293	271	platen bearers
435	288–290	267–268	reiteration
463	303–306	278–279, 281	wetting paper
464	379	343	definition of heap
485	7	12	inkmakers
485	75–77	82–84	inkmakers
485	361	327	inkmakers
493	80	84–85	ink making

[1] *Nineteenth-Century Printing Practices and the Iron Handpress.* New Castle, DE: Oak Knoll Press, 2003.
[2] *Mechanick Exercises.* London: Printed for Joseph Moxon, 1683.
[3] *Mechanick Exercises on the Whole Art of Printing.* Edited by Herbert Davis & Harry Carter. 2nd. ed. London: Oxford University Press, 1962.

Appendix II

Checklist of Descriptions and Illustrations of Iron Handpresses in Printers' Manuals Published between 1808 and 1866

The following checklist provides an at-a-glance guide to descriptions and illustrations of iron handpresses that appeared in printers' manuals published between 1808 and 1866. The first section, under the heading "Descriptions", gives the locations of textual references to specific makes of iron handpresses, as well as a number of descriptions of improved wooden presses. The second section, under the heading "Illustrations," gives the locations of representations of them and/or their parts and mechanisms. Iron handpresses mentioned in passing are not generally noted. Descriptions and illustrations in reprints are not cited unless (1) the text has been modified, (2) the illustrations have changed or been deleted, and (3) the page references are no longer valid.

It should be noted that both James Moran in *Printing Press* (1973) and Stephen O. Saxe in *American Iron Hand Presses* (1991) identify many more iron handpresses in addition to the small number of them that were actually described and illustrated in nineteenth-century printers' manuals.

Descriptions

1808. Stower, Caleb. *The Printer's Grammar.*
　　　Brooke (improved wooden press), pp. 506–511.
　　　Stanhope (first construction), pp.499–507[*].

1818. Van Winkle, Cornelius S. *The Printers' Guide.*
　　　Columbian, pp. 193–196.
　　　Ramage Foolscap (improved wooden press), pp. 201–202.
　　　Ruthven, pp. 196–201.
　　　Wells, p. 202.

1822. Savage, William. *Practical Hints on Decorative Printing.*
　　　Columbian, p. 99.
　　　Ruthven, p. 99.

1824. Johnson, John. *Typographia.*
　　　Albion, vol. II, pp. 553–556.
　　　Church, vol. II, pp. 545–546.
　　　Cogger, vol. II, p. 544.
　　　Columbian, vol. II, pp. 547–552.
　　　Russell, vol. II, p. 546.
　　　Ruthven, vol. II, pp. 544–545.
　　　Sector, vol. II, p. 544.
　　　Stanhope (second construction), vol. II, pp. 536–543.

1825. Hansard, Thomas Curson. *Typographia.*
  Albion (Hansard calls it a *Cope press*), p. 683.
  Barclay, p. 663.
  Brooke (Hansard calls it an *improved manual press*), pp. 647–649.
  Church, pp. 665–668.
  Cogger, pp. 653–655.
  Columbian, pp. 655–657.
  Jedburgh, pp. 663–664.
  Medhurst (improved wooden press), p. 652.
  Ridley (improved wooden press), pp. 652–653.
  Russell (Hansard calls it a *Russel press*), p. 683.
  Ruthven, pp. 650–651.
  Stafford, p. 657.
  Stanhope (first construction), pp. 637–647.

1825. Partington, Charles Frederick. *The Printers' Complete Guide.*
  Stanhope (Rees construction), pp. 262–265.

1828. [Johnson, John, and Thomas F. Adams]. *An Abridgment of Johnson's* Typographia.
  Albion, pp. 298–300.
  Columbian, p. 300.
  Couillard, p. 307.
  Smith, p. 302.
  Stanhope (second construction), pp. 296–298.
  Washington, p. 307.
  Wells, pp. 302–305.

[1833]. *The Printer.*
  Stanhope (first construction), pp. 44–46.

1834. Sherman, Arthur N. *The Printer's Manual.*
  Rust (Washington), pp. 49–50, 83–84.
  Smith, pp. 49–50.

1836. Gazlay, Theodore. *The Practical Printers' Assistant.*
  Rust (Washington), p. 104.
  Smith, pp. 103–104.

1837. Adams, Thomas F. *Typographia.*
  American, p. 331.
  Columbian, pp. [322]–325.
  Philadelphia, pp. 328–331.
  Ramage Foolscap (improved wooden press), pp. 327–328.
  Ruthven, pp. 325–327.
  Smith, p. 332.
  Washington, pp. 332, 335.
  Wells, pp. 335–337.

1838. Timperley, Charles Henry. *The Printers' Manual.*
   Albion (Timperley calls it a *Cope press*), p. 92.
   Britannia, p. 93.
   Church, p. 92.
   Cogger, p. 91.
   Columbian, pp. 91–92.
   Imperial, p. 93.
   Jedburgh, p. 93.
   Russell, p. 91.
   Ruthven, pp. 91, 93.
   Sector, p. 91.
   Stafford, p. 94.
   Stanhope (second construction), pp. 90–91.

1841. Hansard, Thomas Curson, Jr. *Treatises on Printing and Type-Founding.*
   Stanhope (first construction), pp. 100–104.

1841. Houghton, Thomas Shaw. *The Printers' Practical Every-Day-Book.*
   Columbian, pp. 80–82.
   Imperial, pp. 83–84.

1841. Savage, William. *A Dictionary of the Art of Printing.*
   Albion (Savage calls it a *Cope press*), p. 183.
   Cogger, p. 173.
   Columbian (Savage calls it *Clymer's press*), pp. 171–173.
   Imperial (Savage calls it a *Sherwin and Cope press*), pp. 756–757.
   Medhurst (improved wooden press), p. 481.
   Ruthven, p. 719.
   Stanhope (Rees construction), pp. 779–783.

1844. Adams, Thomas F. *Typographia.*
   American, p. 268.
   Columbian, p. [267]
   Philadelphia, p. 272.
   Ramage Foolscap (improved wooden press), p. 272.
   Smith, p. 272.
   Washington, p. 268.
   Wells, p. 270.

1846. Grattan, Edward. *The Printer's Companion.*
   Smith, pp. 77–78.

1855. Abbott, Jacob. *The Harper Establishment.*
   Washington, pp. 115–118.

1855. *The History of Printing.*
   Albion, pp. 89–92.
   Columbian, pp. 92–96.

Imperial, pp. 91–92.
Stanhope (first construction), pp. 87–89.

1856. Adams, Thomas F. *Typographia.*
Columbian, p. [267]
Smith, p. 268.
Washington, p. 268.

[1862]. *The History of Printing.*
Albion, pp. 80–83.
Columbian, pp. 82–86.
Imperial, p. 81.
Stanhope (first construction), pp. 77–80.

1866. MacKellar, Thomas. *The American Printer.*
Columbian, pp. 211–212.
Ramage Foolscap (improved wooden press), p. 211.
Stanhope, p. 211.
Washington, pp. 212, 222.

Illustrations

1808. Stower, Caleb. *The Printer's Grammar.*
Brooke (improved wooden press), facing p. 506; parts, pp. 508–511.
Stanhope (first construction), frontispiece; parts, pp. 500–506 *.

1822. Savage, William. *Practical Hints on Decorative Printing.*
Columbian, second and third plates following p. 98.
Ruthven, first plate following p. 98.

1824. Johnson, John. *Typographia.*
Albion, vol. II, p. 554; parts, pp. 555–557.
Columbian, vol. II, p. 550.
Stanhope (second construction), vol. II, p. 537; parts, pp. 538–543.

1825. Hansard, Thomas Curson. *Typographia.*
Brooke (Hansard calls it an *improved manual press*), parts, pp. 648–649.
Cogger, facing p. 655.
Columbian, p. 655.
Ruthven, p. 651.
Stafford, facing p. 696.
Stanhope (first construction), facing p. 637; parts, pp. 639–645.

1825. Partington, Charles Frederick. *The Printers' Complete Guide.*
Stanhope (Rees construction) elevations and plans, pp. 262–264.

1828. [Johnson, John, and Thomas F. Adams]. *An Abridgment of Johnson's* Typographia.
Albion, p. 299.
Columbian, frontispiece.
Couillard, p. 308.

Smith, p. 301.
Stanhope (second construction), p. 297.
Washington, p. 306.
Wells, p. 303.

[1833]. *The Printer.*
Stanhope (first construction), p. 45.

1834. Sherman, Arthur N. *The Printer's Manual.*
Rust (Washington), p. [82].
Smith, frontispiece.

1836. Gazlay, Theodore. *The Practical Printers' Assistant.*
Rust (Washington), frontispiece, p. 105.
Smith, p. 103.

1836. Van Winkle, Cornelius S. *The Printer's Guide.*
Eagle, p. [242].
Smith, p. [241].
Washington, p. [240].

1837. Adams, Thomas F. *Typographia.*
Columbian, p. [322].
Philadelphia, inserted plate between pp. [329]–[330].
Ramage Foolscap (improved wooden press, mechanism), p. 327.
Ruthven, inserted plate between pp. [323]–[324].
Smith (mechanism), p. 332.
Washington, inserted plate between pp. [333]–[334].
Wells (mechanism), p. 335.

1838. Timperley, Charles Henry. *The Printers' Manual.*
Albion (Timperley calls it a *Cope press*), p. 92
Columbian, p. 91.
Imperial, p. 93.
Stanhope (second construction), p. 90.

1841. Hansard, Thomas Curson, Jr. *Treatises on Printing and Type-Founding.*
Stanhope (first construction), tipped-in plate at the back; mechanism, p. 102.

1841. Houghton, Thomas Shaw. *The Printers' Practical Every-Day-Book.*
Columbian, p. 80.
Imperial, p. 83.

1841. Savage, William. *A Dictionary of the Art of Printing.*
Columbian (Savage calls it *Clymer's press*), p. 172.
Imperial (Savage calls it a *Sherwin and Cope press*), p. 756; mechanism, p. 757.
Medhurst (improved wooden press, mechanism), p. 481.
Stanhope (Rees construction) elevations and plans, p. 780.

1844. Adams, Thomas F. *Typographia.*
American (mechanism), p. 268.

Columbian, p. [267].
Ramage Foolscap (improved wooden press, mechanism), p. 272.
Washington, p. [269].
Wells (mechanism), p. 270.

1846. Grattan, Edward. *The Printer's Companion.*
Smith, frontispiece.
Washington, frontispiece, p. iv.

1846. Trumbull, George. *Pocket Typographia.*
Washington, frontispiece.

1855. Abbott, Jacob. *The Harper Establishment.*
Washington, p. 116.

1855. *The History of Printing.*
Albion, p. 90.
Columbian, p. 93.
Imperial, p. 91; mechanism, p. 92.
Stanhope (first construction), p. 88.

1856. Adams, Thomas F. *Typographia.*
Columbian, p. [267].
Washington, p. 268.

1857. Johnson, L., & Co. *The Printer's General Hand-Book of Needful Information.*
Foster, p. [9].
Hoe's Hand-Lever, p. 11.
Ramage (Philadelphia), p. [9].
Ramage Foolscap (improved wooden press), p. [9].

[1862]. *The History of Printing.*
Albion, p. 81.
Columbian, p. 84.
Imperial, p. 82; mechanism, p. 83.
Stanhope (first construction), p. 78.

1866. MacKellar, Thomas. *The American Printer.*
Bronstrup (Ramage, Philadelphia), p. 311.
Columbian, p. 211.
Washington, p. 212.

Appendix III

Chronological Index of Pre-Twentieth-Century Printers' Manuals

The following short-title index will provide readers with a publishing chronology of printers' manuals from Moxon (1683) through De Vinne (1900–1904). When available, information concerning the probable dates of the four undated entries at the head of the list will be found in the "Bibliographical notes" in the Bibliography of Pre-Twentieth-Century Printers' Manuals beginning on p. 880. Bibliographical ghosts are not included here, although they are listed in the bibliography. Inferred publication dates, authors, and editions are between brackets.

n.d.   *The Art of Printing*, A17.
n.d.   Collingridge. *Collingridge's Pocket Printing Guide*, C2.
n.d.   Crisp. *The General Printers' Book of Practical Recipes*. C18.
n.d.   Read. *Instructions in the Art of Making-Ready Woodcuts*. R5.

1683   Moxon. *Mechanick Exercises*, 2.
1688   Holme. *The Academy of Armory*, 1.
1713   Watson. *The History of the Art of Printing*, 14.
1732   Palmer. *The General History of Printing*, 9.
1733   Palmer. *A General History of Printing*. 2nd ed., 10.
[1755?] Smith. *The Printer's Grammar* (Scott imprint), 13.
1755   Smith. *The Printer's Grammar* (Owen imprint), 12.
1770   [Luckombe]. *A Concise History of the Origin and Progress of Printing*, 7.
1771   Luckombe. *The History and Art of Printing*, 8.
1783   Johnson. *An Introduction to Logography*, 4.
1787   *The Printer's Grammar*, 11.
1797   Lemoine. *Typographic Antiquities*, 5.
1804   Magrath. *The Printers' Assistant*, M21.
1804   Rhynd. *Rhynd's Printers' Guide*. 3rd ed., R6.
1805   Magrath. *The Printers' Assistant*, M22.
1805   Stower. *Typographical Marks, Used in Correcting Proofs*, S45.
1806   Stower. *Typographical Marks, Employed in Correcting Proofs*. 2nd ed., S46.
1808   Stower. *The Compositor's and Pressman's Guide to the Art of Printing*, S40.
1808   Stower. *The Printer's Grammar*, S42.
1809   [Baxter]. *The Sister Arts*, B3.
1809   Brightly. *The Method of Founding Stereotype*, B25.
1810   Mason. *The Printers' Assistant*, M25.
1812   Mason. *The Printers' Assistant*. 2nd ed., M26.
1812   Stower. *The Compositor's and Pressman's Guide to the Art of Printing*. 2nd ed., S41.
1813   Lemoine. *Typographic Antiquities*, 6.

1814   Mason. *The Printers' Assistant*. 3rd ed., M27.

1814   Rose and Evans. *The Printer's Job Price-Book*, R8.

1814   Stower. *The Printer's Price-Book*, S44.

[1816?] *The Printers' Manual*, P12.

1816   Mason. *The Printers' Price Book for Job Work in General*, M30.

1817   Mason. *The Printers' Assistant*. 3rd ed., M28.

1817   [Stower]. *The Printer's Manual*, S43.

1818   Van Winkle. *The Printers' Guide*, V1.

1820   Hodgson. *An Essay on the Origin and Process of Stereotype Printing*, H14.

1820   Mason. *The Printers' Price Book for Job Work in General*. 2nd ed., M31.

[1821]   Mason. *The Printers' Assistant*. 4th ed., M29.

1822   Savage. *Practical Hints on Decorative Printing*, S12.

1822   Stower. *Typographical Marks Used in Correcting Proofs*. 3rd ed., S47.

1824   Johnson. *Typographia*, J9.

[1824]   Rose. *The Printer's Job Price Book*, R9.

1825   Hansard. *Typographia*, H2.

1825   Partington. *The Printer's Complete Guide*, P1.

1826   Simms and M'Intyre. *The Text-Book*, S16.

1827   Van Winkle. *The Printer's Guide*. 2nd ed., V2.

1828   [Johnson/Adams]. *An Abridgment of Johnson's* Typographia, J10.

[183–?] Cowie. *Cowie's Printers' Pocket-Book and Manual*, C9.

[183–?] Cowie. *Cowie's Printer's Pocket-Book and Manual*. [4th ed.], C12.

[1831]   Partington. *The Printers' Complete Guide*. 2nd ed., P2.

1832   Mason. *The Printers' Price Book for Job Work in General*. 4th ed., M32.

1832   Savage. *On the Preparation of Printing Ink*, S11.

[1833]   *The Printer*, P6.

1834   Sherman. *The Printer's Manual*, S15.

[ca.1835] Cowie. *Cowie's Job Master Printers' Price Book*, C8.

[1835?] Cowie. *Cowie's Printer's Pocket-Book and Manual*. 2nd ed., C10.

1835   Dickinson. *A Help to Printers and Publishers*, D6.

[1835]   London Union of Compositors. *The London Scale of Prices for Compositors' Work*, L4.

1836   Gazlay. *The Practical Printers' Assistant*, G4.

1836   Hazen. *The Panorama of Professions and Trades*, H9.

1836   Van Winkle. *The Printer's Guide*. 3rd ed., V3.

[1836/7] Cowie. *Cowie's Printer's Pocket-Book and Manual*. [3rd ed.], C11.

1837   Adams. *Typographia*, A2.

1838   *The Guide to Trade*, G15.

1838   Timperley. *The Printers' Manual*, T3.

[1839?] Cowie. *Cowie's Printer's Pocket-Book and Manual*. [5th ed.], C13.

1839   Saunders. *The Author's Printing and Publishing Assistant* (London imprint), S2.

1839   Saunders. *The Author's Printing and Publishing Assistant* (New York imprint), S9.

1839   Saunders. *The Author's Printing and Publishing Assistant*. 2nd ed., S3.

1839   Timperley. *A Dictionary of Printers and Printing*, T1.

[184–?] Cowie. *Cowie's Printers' Pocket-Book and Manual*. 6th ed., C14.

[ca.1840] Ford. *Printing-Office Pamphlets*, F6.

1840   Saunders. *The Author's Printing and Publishing Assistant*. 3rd ed., S4.

1841   Hansard Jr. *Treatises on Printing and Type-Founding*, H4.

1841   Hazen. *Popular Technology*, H10.

1841   Houghton. *The Printers' Practical Every-Day-Book*, H18.

1841   Savage. *A Dictionary of the Art of Printing*, S10.

1842   Dickinson. *Specimens of Book Printing*, D7.

1842   Houghton. *The Printers' Practical Every-Day-Book*. 2nd ed., H19.

1842   Sampson. *Electrotint*, S1.

1842   Saunders. *The Author's Printing and Publishing Assistant*. 4th ed., S5.

1842   Timperley. *Encyclopædia of Literary and Typographical Anecdote*. 2nd ed., T2.

1843   *The Guide to Trade*, G16.

1843   Houghton. *The Printers' Practical Every-Day-Book*. 3rd ed., H20.

[ca.1844] Cowie. *Cowie's Printers' Pocket Book and Manual*. 7th ed., C15.

1844   Adams. *Typographia*. 2nd ed., A3.

1844   Wilson. *A Treatise on Grammatical Punctuation*, W17.

[1845?] Saunders. *The Author's Printing and Publishing Assistant*. 5th ed., S6.

1845   Adams. *Typographia*. 3rd ed., A4.

1846   Grattan. *The Printer's Companion*, G14.

1846   Holtzapffel. *Printing Apparatus for the Use of Amateurs*. 3rd ed., H17.

1846   Trumbull. *Pocket Typographia*, T6.

1847   *The London Scale of Prices for Compositors' Work*, L2.

1848   Graham. *The Compositor's Text-Book*, G13.

1849   Houghton. *The Printers' Practical Every-Day-Book*. 4th ed., H21.

[1849] Howitt. *The Country Printers' Job Price Book*, H29.

[1849] Howitt. *The Country Printers' Job Price Book*. 2nd ed., H30.

[185–?] Saunders. *The Author's Printing and Publishing Assistant*. 6th ed., S7.

1850   Munsell. *The Typographical Miscellany*, M37.

1850   Wilson. *A Treatise on English Punctuation*. 2nd ed., W18.

1851   Adams. *Typographia*. 4th ed. (Johnson imprint), A5.

1851   Adams. *Typographia*. 4th ed. (Peck & Bliss imprint), A6.

1851   Hansard Jr. *The Art of Printing*, H5.

[1852?] Saunders. *The Author's Printing and Publishing Assistant*. 7th ed., S8.

1852   Tobitt. *Combination Type*, T4.

1853   Adams. *Typographia*. 4th ed. (Johnson imprint), A7.

1853   Adams. *Typographia*. 4th ed. (Peck & Bliss imprint) A8.

1853   Fielding. *The Typographical Ready-Reckoner and Memorandum-Book*, F1.

1854   Adams. *Typographia*. 4th ed., A9.

1854   Beniowski. *Improvements in Printing*, B6.

1854   Ford. *The Compositor's Handbook*, F5.

1855   Abbott. *The Harper Establishment*, A1.

1855   *The History of Printing*, H12.

1855   Summers. *The Art of Printing*, S48.

1855   Wilson. *The Compositor's Assistant*, W20.

1856   Adams. *Typographia* (Conner imprint), A10.

1856   Adams. *Typographia* (Hoe imprint), A11.

1856   Beniowski. *Improvements in Printing*, B7.

[1856] Houghton. *The Printers' Practical Every Day Book*, H22.

1856   Judd & Glass. *Counsels to Authors and Hints to Advertisers*, J13.

1856   Wilson. *A Treatise on English Punctuation*. 6th ed., W19.

1857   Adams. *Typographia*, A13.

1857   Houghton. *The Printers' Practical Every Day Book*. Improved edition, H23.

1857   Johnson.. *The Printer's General Hand-book of Needful Information*, J11.

1857   Judd & Glass. *Counsels to Authors*, J14.

[1857] Ruse. *Imposition Simplified*, R11.

1858   Adams. *Typographia*, A14.

[1858] Fielding. *The Typographical Ready-Reckoner and Memorandum-Book*. 2nd ed., F2.

1859   Beadnell. *The First Part of the Guide to Typography*, B4.

1859   Lynch. *The Printer's Manual*, L5.

1859   *A Manual of Punctuation*, M24.

[1859–1861]   Beadnell. *A Guide to Typography*, B5.

[ca.1860]   Ruse and Straker. *Printing and Its Accessories*, R13.

1860   Hall. *The Art of Printing, Historical and Practical*, H1.

1861   Adams. *Typographia*, A15.

1861   Degotardi. *The Art of Printing in Its Various Branches*, D1.

1861   Summers. *The Art of Printing*, S49[1862]   *The History of Printing*, H13.

1863   Morgan. *A Dictionary of Terms Used in Printing*, M33.

1864   Adams. *Typographia*, A16.

1864   Berri. *The Art of Printing*, B8.

[1864] Crisp. *The Printers' Business Guide and General Price List*, C20.

1864   Lynch. *The Printer's Manual*. [2nd ed.], L6.

1864   New England Franklin Club. *Scale of Prices*, N1.

[ca. 1865]   Houghton. *The Printers' Practical Every Day Book*, H24.

1865   Berri. *The Art of Printing*. 2nd ed., B9.

1865   Bidwell. *Treatise on the Imposition of Forms*, B13.

[1865] Collingridge. *Collingridge's Guide to Printing and Publishing*, C3.

1865   *The Printer*, P7.

1866   Bidwell. *Treatise on the Imposition of Forms*, B14.

[1866] Cowie. *Cowie's Printers' Pocket-Book and Manual*, C16.

1866   Lynch. *The Printer's Manual*, L7.

1866   MacKellar. *The American Printer*, M2.

1866   MacKellar. *The American Printer*. [2nd ed.], M3.

1867   MacKellar. *The American Printer*. [3rd ed.], M4.

1868   Crisp. *The Printers' Business Guide and Ready-Reckoned General Price Lists*. [2nd ed.], C21.

1868   MacKellar. *The American Printer*. [4th ed.], M5.

1869   Collingridge. *Comprehensive Guide to Printing and Publishing*, C4.

[1869] Crisp. *The Printers' Business Guide and Ready-Reckoned General Price Lists*. 3rd ed., C22.

1869   De Vinne. *The Printers' Price List*, D4.

[1869] Hansard. *Typographia*, H3.

[1870] Francis. *Printing at Home*, F7.

1870   Harpel. *Harpel's Typograph*, H7.

1870   Kilvan. *The Typographic Calculator*, K4.

[1870] Lawton. *The Printers' Pocket Companion*, L1.

1870   MacKellar. *The American Printer*. [5th ed.], M6.

[1870]   *A Treatise on Punctuation*, T5.

1871   Berri. *The Art of Printing*. 3rd ed., B10.

1871   De Vinne. *The Printers' Price List*. [2nd ed.], D5.

1871   Gannon. *The Amateur Printer*, G1.

1871   Hoe. *Hints to Stereotypers and Electrotypers*, H15.

1871   MacKellar. *The American Printer*. [6th ed.], M7.

1871   Morrill and Dwight. *The Amateurs' Guide for 1871*, M34.

1871   Myers. *A Few Practical Hints to Printers on the Treatment of Rollers*, M38.

1871   Ringwalt. *American Encyclopædia of Printing*, R7.

1871   Southward. *A Dictionary of Typography and Its Accessory Arts*, S21.

1871   Summers. *The Art of Printing*, S50.

1871   Wightman. *The Amateur Printer's Handbook*, W8.

1872   Lynch. *The Printer's Manual*, L7.

1872   MacKellar. *The American Printer*. [7th ed.], M8.

1872   Morrill. *The Amateur's Guide for 1872*, M35.

1872   [Nicholson.] *Instructions for the Successful Manipulation of the New and Improved "Nicholson" Stereotyping Apparatus*, N2.

1872   *The Printer*, P9.

1872   Southward. *Southward's Dictionary of Typography with Its Auxiliary Arts*, S36.

1872   Watt. *A Few Hints on Colour and Printing in Colours*, W3.

[1873]   Carey. *The History of a Book*, C1.

[1873]   Crisp. *The Printers', Lithographers', Engravers', and Bookbinders' Business Guide*. 4th ed., C23.

1873   Cummins. *The Pressmen's Guide*, C30.

[1873]   Francis. *Printing at Home*. 2nd ed., F8.

1873   MacKellar. *The American Printer*. [8th ed.], M9.

1873   Ramaley. *Employing Printers' Price List for Job Printing*, R1.

1873   Watson. *Instructions for Amateur Printers*, W2.

1874   Bangs. *The Country Printer*, B2.

[1874]   Crisp. *The Printers', Lithographers', Engravers', Bookbinders', and Stationers' Business Guide*. 5th ed., C24.

1874   MacKellar. *The American Printer*. [9th ed.], M10.

1874   [Nicholson.] *Instructions for the Successful Manipulation of the New and Improved "Nicholson" Stereotyping Apparatus*. 2nd ed., N3.

[1874]   *The Typographical Hand Book*, T7.

[ca. 1875]   Ruse. *Imposition Simplified*, R 12.

1875   Bidwell. *The Printers' New Hand-Book*. [2nd ed.], B15.

1875   Bidwell. *The Prompt Computer*, B12.

1875   Crisp. *The General Printers' Book of Practical Recipes*, C19.

[1875]   Crisp. *The Printers' Universal Book*, C25.

[1875]   Crisp. *Punctuation Simplified*, C29.

[1875]   Houghton. *The Printers' Practical Every Day Book*, H25.

1875   Hoe. *Hints on Electrotyping and Stereotyping*, H16.

1875   Munday. *The Cost of Paper*, M36.

1875   Southward. *A Dictionary of Typography and Its Accessory Arts*. 2nd ed., S22.

[1875]   *The Typographical Hand Book*. [2nd ed.], T8.

[ca.1876]   *The Typographical Hand Book*. 3rd ed., T9.

[1876]   Crisp. *The Printers', Lithographers', Engravers', Bookbinders' and Stationers' Business Guide.*
              6th ed., C26.

1876   Ellis and Denton. *The Printers' Calculator*, E5.

1876   Ellis and Denton. *The Printers' Calculator.* 2nd ed. E6.

1876   Gould. *The Letter-Press Printer*, G6.

1876   MacKellar. *The American Printer.* [10th ed.], M11.

[1876]   Raynor. *Printing for Amateurs* (Strand imprint), R3.

[1876]   Raynor. *Printing for Amateurs* (Wellington-Street imprint), R4.

1876   Sawyer. *The Autotype Process*, S13.

[1876–1887] *How to Print* (American imprints), H26.

1877   Collingridge. *Comprehensive Guide to Printing and Publishing.* 10th ed., C5.

1877   Gaskill. *The Printing-Machine Manager's Complete Practical Handbook*, G2.

1877   Machris. *The Printer's Book of Designs*, M1.

1877   Powell. *A Short History of History of the Art of Printing in England*, P5.

[1877]   *The Printer*, P8.

1877   Stevens. *The Roller Guide*, S38.

[ca.1878] Francis. *Printing at Home.* 3rd ed., F9.

1878   Gould. *The Compositor's Guide and Pocket Book*, G5.

1878   MacKellar. *The American Printer.* [10th ed.], M12.

1878   MacKellar. *The American Printer.* [11th ed.], M13.

[1879]   Crisp. *Printers' Prices*, C28.

1879   Herbert. *The Art of Printing*, H11.

1879   MacKellar. *The American Printer.* [12th ed.], M14.

[1879]   Wilson. *Typographic Printing Machines and Machine Printing*, W12.

1880   B. *Women Compositors*, B1.

[1880]   Wilson. *Stereotyping and Electrotyping*, W11.

[1881]   Crisp. *Crisp's Business Guide for Printers, Lithographers, Engravers, Bookbinders, Rulers, Stationers, etc.* 7th ed., C27.

[1881]   Gould. *The Letter-Press Printer.* 2nd ed., G7.

1881   Manning. *The Printers' Vade-Mecum and Ready Reference*, M23.

1881   Noble. *The Principles and Practice of Colour Printing*, N5.

1881   Whybrew. *The Progressive Printer*, W6.

1882   MacKellar. *The American Printer.* [13th ed.], M15.

1882   [Southward]. *Authorship and Publication*, S18.

1882   Southward. *Practical Printing*, S26.

1882   Whybrew. *The Progressive Printer.* 2nd ed., W7.

[1882]   Wilson. *Typographic Printing Machines and Machine Printing.* [2nd ed.], W13.

[1883]   De Vinne. *Office Manual*, D2.

1883   Hart. *Amateur Printer*, H8.

1883   MacKellar. *The American Printer.* [14th ed.], M16.

1883   Noble. *Difficulties in Machine Printing*, N4.

1883   [Southward]. *Authorship and Publication.* [2nd ed.], S19.

[1883]   [Wyman]. *List of Technical Terms Relating to Printing Machinery*, W21.

[1884]   Gould. *The Letter-Press Printer.* 3rd ed., G8.

1884   *How to Print* (British imprint), H27.

1884   Ramaley. *Employing Printers' Price List for Job Printing.* 2nd ed., R2.

1884 [Southward]. *Authorship and Publication.* 5th ed., S20.

1884 Southward. *Practical Printing.* 2nd ed., S27.

[1884] Wilson. *Typographic Printing Machines and Machine Printing.* 3rd ed., W14.

[1885?] [Gaskill]. *The Printing-Machine Manager's Complete Practical Handbook,* G3.

1885 Fielding. *The Typographical Ready-Reckoner and Memorandum-Book,* F3.

1885 MacKellar. *The American Printer.* [15th ed.], M17.

[1885] [Wyman]. *List of Technical Terms Relating to Printing Machinery.* 2nd ed., W22.

[1886?] Wilson. *Typographical Printing Machines and Machine Printing.* 4th ed., W15.

[1886] Böck. *Zincography,* B23.

1886 Government of India, Printing Department. *Hand-Book of the Central Printing Office.* 2nd ed., G11.

[1887] Ellis. *Hints & Tables for the Printing Office and Paper Warehouse,* E3.

1887 Jacobi. *The Printers' Handbook of Trade Recipes,* J2.

1887 MacKellar. *The American Printer.* [16th ed.], M18.

1887 Southward. *Practical Printing.* 3rd ed., S28.

1888 Bishop. *Diagrams of Imposition for the Pocket,* B17.

1888 Cowell. *A Walk through Our Works,* C7.

[1888] Gould. *The Letter-Press Printer.* 4th ed., G9.

1888 Jacobi. *The Printers' Vocabulary,* J4.

1888 Wilson and Grey. *A Practical Treatise upon Modern Printing Machinery and Letterpress Printing,* W16.

1889 Bishop. *The Practical Printer,* B19.

1889 MacKellar. *The American Printer.* [17th ed.], M19.

1889 Weatherly. *The Young Job Printer,* W4.

[ca.1890] Ellis. *Hints and Tables for the Printing Office and Paper Warehouse,* E4.

[ca.1890] Oldfield. *A Practical Manual of Typography and Reference Book for Printers,* O2.

[1890?] Southward. *The Principles and Progress of Printing Machinery.* 2nd ed., S34.

1890 Bishop. *Bishop's Specimens of Job Work,* B16.

1890 Jacobi. *Printing,* J5.

1890 O'Brien. *A Manual for Authors, Printers, and Publishers,* O1.

[1890] Southward. *The Principles and Progress of Printing Machinery,* S33.

1890 Southward. *Type-Composing Machines,* S37.

1890 Warren. *How to Print and Publish a Book,* W1.

1890 Wilkinson. *Photo-Engraving, Photo-Litho, and Collotype,* W9.

1891 Bishop. *Bishop's Practical Printer.* 2nd ed., B20.

1891 Jacobi. *On the Making and Issuing of Books,* J1.

1891 Jacobi. *The Printers' Handbook of Trade Recipes.* 2nd ed., J3.

1891 London Society of Composers. *The London Scale of Prices for Compositors' Work,* L3.

1891 The Printing and Allied Trades Association. *The London Scale of Prices for Compositors' Work,* P13.

[1891] Weatherly. *The Young Job Printer.* [2nd ed.], W5.

1892 Earhart. *The Color Printer,* E1.

1892 Harland. *The Printing Arts,* H6.

1892 Jacobi. *Some Notes on Books and Printing,* J8.

1892 Southward. *Artistic Printing,* S17.

1892 Southward. *Practical Printing.* 4th ed. (Fleet Street imprint), S29.

[1892]   Southward. *Practical Printing*. 4th ed. (Ludgate Hill imprint), S30.

1892   Stewart. *The Printer's Art*, S 39.

1893   Bishop. *The Job Printer's List of Prices and Estimate Guide*, B18.

1893   Bishop. *The Printer's Ready Reckoner*, B22.

1893   Brannt. *Varnishes, Lacquers, Printing Inks, and Sealing-Waxes*, B24.

[1893]   Gould. *The Letter-Press Printer*. 5th ed., G10.

1893   Jacobi. *Printing*, J6.

1893   Krumbholz. *The Country Printer*, K5.

1893   MacKellar. *The American Printer*. [18th ed.], M20.

1894   *The Inland Printer Vest Pocket Manual of Printing*, I1.

1894   Kelly. *Presswork*, K1.

1894   [Pasko]. *American Dictionary of Printing and Bookmaking*, P3.

1895   Bishop. *The Practical Printer*. 3rd ed., B21.

1895   Fisher. *The Elements of Letterpress Printing*, F4.

1895   Joyner. *Fine Printing*, J12.

1895   Powell. *The Printer's Primer*, P4.

[1895]   *The Printer's Estimate Guide*, P10.

1895   Williams. *Hints on Imposition*, W10.

1896   Moxon. *Moxon's Mechanick Exercises* (De Vinne reprint), 3.

[1896]   *The Printer's Estimate Guide*. 3rd ed., P11.

1897   Collingridge. *Comprehensive Guide to Printing and Publishing*. 11th ed., C6.

1897   Earhart. *The Harmonizer*, E2.

1897   *How to Print* (British imprint), H28.

1897   Kelly. *Presswork*, K2.

1897   Southward. *Progress in Printing and the Graphic Arts*, S35.

1897   Rowell. *Hints on Estimating*, R10.

1898   Jacobi. *Printing*. 2nd ed., J7.

1898   Kelly. *Presswork*, K3.

1898   Oldfield. *A Practical Manual of Typography and Reference Book for Printers*, O3.

1898–1899   Southward. *Modern Printing*, S23.

1998–1900   Southward. *Modern Printing*, S24.

1899   Government of India, Printing Department. *Hand-Book of the Central Printing Office*.
            3rd ed., G12.

1900   Sheldon. *The Practical Colorist*, S14.

1900   Southward. *Modern Printing*, S25.

[1900]   Southward. *Practical Printing*. 5th ed., S31.

1900   Southward. *Practical Printing*. 5th ed., S32.

1900–1904   De Vinne. *The Practice of Typography*, D3.

Bibliographies

Bibliography of Pre-Twentieth-Century Printers' Manuals

This annotated bibliography of pre-twentieth-century printers' manuals was compiled primarily to assist contemporary handpress printers and printing historians in their study of historical printing practices. In addition, it will direct them to specific technical information that is usually found only in works intended for use by the trade. Even though there are many fine texts in French and German, this bibliography is limited to monographs in English.

My initial goal was to compile *the* definitive bibliography on the subject; however, upon closer examination, I quickly realized the folly of the task that I had set for myself – right up to the last minute, I was still uncovering additional titles. Accepting the inevitability that this bibliography will never be complete, I would be exceedingly grateful to hear from readers wishing to advise me about overlooked printers' manuals, as well as to point out any errors that may have inadvertently, or through my ignorance, crept into the transcriptions of the titles or my comments on the entries.

This list began to take shape slowly in the late 1970s, starting with entries culled from the reference works cited on pp. 877–878, and then moving on to the catalogs of the various institutions listed on pp. 878–880. I would never have been able to complete this bibliography without the assistance of a small army of collaborators who persistently tracked down hard-to-find editions or brought to my attention texts that were previously unknown to me. They also very generously supplied me with voluminous photocopies that enabled me to analyze in depth a number of texts to which I would not otherwise have had direct access, and when applicable, to compare subsequent editions of works at my leisure. My debt to all of these collaborators is individually acknowledged on pp. xxv–xxxvii.

For the purpose of this bibliography, a printer's manual is defined as any text intended to instruct or help printers, whether professional or amateur, in the practice of their craft, as well as works explaining the printing and publishing processes to prospective authors. Thus, in addition to such obvious works as manuals on composition, presswork, machine work, and practical printing, this list also includes works on imposition, proofreading, scales of prices, and trade recipes – all of which are usually found in library catalogs under the Library of Congress subject heading: "Printing, Practical." Printing dictionaries, encyclopedias, and glossaries have also been included in this list, as have a few titles, which in fact are not manuals, but predominantly histories of the art of printing, since they have traditionally been listed with printers' manuals in previous bibliographies.

Articles in periodicals and encyclopedias, another excellent and valuable source of information on practical printing, have not been included in this bibliography unless they were also published separately as monographs. However, full reference citations are noted in the text whenever an article is quoted. An extensive list of pre-twentieth-century trade periodicals and bibliophilic journals may be found in *A Bibliography of Printing* (1880–1886, vol. II, pp. 153–195) by E. C. Bigmore and C. W. H. Wyman, as well as *Books and Printing: A Selected List of Periodicals, 1800–1942* by Carolyn Ulrich and Karl Küp. Woodstock, VT: William E. Rudge; New York: New York Public Library, 1942.

Seventeenth- and eighteenth-century works are arranged alphabetically by century and numbered together consecutively 1 through 14. Nineteenth-century works are also arranged alphabetically; however, the numbering sequence differs. Within each alphabetical subdivision, a new numbering sequence starts, beginning with number 1 with its appropriate letter prefix. A chronological index of pre-twentieth-century printers' manuals will be found in *Appendix III* on p. 865.

Notes on the Bibliographical Descriptions

Unless otherwise noted, I have personally examined the originals or facsimiles of all the titles listed. In some instances, I have arbitrarily assigned a main entry heading to a work; in which case, I have justified my choice in the "Bibliographical note." When that choice varies from the one given by any of the bibliographical sources listed on pp. 877–878, I have noted their choices in the notes and cross-referenced them in the list.

1. *Authors.* The names of authors have been given in their most complete form regardless of how they appear on the title page. Inferred names are between brackets.

2. *Titles.* Titles are uniformly set in italics, and unless otherwise noted, have been transcribed directly from the books themselves or facsimiles thereof. In all cases, the spelling of the original title has been strictly adhered to, although the capitalization and punctuation may have been altered in favor of modern bibliographical continuity. The source for a title transcription not taken directly from the book is always given in the "Bibliographical note" immediately following the title.

3. *Editions.* Unless otherwise noted, all editions are the first. Subsequent editions of a work issued with variant titles are arranged in *edition sequence* rather than in alphabetical order by title. Unrecorded earlier editions of a work are not listed, although they are acknowledged in the "Bibliographical note" of the first recorded edition. Inferred edition statements are between brackets.

4. *Imprints.* All the information found in the imprints has been transcribed even though the sequence of the data, as well as the capitalization and punctuation, may vary to conform to the modern bibliographical format used throughout this bibliography. Inferred imprints are between brackets.

5. *Publication dates.* For title pages without a publication date, an inferred date has been supplied whenever possible. The source of an inferred date is: (1) the copyright date; (2) dated material in the text itself; and (3) a standard printed or online bibliographical reference. When the inferred date of an entry differs from an inferred date used by an institution, the institution's inferred date is between brackets following its name in the list of locations. Because of these variant inferred dates, some of these items have occasionally been listed as separate items in one or more of the standard bibliographical references, when in fact, they are the same item with different inferred dates. These discrepancies have also been noted.

6. *Bibliographical notes.* Whenever available, bibliographical information, including the source of all inferred dates, editions, and imprints will be found in this note, which immediately follows the title.

7. *Bibliographical citations.* Bibliographical citations have been given for most of the entries. A key to the bibliographical citations begins on p. 877, followed by a list of additional references on p. 878.

8. *Locations.* It should be pointed out that the present list of locations is by no means definitive. Locations for copies have been limited to those institutions in Australia, Canada, Japan, the United Kingdom, and the United States that verified their holdings by responding directly to my queries. Some institutions checked the whole bibliography while others noted specific items only. Therefore, it is possible for an institution to have an item even though it is not cited in this bibliography. Among those institutions responding to my queries, a few reported that some items ascribed to them in the NUC were no longer in their collections, having been destroyed or lost. A key to the locations begins on p. 878.

9. *Annotations.* The contents of each work are briefly described in these notes with the emphasis being placed on the amount of text that pertains specifically to handpresses, presswork, and practical printing, as well as any pertinent illustrations. In most cases, the title page transcription will give additional information about the contents of an item. A number of "first" appearances in a printers' manual have been noted. I should also mention that my pointing out discrepancies in existing bibliographies and catalogs is intended to help readers avoid the frustration I experienced in a number of fruitless searches.

 A few of the terms used in the annotations have specific meanings that are germane to the overall scope of the present work:

  press is limited to wooden presses;

  handpress denotes horizontal flatbed presses activated by pulling a bar;

  printing machine refers to any other printing apparatus whether powered manually or by steam, such as cylinder, rotary, and vertical platen job presses;

  presswork is restricted to work done on a wooden press or an iron handpress;

  machine printing designates any work done on a printing machine;

  practical printing encompasses all the procedures and processes necessary to print on wooden presses, iron handpresses, and printing machines;

  pressmen describes those working at a wooden press or an iron handpress;

  machine men describes those working on printing machines.

10. *Twentieth-century editions.* Twentieth-century editions follow the annotated note. They are cited by short title.

11. *Facsimile reprints.* Facsimile reprints follow the annotated note. Unless otherwise noted, they are complete.

Key to the Bibliographical Citations

Bigmore & Wyman: Edward Clements Bigmore and Charles William Henry Wyman, ed. *A Bibliography of Printing.* 3 vols. London: Bernard Quaritch, 1880–1886.

Bliss: Anthony S. Bliss, comp. *Printing: History, Forms, and Use.* A catalogue in three parts of the collection formed by Jackson Burke. Catalogs no. 428, 433, and 436. Los Angeles: Dawson's Book Shop, 1974–1975.

Davis & Carter: Herbert Davis and Harry Carter. "Appendix VII: Later Books on Printing and Their Reliance on Moxon" in *Mechanick Exercises on the Whole Art of Printing* by Joseph Moxon. Edited by Herbert Davis and Harry Carter. 2nd ed. London: Oxford University Press, 1962.

Gaskell: Philip Gaskell, Giles Barber, and Georgina Warrilow. "An Annotated List of Printers' Manuals to 1850." *Journal of the Printing Historical Society* (1968), no. 4, pp. 11–31.

Gaskell: Philip Gaskell, Giles Barber, and Georgina Warrilow. Addenda and corrigenda to "An

Annotated List of Printers' Manuals to 1850." *Journal of the Printing Historical Society* (1971), no. 7, pp. 65–66.

Hitchings: Sinclair H. Hitchings, comp. Catalog supplement to "The Art of Printing: Joseph Moxon and His Successors" by Herbert Davis. *Printing & Graphic Arts* (May 1957), vol. 5, no. 2, pp. 23–33.

Marthens: John F. Marthens. *Typographical Bibliography: A List of Books in the English Language on Printing and Its Accessories.* Pittsburgh: Printed by Bakewell & Marthens, 1875.

Wakeman: Geoffrey Wakeman. *The Literature of Letterpress Printing 1849–1900: A Selection.* Kidlington, Oxford: Plough Press, 1986.

Wroth: Lawrence C. Wroth. "Corpus typographicum: A Review of English and American Printers' Manuals." *The Dolphin* (1935), no. 2, pp. 157–170.

Other Bibliographical Sources Cited

ATF: Columbia University Libraries. *The History of Printing from Its Beginnings to 1930: The Subject Catalogue of the American Type Founders Company Library in the Columbia University Libraries.* With an introduction by Kenneth A. Lohf. 4 vols. Millwood, NY: Kraus International Publications, 1980.

British: The British Library. *The British Library General Catalogue of Printed Books to 1975.* 360 vols. London: Clive Bingley; K. G. Saur; Detroit: distributed by Gale Research, 1979–1987. Plus supplements.

NYPL: The New York Public Library. *Dictionary Catalog of Research Libraries of The New York Public Library, 1911–1971.* 800 vols. [New York]: New York Public Library, Astor, Lenox, and Tilden Foundations; [Boston]: Distributed by G.K. Hall & Co., 1979.

NUC: The Library of Congress. *The National Union Catalog, Pre-1956 Imprints: A Cumulative Author List Representing Library of Congress Printed Cards and Titles Reported by Other American Libraries.* Compiled and edited with the cooperation of the Library of Congress and the National Union Catalog Subcommittee of the Resources Committee of the Resources and Technical Services Division, American Library Association. 685 vols. London: Mansell, 1968–1980. Plus supplements.

St. Bride: Saint Bride Foundation. *Catalogue of the Technical Reference Library of Works on Printing and the Allied Arts.* London: printed for the Governors, 1919.

Wing: Newberry Library. *Dictionary Catalogue of the History of Printing from the John M. Wing Foundation in the Newberry Library.* 6 vols. Boston: G. K. Hall, 1961.

Online Databases

Three online databases – OCLC, RLIN, and ESTC – as well as several online library catalogs were consulted to locate copies of printers' manuals, verify holdings, and enhance bibliographical data.

Key to the Locations of Copies

American Antiquarian Society: American Antiquarian Society, Worcester, MA 01609–1634.

Bancroft: The Bancroft Library, University of California, Berkeley, CA 94720.

Berkeley: University of California Libraries, Berkeley, CA 94720.

Birmingham: Birmingham Public Library, Birmingham, AL 35203.

Bodleian: Bodleian Library, University of Oxford, Oxford, UK OX1 3BG.

Boston Athenæum: Library of the Boston Athenæum, Boston, MA 02108–3777.

Boston Public: Boston Public Library, Boston, MA 02117.

Bridwell: Special Collections, Bridwell Library, Southern Methodist University, Dallas, TX 75275–0476.

British: The British Library, London, UK NW1 2DB.

Brown: Brown University Library, Providence, RI 02912.

Cambridge: Cambridge University Library, Cambridge, UK CB3 9DR.

Chicago: The University of Chicago Library, Chicago, IL 60637–1502.

Cincinnati: Public Library of Cincinnati and Hamilton County, Cincinnati, OH 45202–2071.

Clark: William Andrews Clark Memorial Library, University of California, Los Angeles, CA 90018.

Columbia: Columbia University Libraries, New York, NY 10027.

CSULA: John F. Kennedy Memorial Library, California State University, Los Angeles, CA 90032–8302.

Dartmouth: Dartmouth College Library, Hanover, NH 03755.

Delaware: University of Delaware Library, Newark, DE 19717–5267.

Detroit: Detroit Public Library, Detroit, MI 48202.

Glasgow: Glasgow University Library, Glasgow, Scotland, UK G12 8QE.

Grolier: The Grolier Club Library, New York, NY 10022.

Harvard: Harvard University Libraries, Cambridge, MA 02138.

Huntington: The Huntington Library, San Marino, CA 91108.

Illinois: University Library, University of Illinois at Urbana-Champaign, Urbana, IL 61801.

Iowa: The John Springer Collection on Typography, University of Iowa Libraries, Iowa City, IA 52242.

Kemble: Kemble Collection on Western Printing & Publishing, North Baker Library, California Historical Society, San Francisco, CA 94109.

Kentucky: University of Kentucky Libraries, Lexington, KY 40506.

LC: The Library of Congress, Washington, DC 20540.

Louisiana: Hill Memorial Library, Louisiana State University, Baton Rouge, LA 70803–3300.

Massey: Robertson Davies Library, Massey College, Toronto, Ontario M5S 2E1, Canada.

Michigan: University of Michigan Libraries, Ann Arbor, MI 48109–1205.

Minnesota: Wilson Library, University of Minnesota, Minneapolis, MN 55455.

Newberry: The Newberry Library, Chicago, IL 60610–3380.

North Carolina: Louis Round Wilson Library, University of North Carolina, Chapel Hill, NC 27514.

NYPL: The New York Public Library, New York, NY 10018–2788.

Ohio: Ohio State University Library, Columbus, OH 43210.

Pennsylvania: Van Pelt Library, University of Pennsylvania, Philadelphia, PA 19104.

Philadelphia: The Library Company of Philadelphia, Philadelphia, PA 19107–5698.

Pittsburgh: E. H. Wadewitz Memorial Library, Graphic Arts Technical Foundation, Pittsburgh, PA 15213.

Portland: Multnomah County Library, Portland, OR 97212–3708.

Princeton: Princeton University Libraries, Princeton, NJ 08544.

Providence Athenaeum: Providence Athenaeum, Providence, RI 02903.

Providence Public: Providence Public Library, Providence, RI 02903.

RIT: Melbert B. Cary Jr. Graphic Arts Collection, Rochester Institute of Technology, Rochester, NY 14623.

St. Bride: St. Bride Printing Library, London, UK EC4Y 8EE.

Seattle: Seattle Public Library, Seattle, WA 98104.

SFPL: San Francisco Public Library, San Francisco, CA 94102.
Smithsonian: Smithsonian Institution Libraries, Washington, DC 20560.
Sydney: University of Sydney Library, Sydney, NSW 2006, Australia.
Syracuse: Syracuse University Library, Syracuse, NY 13244–2010.
Tennessee: Tennessee State Library and Archive, Nashville, TN 37219.
Tokyo: Printing Museum, Tokyo, Japan 112-8531.
Toronto: Thomas Fisher Rare Book Library, University of Toronto, Ontario M5S 1A5, Canada.
UCLA: University Research Library, University of California, Los Angeles, CA 90024–1575.
Utah: J. Willard Marriott Library, University of Utah, Salt Lake City, UT 84103.
Vermont: Bailey-Howe Library, University of Vermont, Burlington, VT 05405.
Virginia: Alderman Library, University of Virginia, Charlottesville, VA 22903–2498.
Washington: University of Washington Libraries, Seattle, WA 98195.
Wichita: Ablah Library, The Wichita State University, Wichita, KS 67208–1595.
William & Mary: Earl Gregg Swem Library, College of William & Mary, Williamsburg, VA 23187.
Yale: Yale University Libraries, New Haven, CT 06520.

Printers' Manuals – Seventeenth Century

1. Holme, Randle. *The Academy of Armory; or, A Storehouse of Armory and Blazon. Containing the Several Variety of Created Beings, and How Born in Coats of Arms, Both Foreign and Domestick. With the Instruments Used in All Trades and Sciences, Together with Their Terms of Art. Also the Etymologies, Definitions, and Historical Observations on the Same, Explicated and Explained According to our Modern Language. Very Usefel [sic] for All Gentlemen, Scholars, Divines, and All Such As Desire Any Knowledge in Arts and Sciences.* Chester: Printed for the author, 1688.

   Bibliographical citations: Bigmore & Wyman, vol. I, p. 337; Davis & Carter, 1; Hitchings, II.

   Locations: Bodleian; Brown; Cambridge; Columbia; Delaware; Harvard; Michigan; Minnesota; Ohio; Pennsylvania; Philadelphia; Princeton; St. Bride; Syracuse; Utah; Virginia; Yale.

   Despite its title, this is a technological encyclopedia of arts and crafts as they were practiced in the middle of the seventeenth century. In the sections on printing (Book III, Chapter 13, pp. 113–127), Holme aimed at giving a complete, although abbreviated, description of the art of printing and its processes. He also discusses personnel, type, and the press and its parts, demonstrating an astute knowledge of these subjects. Much of his information is taken from Moxon (1683), *see* item 2 below, including eight pages of terms from his "Dictionary."

   Facsimile reprints:
   A Reprint of a Part of Book III of the Academy of Armory. By Randle Holme of the City of Chester, Gentleman Sewer [an official similar to a steward] *in Extraordinary to His Majesty King Charles II; Concerning the Art of Printing and Typefounding.* Men-

   ston, Yorkshire: Reprinted for private distribution to members of the Printing Historical Society by the Scholar Press, 1972.

   Twentieth-century editions:
   The Academy of Armory; or, A Storehouse of Armory and Blazon. Containing the Several Variety of Created Beings, and How Born in Coats of Arms, both Foreign and Domestick. With the Instruments Used in All Trades and Sciences, Together with Their Terms of Art. Also the Etymologies, Definitions, and Historical Observations on the Same, Explicated and Explained According to Our Modern Language. Very Usefel [sic] for All Gentlemen, Scholars, Divines, and All Such as Desire Any Knowledge in Arts and Sciences. Second volume. Edited by I. H. Jeayes. London: Printed for the Roxburghe Club, 1905.

2. Moxon, Joseph. *Mechanick Exercises; or, The Doctrine of Handy-Works. Applied to the Art of Printing.* London: Printed for Joseph Moxon on the West-side of Fleet-ditch, at the Sign of Atlas, 1683.

   Bibliographical citations: Bigmore & Wyman, vol. II, p. 54; Bliss, 944; Gaskell, E1; Hitchings, I; Marthens [1677–1696], p. 25; Wroth, 1.

   Locations: Bodleian; Boston Athenæum; Boston Public; British; Brown; Cambridge; Clark; Dartmouth; Grolier; Huntington; Philadelphia; Providence Public; RIT; St. Bride; SFPL; Virginia; Yale.

   The first comprehensive printers' manual in any language and still one of the most informative regarding wooden presses and seventeenth-century presswork and printing practices; with a dictionary of words and phrases used in typography, doubling as an index. Also contains sections on punchcutting, typecasting, and composing. With thirty-three numbered plates, including illustrations of both the common and the improved (Blaeu) presses as well as the parts of the latter, and workmen wetting paper, knocking up ink balls, and handling paper, plus three pages of imposition schemes.

Nineteenth-century editions:
See item 3 below.

Twentieth-century editions:
Mechanick Exercises on the Whole Art of Printing (1683–4). Edited by Herbert Davis and Harry Carter. London: Oxford University Press, 1958.

A reprint of the 1683 edition, *see* item 2 above; with full explanatory notes and an annotated list of later books on printing and their reliance on Moxon by the editors. Indexed. Includes additional historical illustrations.

Mechanick Exercises on the Whole Art of Printing (1683–4). Edited by Herbert Davis and Harry Carter. 2nd ed. London: Oxford University Press, 1962.

A reprint of the 1958 edition above; with corrections and additions, plus an addenda.

Mechanick Exercises on the Whole Art of Printing (1683–4). Edited by Herbert Davis and Harry Carter. Third edition revised and expanded by John A. Lane. 3rd ed. Nottingham: Plough Press; New York: Mark Batty, 2004.

Facsimile reprint of the 1962 edition:
Mechanick Exercises on the Whole Art of Printing (1683–4). Edited by Herbert Davis and Harry Carter. 2nd ed. New York: Dover Publications, 1978.

3. Moxon, Joseph. *Moxon's Mechanick Exercises; or, The Doctrine of Handy-Works Applied to the Art of Printing.* A literal reprint in two volumes of the first edition published in the year 1683. With Preface and Notes by Theo. L. De Vinne. New-York: The Typothetæ of the City of New-York, 1896.

Bibliographical citations: Bliss, 947, Hitchings, 7.

Locations: Bancroft; Bodleian; British; Dartmouth; Delaware; Huntington; Kentucky; Massey; Michigan; Minnesota; Newberry; NYPL; Philadelphia; RIT; St. Bride; SFPL; Toronto; Virginia; William & Mary; Yale.

A line-for-line, page-for-page resetting of the 1683 edition, *see* item 2 above. Also contains thirty-two pages of notes on Moxon's text by De Vinne. The edition was limited to 450 copies.

Facsimile reprints:
Mechanick Exercises; or, The Doctrine of Handyworks Applied to the Art of Printing. Bristol: Thoemmes Press; Tokyo: Kinokuniya, 1998. Series statement: Nico Editions, Classic Works on the History of the Book. Book Design and Production. First Collection: Pre-Victorian British Typography and Printers' Manuals.

Printers' Manuals – Eighteenth Century

4. Johnson, Henry. *An Introduction to Logography; or, The Art of Arranging and Composing for Printing with Words Intire, Their Radices and Terminations, Instead of Single Letters.* By His Majesty's Royal Letters Patent. London: Printed logographically; and sold by J. Walter, bookseller, Charing-Cross, and J. Sewell, Cornhill, 1783.

Bibliographical citations: Bigmore & Wyman [1783–1786], vol. I, p. 370; Marthens, p. 21.

Locations: Bodleian; British; Cambridge; Delaware; Iowa; St. Bride.

Johnson was the inventor of logography, a method for composing text using combinations of joined letters called logotypes. His system predates Lord Stanhope's, which was not introduced until the beginning of the nineteenth century, *see* Readings 7.5 and 7.6 on pp. 220 and 222, respectively. Johnson's book gives a detailed description of his system. In Section XII, pp. 42–47, he offers a set of "Objections" and "Answers" intended to address certain problems that could arise when composing with logotypes. From the text, it would appear that the letters in his logotypes were not cast on the same body, but "cemented" together.

La Caille, Jean de. *See* item 14 on p. 884.

5. Lemoine, Henry. *Typographic Antiquities. History, Origin, and Progress, of the Art of Printing, from Its First Invention in Germany to the End of the Seventeenth Century; and from Its Introduction into England, by Caxton, to the Present Time; Including, among a Variety of Curious and Interesting Matter, Its Progress in the Provinces; with Chronological Lists of Eminent Printers in England, Scotland, and Ireland: Together with Anecdotes of Several Eminent and Literary Characters, Who Have Honoured the Art by Their Attention to Its Improvement: Also a Particular and Complete History of the Walpolean Press, Established at Strawberry Hill; with an Accurate List of Every Publication Issued Therefrom, and the Exact Number Printed Thereof. At the Conclusion Is Given a Curious Dissertation on the Origin of the Use of Paper; Also, a Complete History of the Art of Wood-Cutting and Engraving on Copper, from Its First Invention in Italy to Its Latest Improvement in Great Britain; Concluding with the Adjudication of Literary Property; or the Laws and Terms to Which Authors, Designers, and Publishers, Are Separately Subject. With a Catalogue of Remarkable Bibles and Common Prayer-Books, from Infancy of Printing to the Present Time. Extracted from the Best Authorities.* London: Printed and sold by S. Fisher, No. 10, St. John's Lane, Clerkenwell; also sold by Lee and Hurst, No. 32, Paternoster Row, 1797.

Bibliographical citations: Bigmore & Wyman, vol. I, p. 431; Bliss, 231; Marthens, p. 22.

Locations: Bancroft; Bodleian; British; Cambridge; Chicago; Delaware; Iowa; Michigan; NYPL; Princeton; St. Bride; Sydney; Toronto; UCLA; Vermont; Virginia; Yale.

Primarily a history of the art of printing. The title page gives a full description of the contents. Lacks specific information on presses and practical printing.

Nineteenth-century editions:
See item 6 below.

6. Lemoine, Henry. *Typographic Antiquities. Origin and History of the Art of Printing, Foreign and Domestic, Including among a Variety of Curious and Interesting Matter, Chronological Lists of Eminent Printers in England, Scotland, and Ireland; a Curious Dissertation on the Origin and Use of Paper; a Complete History of Engraving on Wood and Copper; and a Catalogue of Remarkable Bibles and Common Prayers; from the Infancy of Printing, to the End of the Eighteenth Century.* Extracted from the Best Authorities by a late bibliopolist. 2nd ed., corrected and enlarged by T. A. of the Inner Temple, Esq. London: Printed for the editor; and may be had of J. Bumpus, against Holborn Bars, 1813.

Bibliographical citations: Bigmore & Wyman, vol. I, p. 432; Bliss, 232.

Locations: Delaware; Harvard; Iowa; NYPL; Princeton; Toronto; UCLA; Vermont; Virginia; Yale.

A revised and corrected reprint of the 1797 edition, *see* item 5 above; with a new title page, an unsigned "Preface" by T. A. (whose identity is unknown), and an expanded "Preface" by Lemoine. This edition lacks the section on "Literary Property." Lemoine died in 1812 before this edition was issued.

7. [Luckombe, Philip]. *A Concise History of the Origin and Progress of Printing; with Practical Instructions to the Trade in General. Compiled from Those Who Have Wrote on This Curious Art.* London: Printed and sold by W. Adlard and J. Browne, in Fleet-Street, 1770.

Bibliographical citations: Bigmore & Wyman, vol. I, p. 447; Bliss, 941; Davis & Carter, 5; Gaskell, E3; Hitchings, IV; Marthens, p. 23; Wroth, 5.

Locations: Bodleian; British; Clark; Delaware; Harvard; Huntington; Kentucky; Minnesota; Newberry; Providence Public; St. Bride; SFPL; Sydney; UCLA; Toronto; Vermont; William & Mary; Yale.

A work in two parts: the first, historical; the second, practical. The latter contains sections on the improved wooden press, eighteenth-century presswork and printing practices – mostly from Moxon (1683), *see* item 2 on p. 880 – and composition – mostly from Smith (1755), *see* item 12 on p. 883 and a glossary of "Technical Terms Used in Printing." Adds very little new information on the subject. With specimens of types and printers' flowers from William Caslon and T. Cottrell. Includes illustrations of an improved (Blaeu) press and its parts based on Moxon's plates 5–9, plus twenty-four pages of imposition schemes.

8. Luckombe, Philip. *The History and Art of Printing. In Two Parts. Part I. Containing: I. A Concise History of the Art from its Invention to the Present Time; with the Several Charters Granted to the Company of Stationers. II. Specimens of Printing Types of All Sizes, and Various Languages, Music Types, Flowers and Ornaments. Part II. Treating of: I. The Necessary Materials Made Use of in a Printing Office of the Different Points of Letter, Their Properties, Size, and Application; with Tables to Shew the Difference There Is between the Several Bodies of Letter, and How One Gets In or Drives Out More Than Another. – Of Points, Quadrats, Spaces, Rules, Braces, Quotations, Flowers, &c. &c. II. Of Printing Presses, Their Construction and Use Particularly Described, with a Drawing of a Press, and of Its Several Parts, Cut in Wood. III. Of Wetting Paper, Knocking Up Balls, Pulling, Printing Different Colours, and Other Necessary Rules and Directions for the Pressman. IV. Of the Compositor's Business, Viz. Dressing of Chaces, Composing, Spacing, Tying Up Pages, Imposing, &c., with a Great Variety of Examples and Useful Tables. V. Of Correctors and Correcting, with Directions to Authors How to Mark Corrections in Their Proof Sheets. VI. Of Casting Off Copy. VII. Alphabet; and Characters of Various Languages and Sciences. VIII. Of the Business Requisite to Be Done in the Warehouse, and the Duty of the Warehouseman. IX. An Explanation of Technical Terms Used in Printing. The Whole Forming a More Intelligible and Complete Introduction to the Art of Printing Than Has Been Hitherto Attempted, and Containing a Great Variety of Instructions and Examples That Are Not to Be Found in Any Other Performance.* London: Printed by W. Adlard and J. Browne, Fleet-Street; for J. Johnson, No. 72, St. Paul's Church-Yard, 1771.

Bibliographical citations: Bigmore & Wyman, vol. I, p. 447; Bliss, 942; Davis & Carter, 6; Gaskell, E3; Hitchings, V.

Locations: Bancroft; Bodleian; Boston Public; British; Cambridge; Columbia; Dartmouth; Delaware; Grolier; Harvard; Kemble; Michigan; Minnesota; Newberry; Philadelphia; Providence Public; RIT; St. Bride; SFPL; Tokyo; Toronto; Utah; Virginia; William & Mary; Yale.

A reprint of the 1770 edition, *see* item 7 above, with the author's name added to a new title page, which gives a full description of the contents.

Facsimile reprints:
Philip Luckombe: The History and Art of Printing, 1771. London: Gregg Press, 1965. Series statement: English Bibliographical Sources, edited by D. F. Foxon, British Museum. Series 3: Printers' Manuals, no. 3.

Luckombe, Philip. *See also* item 11 on p. 883.

9. Palmer, Samuel. *The General History of Printing, from Its First Invention in the City of Mentz, to Its First Progress and Propagation thro' the Most Celebrated Cities in Europe. Particularly, Its Introduction, Rise, and Progress Here in England. The Character of the Most Celebrated Printers, from the First Inventors of*

the Art to the Years 1520 and 1550. With an Account of Their Works and of the Most Considerable Improvements Which They Made to It during That Interval. London: Printed by the author, and sold by his widow at his late printing-house in Bartholomew-close; also by J. Roberts in Warwick-lane; and by most booksellers in town and country, 1732.

Bibliographical citations: Bigmore & Wyman, vol. II, p. 110; Bliss, 270.

Locations: Bodleian; British; Harvard; Huntington; LC; Newberry; RIT; St. Bride; William & Mary; Yale (original title page missing but replaced with 4-leaf prospectus dated 1729).

Bigmore & Wyman describe this item as being "entirely historical and of little value, being very inaccurate even for the time in which it was written." Lacks specific information on presses and practical printing. After Palmer's death in 1732, George Psalmanazar finished the work. A four-leaf prospectus issued in 1729 mentions a forthcoming second volume – which was never published – titled *The Practical Art of Printing in Which the Materials Are Fully Describ'd and All the Manual Operations Explain'd*. This prospectus is sometimes bound in with the book which accounts for the misleading date of 1729 found in some bibliographical records.

10. Palmer, Samuel. *A General History of Printing; from the First Invention of It in the City of Mentz, to Its Propagation and Progress thro' Most of the Kingdoms in Europe: Particularly the Introduction and Success of It Here in England. With the Characters of the Most Celebrated Printers, from the First Inventors of This Art to the Years 1520 and 1550. Also an Account of Their Works, and of the Considerable Improvements Which They Made during That Time.* London: Printed for A. Bettesworth, C. Hitch, and C. Davis in Paternoster-row, 1733.

Bibliographical citations: Bigmore & Wyman, vol. II, p. 111; Marthens, p. 27.

Locations: Bodleian; Boston Public; British; Grolier; Harvard; LC; Newberry; Philadelphia; Providence Public; St. Bride; SFPL; Vermont; Yale.

A reprint of the 1732 edition, *see* item 9 above, with a slightly modified title page.

Facsimile reprints:
A General History of Printing; from the First Invention of It in the City of Mentz, to Its Propagation and Progress thro' Most of the Kingdoms in Europe: Particularly the Introduction and Success of It Here in England. With the Characters of the Most Celebrated Printers, from the First Inventors of This Art to the Years 1520 and 1550. Also an Account of Their Works, and of the Considerable Improvements Which They Made during That Time. New York: Burt Franklin, 1972. Series statement: Burt Franklin Bibliography & Reference Series 447.

A complete facsimile with the following exception: the Burt Franklin imprint has replaced the original imprint on the facsimile title page.

11. *The Printer's Grammar: Containing a Concise History of the Origin of Printing; Also, an Examination of the Superficies, Gradation, and Properties of the Different Sizes of Types Cast by Letter Founders; Various Tables of Calculation; Models of Letter Cases; Schemes for Casting Off Copy, and Imposing; and Many Other Requisites for Attaining a Perfect Knowledge Both in the Theory and Practice of the Art of Printing. With Directions to Authors, Compilers, &c. How to Prepare Copy, and to Correct Their Own Proofs. Chiefly Collected from Smith's Edition. To Which Are Added Directions for Pressmen, &c. The Whole Calculated for the Service of All Who Have Any Concern in the Letter Press.* London: Printed by L. Wayland; and sold by T. Evans, Pater-Noster-Row, 1787.

Bibliographical citations: Bigmore & Wyman, vol. II, p. 222; Bliss, 958; Davis & Carter, 7; Gaskell, E4; Hitchings, VI; Marthens, p. 38.

Locations: Bodleian; British; Cambridge; Clark; Columbia; Delaware; Grolier; Harvard; Huntington; Kemble; Kentucky; LC; Massey; Michigan; Newberry; Philadelphia; Providence Public; RIT; St. Bride; SFPL; Tokyo; Vermont; Virginia; William & Mary (lacking title page); Yale. Vermont lists this item under "Smith."

A modified reprint of Luckombe's 1770 version of Smith and Moxon, *see* item 7 on p. 882. Lacks specific information on presses. The glossary of "Technical Terms Used in Printing" was not reprinted, nor were the illustrations of the improved (Blaeu) press and its parts. With specimens of types from Edmund Fry & Co. Includes thirty-two pages of imposition schemes. Bigmore & Wyman (vol. II, p. 403) refer to this item as a first edition of Stower (1808) which is very unlikely since Stower would have been no more than nine years old at the time. In a footnote, Gaskell in the *Journal of the Printing Historical Society*, no. 7 (1971, p. 66) alludes to a 1797 edition of this item offered in Maggs's Catalogue no. 478, (1926, item 377). There is no record of a 1797 edition of *The Printer's Grammar* in OCLC, ESTC, or RLIN databases, nor have I been able to locate a copy of it elsewhere. The 1797 date is most likely a typographical error.

Psalmanazar, George. *See* item 9 on p. 882.

12. Smith, John. *The Printer's Grammar: Wherein Are Exhibited, Examined, and Explained, the Superficies, Gradation, and Properties of the Different Sorts and Sizes of Metal Types, Cast by Letter Founders: Sundry Alphabets, of Oriental, and Some Other Languages; Together with the Chinese Characters: The Figures of Mathematical, Astronomical, Musical, and Physical Signs; Jointly with Abbreviations, Contractions, and Ligatures: The Construction of Metal Flowers – Various Tables, and Calculations – Models of Different Letter-*

Cases; Schemes for Casting Off Copy, and Imposing; and Many Other Requisites for Attaining a More Perfect Knowledge Both in the Theory and Practice of the Art of Printing. With Directions to Authors, Compilers, &c. How to Prepare Copy, and to Correct Their Own Proofs. The Whole Calculated for the Service of All Who Have Any Concern in the Letter Press. London: Printed for the editor; and sold by W. Owen, near Temple Bar; and by M. Cooper, at the Globe in Pater-noster Row, 1755.

Bibliographical citations: Bigmore & Wyman, vol. II, p. 365; Davis & Carter, 4; Gaskell, E2; Hitchings, III; Marthens, p. 30; Wroth, 4.

Locations: Bancroft; Bodleian; British; Cambridge; Columbia; Harvard; Huntington; Newberry; Providence Public; St. Bride; SFPL; UCLA; William & Mary (lacking title page); Yale.

Predominantly practical instructions for compositors. Contains chapters on type, typography, composing, imposing, and correcting, as well as information on Continental practices. Lacks specific information about presses and practical printing. Includes sixteen pages of imposition schemes. Even though not directly concerned with the pressmen's duties, Smith's text was frequently consulted and continued to exert a major influence on the subjects of typography and composition until the end of the nineteenth century.

Facsimile reprints:
John Smith: The Printer's Grammar, 1755. London: Gregg Press, 1965. Series statement: English Bibliographical Sources, edited by D. F. Foxon, British Museum. Series 3: Printers' Manuals, no. 2.

The Printer's Grammar. Bristol: Thoemmes Press; Tokyo: Kinokuniya, 1998.

Series statement: Nico Editions, Classic Works on the History of the Book. Book Design and Production. First Collection: Pre-Victorian British Typography and Printers' Manuals.

13. Smith, John. *The Printer's Grammar: Wherein Are Exhibited, Examined, and Explained, the Superficies, Gradation, and Properties of the Different Sorts and Sizes of Metal Types, Cast by Letter Founders: Sundry Alphabets, of Oriental, and Some Other Languages; Together wtth [sic] the Chinese Characters: the Figures of Mathematical, Astronomical, Musical, and Physical Signs; Jointly with Abbreviations, Contractions, and Ligatures: The Construction of Metal Flowers – Various Tables and Calculations – Models of Different Letter-Cases; Schemes for Casting Off Copy, and Imposing; and Many Other Requisites for Attaining a More Perfect Knowledge Both in the Theory and Practice of the Art of Printing. With Directions to Authors, Compilers, &c. How to Prepare Copy, and to Correct Their Own Proofs. The Whole Calculated for the Service of All Who Have Any Concern in the Letter Press.* London: Printed for J. Scott, at the Black Swan, in Pater-noster-Row, [1755?].

Bibliographical notes: The inferred publication date is taken from the Glasgow University Library record, call number: Sp Coll BDA1-c1.

Bibliographical citations: Bliss, 957.

Locations: CSULA [1755]; Glasgow; Philadelphia [1760?]; Yale [175-?].

An undated reprint of the 1755 edition, *see* item 12 above, with a new title page and imprint.

Not seen.

Smith, John. *See also* item 11 on p. 883.

14. Watson, James. *The History of the Art of Printing, Containing an Account of It's [sic] Invention and Progress in Europe: With the Names of the Famous Printers, the Places of Their Birth, and the Works Printed by Them. And a Preface by the Publisher to the Printers in Scotland.* Edinburgh: Printed by James Watson. Sold at his shop, opposite to the Lucken-Booths; and at the shops of David Scot in the Parliament-Close, and George Stewart a little above the Cross, 1713.

Bibliographical citations: Bigmore & Wyman, vol. III, p. 67; Bliss, 967; Marthens, p. 35; Wroth, 2.

Locations: Bodleian; Boston Public; British; Cambridge; Huntington; Massey (lacking the folding specimen of ornaments); Newberry; RIT; St. Bride; SFPL; Toronto; Vermont; Virginia; Yale. St. Bride lists this item under "La Caille."

The work is in three parts: a "Preface" by Watson primarily on the development and progress of printing in Scotland; a "Specimen of Types in the Printing-House of James Watson"; and an abridged English translation of *Histoire de l'imprimerie et de la librairie* by Jean de La Caille (Paris, 1689). Lacks specific information on practical printing.

Facsimile reprints:
James Watson: The History of the Art of Printing, 1713. London: Gregg Press, 1965. Series statement: English Bibliographical Sources, edited by D. F. Foxon, British Museum. Series 3: Printers' Manuals, no. 1.

Printers' Manuals – Nineteenth Century

A1. Abbott, Jacob. *The Harper Establishment; or, How the Story Books Are Made.* New York: Harper & Brothers, publishers, 1855.

Bibliographical notes: The publication date is taken from the copyright notice on the verso of the title page. The following series page – which reads: *Harper's Story Books. A Series of Narratives, Dialogues, Biographies, and Tales, for the Instruction and Entertainment of the Young. By Jacob Abbott. Embellished with Numerous and Beautiful Engravings* – precedes the title page.

Bibliographical citations: Bigmore & Wyman, vol. I, p. 1; Marthens, p. [9].

Locations: Chicago; Delaware; Detroit; Illinois; NYPL; Providence Public; RIT; Toronto; Vermont; Yale.

Written for juveniles, this work contains a comprehensive description of a mid-nineteenth-century printing establishment, together with all its departments. Lacks specific information on practical printing. With forty-three wood engravings by Karl Emil Döpler, including illustrations of a Washington press with Hoe's automatic inking apparatus set up next to it, Franklin's press (an eighteenth-century wooden press, generally referred to as an English common press), and an Adams platen power press.

Facsimile reprints:
The Harper Establishment; or, How the Story Books Are Made. Epistle Dedicatory by Jacob Blanck. Waltham, MA: Mark Press; Hamden, CT: Shoe String Press, [1956].

A complete facsimile with the following exceptions on the facsimile title page: the Mark Press and Shoestring Press imprints, respectively, have replaced the original imprint.

The Harper Establishment: How the Story Books Are Made. With a new introduction and notes by Joel Myerson and Chris L. Nesmith. New Castle, DE: Oak Knoll Press, 2001.

A complete facsimile with the following exceptions: the original series and copyright pages were omitted.

A2. Adams, Thomas F. *Typographia: A Brief Sketch of the Origin, Rise, and Progress of the Typographic Art; with Practical Directions for Conducting Every Department in an Office.* Philadelphia: Printed and published by the compiler, N. W. corner of Third and Chestnut Sts., 1837.

Bibliographical citations: Bigmore & Wyman, vol. I, p. 3; Bliss, 881; Gaskell, E18; Hitchings, 3; Marthens, p. [9]; Wroth, 10.

Locations: Boston Public; Columbia; Grolier; Harvard; Huntington; Iowa; Kemble; Minnesota; Newberry; NYPL; Philadelphia; RIT; St. Bride; SFPL; Tokyo; Vermont; William & Mary; Yale.

The standard American printers' manual until superseded by MacKellar's, *see* item M2 on p. 912, in 1866. An excellent source of information on nineteenth-century printing practices borrowed mostly from Johnson (1824), *see* item J9 on p. 909, with some sections from Hansard (1825), *see* item H2 on p. 903. Contains descriptions of the Columbian, Ruthven, Philadelphia, American, Smith, Washington, and Wells iron handpresses, as well as the Ramage two-pull screw press. With general instructions for setting up iron handpresses and the roller stand. The procedures for pulling have been modified for one-pull iron handpresses and inking with rollers, instead of balls. Also contains sections on casting rollers, stereotype printing, and the first detailed instructions for preparing overlays; with a glossary of "Technical Terms Used in Printing." The contents of each chapter are individually indexed at the back.

Includes illustrations of the Columbian, Ruthven, Philadelphia, Smith (mechanism only), Washington, and Wells (mechanism only) iron handpresses, the Ramage two-pull screw press (mechanism only), and an allegorical tailpiece, on p. 48, with a Smith-style press, plus fifty pages of imposition schemes, including those for imposing from the center. There is an allegorical frontispiece with a Columbian press and a vignette on the title page with a Washington press in the background. This vignette was used in all fourteen editions of Adams's manual. He was the first to mention girls working in a printing office, more specifically, in the warehouse where they were used to fill in and press the printed sheets.

A3. Adams, Thomas F. *Typographia; or, The Printer's Instructor; a Brief Sketch of the Origin, Rise, and Progress of the Typographic Art, with Practical Directions for Conducting Every Department in an Office, Hints to Authors, Publishers, &c.* 2nd ed., with numerous emendations and additions. Philadelphia: Published at No. 118 Chestnut St. and No. 8 Franklin Place; and for sale at the principal type foundries, 1844.

Bibliographical citations: Bliss, 882; Gaskell, E18; Hitchings, 3c.

Locations: Columbia; Iowa; Kemble; LC; Philadelphia; Tokyo; Utah; Yale.

A revised and abridged resetting of the 1837 edition, *see* item A2 above. A few sections in the chapters on improved presses and the warehouse were modified. Contains descriptions of the Columbian, American, Washington, Wells, Philadelphia, and Smith iron handpresses, as well as the Ramage two-pull screw press. The chapter on stereotype printing was deleted. New sections were added on "Printing Engravings on Wood," "Ornamental Printing," "Polychromatic Printing," "Machine Printing," and "Sizes of Paper Made by Machinery." Includes illustrations of the Columbian, American (mechanism only), Washington, Wells (mechanism only) iron handpresses, the Ramage two-pull screw press (mechanism only), and a wood engraving, on the last printed leaf and repeated as the frontispiece, showing four lads working at an A. B. Taylor double cylinder press, plus fifty pages of imposition schemes. There is another wood engraving, on p. [271], showing a lad and a woman working at an Adams platen power press. The lad is manually cranking the flywheel, which could also be activated by steam power, while the woman is handling the paper – the first depiction in a printers' manual of a woman working in a pressroom.

Facsimile reprints:
Typographia: or The Printer's Instructor. With a new introduction by John Bidwell. New York: Garland Publishing, 1981. Series Statement: Nineteenth-Century Book Arts and Printing History.

A4. Adams, Thomas F. *Typographia; or, The Printer's Instructor; a Brief Sketch of the Origin, Rise, and Progress of the Typographic Art, with Practical Directions for Conducting Every Department in an Office, Hints to Authors, Publishers, &c.* 3rd ed., with numerous emendations and additions. Philadelphia: James Kay, Jun. & Brother, 183 1/2 Market Street; Pittsburgh: C. H. Kay, 1845.

Bibliographical citations: Bigmore & Wyman, vol. I, p. 3; Gaskell, E18; Hitchings, 3d.

Locations: Columbia; Grolier; Huntington; Iowa; Kemble; Newberry; NYPL; Providence Athenæum; RIT; St. Bride; Toronto; Yale.

A reprint of the 1844 edition, *see* item A3 above, with a slightly modified title page. The contents, still indexed by chapter, were moved forward to p. [iii]. The frontispiece was deleted from this and all future editions.

A5. Adams, Thomas F. *Typographia; or, The Printer's Instructor; a Brief Sketch of the Origin, Rise, and Progress of the Typographic Art, with Practical Directions for Conducting Every Department in an Office, Hints to Authors, Publishers, &c.* 4th ed., with numerous emendations and additions. Philadelphia: L. Johnson & Co., No. 6 Sansom Street, 1851.

Bibliographical notes: The copyright notice, on the verso of the title page, is dated 1845.

Bibliographical citations: Gaskell, E18.

Locations: Boston Public; Harvard; LC.

A reprint of the 1845 edition, *see* item A4 above, with a slightly modified title page.

A6. Adams, Thomas F. *Typographia; or, The Printer's Instructor; a Brief Sketch of the Origin, Rise, and Progress of the Typographic Art, with Practical Directions for Conducting Every Department in an Office, Hints to Authors, Publishers, &c.* 4th ed., with numerous emendations and additions. Philadelphia: Peck & Bliss, N. Third Street, 1851.

Bibliographical citations: Gaskell, E18; Hitchings, 3e.

Locations: Yale.

A reprint of the 1845 edition, *see* item A4 above, with a slightly modified title page.

Not seen.

A7. Adams, Thomas F. *Typographia; or, The Printer's Instructor; a Brief Sketch of the Origin, Rise, and Progress of the Typographic Art, with Practical Directions for Conducting Every Department in an Office, Hints to Authors, Publishers, &c.* 4th ed., with numerous emendations and additions. Philadelphia: L. Johnson & Co., No. 6 Sansom Street, 1853.

Bibliographical notes: The copyright notice, on the verso of the title page, is dated 1845.

Bibliographical citations: Gaskell, E18.

Locations: Berkeley; Harvard; Smithsonian; Virginia; Yale.

A reprint of the 1845 edition, *see* item A4 above, with a slightly modified title page.

A8. Adams, Thomas F. *Typographia; or, The Printer's Instructor; a Brief Sketch of the Origin, Rise, and Progress of the Typographic Art, with Practical Directions for Conducting Every Department in an Office, Hints to Authors, Publishers, &c.* 4th ed., with numerous emendations and additions. Philadelphia: Peck & Bliss, N. Third Street, 1853.

Bibliographical notes: The copyright notice, on the verso of the title page, is dated 1845.

Bibliographical citations: Gaskell, E18.

Locations: Columbia; Delaware; Providence Public; Yale.

A reprint of the 1845 edition, *see* item A4 above, with a slightly modified title page.

A9. Adams, Thomas F. *Typographia; or, The Printer's Instructor; a Brief Sketch of the Origin, Rise, and Progress of the Typographic Art, with Practical Directions for Conducting Every Department in an Office, Hints to Authors, Publishers, &c.* 4th ed., with numerous emendations and additions. Philadelphia: L. Johnson & Co., No. 6 Sansom Street, 1854.

Bibliographical notes: The copyright notice, on the verso of the title page, is dated 1845.

Bibliographical citations: Bliss, 883.

Locations: Kemble; NYPL; Princeton; William & Mary.

A reprint of the 1845 edition, *see* item A4 above, with a slightly modified title page.

A10. Adams, Thomas F. *Typographia; or, The Printer's Instructor: A Brief Sketch of the Origin, Rise, and Progress of the Typographic Art, with Practical Directions for Conducting Every Department in an Office, Hints to Authors, Publishers, &c.* New-York: James Conner & Sons, 1856.

Bibliographical notes: The copyright notice, on the verso of the title page, is dated 1851.

Bibliographical citations: Gaskell, E18.

Locations: St. Bride.

A reprint of the 1845 edition, *see* item A4 above, with a slightly modified title page and several revisions in the sections on iron handpresses and machine printing. Contains brief descriptions of the Columbian, Washington, and Smith iron handpresses. The section on "Polychromatic Printing" was deleted. A new section on machine job presses was added. Includes an illustration of a Columbian press taken from the 1844 edition and new illustrations of the Washington press, Hoe's single cylinder press, Adams power press, and Gordon and Ruggles job presses. At the back, there are two pages of advertisements for Hoe's machine presses.

A11. Adams, Thomas F. *Typographia; or, The Printer's Instructor: A Brief Sketch of the Origin, Rise, and Progress of the Typographic Art, with Practical Directions for Conducting Every Department in an Office, Hints to Authors, Publishers, &c.* New-York: Published by R. Hoe & Co., 1856.

Bibliographical notes: The copyright notice, on the verso of the title page, is dated 1845.

Bibliographical citations: Bliss, 884; Gaskell, E18.

Locations: Columbia; Iowa; LC; NYPL; RIT; SFPL.

A reprint of the 1856 edition, *see* item A10 above, with a slightly modified title page.

A12. Adams, Thomas F. *Typographia.* Philadelphia: L. Johnson & Co., 1856.

Bibliographical notes: The bibliographical data is taken from pp. xi–xii of John Bidwell's introduction to the facsimile reprint of the 1844 edition, *see* item A3 on p. 885. This item is most likely a bibliographical ghost.

No copies located.

A13. Adams, Thomas F. *Typographia; or, The Printer's Instructor: A Brief Sketch of the Origin, Rise, and Progress of the Typographic Art, with Practical Directions for Conducting Every Department in an Office, Hints to Authors, Publishers, &c.* Philadelphia: Published by L. Johnson & Co., 1857.

Bibliographical notes: The copyright notice, on the verso of the title page, is dated 1845.

Bibliographical citations: Bliss, 885; Gaskell, E18.

Locations: Columbia; Delaware; Harvard; Huntington; Pennsylvania; UCLA.

A reprint of the 1856 edition (Hoe imprint), *see* item A11 above, with a slightly modified title page.

A14. Adams, Thomas F. *Typographia; or, The Printer's Instructor: A Brief Sketch of the Origin, Rise, and Progress of the Typographic Art, with Practical Directions for Conducting Every Department in an Office, Hints to Authors, Publishers, &c.* Philadelphia: Published by L. Johnson & Co., 1858.

Bibliographical notes: The copyright notice, on the verso of the title page, is dated 1845.

Bibliographical citations: Bliss, 886; Gaskell, E18, addenda, p. 66.

Locations: Iowa; LC; Massey.

A reprint of the 1856 edition (Hoe imprint), *see* item A11 above, with a slightly modified title page and minor textual changes.

A15. Adams, Thomas F. *Typographia; or, The Printer's Instructor: A Brief Sketch of the Origin, Rise, and Progress of the Typographic Art, with Practical Directions for Conducting Every Department in an Office, Hints to Authors, Publishers, &c.* Philadelphia: Published by L. Johnson & Co., 1861.

Bibliographical notes: The copyright notice, on the verso of the title page, is dated 1845.

Bibliographical citations: Bliss, 887; Gaskell, E18.

Locations: Columbia; Dartmouth; Kentucky; Minnesota; NYPL; Toronto; Yale.

A reprint of the 1858 edition, *see* item A14 above, with a slightly modified title page.

A16. Adams, Thomas F. *Typographia; or, The Printer's Instructor: A Brief Sketch of the Origin, Rise, and Progress of the Typographic Art, with Practical Directions for Conducting Every Department in an Office, Hints to Authors, Publishers, &c.* Philadelphia: Published by L. Johnson & Co., 1864.

Bibliographical notes: The copyright notice, on the verso of the title page, is dated 1845.

Bibliographical citations: Gaskell, E18; Hitchings, 3g.

Locations: Grolier; Huntington; NYPL; RIT.

A reprint of the 1858 edition, *see* item A14 above, with a slightly modified title page.

Adams, Thomas F. *See also* item J10 on p. 910. The new material in this work is generally attributed to Adams.

A17. *The Art of Printing, Historical and Practical. Combining Historical Digest and Young Printer's Elementary Guide; Being Easy Schemes for Economization of Labour.* Manchester: Published by the author, 13, Nesbit-street, Hulme, n.d.

Bibliographical notes: The bibliographical data is taken from Bigmore & Wyman, vol. I, p. 15. No additional information was given.
No copies located.

B1. B., H. G. *Women Compositors: A Guide to the Composing Room.* London: The Victoria Press, 117, Praed Street, W., Office for the Employment of Women, under the patronage of Her Majesty, 1880.

Bibliographical citations: Bliss, 930.

Locations: Newberry.

Not seen.

B2. Bangs, Charles. *The Country Printer.* St. Louis: 1874.

Bibliographical notes: The bibliographical data is taken from Bigmore & Wyman, vol. I, p. 33. No additional information is given.

No copies located.

B3. [Baxter, John]. *The Sister Arts; or, A Concise and Interesting View of the Nature and History of Paper-Making, Printing, and Bookbinding: Being Designed to Unite Entertainment with Information Concerning Those Arts, with Which the Cause of Literature Is Peculiarly Connected.* Embellished with three engravings. Lewes, UK: Sussex Press; printed and published by J. Baxter; and sold by the principal booksellers in London, 1809.

Bibliographical citations: Bigmore & Wyman, vol. II, p. 363; Bliss, 133; Marthens, p. 39. All of these compilers use *Sister Arts* for the main entry, although Marthens lists it in his section on anonymous works following the alphabetical entries.

Locations: Bodleian; Bridwell; British; Cambridge; Grolier; Harvard; Michigan; SFPL; Yale.

A brief description of the printing trades for young readers. Not intended as a manual to teach the arts. Lacks specific information on iron handpresses. Includes three plates illustrating papermaking, printing – with the pressmen working at a wooden press – and bookbinding. Bigmore & Wyman's pagination of 92 pages for this item is slightly misleading since it actually has 104 pages. The section on printing begins on p. 32 and ends on p. 92. There is at least one known variant title page with the imprint set in an alternate typeface.

B4. Beadnell, Henry. *The First Part of the Guide to Typography, Literary and Practical.* London: F. Bowering, 211, Blackfriars Road; and all booksellers, 1859.

Bibliographical notes: The "Preface" is dated July, 1859. This item presents certain bibliographical problems since it was later reissued as Part I of a work in two parts, *see* item B5 below. However, as an individual work, it is usually found with either the above title page or the title page for Part I from the following entry. In some cases, both title pages were used.

Locations: Columbia; LC (with 1861 title page); St. Bride; Sydney; William & Mary.

Primarily intended for authors and compositors. Lacks specific information on iron handpresses and practical printing.

B5. Beadnell, Henry. *A Guide to Typography, in Two Parts, Literary and Practical; or, The Reader's Handbook and the Compositor's Vade-Mecum.* 2 vols. Part I, Literary; Part II, Practical. London: F. Bowering, 211, Blackfriars Road; and all booksellers, [1859–1861].

Bibliographical notes: The inferred publication dates are taken from the prefaces. The "Preface" to Part I is dated July, 1859; the "Preface" to Part II is dated Aug. 20, 1861. This item is generally found with both parts bound together in one volume.

Bibliographical citations: Bigmore & Wyman, vol. I, p. 41; Marthens [undated], p. 10.

Locations: Bancroft (2 parts in one); British; Columbia; Delaware (2 parts in one); Huntington (2 parts in one); Massey (2 parts in one); Newberry (2 parts in one); St. Bride (2 parts in one); Sydney (part 2 only); Yale (2 parts in one).

Part II contains practical instructions primarily intended for compositors. Indexed. Lacks specific information on handpresses and presswork. With thirteen imposition schemes.

B6. Beniowski, [Bartlomiej]. *Improvements in Printing, Invented and Patented by Major Beniowski.* London:

Printed and published by the author, No. 8, Bow-Street, Covent Garden, 1854.

Bibliographical citations: Bigmore & Wyman, vol. I, p. 44.

Locations: Bodleian; Chicago; Columbia; Detroit; Harvard; Iowa; St. Bride.

The author, who was also an inventor, was responsible for a number of innovations in the printing industry, including air balls and air rollers, a composing machine, and a printing machine, all of which are described and illustrated in this book. Contains sections on "Logotypes" and "Polycomposing," a system for composing and printing identical settings of type together in a single form. Lacks specific information on iron handpresses. The title page carries the following notice: "The Letter-press and Wood-cuts have been worked with inking rollers filled with compressed air, exposed during many months, to dry and wet weather, and also to various extreme temperatures, without ever wanting more than a few minutes to make them ready for use."

B7. Beniowski, [Bartlomiej]. *Improvements in Printing, Invented and Patented by Major Beniowski.* London: Printed and published by the author, No. 8, Bow-Street, Covent Garden, 1856.

Locations: Newberry; St. Bride.

A reprint of the 1854 edition, *see* item B6 above, with a slightly modified title page.

B8. Berri, David Garden. *The Art of Printing.* London: published by the author, at the British and Foreign Heraldic Office, 36, High Holborn, (Opposite Chancery Lane), 1864.

Bibliographical citations: Wakeman, 12.

Locations: Bodleian; Columbia.

Not seen.

B9. Berri, David Garden. *The Art of Printing.* 2nd ed. London: Published by the author at the British and Foreign Heraldic Office, 36, High Holborn, (Opposite Chancery Lane), 1865.

Bibliographical citations: Bigmore & Wyman, vol. I, p. 52.

Locations: Bodleian; Columbia; Huntington; NYPL; Newberry; St. Bride; William & Mary.

Predominantly a manual of practical instructions for amateur printers in the use of tabletop presses. Also contains information on the mechanics of a Stanhope press. Includes a frontispiece showing a woman at work on Berri's New Patent People's Printing Press – a small cylinder press that could be used for letterpress, lithographic, and intaglio printing – and illustrations of two of these presses, as well as a plan for a double case, a Stanhope press, and a facsimile of a 1478 woodcut of a wooden press; plus three pages of imposition schemes. "A guide, intended for the use of mere amateurs." – Bigmore & Wyman.

B10. Berri, David Garden. *The Art of Printing.* 3rd ed. London: Published by the author, at 36, High Holborn, (Opposite Chancery Lane), 1871.

Locations: British; Iowa; Harvard; St. Bride.

A significantly enlarged reprint of the 1865 edition, *see* item B9 above, with a slightly modified title page.

B11. Bidwell, George H. *Printer's New Handbook: A Treatise on the Imposition of Forms, Embracing a System of Rules and Principles for Laying the Pages, Applicable to All Forms, with Instructions for Making Margin and Register, Turning and Folding the Sheets, &c., and Diagrams of All the Standard Forms, Showing Their Relation to Each Other, with Explanations of Their Variations and Transpositions; Also Tables of Signatures, &c., Useful to Compositors, Pressmen, and Publishers.* New York: 1866.

Bibliographical notes: The bibliographical data is taken from Bigmore & Wyman, vol. I, p. 60. This item is most likely a bibliographical ghost. They are probably referring to item B14 below.

No copies located.

Bidwell, George H. *The Printers' New Hand-Book. A Treatise on the Imposition of Forms. See* item B15 below.

B12. Bidwell, George H. *The Prompt Computer for the Use of Book, Newspaper, and Job Printers in Computing Earnings of Employés.* New York: Published by the author, 33 Park Row, 1875.

Bibliographical notes: The publication date is taken from the copyright notice on the verso of the title page. The "Explanatory Preface" is also dated 1875.

Bibliographical citations: Bigmore & Wyman, vol. I, p. 60.

Locations: British; LC.

Consists mainly of scales of prices. Lacks specific information on iron handpresses and practical printing.

B13. Bidwell, George H. *Treatise on the Imposition of Forms: Embracing a System of Rules and Principles for Laying the Pages, Applicable to All Forms; with Instructions for Making Margin and Register, Turning and Folding the Sheets, etc.; and Diagrams of All the Standard Forms Showing Their Relation to Each Other, with Explanations of Their Variations and Transpositions. Also, Tables of Signatures, etc., Useful to Compositors, Pressmen, and Publishers.* New York: Raymond & Caulon, 88 Cedar Street, 1865.

Bibliographical notes: The copyright notice, on the verso of the title page, is dated 1864. The "Preliminary Note" is dated 1865.

Locations: Columbia; Kemble; LC; Toronto.

A comprehensive work on imposing primarily intended for compositors. Consists mainly of imposition schemes, as well as instructions for making ready and making register. Lacks specific information on iron handpresses and presswork.

B14. Bidwell, George H. *Treatise on the Imposition of Forms: Embracing a System of Rules and Principles for Laying the Pages, Applicable to All Forms; with Instructions for Making Margin and Register, Turning and Folding the Sheets, etc.; and Diagrams of All the Standard Forms Showing Their Relation to Each Other, with Explanations of Their Variations and Transpositions. Also, Tables of Signatures, etc., Useful to Compositors, Pressmen, and Publishers.* New York: Published by Dick & Fitzgerald, 1866.

Bibliographical notes: The copyright notice, on the verso of the title page, is dated 1864. The "Preliminary Note" is dated 1865.

Bibliographical citations: Bigmore & Wyman, vol. I, p. 61; Bliss, 927; Marthens, 11.

Locations: Boston Public; British; St. Bride; SFPL.

A reprint of the 1865 edition, *see* item B13 above, in a smaller format with a slightly modified title page.

B15. Bidwell, George H. *The Printers' New Hand-Book. A Treatise on the Imposition of Forms, with Tables of Signatures, etc.* [2nd ed.] New York: Published by the author, 33 Park Row, 1875.

Bibliographical notes: The publication date is taken from the copyright notice on the verso of the title page. The British Library gives this item an inferred publication date of [1877]. The "Preliminary Note" is dated 1865. The inferred edition statement is taken from the Library of Congress record, call number: Z255 .B581.

Bibliographical citations: Bigmore & Wyman, vol. I, p.60.

Locations: British [1877]; Chicago; Columbia; Delaware; Harvard; Huntington; LC; RIT; St. Bride.

A new edition of *A Treatise on the Imposition of Forms* (1865), *see* item B13 above, with additional material, including a "Preface to the New Edition."

Bishop, Henry Gold. *Bishop's Practical Printer. See* item B20 on p. 890.

B16. Bishop, Henry Gold. *Bishop's Specimens of Job Work for Printers, Being Suggestions for Setting Up Business Cards, Letter Heads, Bill Heads, Circulars, and All Kinds of Display Advertising.* Oneonta, N. Y.: To be obtained from H. G. Bishop, and from all type foundries, 1890.

Locations: Chicago [189–]; LC [ca. 1890].

A short text on job composition followed by 116 pages of specimens of job work and 6 pages of advertisements. Lacks specific information of iron handpresses and presswork.

B17. Bishop, Henry Gold. *Diagrams of Imposition for the Pocket. A Book of Reference for Printers. Containing All the Fastest and best Schemes for Imposing All Kinds of Forms.* [Albany]: Through all type-founders, 1888.

Bibliographical notes: The publication date is taken from the copyright notice on the verso of the title page. The inferred place of publication is taken from the Library of Congress record, call number: Z255.B62.

Locations: LC.

A small pocket guide consisting mainly of eighteen pages of imposition schemes. The title page notes that this item was "Printed on Bond Paper," which would imply that it was intended to be consulted with some frequency.

B18. Bishop, Henry Gold. *The Job Printer's List of Prices and Estimate Guide: Containing Prices to Be Charged for All Kinds of Job and Book Work, from a Small Card to a Large Volume.* New York: H. G. Bishop, 128 Duane Street, 1893.

Locations: Delaware; Minnesota; NYPL; Yale.

Consists mainly of scales of prices. Lacks specific information on iron handpresses and practical printing.

Twentieth-century editions:

The Job Printer's List of Prices and Estimate Guide: Containing Prices to Be Charged for All Kinds of Job and Book Work, from a Small Card to a Large Volume. Oneonta, NY: Henry G. Bishop, 1904.

B19. Bishop, Henry Gold. *The Practical Printer. A Book of Instruction for Beginners: A Book of Reference for the More Advanced. Containing Information on All the Various Parts of the Printing Business. With Diagrams of Imposition and Useful Tables.* Illustrated. Albany: H. G. Bishop, 37 North Pearl Street, 1889.

Bibliographical notes: There is a "Note by A. C. Cameron" on p. [xv], which is dated April 1, 1899.

Bibliographical citations: Bliss, 888.

Locations: Columbia; Dartmouth; Grolier; Huntington; Newberry; Providence Public; RIT; St. Bride; Sydney; Virginia.

Contains sections on printing on cylinder and job presses, as well as a list of technical terms. Indexed. Lacks specific information on iron handpresses and presswork. Includes progressive facsimiles of a three-step makeready, plus twenty-six specimens of composition.

B20. Bishop, Henry Gold. *Bishop's Practical Printer: A Book of Instruction for Beginners, a Book of Reference for the More Advanced. Information on All the Various Parts of the Printing Business. With Diagrams of Imposition and Useful Tables.* 2nd ed. Oneonta, N. Y.: To be obtained from H. G. Bishop; and through all type founders, 1891.

Bibliographical notes: The publication date is taken from the most recent copyright notice on the verso of the title page, which also includes an earlier copyright notice dated 1887 (i.e., 1889). The edition statement is also on the verso of the title page.

Locations: Delaware; Iowa; Kemble; LC; NYPL; St. Bride.

A reprint of the 1889 edition of *The Practical Printer* (1889), *see* item B18 above, with a new title page. Lacks specific information on iron handpresses and presswork. Includes an advertisement at the back for the Lux Engraving Co. showing a "Half-Tone Relief Plate direct from Photograph."

B21. Bishop, Henry Gold. *The Practical Printer: A Book of Instruction For Beginners; a Book of Reference for the More Advanced. Containing Information on All the Various Parts of the Printing Business. With Diagrams of Imposition and Useful Tables.* 3rd ed. Oneonta, N. Y.: Henry G. Bishop, publisher; through all type-founders, 1895.

Bibliographical notes: The publication date is taken from the most recent copyright notice on the verso of the title page, which also includes two earlier copyright notices dated 1887 (i.e., 1889) and 1891, respectively.

Bibliographical citations: Bliss, 889.

Locations: Bancroft; Chicago; Harvard; Kemble; LC; Newberry; NYPL; RIT; Smithsonian; Virginia; Yale.

A reprint of the 1891 edition, *see* item B19 above, with a new title page. In his "Preface," the author says that an entirely new chapter on "Proof Reading," pp. 153–164, has been added, although it is not listed in the contents. The "Specimens of Composition" begin on p. 165, not on p. 153 as stated in the contents.

Twentieth-century editions:

The Practical Printer: A Book of Instruction for Beginners, a Book of Reference for the More Advanced. 4th ed. Oneonta, NY: Henry G. Bishop, 1903.

The Practical Printer: A Book of Instruction for Beginners, a Book of Reference for the More Advanced. 5th ed. Oneonta, NY: Henry G. Bishop, 1906.

B22. Bishop, Henry Gold. *The Printer's Ready Reckoner, Containing Many Useful Tables Showing the Cost of Stock Used on Small Jobs, Quantity of Paper to Give Out, Comparative Weights of Paper, Relative Sizes of Type, and Other Useful Information for Printers.* 4th ed. New York: Published by H. G. Bishop, 128 Duane Street; sold by all type founders and dealers, 1893.

Bibliographical notes: The publication date is taken from the most recent copyright notice on the verso of the title page, which also includes an earlier copyright notice dated 1884. The edition statement is also on the verso of the title page.

Locations: Chicago.

Not seen.

B23. Böck, Josef. *Zincography: A Practical Guide to the Art As Practiced in Connexion with Letterpress Printing.* [1st English ed.], revised and enlarged. Translated by E. Menken. London: Wyman & Sons, 74–6, Great Queen Street, Lincoln's-Inn Fields, [1886].

Bibliographical notes: The inferred publication date is taken from the British Library record, shelfmark: 11899.b.39. On the verso of the title page in the Bodleian Library's copy, there is an acquisition stamp dated 13 March 1886. The inferred edition statement is taken from p. 4 of the "Preface" in which the author mentions that this is the first English edition.

Locations: Bodleian; British; Providence Public [1885?].

The first major text on zinc etching. Translation of *Die Zincographie in der Buchdruckerkunst.* Leipzig: Alexander Waldow, 1885. Based on an article first published in *Illustrierte Encyklopädie der graphischen Künste.* Leipzig: Alexander Waldow, 1884. Includes fifteen illustrations of apparatus and tools.

Between 1886 and 1907, five more editions were issued.

Twentieth-century editions:

Zincography: A Practical Guide to the Art As Practiced in Connexion with Letterpress Printing. Translated by E. Menken. 6th ed., revised and enlarged. London: Menken, 1907.

B24. Brannt, William T. *Varnishes, Lacquers, Printing Inks, and Sealing-Waxes: Their Raw Materials and Their Manufacture. To Which Is Added the Art of Varnishing and Lacquering, Including the Preparation of Putties and of Stains for Wood, Ivory, Bone, Horn, and Leather.* Illustrated by thirty-nine engravings. Philadelphia: Henry Carey Baird & Co., industrial publishers, booksellers, and importers, 810 Walnut Street, 1893.

Locations: Columbia; LC; NYPL; Seattle; Smithsonian.

Contains extensive information on the manufacture of varnishes and lacquers. Chapter IX, pp. 238–261, deals with printing inks and includes formulas for both black and colored inks for specific types of work and presses, as well as a resin soap varnish for printing gold. The illustrations in this chapter include two cross sections of furnaces for boiling oil, a mixing mill, and a grinding mill.

B25. Brightly, Charles. *The Method of Founding Stereotype, as Practiced by Charles Brightly, of Bungay, Suffolk.* Bungay: Printed by C. Brightly, for R. Phillips Bridge-Street, London, 1809.

Bibliographical citations: Bigmore & Wyman, vol. I., p. 83.

Locations: Philadelphia.

A first-hand account of printing from stereotypes. Brightly's system was similar to Stanhope's with minor variations. Includes three pages of plates showing the front and back parts of the frame, a cast-iron pan, and two views of the oven.

Facsimile reprints:
The Method of Founding Stereotype, as Practiced by Charles Brightly, of Bungay, Suffolk. With a new introduction by Michael L. Turner. New York: Garland Publishing, 1982. Series Statement: Nineteenth-Century Book Arts and Printing History.

Bound together with *An Essay on the Origin and Progress of Stereotype Printing* by Thomas Hodgson (1820), *see* item H14 on p. 905.

C1. Carey, Annie. *The History of a Book.* London, Paris, and New York: Cassell, Petter, & Galpin, [1873].

Bibliographical notes: The inferred publication date is taken from the British Library record, shelfmark: 11899.ee.10.

Bibliographical citations: Bigmore & Wyman, vol. I, p. 102; Marthens, p. 12; Wakeman, 20.

Locations: British; Massey; RIT; St. Bride [ca. 1873].

Even though intended primarily for a juvenile audience, this book contains an excellent description of every department in a printing office, as well as the processes of stereotyping, engraving, electrotyping, bookbinding, and papermaking, presented in the form of a conversation at the back of an auction house in which a number of old books – with fanciful names like Quarto, Virgil, French MS., and Law Book – "explain" in great detail to the New Book how they were made. Chapter VI, pp. 96–107, on The Press-Room, includes illustrations of a "modern hand-press" (an Albion), a locked-up forme, bank and horse, an inking-roller, and an inking table. Chapter IX, pp. 136–155, on The Binding-Shop, includes illustrations of a book and magazine folding-machine, a rolling-machine, a hand blocking-machine, and a "Guillotine" cutting-machine. Carey was one of the first women to write about printing. An earlier example is *Gutenberg, and the Art of Printing* (a fictional account) by Mrs. Emily Clemens Pearson, Boston: Noyes, Holmes, 1871.

City Press. *See* entries under Collingridge, William Hill, pp. 891–892.

Collingridge, L. *See* items C5 and C6 on p. 892.

Collingridge, William Hill. *Collingridge's Guide to Printing and Publishing. See* item C3 on p. 892.

C2. Collingridge, [William Hill]. *Collingridge's Pocket Printing Guide.* London: City Press, 1, Long Lane, n.d.

Bibliographical notes: This item would have been issued no earlier than 1857, the year the City Press was established, and no later than 1865, the year item C3, on p. 892 was published.

Bibliographical citations: Wakeman, 10.

Locations: Delaware.

A small sixteen-page pamphlet. Primarily a promotional piece for the City Press. Includes specimens of types, an example of a proof before and after being corrected, descriptions of the printing services available from the City Press, and a list of prices for job work. Lacks specific information on iron handpresses and practical printing.

C3. Collingridge, William Hill. *Collingridge's Guide to Printing and Publishing: A Manual of Information on Everything Connected with Printing, Publishing, etc., etc.* London: W. H. Collingridge, City Press, 117 to 119, Aldersgate Street, (Corner of Long Lane) E.C., [1865].

Bibliographical notes: The inferred publication date is taken from the British Library record, shelfmark: 11899.c.20.(6).

Locations: Bodleian; British.

A greatly expanded reprint of *Collingridge's Pocket Printing Guide, see* item C2 above. Intended as a guide for clients – especially, authors wanting to publish their works. Consists of a detailed account of the procedures and processes of book production. Includes twelve specimen leaves of printing and one leaf of ornamental borders at the back, plus thirteen leaves of wood engravings, including three views of the City Press premises: a pressroom with a Columbian press, five Albion presses, and four cylinder machines; a composing room with a Columbian press; and a composing room with a hand-lever proof press.

C4. Collingridge, William Hill. *Comprehensive Guide to Printing and Publishing: A Manual of Information on Matters Connected with Printing, Publishing, etc., etc.* London: W. H. Collingridge, City Press, 117 to 120, Aldersgate Street, 1869.

Locations: Delaware; St. Bride; SFPL; Yale.

An expanded and improved reprint of the [1865] edition, *see* item C3 above. Includes ten leaves of wood engravings at the back, including an interior view of W. H. & L. Collingridge's Steam Printing Works.

C5. Collingridge, William Hill. *Comprehensive Guide to Printing and Publishing: A Manual of Information on Matters Connected with Printing, Publishing, etc., etc.* 10th ed. London: W. H. & L. Collingridge, City Press, 128 & 129, Aldersgate Street, New Street, Long Lane, & 78, Old Broad Street, 1877.

Bibliographical notes: With this edition, L. Collingridge was added as co-publisher.

Locations: Bodleian; Iowa; Newberry; St. Bride.

An expanded reprint of the 1869 edition, *see* item C4 above, with a slightly modified title page. Primarily intended for authors and print buyers. Lacks specific information on iron handpresses and presswork.

It can reasonably be assumed that item C3 above was the first edition and that item C4 above was the second. No copies of the third through the ninth edition were located.

C6. Collingridge, William Hill. *Comprehensive Guide to Printing and Publishing: A Manual of Information on Matters Connected with Printing, Publishing, etc., etc.* 11th ed. London: W. H. & L. Collingridge, City Press, 148 & 149, Aldersgate Street, 1897.

Locations: Massey; NYPL; St. Bride.

A reprint of the 1877 edition, *see* item C5 above, with a new title page.

A Compositor. *The Text-Book; or, Easy Instructions in the Elements of the Art of Printing. See* item S16 on p. 925.

Comprehensive Guide to Printing and Publishing. See items C4 through C6 above.

Counsels to Authors; and, Hints to Advertisers. See items J13 and J14 on p. 910.

C7. Cowell, Samuel Harrison. *A Walk through Our Works: A Short Account of a Visit to the Printing, Stationery, and Bookbinding Manufactory of S. H. Cowell.* With illustrations of printing and its auxiliary processes. Ipswich: S. H. Cowell, 1888.

Bibliographical citations: Wakeman, 35.

Locations: St. Bride.

Primarily a promotional piece for S. H. Cowell. Describes the interdisciplinary nature of letterpress, lithography, and intaglio printing, all of which were done at Cowell's. Contains sections on proofing on an Albion press, making ink rollers, and the machine room. Lacks specific information on iron handpresses and presswork. Includes illustrations of an Albion press, a two-handle roller, and various letterpress and lithographic printing machines, as well as a copperplate press and binding equipment. Cowell is also the author of *A Brief Description of the Art of Anastatic Printing, and of the Uses to Which It May Be Applied, As Practiced by S. H. Cowell* (1872).

C8. Cowie, [George]. *Cowie's Job Master Printers' Price Book; Containing a Fair and Comprehensive Scale of Charges to the Public for Broadsides, Cards, Pamphlets, and Jobs of Every Description: To Which Is Appended, Copious Directions for Working in Gold and Other Colours, and the Manufacturing of Composition Balls or Rollers.* London: William Strange, Paternoster Row; and all booksellers, [ca. 1835].

Bibliographical notes: The inferred publication date is taken from the Bodleian Library record, call number: Johnson f.2219.

Bibliographical citations: Bigmore & Wyman, vol. I, p. 146.

Locations: Bodleian.

A ready-reference guide for compositors and pressmen based on Mason ([1821]), *see* item M29 on p. 916.

Lacks specific information on iron handpresses and practical printing. Includes thirty pages of imposition schemes.

C9. Cowie, George. *Cowie's Printers' Pocket-Book and Manual, Containing the Compositors' and Pressmen's Scale of Prices, Agreed Upon in 1810 and Modified in 1816: The Newsmen's Scale, Numerous Valuable Tables; All the Schemes of Impositions from Folio to Hundred and Twenty-Eights Inclusive; the Hebrew, Greek, and Saxon Alphabets; with Plans of the Respective Cases; an Explanation of Mathematical, Algebraical, Physical, and Astronomical Signs. To Which Is Added a Table for Giving Out Paper, and an Useful Abstract of the Various Acts of Parliament Connected with the Trade. Also, a List of Master Printers, Arranged on a New Plan, and Corrected to the Present Time.* London: W. Strange, 21 Paternoster Row; G. Cowie, 312 Strand; and G. Purkess, 60, Compton Street, Soho, [183–?]

Bibliographical notes: The inferred publication date is taken from the Bancroft Library record, call number: Z244.3 .C68 1830z. Various editions of this item, *see* items C10 through C16 below, were published in the 1830s through the 1860s. None of them were dated. For this reason, some of the inferred publication dates may be out of chronological order since they were supplied by the holding institutions. Nigel Roche, at St. Bride Printing Library, has kindly helped me unravel the publishing history of this work.

Bibliographical citations: Bigmore & Wyman [n.d.], vol. I, p. 146.; Gaskell, E17 [various dates]; Marthens [n.d.], p. 13.

Locations: Bancroft.

The title page gives a full description of the contents.

C10. Cowie, George. *Cowie's Printer's Pocket-Book and Manual, Containing the Compositors' and Pressmen's Scale of Prices, Agreed Upon in 1810 and Modified in 1816: The Newsmen's Scale, Numerous Valuable Tables; All the Schemes of Impositions from Folio to Hundred and Twenty-Eights Inclusive; the Hebrew, Greek, and Saxon Alphabets; with Plans of the Respective Cases; an Explanation of Mathematical, Algebraical, Physical, and Astronomical Signs. To Which Is Added a Table for Giving Out Paper, and an Useful Abstract of the Various Acts of Parliament Connected with the Trade. Also, a List of Master Printers, Arranged on a New Plan, and Corrected to the Present Time.* 2nd ed. London: W. Strange, 21 Paternoster Row; G. Cowie, 312 Strand; and G. Purkess, 60, Compton Street, Soho, [1835?]

Bibliographical notes: The inferred publication date is taken from the British Library record, shelfmark: 619.b.33.

Locations: Bodleian [1836]; British; Harvard.

A reprint of the [183–?] edition, *see* item C9 above, with a slightly modified title page.

C11. Cowie, [George]. *Cowie's Printer's Pocket-Book and Manual, Containing the Compositors' and Pressmen's Scale of Prices, Agreed Upon in 1810 and Modified in 1816: The Newsmen's Scale, Numerous Valuable Tables; All the Schemes of Impositions from Folio to Hundred and Twenty-Eights Inclusive; the Hebrew, Greek, and Saxon Alphabets; with Plans of the Respective Cases; an Explanation of Mathematical, Algebraical, Physical, and Astronomical Signs. To Which Is Added a Table for Giving Out Paper, and an Useful Abstract of the Various Acts of Parliament Connected with the Trade. Also, a List of Master Printers, Arranged on a New Plan, and Corrected to the Present Time.* [3rd ed.] London: W. Strange, 21 Paternoster Row, [1836/7]

Bibliographical notes: The inferred publication date is taken from the St. Bride Printing Library record, call number: 20332. Roche notes that mention is made on p. 100 of the Scale for Parliamentary Printing agreed to on 16 May 1836 and that the *True Sun* newspaper, which ceased publication on 23 December 1837, is listed on p. 99. The inferred edition statement was supplied by the compiler.

Locations: Newberry [183–?]; St. Bride.

A reprint of the [1835?] edition, *see* item C10 above, with a slightly modified title page.

C12. Cowie, [George]. *Cowie's Printer's Pocket-Book and Manual, Containing the Compositors' and Pressmen's Scale of Prices, Agreed Upon in 1810 and Modified in 1816: The Newsmen's Scale, Numerous Valuable Tables; All the Schemes of Impositions from Folio to Hundred and Twenty-Eights Inclusive; the Hebrew, Greek, and Saxon Alphabets; with Plans of the Respective Cases; an Explanation of Mathematical, Algebraical, Physical, and Astronomical Signs. To Which Is Added a Table for Giving Out Paper, and an Useful Abstract of the Various Acts of Parliament Connected with the Trade. Also, a List of Master Printers, Arranged on a New Plan, and Corrected to the Present Time.* 4th ed. London: W. Strange, 21 Paternoster Row, [183–?]

Bibliographical notes: The inferred publication date is taken from the University of Minnesota Library record, call number: 019.3 C839 9ZAR10D15S07TFL. The edition statement is on the front cover.

Locations: Minnesota.

A reprint of the [1835?] edition, *see* item C10 above, with a slightly modified title page.

C13. Cowie, [George]. *Cowie's Printer's Pocket-Book and Manual, Containing the Compositors' and Pressmen's Scale of Prices, Agreed Upon in 1810 and Modified in 1816: The Newsmen's Scale, Numerous Valuable Tables; All the Schemes of Impositions from Folio to Hundred and Twenty-Eights Inclusive; the Hebrew, Greek, and Saxon Alphabets; with Plans of the Respective Cases; an Explanation of Mathematical, Algebraical, Physical, and Astronomical Signs. To Which Is Added a Table for Giving Out Paper, and an Useful Abstract of the Vari-*

ous Acts of Parliament Connected with the Trade. Also, a List of Master Printers, Arranged on a New Plan, and Corrected to the Present Time. 5th ed. London: W. Strange, 21 Paternoster Row, [1839?]

Bibliographical notes: The inferred publication date is taken from the British Library record, shelfmark: RB.23.a.18415. The edition statement is on the front cover.

Locations: British; Columbia [prior to 1860]; Michigan; NYPL [184–?]; St. Bride [1839/40]; Toronto [ca. 1840].

A reprint of the [1835?] edition, *see* item C10 above, with a slightly modified title page. Includes an illustration of an Improved Albion press on the cover.

C14. Cowie, George. *Cowie's Printers' Pocket-Book and Manual.* 6th ed., enlarged and improved. London: W. Strange, 21, Paternoster Row; G. Cowie, 110, Shoe Lane; and all booksellers, [184–?].

Bibliographical notes: The inferred publication date is taken from the New York Public Library record, call number: *IBP (Cowie's printer's pocket-book).

Locations: Columbia; NYPL.

An enlarged and improved reprint of the [1835?] edition, *see* item C10 above, with a slightly modified title page.

Not seen.

C15. Cowie, George. *Cowie's Printers' Pocket Book and Manual: Including the American Scale of Prices, for Compositors and Pressmen.* 7th ed. London: W. Strange, 21, Paternoster Row; G. Cowie, 110, Shoe Lane; and all booksellers, [ca. 1844].

Bibliographical notes: The inferred publication date is taken from the Bodleian Library record, call number: 25835 f.62.

Locations: Bodleian; Columbia [1850?].

It is possible that this edition was intended for American printers. The first comprehensive American scale of prices, Theodore Low De Vinne's *The Printers' Price List, see* item D4 on p. 897, was not published until 1869.

C16. Cowie, [George]. *Cowie's Printers' Pocket-Book and Manual.* London: Simpkin, Marshall, and Co., Stationers' Hall Court, [1866].

Bibliographical notes: The inferred publication date is taken from the British Library record, shelfmark: 11899.a.8.

Bibliographical citations: Bigmore & Wyman, vol. I, p. 146.

Locations: Bodleian; British; Columbia; Iowa; LC; Michigan; St. Bride [ca.1850].

A new edition of the [1844] edition, *see* item C15 above, with alterations, deletions, and additions. Contains sections on composing and imposition.

The "List of Master Printers" was omitted. Lacks specific information on iron handpresses and presswork.

Cowie, George. *See also* item P12 on p. 920. Cowie is listed as one of the publishers.

Crisp, William Finch. *Crisp's Business Guide for Printers, Lithographers, Engravers, Bookbinders, Rulers, Stationers, &c. See* item C27 on p. 895.

Crisp, William Finch. *Dialogue on Printers' Prices. See* item C28 on p. 896.

C17. Crisp, William Finch. *An Easy Catechism of Punctuation for the Use of Newspaper Correspondents, Printers, Juvenile Students, &c.* 1875.

Bibliographical notes: The bibliographical data is taken from Bigmore & Wyman, vol. I., p. 149. This item may be a bibliographical ghost. It was published in the same year as item C29, which has a similar title.

No copies located.

C18. Crisp, William Finch. *The General Printers' Book of Practical Recipes, &c.* Great Yarmouth: n.d.

Bibliographical notes: Bibliographical data taken from Bigmore & Wyman, vol. I, p. 149. This item would have been published prior to 1875.

No copies located.

C19. Crisp, William Finch. *The General Printers' Book of Practical Recipes, &c.* London: 1875.

Bibliographical notes: The bibliographical data is taken from Bigmore & Wyman, vol. I, p. 149.

No copies located.

C20. Crisp, William Finch. *The Printers' Business Guide And General Price List.* London: [1864].

Bibliographical notes: Apart from the inferred publication date, the bibliographical data is taken from Bigmore & Wyman, *see* below. The inferred publication date is taken from Crisp, who in the "Preface" to his *The Printers' Universal Book of Reference* ([1875]), *see* item C25 on p. 895, gives 1864 as the publication date of *The Printers' Business Guide.*

Bibliographical citations: Bigmore & Wyman [1866], vol. I, p. 149.

No copies located.

C21. Crisp, William [Finch]. *The Printers' Business Guide and Ready-Reckoned General Price Lists for Printing Cards, Circulars, Hand Bills, Memorandums, Posters, Cheque Books, Labels, Bill Heads, &c.; to Which Is Added Miscellaneous Receipts, Copious Trade Directory, &c.* [2nd ed.] Great Yarmouth: Printed by Crisp & Maryson, Rows 33 & 101, 1868.

Bibliographical notes: The inferred edition statement was supplied by the compiler.

Locations: Columbia.

An excellent manual on general printing practices intended primarily for job printers, although much of this information is also applicable to printing on the iron handpress.

C22. Crisp, William [Finch]. *The Printers' Business Guide and Ready-Reckoned General Price Lists, for Printing Cards, Circulars, Hand Bills, Memorandums, Posters, Cheque Books, Labels, Bill Heads, &c.; to Which Are Added Miscellaneous Receipts, Copious Trade Directories, &c.* 3rd ed. London: Brace, Brace & Co.; 6, Red Lion Court, Fleet Street, E.C.; Yarmouth: W. Crisp, "Independent" Office, [1869].

Bibliographical notes: The inferred publication date is taken from the "Preface," which is dated July, 1869.

Bibliographical citations: Wakeman, 15.

Locations: Bodleian; British; Massey; St. Bride.

An expanded reprint of the 1868 edition, *see* item C21 above, with a new title page.

C23. Crisp, William Finch. *The Printers', Lithographers', Engravers', and Bookbinders' Business Guide, with Ready-Reckoned General Price Lists; to Which Are Added Legal & Commercial Information, Miscellaneous Recipes, and Practical Advice for Every Member of the Combined Trades.* Edited by William Finch Crisp. 4th ed., extended and improved. London: J. Haddon & Co., 3, Bouverie Street, Fleet Street; Great Yarmouth: W. F. Crisp, 30, Crown Road, [1873].

Bibliographical notes: The inferred publication date is taken from the "Preface," which is dated March, 1873.

Bibliographical citations: Bigmore & Wyman, vol. I, p. 149.

Locations: Bodleian; British; Delaware; Massey; St. Bride; Sydney.

An expanded reprint of the [1869] edition, *see* item C22 above, with a new title.

C24. Crisp, William Finch. *The Printers', Lithographers', Engravers', Bookbinders', and Stationers' Business Guide, with Ready-Reckoned General Price Lists, to Which Are Added Legal & Commercial Information, Miscellaneous Recipes, and Practical Advice for Every Member of the Combined Trades.* Edited by William Finch Crisp. 5th ed., extended and improved. London: J. Haddon & Co., 3, Bouverie Street, Fleet Street; Great Yarmouth: W. F. Crisp, 30, Crown Road, [1874].

Bibliographical notes: The inferred publication date is taken from the "Preface," which is dated July, 1874.

Bibliographic citations: Marthens, p. 13.

Locations: Bodleian; British; Illinois; LC; St. Bride; William & Mary.

An expansion of the [1873] edition, *see* item C23 above, with a new title page.

C25. Crisp, William Finch. *The Printers' Universal Book of Reference and Every-Hour Office Companion. An Addendum to "The Printers', etc., Business Guide."* Edited by William Finch Crisp. London: J. Haddon & Co., 3, Bouverie Street, Fleet Street, E.C.; Great Yarmouth: W. F. Crisp, 30, Crown Road, [1875].

Bibliographical notes: The inferred publication date is taken from the "Preface," which is dated March, 1875.

Bibliographical citations: Bigmore & Wyman [1874], vol. I, p. 150; Marthens [1874], p. 13; Wakeman, 17.

Locations: Bancroft; Bodleian; British; Cambridge; Columbia; Iowa; LC; Newberry; NYPL; St. Bride; William & Mary.

Sound instructions in practical printing. Contains information on setting up the Columbian and Albion presses and sections on bringing up woodcuts, making ready, composition rollers, rolling and printing forms, book work, news work, and numerous trade recipes. Crisp describes several new printing technologies including the Vial and Graphotype (mechanical processes for producing relief plates) and Zincography (zinc plate lithography). The following note is printed on the title page: "The information includes many essentials not generally known, connected with the composing and machine rooms, warehouse, bookbinding, engraving, and ruling departments; thousands of reference notes, and much practical and theoretical advice." Includes a wood engraving on the title page showing *putti* as pressmen at work on opposite sides of the press.

C26. Crisp, William Finch. *The Printers', Lithographers', Engravers', Bookbinders', and Stationers' Business Guide. With Ready-Reckoned General Price Lists, to Which Are Added Legal and Commercial Information, Miscellaneous Recipes, and Practical Advice for Every Member of the Combined Trades.* Edited by William Finch Crisp. 6th ed., extended and improved. London: J. Haddon & Co., 3, Bouverie Street, Fleet Street; Great Yarmouth: W. F. Crisp, 30, Crown Road, [1876].

Bibliographical notes: The inferred publication date is taken from the Bodleian Library record, call number: 170 f.6 (12). The "Preface for the Fifth Edition," which is dated July, 1874, was also used for the sixth.

Locations: Bodleian; St. Bride.

A reprint of the [1874] edition, *see* item C24 above, with a new title page.

C27. Crisp, William Finch. *Crisp's Business Guide for Printers, Lithographers, Engravers, Bookbinders, Rulers, Stationers, &c., with Ready-Reckoned General Price Lists, to Which Are Added Legal and Commercial Information, and Practical Advice for Every Member of the Combined Trades, Including Nearly Two Hundred Ancient and Modern Trade Recipes.* Edited by William Finch Crisp. 7th ed., extended and improved. London: J. Haddon & Co., 3, Bouverie Street, Fleet Street; Great Yarmouth: W. F. Crisp, Independent Office, [1881].

Bibliographical notes: The inferred publication date is taken from the "Preface," which is dated July, 1881.

Locations: Chicago; Massey; Providence Public; St. Bride.

A reprint of the [1874] edition, *see* item C24 on p. 895, with a new title.

C28. Crisp, William Finch. *Printers' Prices, or Estimates Made Easy. 130 Ready-Reckoned Jobs, and Much Other Useful Information. A Dialogue between Mr. Practical and Mr. Novice.* Great Yarmouth: W. F. Crisp, 30, Crown Road, [1879].

Bibliographical notes: The inferred publication date is taken from a testimonial letter, on p. 16, to Crisp from William Prendergast. The letter, in praise of another of Crisp's works, is dated January 11, 1879. Variant title on the cover: *Dialogue on Printers' Prices.*

Bibliographical citations: Wakeman, 26.

Locations: Delaware [1879?]; UCLA.

A sixteen-page pamphlet of which only ten pages are devoted to printers' prices, the remainder being testimonials or reviews of Crisp's earlier books.

Crisp, William Finch. *The Printers' Universal Book of Reference and Every-Hour Office Companion. See* item C25 on p. 895.

C29. Crisp, William Finch. *Punctuation Simplified. Crisp's Catechism of Punctuation; a Simple Mode of Learning the Proper Use of the* , ; : . — ! ? ' ([* † ‡ || § ¶ ç &c., *for the Guidance of Printers, Painters, Newspaper Correspondents, and Also for the Use of Schools.* Great Yarmouth: W. F. Crisp, 30, Crown Road; London: J. Haddon & Co., 3, Bouverie Street, Fleet Street, E.C., [1875].

Bibliographical notes: The inferred publication date is taken from a statement praising this work that originally appeared in the January 5, 1875, issue of *Buck's Advertiser and Aylesbury News,* and was reprinted on p. 13 in Crisp's *Printers' Prices, or Estimates Made Easy* ([1879]), *see* item C28 above.

Bibliographical citations: Marthens, p. 13.

Locations: St. Bride.

In his "Preface," Crisp says the book was written for "the young aspirants to typographical fame, the letter painter, and others in need of a perfect knowledge of punctuation."

C30. Cummins, Richard. *The Pressmen's Guide. Containing Valuable Instructions, and Recipes for Pressmen and Apprentices in City and Country Printing Offices.* Brooklyn: R. Cummins & Co., No. 81 & 83 Court Street, 1873.

Bibliographical citations: Bigmore & Wyman, vol. I, p. 150; Bigmore & Wyman, vol. II, p. 220; Marthens, p. 38. Bigmore & Wyman use *The Pressmen's Guide* for the main entry; Marthens also uses it for the main entry, but lists it under anonymous works at the back.

Locations: LC; Minnesota.

Very good instructions for job work on cylinder presses. Contains a detailed section on making ready wood engravings. Lacks specific information on iron handpresses and presswork.

Daughaday & Co. *See* item H26 on p. 907.

D1. Degotardi, J. *The Art of Printing in Its Various Branches. With Specimens & Illustrations.* Sydney: Published by J. Degotardi, Robin Hood Lane, off George Street, between Hunter and Bridge Streets, 1861.

Locations: British.

More than just a promotional piece for J. Degotardi, who was also the printer, this short book was intended to give the general public a historical background in the art of printing, as well as an overview in the latest improvements and developments in practical printing. Contains a brief description of printing on the iron handpress. Includes ten specimens of printing at the back. This is the only printers' manual in this bibliography with an Australian imprint.

Denton, William. *See* item E5 on p. 898.

D2. De Vinne, Theodore Low. *Office Manual, for the Use of Workmen in the Printing House of Theo. L. De Vinne & Co.* New York: 63 Murray Street, [1883].

Bibliographical notes: The inferred publication date is taken from the cover.

Locations: Iowa.

Gives practical instructions to compositors and pressmen employed in De Vinne's New York printing office.

Twentieth-century editions:

Manual of Printing Office Practice. Reprinted from the original edition of 1883, with an introductory note by Douglas C. McMurtrie. New York: Press of Ars Typographica, 1926.

Facsimile reprint of the 1926 edition:

Manual of Printing Office Practice. Forest Hills, NY: Battery Park Book Company, 1978.

D3. De Vinne, Theodore Low. *The Practice of Typography.* 4 vols. New York: Century Co., 1900–1904.

Bibliographical citations: Bliss (1900), 893; Bliss (1901); 893, 894; Bliss (1902), 895; Bliss (1904), 896; Wroth, 12.

Locations: A Treatise on the Processes of Type-Making, British; Vermont; William & Mary; *Correct Composition,* Massey; Toronto; *A Treatise on Title-Pages,* British; Massey; Toronto; Vermont; William & Mary; *Modern Methods of Book Composition,* Toronto.

Of primary interest to compositors and typographers. The volumes are titled: *A Treatise on the Processes of Type-Making, the Point System, the Names, Sizes, Styles, and Prices of Plain Printing Types*

(1900); *Correct Composition. A Treatise on Spelling, Abbreviations, the Compounding and Division of Words, the Proper Use of Figures and Numerals, Italic and Capital Letters, Notes, etc., with Observations on Punctuation and Proof-Reading* (1901); *A Treatise on Title-Pages. With Numerous Illustrations in Facsimile and Some Observations on the Early and Recent Printing of Books* (1902); and *Modern Methods of Book Composition. A Treatise on Type-Setting by Hand and by Machine and on the Proper Arrangement and Imposition of Pages* (1904). Sound typographical advice with many examples. Lacks specific information on iron handpresses and presswork.

Twentieth-century editions:

The Practice of Typography. 4 vols. New York: Oswald Publishing, 1914–1924.

D4. De Vinne, Theodore Low. *The Printers' Price List. A Manual for the Use of Clerks and Book-Keepers in Job Printing Offices.* New-York: Francis Hart & Company, 63 Cortlandt Street, 1869.

Bibliographical citations: Bigmore & Wyman, vol. I, p. 167.

Locations: Columbia (proof copy); Grolier; Harvard; Toronto; Virginia (De Vinne's proof copy).

First major American publication devoted exclusively to pricing. Primarily concerned with the scale of prices for labor, jobs, and materials in the printing industry. Also contains a considerable amount of sound information on practical printing.

Not seen.

D5. De Vinne, Theodore Low. *The Printers' Price List: A Manual for the Use of Clerks and Book-Keepers in Job Printing Offices.* [2nd ed.] New-York: Francis Hart and Company, 63 Cortlandt St., 1871.

Bibliographical notes: The copyright notice, on the verso of the title page, is dated 1870. The inferred edition statement is taken from p. 16 of the "Preface," which is dated December 21, 1870. In his "Preface," De Vinne refers to an earlier "first edition."

Bibliographical citations: Bigmore & Wyman, vol. I, p. 167; Bliss, 892; Marthens, p. 14.

Locations: Chicago; Columbia; Dartmouth; Delaware; Grolier (De Vinne's marked copy); Harvard; Huntington; Iowa; Kemble; LC; Massey; Newberry; NYPL; Philadelphia; Providence Public (with Robert Hoe's book label); St. Bride; SFPL; Toronto; UCLA; Yale.

A greatly expanded reprint of the 1869 edition, *see* item D4 above, with a new title page.

Facsimile reprints:

The Printers' Price List. With a new introduction by Irene Tichenor. New York: Garland Publishing, 1980. Series Statement: Nineteenth-Century Book Arts and Printing History.

De Vinne, Theodore Low. *See also* item 3 on p. 881.

Dialogue on Printers' Prices. See item C28 on p. 896.

D6. Dickinson, Samuel Nelson. *A Help to Printers and Publishers: Being a Series of Calculations, Showing the Quantity of Paper Required for a Given Number of Signatures in Book Work, and the Number of Tokens Contained Therein; Carried Out to an Extent That Will Seldom, If Ever, Fail to Embrace the Largest Jobs. Also an Extensive Table for Job Work, Showing the Quantity of Paper Required for a Given Number of Bills, Labels, Duplicates of Book Work, etc. etc.* Boston: Printed and published at 52 Washington Street, 1835.

Bibliographical citations: Bigmore & Wyman, vol. I, p. 173; Gaskell, E16; Marthens, p. 15.

Locations: Boston Athenæum; British; Clark; Columbia; Grolier; Harvard; Huntington; Kemble; Massey; Minnesota; Newberry; NYPL; Philadelphia; RIT; Virginia; Yale.

Consists of over 200 tables showing the quantity of paper needed for any given number of signatures. Lacks specific information on iron handpresses and practical printing.

D7. Dickinson, Samuel Nelson. *Specimens of Book Printing.* Boston: 1842.

Bibliographical notes: The bibliographical data is taken from Bigmore & Wyman, vol. I, p. 173.

No copies located.

Dwight, Walter T. *See* item M34 on p. 917.

E1. Earhart, John Franklin. *The Color Printer: A Treatise on the Use of Colors in Typographic Printing.* Cincinnati, Ohio: Earhart & Richardson, 1892.

Bibliographical citations: Bliss, 1167.

Locations: British; Cambridge; Grolier; Huntington; Kemble; LC; Massey; Newberry; Portland; Providence Public; RIT; SFPL; Sydney; Virginia; Yale.

A major work on the subject of mixing colored inks and color printing, requiring 625 different forms to produce. Lacks specific information on iron handpresses and presswork. Includes 90 color plates showing 166 colors, hues, tints, and shades together with the formulas for mixing them.

E2. Earhart, John Franklin. *The Harmonizer.* Cincinnati, Ohio: Earhart & Richardson, 1897.

Locations: Grolier; Huntington; Kemble; Massey; Providence Public; Vermont.

Primarily concerned with colored inks. Consists of a short introduction followed by numerous examples of colored inks mostly printed on colored papers. Lacks specific information on iron handpresses and practical printing.

E3. Ellis, John B. *Hints & Tables for the Printing Office and Paper Warehouse.* Leeds: Published by J. B. Ellis, 9,

Woodbine Square.; may also be had of W. Denton, 7, Briggate; and George Pallister, Printers' Furnisher, Top of Albion Street; printed by Fred. R. Spark, "Leeds Express" Office, [1887].

Bibliographical notes: The inferred publication date is taken from the "Preface," which is dated October, 1887.

Bibliographical citations: Wakeman, 33.

Locations: British; Cambridge [1888]; St. Bride.

A ready-reference guide for printers and compositors. Contains a section on "Hints for Printing Office Management," taken from *The Paper and Printing Trades Journal* and another on "Wood Letter Cutting," taken from Southward (1882), *see* item S26 on p. 927. Lacks specific information on iron handpresses and practical printing.

E4. Ellis, John B. *Hints & Tables for the Printing Office and Paper Warehouse.* Leeds: Published by J. B. Ellis, 10, Woodbine Square; printed by Fred. R. Spark and Son, [ca. 1890].

Bibliographical notes: The inferred publication date is taken from the St. Bride Printing Library record, call number: 191A. The "Preface" is dated October, 1887.

Locations: Bodleian; Delaware; St. Bride.

A reprint of the [1887] edition, *see* item E3 above, with a new title page, which also serves as the "Contents."

E5. Ellis, John B., and William Denton. *The Printers' Calculator and Practical Companion, Comprising a Scale of Wages on the Fifty-Four Hours' System, from 5s to £2; Table for Calculating Piece-Work; Sizes of Paper, with the Lengths of Reglets and Leads Required for Ordinary Jobbing Purposes; Table for Giving Out Paper; Lengths and Widths of Pages for Ordinary Book-Work, with the Number of Ens Contained in Each Page, from Pica to Nonpareil Inclusive; Series of Imposition Schemes; Abstract of the Leeds Compositors' Scale of Prices for News & Book-Work; Together with Numerous Other Useful Tables, &c.* Leeds: T. Barmby, publisher, 18, Briggate; may also be had of George Pallister, printers' broker, etc., Belgrave Street; Bernard and Co., Woodhouse Lane and Meadow Lane; printed by Fred. R. Spark, "Express" Office, Swinegate, 1876.

Bibliographical citations: Bigmore & Wyman, vol. I, p. 195.

Locations: British.

Primarily a guide to prices and calculations for printers. Contains ready references on wages, paper sizes, relative sizes of types, and length and width of pages for book work. Lacks specific information on iron handpresses and practical printing. Includes twenty pages of imposition schemes.

E6. Ellis, John B., and William Denton. *The Printers' Calculator and Practical Companion.* 2nd ed. Leeds: T. Barmby, publisher, 18, Briggate; may also be had of George Pallister, printers' broker, etc., Belgrave Street;

Bernard and Co., Woodhouse Lane and Meadow Lane; printed by Fred. R. Spark, "Express" Office, Swinegate, 1876.

Locations: St. Bride.

A reprint of item E5 above with a new title page, which also serves as the "Contents."

Evans, John. *See* item R8 on p. 922.

F1. Fielding, David. *The Typographical Ready-Reckoner and Memorandum-Book for the Use of Compositors, Pressmen, Machine-Men and Warehousemen; Showing the Number of Pica Ems in Width and Lines Containing a Thousand Ens from Pica, Small Pica, Long Primer, Bourgeois, Brevier, and Minion to Nonpareil; Lines per Hour, and the Number of Hours Produced in Composition from 1 to 1,000; the Price of Composition per Hour, from 5d. to 11d. and 1 to 1,000 hours; and the Quantity of Paper Required in Sheets for Any Job from 25 to 5,000 Copies, and from 2 to 118 on the Sheet.* London: 1853.

Bibliographical notes: The bibliographical data is taken from Bigmore & Wyman, vol. I, p. 217.

No copies located.

F2. Fielding, David. *The Typographical Ready-Reckoner and Memorandum-Book, for the Use of Compositors, Pressmen, Machinemen, and Warehousemen, Showing the Number of Pica Ems in Width, and Lines Containing a Thousand Ens, from Pica, Small Pica, Long Primer, Bourgeois, Brevier, and Minion, to Nonpareil; Lines per Hour, and the Number of Hours Produced in Composition, from One to One Thousand; the Price of Composition per Hour, from 5d. to 11d., and from One to a Thousand Hours; and the Quantity of Paper Required, in Quires and Sheets, for Any Job from 25 to 5000 Copies, and from 2 to 128 on the Sheet.* [2nd ed.] London: Printed by S. Whitwell, 10, Northumberland Terrace, Bagnigge Wells Road, [1857].

Bibliographical notes: The inferred publication date is taken from the author's note, which is dated May 1, 1857. The inferred edition statement was supplied by the compiler.

Locations: St. Bride.

Not seen.

F3. Fielding, David. *The Typographical Ready-Reckoner and Memorandum-Book, for the Use of Compositors, Pressmen, Machinemen, and Warehousemen, Showing the Number of Pica Ems in Width, and Lines Containing a Thousand Ens, from Pica, Small Pica, Long Primer, Bourgeois, Brevier, and Minion, to Nonpareil; Lines per Hour, and the Number of Hours Produced in Composition, from One to One Thousand; the Price of Composition per Hour, from 5d. to 11d., and from One to a Thousand Hours; and the Quantity of Paper Required, in Quires and Sheets, for Any Job from 25 to 5000 Copies, and from 2 to 128 on the Sheet.* [3rd ed.] London: Printed for the London Society of Compositors, by Blades, East & Blades, 23, Abchurch Lane, E.C., [1885].

Bibliographical notes: The inferred publication date is taken from the St. Bride Printing Library record, call number: 22629. The inferred edition statement was supplied by the compiler.

Locations: St. Bride.

Not seen.

Finch-Crisp, William. *See* Crisp, William Finch.

F4. Fisher, T. *The Elements of Letterpress Printing, Composing, and Proof-Reading. A Practical Manual for Indian Artisans.* With over sixty illustrations. Madras: Published by Higginbotham & Co., Mount Road; Bombay: Lukhmidass & Co. (late Karani & Co., Ltd.), Parsi Bazaar Street, Fort, 1895.

Bibliographical citations: Bliss, 1001.

Locations: Newberry; NYPL; RIT; St. Bride.

Primarily intended to train Indian artisans in all aspects of the printing trades. Contains sections on book work and Linotype composition. Indexed. Lacks specific information on iron handpresses and presswork.

Twentieth-century editions:

The Elements of Letterpress Printing Composing and Proof-Reading. A Practical Manual for Indian Artisans. 2nd ed., enlarged and revised. Madras: Published by Higginbotham & Co., Mount Road, 1906.

F5. [Ford, Thomas]. *The Compositor's Handbook: Designed As a Guide in the Composing Room. With the Practice As to Book, Job, Newspaper, Law, and Parliamentary Work; the London Scale of Prices; Appendix of Terms, etc.* London: Simpkin, Marshall, and Co., Stationers' Hall Court, 1854.

Bibliographical notes: The "Preface" is dated September 23, 1854.

Bibliographical citations: Bigmore & Wyman , vol. I, p. 224; Bliss, 962; Wakeman, 5.

Locations: Bodleian; Cambridge; Chicago; Columbia; Delaware; Iowa; Kemble; LC; Newberry; St. Bride.

Predominantly practical instructions for compositors. Also contains a section on the Columbian press used for job work, as well as excellent directions for imposing book work, making margin, and locking up the form. The section on brass rules was "extracted" from *Printing-Office Pamphlets* ([ca. 1840]), *see* item F6 below. Indexed. Includes thirty pages of imposition schemes.

F6. Ford, Thomas. *Printing-Office Pamphlets: Addressed to Master Printers, Overseers, Compositors, and the Trade Generally, on Subjects Relating to Management, Economy of Materials, etc. With Suggestions to Typefounders, Brass Rule Cutters, Printers' Joiners, &c., As to Improvements in Articles of Their Manufacture. No. 1. Brass Rule.* London: C. Mitchell, Newspaper Press Directory Office, [ca. 1840].

Bibliographical notes: The publication date is taken from the Bodleian Library record, call number: 25835 e.7 (12).

Bibliographical citations: Bigmore & Wyman [n.d.], vol. I, p. 224; Wakeman [1851], 2.

Locations: Bodleian.

This was the first in a projected series of short pamphlets on printing practices and was the first work devoted exclusively to the subject of brass rules. Ford advocated cutting brass rules to uniform sizes. It was followed by No. 2. on furniture, the only other known pamphlet in the series to be published, of which no copies were located.

Not seen.

F7. Francis, Jabez. *Printing at Home, with Full Instructions for Amateurs: Containing Illustrations of the Necessary Materials, with Explanatory Key. Specimens of Type, etc.* Rochford, Essex: Printed and published by Jabez Francis, [1870]

Bibliographical notes: The inferred publication date is taken from the copyright receipt stamp in the British Library's copy, shelfmark: 11899.b.40.(4.).

Bibliographical citations: Bigmore & Wyman, vol. I, p. 230.

Locations: British; Louisiana.

Primarily intended to instruct amateurs in the use of tabletop presses. Contains instructions for printing on four different models of small flatbed and platen presses manufactured by Francis. Lacks specific information on iron handpresses and presswork. Includes a frontispiece showing a family printing on a parlour-style press and an engraving of printing accessories, including the first depiction of a chase with screw quoins for tightening the side and footsticks, plus thirteen pages of type specimens.

F8. Francis, Jabez. *Printing at Home, with Full Instructions for Amateurs, Containing Illustrations of the Necessary Materials, with Explanatory Key, Specimens of Type, etc.* 2nd ed. Rochford, Essex: Printed and published by J. Francis & Son, [1873]

Bibliographical notes: The inferred publication date is taken from the St. Bride Printing Library record, call number: 23029.

Bibliographical citations: Marthens, p. 16.

Locations: Bodleian [1876]; St. Bride.

A reprint of the [1870] edition, *see* item F7 above, with a slightly modified title page and a new introduction, plus twelve pages of type specimens.

F9. Francis, Jabez. *Printing at Home, with Full Instructions for Amateurs, Containing Illustrations of the Nec-*

essary Materials, with Explanatory Key, Specimens of Type, &c. 3rd ed. Rochford, Essex: Printed and published by J. Francis and Sons, [ca. 1878].

Bibliographical notes: The inferred publication date is taken from the St. Bride Printing Library record, call number: 18015.

Bibliographical citations: Wakeman, 24.

Locations: British [1880]; Delaware; St. Bride.

A reset and expanded reprint of the [1873] edition, *see* item F8 above, with a slightly modified title page and a new introduction. Includes numerous illustrations in the text, as well as depictions of four of Francis's tabletop presses at the back of the book. The plate of printing accessories has been replaced by a smaller and modified wood engraving of it.

G1. Gannon, William. *The Amateur Printer: I. – The Compositor. A Manual of Instruction in the Typographic Art, with an Account of its Rise and Progress.* New York: Published by the Petersen Pub. Co., 102 Nassau Street, 1871.

Bibliographical notes: The copyright notice, on the verso of the title page, is dated 1870.

Locations: Iowa.

Even though intended for amateur printers, this is an exceedingly detailed manual, making it equally instructive for professional compositors. Lacks specific information on iron handpresses and presswork. Includes a frontispiece with a Washington press as well as numerous illustrations in the text, including the first use of a vignette with *putti* working at a Washington press. This image was the inspiration for the *putti* working at an Albion press used by Crisp ([1875]), *see* item C25 on p. 895. Gannon's image was later modified by MacKellar (1878), *see* item M13 on p. 914.

G2. Gaskill, Jackson. *The Printing-Machine Manager's Complete Practical Handbook; or, The Art of Machine Managing Fully Explained. for the Use of Master Printers, As Well As for the Practical Instruction and Special Guidance of Machine Managers.* London: J. Haddon & Co., 3, Bouverie Street, Fleet Street, E.C.; Edinburgh: Edinburgh Publishing Co., 22, Howe Street; Belfast: W. W. Cleland, 20, Great Victoria Street, 1877.

Bibliographical notes: The "Preface" is dated March, 1877.

Bibliographical citations: Bigmore & Wyman, vol. I, p. 255; Wakeman, 22.

Locations: Bodleian; British; Cambridge; Columbia; Grolier; Iowa; Princeton; St. Bride.

The first manual devoted entirely to machine printing, Contains current practices for book work on printing machines, making ready, printing wood blocks and electrotypes, and color printing, as well as an informative section on printing a six-block relief illustration. Lacks specific information on iron hand-

presses and presswork. Includes an illustration of a paper-wetting machine.

G3. [Gaskill, Jackson]. *The Printing-Machine Manager's Complete Practical Handbook, Specially Designed for the Use of the Young Machine Printer.* By an Old Machine Manager. 2nd. ed. London: J. Gaskill, 5, Paternoster Square, E.C.; and sold by all booksellers and printers' brokers, [1885?].

Bibliographical notes: The inferred publication date is taken from an advertisement pasted on the front endpaper of the copy in the Robertson Davies Library at Massey College. The edition statement is on the front cover.

Locations: Massey; St. Bride [ca. 1880].

A reprint of the 1877 edition, *see* item G2 above, with a new title page without the author's name. Two topics from the first edition were deleted, and fifteen new topics were added to the second. Lacks specific information on iron handpresses and presswork.

Not seen.

G4. Gazlay, Theodore. *The Practical Printers' Assistant: Containing Numerous Schemes of Imposition. Definite Directions for Making Composition Rollers, and Many Useful Tables.* Cincinnati: Stereotyped and published by J. A. James & Co., 1836.

Bibliographical citations: Gaskell, addendum, p. 31.

Locations: Cincinnati; LC; NYPL.

Intended primarily for American printers, with information on composing and practical presswork. Contains sections on preparing forms, new methods of imposing adapted specifically for American book work, and directions for making rollers. There are extensive instructions regarding inking with rollers, including the first mention of using roller bearers to elevate and level the roller. Indexed. Includes illustrations of Rust (Washington) and Smith presses made by the Cincinnati Type Foundry, plus fifty pages of imposition schemes. Gazlay was the first to give specific instructions for setting up Rust (Washington) and Smith presses.

Glass, Alexander Henry. *See* items J13 and J14 on p. 910.

G5. Gould, Joseph. *The Compositor's Guide and Pocket Book; Being the Whole Routine of Work As Practiced in Various Offices: Including Practical Instructions in Book, News, and Jobbing Composition; Casting-Up News and Book Work; Making-Up. Making Margin, Making Out Bills, and Other Necessary Information. Also, Complete Diagrams of Impositions.* London: Farrington & Co., Fetter Lane, Fleet St.; E. Marlborough & Co., 51, Old Bailey, E.C.; Middlesbrough: J. Gould, printer, 24, South Street, 1878.

Bibliographical citations: Wakeman, 25.

Locations: Bancroft: Bodleian; British; Huntington; Massey; Newberry; St. Bride.

Published as an inexpensive, ready-reference guide for compositors and pressmen working in small printing offices. Lacks specific information on iron handpresses and presswork.

Twentieth-century editions:

Wakeman, *see* above, mentions that there was a 1928 edition; however, no copies were located.

G6. Gould, Joseph. *The Letter-Press Printer: A Complete Guide to the Art of Printing; Containing Practical Instructions for Learners at Case, Press, and Machine. Embracing the Whole Practice of Book Work, with Diagram and Complete Schemes of Impositions; Job Work with Examples; News Work, Colour Work, to Make Coloured Inks, to Work Press and Machine, to Make Rollers, and Other Valuable Information.* London: Farrington & Co., 31, Fetter Lane, Fleet Street; Middlesbrough: J. Gould, printer, South Street, 1876.

Bibliographical notes: The "Preface" is dated November, 1876. It was also reprinted with an impression statement of "Third Thousand" on the title page. Both the first and second printings of this item were issued in editions of 1000 copies.

Bibliographical citations: Bigmore & Wyman, vol. I, p. 274; Bliss, 928; Wakeman, 18.

Locations: Bodleian; British; Columbia; Delaware; Harvard; Huntington; Iowa; Newberry; RIT; SFPL; Virginia; William & Mary; Yale.

An excellent manual on general printing practices. Contains sections on book, job, and news work, and handpress and machine work; with a glossary of "Technical Terms." Gould was the first to mention cleaning the form with "benzoline" instead of lye and water.

G7. Gould, Joseph. *The Letter-Press Printer: A Complete Guide to the Art of Printing; Containing Practical Instructions for Learners at Case, Press, and Machine. Embracing the Whole Practice of Book Work, with Diagram and Complete Schemes of Impositions; Job Work with Examples; News Work, Colour Work, to Make Coloured Inks, to Work Press and Machine, to Make Rollers, Instructions in Stereotyping and Other Valuable Information.* 2nd ed. London: Farrington & Co., 31, Fetter Lane, Fleet Street; E. Marlborough & Co., 51, Old Bailey, E.C.; Middlesbrough: J. Gould, printer, South Street, [1881].

Bibliographical notes: The inferred publication date is taken from the "Preface," which is dated May, 1881. This item was issued with an impression statement of "Fourth Thousand," "Fifth Thousand," or "Sixth Thousand" on the title page.

Locations: Bodleian; Chicago; Delaware; LC; Massey; Michigan; RIT; St. Bride; UCLA; Virginia; Yale.

A corrected and expanded reprint of the 1876 edition, of item G6 above, with a slightly modified title page. Contains a new section on stereotype printing.

G8. Gould, Joseph. *The Letter-Press Printer: A Complete Guide to the Art of Printing; Containing Practical Instructions for Learners at Case, Press, and Machine. Embracing the Whole Practice of Book Work, with Diagram and Complete Schemes of Impositions; Job Work with Examples; News Work, Colour Work, to Make Coloured Inks, to Work Press and Machine, to Make Rollers, Instructions in Stereotyping, and Other Valuable Information.* 3rd ed. London: Farrington & Co., 31, Fetter Lane, Fleet Street; E. Marlborough & Co., 51, Old Bailey, E.C.; Middlesbrough: J. Gould, printer, South Street, [1884].

Bibliographical notes: The inferred publication date is taken from the "Preface," which is dated May, 1884. It was issued with an impression statement of "Seventh Thousand," "Eighth Thousand," or "Ninth Thousand" on the title page.

Locations: Chicago; Delaware; Iowa; Kemble; LC; Michigan; Newberry; St. Bride; Sydney; Utah; Virginia; Yale.

A reprint of the [1881] edition, *see* item G7 above, with a slightly modified title page.

G9. Gould, Joseph. *The Letter-Press Printer: A Complete Guide to the Art of Printing; Containing Practical Instructions for Learners at Case, Press, and Machine. Embracing the Whole Practice of Book-Work, with Diagram and Complete Schemes of Impositions; Job Work with Examples; News-Work, Colour Work, to Make Rollers, Instructions in Stereotyping, and Other Valuable Information.* 4th ed. London: E. Marlborough & Co., 51, Old Bailey, E.C.; Farrington & Co., 31, Fetter Lane, Fleet Street; Middlesbrough: J. Gould, printer, South Street, [1888].

Bibliographical notes: The inferred publication date is taken from the "Preface," which is dated November, 1888. It was reprinted in 1890 with an impression statement of "Tenth Thousand" on the title page.

Locations: Bancroft; Cambridge; Delaware [1890]; Harvard; St. Bride; Virginia [1890].

A reprint of the [1881] edition, *see* item G7 above, with a slightly modified title page.

G10. Gould, Joseph. *The Letter-Press Printer: A Complete Guide to the Art of Printing; Containing Practical Instructions for Learners at Case, Press, and Machine. Embracing the Whole Practice of Book-Work, with Diagram and Complete Schemes of Impositions; Job Work with Examples; News-Work, Colour Work, to Make Rollers, Instructions in Stereotyping, and Other Valuable Information.* 5th ed. London: E. Marlborough & Co., 51, Old Bailey, E.C.; Farrington & Co., 31, Fetter Lane, Fleet Street; Middlesbrough: J. Gould, printer, South Street, [1893].

Bibliographical notes: The inferred publication date is taken from the "Preface," which is dated June, 1893.

Locations: Bodleian; British; Massey; Newberry; RIT; Virginia.

A reprint of the [1881] edition, *see* item G7 above, with a slightly modified title page.

Twentieth-century editions:

The Letter-Press Printer: A Complete Guide to the Art of Printing; Containing Practical Instructions for Learners at Case, Press, and Machine. Embracing the Whole Practice of Book-Work, with Diagram and Complete Schemes of Impositions; Job Work with Examples; News Work, Colour Work, to Make Coloured Inks, to Work Press and Machine, to Make Rollers, Instructions in Stereotyping, and Other Valuable Information. 6th ed. London: E. Marlborough & Co., 51, Old Bailey, E.C., [1904].

Bibliographical notes: The inferred date for this item varies. Delaware and NYPL use [ca. 1894]; Bodleian and St. Bride use [1903]; and British uses [1904].

The Letter-Press Printer: A Complete Guide to the Art of Printing. Containing Practical Instructions for Learners at Case, Press, and Machine. Embracing the Whole Practice of Book-Work. With Diagram and Complete Schemes of Impositions; Job Work with Examples; News Work, Colour Work, to Make Coloured Inks, to Work Press and Machine, to Make Rollers, Instructions in Stereotyping, and Other Valuable Information. 6th ed. London: E. Marlborough & Co., Ltd., 51, Old Bailey, E.C. 4, [1927].

G11. Government of India, Printing Department. *Hand-Book of the Central Printing Office.* 2nd ed. Calcutta: Printed by the Superintendent of Government Printing, 1886.

Bibliographical notes: The "Preface to the Second Edition" is signed by A. Sanderson and E. J. Dean, and is followed by the "Preface to the First Edition," which is dated January 1, 1880, and also signed by Sanderson and Dean.

Locations: St. Bride.

An expanded reprint of the 1880 edition. Contains very detailed information on every aspect of the printing business, including the iron handpress and presswork. New divisions on the "Bindery" and "Foundries" were added. Includes fourteen imposition schemes.

No copies of the first edition were located.

G12. Government of India, Printing Department. *Hand-Book of the Central Printing Office.* 3rd ed., corrected to 1st April 1899. Calcutta: Office of the Superintendent, Government Printing, India, 1899.

Bibliographical notes: The "Preface" is signed by Charles Sanderson and William Ross.

Locations: Providence Public; St. Bride.

An abridged reprint of the 1886 edition, *see* item G11 above.

G13. Graham, John. *The Compositor's Text-Book; or, Instructions in the Elements of the Art of Printing: Con-sisting of an Essay on Punctuation, with Rules and Examples; Directions on the Use of Capitals; Greek and Hebrew Alphabets; Rules for Distributing and Composing; with Various Schemes of Imposition, &c.* Glasgow: Richard Griffin and Company; London: John Joseph Griffin & Co., 1848.

Bibliographical notes: The "Preface" is signed by John Wilson and John Graham.

Bibliographical citations: Bigmore & Wyman, vol. I, p. 277.

Locations: Bodleian; British; Huntington; Newberry; NYPL; St. Bride; Virginia.

A new edition of *The Text-Book* (1826), *see* item S16 on p. 925. Primarily intended for compositors. Lacks specific information on handpresses and practical printing. Includes twenty-five pages of imposition schemes.

G14. Grattan, Edward. *The Printer's Companion: Being Practical Directions for Filling the Various Situations in a Printing Office: Embodying a System of Punctuation, and Copious Original Directions for Composing Greek and Hebrew.* Philadelphia: Printed and published by the proprietor; and for sale by all type founders, 1846.

Bibliographical citations: Bigmore & Wyman, vol. I, p. 279; Gaskell, E23; Marthens, p. 18.

Locations: Columbia; Huntington; Toronto; Virginia; William & Mary.

A short, but comprehensive, manual containing considerable new material on general printing practices. Intended primarily for the use of apprentices and journeymen. Contains sections on printing on job and power presses, although the emphasis is on working at the iron handpress. Also contains sections on the making, care, and use of rollers, as well as the arrangement of a job office. Among the firsts that Grattan mentions are the use of figures for signatures, closets for dampened paper (humidors), pins for paper guides, detailed directions for preparing a makeready, frisket bearers, and metal roller and platen bearers. Includes illustrations of Washington (two different views) and Smith presses, plus five pages of imposition schemes.

Facsimile reprints:

The Printer's Companion. With a new introduction by Clinton Sisson. New York: Garland Publishing, 1981. Series Statement: Nineteenth-Century Book Arts and Printing History.

Bound together with *The Printer's Manual* by Caleb Stower (1817), *see* item S43 on p. 929.

G15. *The Guide to Trade: The Printer.* London: Charles Knight and Co., Ludgate Street, 1838.

Bibliographical citations: Marthens, p. 37; Wakeman [1838–1856], 6. Marthens uses the title for the main entry, listing it under anonymous works at the back. In some bibliographies, this item is listed under Charles Knight.

Locations: Delaware; Huntington; LC; Massey; St. Bride.

A reprint of *The Printer* ([1833]) by Houlston and Stoneman with a different title page, *see* item P6 on p. 920.

G16. *The Guide to Trade: The Printer.* London: Charles Knight and Co., Ludgate Street, 1843.

Locations: St. Bride.

A reprint of the 1838 edition, *see* item G15 above.

H1. Hall, Charles Carter. *The Art of Printing, Historical and Practical: Embracing an Outline of the Antecedents, Rise, and Progress of the Art, with Brief Biographical Sketches of Its Founders. To Which Is Added a Concise Elementary Guide: Being a Series of Practical Schemes for the Economization of Labour.* Sheffield: Pawson and Brailsford, No. 5, High-Street; published by the author, Britannia Office, Castle-Street, 1860.

Bibliographical citations: Bigmore & Wyman, vol. I, p. 296.

Locations: St. Bride.

An excellent and useful guide. The first fifty pages are devoted to the history of the art of printing; the remaining thirty-eight consist of brief, but concise, descriptions of practical printing. Contains short paragraphs on the Stanhope, Sector, Albion, Columbian, Imperial, and Britannia presses. The iron handpress is recommended for the majority of small jobs. The emphasis is on the "economization of labour."

H2. Hansard, Thomas Curson. *Typographia: An Historical Sketch of the Origin and Progress of the Art of Printing; with Practical Directions for Conducting Every Department in an Office: With a Description of Stereotype and Lithography.* Illustrated by engravings, biographical notices, and portraits. London: Printed for Baldwin, Cradock, and Joy, 1825.

Bibliographical citations: Bigmore & Wyman, vol. I, p. 301; Bliss, 931; Davis & Carter, 10; Gaskell, E13; Hitchings, XI; Marthens, p. 18; Wroth, 8.

Locations: Bancroft; Bodleian; Boston Public; Cambridge; Clark; Columbia; Dartmouth; Delaware; Grolier; Harvard; Huntington; Kemble; Massey; Michigan; Minnesota; Newberry; RIT; St. Bride; SFPL; Toronto; Vermont; Virginia; William & Mary; Yale.

The most comprehensive manual of its period, with a lengthy historical introduction. Contains sections on composition, handpresses – including the Blaew (Blaeu) wooden press; three late-eighteenth-century wooden presses: the Ridley, Prosser, and Moore presses; four early-nineteenth-century wooden presses: the Medhurst, Roworth, Brown, and Sector presses, as well as the Brooke press with the Stanhope application; and eight iron handpresses including the Stanhope (first construction), Cogger, Columbian, Barclay, Stafford, Jedburgh, Dr. Church's, Russel (i.e., Russell), and Cope (Albion) presses – printing machines (described in great detail), presswork, decorative printing, stereotype printing, making composition rollers, inking, and improved printing accessories such as metal furniture and adjustable tympans; with a glossary of "Technical Terms Used in Printing." Indexed. Hansard was the first to include information on copperplate and lithographic printing in a manual on letterpress printing. He was also the first to elaborate on the new division of labor that existed between the puller and the roller-boy brought about by the widespread use of rollers. Includes illustrations of the "printing press of the original construction" and its parts, the "common press and the application of the Stanhope power" and its parts – this is the same cut of Brooke's press in Stower (1808), *see* item S42 on p. 929, with the addition of an ear on the frisket – the Stanhope press and its parts, the Ruthven, Cogger, and Columbian presses, as well as several printing machines, including Rutt's Printing Machine, which first appeared in Savage (1822), *see* item S12 on p. 924, plus twenty-eight pages of imposition schemes.

Facsimile reprints:
Thomas C. Hansard: Typographia, 1825. London: Gregg Press, 1966. Series statement: English Bibliographical Sources, edited by D. F. Foxon, British Museum. Series 3: Printers' Manuals, no. 6.

Typographia: An Historical Sketch of the Origin and Progress of the Art of Printing. 2 vols. Bristol: Thoemmes Press; Tokyo: Kinokuniya, 1998. Series statement: Nico Editions, Classic Works on the History of the Book. Book Design and Production. First Collection: Pre-Victorian British Typography and Printers' Manuals.

A complete facsimile with the following exceptions: the two-page list of engravings is missing; additional colors in the original were printed in black; and most of the plates are out of sequence.

H3. [Hansard, Thomas Curson]. *Typographia: An Historical Sketch of the Origin and Progress of the Art of Printing; with Practical Directions for Conducting an Office.* [abridged] London: Plackett & Moody, St. Bride's Press, St. Bride's Avenue, Fleet Street, [1869].

Bibliographical notes: The inferred publication date is taken from the "Preface," which is dated March 10, 1869. The inferred edition statement is taken from a comment on p. [i] of the "Preface," "It was determined to use such portions only as would be valuable to the practical reader."

Bibliographical citations: Bigmore & Wyman, vol. I, p. 301; Hitchings, XII; Gaskell, E13; Bliss, 932.

Locations: LC; Michigan; St. Bride; UCLA.

A severely abridged reprint of the 1825 edition, *see* item H2 above.

H4. Hansard, Thomas Curson, Jr. *Treatises on Printing and Type-Founding; from the Seventh Edition of the* Encyclopædia Britannica [1842]. Edinburgh: Adam and Charles Black, North Bridge, booksellers to Her Majesty, 1841.

Bibliographical citations: Bigmore & Wyman, vol. I, p. 305; Bliss, 933; Marthens, p. 18. When describing this item, Marthens confuses Hansard Sr. with Hansard Jr.

Locations: Berkeley; Boston Public; Cambridge; Chicago; Grolier; Huntington; Iowa; Kemble; LC; Michigan; Newberry; NYPL; Providence Public (three copies); RIT; St. Bride; SFPL; Toronto; UCLA; Virginia; William & Mary; Yale.

Primarily an overview for the lay person written by the son of the author of *Typographia* (1825), *see* item H2 above. Excellent information on iron handpresses and presswork. Contains the first description of printing on a Stanhope press. Also contains a section on wood blocks taken from Houghton (1841), *see* item H18 on p. 906, and one on lithographic printing by William Nichol taken from the seventh edition of the *Encyclopædia Britannica* (1842). Includes illustrations of a Stanhope press (first construction) and a detail of its mechanism, as well as Cowper's printing machine, plus three pages of imposition schemes. This item was published in book form before the *Encyclopædia* was issued.

H5. Hansard, Thomas Curson, Jr. *The Art of Printing: Its History and Practice from the Days of John Gutenberg.* Edinburgh: Adam and Charles Black, North Bridge, booksellers to Her Majesty, 1851.

Bibliographical citations: Bigmore & Wyman, vol. I, p. 305.

Locations: Boston Public; Chicago; Clark; Delaware; Massey; Newberry; North Carolina; St. Bride; Sydney; UCLA; Virginia; William & Mary.

A reprint of the 1841 edition, *see* item H4 above, with a new title. Hansard's contribution on printing for the eighth edition of the *Encyclopædia Britannica* (1861) was also condensed and issued as an essay in *Five Black Arts* (Columbus, OH: Follett, Foster, 1861), and later reprinted as *History of the Processes of Manufacture and Uses of Printing, Gas-light, Pottery, Glass, and Iron. From the* Encyclopædia Britannica (New York: John Bradburn, 1864).

H6. Harland, John Whitfield. *The Printing Arts: An Epitome of the Theory, Practice, Processes, and Mutual Relations of Engraving, Lithography, & Printing in Black and in Colours.* With illustrations. London: Ward, Lock, Bowden and Co., Warwick House, Salisbury Square, E.C.; New York: East 12th Street; Melbourne: 3 and 5, St. James's Street, 1892.

Locations: Delaware; Iowa; LC; Massey; North Carolina; NYPL; St. Bride; UCLA

Detailed descriptions of graphic arts techniques.

Indexed. Lacks specific information on iron handpresses.

H7. Harpel, Oscar Henry. *Harpel's Typograph; or, Book of Specimens. Containing Useful Information, Suggestions and a Collection of Examples of Letterpress Job Printing Arranged for the Assistance of Master Printers, Amateurs, Apprentices, and Others.* Cincinnati: Printed and published by the author, 1870.

Bibliographical citations: Bigmore & Wyman, vol. I, p. 306; Bliss, 898; Marthens, p. 18.

Locations: Boston Public; Delaware; Grolier; Huntington; Kemble; Kentucky; Massey; Newberry; NYPL; Providence Public; RIT; SFPL; Toronto; Utah; William & Mary (two copies, both imperfect); Yale.

Features design and color work. Contains excellent instructions for practical printing and the printing of wood engravings; with a glossary of "Technical Terms Used by Printers." Harpel added V and W to his signature tables. He was the first to mention mechanical quoins, drying racks, "typographic design," and printing on parchment. Indexed. Lacks specific information on iron handpresses. Includes numerous illustrations of printing accessories including mechanical quoins, plus six pages of imposition schemes and fourteen pages of advertisements in an addenda at the back. This superb example of nineteenth-century color printing required 476,000 impressions for an edition of less than three thousand copies.

H8. Hart, M. C. *The Amateur Printer; or, Type-Setting at Home. A Complete Instructor for the Amateur in All the Details of the Printer's Art.* With explanatory engravings. New York: Dick & Fitzgerald, publishers, 1883.

Bibliographical notes: The copyright notice, on the verso of the title page, is dated 1883.

Locations: LC.

Even though intended for boys using tabletop presses, this is a thorough and informative handbook for anyone engaged in composing type. Contains numerous illustrations related to composing, including cases, the composing stick, setting type, emptying the stick, and distributing type.

H9. Hazen, Edward. *The Panorama of Professions and Trades; or, Every Man's Book.* Embellished with eighty-two engravings. Philadelphia: Published by Uriah Hunt; sold by the booksellers generally, 1836.

Bibliographical notes: Reprinted in 1837, 1839, 1841, 1845, and 1863. The words "& Son" were added to the imprint in 1863.

Bibliographical citations: Bliss, 206.

Locations: Chicago, [1836], [1837], [1863]; Vermont [1836]; Washington, [1836].

Intended for the general public, but more specifically for school children, as a guide to various professions and trades as a means to encourage the latter to make enlightened decisions about their futures careers. The section on printing gives a brief history of the art of printing as well as a short description of early-nineteenth-century printing practices. Includes an illustration of printers working at a wooden press.

Facsimile of the 1837 edition:
The Panorama of Professions and Trades or Every Man's Book. Embellished with eighty-two engravings. Watkins Glen, NY: Century House, 1970.

A complete facsimile with the following exceptions: the words "Encyclopedia of E.A. Trades" were inserted between the top pair of rules and the Century House imprint was inserted between the bottom pair of rules; and the original copyright page was replaced by a new one.

H10. Hazen, Edward. *Popular Technology; or, Professions and Trades.* Embellished with eighty-one engravings. 2 vols. New-York: Harper and Brothers, 82 Cliff-St., 1841.

Bibliographical notes: Reprinted in 1842, 1843, 1844, 1845, 1846, 1850, 1857, and 1859.

Locations: Bancroft, [1857]; British, [1843], [1844]; LC, 1846].

A resetting in one column of the 1836 edition, *see* item H9 above, with a new title.

Facsimile of the 1846 edition:
Popular Technology; or, Professions and Trades. (Hazen's Panorama.) Embellished with eighty-one engravings. 2 vols. [Albany, NY]: Early American Industries Association, 1981.

H11. Herbert, A. *The Art of Printing. A Practical Guide for the Use of Amateurs: In Which All the Details and Processes Are Fully and Clearly Explained.* Illustrated. London: Printed on the Optimus Press, 1879.

Bibliographical citations: Wakeman, 27.

Locations: Delaware.

Primarily intended for amateurs working on tabletop presses. This item was printed on the Optimus press, which is described in the text; with a "Glossary." Indexed. Lacks specific information on iron hand-presses and presswork. In addition to two views of the press a wooden flatbed platen press activated by a lever – there are a number of illustrations of printing accessories, including a planer, an ink roller, and an ink slab.

H12. *The History of Printing.* Published under the Direction of the Committee of General Literature and Education Appointed by the Society for Promoting Christian Knowledge. London: Printed for the Society for Promoting Christian Knowledge; sold at the depositories, Great Queen Street, Lincoln's Inn Fields; 4, Royal Exchange; 16, Hanover Street, Hanover Square; and by all booksellers, 1855.

Bibliographical citations: Marthens [1852], p. 37; Wakeman, 7.

Locations: Bodleian; Cambridge; Grolier; Providence Public; St. Bride; SFPL (2 variant copies, one with 2 leaves of advertisements).

Primarily a survey of printing practices. Contains sections on handpresses and printing machines, stereotype, color and lithographic printing, and wood engravings. Lacks specific information on presswork. Includes illustrations of the Blaen (i.e., Blaeu) wooden press, the Stanhope (first construction), and Albion presses, as well as the Imperial press with a detail of the lever in the head of its frame, the Columbian press with a diagram of how its levers work, and an ink stand and hand roller.

H13. *The History of Printing.* Published under the Direction of the Committee of General Literature and Education, Appointed by the Society for Promoting Christian Knowledge. London: Society for Promoting Christian Knowledge; sold at the depositories, 77, Great Queen Street, Lincoln's Inn Fields; 4, Royal Exchange; 16, Hanover Street, Hanover Square; and by all booksellers, [1862].

Bibliographical notes: The inferred publication date is taken from the British Library record, shelfmark: 11899.b.35. This same record gives Charles Tomlinson as the inferred author.

Bibliographical citations: Bigmore & Wyman, vol. I, p. 330.

Locations: Bodleian; Bridwell; Cambridge; Delaware; Huntington; St. Bride; Tokyo.

A revised and expanded reprint of the 1855 edition, *see* item H12 above, with a new title page. The spelling of *Blaeu* was corrected in this edition. According to Bigmore & Wyman, below, the book is very "inexact, and behind the times, in its statements."

H14. Hodgson, Thomas. *An Essay on the Origin and Process of Stereotype Printing; Including a Description of the Various Processes.* Newcastle: Printed by and for S. Hodgson, Union-Street; and sold by E. Charnley, Bigg-Market, 1820.

Bibliographical citations: Bigmore & Wyman, vol. I, p. 330; Bliss, 1020; Marthens, p. 19.

Locations: Massey; Toronto; Sydney; Washington.

A meticulous and interesting account of the art of stereotyping up to 1820.

Facsimile reprints:
An Essay on the Origin and Progress of Stereotype Printing. With a new introduction by Michael L. Turner. New York: Garland Publishing, 1982. Series Statement: Nineteenth-Century Book Arts and Printing History.

Bound together with *The Method of Founding Stereotype, as Practiced by Charles Brightly, of Bungay, Suffolk.* by Charles Brightly (1809), *see* item B25 on p. 891.

H15. Hoe, R., & Co. *Hints to Stereotypers and Elec-*

trotypers. New York: R. Hoe & Co., 1871

Bibliographical notes: The bibliographical data is taken from Bigmore & Wyman, vol. I, p. 331.

No copies located

H16. Hoe, R., & Co. *Hints on Electrotyping and Stereotyping.* New York: R. Hoe & Co., Grand, Sheriff, Broome and Columbia Streets, and Nos. 29 & 31 Gold Street; Chicago, Ill.: 84 Dearborn St.; London, E.C.: Tudor Street, 1875

Bibliographical citations: Bigmore & Wyman, vol. I, p. 332.

Locations: Columbia; Delaware; Iowa; LC; NYPL.

A very detailed step-by-step description of the processes for making electrotype and stereotype plates. Contains instructions for stereotyping with plaster and clay molds, as well as the "papier mache" process. Includes twenty-seven illustrations of accessories and machines – manufactured by R, Hoe & Co. – for each phase of the operation.

H17. Holtzapffel & Co. *Printing Apparatus for the Use of Amateurs. Containing Full and Practical Instructions for the Use of Cowper's Parlour Printing Press. Also the Description of Larger Presses on the Same Principle and Various Other Apparatus for the Amateur Typographer. The Whole Manufactured and Sold Only by Holtzapffel & Co., Engine, Lathe, and Tool Manufacturers, London. The Pamphlet Contains Likewise, Numerous Specimens of Plain and Ornamental Types, Brass Rules, Checks, Borders, Ornaments, Corners, Arms, &c., &c.* 3rd ed., greatly enlarged. London: Published by Holtzapffel & Co., 64, Charing Cross and 127, Long Acre; and to be had of all booksellers, 1846.

Bibliographical citations: Bigmore & Wyman, vol. I, p. 342; Bliss 1147.

Locations: Bancroft; British; Columbia; Grolier; Harvard; Illinois; Massey; Newberry; RIT; Yale.

No copies of the first and second editions were located.

Primarily intended for amateurs using Cowper's Parlour press. Lacks specific information on handpress printing, but contains good advice on general printing practices that can be applied to the handpress. This is the first manual to recommend turpentine as an alternative to lye and water for cleaning type. Includes two illustrations of the Parlour press, one open, the other closed.

Facsimile reprints:
Charles Holtzapffel's *Printing Apparatus for the Use of Amateurs.* Reprinted from the third greatly enlarged edition of 1846 and edited by James Mosley and David Chambers. [Pinner, Middlesex]: Private Libraries Association, 1971.

Hoover, H. *See* item H26 on p. 907.

H18. Houghton, Thomas Shaw. *The Printers' Practical Every-Day-Book, Calculated to Assist the Young Printer to Work with Ease and Expedition.* London: Simpkin, Marshall, & Co., Stationers' Hall Court; Preston: H. Oakey, Fishergate, 1841.

Bibliographical citations: Bigmore & Wyman, vol. I, p. 346; Gaskell, E20; Marthens, p. 19. Gaskell refers to separate London and Preston editions.

Locations: British; Bodleian; LC; Newberry; St. Bride.

A comprehensive manual with much new information on presswork and general printing practices, including advice on the proper use of rollers. Contains instructions for setting up the Columbian and Imperial presses, chapters on composing news, job, and book work, machine printing, printing in colors and gold, and descriptions of improved materials; with a glossary of "Technical Terms used in Printing." Houghton was the first to give hints on the use of labor-saving furniture, rules, and leads. Includes illustrations of the Columbian and Imperial presses, plus fourteen pages of imposition schemes with instructions for "burying" light or blank pages in the middle of a form.

H19. Houghton, Thomas Shaw. *The Printers' Practical Every-Day-Book, Calculated to Assist the Young Printer to Work with Ease and Expedition.* 2nd ed. London: Simpkin, Marshall, & Co., Stationers' Hall Court; Preston: H. Oakey, Fishergate, 1842.

Bibliographical citations: Gaskell, E20.

Locations: British.

A reprint of the 1841 edition, *see* item H18 above, with a new title page and minor changes. Includes illustrations of the Imperial and Columbian presses, as well as an illustration of the frame of the latter.

H20. Houghton, Thomas Shaw. *The Printers' Practical Every-Day-Book, Calculated to Assist the Young Printer to Work with Ease and Expedition.* 3rd ed. London: Simpkin, Marshall, & Co., Stationers' Hall Court; Preston: H. Oakey, Fishergate, 1843.

Bibliographical citations: Gaskell, E20.

Locations: British; Delaware; Iowa; St. Bride.

A reprint of the 1842 edition, *see* item H19 above, with a new title page.

H21. Houghton, Thomas Shaw. *The Printers' Practical Every-Day-Book, Calculated to Assist the Young Printer to Work with Ease and Expedition.* 4th ed. London: Simpkin, Marshall, & Co., Stationers' Hall Court; Preston: H. Oakey, Fishergate, 1849.

Bibliographical citations: Bigmore & Wyman, vol. I, p. 346; Gaskell, E20.

Locations: Columbia; St. Bride.

A reprint of the 1842 edition, *see* item H19 above, with a new title page.

H22. Houghton, Thomas Shaw. *The Printers' Practical Every Day Book.* Lancashire: To be had only from the author, Slope Bank, Fulwood Park, near Preston; where all communications must be addressed, [1856].

Bibliographical notes: The inferred publication date is taken from the British Library record, shelfmark: D–7942.aa.6. This copy was destroyed during World War II.

Bibliographical citations: Gaskell, E20.

Locations: Yale [185–?].

A reprint of the 1842 edition, *see* item H19 above, with a new title page.

Not seen.

H23. Houghton, Thomas Shaw. *The Printers' Practical Every Day Book.* [Improved edition.] Lancashire: To be had only from the author, Slope Bank Cottage, Freehold Park, near Preston; where all communications must be addressed, 1857.

Bibliographical notes: The edition statement is taken from the "Advertisement to Improved Edition" on p. [v]. The word *improved* also appears on the half-title page.

Bibliographical citations: Bigmore & Wyman, vol. I, p. 346; Gaskell, E20.

Locations: Columbia.

Largely rewritten reprint of the 1842 edition, *see* item H19 above. Contains information on new developments in printing accessories and equipment; with a glossary of "Technical Terms used in Printing." The chapter on machine printing was omitted in this edition.

H24. Houghton, Thomas Shaw. *The Printers' Practical Every Day Book.* Southport, Lancashire: To be had only from the author, Lily Bank, Tulketh Street; where all communications must be addressed, [ca. 1865].

Bibliographical notes: The inferred publication date is taken from the British Library record, shelfmark: 1568/1237.

Bibliographical citations: Gaskell, E20.

Locations: British; Massey; St. Bride [1854].

An expanded reprint of the 1857 edition, *see* item H23 above, with a new title page.

H25. Houghton, Thomas Shaw. *The Printers' Practical Every Day Book.* With emendations and additions by George Marshall. Preston: Published by G. Marshall, 12, St. Wilfrid St., [1875]

Bibliographical notes: The inferred publication date is taken from a testimonial letter – dated Jan. 17th, 1875 – on p. [152], to Geo. Marshall from Joseph Huntington.

Bibliographical citations: Bigmore & Wyman, vol. I, p. 346.

Locations: Columbia; Huntington; NYPL; St. Bride.

"This is a stereotype reprint of the major parts of Houghton's Manual, with several serious omissions and a few unimportant and valueless interpolations by Mr. Marshall." – Bigmore & Wyman, above.

H26. *How to Print: A Descriptive Catalogue of the Celebrated Model Printing Press, with Samples of Its Work, Specimens of Type, Instructions in Printing, Particulars about Outfits, General Price-List of Materials, &c., &c.* Revised ed. Various American imprints between 1876 and 1887.

Bibliographical notes: The publication dates were supplied by Stephen O. Saxe.

Bibliographical citations: Bliss, 899.

Locations: Huntington (Daughaday); Newberry (Hoover); Philadelphia (Daughaday).

Intended for amateurs, the American imprints are primarily catalogs for tabletop vertical platen presses, printing accessories, and foundry type. Contains just a few pages on how to print on the Model Printing Press. Lacks specific information on iron handpresses and presswork. Includes numerous illustrations of the presses, printing accessories, and type specimens.

H27. *How to Print. Model Self-Inking Printing Press, Type, and Printing Material.* Revised and enlarged edition, cancelling previous publications. London: C.G. Squintani & Co., 3, Ludgate Circus Building, E.C., 1884.

Locations: British.

A combination handbook and catalog similar to the American imprints, *see* item H26 above. The English imprints have longer sections on practical printing on both tabletop vertical platen presses and the Albion press.

H28. *How to Print.* Revised and enlarged edition, cancelling previous publications. London: The Model Printing Press Co., Ltd., 63, Farringdon Street, E.C., 1897.

Bibliographical citations: Wakeman, 51.

Locations: Delaware.

A revised and enlarged reprint of the 1884 edition, *see* item H27 above, with a new title page.

H29. Howitt, Felix H. *The Country Printers' Job Price Book Containing the Master Printer's Charges to the Public for Various Descriptions of Jobs, Together with Several Valuable Receipts.* London: Simpkin, Marshall, & Co., Stationer's Hall Court, [1849].

Bibliographical notes: The inferred publication date is taken from the author's prefatory note, which is dated May, 1849.

Bibliographical citations: Bigmore & Wyman, vol. I, p. 346; Wakeman, 1.

Locations: British

Mainly for small job offices. Contains prices for all types of job work. Lacks information on iron handpresses and presswork. Intended to replace Philip Rose's *The Printer's Job Price Book* ([1824]), *see* item R9 on p. 922.

H30. Howitt, Felix H. *The Country Printers' Job Price Book Containing the Master Printer's Charges to the Public for Various Descriptions of Jobs, Together with Several Valuable Receipts.* 2nd ed. Revised and corrected by the author. London: Longman & Co.; Simpkin & Co.; Hamilton, Adams & Co.; Orr & Co.; and Strange, [1849].

Bibliographical notes: The inferred publication date is taken from the author's prefatory note, which is dated September, 1849.

Locations: St. Bride.

A revised and enlarged reprint of item H29 above with a slightly modified title page.

I1. The Inland Printer. *The Inland Printer Vest Pocket Manual of Printing: A Convenient Reference Book for Employing Printers, Pressmen, Compositors, Newspaper Men, and Others. Containing Rules of Punctuation and Capitalization, Valuable Tables, and a Complete and Accurate Series of Diagrams of Imposition.* Chicago: The Inland Printer, 212–214 Monroe St., 1894.

Locations: Bancroft.

A pocket reference book of useful information for printers. Lacks specific information on iron handpresses and practical printing.

Instructions for Amateur Printers. See item W2 on p. 932.

J1. Jacobi, Charles Thomas. *On the Making and Issuing of Books.* London: Made at The Chiswick Press, and issued from The Bodley Head, by Elkin Mathews, Vigo St. W., 1891.

Bibliographical citations: Bliss, 216.

Locations: Bodleian (small paper); British (large and small paper); Providence Public (small paper); Sydney; Tokyo; Toronto.

A guide for authors. Indexed. Lacks information on practical printing. This item was issued in a large paper edition of 50 copies and a small paper edition of 435 copies.

J2. Jacobi, Charles Thomas, comp. *The Printers' Handbook of Trade Recipes, Hints, & Suggestions Relating to Letterpress and Lithographic Printing, Bookbinding, Stationery Engraving, etc. With Many Useful Tables and an Index.* London: The Chiswick Press, 21, Tooks Court, Chancery Lane, 1887.

Bibliographical citations: Bliss, 936; Wakeman, 34.

Locations: Berkeley; Bodleian; British; Cambridge; Clark; Delaware; Grolier; Massey; NYPL; Philadelphia; Providence Public; St. Bride; SFPL; Toronto; Vermont; Yale.

Contains numerous tips, including advice on such diverse topics as protection against cockroaches, siz-

ing and dampening paper, and cleaning forms with steam. Indexed.

J3. Jacobi, Charles Thomas, comp. *The Printers' Handbook of Trade Recipes, Hints, & Suggestions Relating to Letterpress and Lithographic Printing, Bookbinding, Stationery Engraving, etc. With Many Useful Tables and an Index.* 2nd ed., enlarged and classified. London: The Chiswick Press, 20 & 21, Tooks Court, Chancery Lane, 1891.

Locations: Bodleian; Boston Public; British; Cambridge; Grolier; Providence Public; RIT; St. Bride; Sydney; UCLA; Virginia; Yale.

An expanded – almost doubled in size – and better organized reprint of the 1887 edition, *see* item J2 above. The information is arranged by department or trade. Contains sections on setting up the Columbian and Albion presses, hard packing, and fine printing.

Twentieth-century editions:

The Printers' Handbook of Trade Recipes, Hints, and Suggestions Relating to Letterpress and Lithographic Printing, Bookbinding, Stationery, Process Work, etc. 3rd ed., revised and enlarged. London: Charles Thomas Jacobi, 1905.

J4. Jacobi, Charles Thomas. *The Printers' Vocabulary: A Collection of Some 2500 Technical Terms, Phrases, Abbreviations, and Other Expressions Mostly Relating to Letterpress Printing, Many of Which Have Been in Use Since the Time of Caxton.* London: Chiswick Press, 21, Tooks Court, Chancery Lane, 1888.

Bibliographical citations: Wakeman, 36.

Locations: Bodleian; LC; Massey; Providence Public; Sydney.

By far the most comprehensive nineteenth-century printers' vocabulary. Contains short definitions of printing terms from Moxon through the late 1880s.

J5. Jacobi, Charles Thomas. *Printing: A Practical Treatise on the Art of Typography As Applied More Particularly to the Printing of Books. And Many Useful Tables, Together with Glossarial Index of Technical Terms and Phrases.* With upwards of 150 illustrations. Technical Handbooks. London: George Bell and Sons, York Street, Covent Garden, 1890.

Bibliographical citations: Wakeman, 40.

Locations: Bodleian; Boston Public; Brown; Cambridge; Delaware; Huntington; Massey; Providence Public; St. Bride; UCLA; Utah; William & Mary; Yale.

A comprehensive manual focusing on book work. Contains eight chapters on handpresses and presswork, sections on type, composition, machine printing, and the operation of the warehouse; with a "Glossarial Index." Jacobi was the first to mention Linotype. Includes illustrations of the action of the Stanhope levers, the Columbian and Albion presses with two diagrams of the Albion chill, as well as numerous illustrations of printing accessories, plus nine pages of imposition schemes.

J6. Jacobi, Charles Thomas. *Printing: A Practical Treatise on the Art of Typography As Applied More Particularly to the Printing of Books. And Many Useful Tables, Together with Glossarial Index of Technical Terms and Phrases.* With upwards of 150 illustrations. Technical Handbooks. London and New York: George Bell & Sons, York St., Covent Garden, 1893.

Locations: Cambridge; NYPL; RIT; St. Bride.

A reprint of the 1890 edition, *see* item J5 above, with a slightly modified title page.

J7. Jacobi, Charles Thomas. *Printing: A Practical Treatise on the Art of Typography As Applied More Particularly to the Printing of Books. And Many Useful Tables, Together with the C. & G.L.I. Examination Questions (1892–7) and Glossarial Index.* With upwards of 150 illustrations. Technical Handbooks. 2nd ed. London: George Bell & Sons, York St., Covent Garden, and New York, 1898.

Locations: Delaware; Grolier; Kentucky; Massey; Providence Public; RIT; Utah; Virginia; Yale.

A reprint of the 1890 edition, *see* item J5 above, with a new title page and a new section on examination questions. Includes sixteen samples of paper at the back.

Twentieth-century editions:
Printing: A Practical Treatise on the Art of Typography As Applied More Particularly to the Printing of Books. 3rd ed., revised and enlarged. London: George Bell and Sons, 1904.

Printing: A Practical Treatise on the Art of Typography As Applied More Particularly to the Printing of Books. 4th ed., revised. London: George Bell and Sons, 1908.

Printing: A Practical Treatise on the Art of Typography As Applied More Particularly to the Printing of Books. 5th ed., revised. London: G. Bell and Sons, 1913.

Printing: A Practical Treatise on the Art of Typography As Applied More Particularly to the Printing of Books. 6th ed., revised and enlarged. London: G. Bell and Sons, 1919.

Printing: A Practical Treatise on the Art of Typography As Applied More Particularly to the Printing of Books. 6th ed., reprinted. London: G. Bell and Sons, 1925.

J8. Jacobi, Charles Thomas. *Some Notes on Books and Printing: A Guide for Authors and Others.* London: Chiswick Press, Charles Whittingham and Co., Tooks Court, Chancery Lane, 1892.

Locations: Bodleian; British; Brown; Massey; Tokyo; Vermont; William & Mary.

A revised reprint of item J1 on p. 908 with a new title. Primarily a guide to acquaint authors with the various aspects of book production; with a "Glossary." Indexed. Lacks specific information on iron hand-

presses and practical printing. Includes typographical specimens and samples of papers at the back.

Twentieth-century editions:
Some Notes on Books and Printing: A Guide for Authors, Publishers & Others. New and enlarged edition. London: Charles Whittingham and Co., 1902.

J9. Johnson, John. *Typographia; or, The Printers' Instructor: Including an Account of the Origin of Printing, with Biographical Notices of the Printers of England, from Caxton to the Close of the Sixteenth Century: A Series of Ancient and Modern Alphabets, and Domesday Characters: Together with an Elucidation of Every Subject Connected with the Art.* 2 vols. London: Published by Messrs. Longman, Hurst, Rees, Orme, Brown & Green, Pater-noster Row, 1824.

Bibliographical citations: Bigmore & Wyman, vol. I, p. 371; Bliss, 938; Davis & Carter, 9; Gaskell, E12; Hitchings, X; Marthens, p. 21; Wroth, 7.

Locations: Bodleian (large and small paper); Boston Athenæum (large paper); Cambridge (large and small paper); Clark (large paper); Columbia (large paper); Dartmouth (small paper); Grolier (large and small paper); Harvard (small paper); Huntington (large and small paper); Kemble (small paper); Massey (large and small paper); Michigan (small paper); Newberry (large and small paper); Philadelphia (large paper); Providence Public (large and small paper); RIT (large and small paper); St. Bride (large and small paper); SFPL (large and small paper); Sydney (large and small paper); Utah (large and small paper); Toronto (small paper); Vermont (large paper); Virginia (large paper); William & Mary (one large and two small paper); Yale (large and small paper).

A work in two volumes: the first, historical; the second, practical. The latter contains sections on composition, presswork, and general printing practices, much of which is derived from Moxon (1683), *see* item 2 on p. 880; Smith (1755), *see* item 12 on p. 883; and Stower (1808), *see* item S42 on p. 929. Johnson describes the improved wooden press, the Stanhope, Columbian, and Ruthven presses, as well as composition balls, hand rollers, and overlays. He was also the first to mention the Sector, Cogger, Russell, and Albion presses; with numerous examples of exotic and ancient types and a glossary of "Technical Terms Made Use of by the Profession." Indexed. Includes illustrations of the "working part" of the largest wooden press in England, a Blaew (Blaeu) press, and an improved wooden press and its parts and accessories, the Stanhope press (second construction) and its parts, the Columbian press, and the Albion press and its parts, as well as a hand roller and inking frame (ink table), plus forty-six pages of imposition schemes. In Volume I, p. 555, and Volume II, p. 498, there are facsimiles of two sixteenth-century woodcuts, each showing a beater and a puller working at a wooden press.

Facsimile reprints:
John Johnson: Typographia or the Printer's Instructor, 1824. 2 vols. London: Gregg Press, 1966. Series statement: English Bibliographical Sources, edited by D. F. Foxon, British Museum. Series 3: Printers' Manuals, no. 5.

J10. [Johnson, John, and Thomas F. Adams]. *An Abridgment of Johnson's Typographia; or, The Printers' Instructor: With an Appendix.* Boston: C. L. Adams, print., 1828.

Bibliographical citations: Bigmore & Wyman, vol. I, p. 373; Bliss, 880; Gaskell, E12; Hitchings, 2; Marthens, p. 36. Bliss and Hitchings use Thomas F. Adams for the main entry; Marthens uses the title for the main entry, listing it under anonymous works at the back.

Locations: American Antiquarian Society; Columbia; Grolier; Harvard; Huntington; Iowa; Newberry; Philadelphia; William & Mary (two copies).

An abridgment of Johnson (1824), *see* item J9 above, along with an appendix of new American material attributed to Thomas F. Adams. The sections on practical presswork are limited to the wooden press. The appendix contains descriptions of Stanhope, Columbian, Albion, Smith, Wells, Couillard, and Washington presses, as well as the Williams four-cylinder printing machine. The appendix also contains information on skin rollers and compo balls and advocates the use of rollers; with a glossary of "Technical Terms." Indexed. Includes illustrations of the Columbian (on the frontispiece), Stanhope, Albion, Smith, Wells, Washington (in an acorn frame), and Couillard presses, as well as inking frames, plus forty-six pages of imposition schemes. The description of the Washington press – its first appearance in a printers' manual – reads in its entirety more like a caption: "Was invented by Mr. Rust of New York; and is manufactured by Messrs. Rust & Turney." The facsimile of a 1548 woodcut, on p. 296, showing a beater and a puller at a wooden press and a lad in the drying room handling paper, is repeated from the 1824 edition mentioned above.

J11. Johnson, L. & Co. *The Printer's General Hand-Book of Needful Information Respecting Types, Presses, and Other Essentials of a Printing Office with Valuable Tables, Directions, Etc.* Philadelphia: L. Johnson & Co., 6 Sansom Street, above Sixth, 1857.

Locations: William & Mary.

Not seen.

J12. Joyner, George. *Fine Printing: Its Inception, Development, and Practice.* With twelve artistic supplements illustrating the tendency of fine work. London: Printed and published by Cooper and Budd, High Street, Peckham, 1895.

Bibliographical citations: Wakeman, 49.

Locations: Bodleian; British; Delaware; Grolier; Massey; St. Bride; SFPL; Sydney; UCLA; William & Mary.

Joyner, who was greatly influenced by Earhart (1892), *see* item E1 on p. 897, defines fine printing and gives practical instructions on how to achieve it. Contains sections on making ready wood and halftone engravings, embossing, and selecting the proper equipment and materials necessary for quality printing. Lacks specific information on iron handpresses and presswork. Includes twelve inserted examples of "artistic printing."

J13. Judd & Glass. *Counsels to Authors and Hints to Advertisers.* [Compiled by James Judd and Alexander Henry Glass.] London: Judd & Glass, Gray's Inn Road; and sold by Simpkin, Marshall & Co., Paternoster Row, 1856.

Bibliographical citations: Wakeman, 8. Wakeman uses the title for the main entry.

Locations: British; Delaware.

A printers' promotional piece offering their services to co-publish authors' manuscripts. Lacks information on iron handpresses and practical printing. Includes many examples of sample pages set in various typefaces, as well as designs for title pages and book covers. In the section on "Hints to Advertisers," there are three wood engravings showing their Composing Room, Press Room, with three iron handpresses and a lithographic press, and Binding Room.

J14. Judd & Glass. *Counsels to Authors.* [Compiled by James Judd and Alexander Henry Glass.] London: Judd & Glass, 38 New Bridge Street, and 16 Gray's Inn Road, 1857.

Locations: Chicago; Glasgow; St. Bride.

A modified reprint of the 1856 edition, *see* item J13 above.

Judd, James. *See* items J13 and J14 above.

K1. Kelly, William J. *Presswork. A Practical Handbook for the Use of Pressmen and Their Apprentices.* Chicago, Ill.: The Inland Printer Company, 212–214 Monroe Street, 1894.

Locations: Chicago; Huntington; Iowa; Kemble; LC; Newberry; NYPL; Providence Public.

A good beginner's manual with sound general printing practices for cylinder presses. Contains sections on making ready, preparing under- and overlays, and hard packing. Kelly extols the virtues of the iron handpress and has a short chapter devoted to printing on it. The contents page is in the form of an index of subject headings.

K2. Kelly, William J. *Presswork. A Practical Handbook for the Use of Pressmen and Their Apprentices.* Chicago, Ill.: The Inland Printer Company, 212–214 Monroe Street, 1897.

Bibliographical notes: The copyright notice, on the verso of the title page, is dated 1894.

Locations: Bodleian.

A reprint of the 1894 edition, *see* item K1 above.

K3. Kelly, William J. *Presswork. A Practical Handbook for the Use of Pressmen and Their Apprentices.* Chicago, Ill.: The Inland Printer Company, 212–214 Monroe Street, 1898.

Bibliographical notes: The copyright notice, on the verso of the title page, is dated 1894.

Locations: Bodleian; Delaware.

A reprint of the 1894 edition, *see* item K1 above.

Twentieth-century editions:
Presswork: A Practical Handbook for the Use of Pressmen and Their Apprentices. 2nd ed., revised and enlarged. Chicago: Inland Printer, 1902.

K4. Kivlan, William. *The Typographic Calculator for the Use of Printers. A Ready-Reckoner for Ascertaining with Certainty and without Computation the Exact Contents of Any Page or Piece of Matter of Which the Length and Width Are Known.* Cambridge, [MA]: Riverside Press, 1870.

Bibliographical notes: The bibliographical data is taken from the Harvard Library record, call number: B 6008.8*.

Bibliographic citations: Bigmore & Wyman, vol. I, p. 383; Marthens, p. 22. Both Bigmore & Wyman and Marthens use "Kilvan" for the author's surname and "1871" for the publication date.

Locations: Harvard.

Not seen.

Knight, Charles. *See* items G15 and G16 on pp. 902 and 903 respectively.

K5. Krumbholz, G. *The Country Printer. A Manual, Containing Valuable Recipes and Useful Information Gathered among Recognized Practical Men and Extracted from Our Leading Trade Journals.* North Greenfield, Milwaukee County, Wis.: G. Krumbholz, publisher, 1893.

Bibliographical notes: The publication date is taken from the copyright notice on the title page.

Locations: Iowa; LC; NYPL; RIT.

A short manual full of good tips for printing on vertical platen and cylinder presses. Contains sections on making ready, as well as more exotic topics, such as printing in gold leaf on silk or satin and making flong for stereotypes. The contents page, at the back of the book, is in the form of an index of subject headings. Lacks specific information on iron handpresses and presswork, although many of these hints are also applicable to handpress printing.

L1. Lawton, J. W. *The Printers' Pocket Companion: Contain-*

ing Imposition and Other Valuable Tables; New and Comprehensive Job Price List, etc., etc. Rochdale: Published by J. W. Lawton, 12, Old Market-Place, [1870].

Bibliographical notes: The inferred publication date is taken from the St. Bride Printing Library record, call number: 23488.

Bibliographical citations: Bigmore & Wyman, (Lawton) vol. I, p. 423; Bigmore & Wyman, (*Pocket Companion*) vol. II, p. 214; Bigmore & Wyman, (*The Printers' Pocket Companion*) vol. II, p. 222. The St. Bride Printing Library record lists the same item under Lawton, but the format is not the same as those listed in Bigmore & Wyman.

Locations: St. Bride.

A compendium of hard-to-remember facts such as signatures, sizes, prices, etc., plus fourteen pages of imposition schemes. Lacks specific information on iron handpresses and practical printing. Half of the book consists of advertisements.

L2. *The London Scale of Prices for Compositors' Work, Agreed upon April 16th, 1810 with Additions, Definitions, and Explanations, As Arranged between the Master Printers and Compositors at a Conference Held in the Months of July, August, September, and October, 1847.* London: Printed by J. & H. Cox (Brothers), Great Queen Street, Lincoln's-Inn Fields, 1847.

Locations: Toronto.

A mid-century scale of prices. Lacks specific information on iron handpresses and practical printing.

Not seen.

L3. London Society of Compositors. *The London Scale of Prices for Compositors' Work: Agreed upon February 18, 1891, by the Representatives of the Printing and Allied Trades' Association and the London Society of Compositors, at a Conference Held at Stationers' Hall.* London: Printed for the London Society of Compositors, 3, Raquet Court, Fleet Street, E.C., by C. F. Roworth, 5–11, Great New Street, Fetter Lane, E.C., 1891.

Locations: St. Bride.

The Society's first scale was published in 1879; its last nineteenth-century scale was published in 1899. Lacks specific information on iron handpresses and practical printing.

L4. London Union of Compositors. *The London Scale of Prices for Compositors' Work: Agreed upon, April 16th, 1810, with Explanatory Notes, and the Scales of Leeds, York, Dublin, Belfast, and Edinburgh.* London: Printed under the superintendence of the Trade Council of the London Union of Compositors, by R. Thompson & Co., Elim Place, Fetter Lane; and sold by W. Lambert, Red Lion Court, Fleet Street, [1835].

Bibliographical notes: The inferred publication date is taken from p. vii of the "Preface," in which reference is made to "the Scale of 1835."

Locations: British; Delaware; Massey; St. Bride; Vermont [1810?].

A scale of prices. Lacks specific information on iron handpresses and practical printing.

L5. Lynch, Thomas. *The Printer's Manual: A Practical Guide for Compositors and Pressmen. To Which Is Appended the Manner of Putting Together and Using Printing-Machines.* Cincinnati: Published by the Cincinnati Type-Foundry, 1859.

Bibliographical citations: Hitchings, p. 30; Marthens, p. 23.

Locations: Berkeley; Boston Public; Cincinnati; Columbia; Huntington; LC; Newberry; Pittsburgh; St. Bride; Yale.

For the most part, this is an original work with an emphasis on book and job printing. Contains excellent sections on preparing forms, printing wood engravings, mixing inks, printing in colors, and a short paragraph on setting up a handpress; with a glossary of "Technical Terms," which doubles as an index. In the section on colored inks, Lynch quotes extensively from Savage (1832), *see* item S11 on p. 924, interjecting his own comments about Savage's procedures. Lynch was the first to give directions for dampening vellum for printing and to mention ink in cans. Includes fifty imposition schemes.

Facsimile reprints:
The Printer's Manual: A Practical Guide for Compositors and Pressmen. With an introduction by Peter M. Van Wingen. New York: Garland Publishing, 1981. Series Statement: Nineteenth-Century Book Arts and Printing History.

L6. Lynch, Thomas. *The Printer's Manual: A Practical Guide for Compositors and Pressmen.* [2nd ed.] Cincinnati: Published by the Cincinnati Type-Foundry, 1864.

Bibliographical notes: The inferred edition statement is taken from comments made by the author in the "Preface."

Bibliographical citations: Bliss, 903.

Locations: Boston Public; Cincinnati; Harvard; Kemble; Providence Public.

An abridgment of the 1859 edition, *see* item L5 above, with a new "Preface." The sections on "erecting and using printing presses" and the "paper-use tables" were deleted. Includes forty-seven imposition schemes.

L7. Lynch, Thomas. *The Printer's Manual: A Practical Guide for Compositors and Pressmen.* Cincinnati: Published by the Cincinnati Type-Foundry, 1866.

Bibliographical citations: Bliss, 904.

Locations: Clark; Delaware; NYPL; RIT; William & Mary.

A reprint of the 1864 edition, *see* item L6 above, with a slightly modified title page.

L8. Lynch, Thomas. *The Printer's Manual: A Practical Guide for Compositors and Pressmen.* Cincinnati: Published by the Cincinnati Type-Foundry, 1872.

Bibliographical citations: Bigmore & Wyman, vol. I, p. 448.

Locations: Cincinnati; Columbia; Delaware; Grolier; Harvard; Iowa; LC; Newberry; NYPL; RIT; St. Bride; Sydney; Syracuse; Utah; William & Mary; Yale.

A reprint of the 1866 edition, *see* item L7 above, with a slightly modified title page.

Machris & Aveling. *See* item M1 below and items T8 and T9 on p. 932.

M1. Machris, Charles, comp. *The Printer's Book of Designs. Containing Various and Sundry Designs, Executed with Brass Rule.* Detroit, Mich.: Published by Endriss & Machris, 1877.

Bibliographical citations: Bigmore & Wyman, vol. II, p. 3

Locations: Providence Public; St. Bride.

Consists of numerous designs created with brass rules for job printers.

M2. MacKellar, Thomas. *The American Printer: A Manual of Typography, Containing Complete Instructions for Beginners, As Well As Practical Directions for Managing All Departments of a Printing Office. With Several Useful Tables, Schemes for Imposing Forms in Every Variety, Hints to Authors and Publishers, etc., etc.* Philadelphia: Published by L. Johnson & Company, 1866.

Bibliographical citations: Bigmore & Wyman, vol. II, p. 3; Bliss, 905; Hitchings, 5; Marthens, p. 24; Wroth, 11.

Locations: British; Columbia; Grolier; Huntington; Iowa; Philadelphia; Providence Public; UCLA; Yale.

This easy-to-read, well organized printers' manual replaced Adams's manuals (1837–1864), *see* items A2 through A16 beginning on p. 885. It prevailed as the standard American manual until the end of the 19th century. Contains excellent information on both iron handpresses and printing machines, as well as general printing practices for book and job work. Also contains sections on setting up the Washington press, the roller stand, making ready a form, dampening paper, rolling and pulling on handpresses, printing wood engravings, color printing, fine handpress work, and the warehouse; with a glossary of "Technical Terms of the Craft." MacKellar was the first to show signature tables with both letters and figures. His imposition schemes indicate letters, but his manuals continued to use figures. He was also the first to give specific dimensions for the wetting trough and to describe hard packing. Indexed. Includes illustrations of the Columbian, Washington, and Bronstrup presses, and various printing machines and accessories, such as labor saving quotations, plus fifty pages of imposition schemes.

M3. MacKellar, Thomas. *The American Printer: A Manual of Typography, Containing Complete Instructions for Beginners, As Well As Practical Directions for Managing All Departments of a Printing Office. With Several Useful Tables, Schemes for Imposing Forms in Every Variety, Hints to Authors and Publishers, etc., etc.* 2nd ed. Philadelphia: Published by L. Johnson & Company, 1866.

Bibliographical notes: The edition statement is on the verso of the title page.

Bibliographical citations: Hitchings, 5b.

Locations: Columbia; Harvard; Huntington; Kemble; Newberry; William & Mary; Yale.

A reprint, from electrotypes, of the 1866 edition, *see* item M2 above, with a slightly modified title page and minor changes.

M4. MacKellar, Thomas. *The American Printer: A Manual of Typography, Containing Complete Instructions for Beginners, As Well As Practical Directions for Managing All Departments of a Printing Office. With Several Useful Tables, Schemes for Imposing Forms in Every Variety, Hints to Authors and Publishers, etc., etc.* 3rd ed. Philadelphia: MacKellar, Smiths & Jordan, 1867.

Bibliographical notes: The edition statement is on the verso of the title page.

Locations: Columbia; Kemble; Newberry; NYPL; St. Bride; SFPL; Virginia; Yale.

A reprint of the 1866 edition, *see* item M2 above, with a slightly modified title page and minor changes.

M5. MacKellar, Thomas. *The American Printer: A Manual of Typography, Containing Complete Instructions for Beginners, As Well As Practical Directions for Managing All Departments of a Printing Office. With Several Useful Tables, Schemes for Imposing Forms in Every Variety, Hints to Authors and Publishers, etc., etc.* 4th ed. Philadelphia: MacKellar, Smiths & Jordan, 1868.

Bibliographical notes: The edition statement is on the verso of the title page.

Bibliographical citations: Hitchings, 5c.

Locations: Columbia; Grolier; Huntington; Kemble; Portland; Yale.

A reprint of the 1866 edition, *see* item M2 above, with a slightly modified title page and minor changes.

M6. MacKellar, Thomas. *The American Printer: A Manual of Typography: Containing Complete Instructions for Beginners, As Well As Practical Directions for Managing All Departments of a Printing Office. With Several Useful Tables, Schemes for Imposing Forms in Every Variety, Hints to Authors and Publishers, etc.* 5th ed. Philadelphia: MacKellar, Smiths & Jordan, 1870.

Bibliographical notes: The edition statement is on the verso of the title page.

Locations: Columbia; Grolier; Harvard; Iowa; Kemble; LC; RIT; SFPL; Yale.

A reprint of the 1866 edition, *see* item M2 above, with a slightly modified title page and minor changes.

M7. MacKellar, Thomas. *The American Printer: A Manual of Typography, Containing Complete Instructions for Beginners, As Well As Practical Directions for Managing Every Department of a Printing Office. With Several Useful Tables, Numerous Schemes for Imposing Forms in Every Variety, Hints to Authors, etc.* 6th ed. Philadelphia: MacKellar, Smiths & Jordan, 1871.

Bibliographical notes: The edition statement is on the verso of the title page.

Bibliographical citations: Bliss, 906.

Locations: Columbia; Harvard; Iowa; Kemble; LC; Minnesota; NYPL; SFPL; Toronto; William & Mary (lacking title page); Yale.

A reprint of the 1866 edition, *see* item M2 above, with a slightly modified title page and minor changes.

M8. MacKellar, Thomas. *The American Printer: A Manual of Typography, Containing Complete Instructions for Beginners, As Well As Practical Directions for Managing Every Department of a Printing Office. With Several Useful Tables, Numerous Schemes for Imposing Forms in Every Variety, Hints to Authors, etc.* 7th ed. Philadelphia: MacKellar, Smiths & Jordan, 1872.

Bibliographical notes: The edition statement is on the verso of the title page.

Bibliographical citations: Bliss, 907.

Locations: Columbia; Harvard; Iowa; NYPL; Virginia; Yale.

A reprint of the 1866 edition, *see* item M2 above, with a slightly modified title page and minor changes.

M9. MacKellar, Thomas. *The American Printer: A Manual of Typography, Containing Complete Instructions for Beginners, As Well As Practical Directions for Managing Every Department of a Printing Office. With Several Useful Tables, Numerous Schemes for Imposing Forms in Every Variety, Hints to Authors, etc.* 8th ed. Philadelphia: MacKellar, Smiths & Jordan, 1873.

Bibliographical notes: The edition statement is on the verso of the title page.

Bibliographical citations: Bliss, 908; Hitchings, 5d.

Locations: Columbia; Iowa; Kemble; Massey; RIT; St. Bride; Utah; Yale.

A reprint of the 1866 edition, *see* item M2 above, with a slightly modified title page and minor changes.

M10. MacKellar, Thomas. *The American Printer: A Manual of Typography, Containing Complete Instructions for Beginners, As Well As Practical Directions for Managing Every Department of a Printing Office. With Several Useful Tables, Numerous Schemes for Imposing Forms in Every Variety, Hints to Authors, etc.* 9th ed. Philadelphia: MacKellar, Smiths & Jordan, 1874.

Bibliographical notes: The edition statement is on the verso of the title page.

Bibliographical citations: Bigmore & Wyman, vol. II, p. 3; Bliss, 909.

Locations: Chicago; Columbia; Iowa; Kemble; Newberry; SFPL; Yale.

A reprint of the 1866 edition, *see* item M2 above, with a slightly modified title page and minor changes.

M11. MacKellar, Thomas. *The American Printer: A Manual of Typography, Containing Complete Instructions for Beginners, As Well As Practical Directions for Managing Every Department of a Printing Office. With Several Useful Tables, Numerous Schemes for Imposing Forms in Every Variety, Hints to Authors, etc.* 10th ed. Philadelphia: MacKellar, Smiths & Jordan, 1876.

Bibliographical notes: The edition statement is on the verso of the title page.

Bibliographical citations: Bliss, 910.

Locations: Columbia; Harvard; Kemble; Providence Public; RIT; Yale.

A reprint of the 1866 edition, *see* item M2 above, with a slightly modified title page and minor changes.

M12. MacKellar, Thomas. *The American Printer: A Manual of Typography, Containing Complete Instructions for Beginners, As Well As Practical Directions for Managing Every Department of a Printing Office. With Several Useful Tables, Numerous Schemes for Imposing Forms in Every Variety, Hints to Authors, etc.* 10th ed. Philadelphia: MacKellar, Smiths & Jordan, 1878.

Bibliographical notes: The edition statement is on the verso of the title page.

Locations: St. Bride; SFPL.

A reprint of the 1876 edition, *see* item M11 above, with a publication date of 1878 on the title page.

M13. MacKellar, Thomas. *The American Printer: A Manual of Typography, Containing Practical Directions for Managing All Departments of a Printing Office, As Well As Complete Instructions for Apprentices: With Several Useful Tables, Numerous Schemes for Imposing Forms in Every Variety, Hints to Authors, etc.* 11th ed., revised and enlarged. Philadelphia: MacKellar, Smiths & Jordan, 1878.

Bibliographical notes: The edition statement is on the verso of the title page.

Bibliographical citations: Bliss, 911.

Locations: Boston Public; Columbia; Iowa; Kemble; LC; Sydney; Syracuse; William & Mary; Yale.

First revised edition. Contains new sections on jobbing facilities, useful "receipts," and the metric system. The illustrations of the printing machines and job presses have been updated. Also includes illustrations of a woman working at a book folding machine, a lad at a roller stand, an improved standing press, a proof press, and a vignette on p. 149 of *putti* as pressmen working on opposite sides of the bed of the press.

M14. MacKellar, Thomas. *The American Printer: A Manual of Typography, Containing Practical Directions for Managing All Departments of a Printing Office, As Well As Complete Instructions for Apprentices: With Several Useful Tables, Numerous Schemes for Imposing Forms in Every Variety, Hints to Authors, etc.* 12th ed., revised and enlarged. Philadelphia: MacKellar, Smiths & Jordan, 1879.

Bibliographical notes: The edition statement is on the verso of the title page. The note to "The Twelfth Edition" is dated March, 1880.

Bibliographical citations: Bigmore & Wyman, vol. II, p. 3; Bliss, 912.

Locations: Harvard; Iowa; Kemble; Providence Public; RIT; St. Bride; SFPL; Tokyo; Utah; Virginia; Yale.

A reprint of the 1878 edition, *see* item M13 above, with a slightly modified title page and minor changes.

M15. MacKellar, Thomas. *The American Printer: A Manual of Typography, Containing Practical Directions for Managing All Departments of a Printing Office, As Well As Complete Instructions for Apprentices: With Several Useful Tables, Numerous Schemes for Imposing Forms in Every Variety, Hints to Authors, etc.* 13th ed., revised and enlarged. Philadelphia: MacKellar, Smiths & Jordan, 1882.

Bibliographical notes: The edition statement is on the verso of the title page.

Locations: Grolier; Kemble; Yale.

A reprint of the 1878 edition, *see* item M13 above, with a slightly modified title page and minor changes.

M16. MacKellar, Thomas. *The American Printer: A Manual of Typography, Containing Practical Directions for Managing All Departments of a Printing Office, As Well As Complete Instructions for Apprentices: With Several Useful Tables, Numerous Schemes for Imposing Forms in Every Variety, Hints to Authors, etc.* 14th ed., revised and enlarged. Philadelphia: MacKellar, Smiths & Jordan, 1883.

Bibliographical notes: The edition statement is on the verso of the title page.

Bibliographical citations: Bliss, 913.

Locations: Columbia; Harvard; Iowa; Kemble; Massey; Michigan; Newberry; NYPL; Utah; Yale.

A reprint of the 1878 edition, *see* item M13 above, with a slightly modified title page and minor changes. Includes illustrations of mechanical quoins.

M17. MacKellar, Thomas. *The American Printer: A Manual of Typography, Containing Practical Directions for Managing All Departments of a Printing Office, As Well As Complete Instructions for Apprentices: With Several Useful Tables, Numerous Schemes for Imposing*

Forms in Every Variety, Hints to Authors, etc. 15th ed., revised and enlarged. Philadelphia: MacKellar, Smiths & Jordan, 1885.

Bibliographical notes: The edition statement is on the verso of the title page.

Bibliographical citations: Hitchings, 5e.

Locations: British; Brown; Columbia; Iowa; Massey; Newberry; NYPL; Providence Public; Yale.

A reprint of the 1878 edition, *see* item M13 above, with a slightly modified title page and minor changes. Includes illustrations of Hempel's quoins and standard metal furniture.

Facsimile reprint of the 1885 edition:

The American Printer: A Manual of Typography, Containing Practical Directions for Managing All Departments of a Printing Office, As Well As Complete Instructions for Apprentices: With Several Useful Tables, Numerous Schemes for Imposing Forms in Every Variety, Hints to Authors, etc. With a new Preface by Terry Belanger. Nevada City, CA: Harold A. Berliner, 1977.

The facsimile edition copyright notice, on the verso of the facsimile title page, is dated 1976.

A complete facsimile, with the following exception: a portrait of MacKellar taken from an original photograph, owned by Columbia University, was used for the frontispiece.

M18. MacKellar, Thomas. *The American Printer: A Manual of Typography, Containing Practical Directions for Managing All Departments of a Printing Office, As Well As Complete Instructions for Apprentices: With Several Useful Tables, Numerous Schemes for Imposing Forms in Every Variety, Hints to Authors, etc.* 16th ed., revised and enlarged. Philadelphia: The MacKellar, Smiths & Jordan Co., 1887.

Bibliographical notes: The edition statement is on the verso of the title page. The note to the "Sixteenth Edition" is dated December, 1886.

Bibliographical citations: Bliss, 914; Hitchings, 5f.

Locations: Bodleian; British; Columbia; Iowa; Kemble; LC; RIT; Utah; Yale.

A reprint of the 1878 edition, *see* item M13 above, with a slightly modified title page and minor changes.

M19. MacKellar, Thomas. *The American Printer: A Manual of Typography, Containing Practical Directions for Managing All Departments of a Printing Office, As Well As Complete Instructions for Apprentices: With Several Useful Tables, Numerous Schemes for Imposing Forms in Every Variety, Hints to Authors, etc.* 17th ed., revised and enlarged. Philadelphia: The MacKellar, Smiths & Jordan Co., 1889.

Bibliographical notes: The edition statement is on the verso of the title page.

Bibliographical citations: Bliss, 915; Hitchings, 5g.

Locations: Boston Public; Columbia; Delaware; Grolier; Iowa; Kemble; Newberry; SFPL; Toronto; Virginia; Utah; Yale.

A reprint of the 1878 edition, *see* item M13 above, with a slightly modified title page and minor changes, including two additional pages on photoengraving.

M20. MacKellar, Thomas. *The American Printer: A Manual of Typography, Containing Practical Directions for Managing All Departments of a Printing Office, As Well As Complete Instructions for Apprentices: With Several Useful Tables, Numerous Schemes for Imposing Forms in Every Variety, Hints to Authors, etc.* 18th ed., revised and enlarged. Philadelphia: MacKellar, Smiths & Jordan Foundry, 1893.

Bibliographical notes: The edition statement is on the verso of the title page.

Bibliographical citations: Hitchings, 5h.

Locations: Boston Public; Columbia; Huntington; Iowa; Kemble; Kentucky; Newberry; UCLA; Virginia; Yale.

A reprint of the 1878 edition, *see* item M13 above, with a slightly modified title page and minor changes.

M21. Magrath, William. *The Printers' Assistant; Containing Typographical Tables, and a Few Select Schemes of Difficult Impositions; Together with Scales of Prices for Compositors and Pressmen. To Which Is Added, a Correct List of Master Printers, Letter Founders, Joiners, and Printers' Smiths, &c. &c. in London and Its Vicinity.* Compiled and calculated by William Magrath. London: Printed for, and sold by, the Compiler, No. 40, St. Martin's-le-grand, Newgate-Street, 1804.

Bibliographical citations: Gaskell, E5; Marthens, p. 24.

Locations: St. Bride.

Primarily a ready-reference handbook for the trade. Contains type tables and tables of signatures and folios. Lacks specific information on iron handpresses and practical printing. Includes four pages of imposition schemes. Gaskell describes this item as the "first of the concise pocket reference-books for journeymen," although the first edition of Rhynd's *Printers' Guide*, *see* item R6 on p. 921, probably predates this edition of Magrath's work.

M22. Magrath, William. *The Printers' Assistant; Containing Typographical Tables, and a Few Select Schemes of Difficult Impositions; Together with Scales of Prices for Compositors and Pressmen. To Which Is Added, a Correct List of Master Printers, Letter Founders, Joiners, and Printers' Smiths, &c. &c. in London and Its Vicinity.* Compiled and calculated by William Magrath. London: Printed for the compiler; and may be had at Mr. Flindall's, Hole-in-the-wall, Fleet-street, 1805.

Bibliographical citations: Bigmore & Wyman, vol. II, p. 12; Gaskell, E5.

Locations: Bodleian.

A revised reprint of the 1804 edition, *see* item M21 above.

M23. Manning, J. *The Printers' Vade-Mecum and Ready Reference.* Aberdeen: Printed by John Avery and Co., 1881.

Locations: Newberry; Providence Public; St. Bride.

A practical guide in managing a jobbing office. Lacks specific information on iron handpresses and practical printing. Includes eight pages of imposition schemes.

M24. *A Manual of Punctuation. For Self-Teaching and for Schools.* By a practical printer. Manchester: Dunnill, Palmer, & Co.; London: Trübner & Co., 1859.

Locations: British.

One of many nineteenth-century guides to help printers standardize punctuation in their composing rooms.

Marshall, George. *See* item H25 on p. 907.

M25. Mason, William. *The Printers' Assistant; Containing a Sketch of the History of Printing, an Essay on Punctuation, Typographical Tables, Select Schemes of Difficult Impositions, the Greek & Hebrew Alphabets, and the New Scale of Prices for Compositors and Pressmen; Together with a Correct List of Printers, Letter Founders, Printers' Smiths and Joiners, Ink Makers, Wood Engravers, Type Cutters, &c., &c.* London: Printed and sold by W. Mason, 3, Spa Fields, Clerkenwell; J. S. Dickson, 18, Ivy Lane, Paternoster Row; and at the Hole in the Wall, Fleet Street, 1810.

Bibliographical citations: Bigmore & Wyman, vol. II, p. 222; Bliss, 943; Gaskell, E8. Bigmore & Wyman use the title for the main entry.

Locations: Bodleian; Providence Public; St. Bride.

Primarily a ready-reference handbook for compositors and pressmen. Similar in contents to Magrath (1804) and (1805), *see* items M21 and M22 above. Lacks specific information on iron handpresses and practical printing. Includes four pages of imposition schemes.

M26. Mason, William. *The Printers' Assistant; Containing a Sketch of the History of Printing, an Essay on Punctuation, Various Typographical Tables, Select Schemes of Difficult Impositions, the Greek & Hebrew Alphabets, Scales of Prices for Compositors & Pressmen, Advice to Young Men Commencing Business, Abstracts of Acts Relative to Printers, Present Price of Materials, and a List of Masters, Letter Founders, Printers' Smiths and Joiners, Ink Makers, Wood Engravers, Type Cutters, &c.* 2nd ed. London: Printed and sold by W. Mason, 21, Clerkenwell Green; and at the Hole in the Wall, Fleet Street, 1812.

Bibliographical citations: Gaskell, E8; Hitchings, IX.

Locations: NYPL.

A reprint of the 1810 edition, *see* item M25 above.

M27. Mason, William. *The Printers' Assistant; Containing a Sketch of the History of Printing, an Essay on Punctuation, Various Typographical Tables, Select Schemes of Difficult Impositions, the Greek & Hebrew Alphabets, Scales of Prices for Compositors & Pressmen, Advice to Young Men Commencing Business, Abstracts of Acts Relative to Printers, Present Price of Materials, and a List of Masters, Letter Founders, Printers' Smiths and Joiners, Ink Makers, Wood Engravers, Type Cutters, &c.* 3rd ed. London: Printed and sold by W. Mason, 21, Clerkenwell Green; and at the Hole in the Wall, Fleet Street, 1814.

Bibliographical citations: Bigmore & Wyman, vol. II, p. 29; Gaskell, E8.

Locations: Delaware.

A reprint of the 1810 edition, *see* item M25 above.

M28. Mason, William. *The Printers' Assistant; Containing a Sketch of the History of Printing, an Essay on Punctuation, Various Typographical Tables, Select Schemes of Difficult Impositions, the Greek & Hebrew Alphabets, Instructions to Compose Clean & Quick, Scales of Prices for Compositors & Pressmen, Advice to Young Men Commencing Business, Abstracts of Acts Relative to Printers, Directions for Making Black, Red, and Blue Inks, and Composition Balls, Present Price of Materials, and a List of Masters, Letter Founders, Printers' Smiths and Joiners, Ink Makers, Wood Engravers, Type Cutters, &c.* 3rd ed. London: Printed and sold by W. Mason, 21, Clerkenwell Green; also, by Simpkin & Marshall, 4, Stationers' Court, 1817.

Bibliographical citations: Hitchings, IXb.

Locations: Harvard.

An expansion of the 1810 edition, *see* item M25 above. Contains new sections on making inks and composition balls. Lacks specific information on iron handpresses and practical printing.

Not seen.

M29. Mason, William. *The Printers' Assistant; Containing a Sketch of the History of Printing, an Essay on Punctuation, Various Typographical Tables, Select Schemes of Difficult Impositions, the Greek & Hebrew Alphabets, Instructions to Compose Clean & Quick, Scales of Prices for Compositors & Pressmen, Advice to Young Men Commencing Business, Abstracts of Acts Relative to Printers, Directions for Making Black, Red, and Blue Inks, and Composition Balls, a Table Showing the Quantity of Paper to Be Given Out for Jobs, from 50 to 10,000 Number, Present Price of Materials, and a List of Masters, Letter Founders, Printers' Smiths and Joiners, Ink Makers, Wood Engravers, Type Cutters, &c.* 4th ed. London: Printed and sold by W. Mason, 21, Clerkenwell Green; also, by Simpkin & Marshall, 4, Stationers' Court, London: [1821].

Bibliographical notes: The inferred publication date is taken from the cover.

Bibliographical citations: Bigmore & Wyman [1823], vol. II, p. 29; Gaskell, E8; Marthens, p. 24.

Locations: Columbia [1823]; St. Bride.

An expanded reprint of the 1817 edition, *see* item M28 above. Contains new sections on composition, inkmaking, the organization of a printing office, and paper handling. Lacks specific information on iron handpresses and practical printing. Gaskell notes that there were two issues of this item.

M30. Mason, William. *The Printers' Price Book for Job Work in General, Containing the Master Printers' Charge to the Public for Cards, Bill Heads, Hand Bills, Posting Bills, Circular Letters, Circular Notes, Receipts, Labels, Auctioneers' Particulars, Auctioneers' Catalogues, Club Articles, Account Book Headings, Pamphlets, Booksellers' Catalogues, Library Ditto, Bills in Parliament, Admiralty Cases, &c. &c.* London: Printed and published by the editor, 21, Clerkenwell Green; sold, also, by Simpkin and Marshall, 4 Stationers' Court, 1816.

Locations: St. Bride.

Primarily a price book for job work. Lacks specific information on iron handpresses and practical printing.

M31. Mason, William. *The Printer's Price Book for Job Work in General, Containing the Master Printer's Charge to the Public for Cards, Bill Heads, Hand Bills, Posting Bills, Circular Letters, Circular Notes, Receipts, Labels, Auctioneers' Particulars, Auctioneers' Catalogues, Club Articles, Account Book Headings, Pamphlets, Booksellers' Catalogues, Library Ditto, Bills in Parliament, Admiralty Cases, &c. &c.* 2nd ed. London: Printed and published by the editor, 21, Clerkenwell Green; sold, also, by Simpkin and Marshall, 4 Stationers' Court, 1820.

Bibliographical notes: Bigmore & Wyman, vol. II, p. 29, and Marthens, p. 24, have a listing for an 1821 edition of this item under the title *Price-Book for Job-Work,* which might be a third edition.

Locations: British; St. Bride.

A reprint of the 1816 edition, *see* item M30 above, with a slightly modified title page.

No copies of the third edition were located.

M32. Mason, William. *The Printers' Price Book for Job Work in General, Containing the Master Printers' Charge to the Public for Cards, Bill Heads, Hand Bills, Posting Bills, Circular Letters, Circular Notes, Receipts, Labels, Auctioneers' Particulars, Auctioneers' Catalogues, Club Articles, Account Book Headings, Pamphlets, Booksellers' Catalogues, Library Ditto, Bills in Parliament, Admiralty Cases, &c. &c.* 4th ed., revised and corrected to the present time, with additions. London: Printed and published by the editor, 21, Clerkenwell Green, 1832.

Locations: Huntington.

A revised and corrected reprint of item M30 above.

Model Press Company. *See* items H26 through H28 beginning on p. 907.

M33. Morgan, H. *A Dictionary of Terms Used in Printing.* Madras: Printed at the Military Male Orphan Asylum Press by William Thomas, 1863.

Locations: St. Bride.

In addition to giving definitions of printing terms, the author "has endeavoured to give instructions which may help to make good workmen, or enable persons in charge of presses, who are not Printers, to understand better what are the duties of workmen in their employ" – from the introductory note.

M34. Morrill, Frederick K., and Walter T. Dwight. *The Amateurs' Guide for 1871. A Complete Book of Reference Relative to the Amateur Editors, Authors, Printers, and Publishers of America. With Biographical Sketches.* Chicago: Amateur Publishing Company, 1871.

Locations: Brown.

Primarily for amateur journalists and printers. Lacks specific information on iron handpresses and practical printing.

M35. Morrill, Frederick K. *The Amateurs' Guide for 1872. A Complete Book of Reference, Relative to the Amateur Editors, Authors, Printers, and Publishers of America.* Written and compiled by Fred. K. Morrill. Chicago: Amateur Publishing Company, 1872.

Bibliographical citations: Bigmore & Wyman, vol. II, p. 52; Marthens, p. 24.

Locations: American Antiquarian Society.

An expanded reprint of the 1871 edition, *see* item M34 above, with a brief account of amateur journalism and printing. Contains sections on various amateur press associations.

M36. Munday, Eugene H. *The Cost of Paper Computed and Tabulated for the Printer and the Publisher.* Philadelphia: Published by Collins & M'Leester, Letter Founders, No. 705 Jayne Street, 1875.

Bibliographical citations: Bigmore & Wyman, vol. II, p. 64; Marthens, p. 25.

Locations: British.

The first book devoted entirely to this subject. Consists primarily of tables for computing the cost of paper.

M37. Munsell, Joel. *The Typographical Miscellany.* Albany: Joel Munsell, 58 State Street. 1850.

Bibliographical citations: Bigmore & Wyman, vol. II, p. 65; Marthens, p. 25.

Locations: Boston Public; Grolier; Huntington; Kemble; LC; Newberry; Philadelphia; St. Bride; SFPL; Toronto; William & Mary; Yale.

Even though not strictly a printers' manual, this book contains several hints regarding practical printing compiled from a variety of sources including books and periodicals.

Facsimile reprints:
The Typographical Miscellany. New York: Burt Franklin, 1972. Series statement: Burt Franklin Research & Source Works Series, Art History & Reference Series 34.

A complete facsimile, with the following exception: the Burt Franklin imprint has replaced the original imprint on the facsimile title page.

M38. Myers, J. *A Few Practical Hints to Printers on the Treatment of Rollers. How to Wash Rollers; How to Make Rollers. On Wetting-down Paper. General Remarks to Machine-minders. How to Clean Wood Letter.* By "Caxton." [Southampton]: 1871.

Bibliographical notes: The bibliographical data is taken from Bigmore & Wyman, vol. II, p. 67.

No copies located.

N1. New England Franklin Club. *Scale of Prices As Adopted by the New England Franklin Club, July 1, 1864.* Boston: Printed by Alfred Mudge & Son, 34 School St., 1864.

Locations: Grolier.

A price book. Lacks specific information on handpresses and practical printing.

Not seen.

Nichol, William. *See* item H4 on p. 904.

N2. [Nicholson, Thomas]. *Instructions for the Successful Manipulation of the New and Improved "Nicholson" Stereotyping Apparatus.* London: Printed by Blades, East & Blades, 11, Abchurch Lane, E.C., 1872.

Locations: St. Bride.

Not seen.

N3. [Nicholson, Thomas]. *Instructions for the Successful Manipulation of the New and Improved "Nicholson" Stereotyping Apparatus.* 2nd ed. London: Printed by Blades, East & Blades, 11, Abchurch Lane, E.C., 1874.

Bibliographical citations: Bigmore & Wyman, vol. II, p. 78.

Locations: St. Bride.

A reprint of the 1872 edition, *see* item N2 above, with a slightly modified title page.

N4. Noble, Frederick. *Difficulties in Machine Printing, and How to Overcome Them.* London: "Printers Register" Office, Ludgate Hill, 1883.

Locations: Chicago; St. Bride.

Not seen.

N5. Noble, Frederick. *The Principles and Practice of Colour Printing Stated and Explained.* London: Office

of "Printers' Register," St. Bride St., E.C., 1881.

Locations: Minnesota; St. Bride.

A major work on color theory for printers. Includes fifty plates, printed in as many colors, with simple instructions on how to match or vary each of them.

Noble, Frederick. *See also* item S31 and S32 on pp. 927 and 928 respectively.

O1. O'Brien, M. B. *A Manual for Authors, Printers, and Publishers. Being a Guide in All Matters Pertaining or Incidental to Printing and Publishing.* Illustrated with specimens of chromo-lithography, woodcuts, process blocks, photophane, fine art illustrations, electrotyping, and stereotyping. London: Printed and published by Gee & Co., 34, Moorgate Street, E.C., 1890.

Bibliographical citations: Wakeman, 43.

Locations: St. Bride.

Intended as a guide to assist authors in the publication of their work by acquainting them with the various processes of the printing trade. Contains several short chapters on all aspects of the subject including printing, paper, inks, electrotypes, and photomechanical processes, as well as copyright law and the preparation of the manuscript; with a special chapter on the newly invented typewriter. Also contains chapters on most of the known illustration techniques together with examples of them. Includes twenty-two specimen pages of type.

O2. Oldfield, Arthur. *A Practical Manual of Typography, and Reference Book for Printers. Specially Prepared As a Text Book for Technical Classes in Typography. A List of Technical Questions Calculated to Draw Out the Information of the Student Is Appended.* London: E. Menken, 65 & 66, Chancery Lane, W.C., [ca. 1890]

Bibliographical notes: The inferred publication date is taken from the British Library record, shelfmark: YA.1999.a.3185.

Bibliographical citations: Bliss, 949; Wakeman, 41.

Locations: Bodleian [1892]; British; Delaware[1890]; Iowa [1890]; Massey; NYPL [1890]; Philadelphia [1890]; Providence Public [n.d.]; St. Bride; UCLA [1890]; Virginia [1890].

A comprehensive manual covering all phases of printing. Contains chapters on handpresses (used as proof presses) and presswork, process blocks, inks, color printing, making up pages, and imposing. Includes seven pages of imposition schemes and six pages of type specimens. Originally conceived of as a text for the students at the City and Guilds of London Institute.

O3. Oldfield, Arthur. *A Practical Manual of Typography, and Reference Book for Printers. Specially Prepared As a Text Book for Technical Classes in Typography. A List of Technical Questions Calculated to Draw Out the Information of the Student Is Appended.* 2nd. ed., revised. London: E. Menken, Bury Street, New Oxford Street, W.C., 1898.

Locations: St. Bride.

A reprint of the [1890] edition, *see* item O2 above.

Twentieth-century editions:
A Practical Manual of Typography and Reference Book for Printers. Specially Prepared As a Text Book for Technical Classes in Typography. A List of Technical Questions Calculated to Draw Out the Information of the Student is Appended. 3rd. ed., revised and enlarged. London: E. Menken, 50, Great Russell Street, British Museum, W.C. [1906].

Practical Manual of Typography and Reference Book for Printers. 3rd ed., revised and enlarged. London: Myers & Co., 1914.

P1. Partington, Charles Frederick. *The Printer's Complete Guide; Containing a Sketch of the History and Progress of Printing, to Its Present State of Improvement; Details of Its Several Departments; Numerous Schemes of Imposition; Modern Improvements in Stereotype, Presses, and Machinery, &c. &c.* Illustrated by engravings. London: Printed for Sherwood, Gilbert, and Piper, Paternoster Row, 1825.

Bibliographical citations: Bigmore & Wyman, vol. II, p. 145; Gaskell, E14; Hitchings, XIII.

Locations: British; Cambridge; Columbia; Harvard; Huntington; LC; Princeton; Providence Public; St. Bride; William & Mary (bound with Partington's *Engraver's Complete Guide,* 1825); Yale.

An abridgment of Stower (1808), *see* item S42 on p. 929. The section on practical printing was adapted for the iron handpress. Contains information on printing machines and machine printing. Includes illustrations of a wooden press and technical diagrams of the Stanhope press (taken from Abraham Rees's *Cyclopædia* (1820, vol. 4, plate I), plus twenty-two pages of imposition schemes. Intended as Part 4 of Volume I in his *The Mechanics' Gallery of Science and Art* (London: Sherwood, Gilbert, and Piper, 1825), but issued separately here, which is why the first page of the text begins on p. 193.

P2. Partington, Charles Frederick. *The Printers' Complete Guide; Containing a Sketch of the History and Progress of Printing, to Its Present State of Improvement; Details of Its Several Departments; Numerous Schemes of Imposition; Modern Improvements in Stereotype, Presses, and Machinery, &c.; with Familiar Instructions to Authors Illustrative of the Art of Correcting Proof-Sheets.* Illustrated by engravings. The Mechanics' Library, or Book of Trades. London: Printed for Sherwood, Gilbert, and Piper, Paternoster- Row, [1831].

Bibliographical notes: The inferred publication date is taken from the St. Bride Printing Library record, call number: 22503.

Bibliographical citations: Bigmore & Wyman, vol. II, p. 145; Gaskell, E14; Marthens [n.d.], p. 27.

Locations: Bodleian [1825?]; Columbia; Kemble; St. Bride.

A reprint of the 1825 edition, *see* item P1 above, with a new title page.

P3. [Pasko, Wesley Washington]. *American Dictionary of Printing and Bookmaking, Containing a History of These Arts in Europe and America, with Definitions of Technical Terms and Biographical Sketches.* Illustrated. New York: Howard Lockwood & Co., publishers, 1894.

Bibliographical citations: Bliss, 917.

Locations: Boston Athenæum; Bridwell; Brown; Cambridge; Chicago; Columbia; Delaware; Harvard; Massey; Minnesota; NYPL; Princeton; Providence Public; RIT; St. Bride; Seattle; Smithsonian; Toronto; UCLA; Virginia; William & Mary; Yale.

Excellent source for information on pre-twentieth-century printing. Encyclopedic articles on many subjects, including typecasting, papermaking, printing, and inks. Emphasis on American practices. Also includes biographical notes on many persons associated with the printing industry. Profusely illustrated.

Facsimile reprints:
American Dictionary of Printing and Bookmaking, Containing a History of These Arts in Europe and America, with Definitions of Technical Terms and Biographical Sketches. Illustrated. With a new introduction by Robert E. Runser. Detroit: Gale Research, 1967.

A complete facsimile with the following exceptions on the facsimile title page: information regarding the new material has been inserted between two new ornaments and the Gale research imprint has been added below the original imprint. New information has been added to the original copyright page.

American Dictionary of Printing and Bookmaking. New York: Burt Franklin, 1970. Series statement: Burt Franklin Bibliography and Reference Series 382, American Classics in History and Social Science 158.

A complete facsimile with the following exceptions on the facsimile title page: the Burt Franklin imprint has replaced the original imprint, and the phrase "Biographical Sketches" was omitted. The original copyright page was replaced by a new one.

P4. Powell, Arthur [Charles Joseph]. *The Printer's Primer. Extracted from Southward's "Practical Printing," with Additions and Amendments. Part I. Composition.* London: "Printers' Register" Office, 4, Bouverie Street, E.C., 1895.

Bibliographical citations: Wakeman, 50.

Locations: Delaware; Providence Public.

Intended as a larger work. Contains the first twenty chapters from *Practical Printing* (1892), *see* item S29 on p. 927, and another two abridged chapters on "Making Up and Imposing" and "Jobbing Work." Includes ten pages of examination questions at the back.

P5. Powell, Arthur Charles Joseph. *A Short History of the Art of Printing in England.* London: Joseph M. Powell, "Printers' Register" Office, 1877.

Bibliographical citations: Bigmore & Wyman, vol. II, p. 217; Bliss, 282.

Locations: British; Providence Public; Tokyo; William & Mary.

Issued as a supplement to the *Printers' Register,* in commemoration of the four hundredth anniversary of the introduction of printing into England. Includes illustrations of the Stanhope (second construction), Columbian, and Albion presses.

Powell, Arthur Charles Joseph. *See also* items S27 through S32 beginning on p. 927.

A Practical Printer. *Instructions for Amateur Printers. See* item W2 on p. 932.

A Practical Printer. *A Manual of Punctuation. For Self-Teaching and for Schools. See* item M24 on p. 916.

A Practical Printer. *The Printer. See* item P9 below.

A Practical Printer. *The Typographical Hand Book. See* items T7 through T9, beginning on pp. 931.

The Pressmen's Guide. See item C30 on p. 896.

Price-Book for Job-Work. See items M30 through M32 beginning on pp. 917.

P6. *The Printer.* London: Houlston and Stoneman, 65, Paternoster Row, [1833].

Bibliographical notes: The inferred publication date is taken from p. 37 of the text. Bigmore & Wyman also give [1833] as the inferred publication date.

Bibliographical citations: Bigmore & Wyman, vol. II, p. 221; Bliss [n.d. – 1838 or shortly thereafter], 950, Wakeman, 9.

Locations: Columbia; Delaware; Harvard [18–]; Newberry [1833?]; Providence Public [1833?]; RIT [1833?].

A detailed overview of the printing industry, primarily intended for apprentices, with specific information on the duties of each member of the labor force in every department. Contains sections on composition, printing on both wooden and iron handpresses and printing machines, newspaper printing (its first mention in a printers' manual), and typecasting. Includes illustrations of the Blaew (Blaeu) and Stanhope presses, compositors at work, typecasting, stereotyping, and the warehouse, as well as machine men working at an Applegath and Cowper's cylinder press. This was the first manual to elaborate on the duties of the paper handler (fly-boy) who joined the puller and the roller boy at the handpress, even though he was more frequently employed at printing machines. This item, with a different title page, was also issued as *The Guide to Trade: The Printer* (1838) and (1843), *see* items G15 and G16 on pp. 902 and 903, respectively.

P7. *The Printer.* London: Houlston and Wright, 65, Paternoster Row, 1865.

Locations: St. Bride.

A reprint of the [1833] edition, *see* item P6 above, with a new title page.

P8. *The Printer: A Description of His Business and All That Pertains to It.* Houlston's Industrial Library, No. 31. London: Houlston and Sons, Paternoster Square, [1877].

Bibliographical notes: The inferred publication date is taken from the British Library record.

Locations: British [1877] and [1884]; Chicago [1879]; Delaware [1884]; Iowa [1879]; NYPL [1884]; St. Bride [ca. 1880]; Virginia [1880?].

An expanded resetting of the [1833] edition, *see* item P6 above. Includes information on both the plaster and paper processes of stereotyping.

P9. *The Printer.* By a practical printer. Bungay: Printed by W. C. Barber, 1872.

Locations: St. Bride.

Intended to give journeymen and apprentices the rudiments of the printing trade in an inexpensive twenty-four page pamphlet.

The Printers' Assistant. See items M25 through M29 beginning on p. 916.

P10. *The Printer's Estimate Guide.* Revised edition. London: Young & Surtees, Millwall, E, [1895].

Bibliographical notes: The inferred publication date is taken from the cover.

Locations: Bodleian; British.

The Bodleian Library has a copy of *The Printer's Estimate Guide* [1894] printed on a single sheet and mounted on card to facilitate hanging it on the wall of a printing office. Originally published as *Multum in parvo* (much in little).

P11. *The Printer's Estimate Guide.* 3rd ed. London: Young & Surtees, Millwall, [1896].

Bibliographical notes: The inferred publication date is taken from the British Library record, shelfmark: 08226.f.40.

Locations: Bodleian; British.

A ready-reference list of suggested prices for general everyday work. Lacks specific information on iron handpresses and practical printing.

P12. *The Printers' Manual, Containing the Compositors' Scale of Prices, Agreed Upon in 1810, and Modified in 1816, an Abstract of the Newsmen's Scale, a Table Show-*

ing the Price of Any Number of Letters, from 16,000, to 100,000, Numerous Schemes of Impositions, the Hebrew, Greek, and Saxon Alphabets, and Instructions for Young Compositors: Also, the Pressmen's Scale of Prices, a Table Showing the Quantity of Paper to Be Given Out for Jobs of Various Sizes, from Twenty-Five to Five Thousand, a List of Master Printers, Arranged on a New Plan, &c. &c. &c.* London: Published by C. Strange, 21, Paternoster Row; and Cowie and Co., 24, Brydges Street, Covent Garden, [1816?]

Bibliographical notes: Bliss suggests [1816?] as the publication date. *See also* the entries under Cowie, George, on p. 892.

Bibliographical citations: Bliss, 951.

Locations: Huntington.

Primarily of interest to compositors. Lacks specific information on iron handpresses and practical printing. Cowie may also be the author of this item. *See also* items C8 through C16 beginning on p. 892.

The Printers' Pocket Companion. See item L1 on p. 911.

P13. The Printing and Allied Trades Association. *The London Scale of Prices for Compositors' Work Agreed upon February 12, 1891, at a Conference of Representatives of the Printing and Allied Trades Association and the London Society of Compositors Held at Stationers' Hall; and the Revised London Rates for Machine Managers and Pressmen.* London: The Printing and Allied Trades Association, 57, Ludgate Hill, E.C., 1891.

Locations: St. Bride.

Contains revised scale of prices for pressmen and machine managers.

Printing Apparatus for the Use of Amateurs. See item H17 on p. 906.

R1. Ramaley, David. *Employing Printers' Price List for Job Printing. Based on a New Plan of Measurement, and with Detailed Prices for All Classes of Work.* Saint Paul: Ramaley & Cunningham, publishers, 1873.

Bibliographical citations: Bigmore & Wyman, vol. II, p. 237; Marthens, p. 28.

Locations: Delaware; Providence Public; St. Bride; William & Mary.

Ramaley's objective was to give printers a ready guide for uniform prices, which included a built-in net profit of fifty percent on labor and materials. An eight-page supplement was issued in 1876.

R2. Ramaley, David. *Employing Printers' Price List for Job Printing. Based on a New Plan of Measurement, and with Detailed Prices for All Classes of Work.* 2nd ed. Saint Paul: David Ramaley, publisher, 1884.

Locations: Grolier.

A reprint of the 1873 edition, *see* item R1 above, with revised prices.

Not seen.

Twentieth-century editions:
Employing Printers' Price List for Job Printing and Binding. 8th ed. St. Paul, MN: Ramaley Publishing, 1907.

R3. Raynor, P. E. *Printing for Amateurs: A Practical Guide to the Art of Printing; Containing Descriptions of Presses and Materials, Together with Details of the Processes Employed; to Which Is Added a Glossary of Technical Terms.* Illustrated. London: "The Bazaar" Office, 170, Strand, W.C., [1876].

Bibliographical notes: The inferred publication date is taken from the British Library record, shelfmark: 11899.b.8.

Bibliographical citations: Bigmore & Wyman, vol. II, p. 242.

Locations: British; Philadelphia [1888].

Considered the most valuable of nineteenth-century manuals for amateurs. Describes and evaluates several of the smaller presses on the market for amateur printers, including Berri's People's Printing Press, Francis's Everybody's Printing Press, Holtzapffel's Cowper's Parlour Press, Malins's Excelsior Press, Myers's Amateur Printing Office, and Wightman's Little Stranger Press, as well as the Albion press; with "A Dictionary of Technical Terms and Phrases used in Printing." Indexed. Includes illustrations of the Francis, Malins, and Wightman tabletop presses and an Albion press.

R4. Raynor, P. E. *Printing for Amateurs: A Practical Guide to the Art of Printing; Containing Descriptions of Presses and Materials, Together with Details of the Processes Employed; to Which Is Added a Glossary of Technical Terms.* Illustrated. London: "The Bazaar" Office, 32, Wellington-Street, Strand, W.C., [1876].

Bibliographical notes: The inferred publication date is taken from Wakeman. *See* below.

Bibliographical citations: Wakeman, 19.

Locations: SFPL.

A reprint of item R3 above with a variant imprint.

R5. Read, Joseph Marsh. *Instructions in the Art of Making-Ready Woodcuts: Being a Comprehensive and Thoroughly Practical Treatise, with Illustrations Showing the Great Contrast between the Two Systems.* Reading: n.d.

Bibliographical notes: The bibliographical data is taken from Bigmore & Wyman, vol. II, p. 242.

No copies located.

R6. Rhynd, M. *Rhynd's Printers' Guide: Being a New and Correct List of Master Printers, in London and Its Vicinity: Together with the Letter-Founders, Joiners, Printers' Smiths, &c. To Which Are Added, the Greek, Hebrew, and Arabic Alphabets, the Scales of Prices, Schemes for Imposing, and Other Important Information.* 3rd ed., considerably enlarged, and very much improved. London: printed and sold by M. Rhynd, 21, Ray Street, Cold Bath Fields, 1804.

Bibliographical citations: Bigmore & Wyman, vol. II, p. 255.

Locations: Berkeley (microfilm).

No copies of the first and second editions were located.

Primarily a ready-reference handbook for the trade. Lacks specific information on iron handpresses and practical printing. The 1804 date of this third edition would indicate that the two earlier editions probably predated the first edition of William Magrath's *The Printers' Assistant* (1804), *see* item M21 on p. 915.

R7. Ringwalt, John Luther, ed. *American Encyclopædia of Printing.* Philadelphia: Menamin & Ringwalt, 517 Minor Street; J.B. Lippincott & Co., 715 Market St., 1871.

Bibliographical citations: Bigmore & Wyman, vol. II, p. 259; Bliss, 285; Hitchings, 6; Marthens, 28.

Locations: Bodleian; Massey; NYPL; Providence Public; Toronto; Utah; William & Mary (two copies).

Informative, well-illustrated encyclopedia with in-depth articles on many aspects of handpress printing. About 1,700 entries. Relies heavily on Southward (1871), *see* item S21 on p. 926.

Facsimile reprints:
American Encyclopædia of Printing. With a new introduction by Daniel Traister. New York: Garland Publishing, 1981. Series Statement: Nineteenth-Century Book Arts and Printing History.

A complete facsimile with the following exceptions: all of the plates in the original have been printed in black by offset; none of the additional colors in the original were used in the facsimile. The embossed leaf facing p. 64 and the leaves of watermarks following p. 490 were printed in black by offset.

R8. Rose, Philip, and John Evans. *The Printer's Job Price-Book, Containing Eighty-one Tables of the Master Printer's Charges to the Public, for Various Descriptions of Jobs, Paper of Different Qualities, with Corresponding Degrees of Workmanship. Also a Table Shewing the Quantity of Paper to Be Given Out for the Respective Sizes and Numbers.* Bristol: Printed by Philip Rose, 20, Broadmead, [1814].

Bibliographical notes: The inferred publication date is taken from the "Preface," which is dated Nov. 5, 1814.

Bibliographical citations: Bigmore & Wyman, vol. II, p. 273.

Locations: LC; Toronto.

A price book and ready-reference guide for printers. Lacks specific information on iron handpresses and practical printing.

R9. Rose, Philip. *The Printer's Job Price Book, Containing the Master Printer's Charges to the Public for Various Descriptions of Jobs. Together with Tables Giving the Quantity of Paper Required for Each Job.* Bristol: Philip Rose, Broadmead; London: Longman and Co., [1824].

Bibliographical notes: The inferred publication date is taken from the ATF catalog, vol. 4, p. 2187.

Bibliographical citations: Bigmore & Wyman, vol. II, p. 273.

Locations: Columbia.

A revised reprint of the [1814] edition, *see* item R8 above. John Evans is not listed on the title page as co-author.

Not seen.

R10. Rowell, G. F. *Hints on Estimating, Including a Useful and Comprehensive Price List and a Chapter on Bronze and Leaf Printing.* London: Published by the author, at 29 Lisburne Road, Hampstead, 1897.

Bibliographical notes: The bibliographical data is taken from Wakeman, 52.

No copies located.

Twentieth-century editions:

Hints on Estimating, Including Hints on Bronze Printing, Embossing, Purchasing Plant, How to Make Printing Pay, etc., etc. 2nd ed. London: Rowell and Sons, 1901.

R11. Ruse, George. *Imposition Simplified: The Most Useful Schemes Pictorially Represented; with Diagrams for the Measurement of Margin, Table of Bookwork Furnitures &c.* London: Published by the author, 80, Bishopsgate within; and may be ordered of any bookseller, [1857].

Bibliographical notes: The inferred publication date is taken from the copyright receipt stamp, dated 1857, in the British Library's copy, shelfmark: 819.a.11.

Locations: Bodleian [ca. 1860]; British; Columbia; St. Bride [ca. 1860].

Bibliographical citations: Bigmore & Wyman [1860], vol. II, p. 280; Marthens [1861], p. 28. Bigmore & Wyman erroneously transcribed this title as *Imposition Simplified: Being a Practical Representation of the Most Useful Schemes, Rendering the System Perfectly Intelligible. Together with Diagrams for the Measurement of Margin, Tables of Bookwork, Furniture, &c.*; however, Stephen O. Saxe suggests that Bigmore & Wyman have been describing another edition of this work.

Includes twenty-four diagrams of imposition schemes.

Not seen.

R12. Ruse, George. *Imposition Simplified: The Most Useful Schemes Pictorially Represented; with Diagrams for the Measurement of Margin, Table of Bookwork Furnitures &c.* Eighty-second thousand. London: Published by the author, 80, Bishopsgate within; and may be ordered of any bookseller, [ca. 1875].

Bibliographical notes: The inferred publication date is taken from the St. Bride Printing Library record, call number: 23478.

Bibliographical citations: Bigmore & Wyman, vol. II, p. 280.

Locations: Bodleian; Providence Public [1875?]; St. Bride.

A reprint of the [1857] edition, *see* item R11 above.

R13. Ruse, George, and C. Straker. *Printing and Its Accessories: A Comprehensive Book of Charges for the Guidance of Letter-Press and Lithographic Printers, Engravers, and Bookbinders, with Notes and Items for Reference; Practical Instructions in Lithography, Ink, Chalk, and Chromo, with Descriptive Illustrations, and Various Receipts in Connection Therewith; Together with 156 Samples of English and Foreign Papers, and Tabular Indexes, Showing Their Comparative Mill Numbers, Weights, etc., etc.* London: Published by S. Straker & Son, Steam Printing Works, 80, Bishopsgate Street within, [ca. 1860].

Bibliographical notes: The inferred publication date is taken from the British Library record, shelfmark: 624.

Bibliographical citations: Bigmore & Wyman, vol. II, p. 280; Bliss, 952; Marthens, p. 28; Wakeman, 11. Marthens misspells Ruse's name, referring to him as *Reese*.

Locations: Bodleian [1860]; Boston Athenæum; British; Columbia [1850]; Delaware; Grolier; Huntington; Iowa; Newberry; NYPL; Providence Public [1860]; St. Bride.

Book I, pp. 1–154, is addressed to the letterpress printer. Book II is devoted to lithographic printing. Most of the letterpress section consists of tables for pricing book and job work. Also makes recommendations for which type of paper to use for each job. Lacks specific information on iron handpresses and presswork. Includes 156 samples of paper.

S1. Sampson, Thomas. *Electrotint; or, The Art of Making Paintings in Such a Manner That Copper Plates and "Blocks" Can Be Taken from Them by Means of Voltaic Electricity.* London: Published by Edward Palmer, philosophical instrument maker, No. 103 Newgate Street, 1842.

Bibliographical citations: Bigmore & Wyman, vol. II, p. 294.

Locations: Harvard; Iowa; Michigan; Smithsonian; UCLA; Yale.

An early work on electrotyping, focusing on reproducing illustrations.

S2. Saunders, [Frederic]. *The Author's Printing and Publishing Assistant, Comprising Explanations of the Process of Printing, Preparation and Calculation of Manuscripts, Choice of Paper, Type, Binding, Illustrations, Publishing, Advertising, &c. With an Exemplification and Description of the Typographical Marks Used in the Correction of the Press.* London: Saunders and Otley, Conduit Street, 1839.

Locations: British: Clark; SFPL; Virginia.

An overview of book production and publishing for authors. Lacks specific information on iron handpresses and practical printing.

S3. Saunders, [Frederic]. *The Author's Printing and Publishing Assistant, Comprising Explanations of the Process of Printing, Preparation and Calculation of Manuscripts, Choice of Paper, Type, Binding, Illustrations, Publishing, Advertising, &c. With an Exemplification and Description of the Typographical Marks Used in the Correction of the Press.* 2nd ed. London: Saunders and Otley, Conduit Street, 1839.

Locations: Boston Public; British; Clark; Harvard; Huntington; Minnesota; Newberry.

An expanded reprint of the 1839 edition, *see* item S2 above.

S4. Saunders, [Frederic]. *Author's Printing and Publishing Assistant, Comprising Explanations of the Process of Printing, Preparation and Calculation of Manuscripts, Choice of Paper, Type, Binding, Illustrations, Publishing, Advertising, &c. With an Exemplification and Description of the Typographical Marks Used in the Correction of the Press.* 3rd ed. London: Saunders and Otley, Conduit Street, 1840.

Locations: British; Columbia; Massey.

A reprint of the 1839 second edition, *see* item S3 above.

Not seen.

S5. Saunders, [Frederic]. *The Author's Printing and Publishing Assistant, Comprising Explanations of the Process of Printing, Preparation and Calculation of Manuscripts, Choice of Paper, Type, Binding, Illustrations, Publishing, Advertising, &c. With an Exemplification and Description of the Typographical Marks Used in the Correction of the Press.* 4th ed. London: Saunders and Otley, Conduit Street, 1842.

Bibliographical notes: NYPL uses Frederick [sic] Saunders for the main entry.

Locations: Massey; NYPL.

An expanded reprint of 1840 edition, *see* item S4 above with a slightly modified title page.

S6. Saunders, [Frederic]. *The Author's Printing and Publishing Assistant, Comprising Explanations of the Process of Printing, Preparation and Calculation of Manuscripts, Punctuation, Choice of Paper, Type, Binding, Illustrations, Publishing, Advertising, &c. With an Exemplification and Description of the Typographical Marks Used in the Correction of the Press.* 5th ed. London: Saunders and Otley, Conduit Street, booksellers, publishers, and printing and publishing agents for authors, [1845?].

Bibliographical notes: The inferred publication date is taken from the Newberry Library record, call number: Z30599 .7873.

Locations: Newberry; NYPL [184–?].

An expanded reprint of the [1842] edition, *see* item S5 above, with a new title page. Contains new sections on punctuation and publication of works for authors.

S7. Saunders, [Frederic]. *The Author's Printing and Publishing Assistant, Comprising Explanations of the Process of Printing, Preparation and Calculation of Manuscripts, Punctuation, Choice of Paper, Type, Binding, Illustrations, Publishing, Advertising, &c. With an Exemplification and Description of the Typographical Marks Used in the Correction of the Press.* 6th ed. London: Saunders and Otley, Conduit Street, booksellers, publishers, and printing and publishing agents for authors, [185–?].

Bibliographical notes: The inferred publication date is taken from the Newberry Library record, call number: Z30599 .7874.

Locations: Newberry.

A reprint of the [1845?] edition, *see* item S6 above, with a slightly modified title page.

Not seen.

S8. Saunders, [Frederic]. *The Author's Printing and Publishing Assistant, Comprising Explanations of the Process of Printing, Preparation and Calculation of Manuscripts, Punctuation, Choice of Paper, Type, Binding, Illustrations, Publishing, Advertising, &c. With an Exemplification and Description of the Typographical Marks Used in the Correction of the Press.* 7th ed. London: Saunders and Otley, Conduit Street, booksellers, publishers, and printing and publishing agents for authors, [1852?].

Bibliographical notes: The inferred publication date is taken from the Library of Congress record, call number: Z124.S25 A7.

Locations: Grolier; LC; NYPL; Yale.

An expanded reprint of the 185–?] edition *see* item S7 above, with a new title page.

Not seen.

S9. Saunders, Frederic. *The Author's Printing and Publishing Assistant: Including Interesting Details Respecting the Mechanism of Books.* New York: Frederic Saunders, 357 Broadway, 1839.

Bibliographical citations: Bigmore & Wyman, vol. II, p. 297; Marthens, p. 29. Marthens also uses the title for the main entry, listing it under anonymous works on p. 37.

Locations: Boston Athenæum; LC; NYPL; Philadelphia; William & Mary; Yale.

The American edition of item S2 on p. 923 with additional information on the state of the typographic arts in the United States. Primarily to help authors understand book production. From the "Advertisement," "The object of this little Work is to afford such a view of the Technical details of Printing and Publishing, as shall enable Authors to form a judgment on all subjects connected with the publication of their productions." Contains sections on stereotyping, lithographic and copperplate printing, and wood engravings.

S10. Savage, William. *A Dictionary of the Art of Printing.* London: Longman, Brown, Green and Longmans, 1841.

Bibliographical citations: Bigmore & Wyman, vol. II, p. 297; Bliss, 955; Davis & Carter, 12; Gaskell, E21; Hitchings, XV; Marthens, p. 29.

Locations: Bancroft; Bodleian; Boston Athenæum; Bridwell; British; Brown; Chicago; Columbia; Delaware; Harvard; Iowa; Kentucky; LC; Massey; NYPL; Providence Public; RIT; Smithsonian; Sydney; Tokyo; Toronto; UCLA; Vermont; Virginia; William & Mary (two copies); Yale.

The most comprehensive and informative of the early nineteenth-century dictionaries on printing. Savage's observations on fine printing and inks were repeated by numerous writers throughout the century. An excellent source for handpress terms and printing practices.

Facsimile reprints:
A Dictionary of the Art of Printing. New York: Burt Franklin, n.d. Series statement: Bibliography and Reference Series #82.

A complete facsimile with the following exceptions: the Burt Franklin imprint has replaced the original imprint on the facsimile title page, and the titles of the author's earlier works were omitted.

William Savage: A Dictionary of the Art of Printing, 1841. London: Gregg Press, 1966. Series statement: English Bibliographical Sources, edited by D. F. Foxon, British Museum. Series 3: Printers' Manuals, no. 8.

S11. Savage, William. *On the Preparation of Printing Ink; Both Black and Coloured.* London: Printed for the author; and sold by Longman, Rees, Orme, Brown, Green, and Longman, 1832.

Bibliographical citations: Bigmore & Wyman, vol. II, p. 301; Marthens, p. 29.

Locations: Bodleian; British; Cambridge; NYPL; Sydney; William & Mary.

The first printers' manual devoted entirely to ink. Gives numerous formulas for making both black and colored inks, as well as describing the materials used for them.

S12. Savage, William. *Practical Hints on Decorative Printing, with Illustrations Engraved on Wood, and Printed in Colours at the Type Press.* London: Published for the proprietor by Messrs. Longman, Hurst, Rees,

Orme, and Brown, Paternoster Row; T. Cadell, Strand; J. Booth, Duke Street, Portland Place; J. Major, Skinner Street; R. Triphook, Old Bond Street; and R. Jennings, Poultry, 1822.

Bibliographical notes: The "Address" (to the reader) is dated March 25, 1823. Vermont has an [1818] edition of the first part of a two-part work issued without a title page.

Bibliographical citations: Bigmore & Wyman, vol. II, p. 297; Bliss, 954; Gaskell, E11; Marthens, p. 29.

Locations: Bodleian; Boston Athenæum; Boston Public (large paper); Bridwell; British; Cambridge; Columbia (large paper); Grolier (large and small paper); Harvard; Huntington; Illinois; Kemble; LC (large paper); Massey (large paper); Michigan; Newberry; Philadelphia; Providence Public (large and small paper); SFPL; Yale.

An important early work on printing illustrations. Intended for master printers and pressmen, not compositors. Chiefly concerned with presswork and color printing. Contains sections on making and mixing colored inks. Savage was also the first manual writer to mention machine printing. Includes the first illustrations in a printers' manual of the Columbian and Ruthven presses, as well as an illustration of printers working at Rutt's printing machine.

S13. Sawyer, J. R. *The Autotype Process; Being a Practical Manual of Instruction in the Art of Printing in Permanent Pigments; with a Notice of the Collotype Printing Process.* 5th ed., revised and partly re-written. London: Autotype Company, 36 Rathbone Place, 1876.

Locations: British.

Sawyer gives detailed instructions for printing illustrations using the Autotype and collotype processes. Both processes use a photographic negative to create the image on a plate. The Autotype Company patented their process on February 3, 1869.

No copies of the first through fourth editions were located.

S14. Sheldon, Frederick Martin. *The Practical Colorist: A Pathfinder for the Artist Printer.* Burlington, Vt.: The Owl Press, 1900.

Locations: Chicago; Columbia; Delaware; LC; Smithsonian; William & Mary; Vermont (author's autographed copy); Yale.

Primarily concerned with color printing in job work. Contains chapters on color theory, mixing colored inks, and making ready, as well as three-color process plates and how to print them. Includes numerous examples in the text, including a set of three-color progressive proofs, plus 106 specimen pages of job printing, some with colored inks.

S15. Sherman, Arthur N. *The Printer's Manual; or, A Brief Practical Treatise on the Art of Printing, Including*

Some New and Important Subjects Not Before Discussed. New-York: West & Trow, printers, 1834.

Bibliographical citations: Bigmore & Wyman, vol. II, p. 354; Gaskell, E15; Hitchings, 4; Marthens, p. 30.

Locations: Columbia; Delaware; Harvard; Huntington; Newberry; St. Bride; Virginia.

A summary of general printing practices intended for young printers taken mostly from Stower (1808), *see* item S42 on p. 929. Contains sections on setting up iron handpresses, practical presswork, inking apparatus, and printing machines. Includes illustrations of the Smith and Rust (Washington) presses, as well as an illustration of Spence's Self-Inking Machine in the "Advertising Appendix," plus thirty-three pages of imposition schemes.

S16. Simms and M'Intyre. *The Text-Book; or, Easy Instructions in the Elements of the Art of Printing: Consisting of an Essay on Punctuation, with Rules and Examples; Directions on the Use of Capitals; Greek & Hebrew Alphabets; Rules for Distributing and Composing; with Various Schemes of Imposition, &c. &c.* By a compositor. Belfast: Simms and M'Intyre, Donegall Street, 1826.

Bibliographical citations: Gaskell, E14A.

Locations: Bodleian; NYPL.

Predominantly practical instructions for compositors. Consists chiefly of an essay on punctuation, as well as rules for composing and distributing type. Lacks specific information on iron handpresses and practical printing. Includes nine pages of imposition schemes. Dedicated to John Graham. *See also* Graham's *The Compositor's Text-Book* (1848), item G13 on p. 902.

The Sister Arts. See item B3 on p. 887.

Society for Promoting Christian Knowledge. *See* items H12 and H13 on p. 905.

S17. Southward, John. *Artistic Printing. A Supplement to the Author's Work on "Practical Printing."* London: "Printers' Register" Office, 33A, Ludgate Hill, E.C., 1892.

Bibliographical citations: Bliss, 960; Wakeman, 45.

Locations: British; Delaware; Chicago; Grolier; Iowa; Newberry; Providence Public; Yale.

Contains excellent chapters on color printing, working red ink, bronze printing, tint work, making ready and working cuts. Indexed. Lacks specific information on iron handpresses. Southward was strongly influenced by *Harpel's Typograph* (1870), *see* item H7 on p. 904.

S18. [Southward, John]. *Authorship and Publication: A Concise Guide for Authors in Matters Relating to Printing and Publishing, Including the Law of Copyright and a Bibliographical Appendix.* London: Wyman & Sons, 74, 75, Great Queen Street, W.C., 1882.

Bibliographical citations: Bigmore & Wyman [1881], vol. II, p. 378.

Locations: British; Massey; St. Bride.

A guide for authors. Contains chapters on the preparation of the manuscript, choice of paper, sizes of type, book illustration, and processes of printing, including the iron handpress. Indexed. Includes two illustrations of wooden presses and a double-cylinder printing machine.

S19. [Southward, John]. *Authorship and Publication: A Concise Guide for Authors in Matters Relating to Printing and Publishing, Including the Law of Copyright, and a Bibliographical Appendix.* [2nd ed.] London: Wyman & Sons, 74–76, Great Queen Street, W.C., 1883.

Bibliographical notes: The inferred edition statement supplied by the compiler.

Locations: Chicago; Columbia; Delaware; Iowa; UCLA.

A reprint of the 1882 edition, *see* item S18 above, with a slightly modified title page.

No copies of the third and fourth editions were located.

S20. [Southward, John]. *Authorship and Publication: A Concise Guide for Authors in Matters Relating to Printing and Publishing, Including the Law of Copyright, and a Bibliographical Appendix.* [5th ed.] London: Wyman & Sons, 74–76, Great Queen Street, W.C., 1884.

Bibliographical notes: The inferred edition statement is taken from an advertisement at the back.

Locations: NYPL; St. Bride.

A reprint of the 1882 edition, *see* item S18 above, with a slightly modified title page.

S21. Southward, John. *A Dictionary of Typography and Its Accessory Arts. Presented to the Subscribers of the "Printers' Register"1870–1871.* London: Joseph M. Powell, "Printers' Register" Office, 3, Bouverie Street, E.C., 1871.

Bibliographical citations: Bigmore & Wyman, vol. II, p. 378; Marthens [1871], p. 32.

Locations: Providence Public; St. Bride.

Issued as a supplement to the *Printers' Register,* September 6, 1871. Southward's *Dictionary* formed the basis for Ringwalt's (1871), *see* item R7 on p. 922.

S22. Southward, John. *A Dictionary of Typography and Its Accessory Arts.* 2nd ed. London: Joseph M. Powell, Printers' Register Office, St. Bride Street, 1875.

Bibliographical citations: Bigmore & Wyman, vol. II, p. 379.

Locations: Bodleian; British; Providence Public; Toronto; William & Mary.

A revised reprint of item S21 above.

S23. Southward, John. *Modern Printing: A Handbook of the Principles and Practice of Typography and the Auxiliary Arts.* By John Southward, assisted by well-known experts. 2 vols. London: Raithby, Lawrence & Company, Limited, 1 Imperial Buildings, Ludgate Circus, E.C., 1898–1899.

Locations: Chicago; SFPL (2 vols. in one); St. Bride; Sydney (vol. 1 only); Yale.

An extensive and informative manual on every aspect of the late-nineteenth-century printing industry. Contains a lengthy section on iron handpresses and presswork, art and fine printing, and the Linotype machine. Draws heavily from earlier editions of *Practical Printing, see* items S27 through S32, beginning on p. 927.

S24. Southward, John. *Modern Printing: A Handbook of the Principles and Practice of Typography and the Auxiliary Arts.* Assisted by well-known experts. 2nd ed. 4 vols. London: Raithby, Lawrence & Company, Limited, 1 Imperial Buildings, Ludgate Circus, E.C., 1898–1900.

Locations: Bodleian; British; Cambridge; Minnesota; Providence Public; RIT; St. Bride; Sydney (vol. 3 only).

An expanded reprint of item S23 above in four volumes with slightly modified title pages. The second edition was reissued in three formats: 4 vols., 2 vols., and 3 vols.

S25. Southward, John. *Modern Printing: A Treatise on the Principles and Practice of Typography and the Auxiliary Arts.* By John Southward, assisted by well-known experts. [2nd ed.] 2 vols. London: Raithby, Lawrence & Company, Limited, 1 Imperial Buildings, Ludgate Circus, E.C., 1900.

Bibliographical notes: The inferred edition statement supplied by the compiler.

Bibliographical citations: Wakeman, 54.

Locations: LC; Newberry; NYPL (2 vols. in one); St. Bride (2 vols. in one); Toronto.

An expanded reprint of item S23 in two volumes with new title pages.

Twentieth-century editions:
Modern Printing: A Handbook of the Principles and Practice of Typography and the Auxiliary Arts. Assisted by well-known experts. 2nd ed. 3 vols. London: Raithby, Lawrence & Co., 1904.

Modern Printing: A Handbook of the Principles and Practice of Typography and the Auxiliary Arts. Assisted by well-known experts. 3rd ed. 2 vols. London: Raithby, Lawrence & Co., 1912–1915.

Modern Printing: A Handbook of the Principles and Practice of Typography and the Auxiliary Arts. Assisted by well-known experts. 3rd ed. 2 vols. London: Raithby, Lawrence & Co., 1915.

Modern Printing: A Handbook of the Principles and Practice of Typography and the Auxiliary Arts. Assisted by well-known experts. 4th ed. 2 vols. London: Raithby, Lawrence & Co., 1922.

Modern Printing: A Handbook of the Principles and Practice of Typography and the Auxiliary Arts. Assisted by well-known experts. 5th ed. 2 vols. London: Raithby, Lawrence & Co., 1915-1921.

Modern Printing: A Handbook of the Principles and Practice of Typography and the Auxiliary Arts. Assisted by well-known experts. 5th ed. 2 vols. London: Raithby, Lawrence & Co., 1924–1925.

Modern Printing: A Handbook of the Principles and Practice of Typography and the Auxiliary Arts. Assisted by well-known experts. 6th ed. 2 vols. London: Raithby, Lawrence & Co., 1933–1936.

Modern Printing: A Handbook of the Principles and Practice of Typography and the Auxiliary Arts. Assisted by well-known experts. 7th ed., revised and re-written. 2 vols. Leicester: De Montfort Press, 1954.

Modern Printing: A Handbook of the Principles and Practice of Typography and the Auxiliary Arts. Assisted by well-known experts. 8th ed. 2 vols. London: Raithby, Lawrence & Co., 1954–.

S26. Southward, John. *Practical Printing. A Handbook of the Art of Typography.* London: "Printers' Register" Office, 1882.

Bibliographical citations: Bigmore & Wyman, vol. II, p. 379; Wakeman, 29.

Locations: British; Cambridge; Delaware; Kemble; LC; St. Bride.

The first comprehensive printers' manual of the machine age. Primarily a compilation of information, arranged by numbered paragraphs, on practical printing taken from the pages of the *Printers' Register*. Contains chapters on presswork and descriptions of the Stanhope (second construction), Albion, and Columbian presses, as well as dampening paper, roller making, inking, and machine printing. Indexed. Profusely illustrated, including wood engravings of the Stanhope, Albion, and Columbian presses, plus sixteen pages of imposition schemes.

Facsimile reprints:
Practical Printing. A Handbook of the Art of Typography. New York: Garland Publishing, 1980. Series Statement: Nineteenth-Century Book Arts and Printing History.

S27. Southward, John. *Practical Printing. A Handbook of the Art of Typography. With an Appendix on Book-Keeping for Printers, by Arthur Powell.* 2nd ed. London: J. M. Powell & Son, "Printers' Register" Office, 33A, Ludgate Hill, 1884.

Bibliographical citations: Bigmore & Wyman, vol. II, p. 379.

Locations: Delaware; Grolier; Michigan; Newberry; St. Bride.

An expanded resetting of the 1882 edition, *see* item S26 above, with a new title page. Contains chapters on presswork and bookkeeping, as well as technical questions on printing for the examinations in connection with the City and Guilds of London Institute. Indexed. Includes illustrations of the Stanhope (second construction), Albion, and Columbian presses.

S28. Southward, John. *Practical Printing. A Handbook of the Art of Typography. With an Appendix on Book-Keeping for Printers, by Arthur Powell.* 3rd ed. London: J. M. Powell & Son, "Printers' Register" Office, 33A, Ludgate Hill, 1887.

Locations: Boston Public; Columbia; Delaware; Iowa (in 2 vols.); Massey; Newberry (in 2 vols.); Ohio; St. Bride.

An expanded reprint of the 1884 edition, *see* item S27 above. Contains a new chapter on composing machines. Indexed. Issued in both one and two volumes with slightly modified title pages. In the two-volume edition, Volume II begins on p. 331.

S29. Southward, John. *Practical Printing: A Handbook of the Art of Typography.* Fourth edition by Arthur Powell, [editor]. 4th ed. London: "Printers' Register" Office, 4, Bouverie Street, Fleet Street, E.C., [1892].

Bibliographical notes: The inferred publication date is taken from the "Editor's Preface," which is dated March, 1892.

Locations: Bodleian; Cambridge; Clark; Delaware; Grolier; St. Bride.

An expanded resetting of the 1887 edition, *see* item S28 above. Contains the first description and illustration of the Linotype machine. Powell advocates using the Anglo-American point system.

S30. Southward, John. *Practical Printing: A Handbook of the Art of Typography.* Fourth edition by Arthur Powell, [editor]. 4th ed. 2 vols. London: "Printers' Register" Office, 33A, Ludgate Hill, E.C., 1892.

Bibliographical notes: The "Editor's Preface" is dated May, 1892.

Locations: Delaware; Massey; St. Bride; UCLA; William & Mary; Yale.

An expanded reprint of item S29 above. Nine new chapters under the heading "The Economy of a Printing Office," four new chapters under the heading "Arts Allied to Printing," and five Appendices" were added.

S31. Southward, John. *Practical Printing: A Handbook of the Art of Typography. The Original Work and Two Following Editions by John Southward (Embracing the Work on Colour Printing by F. Noble).* Fifth edition by Arthur Powell assisted by the experts named in the Preface. 5th ed. 2 vols. London: The "Printers' Register" Office, 62 Fleet Street, [1900].

Bibliographical notes: The inferred publication date is taken from the "Preface," which is dated July, 1900.

Locations: Harvard; LC; SFPL; St. Bride; Utah; Yale.

An expanded reprint of the 1892 edition, *see* item S30 above, with new title pages. The Anglo-American point system is fully described and illustrated. Contains new information on color and the Linotype machine. The chapters on iron handpresses and presswork have remained constant through all five editions.

S32. Southward, John. *Practical Printing: A Handbook of the Art of Typography. The Original Work and Two Following Editions by John Southward (Embracing the Work on Colour Printing by F. Noble).* Fifth edition by Arthur Powell assisted by the experts named in the Preface. 5th ed. 2 vols. London: The "Printers' Register" Office, 62 Fleet Street, 1900.

Bibliographical notes: The publication date is printed on both title pages.

Locations: St. Bride (2 vols. in one).

A reprint of item S31 above.

Twentieth-century editions:
Practical Printing: A Handbook of the Art of Typography. The original work by John Southward. The fourth and fifth editions by Arthur Powell. Sixth edition by George Joyner. 6th ed. 2 vols. London: "Printers' Register" Office, [1911].

S33. Southward, John. *The Principles and Progress of Printing Machinery. With an Account of Modern Printing Machines. (Based upon "Typographic Printing Machines")* by F. J. F. Wilson. London: E. Menken, 65 & 66, Chancery Lane, W.C., [1890].

Bibliographical notes: The inferred publication date is taken from the Bodleian Library record, call number: 25835 e.11. This item was most likely published in 1889 since it carries an advertisement in the back for the *Printing Trades' Diary and Reference-Book for 1890.* Variant title on the cover: *Typographic Printing Machines and Machine Printing.*

Series statement on the cover: Wyman's Technical Series.

Bibliographical citations: Wakeman [1888], 37.

Locations: Bodleian; Delaware; Grolier; LC; Massey; Minnesota; Newberry; Philadelphia; Providence Public [1889]; St. Bride [1888].

Primarily concerned with machine printing. Chapter 1 contains a brief note on the difference between *press* and *machine.* Indexed. Lacks specific information on iron handpresses and presswork.

S34. Southward, John. *The Principles and Progress of Printing Machinery. With an Account of Modern Printing Machines. (Based upon "Typographic Printing Machines")* by F. J. F. Wilson. 2nd ed. London: E. Menken, Bury Street, New Oxford Street, W.C., [1890?].

Bibliographical notes: Inferred publication date taken from the British Library record, shelfmark: 7946.df.47.

Bibliographical citations: Bliss [ca. 1890], 1156.

Locations: British; RIT [1890]; SFPL [1890].

A reprint of item S33 above with a slightly modified title page.

S35. Southward, John. *Progress in Printing and the Graphic Arts during the Victorian Era.* London: Simpkin, Marshall, Hamilton, Kent & Co. Ltd., 1897.

Bibliographical citations: Bliss, 298; Wakeman, 53

Locations: Bancroft; Berkeley; Bodleian; Cambridge; Chicago; Harvard; Huntington; Iowa; Kentucky; LC; Massey; Michigan; Newberry; RIT; St. Bride: Sydney; William & Mary.

Primarily an overview of the printing industry with an emphasis on technological innovations and advancements made since the 1830s. It could also be interpreted as a backlash against the theories of William Morris. Lacks specific information on iron handpresses and presswork. Includes photos of various aspects of the printing trade such as type founding, electrotyping, and papermaking.

S36. Southward, John. *Southward's Dictionary of Typography with Its Auxiliary Arts.* Profusely Illustrated. Part I, February 1872. London: E. W. Allen, 11, Ave Maria Lane, Paternoster Row; and of all booksellers; London, Melbourne, and Sidney: Gordon & Gotch, 1872.

Bibliographical citations: Bigmore & Wyman, vol. II, p. 378; Wakeman, 16.

Locations: Bodleian; British.

Intended to be issued in monthly installments, this is the only part published. Contains instructions for erecting the Albion press. Includes illustrations of the Athol screw press, an arming press, and an Albion press.

S37. Southward, John. *Type-Composing Machines of the Past, the Present, and the Future. A Paper Read before the Balloon Society of Great Britain. At St. James's Hall, October 3rd, 1890.* London: Truslove and Shirley, 143, Oxford Street, W., 1890.

Bibliographical citations: Wakeman, 42.

Locations: Bodleian; Cambridge.

This is the original text of Southward's talk, parts of which were omitted due to shortness of time. His descriptions and evaluations of the machines are precise and to the point. He concludes that composing machines were expensive, unreliable, and fatiguing to operate.

S38. Stevens, Charles P. *The Roller Guide: A Treatise on Rollers and Compositions.* Boston: Wild & Stevens, 28 Hawley Street, 1877.

Bibliographical citations: Bigmore & Wyman, vol. II, p. 401.

Locations: Iowa.

Not seen.

S39. Stewart, Alexander A. *The Printer's Art.* Salem, Massachusetts: Printed and published by the author, 1892.

Locations: British; Huntington; NYPL; St. Bride; SFPL.

A brief manual for compositors and pressmen primarily engaged in job printing on vertical platen and cylinder presses.

S40. Stower, Caleb. *The Compositor's and Pressman's Guide to the Art of Printing; Containing Hints and Instructions to Learners, with Various Impositions, Calculations, Scales of Prices, &c. &c.* London: Printed by the editor, 32, Paternoster-row, for B. Crosby and Co., Stationers'-Court, 1808.

Bibliographical citations: Bigmore & Wyman, vol. II, p. 403; Gaskell, E7; Hitchings, VIII; Marthens, p. 32. Here and in items S41 and S42, Hitchings refers to Stower as *Charles Stower.*

Locations: Bodleian; British; Cambridge; Chicago; Grolier; Huntington; Illinois; Massey; Newberry; NYPL; SFPL; Virginia; William & Mary; Yale.

An abridgment of Stower's *Printer's Grammar* (1808), *see* item S42 below. Primarily intended for apprentices and journeymen. Contains sections on composition and presswork; with a scale of prices, a list of tradesmen, and a glossary of "Technical Terms." Includes illustrations showing the lay of the cases.

S41. Stower, Caleb. *The Compositor's and Pressman's Guide to the Art of Printing; Containing Hints and Instructions to Learners, with Various Schemes of Impositions, Calculations, and the New Scale of Prices for Compositors and Pressmen: Together with a List of Master Printers, Letter-Founders, Printers' Smiths and Joiners, Ink Makers, Wood Engravers, Type Cutters, &c.* 2nd ed. London: Printed by the editor, Brooksby's Walk, Homerton, for B. and R. Crosby and Co., Stationers' Court, Ludgate Street, 1812.

Bibliographical citations: Gaskell, E7; Hitchings, VIII.

Locations: Chicago; Columbia; Delaware; Harvard; St. Bride.

A reprint of the 1808 edition, *see* item S40 above; with a new scale of prices and a revised list of tradesmen.

S42. Stower, Caleb. *The Printer's Grammar; or, Introduction to the Art of Printing: Containing a Concise History of the Art, with the Improvements in the Practice of Printing, for the Last Fifty Years.* London: Printed by the editor, 32, Paternoster Row, for B. Crosby and Co. Stationers'-Court, 1808.

Bibliographical citations: Bigmore & Wyman, vol. II, p. 403; Bliss, 963; Davis & Carter, 8; Gaskell, E6; Hitchings, VII; Marthens, p. 32; Wroth, 6.

Locations: Bancroft; Bodleian; Boston Athenæum; Bridwell; British; Brown; Cambridge; Chicago; Clark; Columbia; Dartmouth; Delaware; Harvard; Huntington; Michigan; Minnesota; Newberry; Providence Public; RIT; St. Bride; SFPL; Toronto; Virginia; William & Mary; Yale.

A very good, comprehensive manual covering all phases of the printing trade taken mostly from Smith (1755), *see* item 12 on p. 883 and Luckombe (1770), *see* item 7 on p. 882. Stower's format influenced all printers' manuals through 1838. Contains descriptions of the Brooke and Stanhope (first construction) presses as well as sections on composition, presswork, printing inks, stereotype printing, and management; with a glossary of "Technical Terms Used in Printing." Indexed. Includes two illustrations of wooden presses, the common and Brooke presses, and their parts and accessories, and the Stanhope press and its parts, plus twenty-eight pages of imposition schemes. There are nineteen pages of exotic types, twenty-nine pages of type flowers from Fry & Steele, and ten pages of type specimens from Caslon & Catherwood. This was the first printers' manual to illustrate and describe an iron handpress. Dedicated to Lord Stanhope. Bigmore & Wyman (vol. II, p. 403) mistakenly attribute *The Printer's Grammar* (1787), *see* item 11 on p. 883, to Stower.

Facsimile reprints:

Caleb Stower: The Printer's Grammar, 1808. London: Gregg Press, 1965. Series statement: English Bibliographical Sources, edited by D. F. Foxon, British Museum. Series 3: Printers' Manuals, no. 4.

S43. [Stower, Caleb]. *The Printer's Manual, an Abridgment of Stower's Grammar; Comprising All the Plans in That Work for Imposing Forms, Several Tables and Other Useful Articles.* With a Copperplate Engraving, Being an Exemplification of Typographical Marks. Boston: Printed and published by R. & C. Crocker, No. 3, Suffolk Buildings, 1817.

Locations: Bodleian; Pittsburgh; RIT; Yale.

A greatly condensed abridgment of Stower's *Printer's Grammar* (1808), *see* item S42 above. Contains instructions for working at the wooden press. There is no mention of iron handpresses; with a glossary of "Technical Terms Used in Printing." Includes twenty-eight pages of imposition schemes. This was the first printers' manual to be printed in the USA and was intended primarily for American printers.

Facsimile reprints:

The Printer's Manual, an Abridgment of Stower's Grammar. With a new introduction by John Bidwell. New York: Garland Publishing, 1981. Series Statement: Nineteenth-Century Book Arts and Printing History.

Bound together with *The Printer's Companion* by Edward Grattan, *see* item G14 on p. 902.

S44. Stower, Caleb. *The Printer's Price-Book, Containing the Master Printer's Charges to the Trade for Printing Works of Various Descriptions, Sizes, Types, and Pages;*

Also, a New, Easy, and Correct Method of Casting Off Manuscript and Other Copy, Exemplified in Specimen Pages of Different Sizes and Types: To Which Is Prefixed Some Account of the Nature and Business of Reading Proof Sheets for the Press, with the Typographical Marks Used for This Purpose, and Their Application Shewn in an Engraving. London: Printed by the editor, Hackney, for C. Cradock and W. Joy, Paternoster-Row, 1814.

Bibliographical citations: Bigmore & Wyman, vol. II, p. 404; Gaskell, E9; Marthens, p. 32. Marthens erroneously inserts the word *Master* before *Printer's Price-Book* in his transcription.

Locations: Bodleian; British; Cambridge; Chicago; Columbia; Dartmouth; Grolier; Harvard; Huntington; LC; Massey; Michigan; Minnesota; Newberry; NYPL; Philadelphia; Providence Public (two copies); St. Bride; Toronto; Virginia; Yale.

A ready-reference handbook designed to calculate the area of type pages in ens. Lacks specific information on iron handpresses and presswork. This item was the first printers' manual to include specimens of type pages – 324 to be exact – showing a variety of typefaces and sizes set to different measures and with varying amounts of leading.

S45. Stower, Caleb. *Typographical Marks, Used in Correcting Proofs, Explained and Exemplified; for the Use of Authors.* London: Printed by C. Stower, Pater-noster Row; for Longman, Hurst, Rees, and Orme, Pater-Noster-Row, 1805.

Bibliographical citations: Bigmore & Wyman, vol. II, p. 404; Marthens, p. 32.

Locations: Bodleian: Cambridge; Minnesota; St. Bride.

A 16-page pamphlet with an engraved plate showing the correct use of typographical marks.

S46. Stower, Caleb. *Typographical Marks, Enployed in Correcting Proofs, Explained and Exemplified; for the Use of Authors.* 2nd ed. London: Printed by C. Stower, Pater-noster-Row, for Longman, Hurst, Rees, and Orme, Pater-Noster-Row, 1806.

Bibliographical citations: Bigmore & Wyman, vol. II, p. 404.

Locations: British; LC.

A reprint of the 1805 edition, *see* item S45 above.

S47. Stower, Caleb. *Typographical Marks, Employed in Correcting Proofs, Explained and Exemplified; for the Use of Authors.* 3rd ed. London: Printed for Longman, Hurst, Rees, Orme, and Brown, Paternoster-Row, 1822.

Bibliographical notes: Bibliographical data taken from Bigmore & Wyman.

Bibliographical citations: Bigmore & Wyman, vol. II, p. 404.

Locations: Cambridge; St. Bride.

A reprint of the 1806 edition, *see* item S46 above.

Stower, Charles. *See* Stower, Caleb.

Straker, C. *See* item R13 on p. 923.

S48. Summers, Thomas Osmond, ed. *The Art of Printing.* Nashville, Tenn.: Published by E. Stevenson & F. A. Owen, agents, for the Methodist Episcopal Church, South, 1855.

Bibliographical notes: The "Preface," dated March 21, 1855, implies that there may have been a previous edition, although no copies of it were located.

Locations: SFPL; Tennessee; Wichita.

Primarily a history of printing. Lacks practical information on iron handpresses and practical printing. Includes a frontispiece showing a woman working at an Adams press.

S49. Summers, Thomas Osmond, ed. *The Art of Printing.* Nashville, Tenn.: Southern Methodist Publishing House, 1861.

Bibliographical notes: The "Preface" is dated March 21, 1855.

Locations: Huntington.

A reprint of the 1855 edition, *see* item S48 above, with a slightly modified title page.

S50. Summers, Thomas Osmond, ed. *The Art of Printing.* Nashville, Tenn.: Published by A. H. Redford, agent, for the M. E. Church, South, 1871.

Bibliographical notes: The "Preface" is dated March 21, 1855.

Locations: Birmingham; Smithsonian.

A reprint of the 1855 edition, *see* item S48 above, with a slightly modified title page.

The Text-Book; or, Easy Instructions in the Elements of the Art of Printing. See item S16 on p. 925.

Thompson, R., & Co. *See* item L4 on p. 911.

T1. Timperley, Charles Henry. *A Dictionary of Printers and Printing, with the Progress of Literature, Ancient and Modern; Biographical Illustrations, etc. etc..* London: H. Johnson, 49, Paternoster-Row; Edinburgh: Fraser & Co.; Glasgow: Symington & Co.; Dublin: Curry & Co.; Manchester: Bancks & Co., 1839.

Bibliographical citations: Bigmore & Wyman, vol. III, p. 12; Bliss, 965; Marthens, p. 33.

Locations: Bancroft; Bodleian; Boston Athenæum; Bridwell; British; Brown; Chicago; Dartmouth; Delaware; Harvard; Iowa; Massey; Michigan; NYPL; Providence Public; Sydney; Toronto; UCLA; Virginia; Washington; William & Mary; Yale.

Consists primarily of historical anecdotes.

T2. Timperley, Charles Henry. *Encyclopædia of Literary and Typographical Anecdote; Being a Chronological Digest of the Most Interesting Facts Illustrative of the*

History of Literature and Printing from the Earliest Period to the Present Time. Interspersed with Biographical Sketches of Eminent Booksellers, Printers, Type-Founders, Engravers, Bookbinders and Paper Makers, of All Ages and Countries, but Especially of Great Britain. With Bibliographical and Descriptive Accounts of Their Principal Productions and Occasional Extracts from Them. Including Curious Particulars of the First Introduction of Printing into Various Countries, and of the Books Then Printed. Notices of Early Bibles and Liturgies of All Countries, Especially Those Printed in England or in English. A History of All the Newspapers, Periodicals, and Almanacks Published in This Country. An Account of the Origin and Progress of Language, Writing and Writing-Materials, the Invention of Paper, Use of Paper Marks, etc. Compiled and Condensed from Nichols's Literary Anecdotes, and Numerous Other Authorities. 2nd ed., to which are added, a continuation to the present time, comprising recent biographies, chiefly of booksellers, and a practical manual of printing. London: Henry G. Bohn, York Street, Covent Garden. 1842.

Bibliographical citations: Bigmore & Wyman, vol. III, p. 13; Bliss, 966.

Locations: Bodleian; British; Brown; Chicago; Kentucky; Massey; RIT; Seattle; Sydney; Virginia; William & Mary; UCLA; Yale.

Essentially the same work as item T1 above with a new title page and his *The Printers' Manual* (1838), *see* item T3 below, inserted between pages 32 and 33.

T3. Timperley, Charles Henry. *The Printers' Manual; Containing Instructions to Learners, with Scales of Impositions, and Numerous Calculations, Recipes, and Scales of Prices in the Principal Towns of Great Britain Together with Practical Directions for Conducting Every Department of a Printing Office.* London: H. Johnson, 44, Paternoster-Row; Manchester: Bancks and Co.; and all other booksellers, 1838.

Bibliographical citations: Bigmore & Wyman, vol. III, p. 12; Bliss, 964; Davis & Carter, 11; Gaskell, E19; Hitchings, XIV; Marthens, p. 33.

Locations: Bodleian; Boston Public; British; Columbia; Delaware; Grolier; Harvard; Huntington; Massey; Newberry; Philadelphia; Providence Public; RIT; St. Bride; SFPL; Toronto: UCLA; Vermont; Virginia; Yale.

A concise, but comprehensive, manual consisting of instructions for compositors and pressmen taken mostly from Hansard (1825), *see* item H2 on p. 903, and Mason (1810), *see* item M25 on p. 916. Also contains directions for making composition rollers. The section on pulling is modified for the one-pull press; with a glossary of "Technical Terms used by Printers." Includes illustrations of a compositor at the case, the Stanhope, Columbian, Albion, and Imperial presses, plus twenty-six pages of imposition schemes. This item is also found bound up as a section in the second

edition of Timperley's *Encyclopaedia of Literary and Typographical Anecdote* (1842), *see* item T2 above.

Facsimile reprints:
Charles H. Timperley: *The Printer's Manual, 1838.* London: Gregg Press, 1965. Series statement: English Bibliographical Sources, edited by D. F. Foxon, British Museum. Series 3: Printers' Manuals, no. 7.

T4. Tobitt, John H. *Combination Type: Their History, Advantages, and Application.* [New York: Published and for sale at 9 Spruce St., 1852].

Bibliographical notes: The inferred imprint is taken from the cover, which also serves as the title page.

Bibliographical citations: Bigmore & Wyman, vol. III, p. 18; Marthens, p. 33.

Locations: Iowa; NYPL.

Not seen.

Tomlinson, Charles. *See* item H13 on p. 905.

T5. *A Treatise on Punctuation, and on Other Matters Relating to Correct Writing and Printing.* By an old printer. London: [1870].

Bibliographical notes: The bibliographical data is taken from Bigmore & Wyman, vol. II, p. 225.

No copies located.

T6. Trumbull, George, comp. *Pocket Typographia; A Brief Practical Guide to the Art of Printing.* Albany: Printed and published by Geo. Davidson, 1846.

Bibliographical citations: Bigmore & Wyman, vol. III, p. 23; Bliss, 921; Gaskell, E22; Marthens, p. 33.

Locations: Boston Public; British; Columbia; Delaware; Grolier; Huntington; Kemble; LC; Massey; Newberry; Providence Public; St. Bride; SFPL; Virginia.

Primarily intended for compositors. Lacks specific information on iron handpresses and presswork. Includes a frontispiece showing a Washington press in an acorn frame; plus forty-three pages of imposition schemes.

T7. *The Typographical Hand Book: A Collection of Useful Information and Valuable Tables of Interest to the Apprentice, the Book and Job Printer, the Newspaper Compositor, the Pressman, &c. Also Memoranda of Important Events Connected with the Art.* Compiled by a practical printer. Detroit, Mich.: [Machris & Aveling, publishers, 1874].

Bibliographical notes: The inferred publication date is taken from Bigmore & Wyman. *See* below. The inferred publisher is taken from the "Preface" on the verso of the title page.

Bibliographical citations: Bigmore & Wyman, vol. III, p. 27; Marthens, p. 40.

No copies located.

T8. *The Typographical Hand Book: A Collection of Useful Information and Valuable Tables of Interest to the Apprentice, the Book and Job Printer, the Newspaper Compositor, the Pressman, &c. Also Memoranda of Important Events Connected with the Art.* Compiled by a practical printer. 2nd ed. Detroit, Mich.: [Machris & Aveling, publishers, 1875].

Bibliographical notes: The inferred publication date is taken from the Library of Congress record, call number: Z244.A2 M13. The inferred publisher is taken from the "Preface" on the verso of the title page.

Locations: LC; Minnesota.

A compilation of practical information taken from various sources, such as Harpel, De Vinne, MacKellar, and trade periodicals. Indexed. Lacks specific information on iron handpresses and presswork. Includes numerous tables and diagrams, plus eight pages of imposition schemes.

T9. *The Typographical Hand Book: A Collection of Useful Information and Valuable Tables of Interest to the Apprentice, the Book and Job Printer, the Newspaper Compositor, the Pressman, &c. Also Memoranda of Important Events Connected with the Art.* Compiled by a practical printer. 3rd ed. Detroit, Mich.: [Machris & Aveling, publishers], [ca. 1876]

Bibliographical notes: The inferred publisher is taken from the "Preface" on the verso of the title page. The inferred publication date is taken from the St. Bride Printing Library record, call number: 23486.

Locations: Huntington [1876?]; St. Bride.

A reprint of the [1875] edition, *see* item T8 above, with a new title page.

V1. Van Winkle, Cornelius S. *The Printers' Guide; or, An Introduction to the Art of Printing: Including an Essay on Punctuation, and Remarks on Orthography.* New-York: Printed and published by C. S. Van Winkle, printer to the University of New-York, 1818.

Bibliographical citations: Bliss, 923; Gaskell, E10; Hitchings, 1; Marthens, p. 34; Wroth, 9.

Locations: Columbia; Delaware; Grolier; Harvard; Huntington; Newberry; Philadelphia; Providence Public; RIT; Yale.

An abridgment of Stower's *Printer's Grammar* (1808), *see* item S42 on p. 929. This was the first printers' manual to be written and printed by an American. Contains sections on composition and presswork, although the printing instructions are limited to the wooden press; with a glossary of "Technical Terms." The Columbian, Ruthven, Ramage Screw, and Wells presses are mentioned, but Van Winkle does not give any details on setting them up or printing on them. Includes a printed scale to calculate the number of ems in a page of type, and type specimens and flowers from the foundries of E. White and D. & G. Bruce, plus nineteen pages of imposition schemes. Van Win-

kle was the first to address the apprentice directly in a printers' manual.

Facsimile reprints:

The Printers' Guide; or, An Introduction to the Art of Printing: Including an Essay on Punctuation, and Remarks on Orthography. Chicago: Lakeside Press, 1970.

The Printers' Guide; or, An Introduction to the Art of Printing. With a new introduction by Carey S. Bliss. New York: Garland Publishing, 1981. Series Statement: Nineteenth-Century Book Arts and Printing History.

V2. Van Winkle, Cornelius S. *The Printer's Guide, or, An Introduction to the Art of Printing: Including an Essay on Punctuation, and Remarks on Orthography.* 2nd ed., with additions and alterations. New-York: Published by White, Gallaher, and White, No. 7 Wall Street, 1827.

Bibliographical citations: Gaskell, E10.

Locations: Columbia; LC; Virginia.

Basically the same as the 1818 edition, *see* item V1 above, although the sequence of some of the material has changed.

V3. Van Winkle, Cornelius S. *The Printer's Guide; or, An Introduction to the Art of Printing: Including an Essay on Punctuation, and Remarks on Orthography.* 3rd ed., with additions and alterations. New-York: Published by White & Hagar, No. 45 Gold Street, 1836.

Bibliographical citations: Bigmore & Wyman, vol. III, p. 42; Bliss, 924; Gaskell, E10; Hitchings, 1b.

Locations: British; Columbia; Harvard; Huntington; Kemble; Newberry; NYPL; RIT; St. Bride; SFPL; Sydney; Virginia (author's copy with annotations for another, although not published, edition); Yale.

Unlike the first two editions of this work, the section on presswork in the third edition focuses on the iron handpress; with a glossary of "Technical Terms." Includes nineteen pages of imposition schemes. The Washington, Smith, and Eagle presses are illustrated in the advertisements in the back.

Vest Pocket Manual of Printing. See item I1 on p. 908.

W1. [Warren, William Thorn]. *How to Print and Publish a Book. Also Information about Printing Generally.* Winchester: Warren & Son, printers and publishers, High Street; London: Simpkin & Co., Limited, Stationers' Hall Court, 1890.

Locations: Bodleian; British; Delaware; Princeton.

Primarily intended as an author's guide to printing and publishing. Lacks practical information on iron handpresses and practical printing.

W2. Watson, Joseph. *Instructions for Amateur Printers: Containing Hints on the Selection of Press and Type; Directions for Setting or Composing Type, Making Ink Rollers, &c. With an Explanation of Technical Terms*

Used by Printers. By a practical printer. Boston: Published by Joseph Watson, 1873.

Locations: NYPL; William & Mary.

Mainly to instruct amateurs on the use of small hobby presses; with a glossary of "Technical terms used by printers." Lacks specific information on iron handpresses. Includes a frontispiece showing a tabletop vertical platen press known as the Young America Press.

W3. Watt, P. B. *A Few Hints on Colour and Printing in Colours.* London: W. J. Adams, 59, Fleet Street; Manchester: Henry Blacklock and Co., Albert Square; Glasgow: J. D. Miller, Argyle Street, 1872.

Bibliographical citations: Bigmore & Wyman, vol. III, p. 68.

Locations: Bodleian; British; Grolier; St. Bride.

Originally appeared in the pages of *The Lithographer*, for July and August 1870 and January 1871. Initially intended for lithographic printers, but the text was later revised for this edition in order to make it applicable to color printing in general.

W4. Weatherly, Sidney M. *The Young Job Printer: A Book of Instructions in Detail on Job Printing for Beginners.* Chicago: S. M. Weatherly, 1889.

Locations: Chicago; Huntington; Newberry; RIT.

A short manual intended mainly to acquaint young printers with the basic aspects of the printing business. Very little information on iron handpresses and practical printing.

W5. Weatherly, Sidney M. *The Young Job Printer: A Book of Instructions in Detail on Job Printing for Beginners.* [2nd ed., revised.] Chicago: S. M. Weatherly, 1889 [i.e., 1891].

Bibliographical notes: The inferred edition statement is taken from p. [iv], which also includes a notice that this edition was "issued in January, 1891."

Bibliographical citations: Bliss, 925.

Locations: Iowa; Michigan; SFPL.

A reprint of the 1889 edition, *see* item W4 above, with a new title page.

Twentieth-century editions:
The Young Job Printer: A Book of Instructions in Detail on Job Printing for Beginners. Tustin, CA.: Garden View Press, 1960.

W6. Whybrew, Samuel. *The Progressive Printer. A Book of Instruction for Journeymen and Apprenticed Printers. Containing Much Practical Information of Value to Compositors and Pressmen, with Instructions on the Art of Mixing Colors – Also Showing Form of Some of the Various Kinds of Commercial Printing and Samples of the Same – Advice to Those Already Apprenticed, and to Prospective Apprentices – Useful Recipes for the Trade, and Numerous Hints to the Craft in General.* Rochester, N. Y.: S. Whybrew, 27 W. Main St., 1881.

Locations: Grolier; Huntington; LC.

Practical instructions for printing on a cylinder job press. Contains chapters on the apprentice system, mixing colored inks, and color printing. Includes a color chart and a sample contract for employing apprentices.

W7. Whybrew, Samuel. *The Progressive Printer, A Book of Instruction for Journeymen and Apprenticed Printers. Containing Much Practical Information of Value to Compositors and Pressmen, with Instructions on the Art of Mixing Colors – Advice to Apprentices – Useful Recipes for the Trade, and Numerous Hints to the Craft in General.* 2nd ed. Rochester, N. Y.: Whybrew & Ripley, publishers, 1882.

Bibliographical citations: Bigmore & Wyman, vol. III, p. 82.

Locations: Delaware; Grolier; Huntington; Iowa; Kemble; Newberry; NYPL; RIT.

A reprint of the 1881 edition, *see* item W6 above, with a new title page.

W8. Wightman, W. *The Amateur Printer's Handbook. Containing Instructions for Making Printing-Presses and How to Work Them to Advantage; with Practical Observations and Illustrations, a Great Many of Which Are Working on This Principle and Giving Every Satisfaction.* Leeds: 1871.

Bibliographical notes: The bibliographical data is taken from Bigmore & Wyman, vol. III, p. 84.

No copies located.

W9. Wilkinson, W. T. *Photo-Engraving, Photo-Litho, and Collotype, A Practical Manual.* 4th ed. London: Hampton, Judd & Co., 14, Duke Street, Adelphi, W.C., 1890.

Locations: Delaware; St. Bride.

In the 1880s and 1890s, Wilkinson wrote several books on photo-mechanical processes, published both in London and New York. This particular item is representative of them.

W10. Williams, Tom Burton. *Hints on Imposition. An Illustrated Guide for Printer and Pressman in the Construction of Book Forms. Also Other Matters Pertaining to Letter-Press Printing.* Buffalo, N. Y.: The Matthews-Northrup Co., 1895.

Locations: Chicago; Columbia; Huntington; Kemble.

Detailed information on imposition schemes. Includes numerous diagrams.

W11. Wilson, Frederick John Farlow. *Stereotyping and Electrotyping. A Guide for the Production of Plates by Papier Maché [sic] and Plaster Processes. With Illustration for Depositing Copper by Battery or by the Dynamo Machine. Also Hints on Steel and Brass Facing, etc.* London: Wyman & Sons, Great Queen Street, Lincoln's Inn Fields, [1880].

Bibliographical notes: The inferred publication date is taken from the Bodleian Library record, call number: 176 f.50. A sixth edition was published in 1898.

Bibliographical citations: Bigmore & Wyman [1882], vol. III, p. 87; Bigmore & Wyman, vol. II, p. 379 (under Southward).

Locations: Bodleian; British; St. Bride.

Detailed instructions for stereotyping and electrotyping. Profusely illustrated.

W12. Wilson, Frederick John Farlow. *Typographic Printing Machines and Machine Printing. A Practical Guide to the Selection of Bookwork, Two-Colour, Jobbing, and Rotary Machines, with Remarks upon Their Construction, Capabilities, and Peculiarities. Also Instructions in Making Ready, the Preparation of Engravings, etc.* With numerous illustrations. London: Wyman & Sons, Great Queen Street, Lincoln's Inn Fields, [1879].

Bibliographical notes: The inferred publication date is taken from the "Preface," which is dated December, 1879. Series statement: Wyman's Technical Series. In a footnote to the "Preface" of the third edition of Wilson's *Stereotyping and Electrotypying*, the publishers gives the publication date of item W12 as 1880.

Bibliographical citations: Bigmore & Wyman, vol. III, p. 88; Wakeman, 28.

Locations: American Antiquarian Society; Bodleian [1880]; British [1880]; Chicago; Columbia; Dartmouth; Delaware; Huntington; Iowa; LC; Minnesota; Newberry; RIT; St. Bride [1880]; William & Mary; Yale.

A guide to selecting printing machines, with remarks on their construction and capabilities. The most comprehensive work on the subject to date. Contains chapters on making ready and preparing wood engravings. Lacks specific information on iron handpress, but includes useful advice on general printing practices that can be applied to presswork. Includes fifteen fold-out plates and numerous illustrations in the text of printing machines and their mechanisms.

W13. Wilson, Frederick John Farlow. *Typographic Printing Machines and Machine Printing. A Practical Guide to the Selection of Bookwork, Two-Colour, Jobbing, and Rotary Machines, with Remarks upon Their Construction, Capabilities, and Peculiarities. Also Instructions in Making Ready, the Preparation of Engravings, etc.* With numerous illustrations. [2nd ed.] London: Wyman & Sons, Great Queen Street, Lincoln's Inn Fields, [1882].

Bibliographical notes: The inferred publication date and edition statement are taken from Bigmore & Wyman. *See* below. The "Preface" is dated December, 1879.

Bibliographical citations: Bigmore & Wyman, vol. III, p. 88.

Locations: RIT.

An expanded reprint of the [1879] edition, *see* item W12 above. Contains information on making ready on platen and perfecting printing machines, as well as mechanized bindery equipment; with a six-page appendix updating the [1879] edition, *see* item W12 above. Includes 207 illustrations of printing and binding machines.

W14. Wilson, Frederick John Farlow. *Typographic Printing Machines and Machine Printing. A Practical Guide to the Selection of Bookwork, Two-Colour, Jobbing, and Rotary Machines, with Remarks upon Their Construction, Capabilities, and Peculiarities. Also Instructions in Making Ready, the Preparation of Engravings, etc.* With numerous illustrations. 3rd ed. London: Wyman & Sons, Great Queen Street, Lincoln's Inn Fields, [1884].

Bibliographical notes: The inferred publication date is taken from the copyright receipt stamp in the British Library's copy, shelfmark: 11899.bb.32. The "Preface" is dated December, 1879.

Bibliographical citations: Bigmore & Wyman, vol. III, p. 88.

Locations: Bodleian; British; St. Bride [ca. 1885].

A reprint of the [1882] edition, *see* item W13 above.

W15. Wilson, Frederick John Farlow. *Typographic Printing Machines and Machine Printing. A Practical Guide to the Selection of Bookwork, Two-Colour, Jobbing, and Rotary Machines, with Remarks upon Their Construction, Capabilities, and Peculiarities. Also Instructions in Making Ready, the Preparation of Engravings, etc.* With numerous illustrations. 4th ed. London: Wyman & Sons, Great Queen Street, Lincoln's Inn Fields, [1886?].

Bibliographical notes: The inferred publication date is taken from the Smithsonian Institution Libraries record, call number: Z249 .W74t 1886.

Locations: Delaware; Smithsonian.

A reprint of the [1882] edition, *see* item W13 above.

W16. Wilson, Frederick John Farlow, and Douglas Grey. *A Practical Treatise upon Modern Printing Machinery and Letterpress Printing.* Illustrated with numerous engravings. London, Paris, New York & Melbourne: Cassell & Company, Limited, 1888.

Bibliographical citations: Bliss, 1158; Wakeman, 38.

Locations: Bodleian; British; Chicago; Clark; Delaware; Harvard; Huntington; Iowa; LC; Massey; Michigan; Minnesota; Providence Public; RIT; Virginia; William & Mary; Yale.

Primarily about printing machines with detailed instructions for operating them. Excellent chapters on making ready and cutting out overlays. Chapter 1 has a brief note on the wooden press and the Stanhope press. Lacks practical information on iron handpresses and presswork. Includes illustrations of progressive proofs taken after each layer of the overlay is added to the makeready.

Wilson, Frederick John Farlow. *See also* items S33 and S34 on p. 928.

W17. Wilson, John. *A Treatise on Grammatical Punctuation; Designed for Letter-Writers, Authors, Printers, and Correctors of the Press; and for the Use of Academies and Schools.* Manchester: Printed and published by the author, Victoria Bridge, Salford, and sold by booksellers, 1844.

Locations: British; NYPL.

Not seen.

W18. Wilson, John. *A Treatise on English Punctuation; Designed for Letter-Writers, Authors, Printers, and Correctors of the Press; and for the Use of Schools and Academies. With an Appendix, Containing Rules on the Use of Capitals, a List of Abbreviations, Hints on the Preparation of Copy and on Proof-Reading, Specimen of Proof-Sheet, Etc.* 2nd ed. Boston: Crosby, Nichols, and Company, 111, Washington Street, 1850.

Bibliographical citations: Bigmore & Wyman, vol. III, p. 88; Marthens, p. 35.

Locations: Chicago; Columbia; Harvard.

Not seen. A fourth edition was published in 1855.

W19. Wilson, John. *A Treatise on English Punctuation; Designed for Letter-Writers, Authors, Printers, and Correctors of the Press; and for the Use of Schools and Academies. With an Appendix, Containing Rules on the Use of Capitals, a List of Abbreviations, Hints on the Preparation of Copy and on Proof-Reading, Specimen of Proof-Sheet, Etc.* 6th ed. Boston: Crosby, Nichols, and Company, 111, Washington Street, 1856.

Locations: British.

The twenty-third edition was published in 1871. The title was slightly modified for the American editions. No copies of the first edition (1826) were located.

W20. Wilson, W. *The Compositor's Assistant. Containing All the Imposition Tables Now in Use.* Exeter: 1855.

Bibliographical notes: The bibliographical data is taken from Bigmore & Wyman, vol. III, p. 89.

No copies located.

W21. [Wyman, Charles William Henry]. *List of Technical Terms Relating to Printing Machinery.* Compiled by the editor of the "Printing Times & Lithographer." London: Wyman & Sons, Great Queen Street, Lincoln's-Inn Fields, [1883].

Series statement on the cover: Wyman's Technical Series.

Bibliographical notes: The inferred publication date is taken from the British Library record, shelfmark: 11899.b.24.

Bibliographical citations: Bigmore & Wyman [1882], vol. III, p. 102; Wakeman [ca. 1885], 30.

Locations: Bodleian; British; Chicago; Columbia [1882]; LC [1882]; Michigan [1882]; NYPL; Providence Public [1882]; Smithsonian; St. Bride; William & Mary [1882].

The most comprehensive list of technical terms relating to printing machinery to be published in the nineteenth century.

W22. [Wyman, Charles William Henry]. *List of Technical Terms Relating to Printing Machinery.* Compiled by the editor of the "Printing Times & Lithographer." 2nd ed. London: E. Menken, 65 & 66 Chancery Lane, Lincoln's-Inn Fields, [1885].

Bibliographical notes: The inferred publication date is taken from the University of Delaware Library record, call number: Z249 .L57x 1885.

Locations: Delaware; Virginia [1882?].

A reprint of the [1883] edition, *see* item W21 above.

Twentieth-century editions:

List of Technical Terms Relating to Printing Machinery. Compiled by the editor of the "Printing Times & Lithographer." London: Myers, 1909.

Bibliography of Selected References

In addition to the works listed in the Bibliography of Pre-Twentieth-Century Printers' Manuals, I consulted the following list of reference works, many of which were in my personal library. For this reason, some of the editions may not be the most recent. These works are representative of the texts that I found most useful when I was still printing on iron handpresses in Italy and Alabama, and later in Los Angeles and Seattle while writing this book. The information in them provided me with innumerable insights concerning the art of printing and its allied crafts.

Books

Allen, Edward Monington, ed. *Harper's Dictionary of the Graphic Arts*. New York: Harper & Row, 1963.

Allen, Lewis M. *Printing with the Handpress*. Kentfield, CA: Allen Press, 1969.

Appleton, D., and Company. *Appletons' [sic] Cyclopædia of American Biography*. Edited by James Grant Wilson and John Fiske. 6 vols. New York: D. Appleton and Co., 1886–1889.

Arnett, John Andrews, pseud. for John Hannett. *Bibliopegia; or, The Art of Bookbinding in All Its Branches*. London: Richard Groombridge; Edinburgh: Oliver and Boyd; Dublin: W. F. Wakeman; New York: W. Jackson, 1835.

Atkins, William, ed. *The Art and Practice of Printing*. 6 vols. London: New Era Publishing Co., [1932–1933].

Audin, Marius. *Histoire de l'imprimerie par l'image*. Paris: Henri Jonquières, 1928.

Barber, Giles. *French Letterpress Printing: A List of French Printing Manuals and Others [sic] Texts in French Bearing on the Technique of Letterpress Printing, 1567–1900*. Compiled by Giles Barber. Occasional Publication no. 5. Oxford: Oxford Bibliographical Society, Bodleian Library, 1969.

Barber, Giles. *See also* Gaskell, Philip.

Barr, Leonard F. *ATA Advertising Production Handbook*. 3rd ed., rev. and enl. Edited by a committee appointed by the Advertising Typographers Association of America, Inc. [New York]: Advertising Typographers Association of America, 1963.

Bartram, Alan. *See* Sutton, James.

Berry, William Turner, and H. Edmund Poole. *Annals of Printing: A Chronological Encyclopædia from the Earliest Times to 1950*. Toronto: University of Toronto Press, 1966.

Berry, William Turner. *See also* Jaspert, W. Pincus.

Biggs, John Reginald. *Basic Typography*. London: Faber and Faber, 1968.

Biggs, John Reginald. *Illustration and Reproduction*. London: Blandford Press, 1950.

Bigmore, Edward Clements, and Charles William Henry Wyman, ed. *A Bibliography of Printing with Notes and Illustrations*. 3 vols. London: Bernard Quaritch, 1880–1886.

Bigus, Richard. *See* Turner, Decherd.

Bland, David. *The Illustration of Books*. London: Faber and Faber, 1951.

Bliss, Anthony S., comp. *Printing: History, Forms, and Use*. A catalogue in three parts of the collection formed by Jackson Burke. Catalogs no. 428, 433, and 436. Los Angeles: Dawson's Book Shop, 1974–1975.

Bloy, Colin H. *A History of Printing Ink, Balls, and Rollers, 1440–1850*. London: Wynkyn de Worde Society, 1967.

Blumenthal, Joseph. *Art of the Printed Book, 1455–1955. Masterpieces of Typography through Five Centuries from the Collections of the Pierpont Morgan Library, New York*. New York: Pierpont Morgan Library; London: Bodley Head, 1974.

The Bookman's Glossary 5th ed.. Edited by Jean Peters. New York: R. R. Bowker, 1975.

British Library. *The British Library General Catalogue of Printed Books to 1975*. 360 vols. London: Clive Bingley; New York: K.G. Saur; Detroit: Distributed by Gale Research, 1979–1987. Plus supplements.

Brunner, Felix. *A Handbook of Graphic Reproduction Processes: A Technical Guide Including the Printmaking Processes for Art Collectors and Dealers, Librarians, Booksellers, Publishers, Artists, Graphic Designers, and the Printing Trade*. 4th ed. London: Alec Tirandi, 1972.

Burke, Jackson. *Prelum to Albion: A History of the Development of the Hand Press from Gutenberg to Morris*. San Francisco: [Printed at the Press of M. L. and J. Burke], 1940.

Cambridge Biographical Encyclopedia. Edited by David Crystal. Cambridge: Cambridge University Press, 1994.

Carter, Harry. *See* Moxon, Joseph.

Carter, Harry. *See* Simon, Herbert.

Carter, John. *ABC for Book-Collectors.* 4h ed., revised and reprinted with corrections. London: Hart-Davis, 1967.

Carter, John. *ABC for Book Collectors.* 7th ed. With corrections, additions, and an introduction by Nicolas Barker. New Castle, DE: Oak Knoll Press, 1997.

Cassell's Dutch-English, English-Dutch Dictionary. Completely revised by J. A. Jockin-La Bastide and G. van Kooten. 1st Cassell ed. London: Cassell, 1981.

Cassell's French-English, English-French Dictionary. Completely revised by Denis Girard, with the assistance of Gaston Dulong, Oliver Van Oss, and Charles Guinness. New York: Macmillan, 1981.

Cassell's German-English, English-German Dictionary. Completely revised by Harold T. Betteridge. New York: Macmillan, 1978.

Cassell's Spanish-English, English-Spanish Dictionary. Completely revised by Anthony Gooch and Angel García de Paredes. New York: Macmillan, 1978.

Chambers, Ephraim. *Cyclopædia: or, An Universal Dictionary of Arts and Sciences.* 4th ed. London: D. Midwinter, 1741–1743.

The Chicago Manual of Style. 14th ed. Chicago: University of Chicago Press, 1993.

Clair, Colin. *A Chronology of Printing.* London: Cassell, 1969.

Clair, Colin. *A History of European Printing.* London: Academic Press, 1976.

Cleeton, Glen U., and Charles W. Pitkin. *General Printing.* Revised by Raymond L. Cornwell. 3rd ed. Bloomington, IL: McKnight & McKnight Publishing Co., 1963.

Cockerell, Douglas. *Bookbinding and the Care of Books: A Text-book for Bookbinders and Librarians.* With an appendix by Sydney M. Cockerell. 5 ed., rev. London: Pittman Publishing, 1973.

Columbia Encyclopedia, The. Edited by Paul Lagassé. New York: Columbia University Press, 2000.

Columbia University Libraries. *The History of Printing from Its Beginnings to 1930: The Subject Catalogue of the American Type Founders Company Library in the Columbia University Libraries.* With an introduction by Kenneth A. Lohf, 4 vols. Millwood, NY: Kraus International Publications, 1980.

Combe, William. *The Tour of Doctor Prosody.* London: Matthew Iley, 1821.

Comparato, Frank E. *Chronicles of Genius and Folly: R. Hoe & Company and the Printing Press as a Service to Democracy.* Culver City: Labyrinthos, 1979.

Curwen, Harold. *Processes of Graphic Reproduction in Printing.* Revised by Charles Mayo. 3rd ed., revised and extended. London: Faber and Faber. 1963.

Davis, Herbert. *See* Moxon, Joseph.

Deller, Jack. *Printers' Rollers: Their Manufacture, Use, and Care.* London: Charles Skilton, 1959.

Dictionary of National Biography, The. London: Oxford University Press, [1921–1922].

Dieterichs, Karl. *Die Buchdruckpresse von Johannes Gutenberg bis Friedrich König.* Mainz: Gutenberg-Gesellschaft, 1930.

Dumont, Jean. *Vade-mecum du typographe.* 2nd. ed. Bibliothèque Technique. Brussels: 1894.

Eichenberg, Fritz. *The Art of the Print: Masterpieces, History, Techniques.* New York: Harry N. Abrams, 1976.

Encyclopædia Londinensis; or, Universal Dictionary of Arts, Sciences, and Literature. Projected and arranged by John Wilkes. 24 vols. London: N.p., 1810–1829.

Etherington, Don. *See* Roberts, Matt T.

Exman, Eugene. *The Brothers Harper: A Unique Publishing Partnership and Its Impact upon the Cultural Life of America from 1817 to 1853.* New York: Harper & Row, [1965].

Franklin, Colin. *See* Turner, Decherd.

Gascoigne, Bamber. *How to Identify Prints: A Complete Guide to Manual and Mechanical Processes from Woodcut to Ink Jet.* New York: Thames and Hudson, 1986.

Gaskell, Philip. *A New Introduction to Bibliography.* Reprinted with corrections. London: Oxford University Press, 1974.

Gaskell, Philip, Giles Barber, and Georgina Warrilow. "An Annotated List of Printers' Manuals to 1850." *Journal of the Printing Historical Society,* 1968, no. 4, pp. 11–31.

Gaskell, Philip, Giles Barber, and Georgina Warrilow. "Addenda and Corrigenda to 'An Annotated List of Printers' Manuals to 1850.'" *Journal of the Printing Historical Society,* 1971, no. 7, pp. 65–66.

Gernsheim, Helmut, in collaboration with Alison Gernsheim. *The History of Photography from the Camera Obscura to the Beginning of the Modem Era.* New York: McGraw-Hill, 1969.

Gerry, Vance. *The Ernest A. Lindner Collection of Antique Printing Machinery.* Pasadena: Weather Bird Press, 1971.

Glaister, Geoffrey Ashall. *An Encyclopedia of the Book: Terms Used in Paper-Making, Printing, Bookbinding, and Publishing. With Notes on Illustrated Manuscripts, Bibliophiles, Private Presses, and Printing Societies.* Cleveland: World Publishing Co., 1960.

Glaister, Geoffrey Ashall. *Encyclopedia of the Book.* With a new introduction by David Farren. New Castle, DE: Oak Knoll Press, 1996.

Glatte, Hans. *Shorthand Systems of the World: A Concise Historical and Technical Review.* New York: Philosophical Library, 1959.

Green, Ralph. *The Iron Hand Press in America.* With illustrations by Robert Galvin after drawings by Ralph Green. Rowayton, CT: [Press in Rowayton], 1948.

Hammer, Carolyn Reading. *Notes on the Two-Color Initials of Victor Hammer.* Lexington, KY: Stamperia del Santuccio, 1966.

Hannnett, John. *See* Arnett, John Andrews.

Harrap, Charles. *Text Book of Metalography (Printed from Metals): Being a Full Consideration of the Nature and Properties of Zinc and Aluminium and Their Treatment As Planographic Printing Surfaces.* Leicester: Raithby, Lawrence & Co. 1909.

Harris, Elizabeth M. *The Common Press. Being a Record,*

Description, and Delineation of the Early Eighteenth-Century Handpress in the Smithsonian Institute. With a history and documentation of the press by Elizabeth Harris and drawings and advice on construction by Clinton Sisson. Boston: David R. Godine, 1978.

Harris, Elizabeth M. *How to Print.* Washington D.C.: Smithsonian Institution Press, 1977.

Harris, Elizabeth M. *Printing Presses in the Graphic Arts Collection: Printing, Embossing, Stamping, and Duplicating Devices.* Washington, DC: National Museum of American History, Smithsonian Institution, 1996.

Hart, Horace. *Charles Earl Stanhope and the Oxford University Press.* Reprinted from *Collectanea, 111,* 1896 of the Oxford Historical Society with notes by James Mosley. Publication no. 2. London: Printing Historical Society, 1966.

Harthan, John. *The History of the Illustrated Book: The Western Tradition.* London: Thames and Hudson, 1981.

Heller, Jules. *Papermaking.* New York: Watson-Guptill Publications, 1978.

Hitchings, Sinclair H., comp. Catalog supplement to "The Art of Printing: Joseph Moxon and His Successors" by Herbert Davis. *Printing & Graphic Art,* May 1957, vol. 5, no 2, pp. 23–33.

Hoe, R., & Co. *Catalogue of Printing Presses and Printers' Materials, Lithographic Presses, Stereotyping and Electrotyping Machinery, Binders' Presses and Materials.* New York: R. Hoe & Co., 1881.

Hopkins, Richard L. *Origin of the American Point System for Printers' Type Measurement.* Terra Alta, WV: Hill & Dale Press, 1976.

Hudson, Graham. *The Victorian Printer.* Princess Risborough, Buckinghamshire: Shire Publications, 1996.

Hunter, Dard. *Papermaking: The History and Technique of an Ancient Craft.* 2nd ed., rev. and enl. New York: Alfred A. Knopf, 1947.

Huss, Richard E. *The Development of Printers' Mechanical Typesetting Methods, 1822–1925.* Published for the Bibliographical Society of the University of Virginia. Charlottesville: University Press of Virginia, 1973.

International Paper Company. *Pocket Pal: A Graphic Arts Production Handbook..* 11th ed. New York: International Paper Co., 1974

International Paper Company. *Pocket Pal: A Graphic Arts Production Handbook..* 16th ed. Memphis: International Paper Co., 1995

International Typographical Union. *I.T.U. Lessons in Printing: Principles and Practice As Approved by the Trade.* 4 units in 38 parts. Indianapolis: Issued by International Typographical Union, 1927–1929.

International Typographical Union. *I.T.U. Lessons in Printing* by I.T.U. Bureau of Education. 4 vols. Indianapolis: International Typographical Union, 1945.

Jaspert, W. Pincus; William Turner Berry; and Alfred Forbes Johnson. *The Encyclopaedia of Type Faces.* 4th ed., entirely restyled and greatly enlarged. London: Blandford Press, 1970.

Jean, Georges. *Writing: The Story of Alphabets and Scripts.* Discoveries. New York: Harry N. Abrams, 1992.

Jennett, Seán. *The Making of Books.* London: Faber and Faber, 1951.

Johnson, Alfred Forbes. *See* Jaspert, W. Pincus.

Johnson, Arthur W. *The Thames and Hudson Manual of Bookbinding.* London: Thames and Hudson, 1978.

Kubler, George Adolf. *The Era of Charles Mahon, Third Earl of Stanhope, Stereotyper, 1750–1825.* New York: [Brooklyn Eagle Press], 1938.

Küp, Karl. *See* Ulrich, Carolyn F.

Lardner, Dionysius. *The Museum of Science and Art.* 12 vols. in 6. London: Walton and Maberly, 1854–1856.

Lawson, Alexander S. *Anatomy of a Typeface.* Boston: David R. Godine, 1990.

Lawson, Alexander S. *The School of Printing: Rochester Institute of Technology, The First Half-Century, 1937–1987.* [Rochester, NY]: Press of the Good Mountain, School of Printing Management and Sciences, 1987.

Lawson, Alexander S., with Dwight Agner. *Printing Types: An Introduction.* Revised and expanded edition. Boston: Beacon Press, 1990.

Levarie, Norma. *The Art and History of Books.* New York: James H. Heineman, 1968.

Lewis, John. *Anatomy of Printing: The Influence of Art and History on Its Design.* London: Faber and Faber, 1970.

Library of Congress. *The National Union Catalog, Pre-1956 Imprints: A Cumulative Author List Representing Library of Congress Printed Cards and Titles Reported by Other American Libraries.* Compiled and edited with the cooperation of the Library of Congress and the National Union Catalog Subcommittee of the Resources Committee of the Resources and Technical Services Division, American Library Association. 754 vols. London: Mansell, 1968–1981.

Liveing, Edward. *The House of Harrild, 1801–1948.* London: Harrild and Sons, 1949.

Logan, Herschel C. *The American Hand Press: Its Origin, Development, and Use.* With a foreword by Ward Ritchie. Illustrated by the author. Whittier, CA: Curt Zoller Press, 1980.

The London Journal of Arts and Sciences. London: Sherwood, Neely, and Jones, 1820–1834.

Marthens, John F. *Typographical Bibliography: A List of Books in the English Language on Printing and Its Accessories.* Pittsburgh: Bakewell & Marthens, 1875.

McLean, Ruari. *The Thames and Hudson Manual of Typography.* Reprinted with corrections. New York: Thames and Hudson, 1980.

McMurtrie, Douglas C. *The Book: The Story of Printing and Bookmaking.* 3rd ed., rev. New York: Oxford University Press, 1943.

McCreery, John. "The Press." Liverpool: J. McCreery, 1803.

Mechanics' Magazine. London: Knight & Lacey, 1825, no. 95.

Merriman, Frank. *A.T.A. Type Comparison Book* [New York]: Advertising Typographers Association of America, 1965.

Mills, George J. *Platen Press Operation.* Pittsburgh: Carnegie Institute of Technology, 1959.

Modern Methods of Illustrating Books. Edited by Henry B. Wheatley. London: Elliot Stock, 1887.

Moran, James. *Printing Presses: History and Development from the Fifteenth Century to Modern Times.* London: Faber and Faber, 1973.

Moxon, Joseph. *Mechanick Exercises on the Whole Art of Printing.* Edited by Herbert Davis and Harry Carter. 2nd ed. London: Oxford University Press, 1962.

Muir, Percy. *Victorian Illustrated Books.* London: B. T. Batsford, 1971.

Newberry Library. *Dictionary Catalogue of the History of Printing from the John M. Wing Foundation in the Newberry Library.* 6 vols. [Boston]: G. K. Hall & Co., 1961.

New York Public Library. *Dictionary Catalog of the Research Libraries of The New York Public Library, 1911–1971.* 800 vols. [New York]: New York Public Library, Astor, Lenox, and Tilden Foundations; [Boston]: Distributed by G. K. Hall & Co., 1979.

Oxford English Dictionary, The. Oxford: Clarendon Press, 1970.

Papermaking: Art and Craft. Washington, DC: Library of Congress, 1968.

Papillon, Jean-Michel. *Traité historique et pratique de la gravure en bois.* Paris: P. G. Simon, 1766.

Pardoe, F. E. *John Baskerville of Birmingham: Letter-Founder and Printer.* London: Frederick Muller, 1975.

Pitkin, Charles W. *See* Cleeton, Glen U.

Pitman, Sir Isaac. *Stenographic Sound-Hand.* London: S. Bagster, [1837].

Polk, Ralph Weiss. *The Practice of Printing.* Peoria, IL: Manual Arts Press, 1926.

Poole, H. Edmund. *See* Berry, William Turner.

Prechtl, Johann Josef. *Technologische Encyklopädie.* Stuttgart: J. G. Cotta, 1830–1855.

Printing Ink Handbook. Compiled by Product and Technical Publications Committee, National Association of Printing Ink Manufacturers, Inc. 3rd ed. Harrison, NY: National Association of Printing Ink Manufacturers, 1976.

Printing Ink Manual. Frederick Anderton Askew, editor-in-chief. Commissioned by the Technical Training Board of the Society of British Printing Ink Manufacturers. 2nd ed. Cambridge: W. Heffer & Sons, 1969.

Printing Metals: Their Production, Nature, and Use by members of Capper Pass & Son Ltd. 3rd ed. Bristol: Capper Pass & Son, 1932

Proceedings of the Fine Printing Conference at Columbia University, Held May 19–22, 1982. New York: School of Library Service, Columbia University, 1983.

Pryor, Lewis A. "The History of the California Job Case." *Journal of the Printing Historical Society,* 1972, no. 7.

Rees, Abraham. *The Cyclopædia; or, Universal Dictionary of Arts, Sciences, and Literature.* 45 vols., including 6 vols. of plates. London: Longman, Hurst, Rees, Orme & Brown, 1819–1820.

Roberts, Matt T., and Don Etherington. *Bookbinding and the Conservation of Books: A Dictionary of Descriptive Terminology.* Washington, DC: Library of Congress, 1982.

Romano, Frank J. *Machine Writing and Typesetting: The Story of Sholes and Mergenthaler and the Invention of the Typewriter and the Linotype.* Salem, NH: Gama, 1986.

Rummonds, Richard-Gabriel. *Printing on the Iron Handpress.* New Castle, DE: Oak Knoll Press; London: British Library, 1998.

Rummonds, Richard-Gabriel. *Problem Solving and Printing on the Cast-Iron Handpress: A Manual for the Rochester Institute of Technology Seminar Taught by Richard-Gabriel Rummonds.* Los Angeles: Ex Ouroboros, 1991.

Ryder, John. *Printing for Pleasure: A Practical Guide for Amateurs.* Foreword by Sir Francis Meynell. London: Phoenix House, 1955.

Ryder, John. *Printing for Pleasure.* With a new foreword by Vivian Ridler. Rev. ed. London: Bodley Head, 1976.

Saint Bride Foundation. *Catalogue of the Technical Reference Library of Works on Printing and the Allied Arts.* London: Printed for the Governors, 1919.

Salamon, Ferdinando. *The History of Prints and Printmaking from Dürer to Picasso: A Guide to Collecting.* New York: American Heritage Press, A Division of McGraw-Hill Book Co., 1972.

Saudé, Jean. *Traité d'enluminure d'art au pochoir.* Paris: L'Ibis, 1925.

Saxe, Stephen O. *American Iron Hand Presses.* Council Bluffs, IA: Yellow Barn Press; Madison, NJ: Fairleigh Dickinson University, 1991.

Sigüenza y Vera, Juan Josef. *Mecanismo del arte de la imprenta.* Madrid: Imprenta de la Campañía, 1811.

Silver, Rollo G. *The American Printer, 1787–1825.* Published for the Bibliographical Society of the University of Virginia. Charlottesville: University Press of Virginia, 1967.

Silver, Rollo G. *Typefounding in America, 1787–1825.* Published for the Bibliographical Society of the University of Virginia. Charlottesville: University Press of Virginia, 1965.

Simon, Herbert. *Introduction to Printing: The Craft of Letterpress.* Illustrated by Tom Hughes. London: Faber and Faber, 1968.

Simon, Herbert, and Harry Carter. *Printing Explained: An Elementary Practical Handbook for School and Amateurs.* Illustrated by G. M. Freebairn. Leicester: Dryad Press, 1931.

Simon, Oliver. *Introduction to Typography.* Edited by David Bland. 2nd ed. London: Faber and Faber, 1963.

Skingsley, T. A. "Technical Training and Education in the English Printing Industry." *Journal of the Printing Historical Society,* 1979/80, no. 14, pp. 1–58.

Slythe, R. Margaret. *The Art of Illustration, 1750–1900.* London: Library Association, 1970.

Steinberg, Sigfrid Henry. *Five Hundred Years of Printing.* 3rd ed. Revised by James Moran. Harmondsworth, Middlesex: Penguin Books, 1974.

Sterne, Harold E. *A Catalogue of Nineteenth Century Printing Presses.* New Castle, DE: Oak Knoll Press; London: British Library, 2001.

Stewart, Alexander A. *Compositors' Tools and Materials.* [Chicago]: Published by the Committee on Education, United Typothetæ of America, 1918.

Stone, Jon R. *Latin for the Illiterati: Exorcizing the Ghosts of a Dead Language.* New York: Routledge, 1996.

Stone, Reynolds. "The Albion Press." *Journal of the Printing Historical Society,* 1966, no. 2, pp. 58–73.

Strauss, Victor. *The Printing Industry: An Introduction to Its Many Branches, Processes, and Products.* Washington, DC: Printing Industries of America; New York: R. R. Bowker, 1967.

Sutton, James, and Alan Bartram. *An Atlas of Typeforms.* London: Lund Humphries, 1968.

Thomas, Isaiah. *The History of Printing in America.* 2 vols. Worcester, MA: From the press of Isaiah Thomas, Jun.; Isaac Sturtevant, printer, 1810.

Turner, Decherd, Colin Franklin, and Richard Bigus. *The Mystique of Vellum: Containing an Introduction by Decherd Turner and a Historical Essay on Vellum Printed Books by Colin Franklin Along with a Manual to Printing Letterpress on Vellum and Parchment by Richard Bigus that's edited by Lester Ferriss.* Boston: Anne and David Bromer; [Cedar Falls, IA?]: Labyrinth Editions, 1984.

Turner, Michael L. "Andrew Wilson: Lord Stanhope's Stereotype Printer." *Journal of the Printing Historical Society,* 1973–4, no. 9, pp. 22–65.

Turner, Silvie. *Which Paper: A Guide to Choosing and Using Fine Papers for Artists, Craftspeople, and Designers.* New York: Design Press, 1992.

Twyman, Michael. *Printing, 1770-1970: An Illustrated History of Its Development and Uses in England.* With a new foreword by Ruari McLean and an additional bibliography. London: British Library in association with Reading University Press; New Castle, NE: Oak Knoll Press, 1998.

Ulrich, Carolyn F., and Karl Küp. *Books and Printing: A Selected List of Periodicals,* 1800–1942. Woodstock: William E. Rudge, 1943.

United Typothetæ of America. *U.T.A. Typographical Library.* 10 parts in 65 vols. Typographical Technical Series for Apprentices. Chicago: United Typothetæ of America, 1818–

Updike, Daniel Berkeley. *Printing Types: Their History, Forms, and Use. A Study in Survivals.* 2 vols. Cambridge, MA: Harvard University Press, 1922.

U.S. Bureau of the Census. *Historical Statistics of the United States, Colonial Times to 1957.* Washington, DC, 1960.

Wakeman, Geoffrey. *The Literature of Letterpress Printing 1849–1900: A Selection.* Kidlington, Oxford: Plough Press, 1986.

Wakeman, Geoffrey, *Victorian Book Illustration: The Technical Revolution.* Newton Abbot, UK.: David & Charles, 1973.

Waldow, Alexander. *Illustrierte Encyklopädie der graphischen Künste und der verwandten Zweige.* Leipzig: A. Waldow, 1884.

Warrilow, Georgina. *See* Gaskell, Philip.

Webster's New World Dictionary of the American Language. David B. Guralnik, editor-in-chief. Second College Edition. New York: World Publishing Co., 1970.

Westcott & Thompson. *Glossary: Photo-Typography and Related Processes.* Philadelphia: Westcott & Thompson, n.d.

Wilborg, Frank B. *Printing Ink: A History with a Treatise on Modern Methods of Manufacture and Use.* New York: Harper & Brothers, 1926.

Wilkes, Walter. *Die Entwicklung der eisernen Buchdruckerpresse: eine Dokumentation.* Pinneberg: Renate Raecke, 1983.

Williamson, Hugh. *Methods of Book Design: The Practice of an Industrial Craft.* London: Oxford University Press, 1956.

Wilson, Thomas A. *The Practice of Collotype.* Boston: American Photographic Publishing Co., 1935.

Wolf, Hans-Jürgen. *Geschichte der Druckverfahren: historische Grundlagen, Portraits, Technologie.* Elchingen, Germany: Historia, 1992.

Wroth, Lawrence C. "Corpus Typographicum: A Review of English and American Printers' Manuals." *The Dolphin,* 1935, no. 2, pp. 157–170.

Wyman, Charles William Henry. *See* Bigmore, Edward Clements.

Online References

The Century Dictionary Online (i.e., *The Century Dictionary and Cyclopedia.* 12 vols. New York: Century Co., 1904 – 1909).<http://www.global-language.com/century>.

Google <http://www.google.com>

Webster's Revised Unabridged Dictionary Online (i.e., *Webster's Revised Unabridged Dictionary of the English Language.* Springfield, MA: G. & C. Merriam Co., 1913) <http://work.ucsd.edu:5141/cgi-bin/http_webster>.

Indexes

Index of Names

The entries in this index are arranged in strict alphabetical order, using the letter-by-letter system, ignoring all spaces and punctuation. Variant spellings of names are cross-referenced. Dates of persons born before 1901 are supplied when known. Titles of books, periodicals, and plays are set in italic; titles of articles, poems, and works of art are set in roman, followed by the publication date in parentheses. The pagination in this work is continuous. The first numbered page in Volume Two is 484.

Glossary/Index

The first printers' manual in English, or in any language, *Mechanick Exercises* (1683) by Joseph Moxon, included a glossary, which its author called a *dictionary*. Many of Moxon's terms are still used today, and a few have even survived the transition from letterpress printing to desktop publishing.

Over the centuries, the inevitable changes brought about by new technologies in the printing industry gave rise to changed or alternate terms. In this index preference has been given to nineteenth-century printing terminology as used in the readings. Since many of these terms have seventeenth- and eighteenth-century precedents, I have not shied away from adopting Moxon's – or his successors' – exact words in defining them.

Since many of the manuals were published in England, there are numerous British terms and variant spellings, which have been listed as entries with referrals to the American form of the words. This has been done to keep all the citations under one heading. Occasionally, the meaning of a term will vary from one printing trade to another. For example, in imposing, the word *signature* is used for a letter or number that identifies a form; in bookbinding, it refers to a section or gathering of a book. These distinctions have been indicated (in this case, by "imp." and "bind.") throughout the glossary.

If I may be permitted a personal note, it took more than a year of concentrated effort, with many long days, to compile this Glossary/Index. Why did it take so long? Because it is my nature to fuss and to be preoccupied with detail. One may also ask why there is a subentry for Benjamin Franklin's abstinence or the use of red chalk to mark bundles of paper? Only because I am fascinated by this kind of trivia.

With the publication deadline approaching, Garrett Boge, Bruce Bond, and Carl Hielscher, volunteered to help me to verify the page citations for the over 8,000 entries, which was eventually winnowed down to around 7,000. Darren Pierce painstakingly entered the data from my near-illegible handwriting. Through it all, Stephen O. Saxe read and revised the definitions, making numerous and invaluable suggestions regarding the terms.

How to Navigate the Glossary/Index

The entries are listed in strict alphabetical order, following the letter-by-letter system. Word spaces and all punctuation have been ignored. Please note that preference has been given to the gerund form of verbs. Thus, "printing" precedes "printer."

Spelling. The main entries follow current American usage, with British or other spelling noted.

Compound words. Since the manual writers themselves were not always consistent – sometimes using a single word, sometimes two words, and sometimes a hyphenated word – I have deferred again to current American usage. The page citations of a main entry refer to all three forms.

Nouns, singular versus plural. Nouns are generally listed in the singular form; however, when it was deemed necessary to also include the plural – as in *printer* and *printers* – the plural immediately follows the singular as an indented main entry. Plurals are most often used for nouns representing a class of objects, such as *spaces* and *leads*.

See also. This phrase refers the reader to related subjects.

Also called. This phrase indicates that some of the citations in the main entry include those for the listed terms.

See. This phrase directs the reader to the main entry.

Manufacturers' names. The names of manufacturers are given in their shortest forms.

Subentries. Many of the subentries are also listed as main entries.

Key to the Abbreviations

Crafts categories

bind.	binding
comp.	composition
imp.	imposition and makeready
ink.	ink, inkmaking, and inking
paper.	paper, papermaking, and paper dampening
press.	handpresses and printing machines
print.	printing and presswork
stereo.	stereotyping
type.	type and typefaces
ware.	warehouse and drying and pressing sheets

General

Cf.	*confer*, compare
e.g.	*exempli gratia*, for example
i.e.	*id est*, that is
n.	noun
v.	verb

Cf. etching.

arabesque, 511. A type ornament or block with an elaborate, intertwined design.

arbor, 116, 171–173; *illustrated*, 116, 172. On a Stanhope press, part of the pressure mechanism consisting of an iron pillar attached to the bar handle. *See also* pillar.

arbor head, 116. On a Stanhope press, part of the pressure mechanism.

arching, *see* springing.

arc lights, 709–710. In halftone engraving, the light source for exposing the plate.

Arding's inking apparatus, 570. A cylinder inking apparatus. *See also* inking apparatus.

  ink box, 570; *illustrated*, 570

arm (bind.), 781. Bar of a standing press.

  (press.), *see* bar.

Armstrong's patent combined mallet and shooting stick, 324; *illustrated*, 325

artotype, 700. A photographic process for printing from glass plates.

ascending letter, 222. A lowercase letter that projects above the mean line, e.g., b, d, f, h, k, l, t.

Athol press, 780; *illustrated*, 781. *See also* standing press.

atlas, 457. Old term for a standard size of printing paper.

  paper size: 36 x 26 in., 450

Austin inking machine, 23, 27. *See also* inking machine.

author's alterations, 385, 389. Changes made by the author on the proofs. Also called author's emendation. *See also* alterations.

  publisher's charges for, 389

author's emendations, *see* author's alterations.

automatic inking apparatus, 531. An attachment to a handpress or a printing machine that inks the rollers during the printing process. *See also* inking apparatus.

axle (ink.), 544, 623. Metal rod running through the wooden roller core. Also called roller rod.

  (press.), 123. On a Stanhope press, the rounce spit. *See also* rounce.

back (bind.), 275, 341. The spine of a book. Also called back edge. *See also* spine.

  (imp.), *see* back margin.

  (imp.), 275, 307, 321, 330–331, 333–335, 337–338, 346–347, 349, 353–356.

  (paper.), 456, 465. The crease made each time a sheet of paper is folded.

  back margin, 333, 341–342, 347. The white space between two facing pages of type. Also called gutter margin, inner margin. *See also* margins.

    determining the width of, 348; *illustrated*, 348

back bar, 176–177. On a Columbian press, part of the pressure mechanism.

backbone, 469. The crease in folded quires.

back edge, *see* back (bind.).

back fold, 793. In binding, the fold along the spine edge through which the sewing thread passes.

back furniture, *see* gutter stick.

backing, 308. In binding, forming the spine of a book.

backing up, *see* reiterating.

  backed up, 605. Said of paper printed on both sides.

backup (n.), *see* reiteration.

backup form, *see* reiteration form.

back side of a sheet, 419, 605. The backup side of a sheet of paper.

  burnishing proofs of woodcuts and wood engravings on, 612

  embossing always done on, 644

back plate, 171, 173, 608; *illustrated*, 173. On a Stanhope press, part of the pressure mechanism.

back-return lever, 176–177. On a Columbian press, part of the pressure mechanism.

backs itself, 288–290. Said of a sheet of paper printed from a work-and-turn form.

backstick, *see* gutter stick.

bagging, 203. Said when the tympan and frisket covering materials are not taut.

balance iron, an arm from which the balance weight hangs. *See also* balance weight.

  on the Russell press, 142

  on the Stanhope press, 173–174; *illustrated*, 173

balance weight, the counterweight on the Stafford and Stanhope presses. *See also* balance iron, counterbalance, counterpoise.

  on a Stafford press, 138

  on a Stanhope press, 171, 173–174; *illustrated*, 173

ball knife, 535. A blunt knife used specifically to scrape ink off pelt balls.

ball rack, 531–532, 607; *illustrated*, 533. A receptacle to hold ink balls when not in use.

  fastened to the near cheek on a wooden press, 531

balls, 50, 119, 136, 529–540, 577–578, 587, 596, 599, 607. Round cushions, about nine and a half inches in diameter, stuffed with wool or hair and nailed to wooden ball stocks. The cushion covering was made of sheepskin, pelts, or leather. At the beginning of the nineteenth century, canvas coated with composition was also used. Ink balls were always used in pairs to ink the form before the invention of rollers. A printer's familiar term for ink balls. Also called inking pads. *See also* air-ink balls, composition balls, pelt balls, skin balls.

  air-ink, 557–559; *illustrated*, 557

  composition-covered canvas, 529, 536, 538–539; *illustrated*, 530

  currying, 534

    currying iron, 534

  for fine work, 801

  inking with, 51

  knocking up, 533–535; *illustrated*, 534

  linings, 534

  maintenance of

    capped, 533

    care of, 608–609

    scraping, 535

    soaking pelts in urine, 533, 535

  materials for

    composition, 533

    pelts, 533

    sheepskins, 533

out ink. Also called furnishing roller, ink brayer. Cf. roller.

composition roller, 529–530, 572, 588; *illustrated*, 530 (ink.), 529, 530–532, 568, 580–582; *illustrated*, 532. A wooden muller for braying out ink.

Foster's bottle-brayer with holes in the bottom, 568–570; *illustrated*, 569

wooden mallet for working up ink, 494

wooden muller, 529–530, 532, 568, 570–571, 578–579; *illustrated*, 532

brayering out ink, variant spelling of braying out ink.

brayer inking table, 530, 570–571, 580, 582; *illustrated*, 571. A table used for braying out the ink, as distinct from a cylinder inking table. *See also* Foster's inking table.

braying out ink, 521, 529, 578–579, 582–583, 606. Distributing ink on a table by means of a brayer prior to taking up ink on the roller. Also spelled brayering out ink.

brazil wood, 699. A red dye used in making watercolors.

break, 230. The surplus metal attached to the bottom of a letter as it comes from the mold.

breaking the back of the paper, 468–469. Flattening the fold in a sheet of paper.

brevier, 24, 230, 233, 248–249. Old term for 8-point type.

nicks, 25

bridges, 572. Runners on a roller stand that support the roller as it inks the form.

as roller bearers, 608

brilliant, 229. Old term for 3-point type.

bringing out, 663. In hand proofing a block, intensifying the color by means of burnisher.

bringing up (print.), 416, 684. Making ready the form by overlaying or patching up the impression.

registering the form prior to making the overlay, 440 (print.), 405, 667. Augmenting the height of a block by adding an underlay and/or an interlay in order to make the printing surface type-high.

for stereotype plates, 743

Bristol board, 461. A fine grade of pasteboard. *See also* boards.

Britannia press, 103, 164. An iron handpress invented by R. Porter in Leeds, ca. 1835.

broad formats, 276. Book formats in which the width is greater than the length, as distinct from vertical formats with long, narrow pages. Also called album formats, landscape formats.

broadside (press.), 165. Press size.

(print.), 523. An unfolded sheet of paper printed on one side only, e.g., posters, handbills.

broadside formats, 368. Single-page impositions.

locked in a large chase with crossbars, 313

locked in a small chase without crossbars, 309

printing, 275, 659

broadside work, the printing of broadsides.

composing stick for, 229

broken type, 258. Said of pied type.

bronze, *see* bronze powders.

bronze brush, 643; *illustrated*, 643. A soft brush used for dusting printed matter with bronzing powders. Also called bronzing brush

bronze dust, *see* bronze powders.

bronze powders, 30, 634, 637, 639–640, 643, 775. Any variety of metallic powders used to simulate gold, silver, or copper printing. They are dusted over the wet ink or gold preparation. Also called bronze, bronze dust.

bronze printing, 637. The art of printing with bronze powders.

burnishing

at press, 639, 643

on a printing machine, 644

on a rolling press, 639

in a standing press, 639

how to improve, 644

bronze work, 643–644. A subdivision of color work in which metallic embellishments are added to the letterpress.

bronzing, 633–635, 637, 643–644. Dusting bronzing powders over wet ink or gold preparation.

with gold preparation, 641

health hazards, 638, 641

causing workers' hair to turn green, 637

bronzing brush, *see* bronze brush.

bronzing machine, 639, 642–644; *illustrated*, 644. Mechanical apparatus for dusting sheets of paper with bronze powders.

Bronstrup press, 161. Same as the Philadelphia press invented by Adam Ramage in 1834, but renamed in the 1850s by its new manufacturer Frederick Bronstrup.

with a figure-four toggle; *illustrated*, 162

Brooke's press, 106–108; *illustrated*, 106. An improved wooden press with Stanhopian improvements, used briefly in England ca. 1819.

parts; *illustrated*, 107–108

Brown press, 105. A wooden press with improvements patented in 1807 and 1809 by John Brown of London.

Bruce typecasting machine, 212. The first successful machine for casting foundry type, invented by David Bruce, Jr. in 1838.

Brunswick black, 195. A color recommended by Southward for painting iron handpresses.

brushing paper, 464, 473–474. The process of dampening paper with a wet brush.

building up, 784. Filling in a standing press.

bulk (comp.), 210, 213, 220, 263, 267; *illustrated*, 210. A low table at the end of a composing frame or type cabinet.

orientation of, 33

(print.), 13. Table.

bulking, determining the mass of a book.

badly, 454

well, 454

Bullock press, 844 n, 480. A high-speed, perfecting web printing machine invented by William Bullock in New York in the 1860s.

with an attachment for dampening rolls of paper, 480

bundle, 71, 456, 762, 764. The form in which paper came from the supplier, usually in two-ream parcels.

bur, variant spelling of burr.

burgeois, variant spelling of bourgeois.

term used to describe a better class of handwork, as distinct from common work.

the art of printing perfect impressions from wood engravings, 799–800

fine printing, 103, 649, 664–665, 795–810. Work combining fine materials with superior craftsmanship.

aesthetics of the craft of, 795

excellence in workmanship, 810–811

printing wood engravings considered hallmark of, 800

balls for, 799

blankets for, 799

cost of, 800

difference between common work and, 802

frisket bearers for, 809

hanging up on poles to dry, 807

ink for, 799, 810

overlays for, 809

packing for

hard, 807

paper for, 799, 807–808, 810

linen rags, 808, 810

platen bearers for, 809

presses for, 799

rollers for, 809–810

Johnson's argument against, 801

tympans for, 799

covered with silk, 807

fine printers

Ritchie personally beat his own forms, 803

fine work, 49, 54, 664, 803

fines, 59, 64

abolishing, 66

finish (paper.), 455. Generic term for the surface properties of a sheet of paper determined by the texture and gloss given to it during the manufacturing process. Also called surface finish.

fire hazards, 9, 13–15

first form, *see* inner form.

first proof, 64, 333, 367, 384, 387, 390–391, 603. The first proof to be pulled after the type has been set.

first pull, 276, 404. Impressing the first half of the form on a two-pull press.

five-em space (5-em space), 213–214, 241. A thin space cast five to the em or one-fifth of the square of the body of the type it accompanies. Also called thin space.

fixing the margins, 344; *illustrated*, 344. Establishing the margins.

flake white, 526. White lead.

flanc, 751, 751 n. Alternate term for flong.

flanches, 108. Part of the pressure mechanism on Brooke's press. Archaic term for flanges.

flanges, 105. On a wooden press, part of the pressure mechanism.

flaring the balls, 535. Drying pelt balls by passing them near a flame or open fire.

flat-bed press, 29

flat impression, 53. Said of impressions made on handpresses. Also called platen impression.

flesh side, 203. The inner side of a hide.

flies, 47. A familiar term for boys who take printed sheets of paper off the tympan. *See also* fly-boy.

flock, 588. Tiny cotton fibers floating in the air that get mixed in with the ink and clog up the type.

flong, 748, 751, 751 n, 752–753. The name of the viscous material used for making stereotype molds. *See also* papier mâché.

Florence flask oil, 179, 196. Olive oil.

flour paste, 206. Used for attaching parchments to tympan frames.

flourishes, 222. Decorative strokes added to the design of letters.

flowers, 231. Type ornaments.

flue, 537–538, 568, 570. Lint.

fluff, 629. An inking defect caused by the clay in the soft paper flaking off.

fly-boy, 41, 48, 76, 843. A lad who removed the printed sheets from the tympan. Also called flies.

wages, 843

foam rubber strips, 206, 411

folded quires, 68, 450, 463–464, 469

folder (bind.), a tool for burnishing the fold in a sheet of paper. Often made of bone.

its use in covering the tympan, 205, 207.

(ware.), 70, 770. A person who folds the gathered sheets.

folding chases, *see* newspaper folding chases.

folding machine, 12, 30, 69, 789, 792–793

book-folding machines, 793; *illustrated*, 793

folding room, 22

folding sheets (imp.), 294–296. Used to determine book formats.

(ware.), 764, 769–770, 790–791; *illustrated*, 790. Doubling a signature one or more times on itself at right angles.

by hand, 789–790

understanding uses of signatures, 790

machine, 789–790

fed to gauges, 790

registering by points (registration guides), 790

rules for, 294; *illustrated*, 294

folds, 275. The backs or spines of unbound books.

in a gathering, 307, 330

pricking through, 334

folio (comp.), 59, 63, 67, 276, 286, 300, 332, 345, 356, 362, 383. A compositor's familiar term for page number.

signing, 286

checking in proofs when correcting in the metal, 391

(imp.), 76, 267, 307. The resulting book format when a sheet of paper is folded once to make two leaves or four pages. Abbreviated fo., 2°. Commonly called twos.

(paper.), 286, 428, 433. Half a sheet of any printing paper.

placement of points for, 403

folio post, 778. Old term for a standard size of printing paper.

sheet size, machinemade: 21 x 16 in., 459

follower, 473, 781, 783–784. The platen of a standing press.

Aligning the printing on the second side of the sheet with the printing on the first side so that all the pages and lines fall exactly on the backs of those on the reverse side of the sheet. *See also* registering.

difficulty of
on Napier's press, 157
on a Rutt printing machine, 167
knocking the points, 437–438, 440
moving the form, 408, 439
with registration guides, 442–445
for stereotype forms, 742

making up into pages, 259, 266, 358. Dividing the composition into pages.

making up furniture, 335–336. Surround the pages of type with furniture.

making up the waste, 772. Said when all of the first quality sheets have been used up in gathering signatures and seconds must be used to complete the order.
burying imperfect sheets in the middle of a book, 763–765

male die, 644, 646. The die with the raised portion of the design corresponding to the recessed portions of the female die. *See also* die, force. Cf. female die.
made of leather, 644

mallet (comp.), 220, 324–325, 328, 332, 337, 351–352, 354, 357–359, 361; *illustrated*, 8, 325, 378. A wooden hammer used together with a shooting stick when locking up a form with wooden wedge quoins.
handle used for planing type, 236, 357, 368
using mallet to plane type, 359
(ink.), *see* brayer (ink.).

manager's room, 13. The master printer's office.

mangle press, 715. Dellagana's apparatus for making flong molds for stereotype plates.

manuscript, 22, 258, 263, 266, 379, 387, 821. The author's text from which a book is set.
pages, 381
manuscripts, 633. Prior to the invention of printing, bound books that were usually hand-written on vellum in scriptoria.
codex, 511

marble slab, 28, 504, 514
for grinding ink, 519–520, 525, 622–623
for inking, 530, 570

margin gauge, 438. A guide made for each new work indicating the margin widths.

marginal notes, 314. Notes printed in the margins. They are called footnotes when they appear at the bottom of the page, side notes when placed on either side of the text, and shoulder notes when they are aligned with the top of the text.

margins, 291, 330–331, 353; *illustrated*, 343. The spaces between the pages of type in a form. *See also* back margin, foot margin, fore-edge margin, head margin, page margins.
anatomy of
back, 308, 330, 333–335, 337–338, 341–343, 346–347, 353, 589
bottom (foot), 333–334

foot, 308, 331, 333, 336–338, 342, 346–347, 362
trimming, 341
fore-edge, 308, 330, 333, 337–338, 342–343, 347
trimming, 341
front (fore-edge), 341–342
gutter (back), 308, 343, 346, 353, 355, 589
head, 308, 331, 333, 335–338, 343, 346–347, 353, 362
trimming, 341
outer (fore-edge), 333
outer edge (fore-edge), 334, 335
side, 59, 63, 331
spine (back), 330, 333
tail (foot), 341–343, 346–347
top (head), 333–334
classical proportions, 333
defined, 339
determining
correct, 340
pricking a folded sheet, 334–335
going to the binder for help, 341
proportions
equal, 333–334, 344; *illustrated*, 343
even-and-odd page, 307
extra large, 334
finding, 288
fixing, 344; *illustrated*, 344
Golden Section, 333
large, 339
for octavo
proper, 341
proportional, 333, 342–343; *illustrated*, 343
ratio to size of type, 339
for sextodecimo (sixteens), half-sheet of, *illustrated*, 347
small, 339
uniform, 340–341; *illustrated*, 343
wide, 339
regulating, 333–335
table of, 339
widths of
backs, 348; *illustrated*, 348
gutters, 348; *illustrated*, 348
heads, 348; *illustrated*, 348
tails, 348; *illustrated*, 348

Marinoni locking-up apparatus, 323, 329–330; *illustrated*, 330.

masking tape
In modern practice, fixed to the roller bearers to elevate the roller, 589

master, *see* master printer.

master printer, 3, 6, 10, 16, 41–42, 56, 66, 68, 73, 105, 814. The owner of a printing office. Also said of any skilled printer. Also called master.

match joint, 200–202, 209, 403. Devices for fastening the frisket to the tympan. Also called iron joints.

matrix (type.), 42, 212, 223, 233. A mold from which individual letters are cast.
for a hand-held mold, 805
for the Monotype composing machine, 269

paper bank, 12, 405, 595, 601; *illustrated*, 528. A printer's worktable or bench on which the paper is placed during the printing process. Also called paper bench. *See also* bank and horse.

paper bars, 206, 406. Narrow paper mullions between the windows or holes cut out of the frisket.

paper bearers, *see* rolled-paper bearers.

paper bench, *see* paper bank.

paper board, 465–467, 475, 618. A flat piece of wood upon which the paper is stacked during the dampening process. Also used as a support when cutting out the frisket.

paper curtains, 31. Window shades.

paper cutter, 12, 30, 787–789. An apparatus with a back gauge that cuts one or more sheets of paper at a time. *See also* guillotine.

paper department, *see* paper warehouse.

papered-up matter, 22, 226, 299. Pages of tied-up type wrapped in paper for storing.

paper handling, 761. Generic term for all aspects of working with paper in a printing office including dampening, folding, laying, pressing.

paper handler (print.), 3, 41, 763. A person who lays on or takes off paper at a handpress or printing machine. Also called layer.

reglets used as, 413–414, 661

    pasted to the frisket, 414, 424

replacing with reglets or cork, 661

sticking to the bed with melted roller composition, 421

platen impression, *see* flat impression

platen press, a printing press or machine that makes an impression when two parallel surfaces are brought together, as distinct from a cylinder press. *See also* hand-press, horizontal platen press, vertical platen press.

    platen machines, 53, 597.

        steam, 597

        treadle (foot-operated), 597

        under construction in a machine foundry, *illustrated*, 168

platin, variant spelling of platen.

platten, variant spelling of platen.

plattin, variant spelling of platen.

ploughing, 230. Reducing or evening up the edges of a sewn book.

plumbago, 758. Graphite used to dust electrotype plates.

ply, 461. A papermaker's unit of measure to indicate the thickness of laminated boards.

pochoir, 699. A manual technique for coloring prints using stencils and brushes. *See also* hand-colored illustrations.

point (comp.), 233, 313. An Anglo-American printer's unit of measure, equal to one-twelfth of a pica, or approximately one-seventy-second of an inch. Also called typographic point. In parts of Europe, the Didot point, slightly different in size, is in use.

points (comp.), 24, 212, 380. Punctuation marks.

    referring specifically to periods, 256, 613

    (print.), 6, 125, 137, 207, 209, 309, 403, 415, 435–437, 440–442, 624–625, 653, 680, 685; *illustrated*, 435–436. Long thin pieces of iron with a pin or spur attached at one end to hold the paper. They are fastened at the other to the tympan frame with point screws. Also called press points. *See also* register points, registration points, screw points, sheet anchors, spring points.

        backup, used for, 405

        care of, 598

        different lengths to facilitate backing up, 439–440

        fastening to the tympan frame, 199

        fixing, 401, 403, 435, 440–442

            directly on the tympan, 441

        guides, used as for folding sheets, 440

        modern practices

            fastening to the front of the tympan covering, 199

        near point

            placing closer to the middle, 402

        position of, 402, 441; *illustrated*, 441

            on the tympan, 275

        registering with, 742

        selecting, 54

        spurs, 408

            gulled, 436

        substitutes for, 409

            thumbtacks, 680

types of

    for cards, 690

    elbow, 437, 441; *illustrated*, 442

    long-shanked, 402, 406

    for multicolor printing, 628–629, 653

    with multiple spurs, 629

    for octavo, 406; *illustrated*, 442

    for process blocks, 682–684

    short-shanked, 402, 406

    spring, 409, 437, 441

    for twelves, 408 n, 441; *illustrated*, 442

    (press.), 407–408, 418. A nick on the platen to indicating its proper orientation in the frame.

pointer, 843. A person who feeds sheets of paper into a printing machine.

    wages, 843

point grooves, 206, 436. Wells in the short cross to accept the point spurs when the platen is lowered.

point holes, 402, 409, 439, 441, 602, 624–625, 629, 690. The punctures made in the paper by the spurs during the first impression. They are also used when returning the paper to the points for the backup.

    near, 402

    off, 402

    position on sheet for octavo, *illustrated*, 441

pointing (comp.), 380, 384, 386. Adding punctuation as the type is being composed.

    (print.), 15, 437, 653, 682. Positioning the points on the tympan to insure proper backup. *See also* knocking up or down the points, registering.

point screw, 199–200, 202–205, 435–437, 441, 685; *illustrated*, 435–437, 442. A bolt and wing nut assembly for attaching the shank of a press point to the tympan frame. The bolt passes through a groove in the frame and is held in place on the back side with a wing nut.

    with a rectangular shank, *illustrated*, 436

    with a washer; *illustrated*, 436

point-screw grooves, 200, 202–207, 436–437. Mortises in the tympan frame to accommodate the point screws.

point size, 233, 252. The back-to-front dimension of a piece of type. Also called type size, type size.

point spur, *see* spur

point system, 212, 233–234, 241, 352. A systematic ordering of type sizes using the point as a basis, agreed upon by the United States Type Founders' Association in 1890. Also called American Point System.

    table of dimensions, 233

    table of names, 234

    table of sizes, 234

pole room, 767. A space in a printing office fitted out with rows of poles near the ceiling. Paper is hung here to dry.

poling, 13–14; *illustrated*, 8, 763–764

    poles, 13, 763, 766, 773, 779. A series of suspended wooden poles on which dampened printed sheets are hung up to dry.

polychromatic printing, 635, 637, 650. Printing multiple colors in one impression.

    Adams's patent for, xxvi

    not to be confused with chiaro scuro printing, 635

safe-room, 12. A locked room for storing stereotype plates.

salt of tartar, 515. A mineral added to red ink to give it a purple tinge.

sap green, 699. A mineral, potassium carbonate (verdigris), dissolved in water and gum arabic to make a green watercolor.

satin, 451. Printing on.

scabbord, 618–619. A strip of metal or wood. *See also* scaboard, scale board.

    thin, 227

scaboard, alternate spelling of scabbord.

scabby, 677. A printing defect resulting in uneven ink coverage.

scale board, 250–251, 262, 307–308, 316, 332, 345, 438, 442, 589, 739. Very thin strips of wood furniture. *See also* scabbord.

    altering the margin with, 332

    justifying the length of a page, 618

    putting next to the short cross, 332

    thin, 332

    underlays, 403

    for woodcuts, 667

scale boarding, 110. Packing the head of a wooden press with thin strips of wood.

scale of prices, 51, 813. Rates charged by printers to their clients.

    for printing, 41

    wages, 41, 56

scale of sizes, 252–253; *illustrated*, 253. A primitive type gauge.

scarifier, 757. A tool, similar to a graver, used for cleaning up stereotype plates.

schools, 42, 46, 95. Technical schools for teaching the printing trades.

scraper, 668. A metal ink eraser.

screen, *see* halftone screen.

screw (press.), *see* regulating screw.

    (press.), *see* screw mechanism

    (ware.), 71, 771. On a standing press.

    screws (print.), *see* point screws.

screw mechanism, 16, 101–102, 137, 187. On a wooden press, the pressure-inducing mechanism using a screw, as distinct from one using a lever or levers. *See also* spindle.

    on an improved wooden press, 112

    on a Ramage press, 110

    on a Stanhope press, 116–117, 123–124, 172, 608; *illustrated*, 116, 123

screw press (press.), a handpress using a screw mechanism.

    Ramage press, 110

    wooden press, 103

    (ware.), 473–474, 561, 757, 780–781, 784. Generic term for a variety of presses used in a warehouse for pressing paper and books in which the pressure is obtained by means of a screw. *See also* bookbinder's press, nipping press, standing press.

screw standing press, *see* standing press.

seal press, 163. A small press with a wrought-iron frame.

second pull, 601. On a wooden handpress, the pull made after the form has been moved forward under the platen following the first pull.

section (bind.), 291. A sewing unit. *See also* collating, cutting, folding sheets, gathering, signature, subsection.

Sector press, 105, 125–126, 157. An improved wooden handpress invented in 1810 by Augustus Frederick de Heine.

    the pressure mechanism, 125

sectors, 157. The inclined planes in the pressure mechanism on some iron handpresses.

    on a Cogger press, 126, 128

    on a Sector press, 126

self-changing inking apparatus, *see* inking apparatus.

self-inking apparatus, *see* inking apparatus.

self-inking machine, *see* inking machine.

sending forms to press, 55, 365. Said of forms that have been corrected and are ready to be put on a press.

separate forms, 617. A method of printing multiple colors using a separate form for each color. The type to be printed in an additional color or colors is removed from the form and replaced with blank spaces and furniture. Also called skeletonized forms, successive forms.

serif, 231, 371–372, 396; *illustrated*, 211. A hairline or light finishing stroke crossing, bracketing, or projecting from the ends of the stems of letters. Also spelled ceriph, seriff.

    hairline, 326, 582

set matter, 212–213, 275, 326, 582. Composed type ready to be printed. Also called composed type, type matter. *See also* matter.

    carrying, *illustrated*, 258

set measure, 319. The physical length of the line in the stick. It is not necessarily the same as the printed length of the line.

set solid, 243. Unleaded composition.

setting off (print.), 21, 508, 629, 659. Inadvertently transferring ink from one sheet to another under pressure.

    (ware.), 778–781, 785, 799. Transferring excess ink from one sheet to another when pressing sheets.

      transferring the key block image to make color blocks, 678

setoff, 497, 600, 605, 657, 775, 781. A printing defect caused by the transfer of ink onto the setoff sheet during the backup process. Cf. offset.

setoff paper, 420, 605

    saturated with benzine, 605

setoff sheet, 408, 605, 810. A piece of paper fastened to the tympan. *See also* slipsheet.

    washing with turpentine, 605

setting of ink, 775, 778–779. Said when the surface film of the ink will not smear.

setting rule, 255–258, 396, 398; *illustrated*, 229, 257 A thin piece of brass or steel placed in a composing stick to expedite the setting of unleaded matter or to justify a stick. The rule is moved forward after each line is set and justified. Setting rules are available in set measures with a beak or nib at one or both upper ends. Also called composing rule

setting type, 24, 75, 81, 84, 228, 358. Composing lines of type in a composing stick. Also called setting up matter.

orientation indentations, 180, 183–184

swell, 109. On a Medhurst press, a collar, part of the pressure mechanism.

swelled gelatine process, 704–706. Photomechanical process to transfer an image to a gelatine plate.

> gelatine plate used as a mold for making a stereotype plate, 704, 706
>
> mold for relief casting, 704
>
> not a halftone, 704
>
> photographic negative, 704
>
> stippled image, 705

symbols, *see* reference marks.

table (press.), alternate term for the bed on some iron handpresses. Also called press table. *See also* bed.

> stationary, 136–137
>
> (press.), 237, 408, 417, 584, 601, 622–623, 807.
>
> > on an Albion press, 155, 185, 187
> >
> > on an Albion press, late-nineteenth-century, 187–188
> >
> > on Church's press, 138, 140–141
> >
> > on a Columbian press, 129, 176–177, 179
> >
> > on an Imperial press, 190
> >
> > on Napier's press, 156–157
> >
> > on a Ruthven press, 134, 136–137
> >
> > on a Rutt printing machine, 167
> >
> > on a Stafford press, 137
> >
> > on a Stanhope press, 115, 118–119, 171, 174–175, 799; *illustrated*, 175

tables (print.), 17, 43, 119. Worktables.

tabletop press, a small printing press that can be set up on a table or a bench.

> Ramage portable foolscap press, 110–111, 365; *illustrated*, 111
>
> Stafford press, 137–138; *illustrated*, 138
>
> Superior vertical platen press, xxxi

tablet work, 694, 696. The art of printing white-letter blocks.

> choice of rollers, 694
>
> managing ink and rollers, 695–696

table work (comp.), 43. The art of constructing typographic elements with curved rules.

> (comp.), 219, 245, 249, 392, 748, 838. Setting matter in columns separated by rules. Also called tabular work.

tabular work, *see* table work (comp.).

tack, 560, 564. The cohesion of ink and its resistance to splitting between separating surfaces.

tacky, 560. Said when the surface of a roller in proper condition is slightly adhesive to the touch.

tail margin, *see* foot margin.

tailpiece, 374, 424, 624, 658. A decorative element placed in the blank bottom half of the type page. Cf. headpiece.

taking down the sheets, 767. Removing dry sheets from the poles.

> brushing, 764, 767

taking in, 333. In composing, reducing the spacing in a line of type in a composing stick.

taking the ink, 373, 606. Said of type when it accepts an even film of ink as it is rolled.

> type not taking the ink. 584

taking-off boy, 48–49, 167; *illustrated*, 48

taking off the paper, 47. Removing the sheet of paper from the points or delivery board after it has been printed. Also called throwing off the paper.

> on a handpress, 47, 603, 626
>
> on a printing machine, 54

taking proofs, *see* pulling proofs.

taking up printed sheets, *illustrated*, 763. Loading the peel with freshly printed sheets prior to hanging them on the poles.

tang, 746. A projection on a stereotype plate at the point where the molten metal entered the mold.

tar, 531. An ingredient sometimes added to roller composition.

Taylor cylinder press, A. B., *illustrated*, 48

tea-chest lead, 752. An ingredient in stereotype metal.

technical education, 42. *See also* technical schools.

technical schools, 42, 95–96. Also called technical education, trade schools.

> first in London, 42

tee, 171–172; *illustrated*, 171. The wooden base on which a Stanhope press stands.

telephones, 21, 34

tempering strew, a screw placed on the inside of the bar that rests against the coupling bar to keep the bar out of the way of the tympan as it is lowered.

> on a Rust Washington press, 182
>
> on a Smith press, 182

ten-cylinder type-revolving printing machine (Bullock), 844 n.

tenons, 608. Of a wooden press, the parts of the head that fit into mortises in the cheeks.

text type, 229, 251. Type used specifically for setting text, as distinct from display type. Text type usually ranges from 6 to 14 points, although larger sizes are frequently used in handpress books.

thin letters, 63. Narrow letters such as i, j, l, and most punctuation marks.

thick space, *see* three-em space.

thin spaces, *see* five-em space, hair spaces.

thirty-twomo, 741. The resulting book format when a sheet of paper is folded five times making thirty-two leaves or sixty-four pages. Commonly called thirty-twos. Abbreviated 32mo, 32°.

thread test, 491, 507. A test for evaluating the tack in an ink.

three-color printing, 651. A photomechanical process for printing halftone images in color from separate plates – yellow, magenta, and cyan. Cf. Four-color printing.

three-em quad (3-em quad), 241. A large quad cast three ems wide on the type body it accompanies.

three-em space (3-em space), 241–242. A space that is cast three to the em or one-third the thickness of the square of the type body it accompanies. Also called thick space.

throwing off the paper, *see* taking off paper.

thumb piece, 106, 201, 598, 601. A protrusion on the near side of the frisket frame to facilitate raising and lowering the frisket. Also called ear, frisket ear.

> hitting the cheek, 598
>
> on a wooden press, 608

press, patented by American Daniel Treadwell in England in 1820. It used a great lever on a pivot to apply the pressure; only one was built, and it does not survive.

trimming, 339–340. Cutting the edges of a book. Cf. cutting.

  on a guillotine, 787, 792

trim sizes, 338. Standard book formats.

  established by back and head margins, 338

trough, (paper.), 71, 466, 471–472, 478; *illustrated*, 471. A tray in which paper is dampened.

  (print.), *see* lye trough

trunion, part of the pressure mechanism on some iron handpresses.

    on an Albion press, 185–186

    on a Columbian press, 177

trying his stick, 228. Said of a compositor testing a composing stick for trueness.

trying tool, 248. A gauge used for finishing leads.

tub-sized paper, 449, 455, 629. Cf. engine-sized paper.

Tufts press, 103, 844 n. An American iron handpress, patented in 1831 by Otis Tufts, a Boston machinist. It is strikingly similar to the Smith press, with equal-length levers in the pressure mechanism and an acorn frame.

tumbler, 189. On an Albion press, late-nineteenth-century, part of the pressure mechanism.

turpentine, 491 n, 493, 495, 507, 524, 680, 687. A solvent used to clean wood type, wood engravings, and woodcuts. Also called turps.

    dried soap, 487, 496, 503, 505

    spirits of, 610, 621, 628

    Venice, 507, 523, 638, 642

tweezers, 389, 395, 399; *illustrated*, 229, 395, 398. A small tool with two pointed prongs used to pull sorts or spacing materials out of composed matter. Also called pincers.

twelvemo, *see* duodecimo.

twelves, *see* duodecimo.

twelve-ways, 602. Imposing in twelves.

two-color initials, 511. A method of printing two colors with one impression. Also called multicolor letters.

  Hammer's method, 636

two-color printing machine, 617

two-em quad (2-em quad), 241. A large quad cast two ems wide on the type body it accompanies.

two-em space, *see* en quad.

two-handled roller. Also called double-handled roller.

  inking with, *illustrated*, 8

two-line double pica, 229. Old term for 48-point type.

two-line English, 229–230, 249. Old term for 28-point type.

two-line great primer, 229–230, 249. Old term for 36-point type.

two-line letters, 24–25. Letters double their regular size.

two-line pica, 229, 249. Old term for 24-point type.

two-pull wooden press, 9, 12, 51, 102–103, 109–110, 601 n; *illustrated*, 2. Alternate term for a wooden press. *See also* first pull, printing press, second pull, wooden press.

    determining the stops of the carriage, 404

two-thirders, 55–56. Independent hired hands.

tying tool, 248. A gauge to verify the dimensions of a lead.

tying up printed sheets, 23

tying up pages of type, 63–64, 213, 220, 259–260, 266–267, 297–299, 307, 330, 354, 358; *illustrated*, 260. Securing composed lines of type with page cord.

tied-up matter, *see* tied-up pages.

tympan (press.), 3, 11, 119, 121, 125, 128, 402. A frame covered with parchment or paper upon which the sheet of printing paper is laid. The tympan is hinged to the bed. Also spelled tinpan. *See also* drawer, outer tympan, packing, tympan/frisket assembly.

  bagging, 199, 202–203, 207, 371, 606

    slack, 607

  blankets in, 112

  covering procedures, 199–208

    alternate methods, 208

      laced to frame with leather strips, 208

      nailed to frame, 199, 201–202

      sewn to frame, 207–208

    pasted to frame, 199, 202, 207

  dampening, 199, 609

  inner, 155, 199–200, 203–204, 206–207, 401

    discarded when pulling proofs, 371

    drying out with blankets, 205

    loose, 604

  laying sheets on, 15

  materials, covering

    cambric, 206–207

    canvas, 203

    cloth, 199

      cotton shirting, 205

      Irish cloth, 199, 202

      linen, 199, 203, 206 n, 207

        for proofing photomechanical plates, 429

      muslin, 199, 203

      rubbed with oil, 204–205

      satin, 199

        for proofing blocks, 199

      silk, 199, 203, 206 n, 661–662

    forrel, 199, 201–202

    paper, 199, 371

    parchment, 199, 201–206, 206 n, 371, 661–662

      dampening after attaching, 199, 201, 206

      dampening before attaching, 204–205, 207

      smooth side out, 207

    vellum, 199, 201–202

  for multicolor printing, 628

  outer, 119, 155, 199–200, 206–207, 401, 436

    covering with canvass, 203

    covering for pulling proofs, 371

      with paper, 371–372

    drying out with blankets, 204

  paste for, 202

  removing when pulling proofs, 369

  taking printed sheet off, 47

  wetting down on a wooden press, 199

  working dry on an iron handpress, 199, 405

  (press.)

    on an Albion press, 155, 187

    on Church's press, 138, 140–141

cheeks. The ribs are hooked to the winter at the platen end of the press.

    on Brooke's press, 107
    on a Cogger press (bed), 127
    on a Smith's press, 180
    on a Washington press, 148, 180
    on a wooden press, 119, 125

wire lines, 449. On a sheet of handmade laid paper, the visible fine lines that generally run parallel to the wide dimension of the mold. They are attached at right angles to the chain lines. Cf. chain lines.

women, 776. *See also* girls.
    compositors, 44–46; *illustrated*, 274, 434
      special conditions for, 46
    employment of, 23, 41, 69
      duration of, 46
    folders in the book warehouse, 69
    interleaving printed sheets, 777
    operating folding machines, 790; *illustrated*, 793
    owners of printing offices, 38
    paper handlers, 41, 48; *illustrated*, 48
    wages, 46

wood block, in relief printing, a printer's familiar term for woodcuts and wood engravings.
    cutting overlays, 661
    glazed pasteboard, 661
    instead of blankets with hard packing, 661
    making ready on India paper, 661
    photo-sensitive, 651
    pulling first proof for overlay, 661
    replaced with electrotypes, 664
    warped, 661–662
    worked separately, 661

woodcut, 49, 55, 403, 557, 649, 659. In relief printing, an image cut with gouges and knives into the plank side of a block of wood. *See also* wood block; woodcut, printing; wood engraving.
    maintenance of
      cleaning, 664
        benzine, 664
        camphene, 664
        no lye, 664
      drying, 774
      storing
        cabinet for, 19
      treating, 268
    making ready, 49
      bringing up, 664–666
      cutting out of tympan sheet, 407
      equalizing the impression, 669–670
      gradations in density of color, 669–670; *illustrated*, 670
      degrees of light and shade, 673–674
      hard packing, 660
      overlaying, 407, 411, 673
        also called make ready, 668
        finished overlays covered with tissue paper, 668
      object of, 669

    paste for, 674
    paper for packing
      smooth, 660
    planing the bottoms of, 407
    soft packing, 659
    type-high, 407
    underlaying, 407, 412

woodcut, printing, 673–676
    bite in paper, 659
    card printing, used in, 635
    difficulties in printing, 798
      climate, 798
      ink, 798
      paper, 798
    from electrotypes of, instead of originals, 668–669, 673
    inking with balls, 529, 657, 802
    inks for , 489
      black, 523
    retaining set of sheets, 774
    rivaling copperplate engravings, 802
    separate block for each color, 678
    setting off when printed first, 659–660
    single-block process, 673
    after the text, 659
    tying the bar to the cheek to prevent the block from warping, 662, 673
    underinking proofs, 673
    use of bearers, 660

wooden base, 124–125. The tee on which a Stanhope press stands.

wood engraving, 407, 411, 513, 649–651, 657, 659–668, 672, 684–685, 804. In relief printing, an image engraved on the end grain of a block of wood. Also called white-line block. *See also* woodcut since that term is sometimes used interchangeably with wood engraving. *See also* wood engraving, printing.
    artist's intention, 49
    blocks
      copper plate of, 663
      drawing with pencil on, 797
      photography used to transfer image to photo-sensitive wood block, 651
      plaster molds of for stereotype plates, 721
      type-metal plate of, 663
      warped, 661, 662, 665, 673
      white-line, 649
    inking
      cleaning edges after inking to reduce the amount of ink on the block, 670, 674
      with a composition roller, 665
      gradation of color, 670; *illustrated*, 670
    maintenance of
      cleaning, 662
        camphene, 665
        lye and water not used, 662, 665
        spirits of turpentine, 662, 665
        turpentine, 673
    making ready, 49, 649, 666